Economic Learning and Social Evolution
General Editor
Ken Binmore, Emeritus Professor of Economics at University College London

Evolutionary Games and Equilibrium Selection, Larry Samuelson, 1997

The Theory of Learning in Games, Drew Fudenberg and David K. Levine, 1998

Game Theory and the Social Contract, Volume 2: Just Playing, Ken Binmore, 1998

Social Dynamics, Steven N. Durlauf and H. Peyton Young, editors, 2001

Evolutionary Dynamics and Extensive Form Games, Ross Cressman, 2003

Moral Sentiments and Material Interests: The Foundations of Cooperation in Economic Life, Herbert Gintis, Samuel Bowles, Robert Boyd, and Ernst Fehr, editors, 2004

Does Game Theory Work? The Bargaining Challenge, Ken Binmore, 2006

Population Games and Evolutionary Dynamics, William H. Sandholm, 2010

Population Games and Evolutionary Dynamics

William H. Sandholm

The MIT Press
Cambridge, Massachusetts
London, England

© 2010 Massachusetts Institute of Technology

All rights reserved. No part of this book may be reproduced in any form by any electronic or mechanical means (including photocopying, recording, or information storage and retrieval) without permission in writing from the publisher.

For information about special quantity discounts, please email special_sales@mitpress.mit.edu

This book was set in Palatino by Westchester Book Composition. Printed and bound in the United States of America.

Library of Congress Cataloging-in-Publication Data

Sandholm, William H., 1970–
Population games and evolutionary dynamics / William H. Sandholm.
  p. cm.—(Economic learning and social evolution)
Includes bibliographical references and index.
ISBN 978-0-262-19587-4 (hbk. : alk. paper)
1. Game theory. 2. Evolution—Mathematical models. I. Title.
HB144.S27 2011
303.4—dc22
                                                                 2010011973

10 9 8 7 6 5 4 3 2 1

Contents in Brief

	Series Foreword	xvii
	Preface	xix
1	Introduction	1
I	**Population Games**	
2	Population Games	21
3	Potential Games, Stable Games, and Supermodular Games	53
II	**Deterministic Evolutionary Dynamics**	
4	Revision Protocols and Evolutionary Dynamics	119
5	Deterministic Dynamics: Families and Properties	139
6	Best Response and Projection Dynamics	177
III	**Convergence and Nonconvergence of Deterministic Dynamics**	
7	Global Convergence of Evolutionary Dynamics	221
8	Local Stability under Evolutionary Dynamics	271
9	Nonconvergence of Evolutionary Dynamics	319
IV	**Stochastic Evolutionary Models**	
10	Stochastic Evolution and Deterministic Approximation	367
11	Stationary Distributions and Infinite-Horizon Behavior	397
12	Limiting Stationary Distributions and Stochastic Stability	451
	References	541
	Notation Index	565
	Index	575

Contents

	Series Foreword	xvii
	Preface	xix
1	**Introduction**	**1**
1.1	Population Games	2
	1.1.1 Modeling Interactions in Large Populations	2
	1.1.2 Definitions and Classes of Population Games	5
1.2	Evolutionary Dynamics	6
	1.2.1 Knowledge, Rationality, and Large Games	7
	1.2.2 Foundations for Evolutionary Dynamics	8
	1.2.3 Deterministic Evolutionary Dynamics	9
	1.2.4 Orders of Limits for Stochastic Evolutionary Models	11
	1.2.5 Stationary Distributions and Stochastic Stability	12
1.3	Remarks on History, Motivation, and Interpretation	13
	Notes	15
I	**Population Games**	
2	**Population Games**	**21**
2.1	Population Games	22
	2.1.1 Populations, Strategies, and States	22
	2.1.2 Payoffs	23
	2.1.3 Best Responses and Nash Equilibria	23
	2.1.4 Prelude to Evolutionary Dynamics	24
2.2	Examples	25
	2.2.1 Matching in Normal Form Games	25
	2.2.2 Congestion Games	27
	2.2.3 Two Simple Externality Models	28
2.3	The Geometry of Population Games and Nash Equilibria	29
	2.3.1 Drawing Two-Strategy Games	29
	2.3.2 Displacement Vectors and Tangent Spaces	31

		2.3.3	Orthogonal Projections	34
		2.3.4	Drawing Three-Strategy Games	36
		2.3.5	Tangent Cones and Normal Cones	38
		2.3.6	Normal Cones and Nash Equilibria	41
	2.A	Appendix: Affine Spaces, Tangent Spaces, and Projections		44
		2.A.1	Affine Spaces	44
		2.A.2	Affine Hulls of Convex Sets	45
		2.A.3	Orthogonal Projections	46
		2.A.4	The Moreau Decomposition Theorem	50
		Notes		51
3	**Potential Games, Stable Games, and Supermodular Games**			**53**
	3.1	Full Potential Games		53
		3.1.1	Full Population Games	54
		3.1.2	Definition and Characterization	54
		3.1.3	Examples	55
		3.1.4	Nash Equilibria of Full Potential Games	58
		3.1.5	The Geometry of Nash Equilibrium in Full Potential Games	64
		3.1.6	Efficiency in Homogeneous Full Potential Games	66
		3.1.7	Inefficiency Bounds for Congestion Games	68
	3.2	Potential Games		71
		3.2.1	Motivating Examples	71
		3.2.2	Definition, Characterizations, and Examples	72
		3.2.3	Potential Games and Full Potential Games	76
		3.2.4	Passive Games and Constant Games	77
	3.3	Stable Games		79
		3.3.1	Definition	79
		3.3.2	Examples	81
		3.3.3	Invasion	85
		3.3.4	Global Neutral Stability and Global Evolutionary Stability	87
		3.3.5	Nash Equilibrium and Global Neutral Stability in Stable Games	90
	3.4	Supermodular Games		94
		3.4.1	Definition	94
		3.4.2	Examples	97
		3.4.3	Best Response Monotonicity in Supermodular Games	98
		3.4.4	Nash Equilibria of Supermodular Games	99
	3.A	Appendix: Multivariate Calculus		100
		3.A.1	Univariate Calculus	100
		3.A.2	The Derivative as a Linear Map	101
		3.A.3	Differentiation as a Linear Operation	103
		3.A.4	The Product Rule and the Chain Rule	103

Contents

		3.A.5	Homogeneity and Euler's Theorem	104
		3.A.6	Higher-Order Derivatives	105
		3.A.7	The Whitney Extension Theorem	106
		3.A.8	Vector Integration and the Fundamental Theorem of Calculus	107
		3.A.9	Potential Functions and Integrability	108
	3.B	Appendix: Affine Calculus		108
		3.B.1	Linear Forms and the Riesz Representation Theorem	109
		3.B.2	Dual Characterizations of Multiples of Linear Forms	110
		3.B.3	Derivatives of Functions on Affine Spaces	111
		3.B.4	Affine Integrability	113
		Notes		115

II Deterministic Evolutionary Dynamics

4 Revision Protocols and Evolutionary Dynamics — 119

	4.1	The Basic Stochastic Evolutionary Model		120
		4.1.1	Inertia and Myopia	120
		4.1.2	Revision Protocols	121
	4.2	Mean Dynamics		122
		4.2.1	Derivation	122
		4.2.2	Target Protocols and Target Dynamics	124
	4.3	Examples		125
		4.3.1	Imitative Protocols and Dynamics	126
		4.3.2	Direct Protocols and Dynamics	128
	4.4	Deterministic Evolutionary Dynamics		129
	4.A	Appendix: Ordinary Differential Equations		131
		4.A.1	Basic Definitions	131
		4.A.2	Existence, Uniqueness, and Continuity of Solutions	133
		4.A.3	Ordinary Differential Equations on Compact Convex Sets	135
		Notes		137

5 Deterministic Dynamics: Families and Properties — 139

	5.1	Information Requirements for Revision Protocols		141
	5.2	Incentives and Aggregate Behavior		144
	5.3	Families of Evolutionary Dynamics		148
	5.4	Imitative Dynamics		153
		5.4.1	Definition	153
		5.4.2	Examples	154
		5.4.3	Biological Derivations of the Replicator Dynamic	158
		5.4.4	Extinction and Invariance	160
		5.4.5	Monotone Percentage Growth Rates and Positive Correlation	162
		5.4.6	Rest Points and Restricted Equilibria	164

	5.5	Excess Payoff Dynamics	165
		5.5.1 Definition and Interpretation	166
		5.5.2 Incentives and Aggregate Behavior	167
	5.6	Pairwise Comparison Dynamics	169
		5.6.1 Definition	170
		5.6.2 Incentives and Aggregate Behavior	170
		5.6.3 Desiderata Revisited	172
	5.7	Multiple Revision Protocols and Hybrid Dynamics	173
		Notes	175
6	**Best Response and Projection Dynamics**		**177**
	6.1	The Best Response Dynamic	178
		6.1.1 Definition and Examples	178
		6.1.2 Construction and Properties of Solution Trajectories	180
		6.1.3 Incentive Properties	186
	6.2	Perturbed Best Response Dynamics	187
		6.2.1 Revision Protocols and Mean Dynamics	188
		6.2.2 Perturbed Optimization: A Representation Theorem	189
		6.2.3 Logit Choice and the Logit Dynamic	191
		6.2.4 Perturbed Incentive Properties via Virtual Payoffs	196
	6.3	The Projection Dynamic	198
		6.3.1 Definition	198
		6.3.2 Solution Trajectories	200
		6.3.3 Incentive Properties	202
		6.3.4 Revision Protocols and Connections with the Replicator Dynamic	202
	6.A	Appendix: Differential Inclusions	205
		6.A.1 Basic Theory	205
		6.A.2 Differential Equations Defined by Projections	207
	6.B	Appendix: The Legendre Transform	208
		6.B.1 Legendre Transforms of Functions on Open Intervals	208
		6.B.2 Legendre Transforms of Functions on Multidimensional Domains	210
	6.C	Appendix: Perturbed Optimization	212
		6.C.1 Proof of the Representation Theorem	212
		6.C.2 Additional Results	215
		Notes	216
III	**Convergence and Nonconvergence of Deterministic Dynamics**		
7	**Global Convergence of Evolutionary Dynamics**		**221**
	7.1	Potential Games	223
		7.1.1 Potential Functions as Lyapunov Functions	223
		7.1.2 Gradient Systems for Potential Games	228

Contents xi

	7.2	Stable Games	232
		7.2.1 The Projection and Replicator Dynamics in Strictly Stable Games	232
		7.2.2 Integrable Target Dynamics	235
		7.2.3 Impartial Pairwise Comparison Dynamics	246
		7.2.4 Summary	248
	7.3	Supermodular Games	249
		7.3.1 The Best Response Dynamic in Two-Player Normal Form Games	251
		7.3.2 Stochastically Perturbed Best Response Dynamics	253
	7.4	Dominance Solvable Games	257
		7.4.1 Dominated and Iteratively Dominated Strategies	258
		7.4.2 The Best Response Dynamic	258
		7.4.3 Imitative Dynamics	259
	7.A	Appendix: Limit and Stability Notions for Deterministic Dynamics	260
		7.A.1 ω-Limits and Notions of Recurrence	261
		7.A.2 Stability of Sets of States	262
	7.B	Appendix: Stability Analysis via Lyapunov Functions	262
		7.B.1 Lyapunov Stable Sets	263
		7.B.2 ω-Limits and Attracting Sets	263
		7.B.3 Asymptotically Stable and Globally Asymptotically Stable Sets	265
	7.C	Appendix: Cooperative Differential Equations	266
		Notes	268
8	**Local Stability under Evolutionary Dynamics**		**271**
	8.1	Non-Nash Rest Points of Imitative Dynamics	272
	8.2	Local Stability in Potential Games	273
	8.3	Evolutionarily Stable States	275
		8.3.1 Single-Population Games	276
		8.3.2 Multipopulation Games	280
		8.3.3 Regular Taylor ESS	281
	8.4	Local Stability via Lyapunov Functions	282
		8.4.1 The Replicator and Projection Dynamics	282
		8.4.2 Target and Pairwise Comparison Dynamics: Interior ESS	283
		8.4.3 Target and Pairwise Comparison Dynamics: Boundary ESS	285
	8.5	Linearization of Imitative Dynamics	290
		8.5.1 The Replicator Dynamic	291
		8.5.2 General Imitative Dynamics	295
	8.6	Linearization of Perturbed Best Response Dynamics	297
		8.6.1 Deterministically Perturbed Best Response Dynamics	297
		8.6.2 The Logit Dynamic	298
	8.A	Appendix: Matrix Analysis	299
		8.A.1 Rank and Invertibility	299

		8.A.2	*Eigenvectors and Eigenvalues*	*300*
		8.A.3	*Similarity, (Block) Diagonalization, and the Spectral Theorem*	*302*
		8.A.4	*Symmetric Matrices*	*304*
		8.A.5	*The Real Jordan Canonical Form*	*305*
		8.A.6	*The Spectral Norm and Singular Values*	*306*
		8.A.7	*Hines's Lemma*	*307*
	8.B	Appendix: Linear Differential Equations		308
		8.B.1	*Examples*	*308*
		8.B.2	*Solutions*	*310*
		8.B.3	*Stability and Hyperbolicity*	*312*
	8.C	Appendix: Linearization of Nonlinear Differential Equations		313
		Notes		315
9	**Nonconvergence of Evolutionary Dynamics**			**319**
	9.1	Conservative Properties of Evolutionary Dynamics		320
		9.1.1	*Constants of Motion in Null Stable Games*	*320*
		9.1.2	*Preservation of Volume*	*324*
	9.2	Games with Nonconvergent Evolutionary Dynamics		327
		9.2.1	*Circulant Games*	*327*
		9.2.2	*Continuation of Attractors for Parameterized Games*	*330*
		9.2.3	*Mismatching Pennies*	*333*
		9.2.4	*The Hypnodisk Game*	*337*
	9.3	Chaotic Evolutionary Dynamics		341
	9.4	Survival of Dominated Strategies		344
		9.4.1	*A General Survival Theorem*	*347*
		9.4.2	*Examples and Discussion*	*351*
	9.A	Appendix: Three Classical Theorems on Nonconvergent Dynamics		356
		9.A.1	*Liouville's Theorem*	*356*
		9.A.2	*The Poincaré-Bendixson and Bendixson-Dulac Theorems*	*358*
	9.B	Appendix: Attractors and Continuation		359
		9.B.1	*Attractors and Repellors*	*359*
		9.B.2	*Continuation of Attractors*	*361*
		Notes		362

IV Stochastic Evolutionary Models

10	**Stochastic Evolution and Deterministic Approximation**			**367**
	10.1	The Stochastic Evolutionary Process		368
	10.2	Finite-Horizon Deterministic Approximation		369
		10.2.1	*Kurtz's Theorem*	*370*
		10.2.2	*Deterministic Approximation of the Stochastic Evolutionary Process*	*372*

Contents

	10.3	Extensions	376
		10.3.1 Discrete-Time Models	*376*
		10.3.2 Finite-Population Adjustments	*377*
	10.A	Appendix: The Exponential and Poisson Distributions	378
		10.A.1 Basic Properties	*378*
		10.A.2 The Poisson Limit Theorem	*381*
	10.B	Appendix: Probability Models and Their Interpretation	382
		10.B.1 Countable Probability Models	*383*
		10.B.2 Uncountable Probability Models and Measure Theory	*384*
		10.B.3 Distributional Properties and Sample Path Properties	*386*
	10.C	Appendix: Countable State Markov Chains and Processes	389
		10.C.1 Countable State Markov Chains	*389*
		10.C.2 Countable State Markov Processes: Definition and Construction	*391*
		10.C.3 Countable State Markov Processes: Transition Probabilities	*393*
		Notes	395
11	**Stationary Distributions and Infinite-Horizon Behavior**		**397**
	11.1	Irreducible Evolutionary Processes	399
		11.1.1 Full Support Revision Protocols	*399*
		11.1.2 Stationary Distributions and Infinite-Horizon Behavior	*401*
		11.1.3 Reversibility	*402*
	11.2	Stationary Distributions for Two-Strategy Games	403
		11.2.1 Birth and Death Processes	*403*
		11.2.2 The Stationary Distribution of the Evolutionary Process	*405*
		11.2.3 Examples	*407*
	11.3	Waiting Times and Infinite-Horizon Prediction	412
		11.3.1 Examples	*412*
		11.3.2 Discussion	*415*
	11.4	Model Adjustments for Finite Populations	417
		11.4.1 Finite-Population Games	*418*
		11.4.2 Clever Payoff Evaluation	*419*
		11.4.3 Committed Agents and Imitative Protocols	*421*
	11.5	Potential Games and Exponential Protocols	423
		11.5.1 Finite-Population Potential Games	*424*
		11.5.2 Exponential Revision Protocols	*428*
		11.5.3 Reversibility and Stationary Distributions	*430*
	11.A	Appendix: Long-Run Behavior of Markov Chains and Processes	434
		11.A.1 Communication, Recurrence, and Irreducibility	*434*
		11.A.2 Periodicity	*436*
		11.A.3 Hitting Times and Hitting Probabilities	*437*
		11.A.4 The Perron-Frobenius Theorem	*440*

	11.A.5	Stationary Distributions for Markov Chains	441
	11.A.6	Reversible Markov Chains	442
	11.A.7	Stationary Distributions and Reversibility for Markov Processes	444
	11.A.8	Convergence in Distribution	445
	11.A.9	Ergodicity	448
	Notes		449

12 Limiting Stationary Distributions and Stochastic Stability — 451

- 12.1 Definitions of Stochastic Stability — 454
  - 12.1.1 Small Noise Limits — 454
  - 12.1.2 Large Population Limits — 455
  - 12.1.3 Double Limits — 458
  - 12.1.4 Double Limits: A Counterexample — 460
- 12.2 Exponential Protocols and Potential Games — 463
  - 12.2.1 Direct Exponential Protocols: The Small Noise Limit — 464
  - 12.2.2 Direct Exponential Protocols: The Large Population Limit — 465
  - 12.2.3 Direct Exponential Protocols: Double Limits — 472
  - 12.2.4 Imitative Exponential Protocols with Committed Agents — 472
- 12.3 Noisy Best Response Protocols in Two-Strategy Games — 474
  - 12.3.1 Noisy Best Response Protocols and Their Cost Functions — 474
  - 12.3.2 The Small Noise Limit — 477
  - 12.3.3 The Large Population Limit — 479
  - 12.3.4 Double Limits — 480
  - 12.3.5 Stochastic Stability: Examples — 482
  - 12.3.6 Risk Dominance, Stochastic Dominance, and Stochastic Stability — 486
- 12.4 Imitative Protocols in Two-Strategy Games — 491
  - 12.4.1 Imitative Protocols with Mutations — 491
  - 12.4.2 Imitative Protocols with Committed Agents — 494
  - 12.4.3 Imitative Protocols, Mean Dynamics, and Stochastic Stability — 496
- 12.5 Small Noise Limits — 499
  - 12.5.1 Noisy Best Response Protocols and Cost Functions — 500
  - 12.5.2 Limiting Stationary Distributions via Trees — 502
  - 12.5.3 Two-Strategy Games and Risk Dominance — 504
  - 12.5.4 The Radius-Coradius Theorem — 510
  - 12.5.5 Half-Dominance — 512
- 12.6 Large Population Limits — 515
  - 12.6.1 Convergence to Recurrent States of the Mean Dynamic — 515
  - 12.6.2 Convergence to Stable Rest Points of the Mean Dynamic — 517
- 12.A Appendix: Trees, Escape Paths, and Stochastic Stability — 519
  - 12.A.1 The Markov Chain Tree Theorem — 520
  - 12.A.2 Limiting Stationary Distributions via Trees — 521

Contents

	12.A.3	Limiting Stationary Distributions via Trees on Recurrent Classes	524
	12.A.4	Radius-Coradius Theorems	526
	12.A.5	Lenient Transition Costs and Weak Stochastic Stability	529
12.B	Appendix: Stochastic Approximation Theory		531
	12.B.1	Convergence to the Birkhoff Center	532
	12.B.2	Sufficient Conditions for Convergence to Stable Rest Points	533
	Notes		537

References	541
Notation Index	565
Index	575

Series Foreword

The MIT Press series on Economic Learning and Social Evolution reflects the widespread renewal of interest in the dynamics of human interaction. This issue has provided a broad community of economists, psychologists, biologists, anthropologists, and others with a sense of common purpose so strong that traditional interdisciplinary boundaries have begun to melt away.

Some of the books in the series will be works of theory. Others will be philosophical or conceptual in scope. Some will have an experimental or empirical focus. Some will be collections of papers with a common theme and a linking commentary. Others will have an expository character. Yet others will be monographs in which new ideas meet the light of day for the first time. But all will have two unifying themes. The first is the rejection of the outmoded notion that what happens away from equilibrium can safely be ignored. The second is a recognition that it is no longer enough to speak in vague terms of bounded rationality and spontaneous order. As in all movements, the time comes to put the beef on the table—and the time for us is now.

Authors who share this ethos and would like to be part of the series are cordially invited to submit outlines of their proposed books for consideration. Within our frame of reference, we hope that a thousand flowers will bloom.

Ken Binmore

Preface

This book is my attempt to provide a systematic, rigorous, and unified presentation of evolutionary game theory.

Evolutionary game theory concerns the behavior of large populations of strategically interacting agents who occasionally reevaluate their choices in light of current payoff opportunities. (This is an economist's description; a biologist might refer to populations of interacting animals whose different genetic programs lead to varying levels of reproductive success.) To some observers, it might seem that the theory offers a collection of loosely related models, with deterministic models (e.g., the replicator dynamic) and stochastic models (e.g., stochastic stability theory) being nearly completely isolated from one another. This point of view is reinforced by the fact that basic techniques used in each case—deterministic dynamical systems and Markov processes—are traditionally viewed as belonging to different branches of mathematics, despite their obvious complementarity from an applied point of view. One might notice further that many researchers in evolutionary game theory work either on deterministic models or on stochastic models, but not on both.

This book, by contrast, presents evolutionary game theory as a coherent whole. Here models of aggregate behavior are derived from explicit microfoundations. By starting with descriptions of how individual agents update their strategies over time, one can derive both the deterministic and the stochastic parts of the theory within a single framework, with the two analyses arising by way of different assumptions about population sizes and the time horizon of interest. The idea that microfoundations can give rise to a unified presentation of evolutionary game theory has been articulated by a number of researchers over the past decade, but this book may be the first to offer this point of view to a broad audience.

Over the years, I have heard many economists express regret that gaps in their mathematical background prevented them from understanding evolutionary game theory in more than a superficial way. While I realize that you were all just being polite, it is still the case that the standard graduate training of economists and game theorists includes very little about ordinary differential equations and Markov processes. To address this gap, and to reduce costs of entry, I supplement the main text of this book with appendices that present the mathematical tools needed to work (or even to read deeply) in evolutionary game theory. These appendices, which account for about one quarter of the book, can be read independently of the main text and may be useful for anyone seeking a quick introduction to the methods of dynamic modeling.

A number of books providing overviews of evolutionary game theory appeared between 1988 and 1998, and there have been important surveys and monographs since that time. But it has been more than ten years since a picture of the field in full has been attempted. New ideas introduced during this interval have made it easier to view evolutionary game theory as a unified whole and to present classic results alongside the most recent developments.

What Is in This Book?

This book contains twelve chapters. The first is an introductory chapter, and the remaining eleven chapters are distributed among four parts:

Part I   Population Games (chapters 2 and 3)

Part II   Deterministic Evolutionary Dynamics (chapters 4–6)

Part III   Convergence and Nonconvergence of Deterministic Dynamics (chapters 7–9)

Part IV   Stochastic Evolutionary Models (chapters 10–12)

Figure 1 describes the logical flow of the chapters. The size of each chapter's box corresponds to the chapter's length, and the size of the box's shaded area to the length of the chapter's math appendices. A detailed overview of the contents of the book is provided in chapter 1, but a brief one is given here.

Part I introduces population games, which serve as a simple, general model for studying strategic interactions among large numbers of agents. Basic definitions and examples are presented in chapter 2. Chapter 3 studies three classes of especially well-behaved games: potential games, stable games, and supermodular games.

Part II introduces deterministic evolutionary dynamics. Basic definitions and examples are presented in chapter 4. The notion of a revision protocol, which underlies the microfoundations uniting all subsequent analyses, first appears here. Chapters 5 and 6 introduce a variety of families of deterministic dynamics, the revision protocols that generate them, and their basic properties.

Preface

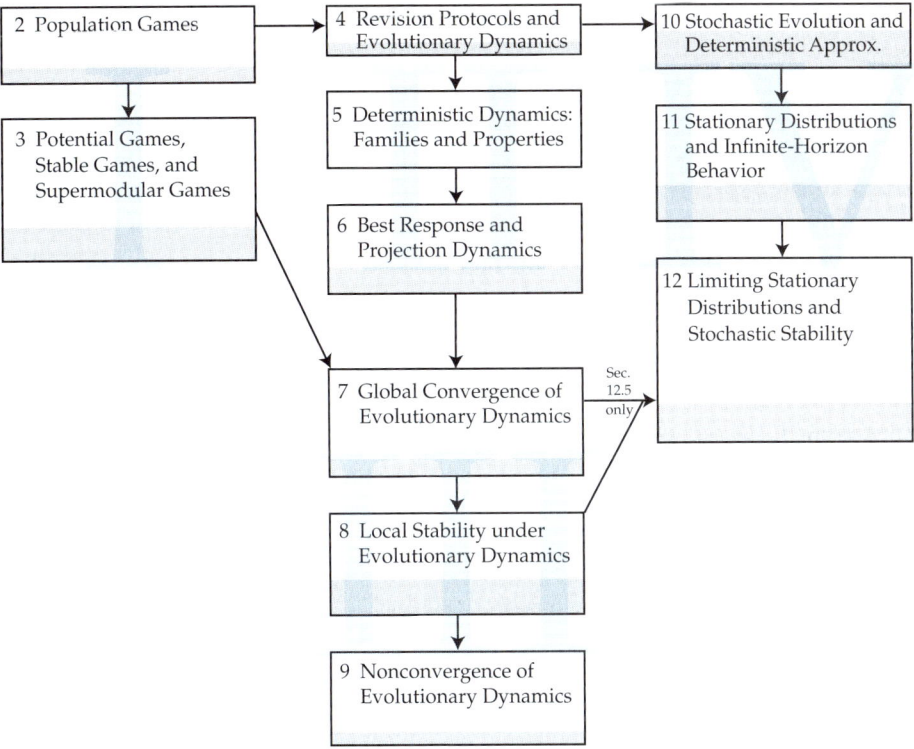

Figure 1

Part III studies convergence and nonconvergence under deterministic evolutionary dynamics. Chapter 7 establishes global convergence results, mainly for combinations of the classes of games from chapter 2 and the families of dynamics from chapters 5 and 6. Chapter 8 considers local stability of rest points and connects local stability with the classic notion of an evolutionarily stable state (ESS). Chapter 9 provides examples of cycling and chaotic behavior and considers the implications of these examples for predicting behavior in games.

Part IV considers models of stochastic evolution. Chapter 10 describes the theory of finite-horizon deterministic approximation, providing a rigorous foundation for the deterministic dynamics studied in parts II and III. Chapters 11 and 12 discuss infinite-horizon behavior of stochastic evolutionary processes, with analyses of stationary distributions, limiting stationary distributions, and stochastic stability.

It is possible to cover all the chapters of the book in a single semester, provided that not every topic is covered in detail, although this path is not for the faint of heart. One alternative is a course that focuses on deterministic dynamics, with emphasis on chapters 2–9. Another is a course focusing on stochastic evolution, which would start with chapters 2, 4, and 10–12, leaving time to return to some topics that initially were passed over.

The reader will discover that many of the analyses and discussions in this book have a decidedly geometric flavor. Each chapter contains a large number of figures, which I believe are necessary to develop a real feeling for many of the topics covered.

The majority of the phase diagrams for deterministic evolutionary dynamics were created using the Dynamo software suite (Sandholm, Dokumacı, and Franchetti 2007). This open source software, which runs within Mathematica, automates the process of drawing phase diagrams for evolutionary dynamics. It is available for download at <http://www.ssc.wisc.edu/~whs/dynamo>. The software is very helpful for running quick numerical experiments, and readers are encouraged to try it out while working through the text and to use it to create figures for their own research.

What Is Not in This Book?

While this book provides a unified treatment of a large swath of evolutionary game theory, there are many important topics that I have omitted entirely. Among them are

- evolution in extensive form games (deterministic models, stochastic models);
- evolution in local interaction games (on lattices, on general graphs);
- evolution in games with continuous strategy sets;
- stochastic evolution via diffusion processes.

Each of these important topics requires new ideas and techniques, and each could easily fill one or more additional chapters. I left them out only to leave myself some hope of finishing the book in finite time.

An area of research with very close connections to evolutionary game theory is heuristic learning. Like models in evolutionary game theory, models of heuristic learning, starting with the classic model of fictitious play, consider the repeated play of a game by players who use simple rules to decide how to act. But these models consider small groups of players—typically, one for each role in a normal form game—and the rules the players employ condition on statistics summarizing the time average of past play rather than on the current play of a large population. The two approaches to disequilibrium game dynamics overlap, with a number of results having formulations in both contexts, but this book maintains the evolutionary point of view.

A basic test of the worth of any theory is its ability to offer insights into applications. Except for certain fundamental examples (for instance, on flows and routing in transportation networks), this book says little about applied topics. Nevertheless, a wide range of applications of evolutionary game theory have been developed in economic and other social science contexts, including

- markets,
- bargaining and hold-up problems,
- signaling and cheap talk,
- public good provision,
- implementation and decentralized control,
- residential segregation,
- preference evolution and cultural evolution.

This list does not mention applications in biology, where evolutionary game theory originated, or more recent applications in engineering, control theory, and computer science. References to applications in all these areas and to the theoretical topics listed earlier can be found in the chapter 1 notes.

What About the Math?

This book is written at a level appropriate for second-year economics graduate students and senior undergraduate mathematics majors. All but the most basic mathematical tools are reviewed in the appendices, which treat the following topics:

Calculus: 3.A

Convex analysis: 2.A, 3.B, 6.B, 6.C

Matrix analysis: 8.A

Dynamical systems: 4.A, 6.A, 7.A, 7.B, 7.C, 8.B, 8.C, 9.A, 9.B

Probability theory and stochastic processes: 10.A, 10.B, 10.C, 11.A, 12.A, 12.B

Appendix 3.A provides a review of the necessary tools from multivariate calculus, but I expect most readers to have the background provided by an undergraduate real analysis sequence. Since most of the action takes place on the simplex or on products of simplices, certain basic tools from convex analysis turn out to be quite useful and are explained as needed. The review of matrix analysis contains what is necessary to understand thoroughly how to linearize a differential equation and thus summarizes a number of results that might be left out of an undergraduate linear algebra course.

The treatments of dynamical systems and stochastic processes assume no prior knowledge in these areas. In both cases the appendices start with basic material and proceed to topics that typically would not be covered until graduate-level courses. A few of the topics treated—for instance, differential inclusions (appendix 6.A), attractors and continuation (appendix 9.B), stochastic stability analysis (appendix 12.A), and stochastic approximation theory (appendix 12.B)—are not treated in typical courses at any level but are very important here.

The appendices can be read independently of the main text. Readers with limited exposure to, say, ordinary differential equations might read the relevant appendices before attempting the chapter texts; others might consult the appendices as necessary. In general, the appendices introduce definitions and notation, state results, and provide intuitions and examples. Results are only proved when the proof aids understanding or when I could not find a proof in the literature.

While I think these overviews are useful, they are pale substitutes for full treatments of their subject matter. For readers looking for mathematics references, I offer a few recommendations here. Lang (1997) provides a clear treatment of calculus and real analysis at about the level of the present book. Hiriart-Urruty and Lemaréchal (2001) provide an excellent reference on convex analysis, and Horn and Johnson (1985) do the same for matrix analysis. Hirsch and Smale (1974) offer a solid undergraduate-level course on dynamical systems, and Robinson (1995) provides a fine graduate-level treatment. My favorite undergraduate-level introduction to Markov chains and processes is the concise account of Norris (1997). Many additional references on a variety of specialized topics are provided in the notes to the chapters where they become relevant.

Thanks

The beginning of my collaboration with Josef Hofbauer in the spring of 2000 was the decisive moment of my research career, and I will always be in his debt.

I had the idea to write this book during a series of lectures that Josef and I gave at the University of Tokyo in June 2002. Portions of the book were written in the collegial atmosphere of the Stockholm School of Economics during May 2005 and May 2008. I thank both institutions for their warm hospitality. I also express my gratitude to the National Science Foundation for supporting my research since 2001.

I was extremely fortunate to have Larry Samuelson as a colleague at Wisconsin from 1998 through 2007; his influence pervades my work. Jörgen Weibull first invited me to speak in Stockholm in the fall of 2000, and he has been a constant source of encouragement and inspiration ever since.

Emin Dokumacı was the original programmer of the Dynamo project, and he created many of the figures in this book; our collaboration is as close as I am likely to come to producing visual art. Joint work with Michel Benaïm, Jeff Ely, and Ratul Lahkar shaped my thinking on various topics presented here. Ignacio Monzón and Danqing Hu gamely undertook the laborious task of file conversion in 2006, when I became the last person on the planet to switch from Microsoft Word to LaTeX. Katsuhiko Aiba, Fernando Louge, Ignacio Monzón, and Ryoji Sawa each read large portions of the manuscript, and their suggestions and corrections have made for a clearer and cleaner presentation.

Many other people provided valuable feedback on this book and on related research projects. I thank Ken Binmore, Ross Cressman, Eddie Dekel, Drew Fudenberg, Ed Hopkins, Bart Lipman, Aki Matsui, Nolan Miller, Daisuke Oyama, Jeroen Swinkels, Peyton Young, and students in many Economics 806 classes at the University of Wisconsin and in a minicourse at the Stockholm School of Economics for stimulating conversations and helpful comments. Many anonymous reviewers provided useful suggestions for improvements, and my editors at MIT Press, John Covell, Deborah Cantor-Adams, and Elizabeth Murry, were patient guides during the seemingly endless process of creating this book.

I dedicate this book to my wife, Leah, and my daughter, Lily. In the words of Lina Lamont, you bring a little joy into my humdrum life, and it makes me feel as though my hard work ain't been in vain for nothin'.

1 Introduction

This book describes an approach to modeling recurring strategic interactions in large populations of small anonymous agents. The approach is built upon two basic elements. The first, called a *population game*, describes the strategic interaction that is to occur repeatedly. The second, called a *revision protocol*, specifies the myopic procedure that agents employ to decide when and how to choose new strategies. Starting with a population game and a revision protocol, one can derive dynamic processes, both deterministic and stochastic, that describe how the agents' aggregate behavior changes over time. These processes are known as *evolutionary game dynamics*.

This introductory chapter begins the work of adding substance to this austere account of evolutionary game theory, providing motivations for and overviews of the analyses to come. For the most part, the chapter is written with an eye toward modeling in economics and other social sciences, although it also discusses the biological origins of the field. But these perspectives should not be viewed as constraints, as the methods presented in this book have ready applications in other disciplines that require models of interacting populations of humans, animals, or machines.

Section 1.1 introduces the notion of a population game by presenting applications, offering informal definitions, and discussing connections with normal form games. It then previews the treatment of population games in chapters 2 and 3. Section 1.2 describes dynamic models of behavior in recurrent play of population games and contrasts this dynamic approach with the equilibrium approach traditionally used in game theory. This section also offers an overview of the presentation of evolutionary dynamics in chapters 4–12. Section 1.3 concludes with some remarks on motivations for and interpretations of evolutionary game theory. References relevant to the discussions in the preface and this chapter can be found in the notes at the end of the chapter.

1.1 Population Games

[O]nly after the theory for moderate numbers of participants has been satisfactorily developed will it be possible to decide whether extremely great numbers of participants simplify the situation.... We share the hope... that such simplifications will indeed occur.
—von Neumann and Morgenstern (1944, 14)

We shall now take up the "mass-action" interpretation of equilibrium points.... It is unnecessary to assume that the participants have full knowledge of the total structure of the game, or the ability and inclination to go through any complex reasoning processes. But the participants are supposed to accumulate empirical information on the relative advantages of the various pure strategies at their disposal.

To be more detailed, we assume that there is a population (in the sense of statistics) of participants for each position of the game. Let us also assume that the "average playing" of the game involves n participants selected at random from the n populations, and that there is a stable average frequency with which each pure strategy is employed by the "average member" of the appropriate population.
—Nash (1950b, 21)

There are many situations, however, in which an individual is, in effect, competing not against an individual opponent but against the population as a whole, or some section of it. Such cases can loosely be described as "playing the field"... [S]uch contests against the field are probably more widespread and important than pairwise contests.
—Maynard Smith (1982, 23)

1.1.1 Modeling Interactions in Large Populations

One can imagine many economic, social, and technological environments in which large collections of small agents make strategically interdependent decisions:

· *Network congestion*   Drivers commute over a highway network. The delay each driver experiences depends not only on the selected route but also on the congestion created by other agents along this route.

· *Public goods and externalities*   A local government maintains a collection of public recreation facilities. The benefit that a family obtains from using a facility depends on the quality of the facility and the number of other families that use it.

· *Industrial organization*   Software developers choose whether to copyright their products or make them freely available under a public license; they can also choose to work within an existing open source framework. The latter options entail a loss of control but allow products to improve through the accumulation of uncoordinated individual efforts.

· *The emergence of conventions, norms, and institutions*   Firms in a developing economy choose among various business practices: for instance, accept credit or require cash, fight or acquiesce to corrupt officials, reward merit or engage in nepotism. Through historical precedent and individual decisions, conventions about business conduct are formed. Whether or not these conventions are efficient, they enable firms to form accurate expectations about how trading partners will act.

· *Cultural integration and assimilation*   The behavior of immigrants settling in a new country is influenced by traditions imported from their home countries, and, to the extent that interactions with the incumbent population require coordination, by the practices of these incumbents as well. At the same time, the choices of the incumbents are influenced by the need to coordinate with the immigrants. The interplay of these forces determines how behavior in the society as a whole evolves.

· *Language and communication*   Agents without a common language interact repeatedly, attempting to communicate their intentions to the others on each occasion. Whether these attempts are ultimately understood, and whether they enable the agents to coordinate on mutually beneficial behavior, depends on meanings determined by the aggregate communication pattern.

· *Task allocation and decentralized control*   The employees of a large firm provide services to customers in a number of distinct locations. To take advantage of the ground-level information possessed by the employees, the firm has them allocate themselves among the customers requiring service, providing incentives to ensure that the employees' choices further the firm's objectives.

· *Markets and bargaining*   Large numbers of buyers and sellers participate in a centralized exchange. Each individual specifies acceptable terms of trade in the hopes of obtaining the greatest benefit from his initial endowment.

These environments are quite varied, but they have certain basic features in common. First, each environment contains a large number of agents capable of making decisions independently. Second, each agent is small, in that his choices have only a minor impact on other agents' outcomes. Third, agents are anonymous: an agent's outcome from the interaction depends on his own strategy and the distribution of others' strategies; further individuation of the opponents is not required.

Simultaneous interactions exhibiting these three properties can be modeled using *population games*. The participants in a population game form a *society* consisting of one or more *populations* of agents. Agents in a given population are assumed to be identical: an agent's population determines his role in the game, the strategies available to him, and his preferences. These preferences are described by a payoff function that conditions on the agent's own strategy and the distribution of strategies in each population. The populations may have either finite numbers of agents or continua of agents, whichever is more convenient. When populations are continuous, the payoffs to each strategy are assumed to depend on the society's aggregate behavior in a continuous fashion, reflecting the idea that very small changes in aggregate behavior do not lead to large changes in the consequences of playing any given strategy.

Aggregate behavior in a population game is described by a *social state*, which specifies the empirical distribution of strategy choices in each population. For simplicity, we assume throughout this book that there are a finite number of populations and that members of each population choose from a finite strategy set. Doing so ensures that the social state is finite-dimensional, expressible as a vector with a finite number of components; if populations are continuous, the set of social states is a polytope.

Except when they are revising (see section 1.2.2), agents in population games are assumed to play pure strategies. One of the main reasons for introducing randomized strategies is moot here: when the populations are continuous, and payoffs are continuous in the social state, pure strategy Nash equilibria always exist. This guarantee may be one of the "simplifications" that von Neumann and Morgenstern had in mind when they looked ahead to the study of games with large numbers of players. But this fact is not as essential to the analysis here as it is to traditional approaches to analyzing games. Whereas traditional approaches are grounded on the assumption of equilibrium play, this book emphasizes the process through which agents adjust their behavior in response to their current strategic environment.

From this point of view, a more important simplification provided by the population games framework is the description of behavior using social states, that is, distributions of agents' choices. To understand the advantages this approach brings, contrast it with the standard framework for modeling simultaneous-move interactions: *normal form games*. To define a normal form game, one must specify a (finite or infinite) set of players, and to describe behavior in such a game, one must stipulate each player's strategy choice. If there are many players, these tasks can be laborious.

One can view a population game as a normal form game that satisfies certain restrictions on the diversity and anonymity of the players. But it is nevertheless preferable to work directly with population games, and so to avoid the extra work involved in individuating the players. Moreover, describing behavior using empirical strategy distributions shifts attention from questions like "Who chose strategy i?" to ones like "How many chose strategy i?" and "What happens to the payoff of strategy j players if some agents switch to strategy i?" This is just where the focus should be: the answers to the last question determine the incentive structure of a population game (see chapter 3).

Introduction

Much research in evolutionary game theory has focused on population games of a particularly simple sort: those generated when populations of agents are matched to play a normal form game. Indeed, Nash informally introduced population games of this sort in 1949 in proposing the "mass action" interpretation of his equilibrium concept, a development that seems to have gone unnoticed for the next 45 years (see the chapter notes). This population-matching interpretation of normal form games has a clear appeal, and normal form games are used as a ready source of simple examples throughout the book.

At the same time, if the main interest is in large population interactions rather than in normal form games, then focusing only on matching in normal form games is quite restrictive. Maynard Smith observed that matching is a rather special sort of interaction in large populations. Instead, interactions in which each agent's payoffs are determined directly from all agents' behavior—what Maynard Smith terms "playing the field"—seem to be the rule rather than the exception. Only a few of the applications listed earlier are most naturally modeled using matching; some, like congestion in highway networks, require payoffs to depend nonlinearly on the population state and so are mathematically inconsistent with a random matching approach. One might expect that moving from linear to nonlinear payoffs would lead to intractable models, but it does not. The dynamics studied here are nonlinear even when payoffs in the underlying game are not, so allowing nonlinear payoffs does not lead to a qualitative increase in the complexity of the analysis.

1.1.2 Definitions and Classes of Population Games

The formal introduction to population games begins in chapter 2, which offers definitions of *population states*, *payoff functions*, and other terms. To reduce the degree of abstraction and illustrate the range of possible applications, the chapter presents basic examples of population games; these include *congestion games*, which provide a general but tractable model of network congestion and of related sorts of multilateral externalities. Finally, by showing how low-dimensional population games can be represented graphically, chapter 2 ushers in the geometric methods of analysis that are emphasized throughout this book.

From a purely formal point of view, a population game is defined by an arbitrary collection of continuous, real-valued functions on an appropriate domain. While some basic results, including existence of Nash equilibrium, can be proved at this level of generality, obtaining more specific conclusions requires focusing on classes of games defined by certain structural properties. Chapter 3 introduces three important classes of population games: *potential games*, *stable games*, and *supermodular games*. Each of these classes of games includes a number of important examples, and each is characterized by restrictions on the nature of the externalities that users of each strategy impose on one another. The structure dictated by these restrictions makes analyses of games in these classes relatively simple. For instance, in games from all three classes, one can prove existence of Nash equilibrium without recourse to fixed point theorems. But more important here is the impact of this structure on disequilibrium behavior: in all three classes of games, broad families of evolutionary dynamics are assured of converging to Nash equilibrium from arbitrary initial conditions (see chapter 7).

1.2 Evolutionary Dynamics

The state of equilibrium... is therefore *stable*; i.e., if either of the producers, misled as to his true interest, leaves it temporarily, he will be brought back to it by a series of reactions, constantly declining in amplitude, and of which the dotted lines of the figure give a representation by their arrangement in steps.
—Cournot (1838)

We repeat most emphatically that our theory is thoroughly static. A dynamic theory would unquestionably be more complete and preferable.
—von Neumann and Morgenstern (1944, 44–45)

An equilibrium would be just an extreme state of rare occurrence if it were not stable—that is, if there were no forces which tended to restore equilibrium as soon as small deviations from it occurred.
   Besides this stability "in the small", one may consider stability "in the large"—that is, the ability of the system to reach an equilibrium from any initial position.
—Beckmann, McGuire, and Winsten (1956, 70)

An obvious weakness of the game-theoretic approach to evolution is that it places great emphasis on equilibrium states, whereas evolution is a process of continuous, or at least periodic, change. It is, of course, mathematically easier to analyse equilibria than trajectories of change. There are, however, two situations in which game theory models force us to think about change as well as constancy. The first is that a game may not have an ESS, and hence the population cycles indefinitely....
   The second situation... is when, as is often the case, a game has more than one ESS. Then, in order to account for the present state of the population, one has to allow for initial conditions—that is, for the state of the ancestral population.
—Maynard Smith (1982, 8)

After modeling a strategic interaction using a population game, one would like to use the game as the basis for predicting how agents in the interaction will behave. Traditionally, most predictions in game theory have been based on equilibrium analysis: one introduces some notion of equilibrium play and then finds all behaviors in the game that agree with the equilibrium notion. The equilibrium approach

Introduction

is standard practice in applications of game theory, but as the preceding quotations emphasize, this approach is incomplete, and should be complemented by an analysis of dynamics. Further, Maynard Smith points out that local stability analysis, which checks whether equilibrium play will be restored after small disturbances in behavior, is only a first step, as it begs the question of how equilibrium is established in the first place. These concerns are most pronounced in settings with large numbers of players, where the interplayer coordination of beliefs and actions associated with equilibrium seems most difficult to achieve.

Most of this book studies dynamic models of behavior in large population games, and so is an attempt to provide some responses to the foregoing concerns.

1.2.1 Knowledge, Rationality, and Large Games

The fundamental solution concept of noncooperative game theory is *Nash equilibrium*, the requirement that each agent choose a strategy that is optimal given the choices of the others. There are many other solution concepts for games, but most of them are refinements of Nash's definition, and are used to reduce the set of predictions in games with multiple Nash equilibria.

Despite the central role of the Nash equilibrium concept, the traditional, rationalistic justification for applying this concept is not especially convincing. It is based on three assumptions about the players in the game. First, each player is assumed to be *rational*, acting to maximize his payoffs given what he knows. Second, players have *knowledge of the game* they are playing: they know what strategies are available and what payoffs result from every strategy profile. Third, the players have *equilibrium knowledge*: they are able to anticipate correctly what their opponents will do. If all players expect a certain strategy profile to be played, and if each player is rational and understands the payoff consequences of switching strategies, then each player is content to play his part in the strategy profile if and only if that profile is a Nash equilibrium.

Of these three assumptions, the equilibrium knowledge assumption is the hardest to accept. Certainly, shared expectations about play can be put into place by a disinterested moderator who guides the players to a particular strategy profile. But without such guidance, it is hard to explain how players can introspectively anticipate how others will act, particularly in games with large numbers of participants.

In fact, when one considers games with many players or strategies, even apparently innocuous conditions for equilibrium play may be called into question. Under the traditional interpretation of equilibrium play in a traffic network, a driver choosing a route to work has a complete mental account of all of the routes she could take and is able to anticipate the delay that would arise on each route for any possible profile of choices by fellow drivers. Evidently, the assumption of knowledge of the game, while seemingly innocent, may actually be quite bold when the game is large.

This discussion suggests that in large games, even the force of seemingly weak solution concepts, ones that do not require equilibrium knowledge, should not be taken for granted. For instance, a basic tenet of traditional game-theoretic analysis holds that a strictly dominated strategy—a strategy that performs worse than some single alternative strategy regardless of how opponents behave—should not be chosen. This requirement is uncontroversial when players have full knowledge of the game. But if players are unable or unwilling to keep the entire game in mind, they may well not notice that one strategy is dominated by another. One might expect that an accumulation of experience would ensure that players eventually avoid dominated strategies, but this is not necessarily so. Section 9.4 presents a set of mild conditions on players' updating rules that are enough to ensure that strictly dominated strategies survive in perpetuity in some games.

Obtaining a convincing rationalistic justification for equilibrium play in games seems an impossible task. But in settings where the same game is played many times, the possibilities become brighter, as one can replace introspection with repetition as the basis for coordination of behavior. In large population settings, repetition may be enough to coordinate behavior even when agents' information and abilities are quite limited. But while dynamic approaches can support and even refine traditional game-theoretic predictions, they also can lead to predictions of cyclical or more complex nonstationary behavior, possibilities that are ignored by traditional analyses.

1.2.2 Foundations for Evolutionary Dynamics

One can take a variety of approaches to studying disequilibrium dynamics in games, depending on the number of players involved, the information the players are expected to possess, and the importance of the interaction to the players. Evolutionary game theory, the approach studied in this book, considers the dynamics of behavior in large, strategically interacting populations. This approach posits that agents only occasionally switch strategies, and then use simple myopic rules to decide how to act. These assumptions are certainly not appropriate for every application, but they seem natural when the interaction in question is just one among many the agent faces, so that the sporadic application of a rule of thumb is a reasonable way for the agent to proceed.

While it is possible to proceed directly with a description of aggregate behavior dynamics, it is preferable to begin by specifying when and how individual agents make decisions. We accomplish this using a modeling device called a *revision protocol*. A revision protocol is a function that takes the strategies' payoffs and utilization levels as inputs; it returns as outputs the overall rate of switching

Introduction

strategies and the probabilities with which each alternative strategy will be chosen.

In defining a revision protocol, one implicitly specifies the informational burden that the agents must bear. Chapters 4–6 show that revision protocols come in many different varieties, from those that embody exact myopic optimization to others that require each agent to know nothing more than his own current payoff. In all cases, though, the protocol only relies on information about current strategic conditions; historical information and counterfactual information about strategies' performances under other conditions are not considered.

Also implicit in the definition of a revision protocol is the method to be used to identify alternative strategies. One can place protocols into two broad categories according to this criterion. Under *imitative protocols*, an agent obtains a candidate strategy by observing the strategy of a randomly chosen member of his population. Under *direct protocols*, agents are assumed to choose candidate strategies directly; a strategy's popularity does not directly influence the probability with which it is considered. (Agents may also meander among different protocols as time passes, in which case they are said to employ a *hybrid protocol*.) After obtaining a candidate strategy, an agent can evaluate its current payoff by briefly experimenting with it. If the strategy is currently in use, its current payoff can also be determined by observing the outcomes of an opponent who employs it.

Aggregate behavior dynamics generated by imitative protocols are very similar to those studied in mathematical biology (see chapter 5). Thus, the *replicator dynamic*, introduced in the mathematical biology literature to model natural selection, also describes the aggregate behavior of agents who use certain imitative protocols. In contrast, dynamics based on direct selection—for instance, the *best response dynamic*, which is based on optimal myopic choices—behave rather differently than those studied in biology. Direct selection allows unused strategies to be introduced to the population, which is impossible under pure imitation (or under biological reproduction without mutations). For its part, imitation generates dynamics with relatively simple functional forms and behavior. But the simple forms and properties of imitative dynamics are rather special. Indeed, when agents use hybrid protocols, their aggregate behavior agrees in qualitative terms with what one would see under direct selection of alternative strategies.

1.2.3 Deterministic Evolutionary Dynamics

Suppose that one or more large populations of agents recurrently play a population game, with each agent occasionally updating his choice of strategies using a fixed revision protocol. Since there are many agents, and since the stochastic elements of the agents' updating procedures are idiosyncratic, one expects these stochastic influences to be averaged away, leaving aggregate behavior to evolve in an essentially deterministic fashion. Chapter 4 explains how such a deterministic evolutionary process can be described by an ordinary differential equation, and how this equation can be derived from the population game and revision protocol. A formal justification for focusing on this differential equation, which we call the *mean dynamic,* is deferred until chapter 10 (see section 1.2.4).

The mean dynamic specifies the rate of change in the use of each strategy i. It is the difference of two terms: an inflow term, which captures agents' switches from other strategies to strategy i, and an outflow term, which captures agents' switches from strategy i to other strategies. Of course, the exact specification of the dynamic depends on the primitives of the model, namely, the protocol the agents employ and the game they play.

For a slightly different point of view, note that any fixed revision protocol defines a map that takes population games as inputs and returns specific instances of mean dynamics as outputs. We call this map from population games to ordinary differential equations an *evolutionary dynamic.*

Chapters 5 and 6 introduce a variety of families of evolutionary dynamics and investigate their properties. Each family of dynamics is generated from a set of revision protocols sharing certain qualitative features, for instance, being based on imitation or on myopic optimization. The main results in chapters 5 and 6 establish properties of evolutionary dynamics that hold regardless of the population game at hand.

One of the basic issues considered in these chapters is the relation between the rest points of the dynamics and the payoff structure of the underlying game. Chapter 5 shows that the rest points of imitative dynamics include all Nash equilibria of the game being played. Further analyses reveal that under many direct and hybrid dynamics, the sets of rest points and Nash equilibria are identical. This latter property, *Nash stationarity,* provides a first link between the population dynamics and traditional equilibrium analyses. A second issue addressed is the connection between out-of-equilibrium dynamics and incentives in the underlying game. Many of the dynamics studied here satisfy a monotonicity property called *positive correlation,* which requires strategies' growth rates to be positively correlated with their payoffs. This property and its relatives are basic ingredients in the subsequent analyses of dynamic stability.

Properties like Nash stationarity only provide a weak justification for the prediction of Nash equilibrium play. To obtain a more convincing defense of this prediction, one must address the questions of stability raised at the start of this section.

Chapter 8 considers local stability of equilibrium: whether equilibrium will be reached if play begins at a nearby social state. It is easy to see that some Nash equilibria are unlikely to be locally stable. For instance, if play begins near the mixed

Introduction

equilibrium of a coordination game, then myopic adjustment will lead the population away from this equilibrium. Additional restrictions beyond Nash's condition are thus needed to obtain general stability results. A main finding in chapter 8 is that the notion of an *evolutionarily stable state* (*ESS*), introduced by Maynard Smith and Price for a model of evolution in populations of mixed strategists, provides a general sufficient condition for local stability under the pure strategist dynamics studied here.

Local stability results only offer a partial justification of equilibrium predictions. To be convinced that equilibrium will be reached, one must look instead for global convergence results, which establish that equilibrium is attained from any initial state. Chapter 7 offers such results, proving that in certain classes of games—namely, the classes of potential games, stable games, and supermodular games (see chapter 3)—there are classes of dynamics that converge to equilibrium from all or almost all initial conditions.

These stability results provide strong support for the Nash prediction in some settings, but they say little about behavior in games outside of the classes the results cover. One might hope that these results would be representative of behavior in most games, but this seems not to be so. Chapter 9 presents a variety of examples in which deterministic dynamics enter cycles far from Nash equilibrium and others in which the dynamics display chaotic behavior. Thus, if one takes the model of myopic adjustment dynamics seriously, one must sometimes accept these more complicated limit behaviors as more credible predictions than equilibrium play. Moreover, as suggested earlier, the possibility of nonconvergent behavior has some counterintuitive consequences; under typical evolutionary dynamics, one can always find simple games in which strictly dominated strategies survive (see section 9.4).

1.2.4 Orders of Limits for Stochastic Evolutionary Models

The deterministic dynamics studied in chapters 4–9 form the largest portion of the literature on evolutionary game dynamics. But another major branch of the literature focuses on the infinite-horizon behavior of stochastic evolutionary dynamics; its central aim is to obtain unique predictions of play in games with multiple equilibria. Chapter 10 brings together these two literatures by showing how deterministic and stochastic evolutionary game dynamics can be derived from a single foundation.

To accomplish this, we consider population games played by large but finite populations of agents. Together, a finite-population game and a revision protocol define a stochastic evolutionary process—in particular, a Markov process—on the now finite set of population states. Which methods are most useful for studying this process depends on the parameter values—the population size N and the time horizon T—that are relevant to the application at hand.

This point is made most clearly by taking limits. To begin, suppose one fixes the time horizon T and takes the population size N to infinity. The main result in chapter 10 shows that once N is large enough, the stochastic evolutionary process is very likely to behave in a nearly deterministic way, mirroring a solution trajectory of the relevant mean dynamic through time T. For intuition, observe that the stochastic aspects of the evolutionary process—the random arrivals of revision opportunities and the randomizations among candidate strategies during these opportunities—are idiosyncratic. When the population size becomes very large, the idiosyncratic noise is averaged away. Thus, the behavior of the process is driven by the expected changes in the state, which are precisely what the mean dynamic captures.

Alternatively, suppose one fixes the population size N and takes the time horizon T to infinity. In this case one is studying the infinite-horizon behavior of a finite-state Markov process. If this process is irreducible—that is, if all states are mutually accessible, as is true under any revision protocol that always places positive probability on each alternative strategy—then results from probability theory imply that every social state will be visited infinitely often, and that the proportion of time spent in each state over the infinite horizon does not depend on the initial state. This invariance property opens the door to obtaining unique predictions of play.

1.2.5 Stationary Distributions and Stochastic Stability

The proportion of time that an irreducible Markov process spends in each state is described by the process's *stationary distribution*. By computing this distribution, one can obtain an exact description of the infinite-horizon behavior of the evolutionary process. Chapter 11 presents some basic results on stationary distributions of stochastic evolutionary models and studies in detail those cases—namely, the models that generate *reversible* Markov processes—in which the stationary distribution can be computed exactly.

These analyses provide a first illustration of a fundamental idea. Even if the underlying game has multiple equilibria, it is nevertheless the case that in the infinite horizon, a stochastic evolutionary dynamic may spend the vast majority of periods in the vicinity of a single state. Still, the amount of time necessary for this analysis to become relevant can be exceedingly long, limiting the range of possible applications.

Once one moves beyond reversible cases, obtaining an exact expression for the stationary distribution is typically impossible. One way of circumventing this difficulty is to take certain parameters of the evolutionary process to their limiting values. If one takes the noise level that parameterizes the agents' revision protocol to zero, or the population size to infinity, one can sometimes describe the limiting stationary distribution even though the stationary distributions for fixed parameter values cannot be computed explicitly. There are many interesting cases in which the limiting stationary distribution places all of its mass on a single state, providing an especially tidy prediction of infinite-horizon play.

States that retain mass in the limiting stationary distribution are said to be *stochastically stable*. Chapter 12 offers a complete presentation of stochastic stability theory. It describes the main analytical techniques used to determine the stochastically stable states and presents key selection results. It also establishes formal connections between the states that are stochastically stable in the large population limit and the recurrent states of the relevant mean dynamic, providing another link between stochastic stability analysis and the deterministic dynamics studied in earlier chapters.

1.3 Remarks on History, Motivation, and Interpretation

Evolutionary game theory dates from the early 1970s, when John Maynard Smith introduced the ESS concept as a way of understanding ritualized animal conflict. In pursuing this line of research, Maynard Smith and other biologists borrowed the standard game-theoretic definitions used by mathematicians and economists but reinterpreted these definitions to suit their own purposes. In a biological model, a strategy is not something that an animal chooses, but a behavior that an animal is hardwired to perform by virtue of its genetic endowment. Similarly, payoffs are not numerical representations of preference relations, but instead represent "Darwinian fitnesses": they describe how the use of the strategy improves an animal's prospects for survival and reproduction. Thus, the development of a biological approach to game theory was marked not only by the invention of new solution concepts and methods of analysis, but also by a recasting of existing definitions.

In the late 1980s, economists surmised that this biological paradigm could be used to address problems with the foundations of traditional game theory. During the heyday of the equilibrium refinements literature, game theorists introduced solution concepts that seemed to impose ever larger demands on the reasoning abilities of the players whose behavior they purported to describe. This development raised the criticism that the solution concepts could only describe the behavior of hyperrational players. If, though, it could be shown that the behavior of populations of preprogrammed creatures could be described by means of these same solution concepts, then this would seem to provide a way of dispelling the hyperrationality critique.

In view of this motivation, it is not surprising that many early efforts by economists in evolutionary game theory adopted the biological paradigm wholesale, with populations of agents hardwired to choose certain strategies, and payoffs interpreted as Darwinian fitnesses. These analyses often found that behavior in these populations, as described by ESS and other biological solution concepts, agreed in a formal sense with the most demanding of the equilibrium refinements introduced by economists.

While these links between the biological and economic approaches to game theory might provide some sense of reassurance, it is important to be mindful of the limitations of this line of reasoning. In many economic applications of game theory, the game in question is played by, say, two or three players. Nash equilibrium and its refinements offer predictions about the mixed strategies these players will employ. For their part, the evolutionary models introduced by biologists concern interactions among large populations of animals, and their solution concepts describe the effects of natural selection on population shares of different genetic types. The fact that economists' predictions about rational agents' choices of mixed strategies formally agree with biologists' predictions about population shares under natural selection is certainly intriguing. But there is no obvious logic by which this agreement enables either analysis to justify the other.

Economists working on population dynamics soon realized that to obtain a modeling tool useful for typical social science environments, the Darwinian assumptions and interpretations of evolutionary game theory would need to be replaced with ones reflecting human decision making. This new vision of evolutionary game theory brought back the original interpretation of the game itself: strategies returned to being objects of choice, and payoffs resumed being descriptions of individual preferences. But other parts of the biologists' approach—in particular, the very idea of population dynamics, with changes in strategies' population shares driven by differences in current payoffs—were retained. Of course, some reinterpretation was necessary here, as the evolution of population shares would no longer be driven by relative rates of reproduction but by conscious decisions to switch from one strategy to another. More intriguing agreements were discovered between the biological and economic approaches. For instance, Taylor and Jonker introduced the replicator dynamic in 1978 to provide a dynamic foundation for Maynard Smith's static approach to natural selection. But in the 1990s economists found that this dynamic could also be derived from models of imitation in populations of economic agents (see section 5.4).

This history has created some understandable confusion about the meaning of the term *evolutionary game theory*. From the origins of the field through the earliest contributions of economists, this phrase referred exclusively to game-theoretic models of natural selection. But since the mid-1990s it has also encompassed models of myopic behavior in games played by large populations of active decision makers. In this interpretation, which predominates in this book, the word *evolution* should not be understood as a direct reference to Darwinian survival of the fittest, but should be taken in its broader sense, referring to a process of gradual change.

As the interpretation of evolutionary game theory has changed, so too has its role within economic modeling. As noted earlier, the initial flush of interest in evolutionary game theory in the economics community stemmed from the theory's potential to provide low-rationality foundations for high-rationality solution concepts. This motivation helps explain why economists working in evolutionary game theory have devoted so much effort to the study of random matching in normal form games. If the point of the theory is to motivate solution concepts for such games, then there is not much reason to move beyond the random matching setting.

As emphasized here, predictions about the aggregate behavior of large populations do not directly address how two players would behave in a two-player normal form game. Such predictions can only play a role that is more than metaphorical in applications that specifically concern the behavior of populations. But once such applications are brought to the fore, restricting attention to matching in normal form games begins to feel artificial. If one is interested in modeling behavior in large populations, the games one should write down are those one believes populations actually play.

Notes

General References on Evolutionary Game Theory

Books: Maynard Smith (1982), Hofbauer and Sigmund (1988; 1998), Bomze and Pötscher (1989), Cressman (1992; 2003), Weibull (1995), Vega-Redondo (1996), Samuelson (1997), Fudenberg and Levine (1998), Young (1998b).

Surveys: Hines (1987), van Damme (1991, ch. 9), Kandori (1997), Mailath (1998), Weibull (2002), Hofbauer and Sigmund (2003), Miękisz (2008), Sandholm (2009a).

References on Omitted Topics

Evolution in extensive form games: Cressman (1996a; 2000; 2003), Cressman and Schlag (1998), Chamberland and Cressman (2000), Binmore, Gale, and Samuelson (1995), Binmore and Samuelson (1999), Ponti (2000) (deterministic models); Samuelson (1994; 1997), Nöldeke and Samuelson (1993), Hart (2002), Kuzmics (2004) (stochastic models).

Local interaction models: Blume (1993; 1995; 1997), Ellison (1993; 2000), Kosfeld (2002), Miękisz (2004); Herz (1994), Ely (2002), Eshel, Samuelson, and Shaked (1998), Anderlini and Ianni (1996), Goyal and Janssen (1997), Alós-Ferrer and Weidenholzer (2006; 2007; 2008), Goyal (2007), Vega-Redondo (2007), Jackson (2008); Nowak and May (1992; 1993), Nowak (2006), Szabó and Fáth (2007), Hauert (2007).

Continuous strategy sets: Eshel (1983), Bomze (1990; 1991), Oechssler and Riedel (2001; 2002), Eshel and Sansone (2003), Cressman (2005; 2009), Cressman and Hofbauer (2005), Cressman, Hofbauer, and Riedel (2006), Hofbauer and Sorin (2006), Friedman and Ostrov (2008; 2010), Lahkar and Seymour (2008), Norman (2008), Hofbauer, Oechssler, and Riedel (2009).

Stochastic evolution via diffusion processes: Foster and Young (1990), Fudenberg and Harris (1992), Cabrales (2000), Imhof (2005), Benaïm, Hofbauer, and Sandholm (2008), Hofbauer and Imhof (2009).

References on Heuristic Learning

Books: Fudenberg and Levine (1998), Young (2004), Cesa-Bianchi and Lugosi (2006). *Survey:* Hart (2005). *Brief overview:* Sandholm (2008b).

References on Applications

Markets: Hopkins and Seymour (2002), Lahkar (2008), Droste, Hommes, and Tuinstra (2002), Sethi (1999), Ben-Shoham, Serrano, and Volij (2004), Agastya (2004), Vega-Redondo (1997), Alós-Ferrer, Ania, and Schenk-Hoppé (2000), Ania, Tröger, and Wambach (2002), Alós-Ferrer and Ania (2005), Alós-Ferrer, Kirchsteiger, and Walzl (2010), Kandori, Serrano, and Volij (2008), Friedman and Ostrov (2008).

Bargaining and hold-up problems: Young (1993b; 1998a; 1998b), Burke and Young (2001), Ellingsen and Robles (2002), Tröger (2002), Binmore, Samuelson, and Young (2003), Abreu and Sethi (2003), Dawid and MacLeod (2008), Robles (2008).

Signaling and cheap talk: Nöldeke and Samuelson (1993; 1997), Jacobsen, Jensen, and Sloth (2001), Robson (1990), Matsui (1991), Wärneryd (1993), Blume, Kim, and Sobel (1993), Kim and Sobel (1995), Bhaskar (1998), Banerjee and Weibull (2000), Trapa and Nowak (2000), Skyrms (2002), Pawlowitsch (2008), Demichelis and Weibull (2008).

Public good provision: Sethi and Somanathan (1996), Myatt and Wallace (2008a; 2008b; 2009).

Implementation and decentralized control: Cabrales (1999), Cabrales and Ponti (2000), Sandholm (2002; 2005b; 2007b), Cabrales and Serrano (2007), Mathevet (2007), Arslan, Marden, and Shamma (2007), Marden, Arslan, and Shamma (2009).

Residential segregation: Young (1998b; 2001), Möbius (2000), Zhang (2004a; 2004b), Dokumacı and Sandholm (2007a).

Preference evolution: Güth and Yaari (1992), Güth (1995), Huck and Oechssler (1999), Koçkesen, Ok, and Sethi (2000), Sethi and Somanathan (2001), Ok and Vega-Redondo (2001), Ely and Yilankaya (2001), Dekel, Ely, and Yilankaya (2007), Heifetz, Shannon, and Spiegel (2007), Herold and Kuzmics (2009).

Cultural evolution: Bisin and Verdier (2001), Sandholm (2001b), Kuran and Sandholm (2008), Montgomery (2009).

Applications in biology: Maynard Smith (1982), Hofbauer and Sigmund (1988), Sigmund (2010) (books); Hammerstein and Selten (1994), Dugatkin and Reeve (1998) (surveys).

Section 1.1
Noncooperative games with a continuum of agents were introduced by Schmeidler (1973), who proved that pure strategy Nash equilibria exist when each player's payoffs only depend on his own action and on the aggregate behavior of all players. Schmeidler used a normal form approach in that he named and described the behavior of each agent separately. Mas-Colell (1984) introduced a simpler formulation based on empirical distributions of strategies rather than on strategy profiles. His formulation can be understood as a population game in which both the set of populations and the set of strategies may be continuous. Mas-Colell also pointed out the overlap between his model and the distributional approach to Bayesian games with a continuum of types (Milgrom and Weber 1985). This connection can be used as the basis for studying evolution in Bayesian games; see Ely and Sandholm (2005). The literature on

Introduction

noncooperative games with large numbers of players was surveyed by Khan and Sun (2002); see Balder (2002) and Carmona and Podczeck (2009) for recent results.

Nash's "mass action" interpretation of his equilibrium concept appeared in his dissertation (Nash 1950b) but not in either of its published versions (Nash (1950a; 1951)). It was later rediscovered by Leonard (1994), Weibull (1994; 1996), and Björnerstedt and Weibull (1996); see also Hofbauer (2000).

Section 1.2

There are many good general references on traditional game-theoretic analysis; see Osborne (2004) at the undergraduate level, and Fudenberg and Tirole (1991), Myerson (1991), Ritzberger (2002), and van Damme (1991) at the graduate level. For an overview of the use of rationality and knowledge assumptions in game theory, see Dekel and Gul (1997).

While evolutionary game theory models assume that agents are myopic, one can imagine large population interactions whose participants are better modeled as forward-looking dynamic optimizers who attempt to maximize discounted flows of future payoffs. The *perfect foresight dynamics* of Matsui and Matsuyama (1995) introduced forward-looking behavior to large population models while retaining the assumption of inertia from the evolutionary approach. For additional references on this model, see the chapter 5 notes.

Section 1.3

A series of papers by John Maynard Smith in the early 1970s (Maynard Smith 1972; 1974; Maynard Smith and Price 1973) are traditionally viewed as heralding the birth of evolutionary game theory. Maynard Smith (1982, 2) himself notes the appearance of game-theoretic ideas in earlier studies of the evolution of sex ratios: they appeared implicitly in the work of Fisher (1930) and explicitly in the work of Hamilton (1967). But it was only with Maynard Smith's contributions that game theory began to take on its role as a standard framework for biological modeling.

I Population Games

2 Population Games

The examples discussed in chapter 1 are among the many important strategic interactions exhibiting the following properties:

1. *The number of agents is large.*
2. *Individual agents are small.* Any one agent's behavior has little or no effect on other agents' payoffs.
3. *Agents interact anonymously.* Each agent's payoffs only depend on opponents' behavior through the distribution of their choices.

While these three properties are basic, two additional restrictions of a more technical nature will sharpen the focus on the environments of most interest here. For the distribution of opponents' choices mentioned in property 3 to exist, there must be collections of agents who share the same set of strategies. This structure and more are ensured by this property:

4. *The number of roles is finite.* Each agent is a member of one of a finite number of populations. Members of a population choose from the same set of strategies, and their payoffs are identical functions of own behavior and the distribution of opponents' behavior.

The final property ensures that very small changes in aggregate behavior do not lead to large changes in strategies' payoffs:

5. *Payoffs are continuous.* The dependence of each agent's payoffs on the distribution of opponents' choices is continuous.

Population games provide a unified framework for studying strategic interactions with the properties listed above. Applications range from economics (externalities, macroeconomic spillovers, centralized markets) to biology (animal conflict, genetic natural selection), transportation science (highway network congestion, mode choice), and computer science (selfish routing of Internet traffic).

This chapter formally defines population games and offers a variety of explicit examples. It introduces some basic tools for the geometric analysis of population games, an approach developed further in subsequent chapters of the book. The mathematics underlying this approach—in particular, the notions of affine spaces, tangent spaces, and orthogonal projections—is reviewed in the chapter appendix.

Until the final chapters of the book, we find it convenient to study games with continuous populations of agents. This framework offers a few distinct advantages: chapter 3 demonstrates the power of tools from analysis in studying continuous-population games, and these games are the natural setting for the differential equation models that are the focus of chapters 4–9. However, one can equally well define large games with finite populations of players. This is done in chapters 11 and 12, where these games provide a tractable environment for defining stochastic evolutionary dynamics. Since continuous-population models can be obtained by taking limits of finite-population models (see section 11.4), the choice between the two settings should be viewed less as a matter of substance than as a matter of convenience.

2.1 Population Games

This section formally defines population games and their equilibria. To reduce the level of abstraction, it may be helpful to look ahead to the presentation of congestion games in example 2.2.4 to see the definitions introduced here in use in an application. Basic mathematical definitions and notations used in the text are summarized in the notation index.

2.1.1 Populations, Strategies, and States

Let $\mathcal{P} = \{1, \ldots, p\}$ be a *society* consisting of $p \geq 1$ *populations* of *agents*. Agents in population p form a continuum of *mass* $m^p > 0$. (Thus, p is the number of populations, whereas p is an arbitrary population.)

The set of *strategies* available to agents in population p is denoted $S^p = \{1, \ldots, n^p\}$, and has typical elements i, j, and (in the context of normal form games) s^p. The total number of pure strategies in all populations is denoted by $n = \sum_{p \in \mathcal{P}} n^p$.

During game play, each agent in population p selects a (pure) strategy from S^p. The set of *population states* (or *strategy distributions*) for population p is $X^p = \{x^p \in \mathbf{R}_+^{n^p} : \sum_{i \in S^p} x_i^p = m^p\}$. The scalar $x_i^p \in \mathbf{R}_+$ represents the mass of players in population p choosing strategy $i \in S^p$. Elements of X_v^p, the set of vertices of X^p, are called *pure population states* because at these states all agents choose the same strategy.

Population Games

Elements of $X = \prod_{p \in \mathcal{P}} X^p = \{x = (x^1, \ldots, x^p) \in \mathbf{R}_+^n : x^p \in X^p\}$, the set of *social states*, describe behavior in all p populations at once. The elements of $X_v = \prod_{p \in \mathcal{P}} X_v^p$ are the vertices of X and are called the *pure social states*.

When there is just one population ($p = 1$), we assume that its mass is 1 and omit the superscript p from all notation. Thus, the strategy set is $S = \{1, \ldots, n\}$; the state space is $X = \{x \in \mathbf{R}_+^n : \sum_{i \in S} x_i = 1\}$, the simplex in $\mathbf{R}^n$; and the set of pure states $X_v = \{e_i : i \in S\}$ is the set of standard basis vectors in $\mathbf{R}^n$.

2.1.2 Payoffs

We generally take the sets of populations and strategies as fixed and identify a game with its payoff function. A *payoff function* $F : X \to \mathbf{R}^n$ is a continuous map that assigns each social state a vector of payoffs, one for each strategy in each population. $F_i^p : X \to \mathbf{R}$ denotes the payoff function for strategy $i \in S^p$, and $F^p : X \to \mathbf{R}^{n^p}$ denotes the payoff functions for all strategies in S^p.

While the standing assumption is that F is continuous, we often impose the stronger requirements that F be Lipschitz continuous or continuously differentiable (C^1). These additional assumptions are made explicit whenever they are used.

Define

$$\bar{F}^p(x) = \frac{1}{m^p} \sum_{i \in S^p} x_i^p F_i^p(x)$$

to be the *(weighted) average payoff* obtained by members of population p at social state x. Similarly, let

$$\bar{F}(x) = \sum_{p \in \mathcal{P}} \sum_{i \in S^p} x_i^p F_i^p(x) = \sum_{p \in \mathcal{P}} m^p \bar{F}^p(x)$$

denote the *aggregate payoff* achieved by the society as a whole.

2.1.3 Best Responses and Nash Equilibria

To describe optimal behavior, we define population p's *pure best response correspondence*, $b^p : X \rightrightarrows S^p$, which specifies the strategies in S^p that are optimal at each social state x:

$$b^p(x) = \operatorname*{argmax}_{i \in S^p} F_i^p(x).$$

Let $\Delta^p = \{y^p \in \mathbf{R}_+^{n^p} : \sum_{i \in S^p} y_i^p = 1\}$ denote the simplex in $\mathbf{R}^{n^p}$. The *mixed best response correspondence* for population p, $B^p : X \rightrightarrows \Delta^p$, is given by

$$B^p(x) = \{y^p \in \Delta^p : y_i^p > 0 \Rightarrow i \in b^p(x)\},$$

that is, $B^p(x)$ is the set of probability distributions in Δ^p whose supports only contain pure strategies that are optimal at x. Geometrically, $B^p(x)$ is the convex hull of the vertices of Δ^p corresponding to elements of $b^p(x)$.

Social state $x \in X$ is a *Nash equilibrium* of the game F if each agent in every population chooses a best response to x:

$$NE(F) = \left\{x \in X : x^p \in m^p B^p(x) \text{ for all } p \in \mathcal{P}\right\}.$$

Equivalently, x is a Nash equilibrium if in each population, every strategy in use earns the maximal payoff:

$$NE(F) = \{x \in X : [x_i^p > 0 \Rightarrow F_i^p(x) \geq F_j^p(x)] \text{ for all } i, j \in S^p, p \in \mathcal{P}\}.$$

In section 2.3.6 this second definition is used to characterize the set of Nash equilibria in a purely geometric way.

Nash equilibria always exist.

Theorem 2.1.1 *Every population game admits at least one Nash equilibrium.*

Theorem 2.1.1 can be proved by applying Kakutani's fixed point theorem to the profile of best response correspondences. But for each of the three classes of games discussed in chapter 3—potential games, stable games, and supermodular games—existence of Nash equilibrium can be established without recourse to fixed point theorems.

2.1.4 Prelude to Evolutionary Dynamics

In traditional game-theoretic analyses, it is usual to assume that players follow some Nash equilibrium of the game at hand. But because population games involve large numbers of agents, the equilibrium assumption is quite strong, making it desirable to rely on less demanding assumptions. Therefore, rather than assuming equilibrium play, it is preferable to suppose that individual agents gradually adjust their choices to their current strategic environment, and to ask whether the induced behavior trajectories converge to Nash equilibrium. When they do, the Nash prediction can be justified; when they do not, the Nash prediction may be unwarranted.

The question of convergence to equilibrium is a central issue in this book. For the three classes of games studied in chapter 3, convergence results can be established with some generality, that is, without being overly specific about the exact nature of the agents' revision protocols. These developments come in chapter 7. In the meantime, this chapter and the next focus on introducing population games and studying their equilibria.

Population Games   25

2.2 Examples

The examples of population games to follow are among the many that are developed and analyzed through the remainder of the book.

2.2.1 Matching in Normal Form Games

Example 2.2.1 is the canonical example of evolutionary game theory.

Example 2.2.1: Matching in a Single Population to Play a Symmetric Game   A symmetric two-player normal form game is defined by a strategy set $S = \{1, \ldots, n\}$ and a payoff matrix $A \in \mathbf{R}^{n \times n}$. A_{ij} is the payoff a player obtains when he chooses strategy i and his opponent chooses strategy j; this payoff does not depend on whether the player in question is called player I or player II. Below is the bimatrix corresponding to A when $n = 3$.

		\multicolumn{3}{c}{Player II}		
		1	2	3
Player I	1	A_{11}, A_{11}	A_{12}, A_{21}	A_{13}, A_{31}
	2	A_{21}, A_{12}	A_{22}, A_{22}	A_{23}, A_{32}
	3	A_{31}, A_{13}	A_{32}, A_{23}	A_{33}, A_{33}

To obtain a population game from this normal form game, suppose that agents in a single (unit mass) population are matched to play A, with each pair of agents meeting exactly once. Aggregating payoffs over all matches, we find that the payoff to strategy i when the population state is x is $F_i(x) = \sum_{j \in S} A_{ij} x_j = (Ax)_i$. Thus, the population game associated with A is described by the linear map $F(x) = Ax$.

Instead of assuming a complete deterministic matching, one can assume alternatively that each agent is randomly matched against a single opponent. Then, if agents evaluate probability distributions over payoffs by taking expectations (i.e., if the entries of the matrix A are von Neumann–Morgenstern utilities), one can again represent the payoffs to the interaction as $F(x) = Ax$. ◆

When we consider foundations for evolutionary dynamics in Chapters 4–6, some of the choice rules will be easiest to interpret when $F_i(x)$ represents a realized payoff rather than an expected payoff. For this reason, we prefer to use complete matchings rather than random matchings to derive population games from normal form games.

Of course, one can also think of the population game $F(x) = Ax$ as describing an interaction that is not based on matching in a normal form game at all. Such interactions are sometimes referred to as "playing the field" models; congestion games (see section 2.2.2) offer one basic example.

Example 2.2.2: Matching in Two Populations   A (possibly asymmetric) two-player game is defined by two strategy sets, $S^1 = \{1,\ldots,n^1\}$ and $S^2 = \{1,\ldots,n^2\}$, and two payoff matrices, $U^1 \in \mathbf{R}^{n^1 \times n^2}$ and $U^2 \in \mathbf{R}^{n^1 \times n^2}$. The corresponding bimatrix when $n^1 = 2$ and $n^2 = 3$ is as follows.

Player II

	1	2	3
1	U^1_{11}, U^2_{11}	U^1_{12}, U^2_{12}	U^1_{13}, U^2_{13}
2	U^1_{21}, U^2_{21}	U^1_{22}, U^2_{22}	U^1_{23}, U^2_{23}

Player I

To define the corresponding population game, suppose there are two unit mass populations, one corresponding to each player role. Each agent is matched with every member of the other population to play the game (U^1, U^2). Alternatively, one can assume that each agent is randomly matched with a single member of the other population (see the previous example). Either way, the payoff functions for populations 1 and 2 are given by $F^1(x) = U^1 x^2$ and $F^2(x) = (U^2)' x^1$, so the entire population game is described by the linear map

$$F(x) = \begin{pmatrix} F^1(x) \\ F^2(x) \end{pmatrix} = \begin{pmatrix} 0 & U^1 \\ (U^2)' & 0 \end{pmatrix} \begin{pmatrix} x^1 \\ x^2 \end{pmatrix} = \begin{pmatrix} U^1 x^2 \\ (U^2)' x^1 \end{pmatrix}.$$ ◆

Example 2.2.3: Matching in p Populations   To generalize the previous example, we define a p-player normal form game. Let $S^p = \{1,\ldots,n^p\}$ denote player p's strategy set and $S = \prod_{q \in \mathcal{P}} S^q$ the set of pure strategy profiles; player p's payoff function U^p is a map from S to $\mathbf{R}$.

In the population game, agents in p unit mass populations are matched to play the normal form game $U = (U^1, \ldots, U^p)$, with each matching of p agents, one from each population, occurring exactly once. This procedure yields a population game with the multilinear (i.e., linear in each x^p) payoff function

$$F^p_{s^p}(x) = \sum_{s^{-p} \in S^{-p}} U^p(s^1,\ldots,s^p) \prod_{r \neq p} x^r_{s^r}, \quad \text{where } S^{-p} = \prod_{q \neq p} S^q.$$ ◆

The following observation relates the Nash equilibria of population games generated by matching to those of the underlying normal form games.

Observation 2.2.1

i. In the single-population case (example 2.2.1), the Nash equilibria of F are the symmetric Nash equilibria of the symmetric normal form game $U = (A, A')$.

ii. In the multipopulation cases (examples 2.2.2 and 2.2.3), the Nash equilibria of F are the Nash equilibria of the normal form game $U = (U^1, \ldots, U^p)$.

2.2.2 Congestion Games

Because of the linearity of the expectation operator, matching in normal form games generates population games with linear or multilinear payoffs. Moreover, when $p \geq 2$, each agent's payoffs are independent of the behavior of other members of his population. Outside of the matching context, neither of these properties need hold. The next class of example provides a case in point.

Example 2.2.4: Congestion Games Consider the following model of highway congestion. A collection of towns is connected by a network of *links* (figure 2.1). For each ordered pair of towns there is a population of agents, each of whom needs to commute from the first town in the pair (where he lives) to the second (where he works). To accomplish this, the agent must choose a *path* connecting the two towns. The payoff the agent obtains is the negation of the delay on the path he takes. The delay on the path is the sum of the delays on its constituent links, and the delay on a link is a function of the number of agents who use that link.

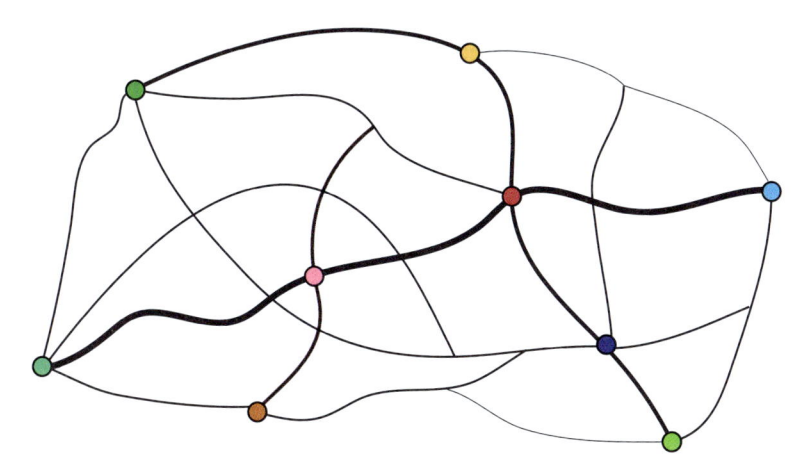

Figure 2.1
A highway network.

Congestion games are used to study not only highway congestion, but also more general settings involving symmetric externalities. To define a congestion game, begin with a finite collection of *facilities* (e.g., links in a highway network), denoted Φ. Every strategy $i \in S^p$ requires the use of some collection of facilities $\Phi_i^p \subseteq \Phi$ (e.g., the links in route i). The set $\rho^p(\phi) = \{i \in S^p : \phi \in \Phi_i^p\}$ contains those strategies in S^p that require facility ϕ.

Each facility ϕ has a *cost function* $c_\phi \colon \mathbf{R}_+ \to \mathbf{R}$ whose argument is the facility's *utilization level* u_ϕ, the total mass of agents using the facility; this is determined from the social state in the following way:

$$u_\phi(x) = \sum_{p \in \mathcal{P}} \sum_{i \in \rho^p(\phi)} x_i^p.$$

Payoffs in the congestion game are obtained by summing the appropriate facility costs and multiplying by -1:

$$F_i^p(x) = -\sum_{\phi \in \Phi_i^p} c_\phi(u_\phi(x)).$$

Since driving on a link increases the delays experienced by other drivers on that link, cost functions in models of highway congestion are increasing; they are typically convex as well. On the other hand, when congestion games are used to model settings with positive externalities (e.g., consumer technology choice), cost functions are decreasing. Evidently, payoffs in congestion games depend on own-population behavior, and need only be linear if the underlying cost functions are linear themselves.

Congestion games are the leading examples of potential games (see sections 3.1 and 3.2); congestion games with increasing cost functions are also stable games (see section 3.3). ◆

2.2.3 Two Simple Externality Models
This section concludes with two simple models of externalities.

Example 2.2.5: Asymmetric Negative Externalities Agents from a single population choose from a set of n activities. There are externalities both within and across activities. The increasing C^1 function $c_{ij} \colon [0,1] \to \mathbf{R}$ represents the cost imposed on agents who choose activity i by agents who choose activity j. Payoffs in this game are described by

$$F_i(x) = -\sum_{j \in S} c_{ij}(x_j).$$

Population Games

If own-activity externalities are strong, in the sense that the derivatives of the cost functions satisfy

$$2c'_{ii}(x_i) \geq \sum_{j \neq i} \left(c'_{ij}(x_j) + c'_{ji}(x_i) \right),$$

then F is a stable game (see section 3.3). ◆

Example 2.2.6: Search with Positive Externalities   Consider this simple model of macroeconomic spillovers. Members of a single population choose levels of search effort from the set $S = \{1, \ldots, n\}$. Stronger efforts increase the likelihood of finding trading partners, so payoffs are increasing in both own-search effort and aggregate search effort. In particular, payoffs are given by

$$F_i(x) = m(i)\, b(a(x)) - c(i),$$

where $a(x) = \sum_{k=1}^{n} k x_k$ represents aggregate search effort, the increasing function $b \colon \mathbf{R}_+ \to \mathbf{R}$ represents the benefits of search as a function of aggregate effort, the increasing function $m \colon S \to \mathbf{R}$ is the benefit multiplier, and the arbitrary function $c \colon S \to \mathbf{R}$ captures search costs. F is an example of a supermodular game (see section 3.4). ◆

2.3 The Geometry of Population Games and Nash Equilibria

In low-dimensional cases, the payoff vectors generated by a population game can be depicted graphically. Doing so provides a way of visualizing the strategic forces at work, and the geometric insights obtained can be extended to games that cannot be drawn.

2.3.1 Drawing Two-Strategy Games

The population games that are easiest to draw are *two-strategy games*, that is, games played by a single population of agents who choose between a pair of strategies. When drawing a two-strategy game, the simplex is represented as a subset of $\mathbf{R}^2$. The drawing is synchronized with the layout of the payoff matrix by using the *vertical* coordinate to represent the mass on the *first* strategy and the *horizontal* coordinate to represent the mass on the *second* strategy. We then select a group of states spaced evenly through the simplex, and from each state x in this grid, we draw an arrow representing the payoff vector $F(x)$ that corresponds to x. (Actually, scaled-down versions of the payoff vectors are used in order to make the diagrams easier to read.)

Figures 2.2 and 2.3 show the payoff vectors generated by the two-strategy coordination game F^{C2} and the Hawk-Dove game F^{HD}:

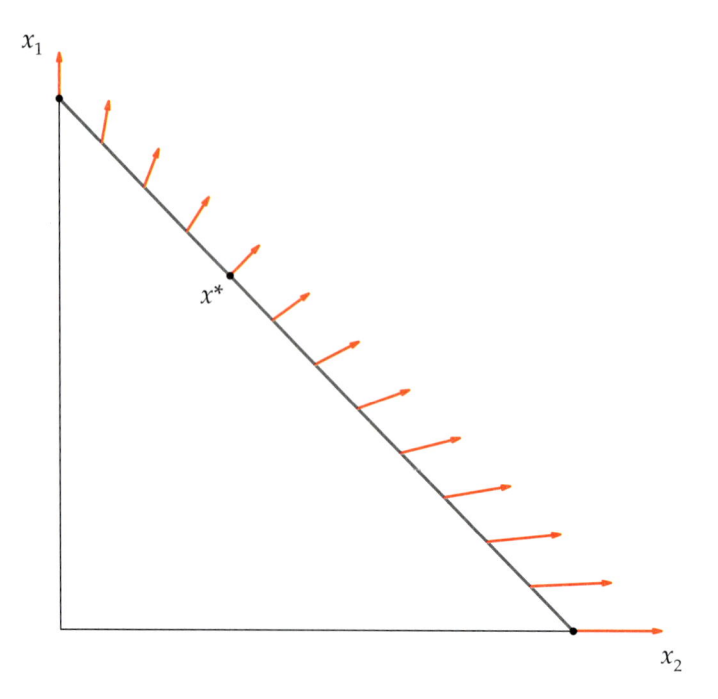

Figure 2.2
Payoffs in 12 Coordination.

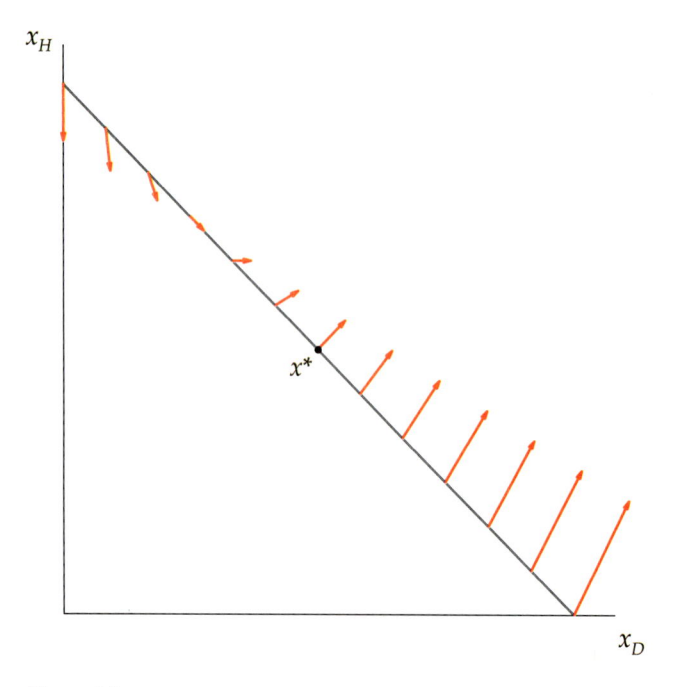

Figure 2.3
Payoffs in the Hawk-Dove game.

Population Games 31

$$F^{C2}(x) = \begin{pmatrix} 1 & 0 \\ 0 & 2 \end{pmatrix}\begin{pmatrix} x_1 \\ x_2 \end{pmatrix} = \begin{pmatrix} x_1 \\ 2x_2 \end{pmatrix}; \qquad F^{HD}(x) = \begin{pmatrix} -1 & 2 \\ 0 & 1 \end{pmatrix}\begin{pmatrix} x_H \\ x_D \end{pmatrix} = \begin{pmatrix} 2x_D - x_H \\ x_D \end{pmatrix}.$$

First, consider the coordination game F^{C2}, called *12 Coordination*. At the pure state $e_1 = (1,0)$ at which all agents play strategy 1, the payoffs to the two strategies are $F_1^{C2}(e_1) = 1$ and $F_2^{C2}(e_1) = 0$; hence, the arrow representing $F^{C2}(e_1)$ points directly *upward* from state e_1. At the interior Nash equilibrium $x^* = (x_1^*, x_2^*) = (\frac{2}{3}, \frac{1}{3})$, each strategy earns a payoff of $\frac{2}{3}$, so the arrow representing payoff vector $F^{C2}(x^*) = (\frac{2}{3}, \frac{2}{3})$ is drawn at a right angle to the simplex at x^*. Similar logic explains how the payoff vectors are drawn at other states, and how the Hawk-Dove figure is constructed as well.

The diagrams of F^{C2} and F^{HD} help one to visualize the incentives faced by agents playing these games. In the coordination game, the payoff vectors push outward toward the two axes, reflecting an incentive structure that drives the population toward the two pure Nash equilibria. In contrast, payoff vectors in the Hawk-Dove game push inward, away from the axes, reflecting forces leading the population toward the interior Nash equilibrium $x^* = (\frac{1}{2}, \frac{1}{2})$.

2.3.2 Displacement Vectors and Tangent Spaces

To draw games with more than two strategies, two new objects must be introduced: TX, the tangent space of the state space X; and $\mathbf{\Phi}$, the orthogonal projection of $\mathbf{R}^n$ onto TX. The relevant concepts are summarized in this section and the next; for a fuller treatment, see appendix 2.A.

To start, we focus on a single-population game F. Imagine that the population is initially at state x, and that a group of agents of mass ε switch from strategy i to strategy j. These revisions move the state from x to $x + \varepsilon(e_j - e_i)$: the mass of agents playing strategy i goes down by ε, and the mass of agents playing strategy j goes up by ε. Vectors like $\varepsilon(e_j - e_i)$, which represent the effects of such strategy revisions on the population state, are called *displacement vectors*. (Since these vectors are tangent to the state space X, they are also called *tangent vectors*.)

Figure 2.4 illustrates displacement vectors for two-strategy games. In this setting, displacement vectors can only point in two directions. When agents switch from strategy 1 to strategy 2, the state moves in direction $e_2 - e_1$, represented by an arrow pointing southeast. When agents switch from strategy 2 to strategy 1, the state moves in direction $e_1 - e_2$, represented by an arrow pointing northwest. Both of these vectors are tangent to the state space X.

(Two clarifications are in order here. First, remember that a vector is characterized by its direction and its length, not where its base is positioned. When drawing an arrow representing the vector z, one uses the context to determine an appropriate position x for the arrow's base; the arrow takes the form of a directed line segment

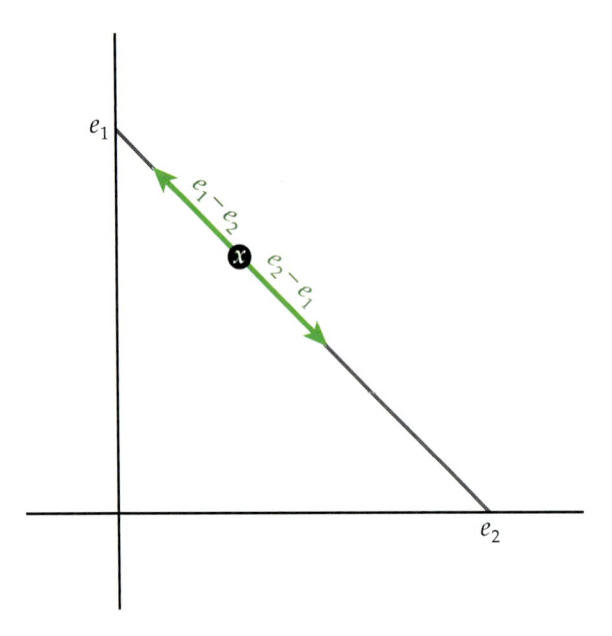

Figure 2.4
Displacement vectors for two-strategy games.

from x to $x + z$. Second, since the main interest lies in displacement vectors' *relative* sizes, they are rescaled before drawing, as was done with payoff vectors in figures 2.2 and 2.3.)

Now consider a *three-strategy game*, a game with one population and three strategies, whose state space X is the simplex in $\mathbf{R}^3$. A "three-dimensional" picture of X is shown in figure 2.5, where X is situated within the plane in $\mathbf{R}^3$ that contains it. This plane is called the *affine hull* of X, and is denoted by $\mathrm{aff}(X)$ (see section 2.A.2). For future reference, note that displacement vectors drawn from states in X are situated in the plane $\mathrm{aff}(X)$.

Instead of representing the state space X explicitly in $\mathbf{R}^3$, it is more common to present it as a two-dimensional equilateral triangle (figure 2.6). Then the sheet of paper itself represents the affine hull $\mathrm{aff}(X)$, and arrows drawn on the paper represent displacement vectors. Figure 2.6 shows arrows describing the $3 \times 2 = 6$ displacement vectors of the form $e_j - e_i$, which correspond to switches between ordered pairs of distinct strategies. Each of these arrows is parallel to some edge of the simplex. For purposes of orientation, note that if the simplex from figure 2.6 is resituated in three-dimensional space (see figure 2.5), then each of the six arrows is obtained by subtracting one standard basis vector from another.

Switches between pairs of strategies are not the only ways of generating displacement vectors. They can also come from switches involving three or more strategies,

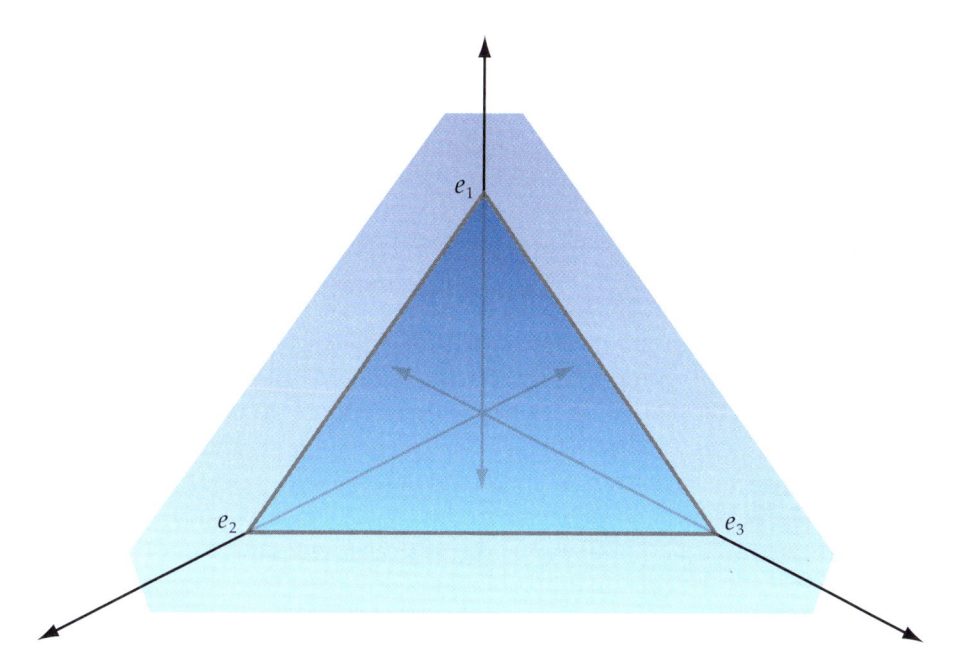

Figure 2.5
The simplex in $\mathbf{R}^3$.

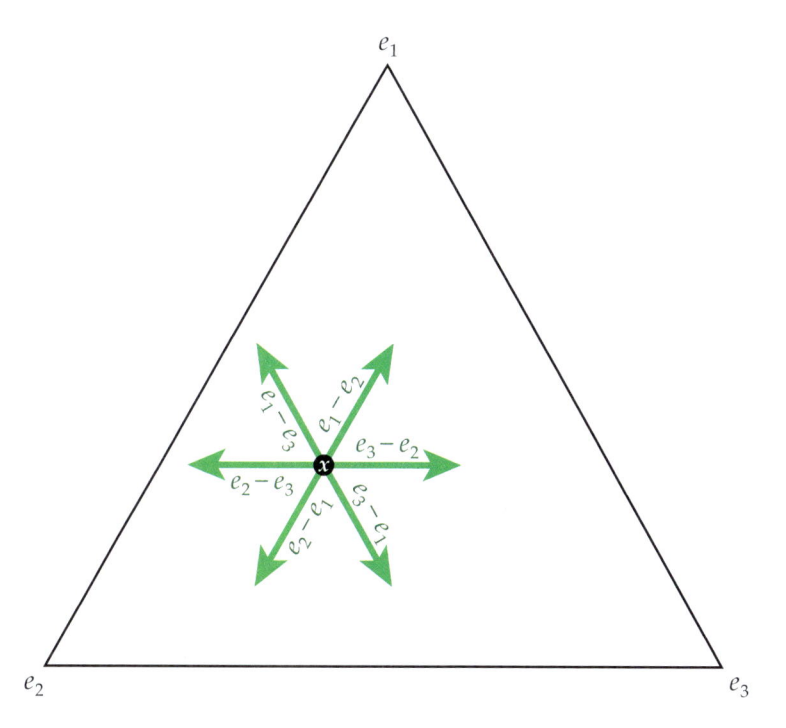

Figure 2.6
Displacement vectors for three-strategy games.

and, in multipopulation settings, from switches occurring within more than one population. The set of all displacement vectors from states in X forms a subspace of $\mathbf{R}^n$; this subspace is called the *tangent space TX*.

To formally define TX, first consider population $p \in \mathcal{P}$ in isolation. The state space for population p is $X^p = \{x^p \in \mathbf{R}_+^{n^p} : \sum_{i \in S^p} x_i^p = m^p\}$. The *tangent space* of X^p, denoted TX^p, is the smallest subspace of $\mathbf{R}^{n^p}$ that contains all vectors describing motions between points in X^p. In other words, if $x^p, y^p \in X^p$, then $y^p - x^p \in TX^p$, and TX^p is the span of all vectors of this form. It is not hard to see that $TX^p = \mathbf{R}_0^{n^p} \equiv \{z^p \in \mathbf{R}^{n^p} : \sum_{i \in S^p} z_i^p = 0\}$, that is, TX^p contains exactly those vectors in $\mathbf{R}^{n^p}$ whose components sum to zero. The restriction on the sum embodies the fact that changes in the population state leave the population's mass constant.

The preceding definition is sufficient for studying single-population games. What if there are multiple populations? In this case, any change in the social state $x \in X = \prod_{p \in \mathcal{P}} X^p$ is a combination of changes occurring within the individual populations. Therefore, the grand tangent space TX is just the product of the tangent spaces for each set X^p, that is, $TX = \prod_{p \in \mathcal{P}} TX^p$.

2.3.3 Orthogonal Projections

How should one draw a diagram representing a three-strategy game F? One possibility is to draw a "three-dimensional" representation of F in the fashion of figure 2.5. As a less demanding alternative, one could instead represent F in just two dimensions. But this simplification would come at a cost. Since three-dimensional payoff vectors $F(x) \in \mathbf{R}^3$ would be presented as two-dimensional objects, some of the information contained in the vectors would be lost.

From a geometric point of view, the most natural way to proceed is pictured in figure 2.7. Instead of drawing an arrow from state x corresponding to the vector $F(x)$ itself, one draws the arrow closest to $F(x)$ among those that lie in the plane aff(X). This arrow represents a vector in the tangent space TX: namely, the orthogonal projection of $F(x)$ onto TX.

Let Z be a linear subspace of $\mathbf{R}^n$. The *orthogonal projection* of $\mathbf{R}^n$ onto Z is a linear map that sends each $\pi \in \mathbf{R}^n$ to the closest point to π in Z. Each orthogonal projection can be represented by a matrix $P_Z \in \mathbf{R}^{n \times n}$ via the map $\pi \mapsto P_Z \pi$, and it is common to identify the projection with its matrix representation. (Further details on orthogonal projections can be found in section 2.A.3.)

Now consider population $p \in \mathcal{P}$ in isolation. The orthogonal projection of $\mathbf{R}^{n^p}$ onto the tangent space TX^p, denoted $\Phi \in \mathbf{R}^{n^p \times n^p}$, is defined by $\Phi = I - \frac{1}{n^p} \mathbf{11}'$, where $\mathbf{1} \in \mathbf{R}^{n^p}$ is the column vector whose entries all equal 1; thus $\frac{1}{n^p} \mathbf{11}'$ is the matrix whose entries are all $\frac{1}{n^p}$.

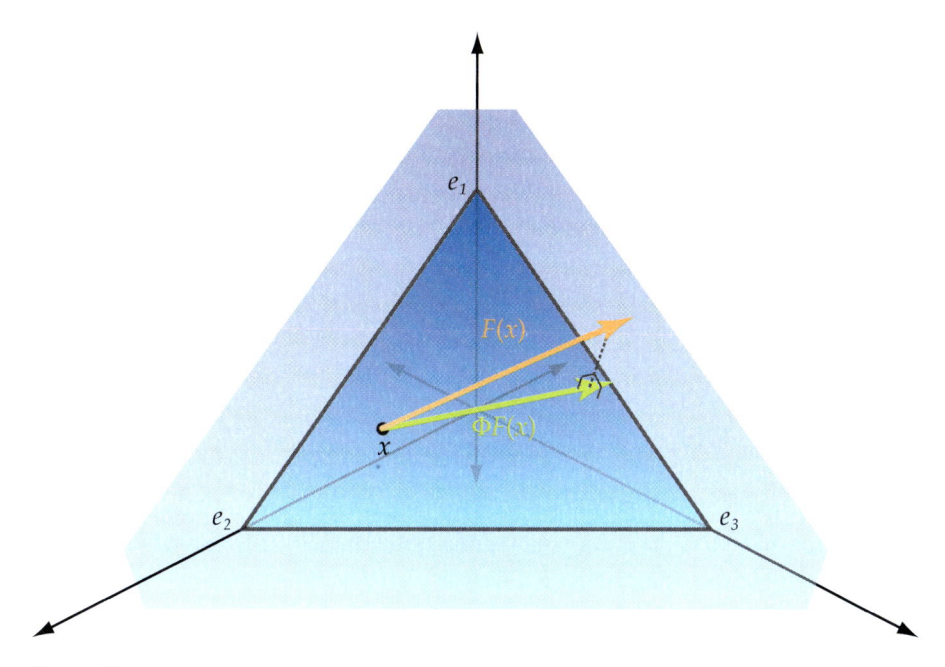

Figure 2.7
Projected payoff vectors for three-strategy games.

If π^p is a payoff vector in $\mathbf{R}^{n^p}$, the projection of π^p onto TX^p is

$$\Phi\pi^p = \pi^p - \frac{1}{n^p}\mathbf{1}\mathbf{1}'\pi^p = \pi^p - \mathbf{1}\left(\frac{1}{n^p}\sum_{k\in S^p}\pi_k^p\right).$$

The ith component of $\Phi\pi^p$ is the difference between the actual payoff to strategy i and the *unweighted* average payoff of all strategies in S^p. Thus, $\Phi\pi^p$ discards information about average payoffs while retaining information about *relative* payoffs of different strategies in S^p. This interpretation is important from a game-theoretic point of view because incentives, and hence Nash equilibria, only depend on payoff differences. Therefore, when incentives (as opposed to, say, efficiency) are the main concern, the actual payoff vectors π^p need not be known; the projected payoff vectors $\Phi\pi^p$ are enough.

In multipopulation settings, the tangent space $TX = \prod_{p\in\mathcal{P}} TX^p$ has a product structure; hence, the orthogonal projection onto TX, denoted $\mathbf{\Phi} \in \mathbf{R}^{n\times n}$, has a block diagonal structure: $\mathbf{\Phi} = \mathrm{diag}(\Phi,\ldots,\Phi)$. (Note that the blocks on the diagonal of $\mathbf{\Phi}$ are generally not the same size: the pth block is an element of $\mathbf{R}^{n^p\times n^p}$.) If $\mathbf{\Phi}$ is applied to the society's payoff vector $\pi = (\pi^1,\ldots,\pi^p)$, the resulting vector $\mathbf{\Phi}\pi = (\Phi\pi^1,\ldots,\Phi\pi^p)$ lists the relative payoffs in each population.

2.3.4 Drawing Three-Strategy Games

Before using orthogonal projections to draw three-strategy games, consider how this device affects pictures of two-strategy games. Applying the projection $\Phi = I - \frac{1}{2}\mathbf{1}\mathbf{1}'$ to the payoff vectors from the coordination game F^{C2} and the Hawk-Dove game F^{HD} yields

$$\Phi F^{C2}(x) = \begin{pmatrix} \frac{1}{2} & -\frac{1}{2} \\ -\frac{1}{2} & \frac{1}{2} \end{pmatrix} \begin{pmatrix} x_1 \\ 2x_2 \end{pmatrix} = \begin{pmatrix} \frac{1}{2}x_1 - x_2 \\ -\frac{1}{2}x_1 + x_2 \end{pmatrix}$$

and

$$\Phi F^{HD}(x) = \begin{pmatrix} \frac{1}{2} & -\frac{1}{2} \\ -\frac{1}{2} & \frac{1}{2} \end{pmatrix} \begin{pmatrix} 2x_D - x_H \\ x_D \end{pmatrix} = \begin{pmatrix} \frac{1}{2}(x_D - x_H) \\ \frac{1}{2}(x_H - x_D) \end{pmatrix}.$$

Both projected payoffs and original payoffs are shown in figures 2.8 and 2.9.

The projected payoff vectors $\Phi F(x)$ lie in the tangent space TX and so are represented by arrows running parallel to the simplex X. Projecting away the orthogonal component of payoffs makes the outward force in the coordination game and the

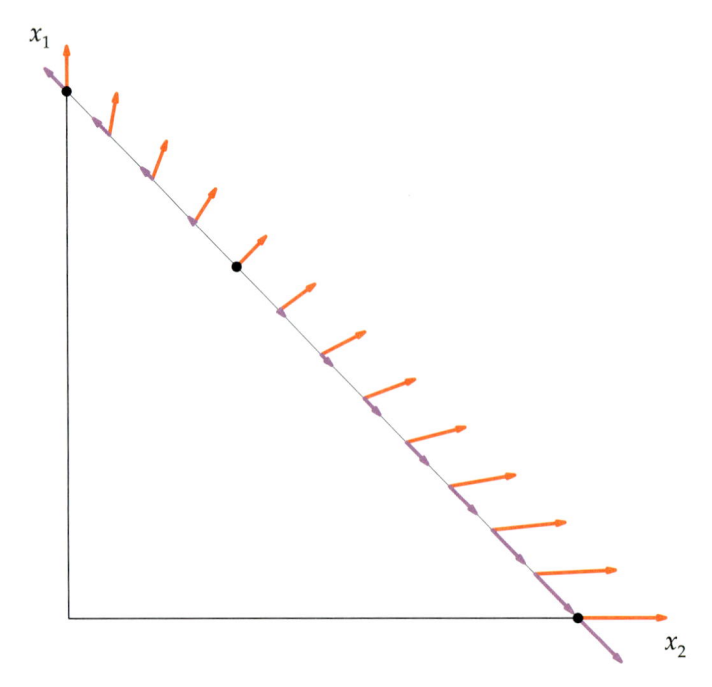

Figure 2.8
Payoffs and projected payoffs in 12 Coordination.

Population Games   37

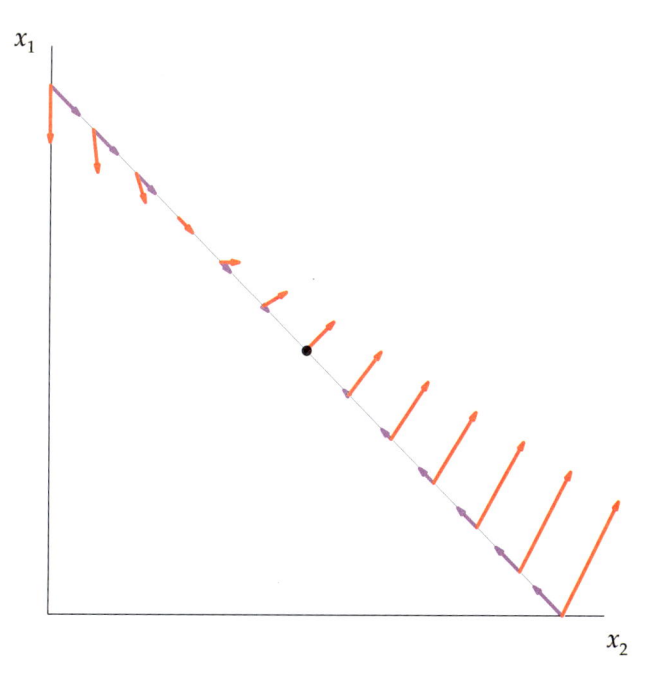

Figure 2.9
Payoffs and projected payoffs in the Hawk-Dove game.

inward force in the Hawk-Dove game more transparent. Indeed, figures 2.8 and 2.9 are suggestive of evolutionary dynamics for these two games (compare exercise 5.2.2).

Now consider the 123 Coordination game F^{C3} and the Rock-Paper-Scissors game F^{RPS}:

$$F^{C3}(x) = \begin{pmatrix} 1 & 0 & 0 \\ 0 & 2 & 0 \\ 0 & 0 & 3 \end{pmatrix} \begin{pmatrix} x_1 \\ x_2 \\ x_3 \end{pmatrix} = \begin{pmatrix} x_1 \\ 2x_2 \\ 3x_3 \end{pmatrix};$$

$$F^{RPS}(x) = \begin{pmatrix} 0 & -1 & 1 \\ 1 & 0 & -1 \\ -1 & 1 & 0 \end{pmatrix} \begin{pmatrix} x_R \\ x_P \\ x_S \end{pmatrix} = \begin{pmatrix} x_S - x_P \\ x_R - x_S \\ x_P - x_R \end{pmatrix}.$$

These games are pictured in figures 2.10 and 2.11. The arrows in figure 2.10 represent the projected payoff vectors $\Phi F^{C3}(x)$, defined by

$$\Phi F^{C3}(x) = \left(I - \tfrac{1}{3}\mathbf{1}\mathbf{1}'\right) \begin{pmatrix} x_1 \\ 2x_2 \\ 3x_3 \end{pmatrix} = \begin{pmatrix} \tfrac{1}{3}(2x_1 - 2x_2 - 3x_3) \\ \tfrac{1}{3}(-x_1 + 4x_2 - 3x_3) \\ \tfrac{1}{3}(-x_1 - 2x_2 + 6x_3) \end{pmatrix}.$$

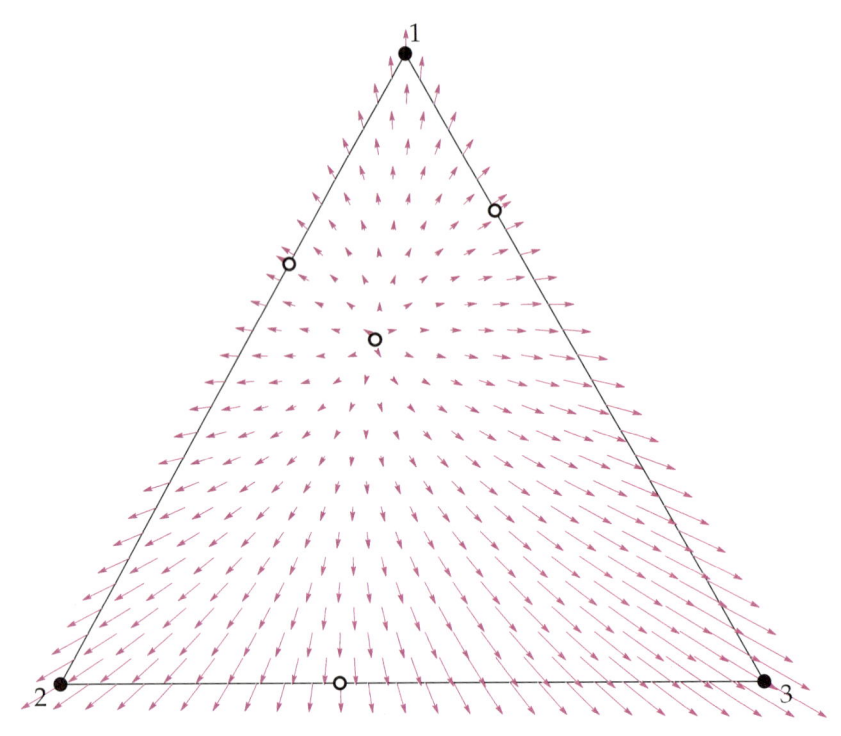

Figure 2.10
Projected payoffs in 123 Coordination.

But in the Rock-Paper-Scissors game, the column sums of the payoff matrix all equal 0, implying that the maps F^{RPS} and ΦF^{RPS} are identical.

As with that of F^{C2}, the diagram of the coordination game F^{C3} shows forces pushing outward toward the extreme points of the simplex. In contrast, figure 2.11 displays a property that cannot occur with just two strategies. Instead of driving toward some Nash equilibrium, the arrows in figure 2.11 cycle around the simplex. Thus, the figure suggests that in the Rock-Paper-Scissors game, evolutionary dynamics need not converge to Nash equilibrium but instead may avoid equilibrium in perpetuity. Questions of convergence and nonconvergence of evolutionary dynamics are the focus of later chapters.

2.3.5 Tangent Cones and Normal Cones

To complete the introduction to the geometric approach to population games, we now explain how to find a game's Nash equilibria by examining a picture of the game.

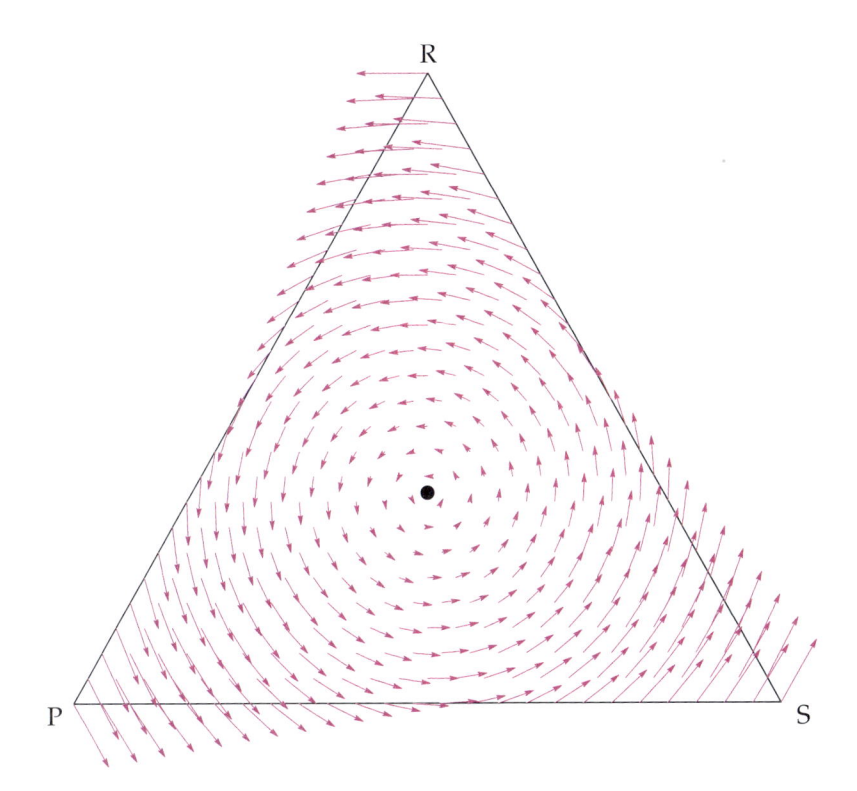

Figure 2.11
Payoffs (= projected payoffs) in Rock-Paper-Scissors.

To begin, note that the constraint defining vectors z as lying in the tangent space TX—the constraint that keeps population masses constant—is not always enough to ensure that motion in direction z is feasible. Motions in every direction in TX are feasible if one begins at a state x in the interior of the state space X. But if $x_i^p = 0$ for some strategy $i \in S^p$, then motion in any direction z with $z_i^p < 0$ would cause the mass of agents playing strategy i to become negative, taking the state out of X.

One can describe the feasible displacement directions from an arbitrary state $x \in X$ by introducing the notion of a tangent cone. Recall that the set $K \subseteq \mathbf{R}^n$ is a *cone* if whenever it contains the vector z, it also contains the vector αz for every $\alpha > 0$. Most often one is interested in convex cones (i.e., cones that are convex sets). The *polar* of the convex cone K is a new convex cone

$$K^\circ = \left\{y \in \mathbf{R}^n : y'z \leq 0 \text{ for all } z \in K\right\}.$$

In words, the polar cone of K contains all vectors that form a weakly obtuse angle with each vector in K (figure 2.12).

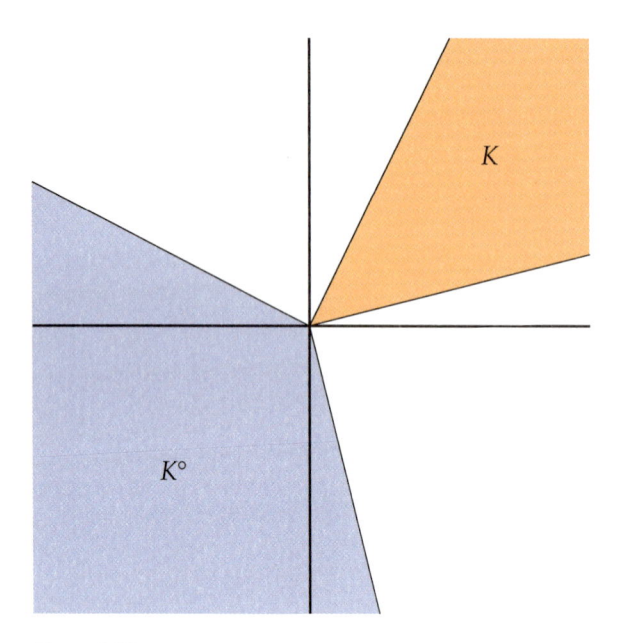

Figure 2.12
A convex cone and its polar cone.

Exercise 2.3.1 Let K be a convex cone.

i. Show that $K°$ is a closed convex cone, and $K° = (\text{cl}(K))°$ (hence, $K°$ contains the origin).

ii. Show that K is a subspace of $\mathbf{R}^n$ if and only if K is symmetric, in the sense that $K = -K$, and that, in this case, $K° = K^\perp$.

iii. Show that $(K°)° = \text{cl}(K)$. (*Hint:* To show that $(K°)° \subseteq \text{cl}(K)$, use the separating hyperplane theorem.) ◇

The last result says that $(K°)° = K$ for any closed convex cone K; thus, polarity defines an *involution* on the set of closed convex cones. Another fundamental result about closed convex cones and their polar cones, the Moreau decomposition theorem, is presented in section 2.A.4.

If $C \subseteq \mathbf{R}^n$ is a closed convex set, then the *tangent cone* of C at state $x \in C$, denoted $TC(x)$, is the closed convex cone

$$TC(x) = \text{cl}(\{z \in \mathbf{R}^n : z = \alpha(y-x) \text{ for some } y \in C \text{ and some } \alpha \geq 0\}).$$

If $C \subset \mathbf{R}^n$ is a *polytope* (i.e., the convex hull of a finite number of points), then the closure operation is redundant. In this case, $TC(x)$ is the set of directions of motion from x that initially remain in C; more generally, $TC(x)$ also contains the limits of

Population Games

such directions. (To see the difference, construct $TC(x)$ for $x \in bd(C)$ when C is a square and when C is a circle.) If x is in the relative interior of C (i.e., the interior of C relative to $aff(C)$), then $TC(x)$ is just TC, the tangent space of C; otherwise, $TC(x)$ is a strict subset of TC.

Finally, define the *normal cone* of C at x to be the polar of the tangent cone of C at x, that is, $NC(x) = (TC(x))°$. By definition, $NC(x)$ is a closed convex cone, and it contains every vector that forms a weakly obtuse angle with every feasible displacement vector at x.

Figures 2.13 and 2.14 present examples of tangent cones and normal cones when X is the state space for a two-strategy game (i.e., the simplex in $\mathbf{R}^2$) and for a three-strategy game (the simplex in $\mathbf{R}^3$). Since the latter figure is two-dimensional, with the sheet of paper representing the affine hull of X, the figure actually displays the projected normal cones $\Phi(NX(x))$.

2.3.6 Normal Cones and Nash Equilibria

At first glance, normal cones might appear to be less relevant to game theory than tangent cones. Theorem 2.3.2 shows that this impression is false; normal cones and Nash equilibria are intimately linked.

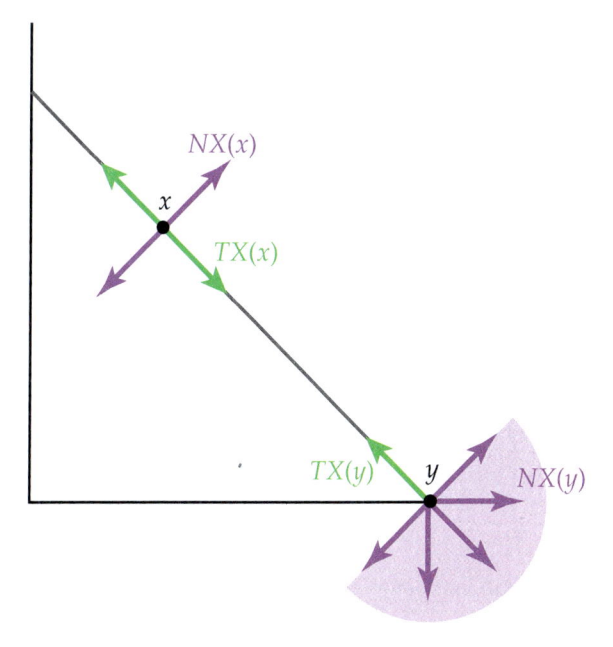

Figure 2.13
Tangent cones and normal cones for two-strategy games.

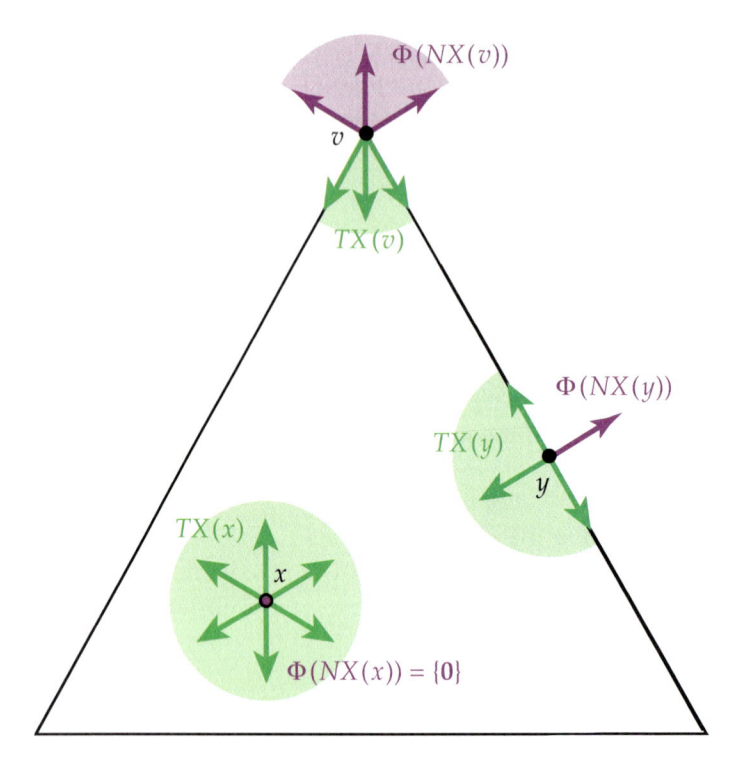

Figure 2.14
Tangent cones and normal cones for three-strategy games.

Theorem 2.3.2 *Let F be a population game. Then $x \in NE(F)$ if and only if $F(x) \in NX(x)$.*

Proof $x \in NE(F) \Leftrightarrow [x_i^p > 0 \Rightarrow F_i^p(x) \geq F_j^p(x)]$ for all $i, j \in S^p, p \in \mathcal{P}$

$\Leftrightarrow (x^p)'F^p(x) \geq (y^p)'F^p(x)$ for all $y^p \in X^p, p \in \mathcal{P}$

$\Leftrightarrow (y^p - x^p)'F^p(x) \leq 0$ for all $y^p \in X^p, p \in \mathcal{P}$

$\Leftrightarrow (z^p)'F^p(x) \leq 0$ for all $z^p \in TX^p(x^p), p \in \mathcal{P}$

$\Leftrightarrow F^p(x) \in NX^p(x^p)$ for all $p \in \mathcal{P}$

$\Leftrightarrow F(x) \in NX(x)$. ∎

Exercise 2.3.3 Justify the second and the last equivalences. ◇

Theorem 2.3.2 says that state x is a Nash equilibrium if and only if the payoff vector $F(x)$ lies in the normal cone of the state space X at x. This result provides a simple geometric description of Nash equilibria of population games. Its

Population Games

straightforward proof shows that x is a Nash equilibrium if and only if it solves a *variational inequality problem*, that is, if it satisfies

$$(y-x)'F(x) \leq 0 \quad \text{for all } y \in X. \tag{2.1}$$

Applying the definitions of tangent and normal cones then yields the result.

In many cases, it is more convenient to speak in terms of projected payoff vectors and projected normal cones. Corollary 2.3.4 restates theorem 2.3.2 in these terms.

Corollary 2.3.4 $x \in NE(F)$ *if and only if* $\Phi F(x) \in \Phi(NX(x))$.

Proof Clearly, $F(x) \in NX(x)$ implies that $\Phi F(x) \in \Phi(NX(x))$. The reverse implication follows from the facts that $NX(x) = \Phi(NX(x)) + (TX)^\perp$ (see exercise 2.3.5) and that $\Phi((TX)^\perp) = \{0\}$ (which is the equation that defines Φ as the *orthogonal* projection of $\mathbf{R}^n$ onto TX). ∎

Exercise 2.3.5

i. Using the notions of relative and average payoffs discussed in section 2.3.3, explain the intuition behind corollary 2.3.4 in the single-population case.

ii. Prove that $NX(x) = \Phi(NX(x)) + (TX)^\perp$.

iii. Only one of the following two statements is equivalent to $x \in NE(F)$: $F(x) \in \Phi(NX(x))$, or $\Phi F(x) \in NX(x)$. Which is it? ◇

In figures 2.8–2.11 the Nash equilibria of the four population games are marked with dots. In the two-strategy games F^{C2} and F^{HD}, the Nash equilibria are those states x at which the payoff vector $F(x)$ lies in the normal cone $NX(x)$, as theorem 2.3.2 requires. In both these games and in the three-strategy games F^{C3} and F^{RPS}, the Nash equilibria are those states x at which the projected payoff vector $\Phi F(x)$ lies in the projected normal cone $\Phi(NX(x))$, as corollary 2.3.4 requires. Even if the dots were not drawn, the Nash equilibria of all four games could be found by examining the arrows alone.

Exercise 2.3.6 Compute the Nash equilibria of the previous four games, and verify that the equilibria appear in the correct positions in figures 2.8–2.11. ◇

Exercise 2.3.7: Two-Population Two-Strategy Games Let F be a game played by two unit mass populations ($p = 2$) with two strategies for each ($n^1 = n^2 = 2$).

i. Describe the state space X, tangent space TX, and orthogonal projection Φ for this setting.

ii. Show that the state space X can be represented on a sheet of paper by a unit square, with the upper left vertex representing the state at which all agents in both populations play strategy 1, and the upper right vertex representing the state at which all agents in population 1 play strategy 1 and all agents in population 2 play strategy 2. Explain how the projected payoff vectors $\Phi F(x)$ can be represented as arrows in this diagram.

iii. At (1) a point in the interior of the square, (2) a nonvertex boundary point, and (3) a vertex, draw the tangent cone $TX(x)$ and the projected normal cone $\Phi(NX(x))$, and give algebraic descriptions of each.

iv. Suppose the projected payoff vectors $\Phi F(x)$ are drawn in the manner you described in part (ii) and the projected normal cones are drawn in the manner you described in part (iii). Verify that in each case considered in part (iii), the arrow representing $\Phi F(x)$ is contained in $\Phi(NX(x))$ if and only if x is a Nash equilibrium of F. ◇

2.A Appendix: Affine Spaces, Tangent Spaces, and Projections

The simplex in $\mathbf{R}^n$, the state space for single-population games, is an $n-1$ dimensional subset of $\mathbf{R}^n$; state spaces for multipopulation games are Cartesian products of scalar multiples of simplices. For this reason, linear subspaces, affine spaces, and orthogonal projections all play important roles in the study of population games.

2.A.1 Affine Spaces

The set $Z \subseteq \mathbf{R}^n$ is a (*linear*) *subspace* of $\mathbf{R}^n$ if it is closed under linear combination: if $z, \hat{z} \in Z$ and $a, b \in \mathbf{R}$, then $az + b\hat{z} \in Z$ as well. Suppose that Z is a subspace of $\mathbf{R}^n$ of dimension $\dim(Z) < n$ and that the set A is a translation of Z by some vector $v \in \mathbf{R}^n$:

$$A = Z + \{v\} = \{x \in \mathbf{R}^n : x = z + v \text{ for some } z \in Z\}.$$

Then A is an *affine space* of dimension $\dim(A) = \dim(Z)$.

Observe that any vector representing a direction of motion through A is itself an element of Z: if $x, y \in A$, then $y - x = (z^y + v) - (z^x + v) = z^y - z^x$ for some z^x and z^y in Z; since Z is closed under linear combinations, $z^y - z^x \in Z$. For this reason, the set Z is called the *tangent space* of A, and one often writes TA in place of Z.

Since the origin is an element of Z, the translation vector v in the definition $A = Z + \{v\}$ can be any element of A. But is there a "natural" choice of v? Recall that the *orthogonal complement* of Z, denoted by $Z^\perp$, contains the vectors in $\mathbf{R}^n$ orthogonal to all elements of Z, that is, $Z^\perp = \{v \in \mathbf{R}^n : v'z = 0 \text{ for all } z \in Z\}$. It is easy to show that the set $A \cap Z^\perp$ contains a single element, denoted by $z_A^\perp$, and that this *orthogonal translation vector* is the closest point in $Z^\perp$ to every point in A (or, as put in section 2.A.3, $P_{Z^\perp} x = z_A^\perp$ for all $x \in A$). For many purposes, this translation vector is the most convenient choice.

Population Games 45

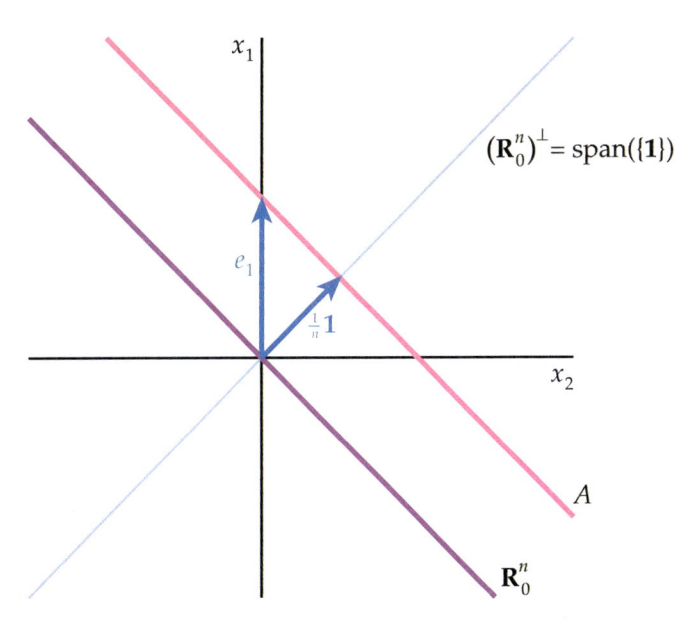

Figure 2.15
The state space and its affine hull for two-strategy games.

Example 2.A.1 Consider the subspace $\mathbf{R}_0^n = \{z \in \mathbf{R}^n: \mathbf{1}'z = 0\}$ and the affine space $A = \mathbf{R}_0^n + \{e_1\} = \{z \in \mathbf{R}^n: \mathbf{1}'z = 1\}$, where $\mathbf{1} = (1,\ldots,1)'$. Since $(\mathbf{R}_0^n)^\perp = \text{span}(\{\mathbf{1}\})$ and $A \cap \text{span}(\{\mathbf{1}\}) = \{\frac{1}{n}\mathbf{1}\}$, the vector $\frac{1}{n}\mathbf{1}$ is the orthogonal translation vector that generates A. In particular, $A = \mathbf{R}_0^n + \{\frac{1}{n}\mathbf{1}\}$, and $\frac{1}{n}\mathbf{1}$ is the closest point in $\text{span}(\{\mathbf{1}\})$ to every $x \in A$. Figure 2.15 illustrates the case in which $n = 2$; note again the convention of using the vertical axis to represent the first component of $x = (x_1, x_2)$. ◆

2.A.2 Affine Hulls of Convex Sets

Let $Y \subseteq \mathbf{R}^n$. The *affine hull* of Y, denoted $\text{aff}(Y)$, is the smallest affine space that contains Y. This set can be described as

$$\text{aff}(Y) = \left\{ x \in \mathbf{R}^n : x = \sum_{i=1}^k \lambda^i y^i \text{ for some } \{y^i\}_{i=1}^k \subset Y \right. \\ \left. \text{and } \{\lambda^i\}_{i=1}^k \subset \mathbf{R} \text{ with } \sum_{i=1}^k \lambda^i = 1 \right\}. \tag{2.2}$$

The vector x is called an *affine combination* of the vectors y^i. If the λ^i were required to be non-negative, x would instead be an *convex combination* of the y^i, and (2.2) would become $\text{conv}(Y)$, the *convex hull* of Y.

Now suppose that Y is itself convex, let $A = \text{aff}(Y)$ be its affine hull, and let $Z = TA$ be the tangent space of A; then $Z = TY$ is also the *tangent space* of Y, as Z contains directions of motion from points in the (relative) interior of Y that stay in Y. Lastly, $\dim(Y) = \dim(Z)$ is the *dimension* of Y.

In constructing the affine hull of a convex set as in (2.2), it is enough to take affine combinations of a fixed set of $\dim(Y)+1$ points in Y. To accomplish this, let $d = \dim(Y)$, fix $y^0 \in Y$ arbitrarily, and choose $y^1, \ldots, y^d$ so that $\{y^1 - y^0, \ldots, y^d - y^0\}$ is a basis for Z. Then, letting $\lambda^0 = 1 - \sum_{i=1}^{d} \lambda^i$,

$$\text{aff}(Y) = Z + \{y^0\}$$
$$= \text{span}(\{y^1 - y^0, \ldots, y^d - y^0\}) + \{y^0\}$$
$$= \left\{ x \in \mathbf{R}^n : x = \sum_{i=1}^{d} \lambda^i(y^i - y^0) + y^0 \text{ for some } \{\lambda^i\}_{i=1}^{d} \subset \mathbf{R} \right\}.$$
$$= \left\{ x \in \mathbf{R}^n : x = \sum_{i=0}^{d} \lambda^i y^i \text{ for some } \{\lambda^i\}_{i=0}^{d} \subset \mathbf{R} \text{ with } \sum_{i=0}^{d} \lambda^i = 1 \right\}.$$

Example 2.A.2: Population States   Let $X^p = \{x^p \in \mathbf{R}_+^{n^p} : \mathbf{1}'x^p = m^p\}$ be the set of population states for a population of mass m^p. This convex set has affine hull $\text{aff}(X^p) = \{x^p \in \mathbf{R}^{n^p} : \mathbf{1}'x^p = m^p\}$ and tangent space $TX^p = \{z^p \in \mathbf{R}^{n^p} : \mathbf{1}'z^p = 0\} = \mathbf{R}_0^{n^p}$ (see example 2.A.1).   ◆

Example 2.A.3: Social States   Let $X = \prod_{p \in \mathcal{P}} X^p$ be the set of social states for a collection of populations $\mathcal{P} = \{1, \ldots, p\}$ with masses $m^1, \ldots, m^p$. This convex set has affine hull $\text{aff}(X) = \prod_{p \in \mathcal{P}} \text{aff}(X^p)$ and tangent space $TX = \prod_{p \in \mathcal{P}} \mathbf{R}_0^{n^p}$. Thus, if $z = (z^1, \ldots, z^p) \in TX$, then each z^p has components that sum to zero.   ◆

2.A.3   Orthogonal Projections

If V and W are subspaces of $\mathbf{R}^n$, their sum is $V + W = \text{span}(V \cup W)$, the set of linear combinations of elements of V and W. If $V \cap W = \{0\}$, every $x \in V + W$ has a unique decomposition $x = v + w$ with $v \in V$ and $w \in W$. In this case, we write $V + W$ as $V \oplus W$, and call it the *direct sum* of V and W. For instance, $V \oplus V^\perp = \mathbf{R}^n$ for any subspace $V \subseteq \mathbf{R}^n$.

Every matrix $A \in \mathbf{R}^{n \times n}$ defines a linear operator from $\mathbf{R}^n$ to itself via $x \mapsto Ax$. To understand the action of this operator, remember that the ith column of A is the image of the standard basis vector e_i, and, more generally, that Ax is a linear combination of the columns of A.

The linear operator $P \in \mathbf{R}^{n \times n}$ is a *projection* onto the subspace $V \subseteq \mathbf{R}^n$ if there is a second subspace $W \subseteq \mathbf{R}^n$ satisfying $V \cap W = \{0\}$ and $V \oplus W = \mathbf{R}^n$ such that $Px = x$ for all $x \in V$ and $Py = 0$ for all $y \in W$. If $W = V^\perp$, P is the *orthogonal projection* onto V, and one writes P_V in place of P.

Population Games

Every projection onto V maps all points in $\mathbf{R}^n$ to points in V. For any given subspace V, there are many projections onto V, but the orthogonal projection onto V is unique. For example,

$$P_1 = \begin{pmatrix} 0 & 0 \\ 1 & 1 \end{pmatrix} \quad \text{and} \quad P_2 = \begin{pmatrix} 0 & 0 \\ 0 & 1 \end{pmatrix}$$

both define projections of $\mathbf{R}^2$ onto the horizontal axis $\{x \in \mathbf{R}^2 : x_1 = 0\}$. (Recall again our convention of representing x_1 on the vertical axis.) However, since P_2 maps the vertical axis $\{x \in \mathbf{R}^2 : x_2 = 0\}$ to the origin, it is the orthogonal projection. The action of the two projections is illustrated in figures 2.16 and 2.17. The latter figure illustrates a geometrically obvious property of orthogonal projections: the orthogonal projection of $\mathbf{R}^n$ onto V maps each point $y \in \mathbf{R}^n$ to the closest point to y in V:

$$P_V y = \operatorname*{argmin}_{v \in V} |y - v|^2.$$

Projections admit simple algebraic characterizations. Recall that the matrix $A \in \mathbf{R}^{n \times n}$ is *idempotent* if $A^2 = A$. It is easy to see that projections are represented by idempotent matrices: once the first application of P projects $\mathbf{R}^n$ onto the subspace V, the second application of P does nothing more. By adding the requirement of symmetry, one characterizes the orthogonal projections.

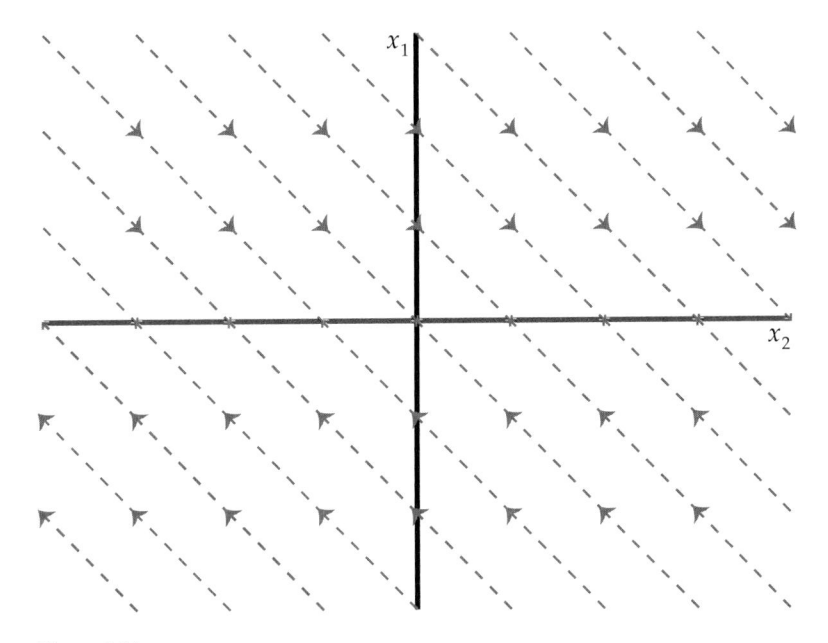

Figure 2.16
A projection.

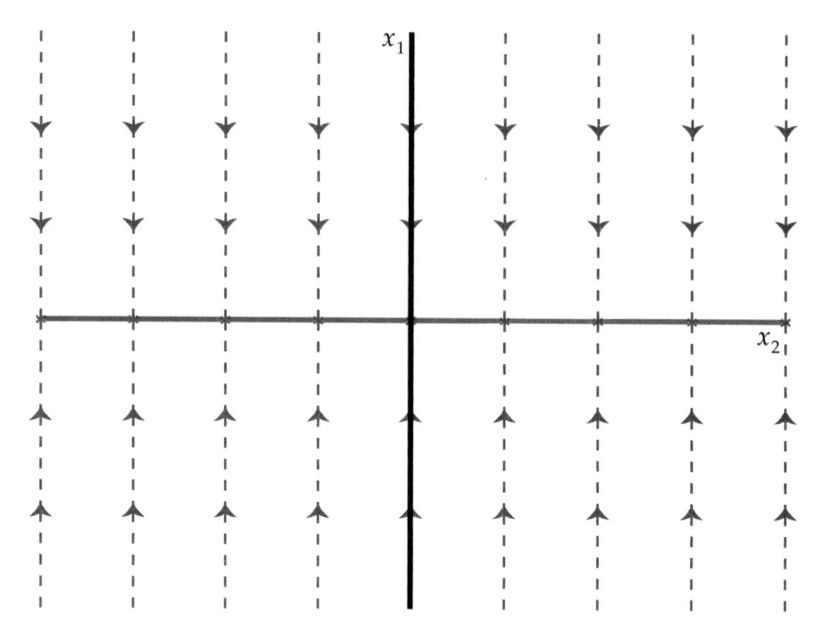

Figure 2.17
An orthogonal projection.

Theorem 2.A.1

i. *P is a projection if and only if P is idempotent.*

ii. *P is an orthogonal projection if and only if P is symmetric idempotent.*

Example 2.A.4: The Orthogonal Projection onto $\mathbf{R}_0^{n^p}$ In example 2.A.2 the set of population states $X^p = \{x^p \in \mathbf{R}_+^{n^p}: \mathbf{1}'x^p = m^p\}$ has tangent space $TX^p = \mathbf{R}_0^{n^p} = \{z^p \in \mathbf{R}^{n^p}: \mathbf{1}'z^p = 0\}$. The space $\mathbf{R}^{n^p}$ can be decomposed into the direct sum $\mathbf{R}_0^{n^p} \oplus \mathbf{R}_1^{n^p}$, where $\mathbf{R}_1^{n^p} = (\mathbf{R}_0^{n^p})^\perp = \text{span}(\{\mathbf{1}\})$. The orthogonal projection of $\mathbf{R}^{n^p}$ onto $\mathbf{R}_1^{n^p}$ is $\Xi = \frac{1}{n^p}\mathbf{11}'$, the matrix whose entries all equal $\frac{1}{n^p}$; to verify this, note that $\Xi z^p = \mathbf{0}$ for $z^p \in \mathbf{R}_0^{n^p}$ and that $\Xi \mathbf{1} = \mathbf{1}$. The orthogonal projection of $\mathbf{R}^{n^p}$ onto $\mathbf{R}_0^{n^p}$ is $\Phi = I - \Xi$, since $\Phi z^p = z^p$ for $z^p \in \mathbf{R}_0^{n^p}$ and $\Phi \mathbf{1} = \mathbf{0}$. (Figure 2.18 shows the case of $n^p = 2$.) Both Ξ and Φ are clearly symmetric, and since $\Xi^2 = (\frac{1}{n^p}\mathbf{11}')(\frac{1}{n^p}\mathbf{11}') = \frac{1}{n^p}\mathbf{11}' = \Xi$ and $\Phi^2 = (I - \Xi)(I - \Xi) = I - 2\Xi + \Xi^2 = I - 2\Xi + \Xi = I - \Xi = \Phi$, both are idempotent as well. ◆

More generally, one can show that if P is the orthogonal projection of $\mathbf{R}^n$ onto V, then $I - P$ is the orthogonal projection of $\mathbf{R}^n$ onto $V^\perp$. Or, in the foregoing notation, $P_{V^\perp} = I - P_V$.

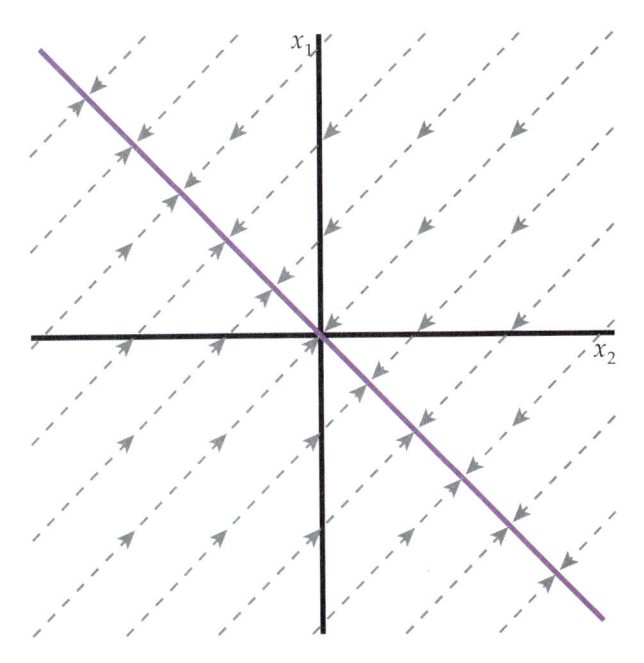

Figure 2.18
The orthogonal projection Φ in $\mathbf{R}^2$.

Example 2.A.5: The Orthogonal Projection onto TX Recall from example 2.A.3 that the set of social states $X = \prod_{p \in \mathcal{P}} X^p$ has tangent space $TX = \prod_{p \in \mathcal{P}} \mathbf{R}_0^{n^p}$. The space $\mathbf{R}^n$ can be decomposed into the direct sum $\prod_{p \in \mathcal{P}} \mathbf{R}_0^{n^p} \oplus \prod_{p \in \mathcal{P}} \mathbf{R}_1^{n^p} = TX \oplus \prod_{p \in \mathcal{P}} \text{span}(\{\mathbf{1}\})$. The orthogonal projection of $\mathbf{R}^n$ onto $\prod_{p \in \mathcal{P}} \text{span}(\{\mathbf{1}\})$ is the block diagonal matrix $\Xi = \text{diag}(\Xi, \ldots, \Xi)$. The orthogonal projection of $\mathbf{R}^n$ onto TX is $\Phi = I - \Xi = \text{diag}(\Phi, \ldots, \Phi)$. Of course, Ξ and Φ are both symmetric idempotent. ◆

Example 2.A.6: Ordinary Least Squares Consider a collection of $n > k$ data points, $\{(x^i, y^i)\}_{i=1}^n$, where each $x^i \in \mathbf{R}^k$ contains k components of explanatory data, and each $y^i \in \mathbf{R}$ is the corresponding component of "explainable" data:

$$X = \begin{pmatrix} (x^1)' \\ \vdots \\ (x^n)' \end{pmatrix} \in \mathbf{R}^{n \times k} \quad \text{and} \quad y = \begin{pmatrix} y^1 \\ \vdots \\ y^n \end{pmatrix} \in \mathbf{R}^n.$$

Assume that the matrix X is of full rank. Our aim is to find the *best linear predictor*, the map $x \mapsto x'\beta$ that minimizes the sum of squared prediction errors $\sum_{i=1}^n (y^i - (x^i)'\beta)^2 = |y - X\beta|^2$.

(The prediction function $x \mapsto x'\beta$ is a truly linear function of x, in the sense that the input vector $\mathbf{0}$ generates a prediction of 0. Typically, one seeks an affine prediction function, which allows for a nonzero constant term. To accomplish this, one sets $x_{k+1}^i = 1$ for all i; in this case, the component β_{k+1} serves as a constant term in the affine prediction function $x \mapsto x'\beta + \beta_{k+1}$.)

Let span$(X) = \{Xb: b \in \mathbf{R}^k\}$ be the column span of X. That $\beta \in \mathbf{R}^k$ minimizes $|y - X\beta|^2$ is equivalent to the requirement that $X\beta$ be the closest point to y in the column span of X:

$$X\beta = \underset{v \in \text{span}(X)}{\text{argmin}} |y - v|^2.$$

Either calculus or geometry can be used to show that for this to be true, the vector of prediction errors $y - X\beta$ must be orthogonal to span(X), and hence to each column of X:

$$X'(y - X\beta) = \mathbf{0}.$$

One can verify that $X \in \mathbf{R}^{n \times k}$ and $X'X \in \mathbf{R}^{k \times k}$ have the same nullspace, and hence the same (full) rank. Therefore, $(X'X)^{-1}$ exists, and the previous equation can be solved for β:

$$\beta = (X'X)^{-1}X'y.$$

Until now, $X \in \mathbf{R}^{n \times k}$ and $y \in \mathbf{R}^n$ were taken as given and used to find the vector $\beta \in \mathbf{R}^k$, which is viewed as defining a map from vectors of explanatory data $x \in \mathbf{R}^k$ to predictions $x'\beta \in \mathbf{R}$. Now, take X alone as given, and consider the map from vectors of "explainable" data $y \in \mathbf{R}^n$ to vectors of predictions $X\beta = X(X'X)^{-1}X'y \in \mathbf{R}^n$. By construction, this linear map $P = X(X'X)^{-1}X' \in \mathbf{R}^{n \times n}$ is the orthogonal projection of $\mathbf{R}^n$ onto span(X). P is clearly symmetric (because the inverse of a symmetric matrix is symmetric), and since $P^2 = X(X'X)^{-1}X'X(X'X)^{-1}X' = X(X'X)^{-1}X' = P$ it is idempotent as well. ◆

2.A.4 The Moreau Decomposition Theorem

A basic fact about orthogonal projection onto subspaces holds that for any vector $v \in \mathbf{R}^n$ and any subspace $Z \subseteq \mathbf{R}^n$, the sum $v = P_Z v + P_{Z^\perp} v$ is the unique decomposition of v into the sum of elements of Z and $Z^\perp$. The *Moreau decomposition theorem* is a generalization of this result that replaces the subspace Z and its orthogonal complement with a closed convex cone and its polar cone. This theorem is used repeatedly in chapter 6 in the analysis of the projection dynamic.

To state this result, one needs an appropriate analogue of orthogonal projection for the context of closed convex sets. To this end, we define $\Pi_C \colon \mathbf{R}^n \to C$, the *(closest point) projection* of $\mathbf{R}^n$ onto the closed convex set C, by

Population Games

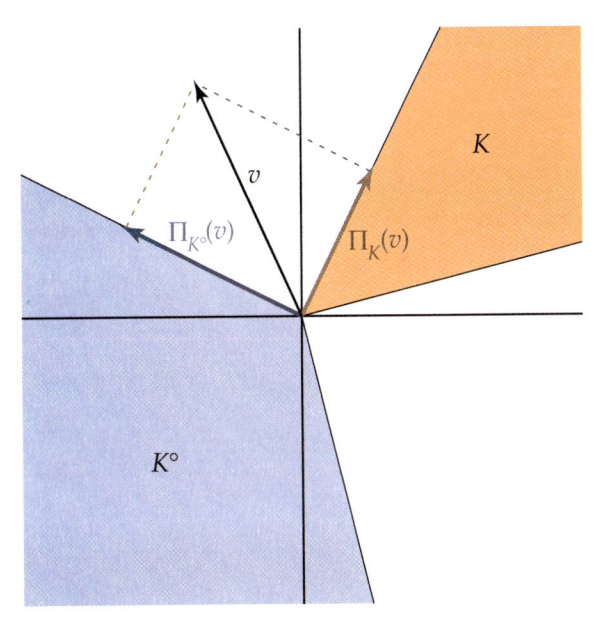

Figure 2.19
The Moreau decomposition theorem.

$$\Pi_C(y) = \underset{x \in C}{\operatorname{argmin}} |y - x|.$$

This definition generalizes that of the projection P_Z onto the subspace $Z \subseteq \mathbf{R}^n$ to cases in which the target set is not linear, but merely closed and convex. With this definition in hand, we can present the decomposition theorem; figure 2.19 provides an illustration.

Theorem 2.A.2 (The Moreau Decomposition Theorem)   *Let $K \subseteq \mathbf{R}^n$ and $K° \subseteq \mathbf{R}^n$ be a closed convex cone and its polar cone, and let $v \in \mathbf{R}^n$. Then the following are equivalent:*

i. $v_K = \Pi_K(v)$ and $v_{K°} = \Pi_{K°}(v)$;

ii. $v_K \in K$, $v_{K°} \in K°$, $v = v_K + v_{K°}$, and $v_K' v_{K°} = 0$.

Notes

Congestion games were introduced by Beckmann, McGuire, and Winsten (1956); see the notes to chapter 3 for additional references. For the biological motivation for the Hawk-Dove game, see Maynard Smith (1982, ch. 2).

Portions of section 2.3 follow Lahkar and Sandholm (2008). The link between normal cones and Nash equilibria is known from the literature on variational inequalities; see Harker and Pang (1990) and Nagurney (1999). For more on affine spaces, tangent cones, normal cones, the Moreau decomposition theorem, and related notions, see Hiriart-Urruty and Lemaréchal (2001). The algebra of orthogonal projections is explained, e.g., in Friedberg, Insel, and Spence (1989, sec. 6.6).

Potential Games, Stable Games, and Supermodular Games

To explain the potential function's role, suppose that $x \in X$ is a population state at which $F_j^p(x) > F_i^p(x)$, so that an agent choosing strategy $i \in S^p$ would be better off choosing strategy $j \in S^p$. Now suppose some small group of agents switch from strategy i to strategy j. These switches are represented by the displacement vector $z = e_j^p - e_i^p$, where e_i^p is the (i,p)th standard basis vector in $\mathbf{R}^n$. The marginal impact that these switches have on the value of potential is therefore

$$\frac{\partial f}{\partial z}(x) = \nabla f(x)' z = \frac{\partial f}{\partial x_j^p}(x) - \frac{\partial f}{\partial x_i^p}(x) = F_j^p(x) - F_i^p(x) > 0.$$

In other words, profitable strategy revisions increase potential. More generally, lemma 7.1.1 shows that the "uphill" directions of the potential function include all directions in which reasonable adjustment processes might lead. This fact underlies the many attractive properties that potential games possess.

If the map $F: \mathbf{R}_+^n \to \mathbf{R}^n$ is C^1 (continuously differentiable), it is well known that F admits a potential function if and only if its derivative matrices $DF(x)$ are symmetric (see section 3.A.9). In the current game-theoretic context, this condition is called *full externality symmetry*.

Observation 3.1.1 *Suppose the population game F is C^1. Then F is a full potential game if and only if it satisfies* full externality symmetry:

$DF(x)$ *is symmetric for all $x \in \mathbf{R}_+^n$.* (3.2)

More explicitly, F is a potential game if and only if

$$\frac{\partial F_i^p}{\partial x_j^q}(x) = \frac{\partial F_j^q}{\partial x_i^p}(x) \quad \text{for all } i \in S^p, j \in S^q,\ p, q \in \mathcal{P}, x \in \mathbf{R}_+^n. \tag{3.3}$$

The preceding observation characterizes smooth full potential games in terms of a simple, economically meaningful property: condition (3.2) requires that the effect on the payoffs to strategy $i \in S^p$ of introducing new agents choosing strategy $j \in S^q$ always equals the effect on the payoffs to strategy j of introducing new agents choosing strategy i.

3.1.3 Examples
The first two examples build on ones introduced in chapter 2.

Example 3.1.1: Matching in Normal Form Games with Common Interests Suppose that agents in a single population are matched to play the symmetric two-player normal form game $A \in \mathbf{R}^{n \times n}$, generating the population game $F(x) = Ax$. While this formula earlier defined F on the state space X, here it defines F on all of $\mathbf{R}_+^n$.

(This choice works very well in the present example, but it is not always innocuous; see section 3.2.)

The symmetric normal form game A has *common interests* if both players always receive the same payoff. This means that $A_{ij} = A_{ji}$ for all i and j, or equivalently, that the matrix A is symmetric. Since $DF(x) = A$, this is precisely what is needed for F to be a full potential game. The full potential function for F is

$$f(x) = \frac{1}{2} x'Ax,$$

which is one-half of $x'Ax = \sum_{i \in S} x_i F_i(x) = \bar{F}(x)$, the aggregate payoff function for F.

To cover the multipopulation case, call the normal form game $U = (U^1, \ldots, U^p)$ a *common interest game* if there is a function $V \colon S \to \mathbf{R}$ such that $U^p(s) = V(s)$ for all $s \in S$ and $p \in \mathcal{P}$. As before, this means that under any pure strategy profile, all p players earn the same payoff. This normal form game generates the full population game

$$F^p_{s^p}(x) = \sum_{s^{-p} \in S^{-p}} V(s) \prod_{r \neq p} x^r_{s^r}$$

on $\mathbf{R}^n_+$. Aggregate payoffs in F are given by

$$\bar{F}(x) = \sum_{p \in \mathcal{P}} \sum_{s^p \in S^p} x^p_{s^p} F^p_{s^p}(x) = p \sum_{s \in S} V(s) \prod_{r \in \mathcal{P}} x^r_{s^r}.$$

Hence, if we let $f(x) = \sum_{s \in S} V(s) \prod_{r \in \mathcal{P}} x^r_{s^r} = \frac{1}{p}\bar{F}(x)$, we obtain

$$\frac{\partial f}{\partial x^p_{s^p}}(x) = \sum_{s^{-p} \in S^{-p}} V(s) \prod_{r \neq p} x^r_{s^r} = F^p_{s^p}(x).$$

So, once again, matching in a common interest game generates a full potential game in which potential is proportional to aggregate payoffs. ◆

Exercise 3.1.2 In the multipopulation case, check directly that condition (3.2) holds. ◇

Example 3.1.2: Congestion Games For ease of exposition, suppose that the congestion game F models behavior in a traffic network. In this environment an agent taking path $j \in S^q$ affects the payoffs of agents choosing path $i \in S^p$ through the marginal increases in congestion on the links $\phi \in \Phi^p_i \cap \Phi^q_j$ that the two paths have in common. But the marginal effect of an agent taking path i on the payoffs of agents choosing path j is identical:

$$\frac{\partial F_i^p}{\partial x_j^q}(x) = -\sum_{\phi \in \Phi_i^p \cap \Phi_j^q} c'_\phi(u_\phi(x)) = \frac{\partial F_j^q}{\partial x_i^p}(x).$$

In other words, congestion games satisfy condition (3.2), and so are full potential games.

The full potential function for the congestion game F is

$$f(x) = -\sum_{\phi \in \Phi} \int_0^{u_\phi(x)} c_\phi(z)\, dz.$$

Hence, potential is typically unrelated to aggregate payoffs, which are given by

$$\bar{F}(x) = \sum_{p \in \mathcal{P}} \sum_{i \in S^p} x_i^p F_i^p(x) = -\sum_{\phi \in \Phi} u_\phi(x) c_\phi(u_\phi(x)).$$

Section 3.1.6 discusses conditions under which potential and aggregate payoffs are directly linked. ◆

Example 3.1.3: Cournot Competition Consider a unit mass population of firms that choose production quantities from the set $S = \{1, \ldots, n\}$. The firms' aggregate production is given by $a(x) = \sum_{i \in S} i\, x_i$. Let $p\colon \mathbf{R}_+ \to \mathbf{R}_+$ denote inverse demand, a decreasing function of aggregate production. Let the firms' production cost function $c\colon S \to \mathbf{R}$ be arbitrary. Then the payoff to a firm producing quantity $i \in S$ at population state $x \in X$ is $F_i(x) = i\, p(a(x)) - c(i)$.

It is easy to check that F is a full potential game with full potential function

$$f(x) = \int_0^{a(x)} p(z)\, dz - \sum_{i \in S} x_i\, c(i).$$

In contrast, aggregate payoffs in F are

$$\bar{F}(x) = \sum_{i \in S} x_i F_i(x) = a(x) p(a(x)) - \sum_{i \in S} x_i c(i).$$

The difference between the two is

$$f(x) - \bar{F}(x) = \int_0^{a(x)} \bigl(p(z) - p(a(x))\bigr)\, dz,$$

which is simply consumers' surplus. Thus, the full potential function $f = \bar{F} + (f - \bar{F})$ measures the total surplus received by firms and consumers. (Total surplus differs from aggregate payoffs because the latter ignores consumers, who are not modeled as active agents.) ◆

Example 3.1.4: Games Generated by Variable Externality Pricing Schemes   Population games can be viewed as models of externalities for environments with many agents. One way to force agents to internalize the externalities they impose upon others is to introduce pricing schemes. Given an arbitrary full population game F with aggregate payoff function $\bar{F}$, define an augmented game $\tilde{F}$ as follows:

$$\tilde{F}_i^p(x) = F_i^p(x) + \sum_{q \in \mathcal{P}} \sum_{j \in S^q} x_j^q \frac{\partial F_j^q}{\partial x_i^p}(x).$$

The double sum represents the marginal effect that an agent choosing strategy i has on other agents' payoffs.

Suppose that when the game F is played, a social planner charges each agent choosing strategy i a tax equal to this double sum, and that each agent's payoff function is separable in this tax. The population game generated by this intervention is $\tilde{F}$.

Now observe that

$$\frac{\partial \bar{F}}{\partial x_i^p}(x) = \frac{\partial}{\partial x_i^p} \sum_{q \in \mathcal{P}} \sum_{j \in S^q} x_j^q F_j^q(x) = F_i^p(x) + \sum_{q \in \mathcal{P}} \sum_{j \in S^q} x_j^q \frac{\partial F_j^q}{\partial x_i^p}(x) = \tilde{F}_i^p(x). \quad (3.4)$$

Equation (3.4) says that the augmented game $\tilde{F}$ is a full potential game, and that its full potential function is the aggregate payoff function of the original game F. Hence, changes in strategy that are profitable in the *augmented* game increase efficiency with respect to the payoffs of the *original* game. ◆

3.1.4 Nash Equilibria of Full Potential Games

We saw in section 3.1.2 that in full potential games, profitable strategy revisions increase potential. It is therefore natural to expect Nash equilibria of full potential games to be related to local maximizers of potential. To investigate this idea, consider the nonlinear program

$$\max f(x) \quad \text{subject to} \quad \sum_{i \in S^p} x_i^p = m^p \quad \text{for all } p \in \mathcal{P},$$

$$x_i^p \geq 0 \quad \text{for all } i \in S^p,\ p \in \mathcal{P}.$$

The Lagrangian for this maximization problem is

$$L(x, \mu, \lambda) = f(x) + \sum_{p \in \mathcal{P}} \mu^p \left(m^p - \sum_{i \in S^p} x_i^p \right) + \sum_{p \in \mathcal{P}} \sum_{i \in S^p} \lambda_i^p x_i^p,$$

Potential Games, Stable Games, and Supermodular Games

so the Kuhn-Tucker first-order necessary conditions for maximization are

$$\frac{\partial f}{\partial x_i^p}(x) = \mu^p - \lambda_i^p \quad \text{for all } i \in S^p, \, p \in \mathcal{P}; \tag{3.5}$$

$$\lambda_i^p x_i^p = 0 \quad \text{for all } i \in S^p, \, p \in \mathcal{P}; \tag{3.6}$$

$$\lambda_i^p \geq 0 \quad \text{for all } i \in S^p, \, p \in \mathcal{P}. \tag{3.7}$$

Let

$$KT(f) = \{x \in X : (x, \mu, \lambda) \text{ satisfies (3.5)–(3.7) for some } \lambda \in \mathbf{R}^n \text{ and } \mu \in \mathbf{R}^p\}.$$

The following theorem shows that the Kuhn-Tucker first-order conditions for maximizing f on X characterize the Nash equilibria of F.

Theorem 3.1.3 *If F is a full potential game with full potential function f, then $NE(F) = KT(f)$.*

Proof If x is a Nash equilibrium of F, then since $F = \nabla f$, the Kuhn-Tucker conditions are satisfied by x, $\mu^p = \max_{j \in S^p} F_j^p(x)$, and $\lambda_i^p = \mu^p - F_i^p(x)$. Conversely, if (x, μ, λ) satisfies the Kuhn-Tucker conditions, then for every $p \in \mathcal{P}$, (3.5) and (3.6) imply that $F_i^p(x) = \frac{\partial f}{\partial x_i^p}(x) = \mu^p$ for all i in the support of x^p. Furthermore, (3.5) and (3.7) imply that $F_j^p(x) = \mu^p - \lambda_j^p \leq \mu^p$ for all $j \in S^p$. Hence, the support of x^p is a subset of $\text{argmax}_{j \in S^p} F_j^p(x)$, and so x is a Nash equilibrium of F. ∎

Note that the multiplier μ^p represents the equilibrium payoff in population p, and that the multiplier λ_i^p represents the "payoff slack" of strategy $i \in S^p$.

Since the set X satisfies constraint qualification, satisfaction of the Kuhn-Tucker conditions is necessary for local maximization of the full potential function. Thus, theorem 3.1.3, along with the fact that a continuous function on a compact set achieves its maximum, yields a simple proof of existence of Nash equilibrium in full potential games.

On the other hand, the Kuhn-Tucker conditions are not sufficient for maximizing potential. Therefore, while all local maximizers of potential are Nash equilibria, not all Nash equilibria locally maximize potential.

Example 3.1.5 Consider again the 123 Coordination game introduced in chapter 2:

$$F(x) = \begin{pmatrix} F_1(x) \\ F_2(x) \\ F_3(x) \end{pmatrix} = \begin{pmatrix} 1 & 0 & 0 \\ 0 & 2 & 0 \\ 0 & 0 & 3 \end{pmatrix} \begin{pmatrix} x_1 \\ x_2 \\ x_3 \end{pmatrix} = \begin{pmatrix} x_1 \\ 2x_2 \\ 3x_3 \end{pmatrix}.$$

The full potential function for this game is the convex function $f(x) = \frac{1}{2}(x_1)^2 + (x_2)^2 + \frac{3}{2}(x_3)^2$. The three pure states, $e_1 = (1,0,0)$, $e_2 = (0,1,0)$, and $e_3 = (0,0,1)$, all locally maximize potential, and so are Nash equilibria. To focus on one instance, note that the Kuhn-Tucker conditions are satisfied at state e_1 by the multipliers $\mu = 1, \lambda_1 = 0$, and $\lambda_2 = \lambda_3 = 1$. The global minimizer of potential, $(\frac{6}{11}, \frac{3}{11}, \frac{2}{11})$, is a state at which payoffs to all three strategies are equal, and is therefore a Nash equilibrium as well; the Kuhn-Tucker conditions are satisfied here with multipliers $\mu = \frac{6}{11}$ and $\lambda_1 = \lambda_2 = \lambda_3 = 0$. Finally, at each of the boundary states $(\frac{2}{3}, \frac{1}{3}, 0)$, $(\frac{3}{4}, 0, \frac{1}{4})$, and $(0, \frac{3}{5}, \frac{2}{5})$, the strategies that are played receive equal payoffs, which exceed the payoff accruing to the unused strategy; thus, these states are Nash equilibria too. These states, coupled with the appropriate multipliers, also satisfy the Kuhn-Tucker conditions: for example, $x = (\frac{2}{3}, \frac{1}{3}, 0)$ satisfies the conditions with $\mu = \frac{2}{3}, \lambda_1 = \lambda_2 = 0$, and $\lambda_3 = \frac{2}{3}$. This exhausts the set of Nash equilibria of F.

Figure 3.1 provides a graph and a contour plot of the full potential function f, illustrating the connection between this function and the Nash equilibria of F. ◆

The previous example demonstrates that in general, potential games can possess Nash equilibria that do not maximize potential. But if the full potential function f is concave, the Kuhn-Tucker conditions are not only necessary for maximizing f; they are also sufficient. This fact yields the following corollary to theorem 3.1.3.

Corollary 3.1.4

i. If f is concave on X, then $NE(F)$ is the convex set of maximizers of f on X.

ii. If f is strictly concave on X, then $NE(F)$ is a singleton containing the unique maximizer of f on X.

Example 3.1.6 A network of highways connects Home and Work. The two towns are separated by a river. Highways A and D are expressways that go around bends in the river and that do not become congested easily: $c_A(u) = c_D(u) = 4 + 20u$. Highways B and C cross the river over two short but easily congested bridges: $c_B(u) = c_C(u) = 2 + 30u^2$. In order to create a direct path between the towns, a city planner considers building a new expressway E that includes a third bridge over the river. Delays on this new expressway are described by $c_E(u) = 1 + 20u$. The highway network as a whole is pictured in figure 3.2.

Before link E is constructed, there are two paths from Home to Work: path 1 traverses links A and B, and path 2 traverses links C and D. The equilibrium driving pattern splits the drivers equally over the two paths, yielding an equilibrium driving time (or negated equilibrium payoff) of 23.5 on each.

After link E is constructed, drivers may also take path 3, which uses links C, E, and B. (Assume that traffic on link E only flows to the right.) The resulting

(a)

(b)

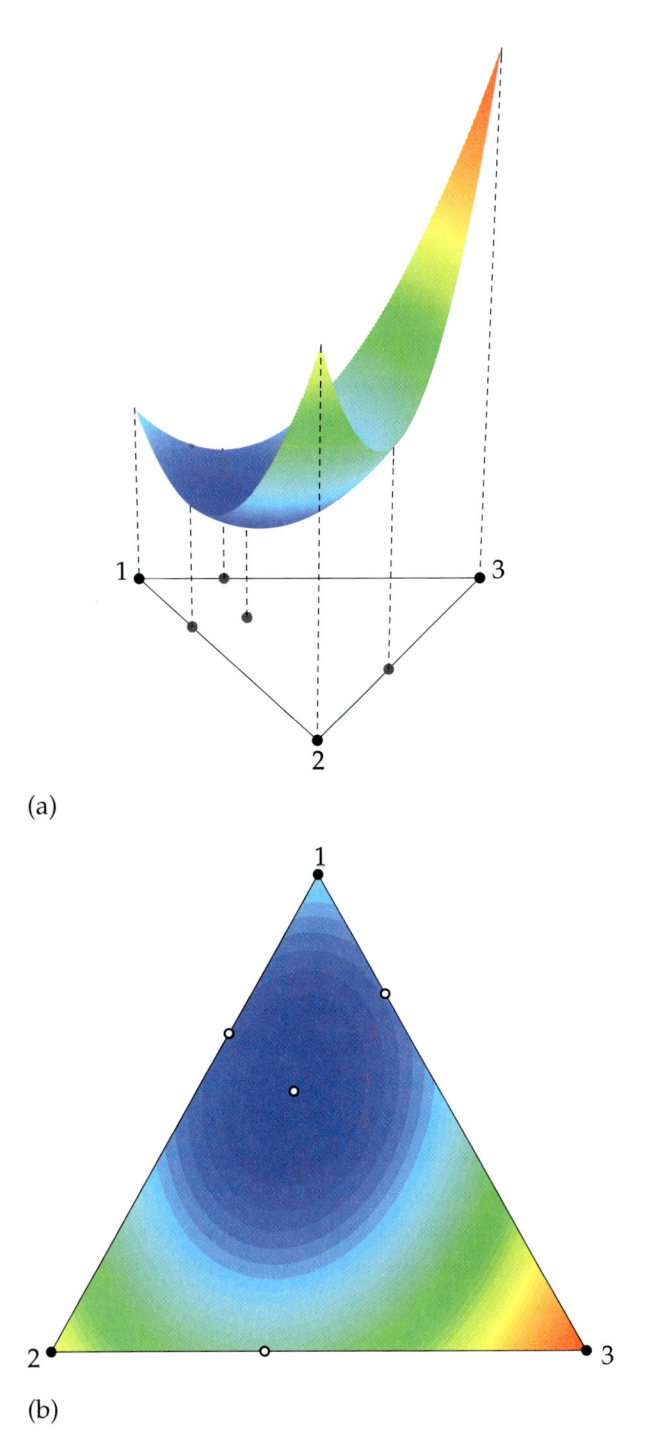

Figure 3.1
Graph (a) and contour plot (b) of the potential function of 123 Coordination.

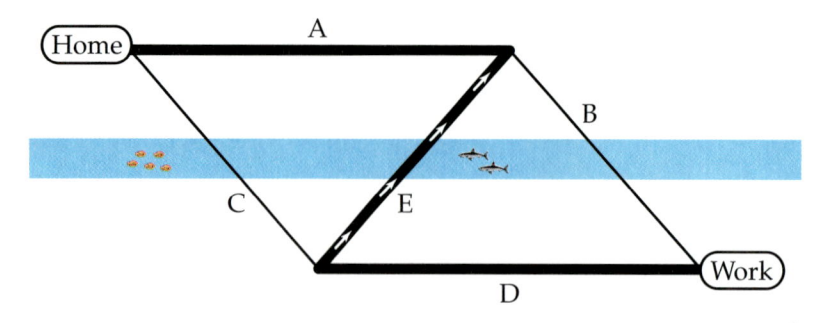

Figure 3.2
A highway network.

population game has payoff functions

$$F(x) = \begin{pmatrix} F_1(x) \\ F_2(x) \\ F_3(x) \end{pmatrix} = \begin{pmatrix} -(6 + 20x_1 + 30(x_1 + x_3)^2) \\ -(6 + 20x_2 + 30(x_2 + x_3)^2) \\ -(5 + 20x_3 + 30(x_1 + x_3)^2 + 30(x_2 + x_3)^2) \end{pmatrix}$$

and full potential function

$$f(x) = -\left(6x_1 + 6x_2 + 5x_3 + 10((x_1)^2 + (x_2)^2 + (x_3)^2 + (x_1 + x_3)^3 + (x_2 + x_3)^3)\right).$$

Figure 3.3 presents a graph and a contour plot of the potential function. Note that the potential function for the two-path game is the restriction of f to the states at which $x_3 = 0$.

Evidently, the potential function f is concave. (This is no coincidence; see exercise 3.1.5.) The unique maximizer of potential on X, the state $x \approx (.4616, .4616, .0768)$, is the unique Nash equilibrium of the game. In this equilibrium, the driving time on each path is approximately 23.93, which exceeds the original equilibrium driving time of 23.5. In other words, adding a link to the network *increases* equilibrium driving times—a phenomenon known as *Braess's paradox*.

The intuition behind this phenomenon is easy to see. Opening up the new link E makes it possible for a single driver on path 3 to use both of the easily congested bridges, B and C. But while using path 3 is bad for the population as a whole, it is appealing to individual drivers, who do not account for the negative externalities that their use of the bridges imposes on others. ◆

Exercise 3.1.5: Uniqueness of Equilibrium in Congestion Games

i. Let F be a congestion game with cost functions c_ϕ and full potential function f. Show that if each c_ϕ is nondecreasing, then f is concave, which implies that $NE(F)$

(a)

(b)

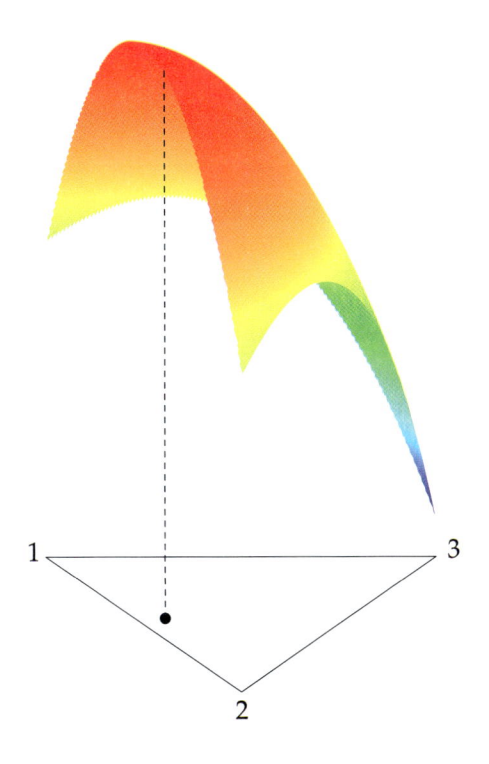

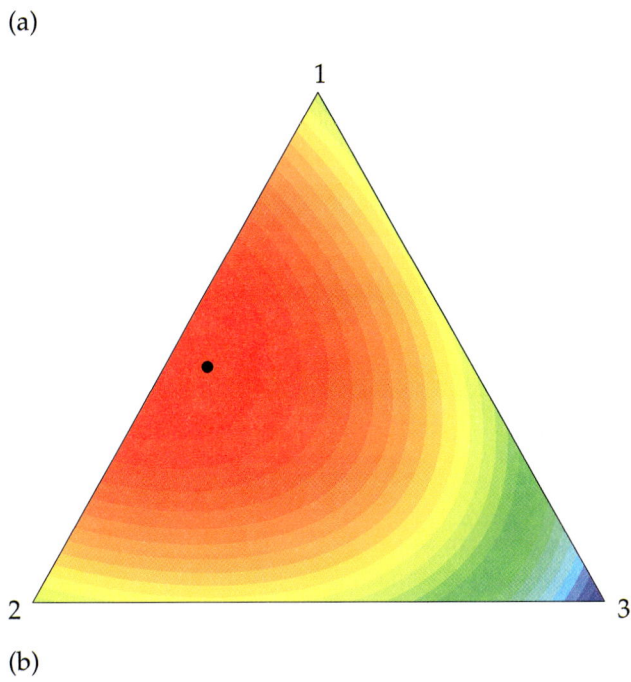

Figure 3.3
Graph (a) and contour plot (b) of the potential function of a congestion game.

is the convex set of maximizers of f on X. (Hint: Fix $y, z \in X$, let $x(t) = (1-t)y + tz$, and show that $g(t) = f(x(t))$ is concave.)

ii. Construct a congestion game in which each c_ϕ is increasing but in which $NE(F)$ is not a singleton.

iii. Show that in case (ii), the equilibrium link utilization levels u_ϕ are unique. (Hint: Since $f(x)$ only depends on the state x through the utilization levels $u_\phi(x)$, one can define a function $g: U \to \mathbf{R}$ on the convex set $U = \{\{v_\phi\}_{\phi \in \Phi}: v_\phi = u_\phi(x)$ for some $x \in \mathbf{R}_+^n\}$ by $g(u_\phi(x)) = f(x)$. Show that x maximizes f on X if and only if $u_\phi(x)$ maximizes g on U.) ◇

Exercise 3.1.6 Example 3.1.4 shows that by adding state-dependent congestion charges to a congestion game, a planner can ensure that drivers use the network efficiently, in the sense of minimizing average travel times. Show that these congestion charges can be imposed on a link-by-link basis, and that the price on each link need only depend on the number of drivers on that link. ◇

Exercise 3.1.7 Show that Cournot competition (example 3.1.3) with a decreasing inverse demand function generates a potential game with a strictly concave potential function and hence admits a unique Nash equilibrium. ◇

Exercise 3.1.8: Entry and Exit When one defines a full population game $F: \mathbf{R}_+^n \to \mathbf{R}^n$, one specifies the payoffs of each of the n strategies for all possible vectors of population masses. It is only a small additional step to allow agents to enter and leave the game. Fixing a vector of population masses $(m^1, \ldots, m^p)$, define a *population game with entry and exit* by assuming that the set of feasible social states is $\bar{X} = \{x = (x^1, \ldots, x^p) \in \mathbf{R}_+^n: \sum_{i \in S^p} x_i^p \leq m^p\}$, and that an agent who exits the game receives a payoff of 0.

i. State an appropriate definition of Nash equilibrium for population games with entry and exit.

ii. A population game with entry and exit is a *potential game* if it satisfies full externality symmetry (3.2). Prove an analogue of theorem 3.1.3 for such games. ◇

3.1.5 The Geometry of Nash Equilibrium in Full Potential Games

Theorem 3.1.3 shows that if F is a potential game with potential function f, then states satisfying the Kuhn-Tucker first-order conditions for maximizing f are precisely the Nash equilibria of F. We now present a geometric proof of this result, and discuss its implications.

The nonlinear program from section 3.1.4 seeks to maximize the function f on the polytope X. What do the Kuhn-Tucker conditions for this program mean?

Potential Games, Stable Games, and Supermodular Games 65

The Kuhn-Tucker conditions adapt the classical approach to optimization based on linearization to settings with both equality and inequality constraints. In the current context, these conditions embody the following construction. To begin, one linearizes the objective function f at the state $x \in X$ of interest, replacing it with the function $l_{f,x}(y) = f(x) + \nabla f(x)'(y-x)$. Then one determines whether the linearized function reaches its maximum on X at state x. Of course, this method can accept states that are not maximizers: for instance, if x is an interior local *minimizer* of f, then the linearization $l_{f,x}$ is a constant function, and so is maximized everywhere in X. But because X is a polytope (in particular, since constraint qualification holds), x must maximize $l_{f,x}$ on X if it is to maximize f on X.

With this interpretation of the Kuhn-Tucker conditions in mind, one can prove geometrically that $NE(F) = KT(f)$. The analysis employs the normal cone characterization of Nash equilibrium from chapter 2.

Theorem 3.1.3 *If F is a full potential game with full potential function f, then $NE(F) = KT(f)$.*

Second proof $x \in KT(f) \Leftrightarrow x$ maximizes $l_{f,x}$ on X

$$\Leftrightarrow [z \in TX(x) \Rightarrow \nabla f(x)'z \leq 0]$$

$$\Leftrightarrow \nabla f(x) \in NX(x)$$

$$\Leftrightarrow F(x) \in NX(x)$$

$$\Leftrightarrow x \in NE(F). \qquad \blacksquare$$

This proof is easy to explain in words. As noted earlier, satisfying the Kuhn-Tucker conditions for f on X is equivalent to maximizing the linearized version of f on X. This in turn is equivalent to the requirement that if z is in the tangent cone of X at x—that is, if z is a feasible displacement direction from x—then z forms a weakly obtuse angle with the gradient vector $\nabla f(x)$, representing the direction in which f increases fastest. But this is precisely what it means for $\nabla f(x)$ to lie in the normal cone $NX(x)$. The definition of potential says that $\nabla f(x)$ can be replaced with $F(x)$, and by theorem 2.3.2, that $F(x) \in NX(x)$ means that x is a Nash equilibrium of F.

This argument sheds new light on theorem 3.1.3. The Kuhn-Tucker conditions, which provide a way of finding the maximizers of the function f, are stated in terms of the gradient vectors $\nabla f(x)$. At first glance, it seems rather odd to replace $\nabla f(x)$ with some nonintegrable map F. After all, what is the point of the Kuhn-Tucker conditions when there is no function to maximize? But from the geometric point of view, replacing $\nabla f(x)$ with F makes perfect sense. When the Kuhn-Tucker conditions are viewed in geometric terms, namely, in the form $\nabla f(x) \in NX(x)$, they become a restatement of the Nash equilibrium condition; the fact that $\nabla f(x)$ is a gradient vector plays no role. To summarize, the Nash equilibrium condition $F(x) \in NX(x)$ is identical to the Kuhn-Tucker conditions, but applies whether or not the map F is integrable.

Exercise 3.1.9 Let F be a full potential game with full potential function f. Let $C \subseteq NE(F)$ be *smoothly connected*, in the sense that if $x, y \in C$, then there exists a piecewise C^1 path $\alpha \colon [0, 1] \to C$ with $\alpha(0) = x$ and $\alpha(1) = y$. Show that f is constant on C. (*Hint:* Use the fundamental theorem of calculus and the fact that $F(x) \in NX(x)$ for all $x \in NE(F)$, along with the fact that when $\alpha(t) = x$ and α is differentiable at x, both $\alpha'(t)$ and $-\alpha'(t)$ are in $TX(x)$.) ◇

3.1.6 Efficiency in Homogeneous Full Potential Games

Section 3.1.3 showed that when agents are matched to play normal form games with common interests, the full potential function of the resulting population game is proportional to the game's aggregate payoff function. How far can one push this connection?

Definition *A full potential game F is homogeneous of degree k if each of its payoff functions $F_i^p \colon \mathbf{R}_+^n \to \mathbf{R}$ is a homogeneous function of degree k (that is, if $F_i^p(tx) = t^k F_i^p(x)$ for all $x \in \mathbf{R}_+^n$ and $t > 0$), where $k \neq -1$.*

Example 3.1.7: Matching in Normal Form Games with Common Interests Under single-population matching, each payoff function $F(x) = Ax$ is linear, so the full potential game F is homogeneous of degree 1. With $p \geq 2$ populations, the payoffs F^p to population p's strategies are multilinear in $(x^1, \ldots, x^{p-1}, x^{p+1}, \ldots, x^p)$, so the full potential game F is homogeneous of degree $p - 1$. ◆

Example 3.1.8: Isoelastic Congestion Games Let F be a congestion game with cost functions c_ϕ. For each facility $\phi \in \Phi$, let

$$\eta_\phi(u) = \frac{u c_\phi'(u)}{c_\phi(u)}$$

denote ϕ's *cost elasticity*, which is well defined whenever $c_\phi(u) \neq 0$. A congestion game is *isoelastic with elasticity* $\eta \in \mathbf{R}$ if $\eta_\phi = \eta$ for all $\phi \in \Phi$. Thus, a congestion game is isoelastic if all facilities in Φ are equally sensitive to congestion at all levels of use.

Isoelasticity implies that all cost functions are of the form $c_\phi(u) = a_\phi u^\eta$, where the a_ϕ are arbitrary (i.e., positive or negative) scalar constants. (Notice that η cannot be negative, because this would force facility costs to become infinite at $u = 0$.) Since each u_ϕ is linear in x, each payoff function F_i^p is a sum of functions that are homogeneous of degree η in x, and so is itself homogeneous of degree η. Therefore, any isoelastic congestion game with elasticity η is a homogeneous potential game of degree η. ◆

The efficiency properties of homogeneous potential games are consequences of the following theorem.

Theorem 3.1.10 *A full potential game F is homogeneous of degree $k \neq -1$ if and only if the normalized aggregate payoff function $\frac{1}{k+1}\bar{F}(x)$ is a full potential function for F and is homogeneous of degree $k+1 \neq 0$.*

Proof If the potential game F is homogeneous of degree $k \neq -1$, then $\frac{1}{k+1}\bar{F}(x) = \frac{1}{k+1}\sum_{p \in \mathcal{P}} \sum_{j \in S^p} x_j^p F_j^p(x)$ is clearly homogeneous of degree $k+1$. Therefore, condition (3.2) and Euler's theorem (see section 3.A.5) imply that

$$\frac{\partial}{\partial x_i^p}\left(\frac{1}{k+1}\bar{F}(x)\right) = \frac{1}{k+1}\left(\sum_{q \in \mathcal{P}} \sum_{j \in S^q} x_j^q \frac{\partial F_j^q}{\partial x_i^p}(x) + F_i^p(x)\right)$$

$$= \frac{1}{k+1}\left(\sum_{q \in \mathcal{P}} \sum_{j \in S^q} x_j^q \frac{\partial F_i^p}{\partial x_j^q}(x) + F_i^p(x)\right)$$

$$= \frac{1}{k+1}\left(kF_i^p(x) + F_i^p(x)\right)$$

$$= F_i^p(x),$$

so $\frac{1}{k+1}\bar{F}$ is a full potential function for F. On the other hand, if $\frac{1}{k+1}\bar{F}$ is homogeneous of degree $k+1 \neq 0$ and is a full potential function for F, then each payoff function $F_i^p = \frac{\partial}{\partial x_i^p}(\frac{1}{k+1}\bar{F})$ is homogeneous of degree k, so the converse statement follows. ∎

To understand the connection between homogeneity and efficiency, consider the expression $\frac{\partial}{\partial x_i^p}\bar{F}(x)$, which represents the impact of an agent who chooses strategy i on aggregate payoffs. Recalling example 3.1.4, we split this impact into two terms. The first term, $\sum_q \sum_j x_j^q \frac{\partial F_j^q}{\partial x_i^p}(x)$, represents the impact of this agent's behavior on his opponents' payoffs. The second term, $F_i^p(x)$, represents the agent's own payoffs. In homogeneous potential games, these two effects are precisely balanced: the payoff an agent receives from choosing a strategy is directly proportional to the social impact of his choice. For this reason, self-interested behavior leads to desirable social outcomes.

Observe that if a potential game is homogeneous of degree less than -1, its full potential function is *negatively* proportional to aggregate payoffs. In this case, self-interested behavior leads to undesirable social outcomes. To remove this case from consideration, call a potential game *positively homogeneous* if its full potential function is homogeneous of positive degree, so that the game itself is homogeneous of degree $k > -1$.

With this definition in hand, we can state a result on the efficiency of Nash equilibria. The social state x is *locally efficient* in game F ($x \in LE(F)$) if there exists an $\varepsilon > 0$ such that $\bar{F}(x) \geq \bar{F}(y)$ for all $y \in X$ within ε of x. If this inequality holds for all $y \in X$, then x is *globally efficient* ($x \in GE(F)$).

Corollary 3.1.11

i. *If a full potential game F is positively homogeneous, then $LE(F) \subseteq NE(F)$.*

ii. *If in addition its full potential function f is concave, then $GE(F) = LE(F) = NE(F)$.*

Exercise 3.1.12 Establish these claims. ◇

Exercise 3.1.13 Let F be a congestion game with nondecreasing affine cost functions: $c_\phi(u) = a_\phi u + b_\phi$. Suppose that within each population, the fixed cost of each route is the same:

$$\sum_{\phi \in \Phi_i^p} b_\phi = b^p \quad \text{for all } i \in S^p, p \in \mathcal{P}.$$

Show that $NE(F) = GE(F)$. ◇

3.1.7 Inefficiency Bounds for Congestion Games

The foregoing results provide stringent conditions under which Nash equilibria of congestion games are efficient. Since exact efficiency rarely obtains, it is natural to ask just how inefficient equilibrium behavior can be. We address this question in the context of congestion games with nondecreasing cost functions, in other words, congestion games in which congestion is a bad.

It will be convenient to use notation tailored to the questions at hand. Given the facilities $\phi \in \Phi$ and the nondecreasing cost functions c_ϕ, let

$$C_i^p(x) = -F_i^p(x) = \sum_{\phi \in \Phi_i^p} c_\phi(u_\phi(x))$$

denote the *cost* of strategy $i \in S^p$ at state x, and let

$$\bar{C}(x) = -\bar{F}(x) = \sum_{p \in \mathcal{P}} \sum_{i \in S^p} x_i^p C_i^p(x) = \sum_{\phi \in \Phi} u_\phi(x) c_\phi(u_\phi(x))$$

denote *social cost* at state x. We refer to the resulting congestion game either as C or as (C, m) (to emphasize the population masses m). When alternative cost functions γ_ϕ are introduced, C is replaced with Γ.

One approach to bounding the inefficiency of equilibria is to compare the equilibrium social cost to the minimal social cost in a game with additional agents.

Potential Games, Stable Games, and Supermodular Games

Proposition 3.1.14 *Let C be a congestion game with nondecreasing cost functions. Let x^* be a Nash equilibrium of (C, m), and let y be a feasible state in $(C, 2m)$. Then $\bar{C}(x^*) \leq \bar{C}(y)$.*

Exercise 3.1.15 This exercise outlines a proof of proposition 3.1.14.

i. Define the cost functions γ_ϕ by $\gamma_\phi(u) = \max\{c_\phi(u_\phi(x^*)), c_\phi(u)\}$. Show that $u(\gamma_\phi(u) - c_\phi(u)) \leq c_\phi(u_\phi(x^*)) u_\phi(x^*)$.

ii. Show that $\Gamma_i^p(y) \geq \min_{j \in S^p} C_j^p(x^*)$.

iii. Use parts (i) and (ii) to show that $\bar{\Gamma}(y) - \bar{C}(y) \leq \bar{C}(x^*)$ and that $\bar{\Gamma}(y) \geq 2\bar{C}(x^*)$, and conclude that $\bar{C}(x^*) \leq \bar{C}(y)$. ◇

Exercise 3.1.16 This exercise applies proposition 3.1.14 to settings with fixed population masses but varying cost functions.

i. Show that the equilibrium social cost under cost functions $\tilde{c}_\phi(u) = \frac{1}{2} c_\phi(\frac{u}{2})$ is bounded above by the minimal social cost under cost functions c_ϕ.

ii. Let C be a congestion game with cost functions $c_\phi(u) = (k_\phi - u)^{-1}$ for some *capacities* $k_\phi > 0$. (Assume that population masses are small enough that no edge can reach its capacity.) Using part (i), show that the equilibrium social cost when capacities are $2k$ is bounded above by the minimal social cost when capacities are k. In other words, doubling the capacities of the edges reduces costs at least as much as enforcing efficient behavior under the original capacities. ◇

A more direct way of understanding inefficiency is to bound a game's *inefficiency ratio*: the ratio between the game's equilibrium social cost and its minimal feasible social cost.

Example 3.1.9 A highway network consisting of two parallel links is to be traversed by a unit mass of drivers. The links' cost functions are $c_1(u) = 1$ and $c_2(u) = u$. In the unique Nash equilibrium of this game, all drivers travel on route 2, creating a social cost of 1. The efficient state, which minimizes $\bar{C}(x) = x_1 + (x_2)^2$, is $x_{\min} = (\frac{1}{2}, \frac{1}{2})$; it generates a social cost of $\bar{C}(x_{\min}) = \frac{3}{4}$. Thus, the inefficiency ratio in this game is $\frac{4}{3}$. ◆

The next result describes an easily established upper bound on inefficiency ratios.

Proposition 3.1.17 *Suppose that the cost functions c_ϕ are nondecreasing and satisfy $uc_\phi(u) \leq \alpha \int_0^u c_\phi(z)\, dz$ for all $u \geq 0$. If $x^* \in NE(C)$ and $x \in X$, then $\bar{C}(x^*) \leq \alpha \bar{C}(x)$.*

Exercise 3.1.18

i. Prove proposition 3.1.17. (*Hint:* Use a potential function argument.)

ii. Show that if cost functions in C are polynomials of degree at most k with nonnegative coefficients, then the inefficiency ratio in C is at most $k+1$. ◇

Exercise 3.1.18 reveals that the inefficiency ratio of a congestion game with affine cost functions cannot exceed 2. Is it possible to establish a smaller upper bound? Example 3.1.9 shows that inefficiency ratios as high as $\frac{4}{3}$ can arise in very simple games with non-negative affine cost functions. Amazingly, $\frac{4}{3}$ is the highest possible inefficiency ratio for congestion games with cost functions of this form.

Theorem 3.1.19 *Let C be a congestion game whose cost functions c_ϕ are non-negative, nondecreasing, and affine: $c_\phi(u) = a_\phi + b_\phi u$ with $a_\phi, b_\phi \geq 0$. If $x^* \in NE(C)$ and $x \in X$, then $\bar{C}(x^*) \leq \frac{4}{3}\bar{C}(x)$.*

Proof Fix $x^* \in NE(C)$ and $x \in X$, and write $v_\phi^* = u_\phi(x^*)$ and $v_\phi = u_\phi(x)$. Let $\Phi_L = \{\phi \in \Phi : v_\phi < v_\phi^*\}$ be the set of facilities that are underutilized at x relative to x^*.

Every $r \in \mathbf{R}$ satisfies $(1-r)r \leq \frac{1}{4}$. Multiplying both sides of this inequality by $b_\phi (v_\phi^*)^2$ and setting $r = v_\phi/v_\phi^*$ yields

$$b_\phi(v_\phi^* - v_\phi)v_\phi \leq \tfrac{1}{4} b_\phi (v_\phi^*)^2 \quad \text{when } \phi \in \Phi_L. \tag{3.8}$$

Thus, since x^* is a Nash equilibrium, and by the assumptions on c_ϕ, we have

$$\bar{C}(x^*) = \sum_{\phi \in \Phi} c_\phi(v_\phi^*) v_\phi^*$$

$$\leq \sum_{\phi \in \Phi} c_\phi(v_\phi^*) v_\phi$$

$$= \sum_{\phi \in \Phi} c_\phi(v_\phi) v_\phi + \sum_{\phi \in \Phi} \left(c_\phi(v_\phi^*) - c_\phi(v_\phi)\right) v_\phi$$

$$\leq \bar{C}(x) + \sum_{\phi \in \Phi_L} b_\phi(v_\phi^* - v_\phi)v_\phi$$

$$\leq \bar{C}(x) + \tfrac{1}{4} \sum_{\phi \in \Phi_L} b_\phi (v_\phi^*)^2$$

$$\leq \bar{C}(x) + \tfrac{1}{4} \sum_{\phi \in \Phi_L} v_\phi^* c_\phi(v_\phi^*)$$

$$= \bar{C}(x) + \tfrac{1}{4}\bar{C}(x^*).$$

Rearranging yields $\bar{C}(x^*) \leq \frac{4}{3}\bar{C}(x)$. ∎

That the highest inefficiency ratio for a given class of cost functions can be realized in a very simple network is true generally. Consider a two-link network with link cost functions $c_1(u) = 1$ and $c_2(u) = u^k$, where $k \geq 1$. With a unit mass population, the Nash equilibrium for this network is $x^* = (0, 1)$, and has social cost $\bar{C}(x^*) = 1$. The efficient state is $x_{\min} = (1 - (k+1)^{-1/k}, (k+1)^{-1/k})$, and has social cost $\bar{C}(x_{\min}) = 1 - k(k+1)^{-(k+1)/k}$. Remarkably, it is possible to show that the resulting inefficiency ratio of $(1 - k(k+1)^{-(k+1)/k})^{-1}$ is the highest possible in any network whose cost functions are polynomials of degree at most k (see the chapter notes for details).

A minor modification of the proof of theorem 3.1.19 improves the bound presented in proposition 3.1.14. The earlier result showed that equilibrium social cost in a congestion game cannot exceed the efficient level of social cost in the game with identical cost functions but with population sizes that are twice as large. Corollary 3.1.20 shows that in the affine case, this multiplicative factor can be reduced from 2 to $\frac{5}{4}$.

Corollary 3.1.20 *Let C be a congestion game whose cost functions c_ϕ are non-negative, nondecreasing, and affine. Let x^* be a Nash equilibrium of (C, m), and let y be a feasible state in $(C, \frac{5}{4}m)$. Then $\bar{C}(x^*) \leq \bar{C}(y)$.*

Exercise 3.1.21 Prove corollary 3.1.20. (*Hint:* The proof of theorem 3.1.19 establishes that $\sum_{\phi \in \Phi} c_\phi(u_\phi(x^*)) u_\phi(y) \leq \bar{C}(y) + \frac{1}{4}\bar{C}(x^*)$ for any $y \in \mathbf{R}_+^n$. Combine this inequality with the fact that x^* is a Nash equilibrium of (C, m).) $\diamond$

While our treatment of inefficiency bounds has focused on congestion games with affine and polynomial cost functions, it is possible to establish such bounds while placing much less structure on the costs. In fact, one can generalize the preceding arguments to obtain inefficiency bounds for general population games (see the chapter notes for relevant references).

3.2 Potential Games

To define full potential games, we first defined full population games by extending the domain of payoffs from the state space X to the positive orthant $\mathbf{R}_+^n$. This device for introducing potential functions is simple, but it is often artificial. By using ideas from affine calculus (appendix 3.B), potential functions for population games can be defined without recourse to changes in domain.

3.2.1 Motivating Examples

The developments to come are motivated not only by parsimony, but also by generality, as the following two examples show.

Example 3.2.1: Matching in Symmetric Normal Form Potential Games Recall that the symmetric normal form game $C \in \mathbf{R}^{n \times n}$ is a common interest game if C is a symmetric matrix, so that both players always receive the same payoff. The symmetric normal form game $A \in \mathbf{R}^{n \times n}$ is a *potential game* if $A = C + \mathbf{1}r'$ for some common interest game C and some arbitrary vector $r \in \mathbf{R}^n$. Thus, each player's payoff is the sum of a common interest term and a term that only depends on her opponent's choice of strategy. (For the latter point, note that $A_{ij} = C_{ij} + r_j$.)

Suppose a population of agents is matched to play game A. Since the second payoff term has no effect on agents' incentives, it is natural to expect the characterization of equilibrium from the previous section to carry over to the current setting. But this does not follow from the previous definitions. Suppose the full population game $F: \mathbf{R}_+^n \to \mathbf{R}^n$ is defined as in example 3.1.1: $F(x) = Ax$. Then the resulting derivative matrix is $DF(x) = A = C + \mathbf{1}r'$, and so

$$\frac{\partial F_i}{\partial x_j}(x) = C_{ij} + r_j, \quad \text{but} \quad \frac{\partial F_j}{\partial x_i}(x) = C_{ji} + r_i.$$

Therefore, unless r is a constant vector (in which case A itself is symmetric), this full population game F is not a full potential game. ◆

Example 3.2.2: Two-Strategy Games Recall that the population game $F: X \to \mathbf{R}^n$ is a two-strategy game if $p = 1$ and $n = 2$. In this setting, the state space X is the simplex in $\mathbf{R}^2$, which can be viewed as a relabeling of the unit interval. Because all functions defined on the unit interval are integrable, it seems natural to expect two-strategy games to admit potential functions. If one wanted to show that F defines a full potential game, one would first need to extend its domain to $\mathbf{R}_+^2$. Once this is done, the domain is no longer one-dimensional, so the intuition about the existence of a potential function is lost. ◆

3.2.2 Definition, Characterizations, and Examples

Example 3.2.2 suggests that the source of the difficulties is the extension of payoffs from the original state space X to the full-dimensional set $\mathbf{R}_+^n$. The definition of full potential games relied on this extension, so the new notion of potential games will require some additional ideas. The key concepts are the tangent spaces and orthogonal projections introduced in chapter 2.

Recall that the state space for population p is given by $X^p = \{x^p \in \mathbf{R}_+^{n^p} : \sum_{i \in S^p} x_i^p = m^p\}$. The tangent space of X^p, denoted TX^p, is the smallest subspace of $\mathbf{R}^{n^p}$ that contains all directions of motion through X^p; it is defined by $TX^p = \mathbf{R}_0^{n^p} \equiv \{z^p \in \mathbf{R}^{n^p} : \sum_{i \in S^p} z_i^p = 0\}$. The matrix $\Phi \in \mathbf{R}^{n^p \times n^p}$, representing the orthogonal projection of $\mathbf{R}^{n^p}$ onto TX^p, is defined by $\Phi = I - \frac{1}{n^p}\mathbf{11}'$. If $\pi^p \in \mathbf{R}^{n^p}$ is a payoff vector, then the projected payoff vector $\Phi\pi^p$ represents relative payoffs under π^p; it preserves the differences between components of π^p while normalizing their sum to zero. Changes in the social state $x \in X = \prod_{p \in \mathcal{P}} X^p$ are represented by elements of $TX = \prod_{p \in \mathcal{P}} TX^p$, the tangent space of X. The matrix $\Phi \in \mathbf{R}^{n \times n}$, representing the orthogonal projection of $\mathbf{R}^n$ onto TX, is the block diagonal matrix $\text{diag}(\Phi, \ldots, \Phi)$. If $\pi = (\pi^1, \ldots, \pi^p) \in \mathbf{R}^n$ is a payoff vector for the society, then $\Phi\pi = (\Phi\pi^1, \ldots, \Phi\pi^p)$ normalizes each of the p pieces of the vector π separately.

With these preliminaries in hand, we can state our new definition.

Potential Games, Stable Games, and Supermodular Games

Definition   Let $F: X \to \mathbf{R}^n$ be a population game. F is a *potential game if it admits a potential function*, a C^1 function $f: X \to \mathbf{R}$ that satisfies

$$\nabla f(x) = \Phi F(x) \quad \text{for all } x \in X. \tag{3.9}$$

Since the potential function f has domain X, the gradient vector $\nabla f(x)$ is by definition an element of the tangent space TX (see section 3.B.3). The definition of potential games requires that this gradient vector always equal $\Phi F(x)$, the projection of the payoff vector $F(x)$ onto the subspace TX.

At the cost of sacrificing parsimony, one can define potential games without affine calculus by using a function defined throughout $\mathbf{R}^n_+$ to play the role of the potential function f. To do so, one simply includes the projection Φ on both sides of the analogue of equation (3.9).

Observation 3.2.1   *If F is a potential game with potential function $f: X \to \mathbf{R}$, then any C^1 extension $\tilde{f}: \mathbf{R}^n_+ \to \mathbf{R}$ of f satisfies*

$$\Phi \nabla \tilde{f}(x) = \Phi F(x) \quad \text{for all } x \in X. \tag{3.10}$$

Conversely, if the population game F admits a function $\tilde{f}$ satisfying condition (3.10), then F is a potential game, and the restriction $f = \tilde{f}\big|_X$ is a potential function for F.

This observation is immediate from the relevant definitions. In particular, if $\tilde{f}$ and f agree on X, then for all $x \in X$ the gradient vectors $\nabla \tilde{f}(x)$ and $\nabla f(x)$ define identical linear operators on TX, implying that $\Phi \nabla \tilde{f}(x) = \Phi \nabla f(x)$. But since $\Phi \nabla f(x) = \nabla f(x)$ by definition, it follows that $\Phi \nabla \tilde{f}(x) = \nabla f(x)$; this equality and definition (3.9) yield the result.

Like full potential games, potential games can be characterized by a symmetry condition on the payoff derivatives $DF(x)$. Since potential games generalize full potential games, the new symmetry condition is less restrictive than the old one.

Theorem 3.2.2   *Suppose the population game $F: X \to \mathbf{R}^n$ is C^1. Then F is a potential game if and only if it satisfies* externality symmetry:

$DF(x)$ *is symmetric with respect to $TX \times TX$ for all $x \in X$.* (3.11)

Proof   Immediate from theorem 3.B.6 in appendix 3.B.   ∎

Condition (3.11) demands that at each state $x \in X$, the derivative $DF(x)$ defines a symmetric bilinear form on $TX \times TX$:

$z' DF(x) \hat{z} = \hat{z}' DF(x) z \quad \text{for all } z, \hat{z} \in TX, x \in X.$

Observation 3.2.3 offers a version of this condition that does not require affine calculus, just as observation 3.2.1 did for definition (3.9).

Observation 3.2.3 *Suppose that the population game $F: X \to \mathbf{R}^n$ is C^1, and let $\tilde{F}: \mathbf{R}^n_+ \to \mathbf{R}^n$ be any C^1 extension of F. Then F satisfies externality symmetry (and so is a potential game) if and only if*

$\Phi D\tilde{F}(x)\Phi$ *is symmetric for all $x \in X$.*

The next exercise characterizes externality symmetry in a more intuitive way.

Exercise 3.2.4 Show that externality symmetry (3.11) holds if and only if the previous equality holds whenever $z = e_j^p - e_i^p$ and $\hat{z} = e_l^q - e_k^q$. In other words, show that (3.11) is equivalent to

$$\frac{\partial(F_j^p - F_i^p)}{\partial(e_l^q - e_k^q)}(x) = \frac{\partial(F_l^q - F_k^q)}{\partial(e_j^p - e_i^p)}(x) \quad \text{for all } i,j \in S^p,\ k,l \in S^q,\ p,q \in \mathcal{P},\ x \in X. \quad \diamond \quad (3.12)$$

The left-hand side of equation (3.12) captures the change in the payoff to strategy $j \in S^p$ relative to strategy $i \in S^p$ as agents switch from strategy $k \in S^q$ to strategy $l \in S^q$. This effect must equal the change in the payoff of l relative to k as agents switch from i to j, as expressed on the right-hand side of (3.12). This description is akin to that of full externality symmetry (3.2) (see the discussion after equation (3.3)), but it only refers to *relative* payoffs and to *feasible* changes in the social state.

Exercise 3.2.5 Let F be a C^1 single-population game. Show that F is a potential game if and only if it satisfies *triangular integrability*:

$$\frac{\partial F_i}{\partial(e_j - e_k)}(x) + \frac{\partial F_j}{\partial(e_k - e_i)}(x) + \frac{\partial F_k}{\partial(e_i - e_j)}(x) = 0 \quad \text{for all } i,j,k \in S,\ x \in X. \quad \diamond$$

Example 3.2.3: Two-Strategy Games Revisited If $F: X \to \mathbf{R}^2$ is a smooth two-strategy game, its state space X is the simplex in $\mathbf{R}^2$, whose tangent space TX is spanned by the vector $d = e_1 - e_2$. If z and $\hat{z}$ are vectors in TX, then $z = kd$ and $\hat{z} = \hat{k}d$ for some real numbers k and $\hat{k}$; thus, however F is defined, $z'DF(x)\hat{z} = k\hat{k}d'DF(x)d = \hat{z}'DF(x)z$ for all $x \in X$. In other words, F is a potential game. Even if F is merely continuous, the function $f: X \to \mathbf{R}$ defined by

$$f(x_1, 1 - x_1) = \int_0^{x_1} (F_1(t, 1-t) - F_2(t, 1-t))\,dt \quad (3.13)$$

is a potential function for F, so F is still a potential game. (If you think that a $\frac{1}{2}$ is needed on the right-hand side of equation (3.13), convince yourself that it is not.) ◆

Exercise 3.2.6: Matching in Symmetric Normal Form Potential Games Let $A = C + \mathbf{1}r'$ be a symmetric normal form potential game: $C \in \mathbf{R}^{n \times n}$ is symmetric, and $r \in \mathbf{R}^n$ is arbitrary. Define the population game $F: X \to \mathbf{R}^n$ by $F(x) = Ax$. Use one of the prior derivative conditions to verify that F is a potential game, and find a potential function $f: X \to \mathbf{R}$ for F. ◇

Exercise 3.2.7: Matching in Normal Form Potential Games The normal form game $U = (U^1, \ldots, U^p)$ is a *potential game* if there is a *potential function* $V: S \to \mathbf{R}$ satisfying

$$U^p(\hat{s}^p, s^{-p}) - U^p(s) = V(\hat{s}^p, s^{-p}) - V(s) \quad \text{for all } s \in S, \hat{s}^p \in S^p, p \in \mathcal{P}.$$

That is, after any unilateral deviation, the change in the deviator's payoffs is equal to the change in potential.

i. Show that pure strategy profile $s \in S$ is a Nash equilibrium of U if and only if it is a local maximizer of the potential function V.

ii. Show that U is a potential game with potential function V if and only if there are auxiliary functions $W^p: S^{-p} \to \mathbf{R}$ such that

$$U^p(s) = V(s) + W^p(s^{-p}) \quad \text{for all } s \in S, p \in \mathcal{P}.$$

That is, each player's payoff function is the sum of a common payoff term given by the value of potential and a term that only depends on opponents' behavior. This characterization accords with the definition of symmetric normal form potential games from the previous exercise.

iii. Define the full population game $\tilde{F}: \mathbf{R}_+^n \to \mathbf{R}^n$ by

$$\tilde{F}^p_{s^p}(x) = \sum_{s^{-p} \in S^{-p}} U^p(s) \prod_{r \neq p} x^r_{s^r} = \sum_{s^{-p} \in S^{-p}} (V(s) + W^p(s^{-p})) \prod_{r \neq p} x^r_{s^r}.$$

Show that in general, $\tilde{F}$ is not a full potential game.

iv. Define the population game $F: X \to \mathbf{R}^n$ using the equation from part (iii). By verifying condition (3.11), show that F is a potential game.

v. Construct a potential function for F. ◇

Exercise 3.2.8 This exercise provides the converse to exercise 3.2.7(iv). Let the population game $F: X \to \mathbf{R}^n$ be generated by matching in a p-player normal form game U. Show that if F is potential game with potential function $f: X \to \mathbf{R}$, then U is a potential game with potential function $V(s) = f(\xi(s))$, where $\xi(s) \in X$ is the pure population state with $\xi(s)^p_{s^p} = 1$ for all $p \in \mathcal{P}$. (*Hint:* To evaluate $f(\xi(\hat{s}^p, s^{-p})) - f(\xi(s))$, use the fundamental theorem of calculus, along with the fact that $F^p(x)$ is independent of x^p.) ◇

3.2.3 Potential Games and Full Potential Games

How are full potential games and potential games related? In the former case, condition (3.1) requires that payoffs be completely determined by the potential function, which is defined on $\mathbf{R}_+^n$; in the latter case, condition (3.9) asks only that relative payoffs be determined by the potential function, now defined just on X.

To understand the relation between the two definitions, take a potential game $F: X \to \mathbf{R}^n$ with potential function $f: X \to \mathbf{R}$ as given, and extend f to a full potential function $\tilde{f}: \mathbf{R}_+^n \to \mathbf{R}$. Theorem 3.2.9 shows that the link between the full potential game $\tilde{F} \equiv \nabla \tilde{f}$ and the original game F depends on how the extension $\tilde{f}$ is chosen.

Theorem 3.2.9 Let $F: X \to \mathbf{R}^n$ be a potential game with potential function $f: X \to \mathbf{R}$. Let $\tilde{f}: \mathbf{R}_+^n \to \mathbf{R}$ be any C^1 extension of f, and define the full potential game $\tilde{F}: \mathbf{R}_+^n \to \mathbf{R}^n$ by $\tilde{F}(x) = \nabla \tilde{f}(x)$. Then

i. The population games F and $\tilde{F}\big|_X$ have the same relative payoffs: $\Phi F(x) = \Phi \tilde{F}(x)$ for all $x \in X$.

ii. One can choose the extension $\tilde{f}$ in such a way that F and $\tilde{F}\big|_X$ are identical.

Part (*i*) of the theorem shows that the full potential game $\tilde{F}$ generated from an arbitrary extension of the potential function f exhibits the same relative payoffs as F on their common domain X. It follows that F and $\tilde{F}$ have the same best response correspondences and Nash equilibria, but may exhibit different average payoff levels. Part (*ii*) of the theorem shows that by choosing the extension $\tilde{f}$ appropriately, one can make $\tilde{F}$ and F identical on X. To accomplish this, the extension $\tilde{f}$ is constructed in such a way (see equation (3.14)) that its derivatives at states in X evaluated in directions orthogonal to TX encode information about average payoffs from the original game F.

In conclusion, theorem 3.2.9(*ii*) demonstrates that if population masses are fixed, so that the relevant set of social states is X, then definition (3.1), while more difficult to check, does not entail a loss of generality relative to definition (3.9).

Proof of theorem 3.2.9 Part (*i*) follows from the fact that $\Phi \tilde{F}(x) = \Phi \nabla \tilde{f}(x) = \nabla f(x) = \Phi F(x)$ for all $x \in X$; compare the discussion following observation 3.2.1.

To prove part (*ii*), we first extend f and F from the state space X to its affine hull aff(X). Let $\hat{f}: \text{aff}(X) \to \mathbf{R}$ be a C^1 extension of $f: X \to \mathbf{R}$, and let $\hat{g}^p: \text{aff}(X) \to \mathbf{R}$ be a continuous extension of population p's average payoff function, $\frac{1}{n^p} \mathbf{1}' F^p: X \to \mathbf{R}$. (The existence of these extensions follows from the Whitney extension theorem—see section 3.A.7.) Then define $\hat{G}: \text{aff}(X) \to \mathbf{R}^n$ by $\hat{G}(x) = \mathbf{1}\hat{g}^p(x)$, so that $F(x) = \Phi F(x) + (I - \Phi)F(x) = \nabla \hat{f}(x) + \hat{G}(x)$ for all $x \in X$. If after this one defines $\hat{F}: \text{aff}(X) \to \mathbf{R}^n$ by $\hat{F}(x) = \nabla \hat{f}(x) + \hat{G}(x)$, then $\hat{F}$ is a continuous extension of F, and $\nabla \hat{f}(x) = \Phi \hat{F}(x)$ for all $x \in \text{aff}(X)$.

Potential Games, Stable Games, and Supermodular Games

With this groundwork complete, we can extend f to all of $\mathbf{R}^n_+$ via

$$\tilde{f}(y) = f(\xi(y)) + (y - \xi(y))'F(\xi(y)), \tag{3.14}$$

where $\xi(y) = \Phi y + z^\perp_{TX}$ is the closest point to y in aff(X). (Here, $z^\perp_{TX}$ is the orthogonal translation vector that sends TX to aff(X), namely, $(z^\perp_{TX})^p = \frac{m^p}{n^p}\mathbf{1}$.) Theorem 3.B.8 shows that $\nabla \tilde{f}\big|_X = \tilde{F}\big|_X$ is identical to F. ∎

Theorem 3.2.9 implies that all the results from sections 3.1.4 and 3.1.5 on Nash equilibria of full potential games apply unchanged to potential games. On the other hand, the efficiency results from section 3.1.6 do not. In particular, the proof of theorem 3.1.10 depends on the game F being a full population game, as the application of Euler's theorem makes explicit use of the partial derivatives of F. In fact, to establish that a potential game F has efficiency properties of the sorts described in section 3.1.6, one must show that F can be extended to a homogeneous full potential game. This should come as no surprise. Since the potential function $f: X \to \mathbf{R}$ only captures relative payoffs, it cannot be used to prove efficiency results, which depend on both relative and average payoffs.

Exercise 3.2.10 Consider population games with entry and exit (see exercise 3.1.8). Which derivative condition is the right one for defining potential games in this context, (3.2) or (3.11)? Why? ◇

Exercise 3.2.11 Prove this simple "converse" to theorem 3.2.9. Suppose $\tilde{F}: \mathbf{R}^n_+ \to \mathbf{R}^n$ is a full potential game with full potential function $\tilde{f}: \mathbf{R}^n_+ \to \mathbf{R}$. Let $F = \tilde{F}\big|_X$ and $f = \tilde{f}\big|_X$. Then F is a potential game with potential function f. ◇

3.2.4 Passive Games and Constant Games

This section introduces two simple classes of population games.

Definition The population game $H: X \to \mathbf{R}^n$ is *a passive game if for each state $x \in X$ and each population $p \in \mathcal{P}$, the payoffs to all of population p's strategies are equal*:

$$H^p_i(x) = H^p_j(x) \quad \text{for all } i, j \in S^p, p \in \mathcal{P}, x \in X.$$

Definition The population game $K: X \to \mathbf{R}^n$ is *a constant game if all strategies' payoffs are independent of the state, that is, if $K(x) = \pi$ for all $x \in X$*, or more explicitly, if

$$K^p_i(x) = \pi^p_i \quad \text{for all } i \in S^p, p \in \mathcal{P}, x \in X.$$

In a passive game, an agent's own behavior has no bearing on her payoffs; in a constant game, each agent's behavior is the sole determinant of her payoffs.

The following two propositions provide some alternative characterizations of these games.

Proposition 3.2.12 *The following statements are equivalent:*

i. H is a passive game.

ii. There are functions $c^p\colon X \to \mathbf{R}$ such that $H^p(x) = c^p(x)\mathbf{1}$ for all $p \in \mathcal{P}$ and $x \in X$.

iii. $H(x) \in (TX)^\perp$ for all $x \in X$.

iv. $\Phi H(x) = \mathbf{0}$ for all $x \in X$.

v. $z'H(x) = \mathbf{0}$ for all $z \in TX$ and $x \in X$.

vi. H is a potential game whose potential function is constant.

Proposition 3.2.13 *The following statements are equivalent:*

i. K is a constant game.

ii. $DK(x) = \mathbf{0}$ for all $x \in X$.

iii. K is a potential game that admits a linear potential function.

In particular, if $K(x) = \pi$ is a constant game, then $k(x) = \pi'x$ is a potential function for K.

One reason that passive and constant games are interesting is that adding them to a population game from a certain class (potential games, stable games, supermodular games) results in a new game from the same class. For instance, suppose that F is a potential game with potential function f, let H be a passive game, and let K be a constant game with potential function k. Evidently, $F + H$ is also a potential game with potential function f; thus, adding H to F leaves the Nash equilibria of F unchanged. $F + K$ is also a potential game, but its potential function is not f but $f + k$; thus, $NE(F)$ and $NE(F + K)$ generally differ. Similar observations are true for stable games and for supermodular games. Adding a passive game or a constant game to a game from either of these classes results in a new game from the same class, but adding only passive games leaves incentives unchanged.

When payoffs are smooth, the invariances just described can be represented in terms of payoff derivatives. As an illustration, recall that the C^1 population game $F\colon X \to \mathbf{R}^n$ is a potential game if and only if it satisfies externality symmetry:

$$DF(x) \text{ is symmetric with respect to } TX \times TX \text{ for all } x \in X. \tag{3.11}$$

The first TX indicates that condition (3.11) constrains the effects of left multiplication of $DF(x)$ by elements of TX; this restricts the purview of (3.11) to *changes in relative payoffs*. The second TX indicates that (3.11) constrains the effects of right multiplication of $DF(x)$ by elements of TX; this reflects that one can only evaluate how payoffs change in response to *feasible changes in the state*. In summary, the action of the derivative matrices $DF(x)$ on $TX \times TX$ captures changes in relative payoffs due to feasible changes in the state. This action is enough to characterize potential games, and we will see that it is enough to characterize stable and supermodular games as well.

It follows from this discussion that the additions to F that do not affect the action of its derivative matrices on $TX \times TX$ are those that do not alter F's class. These additions are characterized by the following proposition.

Proposition 3.2.14 *Let G be a C^1 population game. Then $DG(x)$ is the null bilinear form on $TX \times TX$ for all $x \in X$ if and only if $G = H + K$, where H is a passive game and K is a constant game.*

Exercise 3.2.15 Prove propositions 3.2.12, 3.2.13, and 3.2.14. (*Hint:* For Proposition 3.2.13, prove the equivalence of statements (i) and (iii) using the fundamental theorem of calculus. For proposition 3.2.14, use the previous propositions, along with the fact that $DG(x)$ is the null bilinear form on $TX \times TX$ if and only if $\Phi DG(x) = 0$.) ◇

Exercise 3.2.16

i. Suppose $H(x) = Ax$ is a single-population passive game. Describe A.
ii. Suppose $K(x) = Ax$ is a single-population constant game. Describe A. ◇

3.3 Stable Games

There are a variety of well-known classes of games whose Nash equilibria form a single convex set, for instance, two-player zero-sum games, wars of attrition, games with an interior evolutionarily or neutrally stable state (ESS or NSS), and potential games with concave potential functions. This shared property of these seemingly disparate examples springs from a common source: all these examples are stable games.

3.3.1 Definition

The common structure in the preceding examples is captured by the following definition.

Definition *The population game $F: X \to \mathbf{R}^n$ is a stable game if*

$$(y - x)'(F(y) - F(x)) \leq 0 \quad \text{for all } x, y \in X. \tag{3.15}$$

If the inequality in condition (3.15) *holds strictly whenever $x \neq y$, F is a strictly stable game, whereas if this inequality always binds, F is a null stable game.*

For a first intuition, imagine that $F \equiv \nabla f(x)$ is also a potential game. In this case, condition (3.15) is simply the requirement that the potential function f be concave. The definition of stable games thus extends the defining property of concave potential games to games whose payoffs are not integrable.

Stable games whose payoffs are differentiable can be characterized in terms of the action of their derivative matrices $DF(x)$ on $TX \times TX$.

Theorem 3.3.1 *Suppose the population game F is C^1. Then F is a stable game if and only if it satisfies* **self-defeating externalities:**

$DF(x)$ *is negative semidefinite with respect to TX for all $x \in X$.* (3.16)

Condition (3.16) asks that

$z'DF(x)z \leq 0$ for all $z \in TX$, $x \in X$.

This requirement is in turn equivalent to

$$\sum_{p \in \mathcal{P}} \sum_{i \in S^p} z_i^p \frac{\partial F_i^p}{\partial z}(x) \leq 0 \quad \text{for all } z \in TX, \ x \in X.$$

To interpret this expression, recall that the displacement vector $z \in TX$ describes the aggregate effect on the population state of strategy revisions by a small group of agents. The derivative $\frac{\partial F_i^p}{\partial z}(x)$ represents the marginal effect that these revisions have on the payoffs of agents currently choosing strategy $i \in S^p$. Condition (3.16) considers a weighted sum of these effects, with weights given by the changes in the use of each strategy, and requires that this weighted sum be negative.

Intuitively, a game exhibits self-defeating externalities if the improvements in the payoffs of strategies to which revising agents are switching are always exceeded by the improvements in the payoffs of strategies which revising agents are abandoning. For example, suppose the tangent vector z takes the form $z = e_j^p - e_i^p$, representing switches by some members of population p from strategy i to strategy j. In this case, the requirement in condition (3.16) reduces to $\frac{\partial F_j^p}{\partial z}(x) \leq \frac{\partial F_i^p}{\partial z}(x)$, that is, any performance gains that the switches create for the newly chosen strategy j are dominated by the performance gains created for the abandoned strategy i.

Exercise 3.3.2

i. Characterize the C^1 two-strategy stable games using a derivative condition.

ii. Recall the Hawk-Dove game introduced in chapter 2:

$$F^{HD}(x) = \begin{pmatrix} -1 & 2 \\ 0 & 1 \end{pmatrix} \begin{pmatrix} x_H \\ x_D \end{pmatrix} = \begin{pmatrix} 2x_D - x_H \\ x_D \end{pmatrix}.$$

Verify that F is a stable game. Also, fill in the numerical details of the argument from the previous paragraph for this specific choice of payoff function. ◇

Proof of theorem 3.3.1 To begin, suppose that F is a stable game. Fix $x \in X$ and $z \in TX$; the aim is to show that $z'DF(x)z \leq 0$. Since F is C^1, it is enough to consider x in the interior of X. In this case, $y_\varepsilon = x + \varepsilon z$ lies in X whenever $|\varepsilon|$ is sufficiently small, and so

$$F(y_\varepsilon) = F(x) + DF(x)(y_\varepsilon - x) + o(|y_\varepsilon - x|)$$

by the definition of $DF(x)$. Premultiplying by $y_\varepsilon - x$ and rearranging yields

$$(y_\varepsilon - x)'(F(y_\varepsilon) - F(x)) = (y_\varepsilon - x)'DF(x)(y_\varepsilon - x) + o(|y_\varepsilon - x|^2).$$

Since the left-hand side is nonpositive and since $y_\varepsilon - x = \varepsilon z$, it follows that $\varepsilon^2 z'DF(x)z + o(\varepsilon^2) \leq 0$, and hence that $z'DF(x)z \leq 0$.

Next, suppose that condition (3.16) holds. Then if $\alpha(t) = ty + (1-t)x$, the fundamental theorem of calculus implies that

$$(y-x)'(F(y) - F(x)) = (y-x)'\left(\int_0^1 DF(\alpha(t))(y-x)\,dt\right)$$

$$= \int_0^1 (y-x)'DF(\alpha(t))(y-x)\,dt \leq 0. \qquad \blacksquare$$

Exercise 3.3.3 The derivative condition that characterizes potential games, externality symmetry (3.11), requires that $z'DF(x)\hat{z} = \hat{z}'DF(x)z$. That z and $\hat{z}$ are chosen separately means that $DF(x)$ is treated as a *bilinear form*. Exercise 3.2.4 shows that in order to check that (3.11) holds for all z and $\hat{z}$ in TX, it is enough to show that it holds for all z and $\hat{z}$ in a basis for TX, for example, the set of vectors of the form $e_j^p - e_i^p$.

In contrast, self-defeating externalities (3.16), which requires that $z'DF(x)z \leq 0$, places the same vector z on both sides of $DF(x)$, thus viewing $DF(x)$ as a *quadratic form*. Explain why the conclusion of exercise 3.2.4 does not extend to the present setting. Also, construct a 3×3 symmetric game A such that $z'Az \leq 0$ whenever z is of the form $e_j^p - e_i^p$ but such that $F(x) = Ax$ is not a stable game. ◇

3.3.2 Examples

The following example introduces the notion of an evolutionarily stable state (ESS) in the context of symmetric normal form games. A full treatment of ESSs of general population games is provided in section 8.3.

Example 3.3.1: Matching in Symmetric Normal Form Games with an Interior Evolutionarily or Neutrally Stable State Let $A \in \mathbf{R}^{n \times n}$ be a symmetric normal form game. State $x \in X$ is an *evolutionarily stable state* (or *evolutionarily stable strategy*) of A if

$$x'Ax \geq y'Ax \quad \text{for all } y \in X; \tag{3.17}$$

and

$$[x'Ax = y'Ax \text{ and } y \neq x] \text{ imply that } x'Ay > y'Ay. \tag{3.18}$$

Condition (3.17) says that x is a symmetric Nash equilibrium of A. Condition (3.18) says that x performs better against any alternative best reply y than y performs against itself. (Alternatively, (3.17) says that no $y \in X$ can strictly invade x, and (3.17) and (3.18) together say that if $y \neq x$ can weakly invade x, then x can strictly invade y—see section 3.3.3.) If we weaken condition (3.18) to

$$\text{If } x'Ax = y'Ax, \text{ then } x'Ay \geq y'Ay, \tag{3.19}$$

then a state satisfying conditions (3.17) and (3.19) is called a *neutrally stable state* (*NSS*).

Suppose that the ESS x lies in the interior of X. Then since x is an interior Nash equilibrium, all pure and mixed strategies are best responses to it: for all $y \in X$, we have that $x'Ax = y'Ax$, or equivalently, that $(x-y)'Ax = 0$. Rewrite the inequality in condition (3.18) as $(x-y)'Ay > 0$. Subtracting this last expression from the previous one yields $(x-y)'A(x-y) < 0$. But since x is in the interior of X, all tangent vectors $z \in TX$ are proportional to $x - y$ for some choice of $y \in X$. Therefore, $z'DF(x)z = z'Az < 0$ for all $z \in TX - \{0\}$, and so F is a strictly stable game. Similar reasoning shows that if F admits an interior NSS, then F is a stable game. ◆

Example 3.3.2: Matching in Rock-Paper-Scissors In Rock-Paper-Scissors, Paper covers Rock, Scissors cuts Paper, and Rock smashes Scissors. If a win in a match is worth $w > 0$, a loss $-l < 0$, and a draw 0, one obtains the symmetric normal form game

$$A = \begin{pmatrix} 0 & -l & w \\ w & 0 & -l \\ -l & w & 0 \end{pmatrix}, \quad \text{where } w, l > 0.$$

When $w = l$, A is called (*standard*) RPS; when $w > l$, *good* RPS; and when $w < l$, *bad* RPS. In all cases, the unique symmetric Nash equilibrium of A is $(\frac{1}{3}, \frac{1}{3}, \frac{1}{3})$.

To determine the parameter values for which this game generates a stable population game, define $d = w - l$. Since $y'Ay = \frac{1}{2}y'(A + A')y$, it is enough to see when the symmetric matrix

$$\hat{A} = A + A' = \begin{pmatrix} 0 & d & d \\ d & 0 & d \\ d & d & 0 \end{pmatrix}$$

is negative semidefinite with respect to TX. Now $\hat{A}$ has one eigenvalue of $2d$ corresponding to the eigenvector **1**, and two eigenvalues of $-d$ corresponding to the orthogonal eigenspace TX. Thus, $z'\hat{A}z = -dz'z$ for each $z \in TX$. Since $z'z > 0$ whenever $z \neq \mathbf{0}$, it follows that F is stable if and only if $d \geq 0$. In particular, good RPS is strictly stable, standard RPS is null stable, and bad RPS is not stable. ◆

Exercise 3.3.4: Matching in Wars of Attrition A *war of attrition* is a two-player symmetric normal form game. Strategies represent amounts of time committed to waiting for a scarce resource. If the two players choose times i and $j > i$, then the j player obtains the resource, worth v, while both players pay a cost of c_i: once the first player leaves, the other seizes the resource immediately. If both players choose time i, the resource is split, so payoffs are $\frac{v}{2} - c_i$ each. Show that for any resource value $v \in \mathbf{R}$ and any cost vector $c \in \mathbf{R}^n$ satisfying $c_1 \leq c_2 \leq \ldots \leq c_n$, matching in a war of attrition generates a stable game. ◇

Example 3.3.3: Matching in Symmetric Zero-Sum Games A symmetric two-player normal form game A is *symmetric zero-sum* if A is skew-symmetric, that is, if $A_{ji} = -A_{ij}$ for all $i, j \in S$. This condition ensures that under single-population matching, the total utility generated in any match is zero. Payoffs in the resulting single-population game are $F(x) = Ax$, so $z'DF(x)z = z'Az = 0$ for all vectors $z \in \mathbf{R}^n$, so F is a null stable game. ◆

Example 3.3.4: Matching in Standard Zero-Sum Games A two-player normal form game $U = (U^1, U^2)$ is *zero-sum* if $U^2 = -U^1$, so that the two players' payoffs always add up to zero. Matching of two populations to play U generates the population game

$$F(x^1, x^2) = \begin{bmatrix} 0 & U^1 \\ (U^2)' & 0 \end{bmatrix} \begin{pmatrix} x^1 \\ x^2 \end{pmatrix} = \begin{bmatrix} 0 & U^1 \\ -(U^1)' & 0 \end{bmatrix} \begin{pmatrix} x^1 \\ x^2 \end{pmatrix}.$$

If z is a vector in $\mathbf{R}^n = \mathbf{R}^{n^1+n^2}$, then

$$z'DF(x)z = \begin{pmatrix} (z^1)' & (z^2)' \end{pmatrix} \begin{bmatrix} 0 & U^1 \\ -(U^1)' & 0 \end{bmatrix} \begin{pmatrix} z^1 \\ z^2 \end{pmatrix} = (z^1)'U^1 z^2 - (z^2)'(U^1)'z^1 = 0,$$

so F is a null stable game. ◆

Exercise 3.3.5: Matching in Multi-Zero-Sum Games Let U be a p-player normal form game in which each player $p \in \mathcal{P}$ chooses a single strategy from S^p to simultaneously play a distinct zero-sum contest with each of his $p-1$ opponents. Such a U is a *multi-zero-sum game*.

i. When $p < q$, let $Z^{pq} \in \mathbf{R}^{n^p \times n^q}$ denote player p's payoff matrix for his zero-sum contest against player q. Define the normal form game U in terms of the Z^{pq} matrices.

ii. Let F be the p-population game generated by matching in U. Show that $z'DF(x)z = 0$ for all $z \in \mathbf{R}^n$ and $x \in X$, and hence that F is a null stable game. ◇

The previous example and exercise show that matching across multiple populations can generate a null stable game. Proposition 3.3.6 reveals that null stable games are the only stable games that can be generated in this way.

Proposition 3.3.6 *Suppose F is a C^1 stable game without own-population interactions: $F^p(x)$ is independent of x^p for all $p \in \mathcal{P}$. Then F is a null stable game.*

Proof By theorem 3.3.1, F is stable if and only if for all $x \in X$, $DF(x)$ is negative semidefinite with respect to TX. This requirement on $DF(x)$ can be restated as $\Phi DF(x)\Phi$ is negative semidefinite (with respect to $\mathbf{R}^n$); or as $\Phi(DF(x)+DF(x)')\Phi$ is negative semidefinite; or (since the previous matrix is symmetric) as $\Phi(DF(x)+DF(x)')\Phi$ has all eigenvalues nonpositive. By similar logic, F is null stable if and only if for all $x \in X$, $\Phi(DF(x)+DF(x)')\Phi$ has all eigenvalues zero (and so is the null matrix).

Let $D^q F^p(x)$ be the (p,q)th block of the derivative matrix $DF(x)$. Since F^p is independent of x^p, it follows that $D^p F^p(x) = \mathbf{0}$, and hence that $\Phi(D^p F^p(x)+D^p F^p(x)')\Phi = 0$. Since this product is the (p,p)th block of the symmetric matrix $\Phi(DF(x)+DF(x)')\Phi$, the latter has zero trace, and so its eigenvalues sum to zero. Therefore, the only way $\Phi(DF(x)+DF(x)')\Phi$ can be negative semidefinite is if all of its eigenvalues are zero. In other words, if F is stable, it is null stable. ∎

Proposition 3.3.6 says that within-population interactions are required to obtain a strictly stable game. Thus, strictly stable games can arise when there is matching within a single population to play a symmetric normal form game, but not when there is matching in multiple populations to play a standard normal form game.

On the other hand, strictly stable games can arise in multipopulation matching settings that allow matches both across and within populations. Moreover, in general population games—for instance, in congestion games—within-population interactions are the norm, and strictly stable games are not uncommon. The remaining examples illustrate this point.

Example 3.3.5: (Perturbed) Concave Potential Games $F: X \to \mathbf{R}^n$ is a *concave potential game* if it is a potential game whose potential function $f: X \to \mathbf{R}$ is concave. Since $y - x \in TX$, since the orthogonal projection matrix Φ is symmetric, and since $\nabla f \equiv \Phi F$, it follows that

$$(y-x)'(F(y)-F(x)) = (\Phi(y-x))'(F(y)-F(x))$$

$$= (y-x)'(\Phi F(y) - \Phi F(x))$$

$$= (y-x)'(\nabla f(y) - \nabla f(x))$$

$$\leq 0,$$

Potential Games, Stable Games, and Supermodular Games

so F is a stable game. If these inequalities are satisfied strictly, they will continue to be satisfied if the payoff functions are slightly perturbed. In other words, perturbations of strictly concave potential games remain strictly stable games. ◆

Example 3.3.6: Negative Dominant Diagonal Games A full population game F is a *negative dominant diagonal game* if it satisfies

$$\frac{\partial F_i^p}{\partial x_i^p}(x) < 0 \quad \text{and} \quad \left|\frac{\partial F_i^p}{\partial x_i^p}(x)\right| \geq \frac{1}{2} \sum_{(j,q) \neq (i,p)} \left(\left|\frac{\partial F_j^q}{\partial x_i^p}(x)\right| + \left|\frac{\partial F_i^p}{\partial x_j^q}(x)\right| \right)$$

for all $i \in S^p, p \in \mathcal{P}$, and $x \in X$. The first condition says that choosing strategy $i \in S^p$ imposes a negative externality on other users of this strategy. The second condition requires that this externality exceed the average of (1) the total externalities that users of strategy i impose on users of other strategies, and (2) the total externalities that users of other strategies impose on users of strategy i. These conditions are precisely what is required for the matrix $DF(x) + DF(x)'$ to have a negative dominant diagonal. The dominant diagonal condition implies that all the eigenvalues of $DF(x) + DF(x)'$ are negative; since $DF(x) + DF(x)'$ is also symmetric, it is negative definite. Therefore, $DF(x)$ is negative definite too, and so F is a strictly stable game. ◆

3.3.3 Invasion

Section 3.3.4 introduces new equilibrium concepts that are of basic importance for stable games: global neutral stability and global evolutionary stability. These concepts are best understood in terms of the notion of invasion.

Let $F: X \to \mathbf{R}^n$ be a population game, and let $x, y \in X$ be two social states. State y can *weakly invade* state x ($y \in \bar{I}_F(x)$) if $(y - x)'F(x) \geq 0$. Similarly, y can *strictly invade* x ($y \in I_F(x)$) if $(y - x)'F(x) > 0$.

The intuition behind these definitions is simple. Consider a single population of agents who play the game F and whose initial behavior is described by state $x \in X$. Now imagine that a very small group of agents decide to switch strategies. After these agents select their new strategies, the distribution of choices within their group is described by some $y \in X$, but since the group is so small, the impact of its behavior on the overall population state is negligible. Thus, the average payoff in the invading group is at least as high as that in the incumbent population if $y'F(x) \geq x'F(x)$, or equivalently, if $y \in \bar{I}_F(x)$. Similarly, the average payoff in the invading group exceeds that in the incumbent population if $y \in I_F(x)$.

The interpretation of invasion does not change much when there are multiple populations. Writing $(y - x)'F(x)$ as $\sum_p (y^p - x^p)'F^p(x)$ shows that if $y \in I_F(x)$, the average payoffs across the invading groups exceed the average payoffs across the incumbent populations, where both of these averages are weighted implicitly by the populations' sizes. (See section 8.3.2 for a related discussion of multipopulation versions of ESS.)

These stories suggest a link with evolutionary dynamics. If y is any state in X, then the vector $y - x$ is a feasible displacement direction from state x. If in addition $y \in I_F(x)$, then the direction $y - x$ is not only feasible but also respects the incentives provided by the underlying game.

The invasion conditions also have simple geometric interpretations. When $y \in \bar{I}_F(x)$, the angle between the displacement vector $y - x$ and the payoff vector $F(x)$ is weakly acute; when $y \in I_F(x)$, this angle is strictly acute. Figure 3.4 sketches the set $I_F(x)$ at various states x in a two-strategy game. Figure 3.5 does the same for a three-strategy game. To draw the latter case, one needs the observation that

$$y \in I_F(x) \Leftrightarrow (y - x)'F(x) > 0$$
$$\Leftrightarrow (\Phi(y - x))'F(x) > 0$$
$$\Leftrightarrow (y - x)'\Phi F(x) > 0.$$

In other words, $y \in I_F(x)$ if and only if the angle between the displacement vector $y - x$ and the *projected* payoff vector $\Phi F(x)$ is strictly acute.

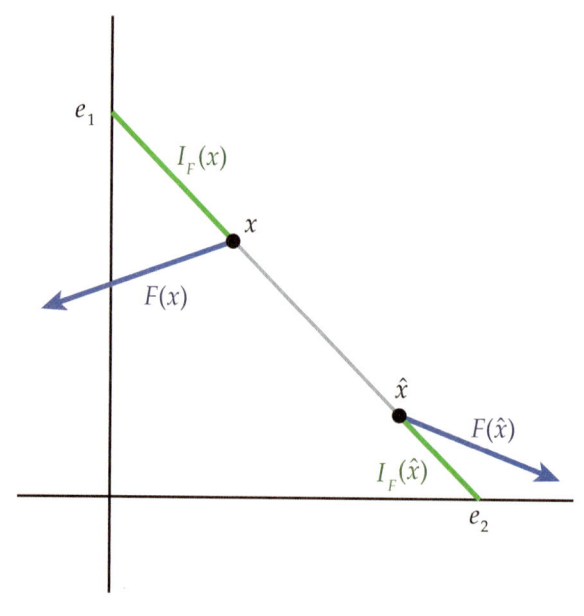

Figure 3.4
Invasion in a two-strategy game.

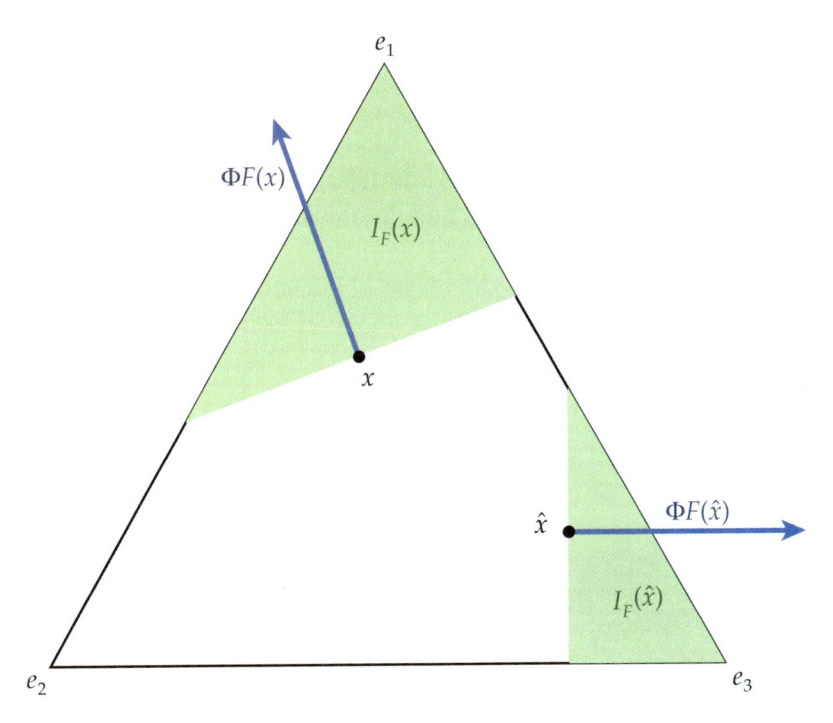

Potential Games, Stable Games, and Supermodular Games

Figure 3.5
Invasion in a three-strategy game.

3.3.4 Global Neutral Stability and Global Evolutionary Stability

Before introducing our new solution concepts, we first characterize Nash equilibrium in terms of invasion: a Nash equilibrium is a state that no other state can strictly invade.

Proposition 3.3.7 $x \in NE(F)$ *if and only if* $I_F(x) = \varnothing$.

Proof $x \in NE(F) \Leftrightarrow (y-x)'F(x) \leq 0$ for all $y \in X \Leftrightarrow I_F(x) = \varnothing$. ∎

With this background in hand, we call $x \in X$ a *globally neutrally stable state* (GNSS) if

$$(y-x)'F(y) \leq 0 \quad \text{for all } y \in X.$$

Similarly, x is a *globally evolutionarily stable state* (GESS) if

$$(y-x)'F(y) < 0 \quad \text{for all } y \in X - \{x\}.$$

Let $GNSS(F)$ and $GESS(F)$ denote the sets of globally neutrally stable states and globally evolutionarily stable states, respectively.

To see the reason for this nomenclature, note that the inequalities used to define GNSS and GESS are the same as those used to define NSS and ESS in symmetric normal form games (see example 3.3.1), but that they are now required to hold not just at those states y that are optimal against x, but at all $y \in X$. NSS and ESS also require a state to be a Nash equilibrium; the new solution concepts implicitly require this as well (see proposition 3.3.9). (The definition of ESS for general population games is deferred until section 8.3.)

It is easy to describe both new concepts in terms of the notion of invasion.

Observation 3.3.8

i. $GNSS(F) = \bigcap_{y \in X} \bar{I}_F(y)$, and so is convex.
ii. $GESS(F) = \bigcap_{y \in X - \{x\}} I_F(y)$.

In words: a GNSS is a state that can weakly invade every state (or equivalently, every other state), and a GESS is a state that can strictly invade every other state.

These new solution concepts can also be described in geometric terms. For example, x is a GESS if a small motion from any state $y \neq x$ in the direction $F(y)$ (or $\Phi F(y)$) moves the state closer to x (figure 3.6). Allowing not only these acute motions but also orthogonal motions yields the weaker notion of GNSS.

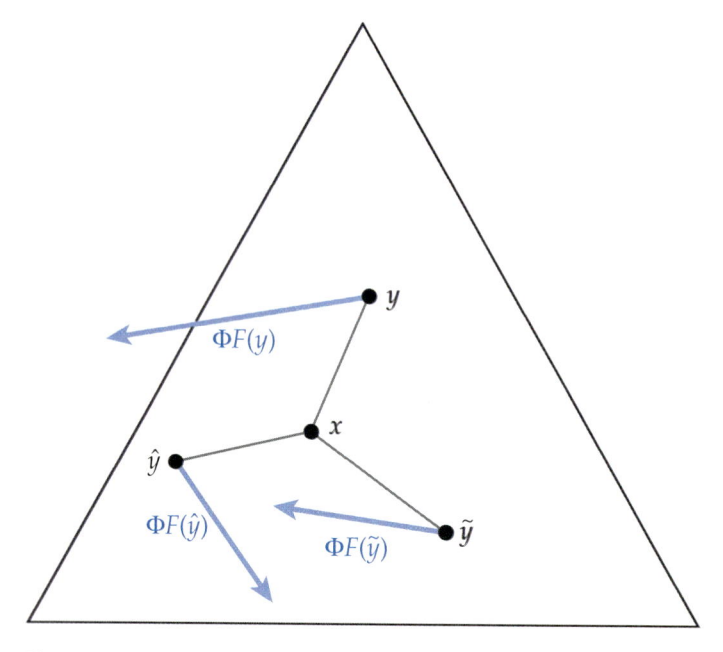

Figure 3.6
The geometric definition of GESS.

We conclude this section by relating the new solution concepts to Nash equilibrium.

Proposition 3.3.9

i. If $x \in GNSS(F)$, then $x \in NE(F)$.

ii. If $x \in GESS(F)$, then $NE(F) = \{x\}$. Hence, if a GESS exists, it is unique.

Proof To prove part (*i*), let $x \in GNSS(F)$ and let $y \neq x$. Define $x_\varepsilon = \varepsilon y + (1-\varepsilon)x$. Since x is a GNSS, $(x - x_\varepsilon)'F(x_\varepsilon) \geq 0$ for all $\varepsilon \in (0, 1]$. Simplifying and dividing by ε yields $(x - y)'F(x_\varepsilon) \geq 0$ for all $\varepsilon \in (0, 1]$, so taking ε to zero yields $(y - x)'F(x) \leq 0$. In other words, $x \in NE(F)$.

To prove part (*ii*), it is enough to show that if x is a GESS, then no $y \neq x$ is Nash. But if $x \in GESS(F)$, then $x \in I_F(y)$; since $I_F(y)$ is nonempty, $y \notin NE(F)$. ∎

Evidently, this proposition implies that in single-population matching settings (see example 3.3.1), every GNSS is an NSS and every GESS is an ESS.

The proof that every GNSS is Nash is easy to explain graphically. Figure 3.7 shows the GNSS x and an arbitrary state y as well as a state x_ε on the segment

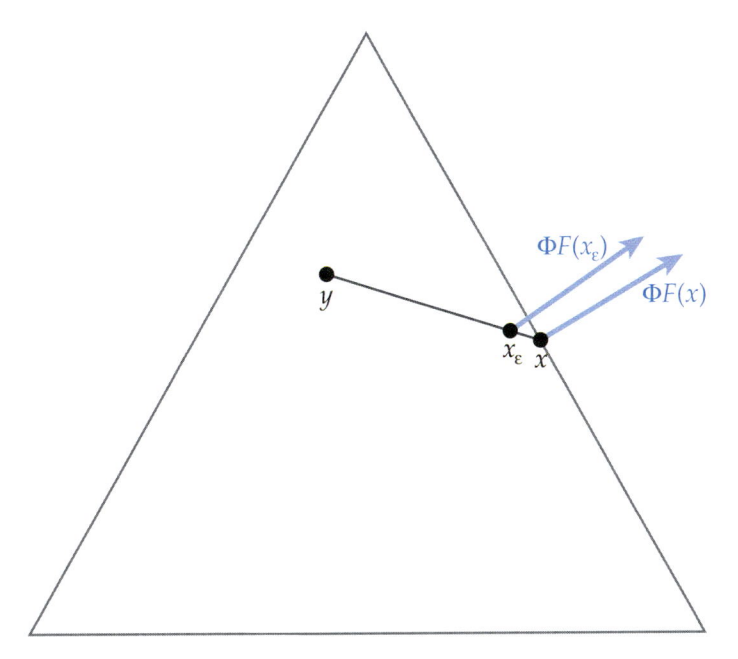

Figure 3.7
Why every GNSS is a Nash equilibrium.

between y and x. Since x is a GNSS, the angle between $F(x_\varepsilon)$ and $x - x_\varepsilon$, and hence between $\Phi F(x_\varepsilon)$ and $x - x_\varepsilon$, is weakly acute. Taking ε to zero, it is apparent that the angle between $\Phi F(x)$ and $y - x$, and hence between $F(x)$ and $y - x$, must be weakly obtuse. Since y was arbitrary, x is a Nash equilibrium.

3.3.5 Nash Equilibrium and Global Neutral Stability in Stable Games

Proposition 3.3.9 says that every GNSS of an arbitrary game F is a Nash equilibrium. Theorem 3.3.10 shows that much more can be said if F is stable. In this case, the sets of globally neutrally stable states and Nash equilibria coincide. Together, this fact and observation 3.3.8 imply that the Nash equilibria of any stable game form a convex set. In fact, if certain of the weak inequalities that define stable games can be replaced with strict ones, then the Nash equilibrium is unique.

Theorem 3.3.10

i. If F is a stable game, then $NE(F) = GNSS(F)$, and so is convex.

ii. If in addition F is strictly stable at some $x \in NE(F)$ (i.e., if $(y - x)'(F(y) - F(x)) < 0$ for all $y \neq x$), then $NE(F) = GESS(F) = \{x\}$.

Proof Suppose that F is stable, and let $x \in NE(F)$. To establish part *(i)*, it is enough to show that $x \in GNSS(F)$. So fix an arbitrary $y \neq x$. Since F is stable,

$$(y - x)'(F(y) - F(x)) \leq 0. \tag{3.20}$$

And since $x \in NE(F)$, $(y - x)'F(x) \leq 0$. Adding these inequalities yields

$$(y - x)'F(y) \leq 0. \tag{3.21}$$

As y was arbitrary, x is a GNSS.

For part *(ii)*, suppose that F is strictly stable at x. Then inequality (3.20) holds strictly, so inequality (3.21) holds strictly as well. This means that x is a GESS of F and hence the unique Nash equilibrium of F. ∎

Example 3.3.7: Rock-Paper-Scissors Revisited Recall from example 3.3.2 that good RPS is a (strictly) stable game, while standard RPS is a zero-sum game and hence a null stable game. The unique Nash equilibrium of both of games is $x^* = (\frac{1}{3}, \frac{1}{3}, \frac{1}{3})$. For a selection of states x, Figure 3.8 shows the projected payoff vectors $\Phi F(x)$ generated by good RPS (with $w = 3$ and $l = 1$), as well as the vector from x to x^*. For each x, the angle between this pair of vectors is acute, reflecting the fact that the Nash equilibrium x^* is a GESS. Figure 3.9 repeats this exercise for standard RPS. In this case, the vectors $\Phi F(x)$ and $x^* - x$ always form a right angle, so x^* is a GNSS but not a GESS. ◆

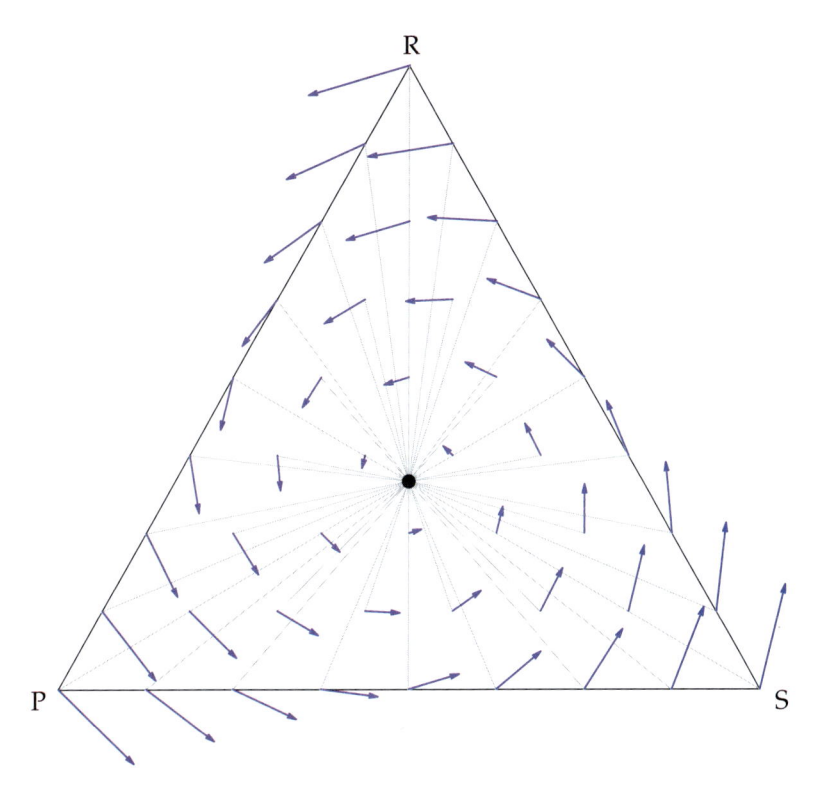

Figure 3.8
The GESS of good RPS.

Exercise 3.3.11 Let F be a stable game. Show that if x^* is a Nash equilibrium of F such that $DF(x^*)$ is negative definite with respect to $TX \times TX$, then x^* is a GESS and hence the unique Nash equilibrium of F. ◇

Exercise 3.3.12: Pseudostable Games A population game F is *pseudostable* if for all $x, y \in X$, $(y-x)'F(x) \leq 0$ implies that $(x-y)'F(y) \geq 0$. In other words, if y cannot strictly invade x, then x can weakly invade y.

i. Show that every stable game is pseudostable.
ii. Show that if F is pseudostable, then $NE(F) = GNSS(F)$ and thus is convex.

(A smooth real-valued function f is *pseudoconcave* if its gradient ∇f is pseudostable. Given facts (i) and (ii) and the discussion in section 3.1.5, it should be no surprise that many results from concave programming (e.g., the convexity of the set of maximizers) remain true when the objective function is only pseudoconcave.) ◇

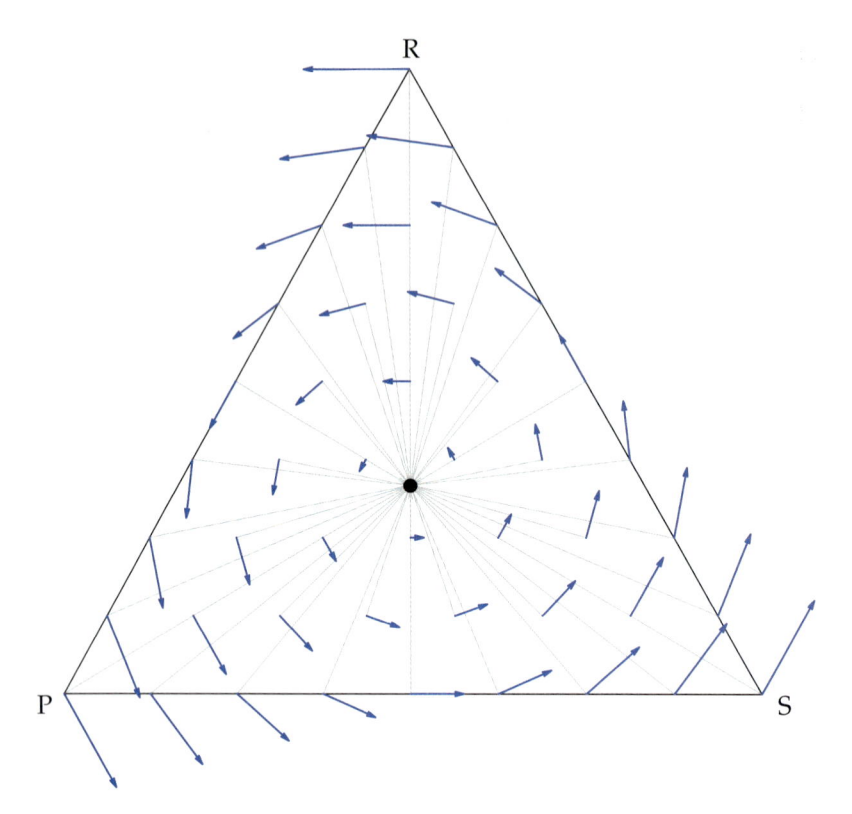

Figure 3.9
The GNSS of standard RPS.

In addition to its role in establishing that the set of Nash equilibria of a stable game is convex, the concept of global neutral stability makes it possible to carry out an important theoretical exercise: devising an elementary proof of existence of Nash equilibrium in stable games, in other words, a proof that does not rely on an appeal to a fixed point theorem. The heart of the proof, proposition 3.3.13, is a finite analogue of the desired result.

Proposition 3.3.13 *Let F be a stable game, and let Y be a finite subset of X. Then there exists a state $x^* \in \text{conv}(Y)$ such that $(y - x^*)'F(y) \leq 0$ for all $y \in Y$.*

In words: if F is a stable game, then given any finite set of states Y, one can always find a state in the convex hull of Y that can weakly invade every element of Y. The proof of this result uses the minmax theorem.

Proof Suppose that Y has m elements. Define a two-player zero-sum game $U = (U^1, U^2) = (Z, -Z)$ with $n^1 = n^2 = m$ as follows:

$Z_{xy} = (x-y)'F(y)$.

In this game, player 2 chooses a status quo state $y \in Y$, player 1 chooses an invader state $x \in Y$, and the payoff Z_{xy} is the invader's relative payoff in F. Split Z into its symmetric and skew-symmetric parts:

$Z^S = \frac{1}{2}(Z+Z')$ and $Z^{SS} = \frac{1}{2}(Z-Z')$.

Since F is stable, equation (3.20) from the previous proof shows that

$Z^S_{xy} = \frac{1}{2}\left((x-y)'F(y) + (y-x)'F(x)\right) = \frac{1}{2}(x-y)'(F(y) - F(x)) \geq 0$ for all $x, y \in Y$.

The minmax theorem states that in any zero-sum game, player 1 has a strategy that guarantees him the value of the game. In the skew-symmetric game $U^{SS} = (Z^{SS}, -Z^{SS}) = (Z^{SS}, (Z^{SS})')$, the player roles are interchangeable, so the game's value must be zero. Since $Z = Z^{SS} + Z^S$ and $Z^S \geq 0$, the value of $U = (Z, -Z)$ must be *at least* zero. In other words, if $\lambda \in \mathbf{R}^m$ is a maxmin strategy for player 1, then

$$\sum_{x \in Y}\sum_{y \in Y} \lambda_x Z_{xy} \mu_y \geq 0$$

for all mixed strategies μ of player 2. So let

$$x^* = \sum_{x \in Y} \lambda_x x \in \text{conv}(Y),$$

and fix an arbitrary pure strategy $y \in Y$ for player 2; then

$$0 \leq \sum_{x \in Y} \lambda_x Z_{xy} = \sum_{x \in Y} \lambda_x (x-y)'F(y) = (x^* - y)'F(y). \quad \blacksquare$$

With this result in hand, existence of Nash equilibrium in stable games follows from a simple compactness argument. Theorem 3.3.10 and observation 3.3.8 yield

$NE(F) = GNSS(F) = \bigcap_{y \in X} \{x \in X : (y-x)'F(y) \leq 0\}$.

Proposition 3.3.13 shows that if one takes the intersection above over an arbitrary finite set $Y \subset X$ instead of over X itself, then the intersection is nonempty. Since X is compact, the finite intersection property (see the chapter notes) allows us to conclude that $GNSS(F)$ is nonempty itself.

Exercise 3.3.14 Exercise 3.1.8 introduced population games with entry and exit. If $F: \mathbf{R}^n_+ \to \mathbf{R}$ is C^1 and defines such a game, what condition on the derivative matrices $DF(x)$ is the appropriate definition of stable games for this context? Argue that all the results in this section continue to hold when entry and exit are permitted. ◇

3.4 Supermodular Games

Of all the classes of games studied in this chapter, the class of supermodular games, which includes models of coordination, search, and Bertrand competition, may be the most familiar to economists. By definition, supermodularity requires that higher choices by one's opponents make one's own higher strategies look relatively more desirable. This complementarity condition imposes a monotone structure on the agents' best response correspondences, which in turn imposes structure on the set of Nash equilibria.

3.4.1 Definition

Each strategy set $S^p = \{1, \ldots, n^p\}$ is naturally endowed with a linear order. To define supermodular games, we introduce a corresponding partial order on the set of population states X^p (and, implicitly, on the set of mixed strategies for population p). Define the matrix $\Sigma \in \mathbf{R}^{(n^p-1) \times n^p}$ by

$$\Sigma = \begin{pmatrix} 0 & 1 & \cdots & 1 \\ \vdots & \ddots & \ddots & \vdots \\ 0 & \cdots & 0 & 1 \end{pmatrix}.$$

Then

$$(\Sigma x^p)_i = \sum_{j=i+1}^{n^p} x_j^p$$

equals the total mass on strategies greater than i at population state x^p. If x^p is viewed as a discrete density function on S^p with total mass m^p, then Σx^p defines the corresponding "decumulative distribution function" for x^p. In particular, $\Sigma y^p \geq \Sigma x^p$ if and only if y^p stochastically dominates x^p.

This partial order is extended to all of X using the matrix $\boldsymbol{\Sigma} \in \mathbf{R}^{(n-p) \times n}$, defined as the block diagonal matrix $\boldsymbol{\Sigma} = \text{diag}(\Sigma, \ldots, \Sigma)$. Note that $\boldsymbol{\Sigma} y \geq \boldsymbol{\Sigma} x$ if and only if y^p stochastically dominates x^p for all $p \in \mathcal{P}$.

Definition A population game $F \colon X \to \mathbf{R}^n$ is a *supermodular game* if it exhibits strategic complementarities:

If $\boldsymbol{\Sigma} y \geq \boldsymbol{\Sigma} x$, then $F_{i+1}^p(y) - F_i^p(y) \geq F_{i+1}^p(x) - F_i^p(x)$ for all $i < n^p$, $p \in \mathcal{P}$, $x \in X$. (3.22)

In words: if y stochastically dominates x, then for any strategy $i < n^p$, the payoff advantage of $i+1$ over i is greater at y than at x.

With a bit more notation, condition (3.22) can be expressed more concisely. Define the matrices $\tilde{\Sigma} \in \mathbf{R}^{n^p \times (n^p-1)}$ and $\tilde{\boldsymbol{\Sigma}} \in \mathbf{R}^{n \times (n-p)}$ by

Potential Games, Stable Games, and Supermodular Games

$$\tilde{\Sigma} = \begin{pmatrix} -1 & 0 & \cdots & 0 \\ 1 & -1 & \ddots & \vdots \\ 0 & 1 & \ddots & 0 \\ \vdots & \ddots & \ddots & -1 \\ 0 & \ddots & 0 & 1 \end{pmatrix} \quad \text{and} \quad \tilde{\boldsymbol{\Sigma}} = \text{diag}(\tilde{\Sigma}, \ldots, \tilde{\Sigma}).$$

Observation 3.4.1 *F is a supermodular game if and only if the following condition holds:*

$$\boldsymbol{\Sigma} y \geq \boldsymbol{\Sigma} x \text{ implies that } \tilde{\boldsymbol{\Sigma}}' F(y) \geq \tilde{\boldsymbol{\Sigma}}' F(x). \tag{3.23}$$

As with potential games and stable games, smooth supermodular games can be characterized in terms of conditions on the derivatives $DF(x)$.

Theorem 3.4.2 *Suppose the population game F is C^1. Then F is supermodular if and only if either of the following equivalent conditions holds.*

$$\frac{\partial (F^p_{i+1} - F^p_i)}{\partial (e^q_{j+1} - e^q_j)}(x) \geq 0 \quad \text{for all } i < n^p, j < n^q, p,q \in \mathcal{P}, \text{ and } x \in X. \tag{3.24}$$

$$\tilde{\boldsymbol{\Sigma}}' DF(x) \tilde{\boldsymbol{\Sigma}} \geq 0 \quad \text{for all } x \in X. \tag{3.25}$$

Condition (3.24) is the most transparent of the four conditions. It requires that if some players in population q switch from strategy j to strategy $j+1$, the performance of strategy $i+1 \in S^p$ improves relative to that of strategy i. On the other hand, condition (3.25) provides the most concise characterization of supermodular games. Moreover, since the range of $\tilde{\boldsymbol{\Sigma}}$ is TX (i.e., since each column of $\tilde{\boldsymbol{\Sigma}}$ lies in TX), condition (3.25) restricts the action of $DF(x)$ on $TX \times TX$, just as conditions (3.11) and (3.16) did for potential games and stable games.

Proof The equivalence of conditions (3.24) and (3.25) is easily verified. Given observation 3.4.1, it is enough to show that (3.22) implies (3.24) and that (3.25) implies (3.23).

So suppose condition (3.22) holds, and fix $x \in X$; since F is C^1, it is enough to consider x in the interior of X. Let $y_\varepsilon = x + \varepsilon(e^q_{j+1} - e^q_j)$, which lies in X whenever $|\varepsilon|$ is sufficiently small and which satisfies $\boldsymbol{\Sigma} y_\varepsilon \geq \boldsymbol{\Sigma} x$. By the definition of $DF(x)$,

$$F^p_{i+1}(y_\varepsilon) - F^p_i(y_\varepsilon) = F^p_{i+1}(x) - F^p_i(x) + \varepsilon \frac{\partial (F^p_{i+1} - F^p_i)}{\partial (e^q_{j+1} - e^q_j)}(x) + o(|y_\varepsilon - x|).$$

Thus, condition (3.22) implies that

$$\varepsilon \frac{\partial (F^p_{i+1} - F^p_i)}{\partial (e^q_{j+1} - e^q_j)}(x) + o(|\varepsilon|) \geq 0,$$

which implies (3.24).

We now show that (3.25) implies (3.23). We consider only the single-population case, leaving the general case as an exercise. The idea behind the proof is simple. If state y stochastically dominates state x, then one can transit from state x to state y by shifting mass from strategy 1 to strategy 2, from strategy 2 to strategy 3, ..., and finally from strategy $n-1$ to strategy n. Condition (3.24) $\equiv$ (3.25) says that each such shift improves the payoff of each strategy $k+1$ relative to that of strategy k. Since transiting from x to y means executing all the shifts, this transition, too, must improve the performance of $k+1$ relative to k, which is exactly what condition (3.22) $\equiv$ (3.23) requires.

Our matrix notation makes it possible to formalize this argument in a streamlined way. Recall the definitions of $\tilde{\Sigma} \in \mathbf{R}^{n \times (n-1)}$ and $\Sigma \in \mathbf{R}^{(n-1) \times n}$, and define $\Omega \in \mathbf{R}^{n \times n}$ as follows:

$$\tilde{\Sigma} = \begin{pmatrix} -1 & 0 & \cdots & & 0 \\ 1 & -1 & \ddots & & \vdots \\ 0 & 1 & \ddots & & 0 \\ \vdots & & \ddots & \ddots & -1 \\ 0 & & \ddots & 0 & 1 \end{pmatrix}; \quad \Sigma = \begin{pmatrix} 0 & 1 & \cdots & & 1 \\ 0 & 0 & 1 & & \vdots \\ \vdots & & \ddots & \ddots & \vdots \\ 0 & \cdots & & 0 & 1 \end{pmatrix}; \quad \Omega = \begin{pmatrix} 1 & 1 & \cdots & & 1 \\ 0 & 0 & \cdots & & 0 \\ 0 & 0 & \ddots & & \vdots \\ \vdots & \vdots & & \ddots & \vdots \\ 0 & 0 & \cdots & & 0 \end{pmatrix}.$$

Then it is easy to verify the next observation.

Observation 3.4.3 $\tilde{\Sigma}\Sigma = I - \Omega \in \mathbf{R}^{n \times n}$.

This observation says that the stochastic dominance operator Σ is "inverted" by the difference operator $\tilde{\Sigma}$, except for a remainder Ω that is a null operator on TX (i.e., that satisfies $\Omega z = \mathbf{0}$ for all $z \in TX$). (For completeness, we also note that $\Sigma \tilde{\Sigma} = I \in \mathbf{R}^{(n-1) \times (n-1)}$.)

Now suppose that $\Sigma x \leq \Sigma y$, and let $\alpha(t) = ty + (1-t)x$, so that $\alpha(0) = x, \alpha(1) = y$, and $\alpha'(t) = y - x \in TX$. Then using the fundamental theorem of calculus, observation 3.4.3, condition (3.25), and the fact that $\Sigma(y - x) \geq 0$, we find that

$$\tilde{\Sigma}'(F(y) - F(x)) = \tilde{\Sigma}' \int_0^1 DF(\alpha(t))(y-x)\,dt$$
$$= \int_0^1 \tilde{\Sigma}' DF(\alpha(t))(\tilde{\Sigma}\Sigma + \Omega)(y-x)\,dt$$
$$= \int_0^1 \left(\tilde{\Sigma}' DF(\alpha(t))\tilde{\Sigma}\right) \Sigma(y-x)\,dt$$
$$\geq 0.$$ ∎

3.4.2 Examples

Exercise 3.4.4: Matching in Supermodular Normal Form Games The normal form game $U = (U^1, \ldots, U^p)$ is *supermodular* if the difference $U^p(s^p + 1, s^q, s^{-\{p,q\}}) - U^p(s^p, s^q, s^{-\{p,q\}})$ is nondecreasing in s^q for all $s^p < n^p, s^{-\{p,q\}} \in \prod_{r \notin \{p,q\}} S^r$ and distinct $p, q \in \mathcal{P}$. Show that matching of p populations to play U generates a supermodular game. ◇

Exercise 3.4.5 Which symmetric normal form games generate supermodular population games? ◇

Example 3.4.1: Bertrand Oligopoly with Differentiated Products A population of firms produce output at zero marginal cost and compete in prices $S = \{1, \ldots, n\}$. Suppose that the demand faced by a firm increases when competitors raise their prices and that this effect does not diminish when the firm itself charges higher prices. More precisely, let $q_i(x)$, the demand faced by a firm that charges price i when the price distribution is x, satisfy

$$\frac{\partial q_i}{\partial (e_{j+1} - e_j)}(x) \geq 0 \quad \text{and} \quad \frac{\partial (q_{k+1} - q_k)}{\partial (e_{j+1} - e_j)}(x) \geq 0 \quad \text{for all } i \leq n,\ j, k < n.$$

The payoff to a firm that charges price i is $F_i(x) = i\, q_i(x)$, and so

$$\frac{\partial (F_{i+1} - F_i)}{\partial (e_{j+1} - e_j)}(x) = (i+1) \frac{\partial q_{i+1}}{\partial (e_{j+1} - e_j)}(x) - i \frac{\partial q_i}{\partial (e_{j+1} - e_j)}(x)$$

$$= i \frac{\partial (q_{i+1} - q_i)}{\partial (e_{j+1} - e_j)}(x) + \frac{\partial q_{i+1}}{\partial (e_{j+1} - e_j)}(x) \geq 0.$$

Therefore, F is a supermodular game. ◆

Example 3.4.2: Search with Positive Externalities A population of agents chooses levels of search effort in $S = \{1, \ldots, n\}$. The payoff to choosing effort i is

$$F_i(x) = m(i)\, b(a(x)) - c(i),$$

where $a(x) = \sum_{k \leq n} k x_k$ is the aggregate search effort, b is some increasing benefit function, m is an increasing multiplier function, and c is an arbitrary cost function. Notice that the benefits from searching are increasing in both own search effort and aggregate search effort. Since

$$\frac{\partial (F_{i+1} - F_i)}{\partial (e_{j+1} - e_j)}(x) = m(i+1)\, b'(a(x))\, ((j+1) - j) - m(i)\, b'(a(x))\, ((j+1) - j)$$

$$= (m(i+1) - m(i))\, b'(a(x)) \geq 0,$$

F is a supermodular game. ◆

Example 3.4.3: Relative Consumption Effects/Arms Races   Agents from a single population choose consumption levels (or armament levels) in $S = \{1, \ldots, n\}$. Payoffs take the form

$$F_i(x) = r(i - a(x)) + u(i) - c(i).$$

Here, r is a concave function of the difference between the agent's consumption level and the average consumption level in the population, and u and c are arbitrary functions of the consumption level. (One would typically assume that r is increasing, but this property is not needed for supermodularity.) Since

$$\frac{\partial (F_{i+1} - F_i)}{\partial (e_{j+1} - e_j)}(x) = r'((i+1) - a(x))\left(-(j+1) + j\right) - r'(i - a(x))\left(-(j+1) + j\right)$$

$$= r'(i - a(x)) - r'((i+1) - a(x)) \geq 0,$$

F is a supermodular game.   ◆

Exercise 3.4.6   Characterize the C^1 two-strategy supermodular games using a derivative condition. Compare them with the C^1 two-strategy stable games (see exercise 3.3.2(i)). Are all C^1 two-strategy games in one class or the other?   ◇

3.4.3   Best Response Monotonicity in Supermodular Games

Recall the definition of the pure best response correspondence for population p:

$$b^p(x) = \underset{i \in S^p}{\mathrm{argmax}}\, F_i^p(x).$$

Theorem 3.4.7 establishes a fundamental property of supermodular games: their pure best response correspondences are increasing.

Theorem 3.4.7   *Let F be a supermodular game with pure best response correspondences b^p. If $\Sigma x \leq \Sigma y$, then $\min b^p(x) \leq \min b^p(y)$ and $\max b^p(x) \leq \max b^p(y)$ for all $p \in \mathcal{P}$.*

This property is intuitively obvious. When opponents choose higher strategies, an agent's own higher strategies look relatively better, so his best strategies must be (weakly) higher as well.

Proof   We consider the case in which $p = 1$, focusing on the first inequality; the remaining cases are left as exercises.

Let $\Sigma x \leq \Sigma y$ and $i < j$. Then condition (3.22) implies that

$$\left(F_j(y) - F_i(y)\right) - \left(F_j(x) - F_i(x)\right) = \sum_{k=i}^{j-1}\left(\left(F_{k+1}(y) - F_k(y)\right) - \left(F_{k+1}(x) - F_k(x)\right)\right) \geq 0.$$

Thus, if $j = \min b(x)$ then $F_j(y) - F_i(y) \geq F_j(x) - F_i(x) > 0$, so i is not a best response to y. Since $i < j \min b(x)$ was arbitrary, we conclude that $\min b(x) \leq \min b(y)$. ∎

To state a version of theorem 3.4.7 for mixed best responses, some additional notation is needed. Let $v_i^p \in \mathbf{R}^{n^p}$ denote the ith vertex of the simplex Δ^p, that is, $(v_i^p)_j$ equals 1 if $j = i$ and equals 0 otherwise. (To summarize the notation to date: $x_i^p \in \mathbf{R}$, $v_i^p \in \mathbf{R}^{n^p}$, and $e_i^p \in \mathbf{R}^n$. Of course, the notation v_i^p is unnecessary in the single-population case.) Population p's mixed best response correspondence can be described in the following equivalent ways:

$$B^p(x) = \{x^p \in \Delta^p : x_i^p > 0 \Rightarrow i \in b^p(x)\}$$
$$= \mathrm{conv}(\{v_i^p : i \in b^p(x)\}),$$

The minimal and maximal elements of $B^p(x)$ can be defined as follows:

$$\underline{B}^p(x) = v_{\min b^p(x)}^p \quad \text{and} \quad \bar{B}^p(x) = v_{\max b^p(x)}^p.$$

To extend this notation to the multipopulation environment, define

$$\underline{B}(x) = (\underline{B}^1(x), \ldots, \underline{B}^p(x)) \quad \text{and} \quad \bar{B}(x) = (\bar{B}^1(x), \ldots, \bar{B}^p(x)).$$

Then the following corollary follows immediately from theorem 3.4.7.

Corollary 3.4.8 *If F is supermodular and $\Sigma x \leq \Sigma y$, then $\Sigma \underline{B}(x) \leq \Sigma \underline{B}(y)$ and $\Sigma \bar{B}(x) \leq \Sigma \bar{B}(y)$.*

3.4.4 Nash Equilibria of Supermodular Games

We now use the monotonicity of the best response correspondence to show that every supermodular game has a minimal and a maximal Nash equilibrium. The derivation of this result includes a finite iterative method for computing the minimal and maximal equilibria, and so provides a simple proof of the existence of equilibrium. We focus attention on the case where each population has mass 1, so that each set of population states X^p is just the simplex in $\mathbf{R}^{n^p}$; the extension to the general case is a simple but notationally cumbersome exercise.

Let $\underline{x}$ and $\bar{x}$ be the minimal and maximal states in $X : \underline{x}^p = v_1^p$ and $\bar{x}^p = v_{n^p}^p$ for all $p \in \mathcal{P}$. Recall that X_v denotes the set of vertices of X, and let $n^* = \#X_v = \prod_{p \in \mathcal{P}} n^p$. Finally, for states $y, z \in X$, define the interval $[y, z] \subseteq X$ by $[y, z] = \{x \in X : \Sigma y \leq \Sigma x \leq \Sigma z\}$.

Theorem 3.4.9 *Suppose F is a supermodular game. Then*

i. $\{\underline{B}^k(\underline{x})\}_{k \geq 0}$ and $\{\bar{B}^k(\bar{x})\}_{k \geq 0}$ are monotone sequences in X_v, and so converge within n^* steps to their limits, $\underline{x}^*$ and $\bar{x}^*$;

ii. $\underline{x}^* = \underline{B}(\underline{x}^*)$ and $\bar{x}^* = \bar{B}(\bar{x}^*)$, so $\underline{x}^*$ and $\bar{x}^*$ are pure Nash equilibria of F;

iii. $NE(F) \subseteq [\underline{x}^*, \bar{x}^*]$. Thus, if $\underline{x}^* = \bar{x}^*$, then this state is the Nash equilibrium of F.

In short, iterating $\underline{B}$ and $\bar{B}$ from the minimal and maximal states in X yields Nash equilibria of F, and all other Nash equilibria of F lie between the two so obtained.

Proof Part (i) follows immediately from corollary 3.4.8. To prove part (ii), note that since $\underline{x}^* = \underline{B}^{n^*}(\underline{x})$ and $\underline{B}^{n^*+1}(\underline{x}) = \underline{B}^{n^*}(\underline{x})$ by part (i), it follows that

$$\underline{B}(\underline{x}^*) = \underline{B}(\underline{B}^{n^*}(\underline{x})) = \underline{B}^{n^*+1}(\underline{x}) = \underline{B}^{n^*}(\underline{x}) = \underline{x}^*.$$

An analogous argument shows that $\bar{B}(\bar{x}^*) = \bar{x}^*$.

To prove part (iii), note that if $Y \subseteq X$ and $\min Y$ and $\max Y$ exist, then the monotonicity of B implies that $B(Y) \subseteq [\underline{B}(\min Y), \bar{B}(\max Y)]$. Iteratively applying B to the set X therefore yields $B^{n^*}(X) \subseteq [\underline{B}^{n^*}(\underline{x}), \bar{B}^{n^*}(\bar{x})] = [\underline{x}^*, \bar{x}^*]$. Also, if $x \in NE(F)$, then $x \in B(x)$, and so $B^{k-1}(x) \subseteq B^{k-1}(B(x)) = B^k(x)$, implying that $x \in B^k(x)$ for all $k \geq 1$. We therefore conclude that $x \in B^{n^*}(x) \subseteq B^{n^*}(X) \subseteq [\underline{x}^*, \bar{x}^*]$. ∎

3.A Appendix: Multivariate Calculus

3.A.1 Univariate Calculus

This section reviews some ideas from univariate calculus. A function f from the real line to itself is *differentiable* at the point x if

$$f'(x) = \lim_{y \to x} \frac{f(y) - f(x)}{y - x}$$

exists; this limit is called the *derivative* of f at x. The following are three useful facts about derivatives:

The product rule: $(fg)'(x) = f(x)g'(x) + g(x)f'(x)$.

The chain rule: $(g \circ f)'(x) = g'(f(x))f'(x)$.

The fundamental theorem of calculus: $f(y) - f(x) = \int_x^y f'(z)\,dz$.

The definition of $f'(x)$ is equivalent to the requirement that

$$f(y) = f(x) + f'(x)(y - x) + o(y - x), \tag{3.26}$$

where $o(z)$ represents a remainder function $r: \mathbf{R} \to \mathbf{R}$ satisfying

$$\lim_{z \to 0} \frac{r(z)}{z} = 0.$$

In words: $r(z)$ approaches zero faster than z approaches zero. In approximation (3.26), $f'(x)$ acts as a linear map from $\mathbf{R}$ to itself: it sends the displacement of the input, $y - x$, to the approximate displacement of the output, $f'(x)(y - x)$.

3.A.2 The Derivative as a Linear Map

Let $L(\mathbf{R}^n, \mathbf{R}^m)$ denote the space of linear maps from $\mathbf{R}^n$ to $\mathbf{R}^m$:

$$L(\mathbf{R}^n, \mathbf{R}^m) = \{\lambda \colon \mathbf{R}^n \to \mathbf{R}^m \mid \lambda(az + b\hat{z}) = a\lambda(z) + b\lambda(\hat{z}) \text{ for all } a, b \in \mathbf{R} \text{ and } z, \hat{z} \in \mathbf{R}^n\}.$$

Each matrix $A \in \mathbf{R}^{m \times n}$ defines a linear map in $L(\mathbf{R}^n, \mathbf{R}^m)$ via $\lambda(z) = Az$, and such a matrix can be found for every map λ in $L(\mathbf{R}^n, \mathbf{R}^m)$ (see section 3.B.1). It is common to identify a linear map with its matrix representation. But it is important to be aware of the distinction between these two objects. If we replace the domain $\mathbf{R}^n$ with a proper subspace of $\mathbf{R}^n$, matrix representations of linear maps are no longer unique (see appendix 3.B).

Let F be a function from $\mathbf{R}^n$ to $\mathbf{R}^m$. (Actually, one can replace the domain $\mathbf{R}^n$ with any open set in $\mathbf{R}^n$, or even with a closed set in $\mathbf{R}^n$; see section 3.A.7.) F is *differentiable* at x if there is a linear map $DF(x) \in L(\mathbf{R}^n, \mathbf{R}^m)$ satisfying

$$F(y) = F(x) + DF(x)(y - x) + o(y - x). \tag{3.27}$$

Here, $o(z)$ represents a remainder function $r \colon \mathbf{R}^n \to \mathbf{R}^m$ that satisfies

$$\lim_{z \to 0} \frac{r(z)}{|z|} = 0.$$

If the function $DF \colon \mathbf{R}^n \to L(\mathbf{R}^n, \mathbf{R}^m)$ is continuous, then F is *continuously differentiable* or of *class* C^1.

When $DF(x)$ is viewed as a matrix in $\mathbf{R}^{m \times n}$, it is called the *Jacobian matrix* or *derivative matrix* of F at x. To express this matrix explicitly, define the *partial derivatives* of F at x by

$$\frac{\partial F_i}{\partial x_j}(x) = \lim_{y_j \to x_j} \frac{F_i(y_j, x_{-j}) - F_i(x)}{y_j - x_j}.$$

Then the derivative matrix $DF(x)$ can be expressed as

$$DF(x) = \begin{pmatrix} \frac{\partial F_1}{\partial x_1}(x) & \cdots & \frac{\partial F_1}{\partial x_n}(x) \\ \vdots & \vdots & \vdots \\ \frac{\partial F_m}{\partial x_1}(x) & \cdots & \frac{\partial F_m}{\partial x_n}(x) \end{pmatrix}.$$

If f is a function from $\mathbf{R}^n$ to $\mathbf{R}$ (i.e., if $m = 1$), then its derivative at x can be represented by a vector. This vector is the *gradient* of f at x, defined by

$$\nabla f(x) = \begin{pmatrix} \frac{\partial f}{\partial x_1}(x) \\ \vdots \\ \frac{\partial f}{\partial x_n}(x) \end{pmatrix}.$$

The notations for derivatives are related by $Df(x) = \nabla f(x)'$, where the prime represents transposition, and also by

$$DF(x) = \begin{pmatrix} \nabla F_1(x)' \\ \vdots \\ \nabla F_m(x)' \end{pmatrix}.$$

Suppose one is interested in how quickly the value of f changes as one moves from the point $x \in \mathbf{R}^n$ in the direction $z \in \mathbf{R}^n - \{0\}$. This rate is described by the *directional derivative* of f at x in direction z, defined by

$$\frac{\partial f}{\partial z}(x) = \lim_{\varepsilon \to 0} \frac{f(x+\varepsilon z) - f(x)}{\varepsilon}. \tag{3.28}$$

It is easy to verify that

$$\frac{\partial f}{\partial z}(x) = \nabla f(x)'z.$$

More generally, the rate of change of the vector-valued function F at x in direction z can be expressed as $DF(x)z$.

It is worth noting that a function can admit directional derivatives at x in every direction $z \neq 0$ without being differentiable at x (i.e., without satisfying definition (3.27)). Amazingly, such a function need not even be continuous at x, as the following example shows.

Example 3.A.1 Define the function $f: \mathbf{R}^2 \to \mathbf{R}$ by

$$f(x_1, x_2) = \begin{cases} \dfrac{x_1(x_2)^2}{(x_1)^2 + (x_2)^4} & \text{if } x_1 \neq 0, \\ 0 & \text{if } x_1 = 0. \end{cases}$$

Using definition (3.28), it is easy to verify that the directional derivatives of f at the origin in every direction $z \neq 0$ exist:

$$\frac{\partial f}{\partial z}(0) = \begin{cases} \dfrac{(z_2)^2}{z_1} & \text{if } z_1 \neq 0, \\ 0 & \text{if } z_1 = 0. \end{cases}$$

But while $f(0) = 0$, $f(x) = \frac{1}{2}$ at all other x that satisfy $x_1 = (x_2)^2$, and so f is discontinuous at $\mathbf{0}$. ◆

On the other hand, if all (or even all but one) of the partial derivatives f exist and are continuous in a neighborhood of x, then f is differentiable at x.

3.A.3 Differentiation as a Linear Operation

Differentiation can be viewed an operation that takes functions as inputs and returns functions as outputs. From this point of view, differentiation is a linear operation between spaces of functions. As an example, suppose that f and g are functions from $\mathbf{R}$ to itself and that a and b are real numbers. Then the scalar product af is a function from $\mathbf{R}$ to itself, as is the linear combination $af + bg$. (In other words, the set of functions from $\mathbf{R}$ to itself is a *vector space*.) The fact that differentiation is linear means that the derivative of the linear combination, $(af+bg)'$, is equal to the linear combination of the derivatives, $af' + bg'$.

This idea can be expressed in a multivariate setting using a simple formula. Suppose that $F\colon \mathbf{R}^n \to \mathbf{R}^m$ is a differentiable function and that A is a matrix in $\mathbf{R}^{l \times m}$. Then AF is the function from $\mathbf{R}^n$ to $\mathbf{R}^l$ defined by $(AF)_k(x) = \sum_{j=1}^m A_{kj} F_j(x)$ for $k \in \{1,\ldots,l\}$. Linearity of differentiation says that $D(AF) = A(DF)$, or more explicitly,

Linearity of differentiation: $D(AF)(x) = A(DF)(x)$ for all $x \in \mathbf{R}^n$.

Put differently, the differential operator D and the linear map A commute.

3.A.4 The Product Rule and the Chain Rule

Suppose f and g are differentiable functions from $\mathbf{R}$ to itself. Then the product rule says that $(fg)'(x) = f(x)g'(x) + g(x)f'(x)$. In other words, to find the effect of changing x on the value $(fg)(x)$ of the product function, first find the effect of changing x on $g(x)$, and scale this effect by $f(x)$; then find the effect of changing x on $f(x)$, and scale this effect by $g(x)$; and finally, add the two terms.

This same idea can be applied in multidimensional cases as well. Let $F\colon \mathbf{R}^n \to \mathbf{R}^m$ and $G\colon \mathbf{R}^n \to \mathbf{R}^m$ be differentiable vector-valued functions. Then $F'G\colon \mathbf{R}^n \to \mathbf{R}$, defined by $(F'G)(x) = F(x)'G(x)$, is a scalar-valued function. The derivative $D(F'G)(x) \in \mathbf{R}^{1 \times n}$ of the new function is described by the following product rule:

Product rule 1: $D(F'G)(x) = (\nabla(F'G)(x))' = F(x)'DG(x) + G(x)'DF(x)$.

(Notice that in the previous paragraph a prime (') denoted the derivative of a scalar-valued function, whereas here it denotes matrix transposition. As long as these scalar and matrix usages are kept separate, no confusion should arise.)

If $a\colon \mathbf{R}^n \to \mathbf{R}$ is a differentiable scalar-valued function, then $aF\colon \mathbf{R}^n \to \mathbf{R}^m$, defined by $(aF)(x) = a(x)F(x)$, is a vector-valued function. Its derivative $D(aF)(x) \in \mathbf{R}^{m \times n}$ is described by the next product rule:

Product rule 2: $D(aF)(x) = a(x)DF(x) + F(x)\nabla a(x)' = a(x)DF(x) + F(x)Da(x)$.

Finally, a vector-valued function can be created from $F\colon \mathbf{R}^n \to \mathbf{R}^m$ and $G\colon \mathbf{R}^n \to \mathbf{R}^m$ by introducing the componentwise product $F \bullet G\colon \mathbf{R}^n \to \mathbf{R}^m$. This function is defined by $(F \bullet G)_i(x) = F_i(x)G_i(x)$, or in matrix notation, by $(F \bullet G)(x) =$

$\text{diag}(F(x))G(x) = \text{diag}(G(x))F(x)$, where $\text{diag}(v)$ denotes the diagonal matrix whose diagonal entries are the components of the vector v. The derivative of the componentwise product, $D(F \bullet G)(x) \in \mathbf{R}^{m \times n}$, is described by the last product rule:

Product rule 3: $\quad D(F \bullet G)(x) = \text{diag}(F(x))DG(x) + \text{diag}(G(x))DF(x)$.

One can verify each of these formulas by expanding them and then applying the univariate product rule term by term. To remember the product rules, bear in mind that the end result must be a sum of two terms of the same dimensions and that each of the terms must end with a derivative, so as to operate on a displacement vector $z \in \mathbf{R}^n$ to be placed on the right-hand side.

In the one-dimensional setting, the chain rule says that $(g \circ f)'(x) = g'(f(x))f'(x)$. In words, the formula says that the effect of changing x on $(g \circ f)(x)$ can be decomposed into two pieces: the effect of changing x on the value of $f(x)$, and the effect of this change in $f(x)$ on the value of $g(f(x))$.

This same idea carries through to multivariate functions. Let $F: \mathbf{R}^n \to \mathbf{R}^m$ and $G: \mathbf{R}^m \to \mathbf{R}^l$ be differentiable, and let $G \circ F: \mathbf{R}^n \to \mathbf{R}^l$ be their composition. The chain rule says that the derivative of this composition at $x \in \mathbf{R}^n$, $D(G \circ F)(x) \in \mathbf{R}^{l \times n}$, is obtained as the product of the derivative matrices $DG(F(x)) \in \mathbf{R}^{l \times m}$ and $DF(x) \in \mathbf{R}^{m \times n}$.

The chain rule: $\quad D(G \circ F)(x) = DG(F(x))\, DF(x)$.

This equation can be stated more explicitly as

$$\frac{\partial (G \circ F)_k}{\partial x_i}(x) = \sum_{j=1}^{m} \frac{\partial G_k}{\partial y_j}(F(x)) \frac{\partial F_j}{\partial x_i}(x).$$

The chain rule can be viewed as a generalization of the earlier formula on linearity of differentiation, with the linear map A replaced by the nonlinear function G.

3.A.5 Homogeneity and Euler's Theorem

Let f be a differentiable function from $\mathbf{R}^n$ to $\mathbf{R}$. (The domain $\mathbf{R}^n$ can be replaced with an open (or even a closed) *convex cone*: a convex set which, if it contains $x \in \mathbf{R}^n$, also contains tx for all $t > 0$.) The function f is *homogeneous of degree k* if

$$f(tx) = t^k f(x) \quad \text{for all } x \in \mathbf{R}^n, t > 0. \tag{3.29}$$

By definition, homogeneous functions are monomials along each ray from the origin. Indeed, when $n = 1$, the homogeneous functions are precisely the monomials: if $x \in \mathbf{R}$, $g(tx) = t^k g(x)$, and $g(1) = a$, then $g(x) = ax^k$. But when $n > 1$, more complicated homogeneous functions can be found.

Nevertheless, the basic properties of homogeneous functions are generalizations of properties of monomials. If one takes the derivative of each side of equation (3.29) with respect to x_i, applying the chain rule on the left-hand side, one obtains

$$\nabla f(tx)'(te_i) = t^k \frac{\partial f}{\partial x_i}(x).$$

Dividing both sides of this equation by t and simplifying yields

$$\frac{\partial f}{\partial x_i}(tx) = t^{k-1} \frac{\partial f}{\partial x_i}(x).$$

In other words, the partial derivatives of a homogeneous function of degree k are themselves homogeneous of degree $k-1$.

If one instead takes the derivative of each side of (3.29) with respect to t, again using the chain rule on the left-hand side, one obtains

$$\nabla f(tx)'x = \begin{cases} 0 & \text{if } k = 0, \\ kt^{k-1}f(x) & \text{otherwise.} \end{cases}$$

Setting $t = 1$ yields *Euler's theorem*: if f is homogeneous of degree k, then

$$\nabla f(x)'x = kf(x) \quad \text{for all } x \in \mathbf{R}^n.$$

In fact, the converse of Euler's theorem is also true: one can show that if f satisfies the previous identity, it is homogeneous of degree k.

3.A.6 Higher-Order Derivatives

As we have seen, the derivative of a function $F: \mathbf{R}^n \to \mathbf{R}^m$ is a new function

$$DF: \mathbf{R}^n \to L(\mathbf{R}^n, \mathbf{R}^m). \tag{3.30}$$

For each $x \in \mathbf{R}^n$, $DF(x)$ describes how the value of F in $\mathbf{R}^m$ changes as one moves away from x in any direction $z \in \mathbf{R}^n$. Notice that in expression (3.30), the point x around which the function F is evaluated inhabits the first $\mathbf{R}^n$, whereas the displacement vector z inhabits the second $\mathbf{R}^n$.

The second derivative of F at x, $D^2F(x) = D(DF(x))$, describes how the value of the first derivative $DF(x) \in L(\mathbf{R}^n, \mathbf{R}^m)$ changes as one moves away from x in direction $\hat{z} \in \mathbf{R}^n$. Thus, $D^2F(x)$ is an element of the set of maps $L(\mathbf{R}^n, L(\mathbf{R}^n, \mathbf{R}^m))$, which we denote by $L^2(\mathbf{R}^n, \mathbf{R}^m)$. Elements of $L^2(\mathbf{R}^n, \mathbf{R}^m)$ are called *bilinear maps* from $\mathbf{R}^n \times \mathbf{R}^n$ to $\mathbf{R}^m$; they take two vectors in $\mathbf{R}^n$ as inputs, are linear in each of these vectors, and return elements of $\mathbf{R}^m$ as outputs.

If F is twice continuously differentiable (i.e., if DF and D^2F are both continuous in x), then it can be shown that $D^2F(x)$ is *symmetric*, in the sense that $D^2F(x)(z, \hat{z}) = D^2F(x)(\hat{z}, z)$ for all $z, \hat{z} \in \mathbf{R}^n$. Therefore, $D^2F(x)$ is an element of $L_s^2(\mathbf{R}^n, \mathbf{R}^m)$, the set of *symmetric bilinear maps* from $\mathbf{R}^n \times \mathbf{R}^n$ to $\mathbf{R}^m$.

More generally, the kth derivative of F is a map $D^k F\colon \mathbf{R}^n \to L^k_s(\mathbf{R}^n, \mathbf{R}^m)$. For each $x \in \mathbf{R}^n$, $D^k F(x)$ is a symmetric multilinear map; it takes k displacement vectors in $\mathbf{R}^n$ as inputs, is linear in each, and returns an output in $\mathbf{R}^m$; this output does not depend on the order of the inputs. If F has continuous derivatives of orders zero through K, it is in *class C^K*.

One can use higher-order derivatives to write the Kth-order version of Taylor's formula, which provides a polynomial approximation of a C^K function F around the point x.

Taylor's formula: $\quad F(y) = F(x) + \sum_{k=1}^{K} \frac{1}{k!} D^k F(x)(y-x, \ldots, y-x) + o\left(|y-x|^K\right).$

Here, $D^k F(x)(y-x, \ldots, y-x) \in \mathbf{R}^m$ is the output generated when the multilinear map $D^k F(x) \in L^k_s(\mathbf{R}^n, \mathbf{R}^m)$ acts on k copies of the displacement vector $(y-x) \in \mathbf{R}^n$. (To see where the factorial terms come from, try expressing the coefficients of a Kth-order polynomial in terms of the polynomial's derivatives.)

The higher-order derivative that occurs most frequently in applications is the second derivative of a scalar-valued function $f\colon \mathbf{R}^n \to \mathbf{R}$. This second derivative, $D^2 f$, sends each $x \in \mathbf{R}^n$ to a symmetric bilinear map $D^2 f(x) \in L^2_s(\mathbf{R}^n, \mathbf{R})$. This map can be represented using a *Hessian matrix* $\nabla^2 f(x) \in \mathbf{R}^{n \times n}$, the elements of which are the second-order partial derivatives of f:

$$\nabla^2 f(x) = \begin{pmatrix} \frac{\partial^2 f}{(\partial x_1)^2}(x) & \cdots & \frac{\partial^2 f}{\partial x_1 \partial x_n}(x) \\ \vdots & \vdots & \vdots \\ \frac{\partial^2 f}{\partial x_n \partial x_1}(x) & \cdots & \frac{\partial^2 f}{(\partial x_n)^2}(x) \end{pmatrix}.$$

When f is C^2, the symmetry of the map $D^2 f(x)$ is reflected in the fact that the Hessian matrix is symmetric: corresponding pairs of mixed partial derivatives are equal.

The value $D^2 f(x)(z, \hat{z})$ is expressed in terms of the Hessian matrix in this way:

$$D^2 f(x)(z, \hat{z}) = z' \nabla^2 f(x) \hat{z}.$$

Using the gradient vector and Hessian matrix, the second-order Taylor approximation of a C^2 scalar-valued function is expressed as follows:

$$f(y) = f(x) + \nabla f(x)'(y-x) + \tfrac{1}{2}(y-x)' \nabla^2 f(x)(y-x) + o\left(|y-x|^2\right).$$

3.A.7 The Whitney Extension Theorem

The K times continuously differentiable functions have been defined to have domain $\mathbf{R}^n$, but nothing discussed so far would change if the functions were defined only on open subsets of $\mathbf{R}^n$. In fact, it is also possible to define C^K functions on *closed* sets $X \subset \mathbf{R}^n$. However, doing so requires some care, as the following example illustrates.

Example 3.A.2 Let $f\colon [0, \infty) \to \mathbf{R}$ be defined by

$$f(x) = \begin{cases} x^2 \sin \frac{1}{x} & \text{if } x > 0, \\ 0 & \text{if } x = 0. \end{cases}$$

Then f is continuous on $[0, \infty)$, and f is continuously differentiable on $(0, \infty)$ with $f'(x) = 2x \sin \frac{1}{x} - \cos \frac{1}{x}$. It is possible to extend f to a differentiable function defined throughout $\mathbf{R}$: for instance, one can set $f(x) = 0$ for $x < 0$, in which case $f'(x) = 0$ for all $x \le 0$. But since f' takes values -1 and 1 at points arbitrarily close to 0, f cannot be extended to a continuously differentiable function defined throughout $\mathbf{R}$. ◆

The *Whitney extension theorem* provides conditions under which a function $F\colon X \to \mathbf{R}^m$ can be extended to a C^K function defined throughout $\mathbf{R}^n$. Example 3.A.2 shows that it is not enough for F to be continuous on X and C^K on $\text{int}(X)$: in addition, F must admit "local uniform Taylor expansions" at each x on $\text{bd}(X)$. In effect, the Whitney extension theorem provides a definition of (K times) continuous differentiability for functions defined on closed sets in $\mathbf{R}^n$.

3.A.8 Vector Integration and the Fundamental Theorem of Calculus

Let $\alpha\colon \mathbf{R} \to \mathbf{R}^n$ be a vector-valued function defined on the real line. Integrals of α are computed componentwise, in other words,

$$\left(\int_a^b \alpha(t)\, dt \right)_i = \int_a^b \alpha_i(t)\, dt. \tag{3.31}$$

It is easy to verify that integration, like differentiation, is linear: if $A \in \mathbf{R}^{m \times n}$, then

$$\int_a^b A\alpha(t)\, dt = A \int_a^b \alpha(t)\, dt.$$

With definition (3.31) in hand, one can state a multivariate version of the fundamental theorem of calculus. Suppose that $F\colon \mathbf{R}^n \to \mathbf{R}^m$ is a C^1 function. Let $\alpha\colon [0, 1] \to \mathbf{R}^n$ be a C^1 function satisfying $\alpha(0) = x$ and $\alpha(1) = y$, and call its derivative $\alpha'\colon \mathbf{R} \to \mathbf{R}^n$.

The fundamental theorem of calculus: $\quad F(y) - F(x) = \int_0^1 DF(\alpha(t))\, \alpha'(t)\, dt.$

3.A.9 Potential Functions and Integrability

When can a continuous vector field $F: \mathbf{R}^n \to \mathbf{R}^n$ be expressed as the gradient of some scalar-valued function f? In other words, when does $F = \nabla f$ for some *potential function* $f: \mathbf{R}^n \to \mathbf{R}$? One can characterize the vector fields that admit potential functions in terms of their integrals over closed curves: if $F: \mathbf{R}^n \to \mathbf{R}^n$ is continuous, it admits a potential function if and only if

$$\int_0^1 F(\alpha(t))' \left(\tfrac{d}{dt}\alpha(t)\right) dt = 0 \tag{3.32}$$

for every piecewise C^1 function $\alpha: [0,1] \to \mathbf{R}^n$ with $\alpha(0) = \alpha(1)$. If C denotes the closed curve through $\mathbf{R}^n$ traced by α, then (3.32) can be expressed more concisely as

$$\oint_C F(x) \cdot dx = 0.$$

When F is not only continuous, but also C^1, the question of the integrability of F can be answered by examining cross-partial derivatives. Note first that if F admits a C^2 potential function f, then the symmetry of the Hessian matrices of f implies that

$$\frac{\partial F_i}{\partial x_j}(x) = \frac{\partial^2 f}{\partial x_i \partial x_j}(x) = \frac{\partial^2 f}{\partial x_j \partial x_i}(x) = \frac{\partial F_j}{\partial x_i}(x), \tag{3.33}$$

and hence that the derivative matrix $DF(x)$ is symmetric for all $x \in \mathbf{R}^n$. The converse statement is also true, and provides the desired characterization of integrability: if F is C^1, with $DF(x)$ symmetric for all $x \in \mathbf{R}^n$ (i.e., whenever the *integrability condition* (3.33) holds), there is a function $f: \mathbf{R}^n \to \mathbf{R}$ such that $\nabla f = F$. This sufficient condition for integrability remains valid whenever the domain of F is an open (or closed) convex subset of $\mathbf{R}^n$. However, condition (3.33) does not ensure the existence of a potential function for vector fields defined on more general domains.

3.B Appendix: Affine Calculus

The simplex in $\mathbf{R}^n$, which serves as the state space in single-population games, is an $n-1$ dimensional set. As a consequence, derivatives of functions defined on the simplex cannot be computed in the manner described in appendix 3.A because partial derivatives of such functions do not exist. To understand differential calculus in this context, and in the more general context of multipopulation games, one must develop the tools of calculus for functions defined on affine spaces.

3.B.1 Linear Forms and the Riesz Representation Theorem

Let Z be a subspace of $\mathbf{R}^n$, and let $L(Z, \mathbf{R})$ be the set of linear maps from Z to $\mathbf{R}$. $L(Z, \mathbf{R})$ is also known as the *dual space* of Z, and elements of $L(Z, \mathbf{R})$, namely, maps $\lambda \colon Z \to \mathbf{R}$ that satisfy $\lambda(az + b\hat{z}) = a\lambda(z) + b\lambda(\hat{z})$, are also known as *linear forms*.

Each vector $y \in Z$ defines a linear form $\lambda \in L(Z, \mathbf{R})$ via $\lambda(z) = y'z$. In fact, the converse statement is also true: every linear form can be uniquely represented in this way.

Theorem 3.B.1 (The Riesz Representation Theorem) *For each linear form $\lambda \in L(Z, \mathbf{R})$, there is a unique $y \in Z$, the* Riesz representation *of λ, such that $\lambda(z) = y'z$ for all $z \in Z$.*

Another way of describing the Riesz representation theorem is to say that Z and $L(Z, \mathbf{R})$ are *linearly isomorphic*: the map from Z to $L(Z, \mathbf{R})$ described above is linear, one-to-one, and onto.

It is crucial to note that when Z is a proper subspace of $\mathbf{R}^n$, the linear form λ can be represented by many vectors in $\mathbf{R}^n$. What theorem 3.B.1 says is that λ can be represented by a unique vector *in Z itself*.

Example 3.B.1 Let $Z = \mathbf{R}_0^2 = \{z \in \mathbf{R}^2 \colon z_1 + z_2 = 0\}$, and define the linear form $\lambda \in L(Z, \mathbf{R})$ by $\lambda(z) = z_1 - z_2$. Then both

$$y = \begin{pmatrix} 1 \\ -1 \end{pmatrix} \quad \text{and} \quad \hat{y} = \begin{pmatrix} 3 \\ 1 \end{pmatrix}$$

represent λ: if $z \in Z$, then $\hat{y}'z = 3z_1 + z_2 = 3z_1 + (-z_1) = 2z_1 = z_1 - z_2 = y'z = \lambda(z)$. But since y is an element of Z, it is the Riesz representation of λ. ◆

In this example, the reason that both y and $\hat{y}$ can represent λ is that their difference,

$$\hat{y} - y = \begin{pmatrix} 2 \\ 2 \end{pmatrix},$$

is orthogonal to Z. This suggests a simple way of recovering the Riesz representation of a linear form from an arbitrary vector representation: eliminate the portion orthogonal to Z by applying the orthogonal projection P_Z.

Theorem 3.B.2 *Let $\lambda \in L(Z, \mathbf{R})$ be a linear form. If $\hat{y} \in \mathbf{R}^n$ represents λ, in the sense that $\lambda(z) = \hat{y}'z$ for all $z \in Z$, then $y = P_Z \hat{y}$ is the Riesz representation of λ.*

Example 3.B.2 Recall that the orthogonal projection onto $\mathbf{R}_0^2$ is $\Phi = I - \tfrac{1}{2}\mathbf{1}\mathbf{1}'$. Thus, in the previous example, y can be recovered from $\hat{y}$ in the following way:

$$y = \Phi\hat{y} = (I - \tfrac{1}{2}\mathbf{1}\mathbf{1}')\begin{pmatrix} 3 \\ 1 \end{pmatrix} = \begin{pmatrix} 3 \\ 1 \end{pmatrix} - \begin{pmatrix} 2 \\ 2 \end{pmatrix} = \begin{pmatrix} 1 \\ -1 \end{pmatrix}.$$

◆

3.B.2 Dual Characterizations of Multiples of Linear Forms

This section presents results characterizing linear forms that are scalar multiples of one another. These results are used when studying imitative dynamics in chapters 5 and 8; see especially exercise 5.4.10 and theorem 8.5.8.

If the vectors $v \in \mathbf{R}^n$ and $w \in \mathbf{R}^n$ are nonzero multiples of one another, then v and w clearly are orthogonal to the same set of vectors in $\mathbf{R}^n$. Conversely, if $\{v\}^\perp = \{y \in \mathbf{R}^n : v'y = 0\}$ equals $\{w\}^\perp$, then v and w must be (nonzero) multiples of one another because they are both normal vectors of the same hyperplane.

When are v and w positive multiples of one another? This is the case if and only if the set $\mathcal{H}(v) = \{y \in \mathbf{R}^n : v'y \geq 0\}$, the closed half-space consisting of those vectors with which v forms an acute or right angle, is equal to the corresponding set $\mathcal{H}(w)$. Clearly, $\mathcal{H}(v) = \mathcal{H}(w)$ implies that $\{v\}^\perp = \{w\}^\perp$, and so that $v = cw$; since $v \in \mathcal{H}(v) = \mathcal{H}(w)$, it must be that $c > 0$.

In summary:

Observation 3.B.3

i. $\{x \in \mathbf{R}^n : v'x = 0\} = \{x \in \mathbf{R}^n : w'x = 0\}$ if and only if $v = cw$ for some $c \neq 0$.

ii. $\{x \in \mathbf{R}^n : v'x \geq 0\} = \{x \in \mathbf{R}^n : w'x \geq 0\}$ if and only if $v = cw$ for some $c > 0$.

Proposition 3.B.4 provides analogues of these characterizations for settings in which one can only compare how v and w act on vectors in some subspace $Z \subseteq \mathbf{R}^n$. Since these comparisons relate v and w as linear forms on Z, theorem 3.B.2 suggests that the characterizations should be expressed in terms of the orthogonal projections of v and w onto Z.

Proposition 3.B.4

i. $\{z \in Z : v'z = 0\} = \{z \in Z : w'z = 0\}$ if and only if $P_Z v = c P_Z w$ for some $c \neq 0$.

ii. $\{z \in Z : v'z \geq 0\} = \{z \in Z : w'z \geq 0\}$ if and only if $P_Z v = c P_Z w$ for some $c > 0$.

Proof The "if" direction of part (i) is immediate. For the "only if" direction, observe that $v'z = 0$ for all $z \in Z$ if and only if $v'P_Z x = 0$ for all $x \in \mathbf{R}^n$. Since the matrix P_Z is symmetric, the second equality can be rewritten as $(P_Z v)'x = 0$. Thus, the conclusion that $P_Z v = c P_Z w$ with $c \neq 0$ (part (i) of the proposition) follows from observation 3.B.3(i). The proof of part (ii) follows similarly from observation 3.B.3(ii). ■

To cap this discussion, we note that both parts of observation 3.B.3 are the simplest cases of more general duality results that link a linear map $A \in L(\mathbf{R}^m, \mathbf{R}^n) \equiv \mathbf{R}^{n \times m}$ with its transpose $A' \in L(\mathbf{R}^n, \mathbf{R}^m) \equiv \mathbf{R}^{m \times n}$. Part (i) is essentially the $m = 1$ case of the *fundamental theorem of linear algebra*:

$$\text{range}(A) = (\text{nullspace}(A'))^\perp. \tag{3.34}$$

In equation (3.34) the set $\text{range}(A) = \{w \in \mathbf{R}^n : w = Ax \text{ for some } x \in \mathbf{R}^m\}$ is the span of the columns of A. The set $\text{nullspace}(A') = \{y \in \mathbf{R}^n : A'y = 0\}$ consists of the vectors that A' maps to the origin; equivalently, it is the set of vectors that are orthogonal to every column of A. Viewed in this light, equation (3.34) says that w is a linear combination of the columns of A if and only if any y that is orthogonal to each column of A is also orthogonal to w. While (3.34) is of basic importance, it is quite easy to derive after taking orthogonal complements:

$$(\text{range}(A))^\perp = \{y \in \mathbf{R}^n : y'Ax = 0 \text{ for all } x \in \mathbf{R}^m\}$$
$$= \{y \in \mathbf{R}^n : y'A = \mathbf{0}'\} = \text{nullspace}(A').$$

Part (ii) of observation 3.B.3 is essentially the $m = 1$ case of *Farkas's lemma*:

$$[w = Ax \text{ for some } x \in \mathbf{R}_+^m] \text{ if and only if } [[A'y \geq \mathbf{0} \Rightarrow w'y \geq 0] \text{ for all } y \in \mathbf{R}^n]. \tag{3.35}$$

In words: w is a *non-negative* linear combination of the columns of A if and only if any y that forms a *weakly acute* angle with each column of A also forms a *weakly acute* angle with w. Despite their analogous interpretations, statement (3.35) is considerably more difficult to prove than statement (3.34) (see the chapter notes).

3.B.3 Derivatives of Functions on Affine Spaces

Before considering calculus on affine spaces, let us briefly review differentiation of scalar-valued functions on $\mathbf{R}^n$. If f is a C^1 function from $\mathbf{R}^n$ to $\mathbf{R}$, then its derivative at x, denoted $Df(x)$, is an element of $L(\mathbf{R}^n, \mathbf{R})$, the set of linear maps from $\mathbf{R}^n$ to $\mathbf{R}$. For each $x \in \mathbf{R}^n$, the map $Df(x)$ takes vectors $z \in \mathbf{R}^n$ as inputs and returns scalars $Df(x)z \in \mathbf{R}$ as outputs. The latter expression appears in the first-order Taylor expansion

$$f(x + z) = f(x) + Df(x)z + o(z) \quad \text{for all } z \in \mathbf{R}^n.$$

By the Riesz representation theorem, there is a unique vector $\nabla f(x) \in \mathbf{R}^n$ satisfying $Df(x)z = \nabla f(x)'z$ for all $z \in \mathbf{R}^n$. We call $\nabla f(x)$ the gradient of f at x. In the present full-dimensional case, $\nabla f(x)$ is the vector of partial derivatives $\frac{\partial f}{\partial x_i}(x)$ of f at x.

Now, let $A \subseteq \mathbf{R}^n$ be an affine space with tangent space TA, and consider a function $f : A \to \mathbf{R}$. (As in appendix 3.A, the ideas to follow can also be applied to functions whose domain is a set that is open (or closed) relative to A.) The function f is *differentiable* at $x \in A$ if there is a linear map $Df(x) \in L(TA, \mathbf{R})$ satisfying

$$f(x + z) = f(x) + Df(x)z + o(z) \quad \text{for all } z \in TA.$$

The *gradient of* f at x is the Riesz representation of $Df(x)$. In other words, it is the unique vector $\nabla f(x) \in TA$ such that $Df(x)z = \nabla f(x)'z$ for all $z \in TA$. If the function $\nabla f \colon A \to TA$ is continuous, then f is *continuously differentiable* or of *class* C^1.

When $A = \mathbf{R}^n$, this definition of the gradient is simply the one presented earlier, and $\nabla f(x)$ is the only vector in $\mathbf{R}^n$ that represents $Df(x)$. But in lower-dimensional cases, there are many vectors in $\mathbf{R}^n$ that can represent $Df(x)$. The gradient vector $\nabla f(x)$ is the only one lying in TA; all others are obtained by summing $\nabla f(x)$ and an element of $(TA)^\perp$.

When $A = \mathbf{R}^n$, the gradient of f at x is just the vector of partial derivatives of f at x. But in other cases the partial derivatives of f may not even exist. How does one compute $\nabla f(x)$ then? Usually, it is easiest to extend the function f to all of $\mathbf{R}^n$ in some smooth way, and then to compute the gradient by way of this extension. In some cases (e.g., when f is a polynomial), obtaining the extension is just a matter of declaring that the domain is $\mathbf{R}^n$. But even in this situation, there is an alternative extension that is often handy.

Proposition 3.B.5 *Let $f \colon A \to \mathbf{R}$ be a C^1 function on the affine set A, and let $Z = TA$.*

i. *Let $\tilde{f} \colon \mathbf{R}^n \to \mathbf{R}$ be any C^1 extension of f. Then $\nabla f(x) = P_Z \nabla \tilde{f}(x)$ for all $x \in A$.*

ii. *Define $\bar{f} \colon \mathbf{R}^n \to \mathbf{R}$ by $\bar{f}(y) = f(P_Z y + z_A^\perp)$, where $z_A^\perp$ is the unique element of $A \cap Z^\perp$. Then $\nabla f(x) = \nabla \bar{f}(x)$ for all $x \in A$.*

In words, $\bar{f}$ assigns the value $f(x)$ to each point in $\mathbf{R}^n$ whose orthogonal projection onto $TA = Z$ is the same as that of $x \in A$; the gradient of $\bar{f}$ is identical to the gradient of f on the set A.

Proof Part (i) follows immediately from the relevant definitions. To prove part (ii), suppose that $x \in A$. Then by the chain and product rules,

$$D\bar{f}(x) = D(f(P_Z x + z_A^\perp)) = Df(x)P_Z.$$

This linear form on $\mathbf{R}^n$ is represented by the (column) vector $\nabla \bar{f}(x) = (\nabla f(x)' P_Z)' \in \mathbf{R}^n$. But since the orthogonal projection matrix P_Z is symmetric, and since $\nabla f(x) \in Z$, we conclude that

$$\nabla \bar{f}(x) = (\nabla f(x)' P_Z)' = P_Z' \nabla f(x) = P_Z \nabla f(x) = \nabla f(x). \quad \blacksquare$$

The fact that P_Z is an *orthogonal* projection makes this proof simple: since P_Z is symmetric, its action can be transferred from the displacement direction $z \in Z$ to the vector $\nabla f(x)$ itself.

Similar considerations arise for vector-valued functions defined on affine spaces, and also for higher-order derivatives. If $F \colon A \to \mathbf{R}^m$ is C^1, its derivative at $x \in A$ is a linear map $DF(x) \in L(Z, \mathbf{R}^m)$, where Z is again written for TA. While there are many matrices in $\mathbf{R}^{m \times n}$ that represent this derivative, applying the logic above to each component of F shows that there is a unique such matrix, called the *Jacobian matrix* or *derivative matrix*, whose rows are elements of Z. As before, we abuse notation by denoting this matrix $DF(x)$, but this time there can be some confusion. If F is "automatically" defined on all of $\mathbf{R}^n$, one must be careful to distinguish between the derivative matrix of $F: \mathbf{R}^n \to \mathbf{R}^m$ at x and the derivative matrix of its restriction $F|_A: A \to \mathbf{R}^m$ at x; they are related by $DF|_A(x) = DF(x)P_Z$.

If the function $f: A \to \mathbf{R}$ is C^2, then its second derivative at $x \in A$ is a symmetric bilinear map $D^2f(x) \in L_s^2(Z, \mathbf{R})$. There are many symmetric matrices in $\mathbf{R}^{n \times n}$ that represent $D^2f(x)$, but there is a unique such matrix whose rows and columns are in Z. This matrix is the *Hessian* of f at x, denoted $\nabla^2 f(x)$. If $\tilde{f}: \mathbf{R}^n \to \mathbf{R}$ is any C^2 extension of f, then the Hessian of f is computed as $\nabla^2 f(x) = P_Z \nabla^2 \tilde{f}(x) P_Z$; if $\bar{f}(y) = f(P_Z y + z_A^\perp)$ is the constant orthogonal extension of f to $\mathbf{R}^n$, then $\nabla^2 f(x) = \nabla^2 \bar{f}(x)$.

3.B.4 Affine Integrability

A necessary and sufficient condition for a C^1 vector field $F: \mathbf{R}^n \to \mathbf{R}^n$ to admit a potential function, that is, a scalar-valued function f satisfying $\nabla f(x) = F(x)$ for all $x \in \mathbf{R}^n$, is that its derivative matrix $DF(x)$ be symmetric for all $x \in \mathbf{R}^n$. We now state a definition of potential functions for cases in which the map F is only defined on an affine space, and show that an appropriate symmetry condition on $DF(x)$ is necessary and sufficient for a potential function to exist. We also relate these notions to their full-dimensional analogues.

Let $A \subseteq \mathbf{R}^n$ be an affine space with tangent space $Z = TA$, and let $z_A^\perp$ be the unique element of $A \cap Z^\perp$. Suppose that the map $F: A \to \mathbf{R}^n$ is continuous. The function $f: A \to \mathbf{R}$ is a *potential function* for F if

$$\nabla f(x) = P_Z F(x) \quad \text{for all } x \in A. \tag{3.36}$$

What does this definition require? Since $\nabla f(x) \in Z$, the action of $\nabla f(x)$ on $Z^\perp$ is null (that is, $(z^\perp)'\nabla f(x) = 0$ whenever $z^\perp \in Z^\perp$). But since $F(x) \in \mathbf{R}^n$, the action of $F(x)$ on $Z^\perp$ is not restricted in this way. Condition (3.36) requires that $F(x)$ have the same action as $\nabla f(x)$ on Z, but places no restriction on how $F(x)$ acts on the complementary set $Z^\perp$.

Theorem 3.B.6 characterizes the smooth maps on A that admit potential functions. The characterization is stated in terms of a symmetry condition on the derivatives $DF(x)$.

Theorem 3.B.6 *The C^1 map $F: A \to \mathbf{R}^n$ admits a potential function if and only if $DF(x)$ is symmetric with respect to $Z \times Z$ for all $x \in A$ (i.e., if and only if $z'DF(x)\hat{z} = \hat{z}'DF(x)z$ for all $z, \hat{z} \in Z$ and $x \in A$).*

Proof To prove the "only if" direction, suppose that F admits a potential function f satisfying condition (3.36). This means that for all $x \in A$, $F(x)$ and $\nabla f(x)$ define identical linear forms in $L(Z, \mathbf{R})$. Taking the derivative of each side of this identity shows that $DF(x) = \nabla^2 f(x)$ as bilinear forms in $L^2(Z, \mathbf{R})$. But since $\nabla^2 f(x)$ is a symmetric bilinear form on $Z \times Z$ (by virtue of being a second derivative), $DF(x)$ is as well.

The "if" direction is a consequence of the following proposition.

Proposition 3.B.7 *Define the map $\bar{F} \colon \mathbf{R}^n \to \mathbf{R}^n$ by $\bar{F}(y) = P_Z F(P_Z y + z_A^\perp)$. Then $\bar{F}$ admits a potential function $\bar{f} \colon \mathbf{R}^n \to \mathbf{R}$ if and only if $DF(x)$ is symmetric with respect to $Z \times Z$ for all $x \in A$. In this case, $f = \bar{f}\big|_A$ is a potential function for F.*

Proof Define the function $\xi \colon \mathbf{R}^n \to A$ by $\xi(y) = P_Z y + z_A^\perp$. Then

$$D\bar{F}(y) = D(P_Z F(\xi(y))) = P_Z(DF(\xi(y)))P_Z. \qquad (3.37)$$

Now $\bar{F}$ admits a potential function if and only if $D\bar{F}(y)$ is symmetric for all $y \in \mathbf{R}^n$. According to equation (3.37), the latter statement is true if and only if $DF(x)$ is symmetric with respect to $Z \times Z$ for all $x \in A$, proving the first statement in the proposition.

To prove the second statement, suppose that $\bar{f}$ is a potential function for $\bar{F}$, and let $f = \bar{f}\big|_A$. Then, since $\xi(x) = x$ for all $x \in A$,

$$\nabla f(x) = P_Z \nabla \bar{f}(x) = P_Z \bar{F}(x) = P_Z(P_Z F(\xi(x))) = P_Z F(x).$$

This completes the proof of theorem 3.B.6. ∎

If the C^1 map $F \colon A \to \mathbf{R}^n$ is integrable (i.e., if it admits a potential function $f \colon A \to \mathbf{R}$), can F be extended to all of $\mathbf{R}^n$ in such a way that the extension is integrable, too? One natural way to proceed is to extend the potential function f to all of $\mathbf{R}^n$. If one does so in an arbitrary way, then the *projected* maps $P_Z F$ and $P_Z \tilde{F}$ will agree regardless of how the extended potential function $\tilde{f}$ is chosen (see observation 3.2.1 and the subsequent discussion). But is it always possible to choose $\tilde{f}$ in such a way that F and $\tilde{F}$ are *identical* on A, so that the function $\tilde{F}$ is a genuine extension of the function F? Theorem 3.B.8 shows one way that this can be done.

Theorem 3.B.8 *Suppose $F \colon A \to \mathbf{R}^n$ is continuous with potential function $f \colon A \to \mathbf{R}$. Define $\tilde{f} \colon \mathbf{R}^n \to \mathbf{R}$ by*

$$\tilde{f}(y) = f(\xi(y)) + (y - \xi(y))' F(\xi(y)), \text{ where } \xi(y) = P_Z y + z_A^\perp,$$

and define $\tilde{F} \colon \mathbf{R}^n \to \mathbf{R}^n$ by $\tilde{F}(y) = \nabla \tilde{f}(y)$. Then $\tilde{F}\big|_A = F$. Thus, any integrable map/potential function pair defined on A can be extended to a vector field/potential function pair defined on all of $\mathbf{R}^n$.

Potential Games, Stable Games, and Supermodular Games

Proof $\tilde F$ can be computed from $\tilde f$ using the chain and product rules:

$$\begin{aligned}
\tilde F(y)' &= \nabla \tilde f(y)' \\
&= \nabla f(\xi(y))' P_Z + (y - \xi(y))' DF(\xi(y)) P_Z + F(\xi(y))'(I - P_Z) \\
&= \big(P_Z F(\xi(y))\big)' P_Z + (y - \xi(y))' DF(\xi(y)) P_Z + F(\xi(y))' - F(\xi(y))' P_Z \\
&= F(\xi(y))' P_Z P_Z + (y - \xi(y))' DF(\xi(y)) P_Z + F(\xi(y))' - F(\xi(y))' P_Z \\
&= F(\xi(y))' + (y - \xi(y))' DF(\xi(y)) P_Z.
\end{aligned}$$

If $x \in A$, then $\xi(x) = x$; thus, $\tilde F(x) = F(x)$. ∎

If F takes values in Z, so that $F(x) = P_Z F(x)$ for all $x \in A$, then $\tilde f(y)$ is simply $f(\xi(y))$, and so $\tilde F(y) = P_Z \nabla f(\xi(y)) = P_Z F(\xi(y))$; in this case, the construction in theorem 3.B.8 is identical to the one introduced in proposition 3.B.7. The novelty in theorem 3.B.8 is that it lets us extend the domain of F to all of $\mathbf{R}^n$ in an integrable fashion even when F takes values throughout $\mathbf{R}^n$.

Notes

Section 3.1
Sections 3.1.1–3.1.6 follow Sandholm (2001a); section 3.1.7 follows Roughgarden and Tardos (2002; 2004) and Correa, Schulz, and Stier-Moses (2004; 2008).

Matching in two-player games with common interests defines a fundamental model from population genetics; the common interest assumption reflects the shared fate of two genes that inhabit the same organism. See Hofbauer and Sigmund (1988; 1998) for further discussion.

Congestion games first appeared in the seminal book of Beckmann, McGuire, and Winsten (1956), who defined a general model of traffic flow with inelastic demand and used a potential function argument to establish the existence and uniqueness of Nash equilibrium. Boyce, Mahmassani, and Nagurney (2005) described this book's influence on later work in transportation science. In this literature, Nash equilibria of congestion games are sometimes referred to as *Wardrop equilibria*, after Wardrop (1952). The textbook of Sheffi (1985) treated congestion games from a transportation science perspective at an undergraduate level; more recently, the monograph of Patriksson (1994) provided a comprehensive treatment of the topic from this point of view.

Important examples of finite-player potential games were introduced by Rosenthal (1973) and Slade (1994), and characterizations of this class of normal form games were provided by Monderer and Shapley (1996b), Ui (2000), Sandholm (2010a), and Hino (2010). Example 3.1.4 and exercise 3.1.6 are due to Sandholm (2005b). Braess's paradox (example 3.1.6) was first reported in Braess (1968). Exercise 3.1.5 is well known in the transportation science literature; it also corrects a mistake(!) in Sandholm (2001a, corollary 5.6). Versions of the efficiency results in section 3.1.6 were established by Dafermos and Sparrow (1969) for a model of traffic congestion and by Hofbauer and Sigmund (1988) for single-population games. For further discussion of constraint qualification and the interpretation of the Kuhn-Tucker-first order conditions, see Avriel (1976, sec. 3.1) and Harker and Pang (1990).

Inefficiency bounds were introduced in the computer science literature by Koutsoupias and Papadimitriou (1999) and by Papadimitriou (2001), who introduced the term "price of anarchy" to refer to these bounds. Most of the results in presented in section 3.1.7 are due to Roughgarden and Tardos (2002; 2004) and were presented in Roughgarden (2005). The simple proof of theorem 3.1.19 presented here is due to Correa, Schulz, and Stier-Moses (2004; 2008), as is corollary 3.1.20. These references present a variety of additional inefficiency bounds for congestion games with general classes of cost functions, as well as inefficiency bounds for general population games; for recent results of the latter sort, see Roughgarden (2005).

Section 3.2
This section follows Sandholm (2009b).
The general definition and basic properties of normal form potential games were established by Monderer and Shapley (1996b). The triangular integrability condition from exercise 3.2.5 is due to Hofbauer (1985). The fact that constant games are potential games in which potential equals aggregate payoffs is important in models of evolutionary implementation; see Sandholm (2002; 2005b; 2007b).

Section 3.3
This section follows Hofbauer and Sandholm (2009).
Evolutionarily stable strategies and neutrally stable strategies were introduced in the single-population random matching context by Maynard Smith and Price (1973) and Maynard Smith (1982), respectively. The connection between interior ESS and negative definiteness of the payoff matrix was first noted by Haigh (1975). See Hines (1987) for a survey of early work on these and related concepts. A version of the GESS concept was used by Hamilton (1967) in his pioneering analysis of sex-ratio selection under the name "unbeatable strategy." See Hamilton (1996, 373–374) for an intriguing discussion of the links between the notions of unbeatable strategy and ESS, and see Kojima (2006b) for a recent treatment. Further discussion of the ESS concept can be found in the notes to chapter 8.

For more on Rock-Paper-Scissors, see Gaunersdorfer and Hofbauer (1995). Wars of attrition are introduced in Bishop and Cannings (1978); for economic applications, see Bulow and Klemperer (1999) and the references therein. Imhof (2005) derives a closed form expression for the Nash equilibrium of the war of attrition in terms of Chebyshev polynomials of the second kind. The dominant diagonal condition used in example 3.3.6 is a consequence of the Geršgorin disk theorem; see Horn and Johnson (1985). This reference also presents the trace condition used in proving proposition 3.3.6.

In the convex analysis literature, functions that satisfy the definition of stability (though typically with the inequality reversed) are called monotone; see Rockafellar (1970) or Hiriart-Urruty and Lemaréchal (2001). For more on pseudomonotonicity and pseudoconvexity, see Avriel (1976, ch. 6) and Crouzeix (1998). The elementary proof of existence of Nash equilibrium in stable games presented in section 3.3.5 is a translation to the present context of work on monotone operators on vector spaces due to Minty (1967). Good references on the minmax theorem and its connection with the separating hyperplane theorem are Kuhn (2003) and Luce and Raiffa (1957). For the finite intersection property, see Folland (1999).

Section 3.4
The definition of supermodular population games comes from Hofbauer and Sandholm (2007). Finite-player analogues of the results presented here are established by Topkis (1979), Vives (1990), and Milgrom and Roberts (1990). Accounts of these results can be found in Fudenberg and Tirole (1991, sec. 12.3) and Vives (2005); Topkis (1998) and Vives (2000) are book-length studies. For macroeconomic applications, see Cooper (1999).

Appendix 3.A
For a textbook treatment of multivariate calculus that emphasizes the notion of the derivative as a linear map, see Lang (1997, ch. 17). For the Whitney extension theorem, see Abraham and Robbin (1967) or Krantz and Parks (1999).

Appendix 3.B
The version of the Riesz representation theorem presented here, along with further discussion of calculus on affine spaces, can be found in Akin (1990). For further discussion of the dual characterizations described at the end of section 3.B.2, see Lax (2007, ch. 13) or Hiriart-Urruty and Lemaréchal (2001, sec. A.4.3).

II Deterministic Evolutionary Dynamics

4 Revision Protocols and Evolutionary Dynamics

The theory of population games developed in the previous chapters provides a simple framework for describing strategic interactions among large numbers of agents. Having explored these games' basic properties, we now turn to modeling the behavior of the agents who play them.

Traditionally, predictions of behavior in games are based on some notion of equilibrium, typically Nash equilibrium or some refinement thereof. These notions are founded on the assumption of equilibrium knowledge, which posits that each player correctly anticipates how his opponents will act. The equilibrium knowledge assumption is difficult to justify, and in contexts with large numbers of agents it is particularly strong.

As an alternative to the equilibrium approach, we introduce an explicitly dynamic model in which each agent occasionally reconsiders his choice of strategy, using myopic rules to adjust his action in response to the current strategic environment. This dynamic model does not assume the automatic coordination of agents' beliefs, and it accommodates a variety of specifications of agents' myopic updating procedures.

We define these updating procedures formally in section 4.1, where we introduce the notion of a *revision protocol*. A revision protocol ρ takes current payoffs and aggregate behavior as inputs; its outputs are *conditional switch rates* $\rho_{ij}^p(\pi^p, x^p)$, which describe how frequently agents playing strategy $i \in S^p$ who are considering switching strategies switch to strategy $j \in S^p$, given that the current payoff vector and population state are π^p and x^p. Revision protocols are flexible enough to accommodate a wide range of choice paradigms, including ones based on imitation, optimization, and other possibilities.

A population game F describes a strategic environment; a revision protocol ρ describes the procedures agents follow in adapting their behavior to that environment. Together, F and ρ define a stochastic evolutionary process, a process whose stochastic elements are independent conditional on the current population state. Since the number of agents is large, intuition from the law of large numbers suggests that the idiosyncratic noise in this process will be averaged away, leaving aggregate behavior to evolve according to an essentially deterministic process. This process, the *mean dynamic* generated by F and ρ, is derived in section 4.2. Section 4.3 presents examples illustrating how well-known dynamics from the literature can be provided with microfoundations by means of this approach.

Taking a different turn, one can investigate the consequences of a particular choice procedure by fixing the revision protocol and letting the game F vary. Doing so generates a map from population games to differential equations. This map, which we call a *deterministic evolutionary dynamic*, is discussed in detail in section 4.4.

The derivation of deterministic evolutionary dynamics in this chapter is informal, based solely on an appeal to the idea that idiosyncratic noise should be averaged away when populations are large. We will formalize this logic in chapter 10, where we introduce a Markov process to describe stochastic evolution in a large but finite population. We prove there that over finite time spans this Markov process converges to a deterministic limit—namely, a solution trajectory of the mean dynamic—as the population size becomes arbitrarily large. This deterministic approximation result does not hold over infinite time spans, but chapter 12 shows that the range of possible infinite-horizon behaviors of the Markov process can still be narrow through an analysis of the mean dynamic.

Chapters 4–9 work directly with the differential equations obtained in the deterministic limit. To provide background, appendix 4.A introduces the rudiments of the theory of ordinary differential equations.

4.1 The Basic Stochastic Evolutionary Model

4.1.1 Inertia and Myopia

There are many possible definitions of behavior dynamics for games played by large populations of agents. The evolutionary approach to population game dynamics is based on two assumptions, inertia and myopia, that dictate the form the dynamics take.

Inertia means that individual agents do not continually reevaluate their choices in the game, but instead reconsider their strategies only sporadically. It is natural to expect inertia when the strategic environment being modeled is just one of many with which the agents simultaneously contend. Such a multiplicity of concerns, rather than a single-minded focus on one problem over days, weeks, months, or years, seems more usual than exceptional.

Myopia means that revising agents condition their choices on current behavior and payoff opportunities; they do not attempt to incorporate beliefs about the future course of play into their decisions. Large population interactions make myopia relatively appealing. When populations are large enough that individual members become anonymous, contingent punishments, reputations, and other possibilities that are central to the theory of repeated games can safely be ignored. Moreover, myopia and inertia are mutually reinforcing, as myopic behavior is most sensible when opponents' behavior adjusts slowly, so that strategies that are appealing now are likely to continue to be so.

4.1.2 Revision Protocols

We now introduce a simple, general model of choice in population games. It is based on the notion of a revision protocol, which describes when and how individual agents update their strategies as time passes. Inertia and myopia are built into the fabric of this model. The model has agents wait a random amount of time before they consider switching strategies, and their decisions at such moments only condition on current payoffs and the current social state.

Let $F: X \to \mathbf{R}^n$ be a population game with pure strategy sets $(S^1, \ldots, S^p)$ and integer-valued population masses $(m^1, \ldots, m^p)$. Suppose that each population is large but finite: population $p \in \mathcal{P}$ has Nm^p members, where N is a positive integer. The set of feasible social states is then $X^N = X \cap \frac{1}{N}\mathbf{Z}^n = \{x \in X: Nx \in \mathbf{Z}^n\}$, a discrete grid embedded in the original state space X. We refer to the parameter N somewhat loosely as the *population size*.

The procedures that agents follow in deciding when to switch strategies and which strategies to switch to are called *revision protocols*.

Definition *A revision protocol ρ^p is a map $\rho^p: \mathbf{R}^{n^p} \times X^p \to \mathbf{R}_+^{n^p \times n^p}$. The scalar $\rho_{ij}^p(\pi^p, x^p)$ is called the conditional switch rate from strategy $i \in S^p$ to strategy $j \in S^p$ given payoff vector π^p and population state x^p.*

For convenience, we write $\rho_{ij}^p(\pi^p)$ in place of $\rho_{ij}^p(\pi^p, x^p)$ when conditional switch rates do not depend directly on x^p, and we refer to the collection $\rho = (\rho^1, \ldots, \rho^p)$ as a revision protocol when no confusion will arise. Analogous simplifications are used whenever it is helpful to do so.

A population game F, a population size N, and a revision protocol ρ define a continuous-time evolutionary process on X^N. A one-size-fits-all interpretation of this process is as follows. Each agent in the society is equipped with a stochastic alarm clock. The times between rings of an agent's clock are independent, each with a rate R exponential distribution. (This modeling device is often called a Poisson alarm clock; see section 10.A.1 and example 10.C.1.) We assume that the rate R satisfies

$$R \geq \max_{x,i,p} \sum_{j \in S^p - \{i\}} \rho_{ij}^p(F^p(x), x^p),$$

and that the ring times of different agents' clocks are independent of one another.

The ringing of a clock signals the arrival of a revision opportunity for the clock's owner. If an agent playing strategy $i \in S^p$ receives a revision opportunity, he switches to strategy $j \neq i$ with probability ρ_{ij}^p/R, and he continues to play strategy i with probability $1 - \sum_{j \neq i} \rho_{ij}^p/R$; this decision is made independently of the timing of the clocks' rings. If a switch occurs, the population state changes accordingly, from the old state x to a new state y that accounts for the agent's choice. As the evolutionary process proceeds, the alarm clocks and the revising agents are only influenced by the prior history of the process by way of the current values of payoffs and the social state.

This interpretation of the evolutionary process can be applied to any revision protocol. Still, simpler interpretations are often available for protocols with additional structure. To motivate one such case, observe that in the foregoing interpretation the diagonal components ρ_{ii}^p of the revision protocol play no role whatsoever. But if the protocol is *exact*, that is, if there is a constant $R > 0$ such that

$$\sum_{j \in S^p} \rho_{ij}^p(\pi^p, x^p) = R \quad \text{for all } \pi^p \in \mathbf{R}^{n^p}, x^p \in X^p, i \in S^p, p \in \mathcal{P}, \tag{4.1}$$

then the values of these diagonal components become meaningful. In this case, $\rho_{ii}^p/R = 1 - \sum_{j \neq i} \rho_{ij}^p/R$ is the probability that a strategy i player who receives a revision opportunity does not switch strategies.

Exact protocols are particularly easy to interpret when $R = 1$: then agents' clocks ring at rate 1, and for every strategy $j \in S^p$, ρ_{ij}^p itself is the probability that an i player whose clock rings proceeds by playing strategy j. We will henceforth assume that protocols described as exact have clock rate $R = 1$ unless a different clock rate is specified explicitly. This focus on unit clock rates is not very restrictive; the only effect of replacing a protocol ρ with its scalar multiple $\frac{1}{R}\rho$ is to change the speed at which the evolutionary process runs by a constant factor.

Other examples of protocols that allow alternative interpretations of the evolutionary process can be found in section 4.3.

4.2 Mean Dynamics

4.2.1 Derivation

The preceding model defines a stochastic process $\{X_t^N\}$ on the state space $\mathcal{X}^N$. We now derive a deterministic process that describes the expected motion of $\{X_t^N\}$. In chapter 10, we will prove that this deterministic process provides a very good approximation of the behavior of the stochastic process $\{X_t^N\}$ as long as the time horizon of interest is finite and the population size is sufficiently large. Chapters 4–9 focus on the deterministic process itself.

Revision Protocols and Evolutionary Dynamics

The times between rings of each agent's stochastic alarm clock are independent and follow a rate R exponential distribution. How many times will this agent's clock ring during the next t time units? A basic result from probability theory shows that the number of rings during time interval $[0, t]$ follows a Poisson distribution with mean Rt. This fact is sufficient to perform the analysis that follows. A detailed account of the exponential and Poisson distributions can be found in appendix 10.A.

Let us now compute the expected motion of the stochastic process $\{X_t^N\}$ over the next dt time units, where dt is small, focusing on the single-population case.

Each agent in the population receives revision opportunities according to an exponential distribution with rate R, and so each expects to receive $R\,dt$ opportunities during the next dt time units. Thus, if the current state is x, the expected number of revision opportunities received by agents currently playing strategy i is approximately

$$N x_i R\,dt.$$

The number is approximate because the value of x_i may change during time interval $[0, dt]$, but this change is very likely to be small if dt is small.

Since an i player who receives a revision opportunity switches to strategy j with probability ρ_{ij}/R, the expected number of such switches during the next dt time units is approximately

$$N x_i \rho_{ij}\,dt.$$

It follows that the expected change in the use of strategy i during the next dt time units is approximately

$$N \left(\sum_{j \in S} x_j \rho_{ji} - x_i \sum_{j \in S} \rho_{ij} \right) dt. \tag{4.2}$$

The first term in expression (4.2) captures switches to strategy i from other strategies, and the second term captures switches to other strategies from strategy i. Dividing expression (4.2) by N yields the expected change in the *proportion* of agents choosing strategy i, that is, in component x_i of the social state. We obtain a differential equation for the social state by eliminating the time differential dt:

$$\dot{x}_i = \sum_{j \in S} x_j \rho_{ji} - x_i \sum_{j \in S} \rho_{ij}.$$

This ordinary differential equation is the *mean dynamic* corresponding to revision protocol ρ (and, implicitly, population game F).

We now describe the mean dynamic for the general multipopulation case.

Definition   *Let F be a population game, and let ρ be a revision protocol. The mean dynamic corresponding to F and ρ is*

$$\dot x_i^p = \sum_{j \in S^p} x_j^p \rho_{ji}^p(F^p(x), x^p) - x_i^p \sum_{j \in S^p} \rho_{ij}^p(F^p(x), x^p). \tag{M}$$

4.2.2   Target Protocols and Target Dynamics

We now introduce a condition on revision protocols that is satisfied in many interesting examples, and that generates mean dynamics easy to describe in geometric terms.

The revision protocol ρ is a *target protocol* if conditional switch rates under ρ do not depend on agents' current strategies; in other words, ρ_{ij}^p may depend on the candidate strategy j but not on the incumbent strategy i. Target protocols can be represented using maps of the form $\tau^p \colon \mathbf{R}^{n^p} \times X^p \to \mathbf{R}_+^{n^p}$, where $\rho_{ij}^p \equiv \tau_j^p$ for all $i \in S^p$. This restriction yields mean dynamics of the form

$$\dot x_i^p = m^p \tau_i^p(F^p(x), x^p) - x_i^p \sum_{j \in S^p} \tau_j^p(F^p(x), x^p), \tag{4.3}$$

called *target dynamics*.

What is the geometric interpretation of these dynamics? If $\tau^p(\pi^p, x^p) \in \mathbf{R}_+^{n^p}$ is not the zero vector, one can define

$$\lambda^p(\pi^p, x^p) = \sum_{i \in S^p} \tau_i^p(\pi^p, x^p) \quad \text{and} \quad \sigma_i^p(\pi^p, x^p) = \frac{\tau_i^p(\pi^p, x^p)}{\lambda^p(\pi^p, x^p)}.$$

Then $\sigma^p(\pi^p, x^p) \in \Delta^p$ is a probability vector, and we can rewrite equation (4.3) as

$$\dot x^p = \begin{cases} \lambda^p(F^p(x), x^p)\left(m^p \sigma^p(F^p(x), x^p) - x^p\right) & \text{if } \tau^p(F^p(x), x^p) \neq \mathbf{0}, \\ 0 & \text{otherwise.} \end{cases} \tag{4.4}$$

The first case of equation (4.4) says that the population state $x^p \in X^p$ moves in the direction of the target state $m^p \sigma^p \in X^p$, the representative of the probability vector $\sigma^p \in \Delta^p$ in the state space $X^p = m^p \Delta^p$; moreover, motion toward the target state proceeds at rate λ^p. Figure 4.1a illustrates this idea in the single-population case; since here the population's mass is 1, the target state is just the probability vector $\sigma^p \in X^p = \Delta^p$.

Now suppose that protocol τ is an *exact target protocol*: a target protocol that is exact with clock rate $R = 1$ (see equation (4.1) and the subsequent discussion). In this case, the resulting mean dynamic is an *exact target dynamic*. Since exactness implies that $\lambda^p \equiv 1$, we often denote exact target protocols by σ rather than τ, emphasizing that the values of $\sigma^p \colon \mathbf{R}^{n^p} \times X^p \to \Delta^p$ are probability vectors. Exact

Revision Protocols and Evolutionary Dynamics

(a) A target dynamic

(b) An exact target dynamic ($\lambda \equiv 1$)

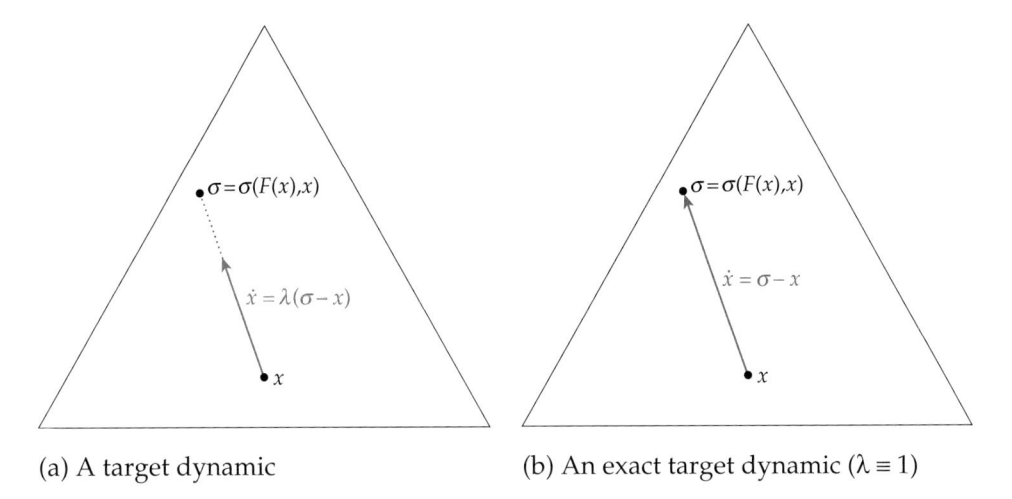

Figure 4.1
Target dynamics in a single population.

target dynamics take the especially simple form

$$\dot{x}^p = m^p \sigma^p(F^p(x), x^p) - x^p. \tag{4.5}$$

The vector of motion in (4.5) can be drawn with its tail at the current state x^p and its head at the target state $m^p \sigma^p$, as illustrated in figure 4.1b in the single-population case.

4.3 Examples

This section provides a number of examples of revision protocols and their mean dynamics that are revisited throughout the remainder of the book. Recall that

$$\bar{F}^p(x) = \frac{1}{m^p} \sum_{i \in S^p} x_i^p F_i^p(x)$$

represents the average payoff obtained by members of population p. It is useful to define the *excess payoff* to strategy $i \in S^p$,

$$\hat{F}_i^p(x) = F_i^p(x) - \bar{F}^p(x),$$

as the difference between strategy i's payoff and the average payoff in population p. The *excess payoff vector* for population p is written

$$\hat{F}^p(x) = F^p(x) - \mathbf{1}\bar{F}^p(x).$$

To conserve on notation, the examples are stated for the single-population setting. When we introduce revision protocols, $\pi \in \mathbf{R}^n$ denotes an arbitrary payoff vector; when the population state $x \in X$ is also given, $\hat{\pi} = \pi - \mathbf{1}x'\pi$ denotes the resulting excess payoff vector.

It is useful to place the revision protocols to follow in one of two categories: imitative protocols and direct protocols.

4.3.1 Imitative Protocols and Dynamics

Imitative protocols are of the form

$$\rho_{ij}(\pi, x) = x_j r_{ij}(\pi, x), \tag{4.6}$$

with additional restrictions placed on the form of the function r_{ij} (see section 5.4.1). Under an imitative protocol, an agent who receives a revision opportunity chooses an opponent at random and observes her strategy. If the agent is playing strategy i and the opponent strategy j, the agent switches from i to j with probability proportional to r_{ij}. Note that the value of x_j need not be observed; instead, the initial term on the right-hand side of (4.6) reflects the agent's observation of a randomly chosen opponent.

Example 4.3.1: Pairwise Proportional Imitation   Suppose that after selecting an opponent, the agent imitates the opponent only if the opponent's payoff is higher than his own, doing so with probability proportional to the payoff difference:

$$\rho_{ij}(\pi, x) = x_j [\pi_j - \pi_i]_+.$$

The mean dynamic generated by this revision protocol is

$$\dot{x}_i = \sum_{j \in S} x_j \rho_{ji}(F(x), x) - x_i \sum_{j \in S} \rho_{ij}(F(x), x)$$

$$= \sum_{j \in S} x_j x_i [F_i(x) - F_j(x)]_+ - x_i \sum_{j \in S} x_j [F_j(x) - F_i(x)]_+$$

$$= x_i \sum_{j \in S} x_j (F_i(x) - F_j(x))$$

$$= x_i \left(F_i(x) - \bar{F}(x) \right).$$

This equation, which we can rewrite as

$$\dot{x}_i = x_i \hat{F}_i(x), \tag{R}$$

defines the *replicator dynamic*, the best known dynamic in evolutionary game theory. Under this dynamic, the percentage growth rate $\dot{x}_i / x_i$ of each strategy currently

Revision Protocols and Evolutionary Dynamics

in use is equal to that strategy's current excess payoff; unused strategies always remain so. ◆

Example 4.3.2: Imitation Driven by Dissatisfaction Suppose that when a strategy i player receives a revision opportunity, she opts to switch strategies with a probability that is linearly decreasing in her current payoff. (For example, agents might revise when their payoffs do not meet a uniformly distributed random aspiration level.) In the event that the agent decides to switch, she imitates a randomly selected opponent. This leads to the revision protocol

$$\rho_{ij}(\pi, x) = (K - \pi_i)x_j,$$

where the constant K is sufficiently large that conditional switch rates are always positive.

The mean dynamic generated by this revision protocol is

$$\dot{x}_i = \sum_{j \in S} x_j \rho_{ji}(F(x), x) - x_i \sum_{j \in S} \rho_{ij}(F(x), x)$$

$$= \sum_{j \in S} x_j(K - F_j(x))x_i - x_i(K - F_i(x))$$

$$= x_i \left(K - \sum_{j \in S} x_j F_j(x) - K + F_i(x) \right)$$

$$= x_i \hat{F}_i(x).$$

Thus, this protocol's mean dynamic is the replicator dynamic as well. ◆

Exercise 4.3.1: Imitation of Success Consider the revision protocol

$$\rho_{ij}(\pi, x) = \tau_j(\pi, x) = x_j(\pi_j - K),$$

where the constant K is smaller than any feasible payoff.

i. Offer an interpretation of this protocol.

ii. Show that this protocol generates the replicator dynamic as its mean dynamic.

iii. Part (ii) implies that the replicator dynamic is a target dynamic. Compute the rate $\lambda(F(x), x)$ and target state $\sigma(F(x), x)$ corresponding to population state x. Describe how these vary as one changes the value of K. ◇

While the three protocols above all generate the replicator dynamic as their mean dynamics, the class of imitative dynamics contains many other members; see section 5.4.2 for additional examples.

Exercise 4.3.2 In the single-population setting, a mean dynamic is an *antitarget dynamic* if it can be expressed as

$$\dot{x} = \tilde{\lambda}(F(x), x)(x - \tilde{\sigma}(F(x), x)),$$

where $\tilde{\lambda}(\pi, x) \in \mathbf{R}_+$ and $\tilde{\sigma}(\pi, x) \in \Delta$.

i. Give a geometric interpretation of antitarget dynamics.
ii. Show that the replicator dynamic is an antitarget dynamic. ◇

4.3.2 Direct Protocols and Dynamics

Under imitative protocols, agents obtain candidate strategies by observing the behavior of randomly chosen opponents. In settings where agents are aware of the full set S of available strategies, one can assume that they choose candidate strategies directly, without having to see the choices of others. The analyses in subsequent chapters show that these *direct protocols* generate dynamics that differ in a number of important ways from those generated by imitative protocols, some fairly obvious, and others less so.

Example 4.3.3: Logit Choice Suppose that choices are made according to the *logit choice protocol*, the exact target protocol defined by

$$\rho_{ij}(\pi) = \sigma_j(\pi) = \frac{\exp(\eta^{-1}\pi_j)}{\sum_{k \in S} \exp(\eta^{-1}\pi_k)}.$$

The parameter $\eta > 0$ is called the *noise level*. If η is large, choice probabilities under the logit protocol are nearly uniform. But if η is near zero, choices are optimal with probability close to 1, at least when the difference between the best and second-best payoff is not too small. By equation (4.5), the exact target dynamic generated by protocol σ is

$$\dot{x}_i = \sigma_i(F(x)) - x_i$$

$$= \frac{\exp(\eta^{-1}F_i(x))}{\sum_{k \in S} \exp(\eta^{-1}F_k(x))} - x_i. \tag{L}$$

This is the *logit dynamic* with noise level η. ◆

Example 4.3.4: Comparison to the Average Payoff Consider the target protocol

$$\rho_{ij}(\pi, x) = \tau_j(\pi, x) = [\hat{\pi}_j]_+ = \left[\pi_j - \sum_{k \in S} x_k \pi_k\right]_+.$$

When an agent's clock rings, he chooses a strategy at random. If that strategy's payoff is above average, the agent switches to it with probability proportional to its excess payoff. By equation (4.3), the induced target dynamic is

$$\dot{x}_i = \tau_i(F(x), x) - x_i \sum_{j \in S} \tau_j(F(x), x)$$

$$= [\hat{F}_i(x)]_+ - x_i \sum_{k \in S} [\hat{F}_k(x)]_+. \tag{BNN}$$

This is the *Brown–von Neumann–Nash* (BNN) *dynamic*. ◆

Example 4.3.5: Pairwise Comparisons   Suppose that

$$\rho_{ij}(\pi) = [\pi_j - \pi_i]_+.$$

When an agent's clock rings, he selects a strategy at random. If the new strategy's payoff is higher than his current strategy's payoff, he switches strategies with probability proportional to the difference between the two payoffs. The resulting mean dynamic,

$$\dot{x}_i = \sum_{j \in S} x_j \rho_{ji}(F(x), x) - x_i \sum_{j \in S} \rho_{ij}(F(x), x)$$

$$= \sum_{j \in S} x_j [F_i(x) - F_j(x)]_+ - x_i \sum_{j \in S} [F_j(x) - F_i(x)]_+, \tag{S}$$

is the *Smith dynamic*. ◆

4.4 Deterministic Evolutionary Dynamics

We conclude the chapter with a formal definition of deterministic evolutionary dynamics. Let $\mathcal{P} = \{1, \ldots, p\}$ be a set of populations with masses m^p and strategy sets S^p. Let X be the corresponding set of social states:

$$X = \{x \in \mathbf{R}^n_+ : x = (x^1, \ldots, x^p), \text{ where } \sum_{i \in S^p} x_i^p = m^p\}.$$

Define the sets $\mathcal{F}$ and $\mathcal{T}$ as follows:

$\mathcal{F} = \{F \colon X \to \mathbf{R}^n | F \text{ is Lipschitz continuous}\};$

$\mathcal{T} = \{\{x_t\}_{t \geq 0} \subseteq X | x_{(\cdot)} \text{ is continuous}\}$

$\mathcal{F}$ is the set of population games with Lipschitz continuous payoffs; $\mathcal{T}$ is the set of continuous forward-time trajectories through the state space X.

Definition   *A deterministic evolutionary dynamic is a set-valued map* $\mathbf{D}\colon \mathcal{F} \Rightarrow \mathcal{T}$. *It assigns each population game* $F \in \mathcal{F}$ *a set of trajectories* $\mathbf{D}(F) \subset \mathcal{T}$ *satisfying*

Existence and forward invariance: For each $\xi \in X$, there is a $\{x_t\}_{t \geq 0} \in \mathbf{D}(F)$ with $x_0 = \xi$.

Thus, for each game F and each initial condition $\xi \in X$, an evolutionary dynamic must specify at least one solution trajectory that begins at ξ and then remains in X at all positive times.

This definition of a deterministic evolutionary dynamic is rather general, in that it does not impose a uniqueness requirement (i.e., since it allows multiple trajectories in $\mathbf{D}(F)$ to emanate from a single initial condition). This generality is useful for dynamics defined by discontinuous differential equations and by differential inclusions (see chapter 6). But for dynamics defined by Lipschitz continuous differential equations, this level of generality is unnecessary, as standard results ensure not only the existence of solutions, but also

Uniqueness: For each $\xi \in X$, there is exactly one $\{x_t\}_{t \geq 0} \in \mathbf{D}(F)$ with $x_0 = \xi$.

Lipschitz continuity: For each t, $x_t = x_t(\xi)$ is a Lipschitz continuous function of ξ.

The basic results on existence and uniqueness of solutions to ordinary differential equations concern equations defined on open sets. To contend with the fact that the mean dynamics here are defined on the compact, convex set X, we need conditions ensuring that solution trajectories do not leave this set. The required conditions are provided by theorem 4.4.1: if the vector field $V_F: X \to \mathbf{R}^n$ is Lipschitz continuous, and if at each state $x \in X$, the growth rate vector $V_F(x)$ is contained in the tangent cone $TX(x)$, the set of directions of motion from x that do not point out of X, then all the desiderata for solution trajectories are satisfied.

Theorem 4.4.1 *Suppose $V_F: X \to \mathbf{R}^n$ is Lipschitz continuous, and let $S(V_F) \subset \mathcal{T}$ be the set of solutions $\{x_t\}_{t \geq 0}$ to $\dot{x} = V_F(x)$. If $V_F(x) \in TX(x)$ for all $x \in X$, then $S(V_F)$ satisfies existence and forward invariance, uniqueness, and Lipschitz continuity.*

Theorem 4.4.1 follows directly from theorems 4.A.1, 4.A.3, and 4.A.5 in section 4.A.

In section 4.2, we showed how a population game F and revision protocol ρ together define a mean dynamic $\dot{x} = V_F(x)$ via equation (M). Viewing this development in the present light, we can think of the revision protocol ρ by itself as defining a map from population games to differential equations, or, going one step further, to sets of forward-time trajectories through the state space X. To conclude this chapter, we show that as long as ρ is Lipschitz continuous, the map so defined is a deterministic evolutionary dynamic in the sense specified above. Indeed, by proposing a Lipschitz continuous revision protocol, one implicitly identifies a unique aggregate behavior trajectory from every initial social state and for every population game.

Theorem 4.4.2 *Fix a Lipschitz continuous revision protocol ρ. For each population game $F \in \mathcal{F}$, let*

$$\dot{x}_i^p = (V_F)_i^p(x) = \sum_{j \in S^p} x_j^p \rho_{ji}^p(F^p(x), x^p) - x_i^p \sum_{j \in S^p} \rho_{ij}^p(F^p(x), x^p). \tag{M}$$

be the mean dynamic defined by F and ρ, and let

$$\mathbf{D}(F) = \{\{x_t\} \in \mathcal{T} : \{x_t\} \text{ solves } \dot{x} = V_F(x)\}$$

be the set of solutions of this dynamic. Then the map $\mathbf{D}: \mathcal{F} \Rightarrow \mathcal{T}$ so defined is a deterministic evolutionary dynamic. Indeed, for each $F \in \mathcal{F}$, the set $\mathbf{D}(F) \subset \mathcal{T}$ satisfies not only existence and forward invariance, but also uniqueness and Lipschitz continuity.

Proof   We begin with a simple observation about the form of the tangent cones $TX(x)$.

Observation 4.4.3   *Let $z \in \mathbf{R}^n$. Then $z \in TX(x)$ if and only if*

i. *For all $p \in \mathcal{P}$, $\sum_{i \in S^p} z_i^p = 0$, and*
ii. *For all $i \in S^p$ and $p \in \mathcal{P}$, $x_i^p = 0$ implies that $z_i^p \geq 0$.*

In words: for z to be a feasible vector of strategy growth rates when the social state is x, the growth rates for each population must sum to zero (so that population masses stay constant over time), and the growth rates of unused strategies must be nonnegative.

Since the population shares x_i^p and conditional switch rates $\rho_{ij}^p(\pi^p, x^p)$ are nonnegative, it is clear from equation (M) that the vector $V_F(x)$ satisfies the conditions from the observation, and so lies in $TX(x)$. Moreover, since F and ρ are Lipschitz continuous, V_F is Lipschitz continuous as well. The conclusions of the theorem thus follow from theorem 4.4.1. ∎

4.A Appendix: Ordinary Differential Equations

4.A.1 Basic Definitions

Every continuous vector field $V: \mathbf{R}^n \to \mathbf{R}^n$ defines an *ordinary differential equation* (*ODE*) on $\mathbf{R}^n$, namely,

$$\frac{d}{dt} x_t = V(x_t).$$

Often we write $\dot{x}_t$ for $\frac{d}{dt} x_t$; we also express the previous equation as

$$\dot{x} = V(x). \tag{D}$$

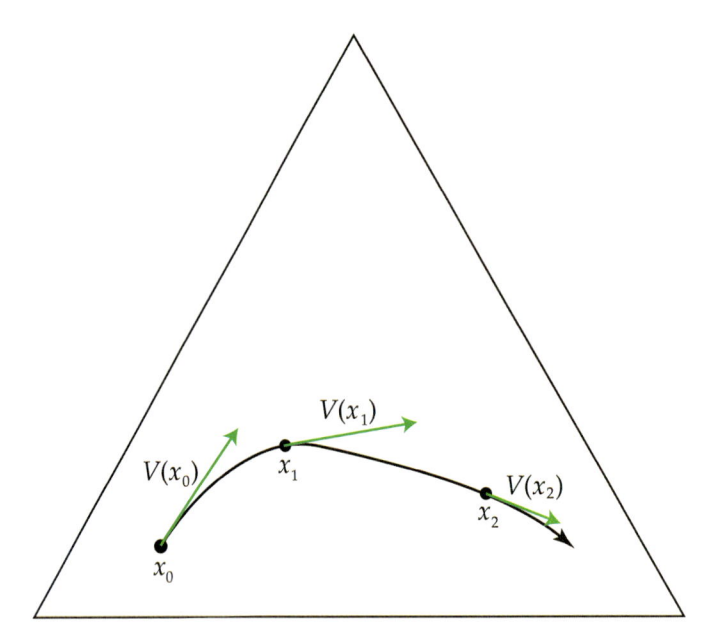

Figure 4.2
A solution of an ordinary differential equation.

Equation (D) describes the evolution of a state variable x_t over time. When the current state is x_t, the current velocity of the state—in other words, the speed and direction of the change in the state—is $V(x_t)$. The trajectory $\{x_t\}_{t \in I}$ is a *solution* to (D) if $\dot{x}_t = V(x_t)$ at all times t in the interval I, so that at each moment, the time derivative of the trajectory is described by the vector field V (figure 4.2).

In many applications, one is interested in solving an *initial-value problem*, that is, in characterizing the behavior of solution(s) to (D) that start at a given initial condition $\xi \in \mathbf{R}^n$.

Example 4.A.1: Exponential Growth and Decay The simplest differential equation is the linear equation $\dot{x} = ax$ on the real line. What are the solutions to this equation starting from initial condition $\xi \in \mathbf{R}$? It is easy to verify that $x_t = \xi \exp(at)$ is a solution to this equation on the full time interval $(-\infty, \infty)$, since

$$\frac{d}{dt} x_t = \frac{d}{dt}(\xi \exp(at)) = a(\xi \exp(at)) = ax_t,$$

as required. This solution describes a process of exponential growth or decay according to whether a is positive or negative.

In fact, $x_t = \xi \exp(at)$ is the only solution to $\dot{x} = ax$ from initial condition ξ. If $\{y_t\}$ is a solution to $\dot{x} = ax$ from any initial condition, then

$$\frac{d}{dt}\left(y_t \exp(-at)\right) = \dot{y}_t \exp(-at) - a y_t \exp(-at) = 0.$$

Hence, $y_t \exp(-at)$ is constant, and so $y_t = \psi \exp(at)$ for some $\psi \in \mathbf{R}$. Since $y_0 = \xi$, it must be that $\psi = \xi$. ◆

4.A.2 Existence, Uniqueness, and Continuity of Solutions

Except in cases where the state variable x is one-dimensional or the vector field V is linear, explicit solutions to ODEs are usually impossible to obtain. To investigate dynamics for which explicit solutions are unavailable, one begins by verifying that a solution exists and is unique, and then uses various indirect methods to determine its properties.

The main tool for ensuring existence and uniqueness of solutions to ODEs is the *Picard-Lindelöf theorem*. To state this result, fix an open set $O \subseteq \mathbf{R}^n$. The function $f: O \to \mathbf{R}^m$ is *Lipschitz continuous* if there exists a scalar K such that

$$|f(x) - f(y)| \leq K|x - y| \quad \text{for all } x, y \in O.$$

More generally, f is *locally Lipschitz continuous* if for all $x \in O$, there exists an open neighborhood $O_x \subseteq O$ containing x such that the restriction of f to O_x is Lipschitz continuous. It is easy to verify that every C^1 function is locally Lipschitz.

Theorem 4.A.1 (The Picard-Lindelöf Theorem) *Let $V: O \to \mathbf{R}^n$ be locally Lipschitz continuous. Then for each $\xi \in O$, there exists a scalar $T > 0$ and a unique trajectory $x: (-T, T) \to O$ with $x_0 = \xi$ such that $\{x_t\}$ is a solution to* (D).

The Picard-Lindelöf theorem is proved using the method of successive approximations. Given a trajectory $x^k: (-T, T) \to O$ with $x_0^k = \xi$, one constructs a new trajectory $x^{k+1}: (-T, T) \to O$ using the map C, defined as follows:

$$x_t^{k+1} = C(x^k)_t \equiv \xi + \int_0^t V(x_s^k)\, ds.$$

It is easy to see that the trajectories $\{x_t\}$ that are fixed points of C are the solutions to (D) with $x_0 = \xi$. Thus, if C has a unique fixed point, the theorem is proved. But it is possible to show that if T is sufficiently small, then C is a contraction in the supremum norm; therefore, the desired conclusion follows from the *Banach* (or *contraction mapping*) *fixed point theorem*.

If V is continuous but not Lipschitz, *Peano's theorem* says that solutions to (D) exist but need not be unique. The following example shows that when V does not satisfy a Lipschitz condition, so that small changes in x can lead to arbitrarily large changes in $V(x)$, it is possible for solution trajectories to escape from states at which the velocity under V is zero.

Example 4.A.2 Consider the ODE $\dot{x} = 3x^{2/3}$ on **R**. The right-hand side of this equation is continuous, but it fails to be Lipschitz continuous at $x = 0$. One solution to this equation from initial condition $\xi = 0$ is the stationary solution $x_t \equiv 0$. Another solution is given by $x_t = t^3$. In fact, for each $t_0 \in [0, \infty)$, the trajectory that equals 0 until time t_0 and satisfies $x_t = (t - t_0)^3$ thereafter is also a solution. ◆

The Picard-Lindelöf theorem guarantees the existence of a solution to (D) over some open interval of times. This open interval need not be the full time interval $(-\infty, \infty)$, even if the domain of the state variable is all of $\mathbf{R}^n$. The following example illustrates this point.

Example 4.A.3 Consider the C^1 ODE $\dot{x} = x^2$ on **R**. The unique solution with initial condition $\xi = 1$ is $x_t = \frac{1}{1-t}$. This solution exists for all negative times, but it explodes in forward time at $t = 1$. ◆

When V is locally Lipschitz, one can always find a maximal open time interval over which the solution to (D) from initial condition ξ exists in the domain O. If V is defined throughout $\mathbf{R}^n$ and is bounded, then the speed of all solution trajectories is bounded as well, which implies that solutions exist for all time.

Theorem 4.A.2 *If $V: \mathbf{R}^n \to \mathbf{R}^n$ is locally Lipschitz continuous and bounded and $\xi \in \mathbf{R}^n$, then $\{x_t\}$, the unique solution to (D) with $x_0 = \xi$, exists for all $t \in (-\infty, \infty)$.*

It is often convenient to discuss solutions to (D) from more than one initial condition at the same time. To accomplish this most easily, we introduce the flow of differential equation (D).

Suppose that $V: \mathbf{R}^n \to \mathbf{R}^n$ is Lipschitz continuous, and let $A \subseteq \mathbf{R}^n$ be an *invariant* set under (D), that is, solutions to (D) with initial conditions in A exist and remain in A at all times $t \in (-\infty, \infty)$. Then the *flow* $\phi: (-\infty, \infty) \times A \to A$ generated by (D) is defined by $\phi_t(\xi) = x_t$, where $\{x_t\}_{t \in (-\infty, \infty)}$ is the solution to (D) with initial condition $x_0 = \xi$. If we fix $\xi \in A$ and vary t, then $\{\phi_t(\xi)\}_{t \in (-\infty, \infty)}$ is the solution orbit of (D) through initial condition ξ; note that ϕ satisfies the group property $\phi_t(\phi_s(\xi)) = \phi_{s+t}(\xi)$. If we instead fix t and vary ξ, then $\{\phi_t(\xi)\}_{\xi \in A'}$ describes the positions at time t of solutions to (D) with initial conditions in $A' \subseteq A$.

Using this last notational device, one can describe the continuous variation of solutions to (D) in their initial conditions.

Theorem 4.A.3 *Suppose that $V: \mathbf{R}^n \to \mathbf{R}^n$ is Lipschitz continuous with Lipschitz constant K, and that $A \subseteq \mathbf{R}^n$ is invariant under (D). Let ϕ be the flow of (D), and fix $t \in (-\infty, \infty)$. Then $\phi_t(\cdot)$ is Lipschitz continuous with Lipschitz constant $e^{K|t|}$: for all $\xi, \chi \in A$, we have that $|\phi_t(\xi) - \phi_t(\chi)| \leq |\xi - \chi| e^{K|t|}$.*

Revision Protocols and Evolutionary Dynamics

The assumption that A is invariant is only made for notational convenience; the theorem is valid as long as solutions to (D) from ξ and χ exist throughout the time interval from 0 to t.

The proof of theorem 4.A.3 is a direct consequence of the following inequality, which is important in its own right.

Lemma 4.A.4 (Grönwall's Inequality) *Let $z: [0, T] \to \mathbf{R}_+$ be continuous. Suppose $C \geq 0$ and $K \geq 0$ are such that $z_t \leq C + \int_0^t K z_s \, ds$ for all $t \in [0, T]$. Then $z_t \leq C e^{Kt}$ for all $t \in [0, T]$.*

If we set $z_t = |\phi_t(\xi) - \phi_t(\chi)|$, then the antecedent inequality in the lemma is satisfied when $C = |\xi - \chi|$ and K is the Lipschitz constant for V, so theorem 4.A.3 immediately follows. Also note that setting $\xi = \chi$ establishes the uniqueness of solutions to (D) from each initial condition.

4.A.3 Ordinary Differential Equations on Compact Convex Sets

The Picard-Lindelöf theorem concerns ODEs defined on open subsets of $\mathbf{R}^n$. In contrast, evolutionary dynamics for population games are defined on the set of population states X, which is compact and convex. Fortunately, existence and uniqueness of *forward-time* solutions can still be established in this setting.

The set $C \subseteq \mathbf{R}^n$ is *forward invariant* under the Lipschitz ODE (D) if every solution to (D) that starts in C at time 0 remains in C at all positive times: if $\{x_t\}$ is the solution to (D) from $\xi \in C$, then x_t exists and lies in C at all $t \in [0, \infty)$. When C is forward invariant but not necessarily invariant under (D), we can speak of the *semiflow* $\phi: [0, \infty) \times C \to C$ generated by (D). While semiflows are not defined for negative times, they resemble flows in many other respects: by definition, $\phi_t(\xi) = x_t$, where $\{x_t\}_{t \geq 0}$ is the solution to (D) with initial condition $x_0 = \xi$; also, ϕ is continuous in t and ξ, and ϕ satisfies the group property $\phi_t(\phi_s(\xi)) = \phi_{s+t}(\xi)$.

Now suppose that the domain of the vector field V is a compact, convex set C. Intuition suggests that as long as V never points outward from C, solutions to (D) should be well defined and remain in C for all positive times.

Theorem 4.A.5 says that if there is a Lipschitz continuous vector field V that is defined on a compact convex set C and that never points outward from the boundary of C, then the ODE $\dot{x} = V(x)$ leaves C forward invariant. If in addition the negation of V never points outward from the boundary of C, then C is both forward and backward invariant under the ODE.

Theorem 4.A.5 *Let $C \subset \mathbf{R}^n$ be a compact convex set, and let $V: C \to \mathbf{R}^n$ be Lipschitz continuous.*

i. Suppose that $V(\hat{x}) \in TC(\hat{x})$ for all $\hat{x} \in C$. Then for each $\xi \in C$, there exists a unique $x: [0, \infty) \to C$ with $x_0 = \xi$ that solves (D).

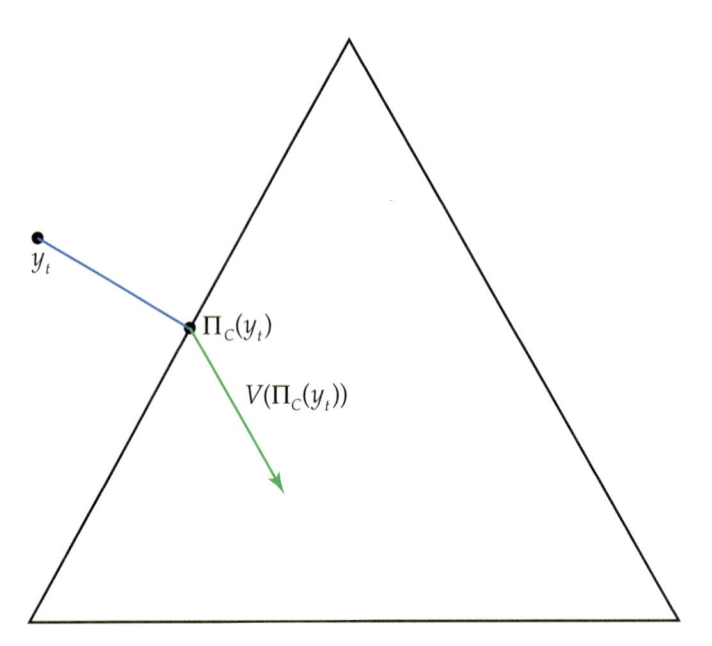

Figure 4.3
The proof of theorem 4.A.5.

ii. *Suppose that $V(\hat{x}) \in TC(\hat{x}) \cap (-TC(\hat{x}))$ for all $\hat{x} \in C$. Then for each $\xi \in C$, there exists a unique $x: (-\infty, \infty) \to C$ with $x_0 = \xi$ that solves* (D).

Proof

i. Let $\bar{V}: \mathbf{R}^n \to \mathbf{R}^n$ be the extension of $V: C \to \mathbf{R}^n$ defined by $\bar{V}(y) = V(\Pi_C(y))$, where $\Pi_C: \mathbf{R}^n \to C$ is the closest point projection onto C (see section 2.A.4). Then $\bar{V}$ is Lipschitz continuous and bounded. Thus, theorem 4.A.2 implies that the ODE

$$\dot{y} = \bar{V}(y) \tag{4.7}$$

admits unique solutions from all initial conditions in $\mathbf{R}^n$, and that these solutions exist for all (forward and backward) time. Now let $\xi \in C$, let $\{x_t\}_{t \in (-\infty, \infty)}$ be the unique solution to (4.7) with $x_0 \in C$, and suppose that $x_t \in C$ for all positive t; then since V and $\bar{V}$ agree on C, $\{x_t\}_{t \geq 0}$ must be the unique forward solution to (D) with $x_0 = \xi$. Thus, to prove the result, it is enough to show that the set C is forward invariant under the dynamic (4.7).

Define the squared distance function $\delta_C: \mathbf{R}^n \to \mathbf{R}$ by

$$\delta_C(y) = \min_{x \in C} |y - x|^2.$$

Revision Protocols and Evolutionary Dynamics

It can be shown that δ_C is differentiable with gradient

$$\nabla \delta_C(y) = 2(y - \Pi_C(y)).$$

Hence, if $\{y_t\}$ is a solution to (4.7), then according to the chain rule,

$$\frac{d}{dt}\delta_C(y_t) = \nabla \delta_C(y_t)' \dot{y}_t = 2(y_t - \Pi_C(y_t))' \bar{V}(y_t) = 2(y_t - \Pi_C(y_t))' V(\Pi_C(y_t)). \quad (4.8)$$

Suppose one could show that this quantity is bounded above by zero (i.e., that when $y_t - \Pi_C(y_t)$ and $V(\Pi_C(y_t))$ are nonzero, the angle between them is weakly obtuse). This would imply that the distance between y_t and C is nonincreasing over time, which would in turn imply that C is forward invariant under (4.7). (The function δ_C is thus a *Lyapunov function* for the set C under the dynamic (4.7); see appendix 7.B.)

The analysis is divided into two cases. If $y_t \in C$, then $y_t = \Pi_C(y_t)$, so expression (4.8) evaluates to zero. On the other hand, if $y_t \notin C$, then the difference $y_t - \Pi_C(y_t)$ is in the normal cone $NC(\Pi_C(y_t))$ (figure 4.3). Since $V(\Pi_C(y_t)) \in TC(\Pi_C(y_t))$, it follows that $(y_t - \Pi_C(y_t))' V(\Pi_C(y_t)) \leq 0$, so the proof is complete.

ii. If $V(\hat{x}) \in TC(\hat{x}) \cap (-TC(\hat{x}))$, then a slight modification of the previous argument shows that $\frac{d}{dt}\delta_C(y_t) = 2(y_t - \Pi_C(y_t))' V(\Pi_C(y_t)) = 0$, so the distance between y_t and C is constant over time under the dynamic (4.7). Therefore, C is both forward and backward invariant under (4.7), and hence under (D) as well. ∎

Notes

Sections 4.1 and 4.2
Björnerstedt and Weibull (1996) introduced a version of the revision protocol model and derived the mean dynamics associated with certain imitative decision rules; see Weibull (1995, secs. 4.4 and 5.3) for a summary. The model studied here builds on Benaïm and Weibull (2003) and Sandholm (2003; 2010d). Versions of target dynamics are considered in Sandholm (2005a) and Hofbauer and Sandholm (2009).

The evolutionary approach is not the only alternative for modeling recurring strategic interactions in large populations. The perfect foresight dynamics of Matsui and Matsuyama (1995) retain the assumption of inertia from evolutionary approach but replace the assumptions of myopia and limited information with those of dynamic optimization and equilibrium knowledge. For recent work on perfect foresight dynamics, see Hofbauer and Sorger (1999), Oyama (2002), Matsui and Oyama (2006), Kojima (2006a), Kojima and Takahashi (2008), Takahashi (2008), Oyama, Takahashi, and Hofbauer (2008), and Oyama and Tercieux (2009).

The traditional approach to studying repeated strategic interactions is the theory of repeated games, which considers equilibrium behavior among small groups of forward-looking, nonanonymous agents. Mailath and Samuelson (2006) provided an excellent and comprehensive presentation of this subject.

Section 4.3
The replicator dynamic was introduced by Taylor and Jonker (1978) but is closely related to a number of older models from mathematical biology, see Schuster and Sigmund (1983). The latter authors coined the term *replicator dynamic*, borrowing the term *replicator* from Dawkins (1976; 1982). Examples 4.3.1

and 4.3.2 and exercise 4.3.1 are due to Helbing (1992), Schlag (1998), Björnerstedt and Weibull (1996), and Hofbauer (1995a), respectively.

The logit dynamic was studied by Fudenberg and Levine (1998) and Hofbauer and Sandholm (2002; 2007). The BNN dynamic was introduced in the context of symmetric zero-sum games by Brown and von Neumann (1950). Nash (1951) used a discrete version of this dynamic to devise a proof of existence of Nash equilibrium in normal form games based on Brouwer's fixed point theorem. The Smith dynamic was introduced by Smith (1984) to study the dynamics of traffic flow. Generalizations of all the dynamics from this section are studied in chapters 5 and 6, where additional references can be found.

Appendix 4.A
Hirsch and Smale (1974) and Robinson (1995) provided fine introductions to ordinary differential equations at the undergraduate and graduate levels, respectively. Theorem 4.A.5 is adapted from Smirnov (2002, theorem 5.7).

5   Deterministic Dynamics: Families and Properties

In the model of stochastic evolution introduced in chapter 4, a large society of agents recurrently play a population game F by applying a revision protocol ρ. Through an informal appeal to the law of large numbers (made formal in chapter 10), we argued that aggregate behavior in the society can be described by a differential equation on the set of social states X. This differential equation, the *mean dynamic*, describes the inflows and outflows of agents to and from each available strategy:

$$\dot{x}_i^p = \sum_{j \in S^p} x_j^p \rho_{ji}^p(F^p(x), x^p) - x_i^p \sum_{j \in S^p} \rho_{ij}^p(F^p(x), x^p). \tag{M}$$

Each revision protocol ρ can be viewed as defining a map from population games F to differential equations (M). This map from games to differential equations is called a *deterministic evolutionary dynamic*.

   This chapter begins to investigate revision protocols and evolutionary dynamics in a systematic fashion. A primary goal is to understand the connections between evolutionary dynamics and the traditional solution concepts of game theory, particularly Nash equilibrium. As we discussed in chapters 1 and 4, the prediction of Nash equilibrium play is commonly justified by strong assumptions about agents' knowledge, both about other agents' behavior and about the game itself. In this chapter, we ask whether and when Nash equilibria correspond to stationary patterns of behavior among agents with limited information about their strategic environment. We thereby obtain a new interpretation of the Nash equilibrium condition, one based not on strong equilibrium knowledge assumptions, but instead on large numbers arguments and weak assumptions about agents' observations of current payoff opportunities.

   Section 5.1 considers the informational demands imposed by different revision protocols. We argue first that revision protocols should be continuous functions of their inputs; in large population environments, very precise information about aggregate behavior may be difficult to obtain, prohibiting agents from implementing revision protocols that are extremely sensitive to the exact values of payoffs or the population state. Next, we categorize revision protocols by the pieces of data they require. One key distinction is between protocols that only condition on payoffs and those that require information about the social state itself. Protocols that respect our continuity and data requirements do not make unrealistic demands on the amount of information that agents in an evolutionary model must possess, and so can provide a compelling low-rationality interpretation of Nash equilibrium.

Section 5.2 takes a further step toward formalizing this goal, introducing conditions that relate aggregate behavior under evolutionary dynamics to incentives in the underlying games. The first such condition, *positive correlation* (PC), requires that whenever a population is not at rest, its strategies' growth rates be positively correlated with their payoffs. This condition demands a weak but fundamental connection between individual incentives and disequilibrium aggregate dynamics, and is a key building block in the analyses of dynamic stability in chapters 7–9. The second condition, *Nash stationarity* (NS), asks that the rest points of the mean dynamic be precisely the Nash equilibria of the game being played. Dynamics satisfying (NS) evince a basic agreement between the evolutionary dynamic and the traditional game-theoretic notion of equilibrium play.

Each revision protocol specifies a particular functional relation between its inputs (payoffs and population states) and its outputs (conditional switch rates). To the extent that the precise form of this functional relation affects the results, the evolutionary interpretation of Nash equilibrium becomes less convincing. Fortunately, many of the results in this book depend only on the qualitative properties of protocols and dynamics, not on details about functional forms. This idea is made precise in section 5.3, which introduces *families of evolutionary dynamics*; these are collections of evolutionary dynamics derived from qualitatively similar revision protocols.

The study of these families begins in section 5.4, which introduces *imitative dynamics*, the most thoroughly studied dynamics in the evolutionary literature. Imitative dynamics, exemplified by the replicator dynamic, have many appealing properties. They can be defined using protocols that require very little information, and they satisfy the disequilibrium condition (PC); the latter fact implies that all Nash equilibria are rest points of these dynamics (see proposition 5.2.1). However, because pure imitation precludes the introduction of unused strategies, imitative dynamics admit rest points that are not Nash equilibria, and so fail Nash stationarity (NS).

Section 5.5 introduces *excess payoff dynamics*. These dynamics are derived from direct protocols (see section 4.3.2) under which agents compare the payoffs of candidate strategies with the average payoff obtained in their population. While excess

Deterministic Dynamics

payoff dynamics satisfy both positive correlation (PC) and Nash stationarity (NS), their strong informational requirements leave them unsuited to provide a broadly applicable interpretaion of Nash equilibrium.

We provide such an interpretation in section 5.6, where we define *pairwise comparison dynamics*. The direct revision protocols that generate these dynamics only require agents to compare the payoffs of their current and candidate strategies. Pairwise comparison dynamics are informationally undemanding, and they satisfy positive correlation (PC) and Nash stationarity (NS). They therefore provide the basis for an appealing interpretation of Nash equilibrium.

Because imitation is a basic feature of human decision processes, the fact that imitative dynamics fail one of the basic desiderata, Nash stationarity (NS), may seem a cause for concern. Fortunately, this conclusion is somewhat misleading. Section 5.7 shows that the failure of Nash stationarity is not due to imitation per se, but rather to its exclusive use. Under hybrid protocols that temper imitation with occasional direct selection of alternative strategies, Nash stationarity (NS) is achieved.

While this chapter focuses on the connection between stationary states and Nash equilibria, a compelling justification of the Nash prediction would go further, showing that evolutionary dynamics lead to Nash equilibrium from disequilibrium states. This fundamental question requires more sophisticated analyses; it is the focus of chapters 7–9.

5.1 Information Requirements for Revision Protocols

In the model of evolution introduced in chapter 4, we used revision protocols to describe the process through which individual agents update their choices over time. By design, the behavior of agents who employ revision protocols is characterized by inertia and myopia. Inertia and myopia are natural assumptions in the context of population games, particularly when the game in question is one of many interactions that agents concurrently face.

In environments of this sort, one might also expect agents to possess limited information about current strategic conditions. In interactions involving large numbers of agents, exact and comprehensive information about payoffs and (especially) opponents' behavior may be difficult or costly to obtain. Agents who are content to revise their choices sporadically and myopically seem unlikely to make the efforts necessary to gain precise knowledge about the current strategic environment. With this concern in mind, we introduce conditions to help assess the informational demands that a revision protocol imposes.

It seems contrary to the evolutionary paradigm to posit revision protocols that are extremely sensitive to the exact values of payoffs or social state. This concern is reflected in the following condition, which requires that agents' revision protocols be continuous functions of payoffs and the state.

Continuity: ρ is Lipschitz continuous. (C)

Condition (C) asks that small changes in aggregate behavior not lead to large changes in players' responses. (We require Lipschitz continuity rather than just continuity because the former implies that solutions to the mean dynamic are unique [see section 4.4 and appendix 4.A].)

Revision protocols also vary in terms of the specific pieces of data needed to implement them. A particularly simple protocol might only condition on the payoff to the agent's current strategy. Others might require agents to gather information about the payoffs to other strategies, whether by briefly experimenting with these strategies or by asking others about their experiences with them. Still other protocols might require data beyond that provided by payoffs alone.

Before introducing the data requirements for revision protocols, we note an important case that requires special handling. Sections 4.3 and 5.4 consider imitative protocols, which take the form

$$\rho^p_{ij}(\pi^p, x^p) = \frac{x^p_j}{m^p} r^p_{ij}(\pi^p, x^p).$$

An imitative protocol can be interpreted as a description of a two-stage revision procedure. When an agent using an imitative protocol receives a revision opportunity, she first selects a member of her population at random and observes this member's strategy; the probability that a strategy j player is observed is x^p_j/m^p. Strategy j becomes the revising agent's candidate strategy. The agent switches to this candidate strategy with probability proportional to $r^p_{ij}(\pi^p, x^p)$. This act of observing the strategy of a randomly chosen opponent does not impose an informational burden. Thus, data requirements for imitative protocols are expressed in terms of the function r^p rather than the full protocol ρ^p.

The data requirements for revision protocols are as follows.

ρ^p_{ij} (or r^p_{ij}) depends only on π^p_i. (D1)

ρ^p_{ij} (or r^p_{ij}) depends only on π^p_j. (D1')

ρ^p_{ij} (or r^p_{ij}) depends only on π^p_i and π^p_j. (D2)

ρ^p_{ij} (or r^p_{ij}) depends on $\pi^p_1, \ldots, \pi^p_{n^p}$ but not on $x^p_1, \ldots, x^p_{n^p}$. (Dn)

ρ^p_{ij} (or r^p_{ij}) depends on $\pi^p_1, \ldots, \pi^p_{n^p}$ and on $x^p_1, \ldots, x^p_{n^p}$. (D+)

Deterministic Dynamics 143

Protocols in classes (D1) and (D1′) require only a single piece of payoff data, either the payoff of the agent's current strategy (under (D1)) or the payoff of the agent's candidate strategy (under (D1′)). Protocols in class (D2) are slightly more demanding, requiring agents to know the payoffs of both these strategies. Protocols in class (Dn) require agents to know the payoffs of additional strategies.

Finally, protocols in class (D+) require not only information about the strategies' payoffs but also information about the strategies' utilization levels. Unless information about these levels is provided by a central planner, it is not readily available to agents in typical large population settings.

These conditions are illustrated with some examples of revision protocols from section 4.3, all of which satisfy continuity (C).

Example 5.1.1 The following three imitative protocols generate the replicator dynamic as their mean dynamics:

$$\rho_{ij}^p(\pi^p, x^p) = (K^p - \pi_i^p)\frac{x_j^p}{m^p}; \tag{5.1}$$

$$\rho_{ij}^p(\pi^p, x^p) = \frac{x_j^p}{m^p}(\pi_j^p - K^p); \tag{5.2}$$

$$\rho_{ij}^p(\pi^p, x^p) = \frac{x_j^p}{m^p}[\pi_j^p - \pi_i^p]_+. \tag{5.3}$$

(In equations (5.1) and (5.2), the constant K^p is chosen so that $\rho_{ij}^p(\pi^p, x^p) \geq 0$.) Protocol (5.1), *imitation driven by dissatisfaction*, is in class (D1). Protocol (5.2), *imitation of success*, is in class (D1′). Protocol (5.3), *pairwise proportional imitation*, is in class (D2). Evidently, each of these imitative protocols makes limited informational demands. ◆

Example 5.1.2 The logit dynamic is derived from the exact target protocol

$$\rho_{ij}^p(\pi^p) = \sigma_j^p(\pi^p) = \frac{\exp(\eta^{-1}\pi_j^p)}{\sum_{k \in S^p} \exp(\eta^{-1}\pi_k^p)}.$$

This protocol conditions on all strategies' payoffs, and so is in class (Dn). ◆

Example 5.1.3 The target protocol

$$\rho_{ij}^p(\pi^p, x^p) = \tau_j^p(\pi^p, x^p) = [\hat{\pi}_j^p]_+ = \left[\pi_j^p - \frac{1}{m^p}\sum_{k \in S^p} x_k^p \pi_k^p\right]_+$$

induces the Brown–von Neumann–Nash (BNN) dynamic as its mean dynamic. This protocol conditions on strategy j's excess payoff $\hat{\pi}_j^p$, and hence on the population average payoff $\frac{1}{m^p}(x^p)'\pi^p$. Since computing this average payoff requires knowledge of the payoffs and utilization levels of all strategies, this protocol is in class (D+). ◆

5.2 Incentives and Aggregate Behavior

The conditions introduced in the previous section provide ways of gauging the informational demands of revision protocols, and so can help determine whether a protocol is appropriate for use in a given application. The properties defined in this section are of a different nature. Rather than appraising the plausibility of a revision protocol for modeling boundedly rational behavior, they assess the extent to which the aggregate dynamics induced by the protocol respect the incentives provided by the underlying game.

We start with the basic restriction on disequilibrium dynamics.

Positive correlation: $\quad V_F^p(x) \neq \mathbf{0}$ implies that $V_F^p(x)'F^p(x) > 0$. $\hfill$ (PC)

Positive correlation requires that whenever a population is not at rest, the covariance between its strategies' growth rates and payoffs is positive; here the covariance is defined with respect to a uniform random draw from the strategies in S^p.

To make this interpretation precise, view the strategy set $S^p = \{1, \ldots, n^p\}$ as a probability space endowed with the uniform probability measure: $\mathbb{P}(\{i\}) = \frac{1}{n^p}$ for all $i \in S^p$. Then for any fixed $x \in X$, view the vectors $V_F^p(x) \in \mathbf{R}^{n^p}$ and $F^p(x) \in \mathbf{R}^{n^p}$ as functions from S^p to $\mathbf{R}$, or in other words, as scalar-valued random variables for the probability model $(S^p, \mathbb{P})$. (For background on probability models, see appendix 10.B.) It is then meaningful to speak of the covariance between $V_F^p(x)$ and $F^p(x)$.

With this background in mind, we can verify that

$$\mathrm{Cov}(V_F^p(x), F^p(x)) = \frac{1}{n^p} V_F^p(x)' F^p(x), \tag{5.4}$$

which implies that condition (PC) admits the preceding interpretation. To establish (5.4), observe that when the vector $V_F^p(x)$ is viewed as a random variable on $(S^p, \mathbb{P})$, its expectation is 0. This follows from the fact that the dynamic V_F keeps population p's mass constant (i.e., that $V_F^p(x) \in TX^p$); indeed,

$$\mathbb{E}(V_F^p(x)) \equiv \sum_{k \in S^p} \mathbb{P}(\{k\}) V_{F,k}^p(x) = \sum_{k \in S^p} \frac{1}{n^p} V_{F,k}^p(x) = 0.$$

A standard formula for the covariance then yields

Deterministic Dynamics 145

$$\text{Cov}(V_F^p(x), F^p(x)) = \mathbb{E}(V_F^p(x) F^p(x)) - \mathbb{E}(V_F^p(x)) \mathbb{E}(F^p(x))$$

$$= \sum_{k \in S^p} \mathbb{P}(\{k\}) V_{F,k}^p(x) F_k^p(x) - 0$$

$$= \frac{1}{n^p} V_F^p(x)' F^p(x),$$

which is equation (5.4).

While the description of condition (PC) in terms of covariances is most natural from a game-theoretic point of view, the condition also has a very useful geometric interpretation. Recall that a pair of vectors emanating from the same point form an acute angle if and only if their inner product is positive. (This follows from the *law of cosines*: if θ is the angle between vectors u and v, then $u'v = |u| |v| \cos(\theta)$.) Viewed in this light, condition (PC) requires that whenever the growth rate vector $V_F^p(x)$ is nonzero, the angle it forms with the payoff vector $F^p(x)$ is acute (see examples 5.2.1 and 5.2.2). Ignoring considerations of feasibility, condition (PC) allows considerable latitude in choosing a direction of motion for population p: the entire half-space of directions forming an acute angle with $F^p(x)$ are permitted.

Of course, this constraint on the direction of motion is in addition to those imposed by forward invariance. In other words, the growth rate vector $V_F^p(x)$ must be an element of the tangent cone $TX^p(x^p)$; the vector's components must sum to zero, and it must not assign negative growth rates to unused strategies (see observation 4.4.3). Because of these constraints, the direction of motion $V_F^p(x)$ often must distort the direction of the payoff vector $F^p(x)$ in order to remain feasible. (The dynamic that minimizes this distortion, the *projection dynamic*, is defined in section 6.3.)

The second condition on evolutionary dynamics asks for exact agreement between stationary behavior and the basic game-theoretic notion of equilibrium play. It opens the door to an interpretation of Nash equilibrium that does not require strong equilibrium knowledge assumptions, but only large populations of agents with limited information about opponents' behavior.

Nash stationarity: $\quad V_F(x) = \mathbf{0}$ if and only if $x \in NE(F)$. $\hfill$ (NS)

Nash stationarity requires that the Nash equilibria of the game F and the rest points of the dynamic V_F coincide. It can be split into two distinct restrictions. First, (NS) asks that every Nash equilibrium of F be a rest point of V_F. If state x is a Nash equilibrium, then no agent benefits from switching strategies; (NS) demands that in this situation, aggregate behavior is at rest under V_F. (This does not imply that individual agents' behavior is also at rest; see the following discussion.)

Second, condition (NS) asks that every rest point of V_F be a Nash equilibrium of F. If the current population state is not a Nash equilibrium, then by definition there are agents who would benefit from switching strategies. Condition (NS) requires that some of these agents eventually avail themselves of this opportunity.

In interpreting condition (NS), it is worth emphasizing that rest points of the mean dynamic V_F need not be states at which the underlying stochastic process is itself at rest. The derivation of the mean dynamic in section 4.2 reveals that $V_F(x)$ captures the *expected* changes in the use of each strategy under the stochastic evolutionary process. It thus entirely possible that a rest point of $V_F(x)$ represents a balancing of stochastic forces rather than the absence of such forces. Indeed, some revision protocols, including the logit protocol (example 4.3.3), always assign positive probabilities to all feasible transitions; under such protocols, all rest points of the mean dynamics must be balance points rather than dead spots of the stochastic evolutionary process.

There is an important link between our two restrictions on aggregate behavior: the out-of-equilibrium condition (PC) implies that all Nash equilibria of F are rest points under V_F. This is easiest to see in the single-population setting. If x is a Nash equilibrium of F, then $F(x)$ is in the normal cone of X at x. Since $V_F(x)$ is a feasible direction of motion from x, it is in the tangent cone of X at x; thus, the angle between $F(x)$ and $V_F(x)$ cannot be acute. Positive correlation therefore implies that x is a rest point of V_F.

More generally, we have the following result.

Proposition 5.2.1 *If V_F satisfies* (PC), *then* $x \in NE(F)$ *implies that* $V_F(x) = \mathbf{0}$.

Proof Suppose that V_F satisfies (PC) and that $x \in NE(F)$. Recall that

$$x \in NE(F) \Leftrightarrow F(x) \in NX(x) \Leftrightarrow [v'F(x) \leq 0 \text{ for all } v \in TX(x)].$$

Now fix $p \in \mathcal{P}$, and define the vector $v \in \mathbf{R}^n$ by $v^p = V_F^p(x)$ and $v^q = \mathbf{0}$ for $q \neq p$. Then $v \in TX(x)$ by construction, and so $V_F^p(x)'F^p(x) = v'F(x) \leq 0$. Condition (PC) then implies that $V_F^p(x) = \mathbf{0}$. Since p was arbitrary, $V_F(x) = \mathbf{0}$. ∎

Example 5.2.1 Consider the two-strategy coordination game

$$F(x) = \begin{pmatrix} F_1(x) \\ F_2(x) \end{pmatrix} = \begin{pmatrix} 1 & 0 \\ 0 & 2 \end{pmatrix} \begin{pmatrix} x_1 \\ x_2 \end{pmatrix} = \begin{pmatrix} x_1 \\ 2x_2 \end{pmatrix}$$

and the replicator dynamic for this game,

$$V(x) = \begin{pmatrix} V_1(x) \\ V_2(x) \end{pmatrix} = \begin{pmatrix} x_1 \hat{F}_1(x) \\ x_2 \hat{F}_2(x) \end{pmatrix} = \begin{pmatrix} x_1 \left(x_1 - ((x_1)^2 + 2(x_2)^2) \right) \\ x_2 \left(2x_2 - ((x_1)^2 + 2(x_2)^2) \right) \end{pmatrix},$$

Deterministic Dynamics

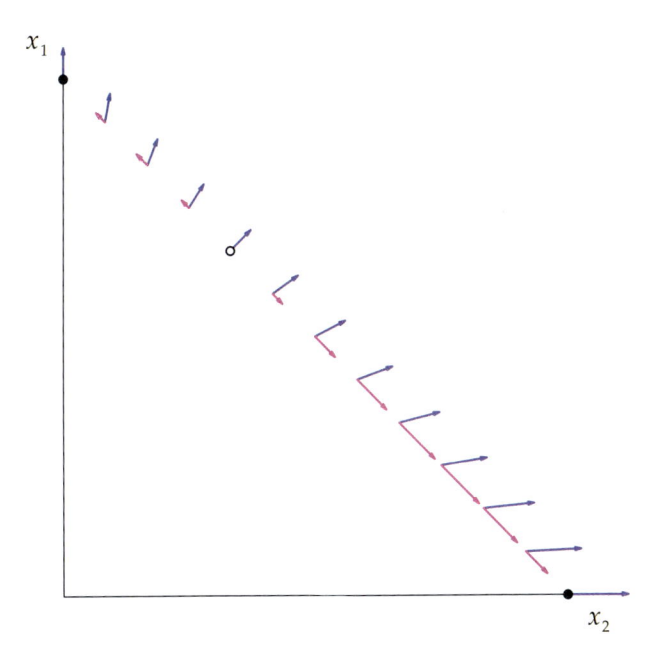

Figure 5.1
Condition (PC) in 12 Coordination.

both of which are graphed in figure 5.1. At each state that is not a rest point, the angle between $F(x)$ and $V(x)$ is acute. At each Nash equilibrium, no vector that forms an acute angle with the payoff vector is a feasible direction of motion; thus, all Nash equilibria must be rest points under V. ◆

Exercise 5.2.2 Suppose that F is a two-strategy game, and let V_F and $\hat{V}_F$ be Lipschitz continuous dynamics that satisfy condition (PC). Show that if neither dynamic is at rest at state $x \in X$, then $\hat{V}_F(x)$ is a positive multiple of $V_F(x)$. Conclude that if V_F and $\hat{V}_F$ also satisfy condition (NS), then $\hat{V}_F(x) = k(x)V_F(x)$ for some positive function $k: X \to (0, \infty)$. In this case, the phase diagrams of V_F and $\hat{V}_F$ are identical, and solutions to V_F and $\hat{V}_F$ differ only by a change in speed (see exercise 5.4.3). ◇

Example 5.2.2 Consider the three-strategy coordination game

$$F(x) = \begin{pmatrix} F_1(x) \\ F_2(x) \\ F_2(x) \end{pmatrix} = \begin{pmatrix} 1 & 0 & 0 \\ 0 & 2 & 0 \\ 0 & 0 & 3 \end{pmatrix} \begin{pmatrix} x_1 \\ x_2 \\ x_2 \end{pmatrix} = \begin{pmatrix} x_1 \\ 2x_2 \\ 3x_2 \end{pmatrix}.$$

Since payoffs are now vectors in $\mathbf{R}^3$, they can no longer be drawn in a two-dimensional picture, so we draw the projected payoff vectors

$$\Phi F(x) = \left(I - \tfrac{1}{3}\mathbf{1}\mathbf{1}'\right) F(x) = \begin{pmatrix} x_1 - \tfrac{1}{3}(x_1 + 2x_2 + 3x_3) \\ 2x_2 - \tfrac{1}{3}(x_1 + 2x_2 + 3x_3) \\ 3x_3 - \tfrac{1}{3}(x_1 + 2x_2 + 3x_3) \end{pmatrix}$$

instead. Since the dynamic V_F also takes values in TX, drawing the growth rate vectors $V_F(x)$ and the projected payoff vectors $\Phi F(x)$ is enough to evaluate property (PC) (see exercise 5.2.3). Figure 5.2a plots the projected payoffs ΦF and the replicator dynamic. Figure 5.2b plots the projected payoffs ΦF and the BNN dynamic. In both cases, except when $V_F(x) = \mathbf{0}$, the angles between $V_F(x)$ and $\Phi F(x)$ are always acute. At each Nash equilibrium x, all directions of motion from x that form an acute angle with $\Phi F(x)$ are infeasible, and so both dynamics are at rest. ◆

Exercise 5.2.3 Let V_F be an evolutionary dynamic for the single-population game F. Show that $\text{sgn}(V_F(x)'F(x)) = \text{sgn}(V_F(x)'\Phi F(x))$. Thus, to check that (PC) holds, it is enough to verify that it holds with respect to projected payoffs. ◇

5.3 Families of Evolutionary Dynamics

In moving from equilibrium to evolutionary analysis of games, one encounters a vast array of plausible assumptions about how agents make decisions. Indeed, an old criticism of the use of bounded rationality in economic modeling holds that in departing from the traditional assumptions of rationality and equilibrium knowledge, one is left with too many possible alternatives. Since it is difficult to know which alternative is most apt for the application at hand, the predictions must be viewed with suspicion.

This criticism can be countered by proving results that are robust to a range of alternative specifications of agents' revision processes. When conclusions hold under any of number of protocols sharing a certain family resemblance, one can argue that they are not artifacts of a particular choice of functional forms but of more fundamental assumptions about how agents make decisions.

Following this principle, this chapter and the next define a variety of families of evolutionary dynamics. Each family is generated from a collection of revision protocols whose members all embody a particular style of decision making. Many of the basic results hold for families of dynamics as a whole, suggesting that there is range of environments in which the results may be of practical relevance.

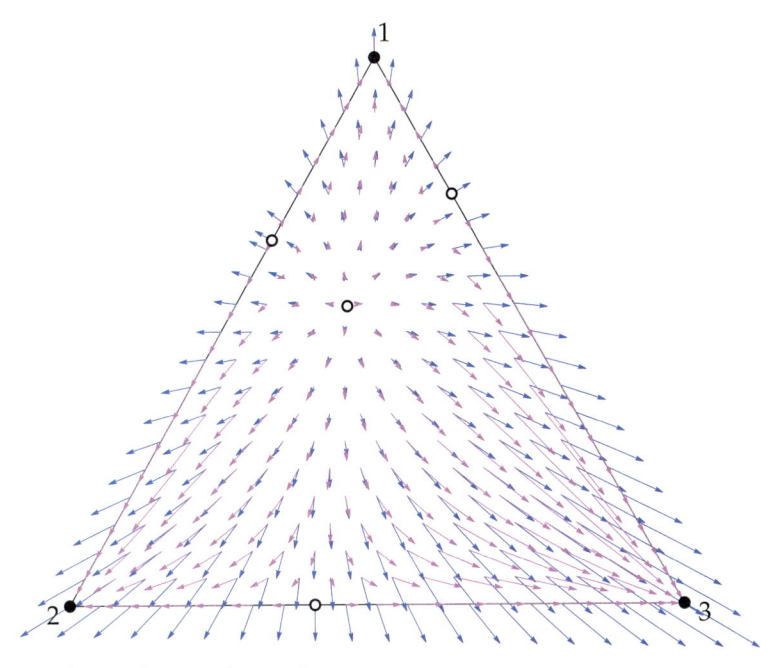

(a) The replicator dynamic

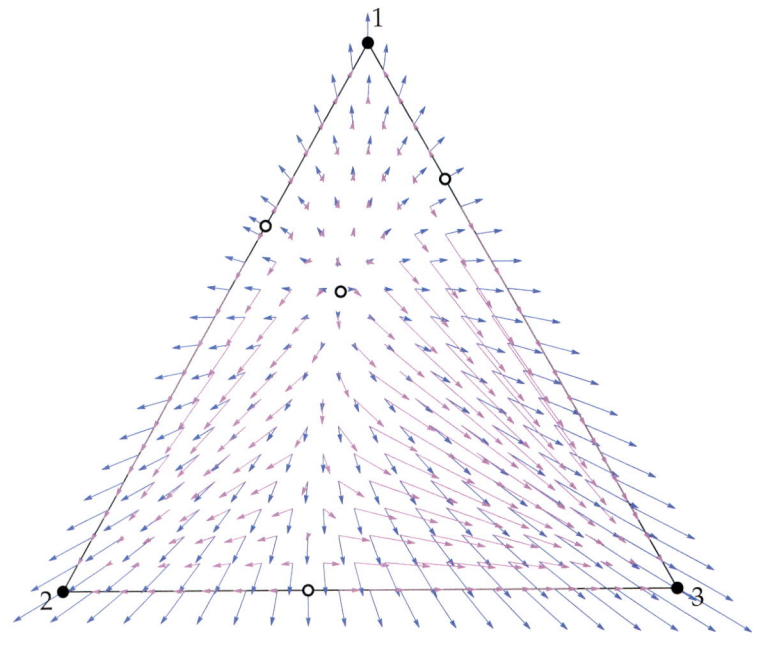

(b) The BNN dynamic

Figure 5.2
Condition (PC) in 123 Coordination.

Table 5.1
Families of Evolutionary Dynamics and Their Properties

Family	Leading Example	(C)	≤ (Dn)	(PC)	(NS)
Imitation	Replicator	yes	yes	yes	no
Excess payoff	BNN	yes	no	yes	yes
Pairwise comparison	Smith	yes	yes	yes	yes
	Best response	no	yes	yes[a]	yes[a]
Perturbed best response	Logit	yes	yes	no	no
	Projection	no	no	yes	yes

a. The best response dynamics satisfy versions of conditions (NS) and (PC) defined for differential inclusions.

Table 5.1 lists various families and examples of evolutionary dynamics and indicates whether they meet the two conditions on revision protocols (continuity (C) and data requirements ((Dn) or weaker)) and the two conditions on aggregate dynamics (positive correlation (PC) and Nash stationarity (NS)). The following remarks capture a few of the main ideas from the analyses that follow.

· Imitative dynamics, including the replicator dynamic, satisfy all the desiderata except for Nash stationarity (NS). These dynamics admit rest points that are not Nash equilibria.

· Excess payoff dynamics, including the BNN dynamic, satisfy all the desiderata except data requirement (Dn). The revision protocols that generate these dynamics involve comparisons between the individual strategies' payoffs and the population's average payoff.

· By introducing revision protocols that only require pairwise comparisons of payoffs, one obtains a family of evolutionary dynamics that satisfies all four desiderata.

· The best response dynamic satisfies versions of all the desiderata except continuity. Its revision protocol depends discontinuously on payoffs.

· The discontinuity of the best response dynamic can be eliminated by introducing perturbations, but at the cost of violating the incentive conditions. In fact, choosing the level of perturbations involves a trade-off between condition (C) and conditions (NS) and (PC). Smaller perturbations reduce the degree of smoothing, whereas larger perturbations make the failures of the incentive conditions more severe.

· The projection dynamic minimizes the discrepancy at each state between the vector of payoffs and the vector representing the direction of motion. It satisfies both incentive conditions but neither limited information condition. There are a variety of close connections between the projection dynamic and the replicator dynamic.

Deterministic Dynamics

Figure 5.3 presents phase diagrams for the six basic dynamics in the standard Rock-Paper-Scissors game

$$F(x) = \begin{pmatrix} F_R(x) \\ F_P(x) \\ F_S(x) \end{pmatrix} = \begin{pmatrix} 0 & -1 & 1 \\ 1 & 0 & -1 \\ -1 & 1 & 0 \end{pmatrix} \begin{pmatrix} x_R \\ x_P \\ x_S \end{pmatrix} = \begin{pmatrix} x_S - x_P \\ x_R - x_S \\ x_P - x_R \end{pmatrix}.$$

The unique Nash equilibrium of RPS places equal mass on each strategy: $x^* = (\frac{1}{3}, \frac{1}{3}, \frac{1}{3})$. In the phase diagrams, colors represent speed of motion; within each diagram, motion is fastest in the red regions and slowest in the blue ones. In this example, the maximum speed under the replicator dynamic is $\frac{\sqrt{2}}{4} \approx .3536$, and the maximum speed under the other five dynamics is $\sqrt{2} \approx 1.4142$. Some remarks on the phase diagrams follow.

· The replicator and projection dynamics exhibit closed orbits around the Nash equilibrium. Under the other four dynamics, the Nash equilibrium is globally asymptotically stable.

· The replicator dynamic has rest points at the Nash equilibrium and at each of the pure states. Under the other dynamics, the only rest point is the Nash equilibrium.

· The phase diagram for the BNN dynamic can be divided into six regions. In the odd regions, exactly one strategy has above-average payoffs, so the dynamic moves directly toward a pure state, just as under the best response dynamic. In the even regions, two strategies have above-average payoffs; as these regions are traversed, the target point of the dynamic passes from one pure state to the next.

· Compared to those of the BNN dynamic, solutions of the Smith dynamic approach the Nash equilibrium at closer angles and at higher speeds.

· Under the best response dynamic, solution trajectories always aim directly toward the state representing the current best response. The trajectories are kinked whenever best responses change.

· Unlike those of the best response dynamic, solution trajectories of the logit dynamic are smooth. The directions of motion under the two dynamics are similar, except at states near the boundaries of the best response regions.

· Under the replicator dynamic, the boundary consists of three rest points and three *heteroclinic orbits* that connect distinct rest points. All told, the boundary forms what is known as a *heteroclinic cycle*.

· Under the projection dynamic, there is a unique forward solution from each initial condition, but backward solutions are not unique. For example, the outermost closed orbit (the inscribed circle) is reached in finite time by every solution trajectory that starts outside it. In addition, there are solution trajectories that start in the

(a) Replicator

(b) Projection

(c) Brown–von Neumann–Nash

(d) Smith

(e) Best response

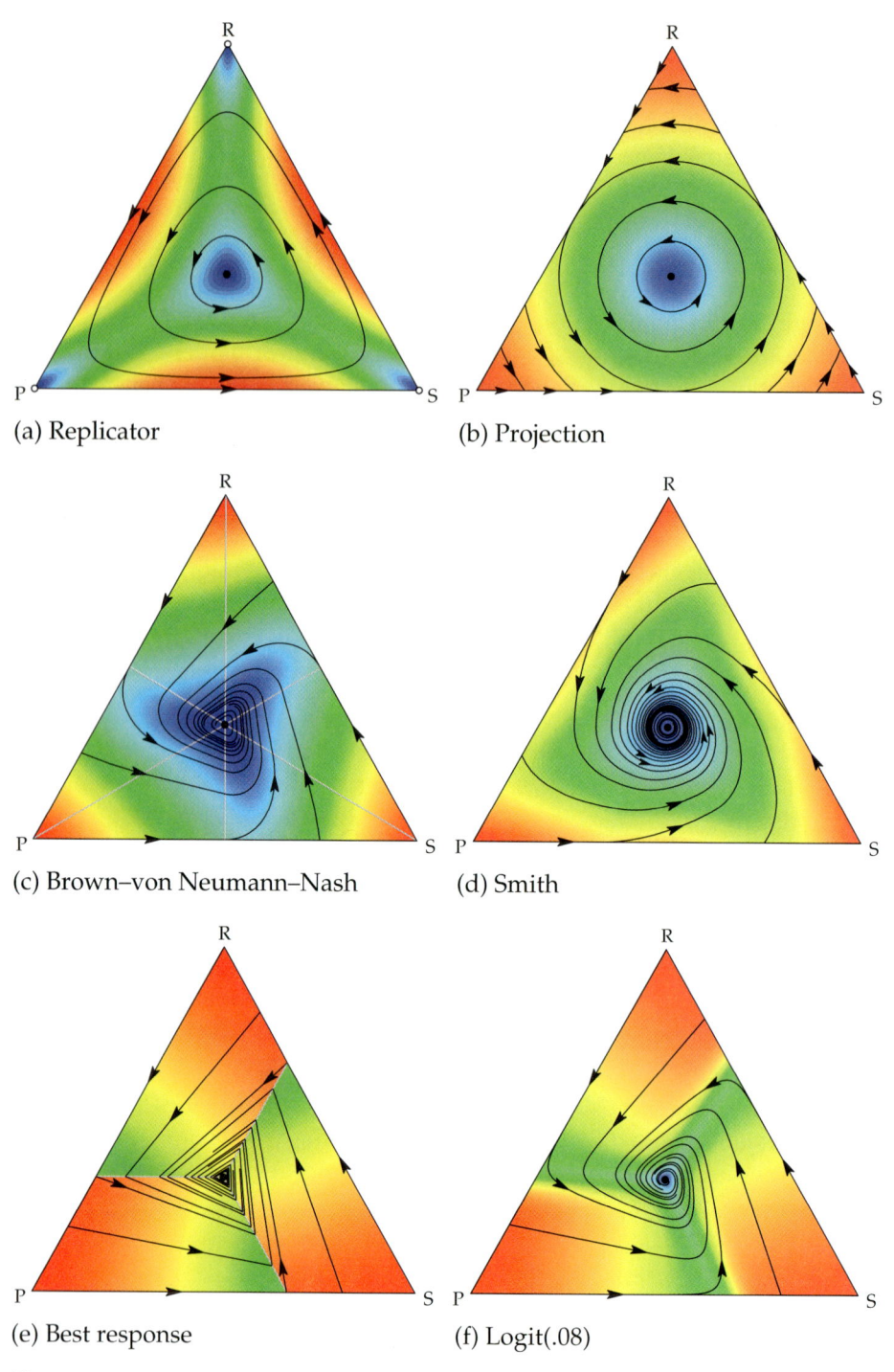

(f) Logit(.08)

Figure 5.3
Six basic dynamics in Rock-Paper-Scissors.

Deterministic Dynamics

interior of the state space and reach the boundary in finite time—an impossibility under any of the other dynamics.

5.4 Imitative Dynamics

5.4.1 Definition

Imitative dynamics are based on revision protocols of the form

$$\rho_{ij}^p(\pi^p, x^p) = \hat{x}_j^p r_{ij}^p(\pi^p, x^p), \tag{5.5}$$

where $\hat{x}_j^p = x_j^p / m^p$ is the proportion of population p members playing strategy $j \in S^p$. These protocols are interpreted as follows. When an agent's clock rings, he randomly chooses an opponent from his population. If the agent is playing strategy $i \in S^p$ and the opponent strategy $j \in S^p$, then the agent imitates the opponent with probability proportional to the *conditional imitation rate* r_{ij}^p.

The revision protocol (5.5) generates a mean dynamic of the form

$$\dot{x}_i^p = \sum_{k \in S^p} x_k^p \rho_{ki}^p(F^p(x), x^p) - x_i^p \sum_{k \in S^p} \rho_{ik}^p(F^p(x), x^p)$$

$$= \sum_{k \in S^p} x_k^p \hat{x}_i^p r_{ki}^p(F^p(x), x^p) - x_i^p \sum_{k \in S^p} \hat{x}_k^p r_{ik}^p(F^p(x), x^p)$$

$$= x_i^p \sum_{k \in S^p} \hat{x}_k^p \left(r_{ki}^p(F^p(x), x^p) - r_{ik}^p(F^p(x), x^p) \right). \tag{5.6}$$

If the revision protocol satisfies the following requirements, the differential equation defines an imitative dynamic.

Definition *Suppose that the conditional imitation rates r_{ij}^p are Lipschitz continuous and that* net conditional imitation rates are monotone:

$$\pi_j^p \geq \pi_i^p \Leftrightarrow r_{kj}^p(\pi^p, x^p) - r_{jk}^p(\pi^p, x^p) \geq r_{ki}^p(\pi^p, x^p) - r_{ik}^p(\pi^p, x^p) \quad \text{for all } i, j, k \in S^p, p \in \mathcal{P}. \tag{5.7}$$

Then the map from population games $F \in \mathcal{F}$ to differential equations (5.6) is called an imitative dynamic.

Condition (5.7) says that whenever strategy $j \in S^p$ has a higher payoff than strategy $i \in S^p$, the net rate of imitation from any strategy $k \in S^p$ to j exceeds the net rate of imitation from k to i. This condition is illustrated in section 5.4.2 using a variety of examples; the condition's implications for aggregate behavior are developed thereafter.

Example 5.4.1: The Replicator Dynamic The fundamental example of an imitative dynamic is the *replicator dynamic*, defined by

$$\dot{x}_i^p = x_i^p \hat{F}_i^p(x). \tag{R}$$

Under the replicator dynamic, the percentage growth rate of each strategy $i \in S^p$ currently in use equals its excess payoff $\hat{F}_i^p(x) = F_i^p(x) - \bar{F}^p(x)$; unused strategies remain so. A variety of derivations of the replicator dynamic follow. ◆

5.4.2 Examples

The following examples are expressed in the setting of a single, unit mass population, so that $\hat{x}_i = x_i$. They are easily recast for multipopulation settings.

Example 5.4.2: Imitation via Pairwise Comparisons Suppose that $\rho_{ij}(\pi, x) = x_j \phi(\pi_j - \pi_i)$, where $\phi \colon \mathbf{R} \to \mathbf{R}_+$ equals 0 on $(-\infty, 0]$ and is increasing on $[0, \infty)$. In this case, an agent only imitates his randomly chosen opponent when the opponent's payoff is higher than the agent's own. Protocols of this form satisfy condition (5.7). Let $\psi(d) = \phi(d) - \phi(-d)$; then the corresponding mean dynamic is

$$\dot{x}_i = x_i \sum_{k \in S} x_k \left(\phi(F_i(x) - F_k(x)) - \phi(F_k(x) - F_i(x)) \right)$$

$$= x_i \sum_{k \in S} x_k \, \psi(F_i(x) - F_k(x)).$$

Setting $\phi(d) = [d]_+$ yields the *pairwise proportional imitation* protocol from example 4.3.1. In this case $\psi(d) = d$, and the mean dynamic is the replicator dynamic (R). ◆

Exercise 5.4.1 Suppose we generalize example 5.4.2 by letting $\rho_{ij}(\pi, x) = x_j \phi_{ij}(\pi_j - \pi_i)$, where each function ϕ_{ij} equals 0 on $(-\infty, 0]$ and is increasing on $[0, \infty)$. Explain why the the protocol need not satisfy condition (5.7), in which case the resulting dynamic is not an imitative dynamic. (For an interesting contrast, see section 5.6.) ◇

Example 5.4.3: Imitation Driven by Dissatisfaction Suppose that $\rho_{ij}(\pi, x) = a(\pi_i) x_j$. Then when the clock of an i player rings, she abandons her current strategy with probability proportional to the *abandonment rate* $a(\pi_i)$. In such instances, she imitates a randomly chosen opponent. In this case, condition (5.7) requires that $a \colon \mathbf{R} \to \mathbf{R}_+$ be decreasing, and the mean dynamic becomes

$$\dot{x}_i = x_i \sum_{k \in S} x_k \left(a(F_k(x)) - a(F_i(x)) \right) = x_i \left(\sum_{k \in S} x_k \, a(F_k(x)) - a(F_i(x)) \right). \tag{5.8}$$

Deterministic Dynamics   155

If abandonment rates take the linear form $a(\pi_i) = K - \pi_i$ (where K is large enough), then (5.8) is again the replicator dynamic (R). ◆

Example 5.4.4: Imitation of Success Suppose $\rho_{ij}(\pi, x) = x_j c(\pi_j)$. Then when an agent's clock rings, he picks an opponent at random; if the opponent is playing strategy j, the player imitates him with probability proportional to the *copying rate* $c(\pi_j)$. In this case, condition (5.7) requires that $c: \mathbf{R} \to \mathbf{R}_+$ be increasing, and the mean dynamic becomes

$$\dot{x}_i = x_i \sum_{k \in S} x_k \big(c(F_i(x)) - c(F_k(x))\big) = x_i \left(c(F_i(x)) - \sum_{k \in S} x_k c(F_k(x)) \right). \tag{5.9}$$

Since ρ is a target protocol (i.e., $\rho_{ij} \equiv \tau_j$), the mean dynamic (5.9) is actually a target dynamic:

$$\dot{x}_i = \begin{cases} \sum_{k \in S} x_k c(F_k(x)) \left(\dfrac{x_i c(F_i(x))}{\sum_{k \in S} x_k c(F_k(x))} - x_i \right) & \text{if } x_j c(F_j(x)) \neq 0 \text{ for some } j \in S, \\ 0 & \text{otherwise.} \end{cases}$$

If copying rates are of the linear form $c(\pi_j) = \pi_j + K$ (for K large enough), then (5.9) is once again the replicator dynamic (R). If in addition payoffs are non-negative and average payoffs are positive, one can choose $c(\pi_j) = \pi_j$, so that (5.9) becomes

$$\dot{x}_i = \bar{F}(x) \left(\dfrac{x_i F_i(x)}{\bar{F}(x)} - x_i \right). \tag{5.10}$$

Here, the target state is proportional to the vector of popularity-weighted payoffs $x_i F_i(x)$, with the rate of motion toward this state governed by average payoffs $\bar{F}(x)$. ◆

Exercise 5.4.2 Why is the restriction on payoffs needed to obtain equation (5.10)? ◇

Example 5.4.5: Imitation of Success with Repeated Sampling Suppose

$$\rho_{ij}(\pi, x) = \dfrac{x_j w(\pi_j)}{\sum_{k \in S} x_k w(\pi_k)}, \tag{5.11}$$

where $\sum_{k \in S} x_k w(\pi_k) > 0$. Here, when an agent's clock rings he chooses an opponent at random. If the opponent is playing strategy j, the agent imitates him with probability proportional to the *copying weight* $w(\pi_j)$. If the agent does not imitate this opponent, he draws a new opponent at random and repeats the procedure, only stopping when imitation occurs. In this case, condition (5.7) requires that

$w: \mathbf{R} \to \mathbf{R}_+$ be increasing. Since ρ is an exact target protocol (i.e., $\rho_{ij} \equiv \sigma_j$ and $\sum_{j \in S} \sigma_j \equiv 1$), it induces the exact target dynamic

$$\dot{x}_i = \frac{x_i \, w(F_i(x))}{\sum_{k \in S} x_k \, w(F_k(x))} - x_i. \qquad \blacklozenge \quad (5.12)$$

Two important instances of repeated sampling follow.

Example 5.4.6: The Maynard Smith Replicator Dynamic If payoffs are non-negative and average payoffs are positive, one can let copying weights equal payoffs: $w(\pi_j) = \pi_j$. The resulting exact target dynamic,

$$\dot{x}_i = \frac{x_i F_i(x)}{\bar{F}(x)} - x_i = \frac{x_i \hat{F}_i(x)}{\bar{F}(x)}, \qquad (5.13)$$

is known as the *Maynard Smith replicator dynamic*.

Example 5.4.4 showed that under the same assumptions on payoffs, the replicator dynamic takes the form (5.10). The Maynard Smith replicator dynamic (5.13) differs from (5.10) only in that the target state is approached at a unit rate rather than at a rate determined by average payoffs. Thus, motion under (5.10) is relatively fast when average payoffs are relatively high. Comparing the protocol here to the one from example 5.4.4 reveals the source of the difference in speeds: under repeated sampling, the overall payoff level has little influence on the probability that a revising agent winds up switching strategies.

In the single-population setting, the phase diagrams of (5.10) and (5.13) are identical, and the dynamics only differ in terms of the speed at which solution trajectories are traversed (see exercise 5.4.3). This is illustrated in figure 5.4, which presents phase diagrams for the two dynamics in 123 Coordination.

When there are multiple populations, the fact that average payoffs differ across populations implies that the phase diagrams of (5.10) and (5.13) no longer coincide. This is illustrated in figure 5.5, which presents phase diagrams for this Matching Pennies game:

	h	t
H	2, 1	1, 2
T	1, 2	2, 1

While interior solutions of (5.10) form closed orbits around the unique Nash equilibrium $x^* = ((\frac{1}{2}, \frac{1}{2}), (\frac{1}{2}, \frac{1}{2}))$, interior solutions of (5.13) converge to x^*. $\blacklozenge$

Deterministic Dynamics

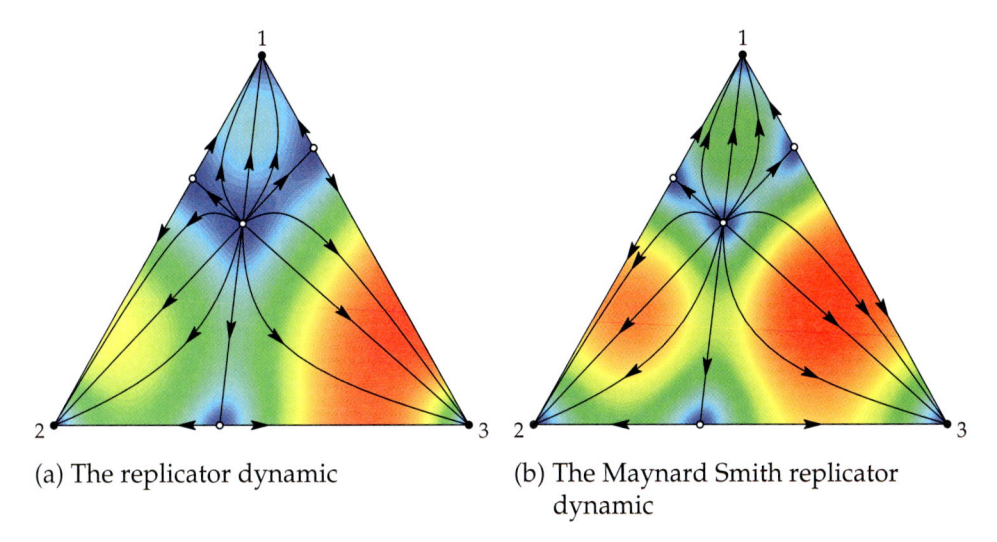

(a) The replicator dynamic

(b) The Maynard Smith replicator dynamic

Figure 5.4
Two imitative dynamics in 123 Coordination.

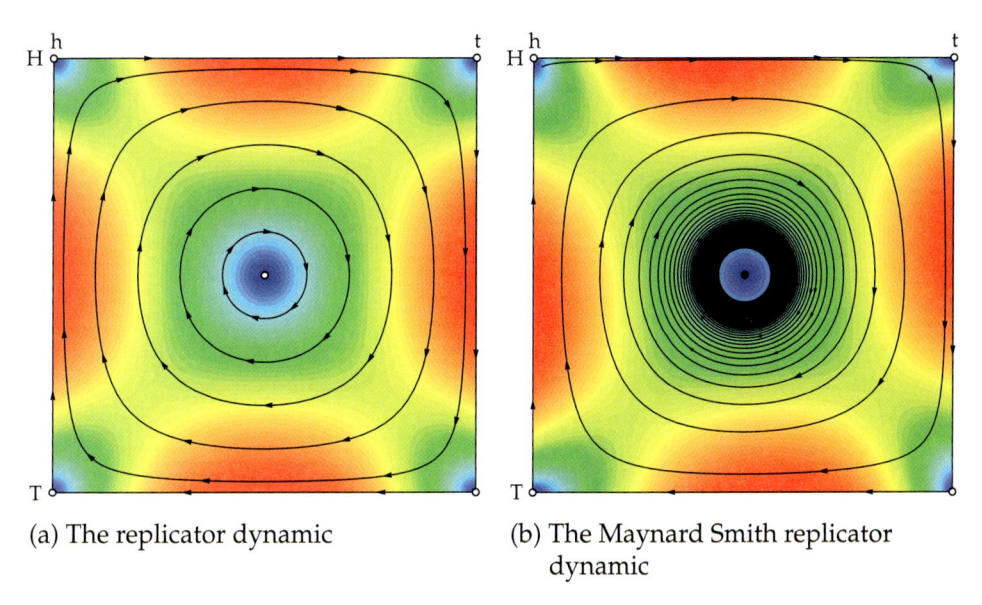

(a) The replicator dynamic

(b) The Maynard Smith replicator dynamic

Figure 5.5
Two imitative dynamics in Matching Pennies.

In the biology literature, the stochastic evolutionary process generated by the revision protocol in the previous example is known as a *frequency-dependent Moran process* (see the chapter notes for further discussion).

Example 5.4.7: The Imitative Logit Dynamic   If the copying weights $w(\pi_j) = \exp(\eta^{-1}\pi_j)$ are exponential functions of payoffs, the exact target dynamic (5.12) becomes the *imitative logit* (or *i-logit*) *dynamic* with *noise level* $\eta > 0$.

$$\dot{x}_i = \frac{x_i \exp(\eta^{-1} F_i(x))}{\sum_{k \in S} x_k \exp(\eta^{-1} F_k(x))} - x_i.$$

Here, the *i*th component of the target state is proportional both to the mass of agents playing strategy *i* and to an exponential function of strategy *i*'s payoff. If η is small, and *x* is not too close to the boundary of *X* or of any best response region, then the target state is close to $e_{b(x)}$, the vertex of *X* corresponding to the current best response. Therefore, in most games, the i-logit dynamic with small η approximates the best response dynamic $\dot{x} \in B(x) - x$ on much of the interior of the simplex. This is illustrated in figure 5.6, which presents four i-logit dynamics (with $\eta = .5, .1, .05,$ and $.01$) and the best response dynamic for the anticoordination game

$$F(x) = Ax = \begin{pmatrix} -1 & 0 & 0 \\ 0 & -1 & 0 \\ 0 & 0 & -1 \end{pmatrix} \begin{pmatrix} x_1 \\ x_2 \\ x_3 \end{pmatrix} = \begin{pmatrix} -x_1 \\ -x_2 \\ -x_3 \end{pmatrix}.$$

The figure reveals that regardless of the value of η, the i-logit dynamic does not resemble the best response dynamic on the boundary of the simplex. Solutions of the best response dynamic starting on the boundary of the simplex immediately enter its interior and move rapidly toward the center of the simplex. For their part, solutions of the i-logit dynamic starting on the boundary remain there forever; by continuity, solutions starting close enough to the boundary initially move away from it quite slowly. These are general properties of imitative dynamics (see section 5.4.4). ◆

Exercise 5.4.3: Changes of Speed and Reparameterizations of Time   Let $V: \mathbf{R}^n \to \mathbf{R}^n$ be a Lipschitz continuous vector field, and let $k: \mathbf{R}^n \to (0, \infty)$ be a positive Lipschitz continuous function. Let $\{x_t\}$ be a solution to $\dot{x} = V(x)$ with initial condition ξ, and let $\{y_t\}$ be a solution to $\dot{x} = k(x)V(x)$, also with initial condition ξ. Show that $y_t = x_{I(t)}$, where $I(t) = \int_0^t k(y_s)\,ds$. ◇

5.4.3   Biological Derivations of the Replicator Dynamic

While we have derived the replicator dynamic from models of imitation, its origins lie in mathematical biology, where it arises from models of intra- and interspecies

(a) The i-logit(.5) dynamic

(b) The i-logit(.1) dynamic

(c) The i-logit(.05) dynamic

(d) The i-logit(.01) dynamic

(e) The best response dynamic

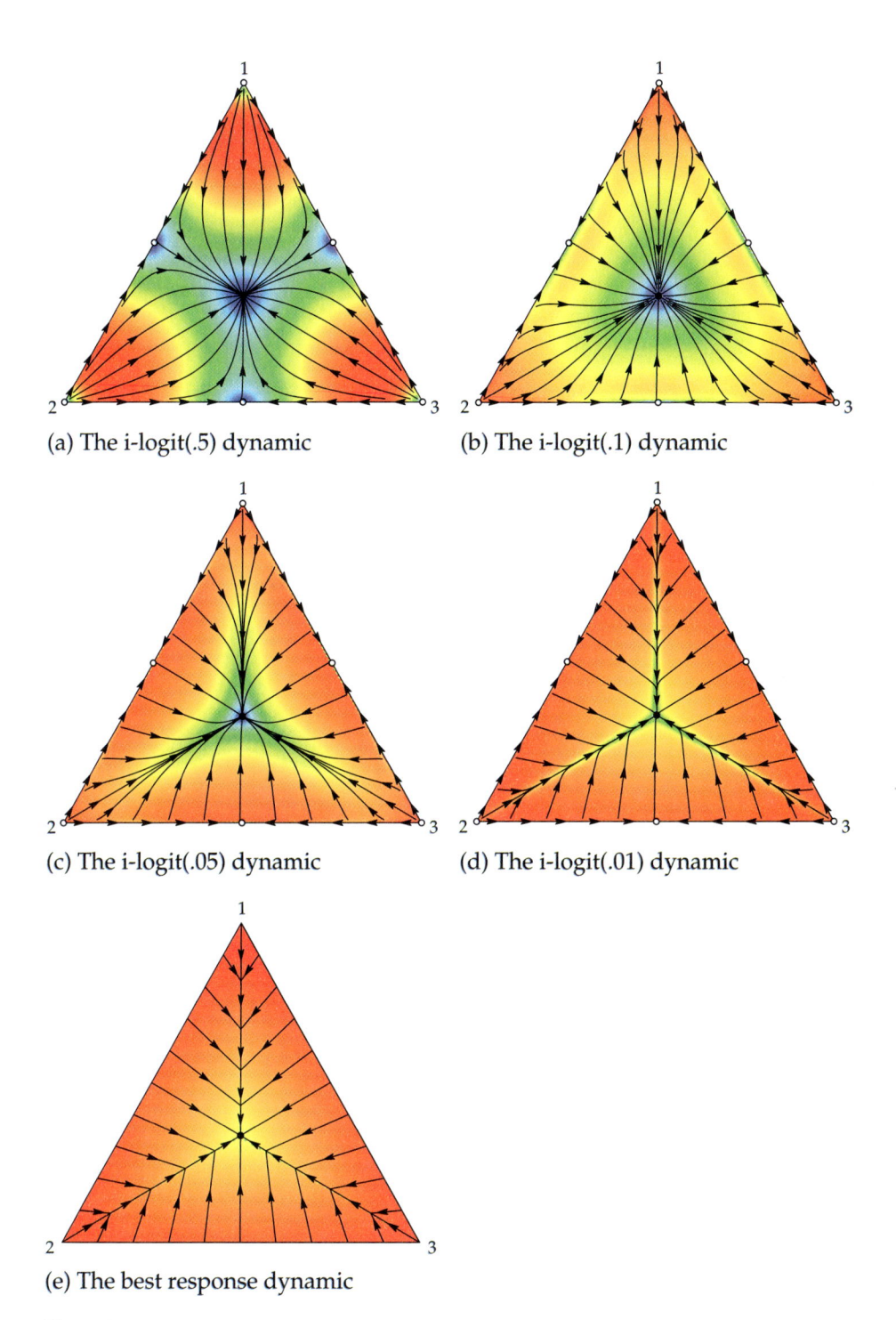

Figure 5.6
Imitative logit and best response dynamics in Anticoordination.

competition. The next two exercises, which are set in a single population, consider the replicator dynamic from this point of view.

Exercise 5.4.4 In the basic game-theoretic model of natural selection within a single animal species, each strategy $i \in S$ represents a behavioral tendency. The value of $F_i(x)$ represents the *(reproductive) fitness* of tendency i when the current proportions of tendencies are described by $x \in \text{int}(X)$. In particular, if $y_i \in (0, \infty)$ represents the (absolute) number of animals of tendency i in the population, then the evolution of the population is described by

$$\dot{y}_i = y_i F_i(x), \quad \text{where } x_i = \frac{y_i}{\sum_{j \in S} y_j}. \tag{5.14}$$

Show that under equation (5.14), the vector x describing the proportions of animals of each tendency evolves according to the replicator equation (R). ◇

Exercise 5.4.5: The Lotka-Volterra Equation The *Lotka-Volterra equation* is a fundamental model of biological competition among members of multiple species. When there are $n-1$ species, the equation takes the form

$$\dot{y}_k = y_k \big(b_k + (My)_k \big), \quad k \in \{1, \ldots, n-1\}, \tag{5.15}$$

where b_k is the baseline growth rate for species k, and the interaction matrix $M \in \mathbf{R}^{(n-1) \times (n-1)}$ governs cross-species effects. Show that after the change of variable

$$x_i = \frac{y_i}{1 + \sum_{l=1}^{n-1} y_l} \quad \text{and} \quad x_n = \frac{1}{1 + \sum_{l=1}^{n-1} y_l},$$

the $n-1$ dimensional Lotka-Volterra equation (5.15) is equivalent up to a change of speed (see exercise 5.4.3) to the n-strategy replicator dynamic

$$\dot{x}_i = x_i((Ax)_i - x'Ax), \quad i \in \{1, \ldots, n\},$$

where the payoff matrix $A \in \mathbf{R}^{n \times n}$ is related to $M \in \mathbf{R}^{(n-1) \times (n-1)}$ and $b \in \mathbf{R}^{n-1}$ by the $\mathbf{R}^{(n-1) \times n}$ matrix equation

$(M\ b) = (I\ (-\mathbf{1}))A.$

If M and b are given, this equation determines A up to an additive constant in each column. Thus, A can always be chosen so that either the elements of its last row or the elements of its diagonal are all zero. ◇

5.4.4 Extinction and Invariance

Some properties are shared by all imitative dynamics. First, it follows immediately from equation (5.6) that all imitative dynamics satisfy *extinction*: if a strategy is unused, its growth rate is zero.

Deterministic Dynamics

If $x_i^p = 0$, then $V_i^p(x) = 0$. (5.16)

Extinction implies that the growth rate vectors $V(x)$ are always tangent to the boundaries of X; formally, $V(x)$ is not only in $TX(x)$, but also in $-TX(x)$ (see observation 4.4.3). Thus, since imitative dynamics are Lipschitz continuous, it follows from theorem 4.A.5 that solutions to imitative dynamics exist for all positive *and negative* times.

Proposition 5.4.6 (Forward and Backward Invariance) *Let $\dot{x} = V_F(x)$ be an imitative dynamic. Then for each initial condition $\xi \in X$, this dynamic admits a unique solution trajectory in $\mathcal{T}_{(-\infty,\infty)} = \{x\colon (-\infty, \infty) \to X | x \text{ is continuous}\}$.*

Extinction also implies a second invariance property: if $\{x_t\}$ is a solution trajectory of an imitative dynamic, then the support of x_t is independent of t. Uniqueness of solution trajectories, which is implied by the Lipschitz continuity of the dynamic, is an essential ingredient of the proof of this result.

Theorem 5.4.7 (Support Invariance) *If $\{x_t\}$ is a solution trajectory of an imitative dynamic, then the sign of component $(x_t)_i^p$ is independent of $t \in (-\infty, \infty)$.*

Proof Let $\{x_t\}$ be a solution to the imitative dynamic $\dot{x} = V(x)$ and let $x_0 = \xi$. Suppose that $\xi_i^p = 0$; the aim is to show that $(x_t)_i^p = 0$ for all $t \in (-\infty, \infty)$. To accomplish this, define a new vector field $\hat{V}\colon X \to \mathbf{R}^n$ as follows:

$$\hat{V}_j^q(x) = \begin{cases} 0 & \text{if } j = i \text{ and } q = p, \\ V_j^q(x) & \text{otherwise.} \end{cases}$$

If $\{\hat{x}_t\} \subset X$ is the unique solution to $\dot{x} = \hat{V}(x)$ with $\hat{x}_0 = \xi$, then $(\hat{x}_t)_i^p = 0$ for all t. But V and $\hat{V}$ are identical whenever $x_i^p = 0$ by extinction (5.16); therefore, $\{\hat{x}_t\}$ is also a solution to $\dot{x} = V(x)$. Since solutions to $\dot{x} = V(x)$ are unique, it must be that $\{\hat{x}_t\} = \{x_t\}$, and hence that $(x_t)_i^p = 0$ for all t.

Now suppose that $\xi_i^p > 0$. If $x_t = \chi$ satisfied $\chi_i^p = 0$, then the preceding analysis would imply that there are two distinct solutions to $\dot{x} = V(x)$ with $x_t = \chi$, one that is contained in the boundary of X and one that is not. As this would contradict uniqueness of solutions, we conclude $(x_t)_i^p > 0$ at all times t. ∎

All the phase diagrams presented in this section illustrate the support invariance property. The next example points out one of its more subtle consequences.

Example 5.4.8 Figure 5.7 presents a phase diagram of the replicator dynamic for a game with a strictly dominant strategy: for all $x \in X$, $F_1(x) = 1$ and $F_2(x) = F_3(x) = 0$. There are two connected components of rest points. One consists solely of the unique Nash equilibrium e_1, and the other contains those states at which strategy 1 is unused. Clearly, the latter component is unstable; all nearby solution trajectories lead away from it and toward the Nash equilibrium. But as the coloring

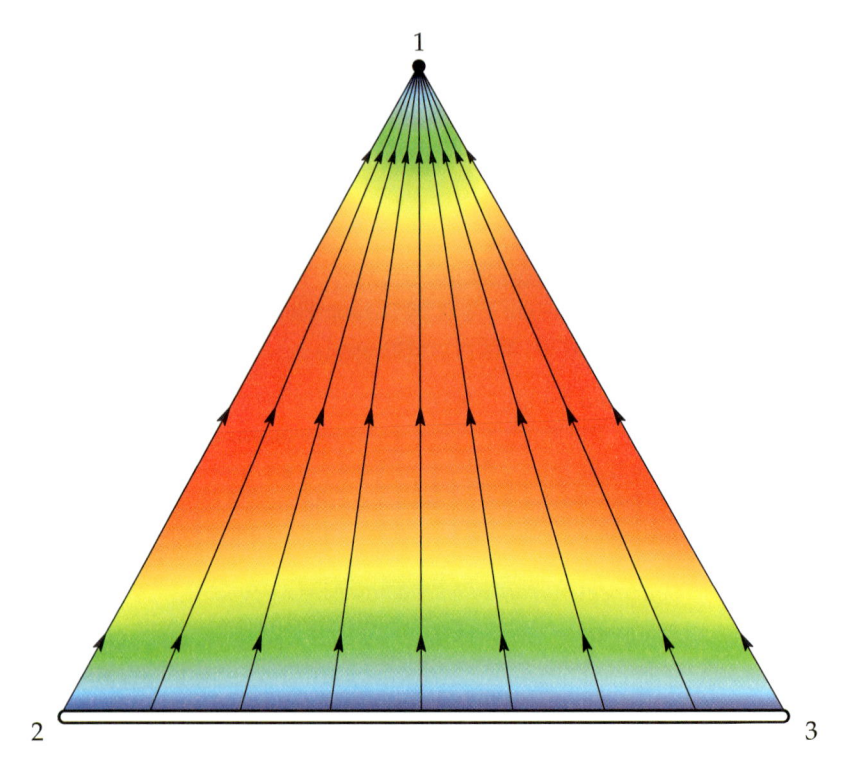

Figure 5.7
The replicator dynamic in a game with a strictly dominant strategy.

of the figure indicates, the speed of motion away from the unstable component is very slow. If a small behavior disturbance pushes the state off the component, it may take a long time before the stable equilibrium is reached. ◆

In general, the speed of motion of imitative dynamics toward or away from the boundary of X must decline exponentially as the boundary is approached. This is an immediate consequence of extinction (5.16) and the Lipschitz continuity of the dynamics.

5.4.5 Monotone Percentage Growth Rates and Positive Correlation

We now turn to the monotonicity properties of imitative dynamics. All dynamics of form (5.6) can be expressed as

$$\dot{x}_i^p = V_i^p(x) = x_i^p G_i^p(x), \quad \text{where } G_i^p(x) = \sum_{k \in S^p} \hat{x}_k^p \left(r_{ki}^p(F^p(x), x^p) - r_{ik}^p(F^p(x), x^p) \right). \quad (5.17)$$

If strategy $i \in S^p$ is in use, then $G_i^p(x) = V_i^p(x)/x_i^p$ represents the *percentage growth rate* of the number of agents using this strategy.

Deterministic Dynamics

Observation 5.4.8 notes that under every imitative dynamic (as defined in section 5.4.1), strategies' percentage growth rates are ordered by their payoffs.

Observation 5.4.8 *All imitative dynamics exhibit* monotone percentage growth rates:

$$G_i^p(x) \geq G_j^p(x) \quad \text{if and only if} \quad F_i^p(x) \geq F_j^p(x). \tag{5.18}$$

This observation is immediate from condition (5.7), which defines imitative dynamics.

Condition (5.18) is a strong restriction on strategies' *percentage* growth rates. It also implies our basic payoff monotonicity condition, which imposes a weak restriction on strategies' *absolute* growth rates.

Theorem 5.4.9 *All imitative dynamics satisfy positive correlation* (PC).

Proof Let x be a social state at which $V^p(x) \neq \mathbf{0}$; the aim is to show that $V^p(x)'F^p(x) > 0$. To do so, define

$$S_+^p(x) = \{i \in S^p : V_i^p(x) > 0\} \quad \text{and} \quad S_-^p(x) = \{j \in S^p : V_j^p(x) < 0\}$$

to be the sets of population p strategies with positive and negative absolute growth rates, respectively. By extinction (5.16), these sets are contained in the support of x^p. It follows that

$$S_+^p(x) = \{i \in S^p : x_i^p > 0 \text{ and } \frac{V_i^p(x)}{x_i^p} > 0\} \quad \text{and}$$

$$S_-^p(x) = \{j \in S^p : x_j^p > 0 \text{ and } \frac{V_j^p(x)}{x_j^p} < 0\}.$$

Since $V(x) \in TX$, it follows from observation 4.4.3 that

$$\sum_{k \in S_+^p(x)} V_k^p(x) = - \sum_{k \in S_-^p(x)} V_k^p(x),$$

and since $V^p(x) \neq \mathbf{0}$, these expressions are positive. Therefore, by observation 5.4.8,

$$V^p(x)'F^p(x) = \sum_{k \in S_+^p(x)} V_k^p(x) F_k^p(x) + \sum_{k \in S_-^p(x)} V_k^p(x) F_k^p(x)$$

$$\geq \min_{i \in S_+^p(x)} F_i^p(x) \sum_{k \in S_+^p(x)} V_k^p(x) + \max_{j \in S_-^p(x)} F_j^p(x) \sum_{k \in S_-^p(x)} V_k^p(x)$$

$$= \left(\min_{i \in S_+^p(x)} F_i^p(x) - \max_{j \in S_-^p(x)} F_j^p(x) \right) \sum_{k \in S_+^p(x)} V_k^p(x) > 0. \quad \blacksquare$$

This section concludes with two other monotonicity conditions that appear in the literature.

Exercise 5.4.10 In the single-population setting, an imitative dynamic (5.17) has *aggregate monotone percentage growth rates* if

$$\hat{y}'G(x) \geq y'G(x) \quad \text{if and only if} \quad \hat{y}'F(x) \geq y'F(x) \tag{5.19}$$

for all population states $x \in X$ and mixed strategies $\hat{y}, y \in \Delta$.

i. Show that any imitative dynamic satisfying condition (5.19) is equivalent to the replicator dynamic up to a reparameterization of time (see exercise 5.4.3). (*Hint:* Use proposition 3.B.4 to show that condition (5.19) implies that $\Phi G(x) = c(x)\Phi F(x)$ for some $c(x) > 0$. Then use the fact that $G(x)'x = 0$ (why?) to conclude that $\dot{x}_i = c(x) x_i \hat{F}_i(x)$.)

ii. If a multipopulation imitative dynamic satisfies the natural analogue of condition (5.19), what can one conclude about the dynamic? ◇

Exercise 5.4.11 A dynamic of form (5.17) has *sign-preserving percentage growth rates* if

$$\text{sgn}(G_i^p(x)) = \text{sgn}(\hat{F}_i^p(x)). \tag{5.20}$$

Show that any such dynamic satisfies positive correlation (PC). (Note that dynamics satisfying condition (5.20) need not satisfy condition (5.7), and so need not be imitative dynamics as defined here. No intuitive restrictions on revision protocols leading to condition (5.20) are known.) ◇

5.4.6 Rest Points and Restricted Equilibria

Since all imitative dynamics satisfy positive correlation (PC), proposition 5.2.1 implies that their rest points include all Nash equilibria of the underlying game F. On the other hand, support invariance says that non-Nash rest points can exist: for instance, pure states in X are not always Nash equilibria of F, but they are necessarily rest points of V_F.

To characterize the set of rest points, recall the definition of Nash equilibrium:

$$NE(F) = \{x \in X : x_i^p > 0 \Rightarrow F_i^p(x) = \max_{j \in S^p} F_j^p(x)\}.$$

Then define the set of *restricted equilibria* of F by

$$RE(F) = \{x \in X : x_i^p > 0 \Rightarrow F_i^p(x) = \max_{j \in S^p : x_j > 0} F_j^p(x)\}.$$

Thus, x is a restricted equilibrium of F if it is a Nash equilibrium of a restricted version of F in which only strategies in the support of x can be played.

Deterministic Dynamics

Exercise 5.4.12: Alternative Definitions of Restricted Equilibrium

i. Show that $x \in RE(F)$ if and only if within each population p, all strategies in the support of x^p achieve the same payoff: $RE(F) = \{x \in X: x_i^p > 0 \Rightarrow F_i^p(x) = \pi^p\}$.

ii. There is also a geometric definition of restricted equilibrium. Let $X_{[\hat{x}]}$ be the set of social states whose supports are contained in the support of $\hat{x}$: $X_{[\hat{x}]} = \{x \in X: \hat{x}_i^p = 0 \Rightarrow x_i^p = 0\}$. Show that $x \in RE(F)$ if and only if the payoff vector $F(x)$ is contained in the normal cone of $X_{[x]}$ at x: $RE(F) = \{x \in X: F(x) \in NX_{[x]}(x)\}$. ◇

Because imitative dynamics exhibit support invariance, strategies that are initially unused are never subsequently chosen. This suggests a link between rest points of imitative dynamics and the restricted equilibria of the underlying game that is established in the following theorem.

Theorem 5.4.13 *If $\dot{x} = V_F(x)$ is an imitative dynamic, then $RP(V_F) = RE(F)$.*

Proof $x \in RP(V) \Leftrightarrow V_i^p(x) = 0 \quad$ for all $i \in S^p, p \in \mathcal{P}$

$$\Leftrightarrow \frac{V_i^p(x)}{x_i^p} = 0 \quad \text{when } x_i^p > 0, p \in \mathcal{P} \quad \text{(by (5.16))}$$

$$\Leftrightarrow F_i^p(x) = \pi^p \quad \text{when } x_i^p > 0, p \in \mathcal{P} \quad \text{(by (5.18))}$$

$$\Leftrightarrow x \in RE(F). \qquad \blacksquare$$

While there are rest points of imitative dynamics that are not Nash equilibria, such rest points are locally unstable (see chapter 8). On the other hand, as example 5.4.8 illustrates, the speed of motion away from these unstable rest points is initially rather slow.

Exercise 5.4.14

i. Suppose that the payoffs of one population game are the negation of the payoffs of another. What is the relation between the replicator dynamics of the two games?

ii. Give an example of a three-strategy game whose Nash equilibrium is unique and whose replicator dynamic admits seven rest points. ◇

5.5 Excess Payoff Dynamics

This section considers revision protocols that are not based on imitation, but rather, on the direct selection of candidate strategies. Under such protocols, good unused strategies will be discovered and chosen, raising the possibility that the dynamics satisfy Nash stationarity (NS).

5.5.1 Definition and Interpretation

In some settings, particularly those in which information about population aggregates is provided by a central planner, agents may know their population's current average payoff. Suppose that each agent's choices are based on comparisons between the various strategies' current payoffs and the population's average payoff, and that these choices do not condition on the agent's current strategy. Then the agents' choice procedure can be described using a target protocol of the form

$$\rho_{ij}^p(\pi^p, x^p) = \tau_j^p(\hat{\pi}^p),$$

where $\hat{\pi}_i^p = \pi_i^p(x) - \frac{1}{m^p}(x^p)'\pi^p$ represents the excess payoff to strategy $i \in S^p$. Such a protocol generates the target dynamic

$$\dot{x}_i^p = m^p \tau_i^p(\hat{F}^p(x)) - x_i^p \sum_{j \in S^p} \tau_j^p(\hat{F}^p(x))$$

$$= \begin{cases} \sum_{j \in S^p} \tau_j^p(\hat{F}^p(x)) \left(m^p \dfrac{\tau_i^p(\hat{F}^p(x))}{\sum\limits_{j \in S^p} \tau_j^p(\hat{F}^p(x))} - x_i^p \right) & \text{if } \tau^p(\hat{F}^p(x)) \neq 0, \\ 0 & \text{otherwise.} \end{cases} \quad (5.21)$$

To obtain the new class of dynamics, we impose a monotonicity condition on the protocol τ. First, observe that the excess payoff vector $\hat{F}^p(x)$ cannot lie in the interior of the negative orthant $\mathbf{R}_-^{n^p}$; for this to happen, every strategy would have to earn a below-average payoff. We can therefore let the domain of the function τ^p be the set $\mathbf{R}_*^{n^p} = \mathbf{R}^{n^p} - \text{int}(\mathbf{R}_-^{n^p})$. Note that $\text{int}(\mathbf{R}_*^{n^p}) = \mathbf{R}^{n^p} - \mathbf{R}_-^{n^p}$ is the set of excess payoff vectors under which at least one strategy earns an above-average payoff, while $\text{bd}(\mathbf{R}_*^{n^p}) = \text{bd}(\mathbf{R}_-^{n^p})$ is the set of excess payoff vectors under which no strategy earns an above-average payoff. This definition of $\mathbf{R}_*^{n^p}$ is quite convenient; see especially lemma 5.5.3.

Now the family of dynamics can be defined.

Definition *Suppose the protocols $\tau^p \colon \mathbf{R}_*^{n^p} \to \mathbf{R}_+^{n^p}$ are Lipschitz continuous and satisfy* acuteness:

If $\hat{\pi}^p \in \text{int}(\mathbf{R}_*^{n^p})$, then $\tau^p(\hat{\pi}^p)'\hat{\pi}^p > 0$. (5.22)

Then the map from population games $F \in \mathcal{F}$ to differential equations (5.21) *is called an* excess payoff dynamic.

Deterministic Dynamics

How should one interpret condition (5.22)? If the excess payoff vector $\hat{\pi}^p$ has a positive component, this condition implies that

$$\sigma^p(\hat{\pi}^p) = \frac{1}{\sum_{i \in S^p} \tau_i^p(\hat{\pi}^p)} \tau^p(\hat{\pi}^p) \in \Delta^p,$$

the probability vector that defines the target state, is well defined. Acuteness requires that if a component of the excess payoff vector $\hat{\pi}^p$ is picked at random according to this probability vector, then the expected value of this randomly chosen component is positive. Put differently, acuteness asks that *on average*, revising agents switch to strategies with above-average payoffs.

There is at least a formal resemblance between acuteness (5.22), which constrains the target protocol τ, and positive correlation (PC), which constrains the dynamic V_F. This resemblance is used to best advantage in lemma 5.5.5.

Example 5.5.1: The BNN Dynamic   Suppose that the conditional switch rate to strategy $i \in S^p$ is given by the positive part of strategy i's excess payoffs: $\tau_i^p(\hat{\pi}^p) = [\hat{\pi}_i^p]_+$. The resulting mean dynamic,

$$\dot{x}_i^p = m^p [\hat{F}_i^p(x)]_+ - x_i^p \sum_{j \in S^p} [\hat{F}_j^p(x)]_+, \tag{BNN}$$

is called the *Brown–von Neumann–Nash* (BNN) *dynamic*.   ◆

Exercise 5.5.1: k-BNN Dynamics   The *k-BNN dynamic* is generated by the revision protocol $\tau_i^p(\hat{\pi}^p) = [\hat{\pi}_i^p]_+^k$, where $k \geq 1$. Argue informally that if k is large, then at typical states, the direction of motion under the k-BNN dynamic is close to that under the best response dynamic, $\dot{x}^p \in m^p B^p(x) - x^p$ (see chapter 6), but the speed of motion is not.   ◇

5.5.2 Incentives and Aggregate Behavior

The goal in this section is to show that every excess payoff dynamic satisfies the two incentive properties.

Theorem 5.5.2   *Every excess payoff dynamic $\dot{x} = V_F(x)$ satisfies positive correlation* (PC) *and Nash stationarity* (NS).

This result is proved under the assumption that τ^p satisfies *sign preservation*:

$$\operatorname{sgn}(\tau_i^p(\hat{\pi}^p)) = \operatorname{sgn}([\hat{\pi}_i^p]_+). \tag{5.23}$$

A proof using only acuteness is outlined in exercise 5.5.7.

Theorem 5.2.2 follows immediately from the following three lemmas. The proofs of the lemmas are given for the single-population case ($p = 1$); the proofs for the multipopulation case are simple extensions.

Lemma 5.5.3 $\hat{F}^p(x) \in \text{bd}(\mathbf{R}_*^n)$ for all $p \in \mathcal{P}$ if and only if $x \in NE(F)$.

Proof ($p = 1$) $\hat{F}(x) \in \text{bd}(\mathbf{R}_*^n) \Leftrightarrow F_i(x) \leq \sum_{k \in S} x_k F_k(x)$ for all $i \in S$

$\Leftrightarrow$ there exists a $c \in \mathbf{R}$ such that $F_i(x) \leq c$ for all $i \in S$, with $F_j(x) = c$ when $x_j > 0$

$\Leftrightarrow F_j(x) = \max_{k \in S} F_k(x)$ when $x_j > 0$

$\Leftrightarrow x \in NE(F)$. ∎

Lemma 5.5.4 *If* $\hat{F}^p(x) \in \text{bd}(\mathbf{R}_*^{np})$, *then* $V_F^p(x) = 0$.

Proof Immediate from sign preservation (5.23). ∎

Lemma 5.5.5 *If* $\hat{F}^p(x) \in \text{int}(\mathbf{R}_*^{np})$, *then* $V_F^p(x)' F^p(x) > 0$.

Proof ($p = 1$) Recall that $\hat{F}(x) = F(x) - \mathbf{1}\bar{F}(x)$ and $V_F(x) = \tau(\hat{F}(x)) - \mathbf{1}'\tau(\hat{F}(x))x$. The first definition implies that x and $\hat{F}(x)$ are always orthogonal:

$$x'\hat{F}(x) = x'(F(x) - \mathbf{1}\bar{F}(x)) = x'F(x) - \bar{F}(x) = 0.$$

Combining this with the second definition, we see that if $\hat{F}(x) \in \text{int}(\mathbf{R}_*^n)$, then

$V_F(x)'F(x) = V_F(x)'(\hat{F}(x) + \mathbf{1}\bar{F}(x))$

$\qquad = V_F(x)'\hat{F}(x)$ (since $V_F(x) \in TX$)

$\qquad = (\tau(\hat{F}(x)) - \mathbf{1}'\tau(\hat{F}(x))x)'\hat{F}(x)$

$\qquad = \tau(\hat{F}(x))'\hat{F}(x)$ (since $x'\hat{F}(x) = 0$)

$\qquad > 0$ (by acuteness (5.22)). ∎

Exercise 5.5.6 Suppose that revision protocol τ^p is Lipschitz continuous, acute, and *separable*:

$\tau_i^p(\hat{\pi}^p) \equiv \tau_i^p(\hat{\pi}_i^p)$.

Show that τ^p also satisfies sign preservation (5.23). ◇

Exercise 5.5.7 This exercise shows how to establish properties (PC) and (NS) using only continuity and acuteness (5.22), that is, without requiring sign preservation

Deterministic Dynamics

(5.23). The proofs of lemmas 5.5.3 and 5.5.5 go through unchanged, but lemma 5.5.4 requires additional work.

Assume that there is single population ($p = 1$), and use acuteness and continuity to establish the following facts.

i. Show that if $\hat{\pi} \in \mathrm{bd}(\mathbf{R}_*^n)$ and $\hat{\pi}_i < 0$, then $\tau_i(\hat{\pi}) = 0$. (*Hint:* Consider $\hat{\pi}^\varepsilon = \hat{\pi} + \varepsilon e_j$, where $\hat{\pi}_j = 0$.)

ii. Show that if $\hat{\pi} \in \mathrm{bd}(\mathbf{R}_*^n)$ and $\hat{\pi}_i = \hat{\pi}_j = 0$, then $\tau(\hat{\pi}) = \mathbf{0}$. (*Hint:* To show that $\tau_i(\hat{\pi}) = 0$, consider $\hat{\pi}^\varepsilon = \hat{\pi} - \varepsilon e_i + \varepsilon^2 e_j$.)

Then use these two facts to prove lemma 5.5.4. ◇

Exercise 5.5.8 This exercise demonstrates that in general, one cannot normalize a target dynamic in order to create an exact target dynamic. This highlights a nontrivial sense in which the former class of dynamics is more general than the latter.

Recall that in the single-population setting, the BNN dynamic is defined by the target protocol $\tau_i(\hat{\pi}) = [\hat{\pi}_i]_+$.

i. It is tempting to try to define an exact target protocol by normalizing τ in an appropriate way. Explain why such a protocol would not be well defined.

ii. To circumvent this problem, one can construct a dynamic that is derived from the normalized protocol whenever the latter is well defined. Show that such a dynamic must be discontinuous in some games. (*Hint:* It is enough to consider two-strategy games.) ◇

5.6 Pairwise Comparison Dynamics

Excess payoff dynamics satisfy Nash stationarity (NS), positive correlation (PC), and continuity (C), but they fall into the quite demanding data requirement class (D+). The revision protocols that underlie these dynamics require agents to compare their current payoff with the average payoff obtained in their population. Without the assistance of a central planner, this information is unlikely to be known to the agents.

A natural way to reduce these informational demands is to replace the population's average payoff with another reference payoff, one whose value agents can directly access. This can be accomplished by considering revision protocols based on pairwise payoff comparisons, which fall into data requirement class (D2). The remainder of this section shows that the resulting evolutionary dynamics can be made to satisfy the other desiderata as well.

5.6.1 Definition

Suppose that the revision protocol ρ^p directly conditions on payoffs, but not on the population state. The induced mean dynamic is then of the form

$$\dot{x}_i^p = \sum_{j \in S^p} x_j^p \rho_{ji}^p(F^p(x)) - x_i^p \sum_{j \in S^p} \rho_{ij}^p(F^p(x)). \tag{5.24}$$

This equation and a mild monotonicity condition on ρ defines the next class of dynamics.

Definition *Suppose that the revision protocol ρ is Lipschitz continuous and sign-preserving:*

$$\operatorname{sgn}(\rho_{ij}^p(\pi^p)) = \operatorname{sgn}([\pi_j^p - \pi_i^p]_+) \quad \text{for all } i, j \in S^p, p \in \mathcal{P}. \tag{5.25}$$

Then the map from population games $F \in \mathcal{F}$ to differential equations (5.24) is called a pairwise comparison dynamic.

Sign preservation (5.25) is a natural property; it says that the conditional switch rate from $i \in S^p$ to $j \in S^p$ is positive if and only if the payoff to j exceeds the payoff to i.

Example 5.6.1: The Smith Dynamic The simplest sign-preserving revision protocol,

$$\rho_{ij}^p(\pi^p) = [\pi_j^p - \pi_i^p]_+,$$

generates the *Smith dynamic*:

$$\dot{x}_i^p = \sum_{j \in S^p} x_j^p [F_i^p(x) - F_j^p(x)]_+ - x_i^p \sum_{j \in S^p} [F_j^p(x) - F_i^p(x)]_+. \qquad \blacklozenge \text{ (S)}$$

Exercise 5.6.1: The k-Smith Dynamic Consider the protocol $\rho_{ij}^p(\pi^p) = [\pi_j^p - \pi_i^p]_+^k$, where $k \geq 1$. Argue informally that in the single-population case, when k is large, the direction of motion from most states x is approximately parallel to an edge of the simplex. How is this edge determined from the payoff vector $F(x)$?   ◇

5.6.2 Incentives and Aggregate Behavior

We now state the main result in this section.

Theorem 5.6.2 *Every pairwise comparison dynamic satisfies positive correlation* (PC) *and Nash stationarity* (NS).

Deterministic Dynamics

The proof of this theorem relies on three equivalences between properties of Nash equilibria and evolutionary dynamics on the one hand, and requirements that sums of terms of the form $\rho_{ij}^p [F_j^p - F_i^p]_+$, or $\rho_{ij}^p [F_j^p - F_i^p]_+$ equal zero on the other. Sign preservation ensures that sums of the three types are identical, allowing us to establish the result.

In what follows, $\dot{x} = V(x)$ is the pairwise comparison dynamic generated by the population game F and the revision protocol ρ.

Lemma 5.6.3 $x \in NE(F) \Leftrightarrow$ For all $i \in S^p$ and $p \in \mathcal{P}$, $x_i^p = 0$ or $\sum_{j \in S^p} [F_j^p(x) - F_i^p(x)]_+ = 0$.

Proof Both statements say that each strategy in use at x is optimal. ∎

Lemma 5.6.4 $V^p(x) = \mathbf{0} \Leftrightarrow$ For all $i \in S^p$, $x_i^p = 0$ or $\sum_{j \in S^p} \rho_{ij}^p(F^p(x)) = 0$.

Proof ($\Leftarrow$) Immediate.

($\Rightarrow$) Fix a population $p \in \mathcal{P}$, and suppose that $V^p(x) = \mathbf{0}$. If j is an optimal strategy for population p at x, then sign preservation implies that $\rho_{jk}^p(F^p(x)) = 0$ for all $k \in S^p$, so there is no outflow from strategy j:

$$x_j^p \sum_{i \in S^p} \rho_{ji}^p(F^p(x)) = 0.$$

Since $V_j^p(x) = 0$, there can be no inflow into strategy j either:

$$\sum_{i \in S^p} x_i^p \rho_{ij}^p(F^p(x)) = 0.$$

This condition is expressed equivalently as

For all $i \in S^p$, either $x_i^p = 0$ or $\rho_{ij}^p(F^p(x)) = 0$.

If all strategies in S^p earn the same payoff at state x, the proof is complete. Otherwise, let i be a second-best strategy, that is, a strategy whose payoff $F_i^p(x)$ is second-highest among the payoffs available from strategies in S^p at x. The last observation in the previous paragraph and sign preservation imply that there is no outflow from i. But since $V_i^p(x) = 0$, there is also no inflow into i:

For all $k \in S^p$, either $x_k^p = 0$ or $\rho_{ki}^p(F^p(x)) = 0$.

Iterating this argument for strategies with lower payoffs establishes the result. ∎

Lemma 5.6.5 *Fix a population $p \in \mathcal{P}$. Then*

i. $V^p(x)'F^p(x) \geq 0$;

ii. $V^p(x)'F^p(x) = 0 \Leftrightarrow$ For all $i \in S^p, x_i^p = 0$ or $\sum_{j \in S^p} \rho_{ij}^p(F^p(x))[F_j^p(x) - F_i^p(x)]_+ = 0$.

Proof The inner product is computed as follows:

$$V^p(x)'F^p(x) = \sum_{j \in S^p} \left(\sum_{i \in S^p} x_i^p \rho_{ij}^p(F^p(x)) - x_j^p \sum_{i \in S^p} \rho_{ji}^p(F^p(x)) \right) F_j^p(x)$$

$$= \sum_{j \in S^p} \sum_{i \in S^p} \left(x_i^p \rho_{ij}^p(F^p(x)) F_j^p(x) - x_j^p \rho_{ji}^p(F^p(x)) F_j^p(x) \right)$$

$$= \sum_{j \in S^p} \sum_{i \in S^p} x_i^p \rho_{ij}^p(F^p(x)) \left(F_j^p(x) - F_i^p(x) \right)$$

$$= \sum_{i \in S^p} \left(x_i^p \sum_{j \in S^p} \rho_{ij}^p(F^p(x))[F_j^p(x) - F_i^p(x)]_+ \right),$$

where the last equality follows from sign preservation. Both claims directly follow. ∎

Theorem 5.6.2 follows easily from these three lemmas and sign preservation (5.25). Sign preservation implies that the second conditions in lemmas 5.6.3, 5.6.4, and 5.6.5(ii) are equivalent. This observation and lemmas 5.6.3 and 5.6.4 imply that $x \in NE(F)$ if and only if $V^p(x) = \mathbf{0}$ for all $p \in \mathcal{P}$; this is condition (NS). In addition, the observation, lemma 5.6.4, and lemma 5.6.5(ii) imply that $V^p(x) = \mathbf{0}$ if and only if $V^p(x)'F^p(x) = 0$; this fact and lemma 5.6.5(i) imply that $V^p(x)'F^p(x) > 0$ whenever $V^p(x) \neq \mathbf{0}$, which is condition (PC). This completes the proof of theorem 5.6.2.

5.6.3 Desiderata Revisited

Pairwise comparison dynamics satisfy all four of the desiderata proposed at the beginning of the chapter. Their revision protocols are continuous (C) and satisfy the mild data requirement (D2), and the dynamics themselves satisfy Nash stationarity (NS) and positive correlation (PC). Some insight into this result can be gained by comparing the revision protocols that generate the three key dynamics in this chapter:

Replicator: $\rho_{ij}^p(\pi^p, x^p) = \hat{x}_j^p [\pi_j^p - \pi_i^p]_+$.

BNN: $\rho_{ij}^p(\pi^p, x^p) = [\pi_j^p - \bar{\pi}^p]_+ = \left[\pi_j^p - \sum_{k \in S^p} \hat{x}_k^p \pi_k^p \right]_+$.

Smith: $\rho_{ij}^p(\pi^p) = [\pi_j^p - \pi_i^p]_+$.

Deterministic Dynamics

From the point of view of the desiderata, the protocol that generates the Smith dynamic combines the best features of the other two. Like the protocol for the BNN dynamic, the Smith protocol is based on direct selection of candidate strategies rather than on imitation, allowing it to satisfy Nash stationarity (NS). Like the protocol for the replicator dynamic, the Smith protocol is based on comparisons of individual strategies' payoffs rather than on comparisons involving aggregate statistics, and so it satisfies data requirement (D2). Thus, whereas the BNN and replicator dynamics each satisfy three of the desiderata, the Smith dynamic satisfies all four.

5.7 Multiple Revision Protocols and Hybrid Dynamics

The preceding results might seem to suggest that dynamics satisfying all four desiderata are rather special, in that they must be derived from a very specific sort of revision protocol. We now argue to the contrary that these desiderata are satisfied rather broadly.

Consider what happens if an agent uses multiple revision protocols at possibly different intensities. If an agent uses the revision protocol ρ^V at intensity a and the revision protocol ρ^W at intensity b, then his behavior is described by the new revision protocol $\rho^H = a\rho^V + b\rho^W$. Moreover, since mean dynamics are linear in conditional switch rates, the mean dynamic for the hybrid protocol is a linear combination of the two original mean dynamics: $H_F = aV_F + bW_F$.

Theorem 5.7.1 links the properties of the original and hybrid dynamics.

Theorem 5.7.1 *Suppose that the dynamic V_F satisfies* (PC), *that the dynamic W_F satisfies* (PC) *and* (NS), *and that $a, b > 0$. Then the hybrid dynamic $H_F = aV_F + bW_F$ also satisfies* (PC) *and* (NS).

Proof To show that H_F satisfies (PC), suppose that $H_F^p(x) \neq \mathbf{0}$. Then either $V_F^p(x)$, $W_F^p(x)$, or both are not $\mathbf{0}$. Since V_F and W_F satisfy (PC), it follows that $V_F^p(x)'F^p(x) \geq 0$, that $W_F^p(x)'F^p(x) \geq 0$, and that at least one of these inequalities is strict. Consequently, $H_F^p(x)'F^p(x) > 0$, and therefore H_F satisfies (PC).

The proof that H_F satisfies (NS) is divided into three cases. First, if x is a Nash equilibrium of F, then it is a rest point of both V_F and W_F by proposition 5.2.1 and hence a rest point of H_F as well. Second, if x is a non-Nash rest point of V_F, then it is not a rest point of W_F. Since $V_F(x) = \mathbf{0}$ and $W_F(x) \neq \mathbf{0}$, it follows that $H_F(x) = bW_F(x) \neq \mathbf{0}$, so x is not a rest point of H_F. Finally, suppose that x is not a rest point of V_F. Then by proposition 5.2.1, x is not a Nash equilibrium, and so x is not a rest point of W_F either. Since V_F and W_F satisfy condition (PC), we know that $V_F(x)'F(x) = \sum_{p \in \mathcal{P}} V_F^p(x)'F^p(x) > 0$ and that $W_F(x)'F(x) > 0$. Consequently, $H_F(x)'F(x) > 0$, implying that x is not a rest point of H_F. Thus, H_F satisfies (NS). ∎

A key implication of theorem 5.7.1 is that imitation and Nash stationarity are not incompatible. If agents usually rely on imitative protocols but occasionally follow protocols that directly evaluate strategies' payoffs, then the rest points of the resulting mean dynamics are precisely the Nash equilibria of the underlying game. Indeed, if we combine an imitative dynamic V_F with any small amount of a pairwise comparison dynamic W_F, we obtain a hybrid dynamic H_F that satisfies all four desiderata.

Example 5.7.1 Figure 5.8 presents a phase diagram for the $\frac{9}{10}$ replicator + $\frac{1}{10}$ Smith dynamic in standard Rock-Paper-Scissors. Comparing this diagram to those for the replicator and Smith dynamics alone (see figures 5.3a and 5.3d), we see that the diagram for the hybrid dynamic more closely resembles the Smith phase diagram than the replicator phase diagram, and in more than one respect: the combined dynamic has exactly one rest point, the unique Nash equilibrium $x^* = (\frac{1}{3}, \frac{1}{3}, \frac{1}{3})$, and all solutions to the combined dynamic converge to this state. This fragility of

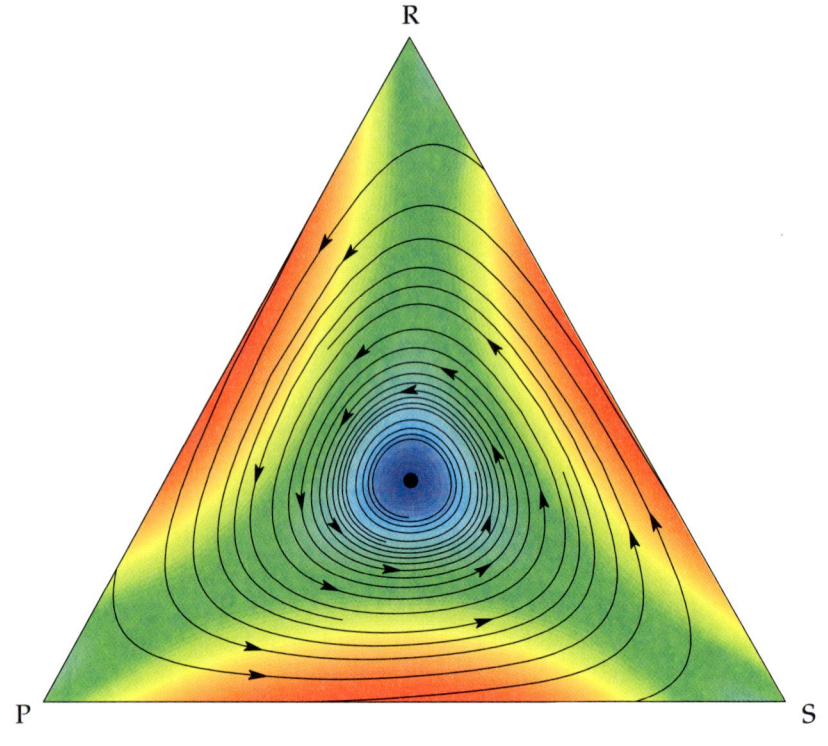

Figure 5.8
The $\frac{9}{10}$ replicator $+\frac{1}{10}$ Smith dynamic in Rock-Paper-Scissors.

Deterministic Dynamics

imitative dynamics is revisited in chapter 9, where it appears in a much starker form. ◆

Notes

Section 5.1
This section follows Sandholm (2010d).

Section 5.2
A wide variety of payoff monotonicity conditions have been considered in the literature; for examples, see Nachbar (1990), Friedman (1991), Samuelson and Zhang (1992), Swinkels (1993), Ritzberger and Weibull (1995), Hofbauer and Weibull (1996), and Sandholm (2001a). Positive correlation is essentially the weakest condition that has been proposed; see the section 5.4 notes for related references. Friedman's (1991) *weak compatibility* is positive correlation plus the additional restriction that unused strategies are never subsequently chosen. Swinkels (1993) called a dynamic a *myopic adjustment dynamic* if it satisfies positive correlation, but he allowed $F^p(x)'V^p(x) = 0$ even when $V^p(x) \neq \mathbf{0}$.

Section 5.4
The approach to imitative revision protocols and dynamics in this section builds on the work of Björnerstedt and Weibull (1996), Weibull (1995), and Hofbauer (1995a).

Taylor and Jonker (1978) introduced the replicator dynamic to provide a dynamic analogue of Maynard Smith and Price's (1973) equilibrium (ESS) model of animal conflict. Exercise 5.4.5, which shows that the replicator dynamic is equivalent after a nonlinear (barycentric) change of variable to the Lotka-Volterra equation, is due to Hofbauer (1981b). Schuster and Sigmund (1983) observed that fundamental models of population genetics (e.g., Crow and Kimura 1970) and of biochemical evolution (e.g., Eigen and Schuster 1979) could be viewed as special cases of the replicator dynamic. Schuster and Sigmund (1983) were the first to refer to the dynamic by this name. For more on biological models, see Hofbauer and Sigmund (2003). For a detailed analysis of the replicator dynamic from an economic point of view, see Weibull (1995, ch. 3). The derivations of the replicator dynamic in examples 5.4.2, 5.4.3, and 5.4.4 are due to Helbing (1992) and Schlag (1998), Björnerstedt and Weibull (1996), and Hofbauer (1995a), respectively.

The Maynard Smith replicator dynamic can be found in Maynard Smith (1982, appendices D and J). For a contrast between the standard and Maynard Smith replicator dynamics from a biological point of view, see Hofbauer and Sigmund (1988, sec. 27.1). The imitative logit dynamic is due to Björnerstedt and Weibull (1996) and Weibull (1995).

In the biology literature, the stochastic evolutionary process generated by the revision protocol in example 5.4.6 (i.e., protocol (5.11) with $w(\pi_j) = \pi_j$) is called a *frequency-dependent Moran process*, after Moran (1962). In this context, each animal is programmed to play a particular pure strategy; the arrival of a revision opportunity corresponds to the death of one of the animals in the population, and the revision protocol (5.11) determines which animal will reproduce asexually to fill the vacancy. This process is usually studied in finite populations, often after the addition of mutations, in order to focus on its stochastic aspects. See Nowak (2006) and the notes to section 12.4 for further references.

Most early work by economists on deterministic evolutionary dynamics focused on generalizations of the replicator dynamic expressed in terms of percentage growth rates, as in equation (5.17). The condition we call monotone percentage growth rates (5.18) has appeared in many places under a variety of names: *relative monotonicity* (Nachbar 1990), *order compatibility of predynamics* (Friedman 1991), *monotonicity* (Samuelson and Zhang 1992), and *payoff monotonicity* (Weibull 1995). Aggregate monotone percentage growth rates (5.19) and exercise 5.4.10 are due to Samuelson and Zhang (1992). Sign-preserving percentage growth rates (5.20) is a condition due to Nachbar (1990); see also Ritzberger and Weibull (1995), who called this condition *payoff positivity*. For surveys of the literature referenced here, see Weibull (1995, chs. 4, 5) and Fudenberg and Levine (1998, ch. 3).

Sections 5.5, 5.6, 5.7
These sections follow Sandholm (2005a; 2010d).

The Brown–von Neumann–Nash dynamic was introduced in the context of symmetric zero-sum games by Brown and von Neumann (1950). Nash (1951) used a discrete-time analogue of this dynamic as the basis for his simple proof of existence of equilibrium based on Brouwer's theorem. More recently, the BNN dynamic was reintroduced by Skyrms (1990), Swinkels (1993), and Weibull (1996), and by Hofbauer (2000), who gave the dynamic its name. The Smith dynamic was introduced in the transportation science literature by Smith (1984).

6 Best Response and Projection Dynamics

This chapter continues the procession of deterministic evolutionary dynamics. In the first two sections, the step from payoff vector fields to evolutionary dynamics is traversed through a traditional game-theoretic approach, by employing best response correspondences and perturbed versions thereof. The third section follows a geometric approach, defining an evolutionary dynamic via closest point projections of payoff vectors.

The *best response dynamic* embodies the assumption that revising agents always switch to their current best response. Because the best response correspondence is discontinuous and multivalued, the basic properties of solution trajectories under the best response dynamic are quite different from those studied earlier. Multiple solution trajectories can sprout from a single initial condition, and solution trajectories can cycle in and out of Nash equilibria. Despite these difficulties, analogues of incentive properties (NS) and (PC) still hold true.

While the discontinuity of the best response protocol stands in violation of a basic desideratum from chapter 5, one can obtain a continuous protocol by working with perturbed payoffs. The resulting *perturbed best response dynamics* are continuous (and even differentiable) and so have well-behaved solution trajectories. Although the payoff perturbations prevent our incentive conditions from holding exactly, appropriately perturbed versions of these conditions, defined in terms of so-called virtual payoffs, can be established.

The final evolutionary dynamic, the *projection dynamic*, is motivated by geometric considerations. The growth rate vector under the projection dynamic is defined to be the closest approximation of the payoff vector by a feasible vector of motion. The resulting dynamic is discontinuous, but its solutions still exist, are unique, and are continuous in their initial conditions; moreover, both of our incentive conditions are easily verified. The projection dynamic can be derived from protocols that reflect "revision driven by insecurity." These protocols also reveal surprising connections between the projection dynamic and the replicator dynamic, connections we develop further when studying the global behavior of evolutionary dynamics in chapter 7.

The dynamics studied in this chapter require new mathematical techniques. Determining the basic properties of the best response dynamic and the projection dynamic requires ideas from the theory of differential inclusions (i.e., set-valued differential equations), discussed in appendix 6.A. A key tool for analyzing perturbed best response dynamics is the Legendre transform, whose basic properties are explained in appendix 6.B. These properties are central to the analysis of perturbed maximization, presented in appendix 6.C.

6.1 The Best Response Dynamic

6.1.1 Definition and Examples

Traditional game-theoretic analysis is based on the assumption of equilibrium play. This assumption can be split into two distinct parts: agents have correct beliefs about their opponents' behavior, and they choose their strategies optimally given those beliefs. When all agents simultaneously have correct beliefs and play optimal responses, their joint behavior constitutes a Nash equilibrium.

It is natural to introduce an evolutionary dynamic based on similar principles. To accomplish this, suppose that each agent's revision opportunities arrive at a fixed rate, and that when an agent receives such an opportunity, he chooses a best response to the current population state. Thus, each agent responds optimally to correct beliefs whenever he is revising but not necessarily at other points in time.

Before taking up the best response dynamic, let us review the notions of exact target protocols and dynamics introduced in section 4.2.2. Under an exact target protocol, conditional switch rates $\rho_{ij}^p(\pi^p, x^p) \equiv \sigma_j^p(\pi^p, x^p)$ are independent of an agent's current strategy. These rates also satisfy $\sum_{j \in S} \sigma_j^p(\pi^p, x^p) \equiv 1$, so that $\sigma^p(\pi^p, x^p) \in \Delta^p$ is a mixed strategy. Such a protocol induces the exact target dynamic

$$\dot{x}^p = m^p \sigma^p(F^p(x), x^p) - x^p. \tag{6.1}$$

Under (6.1), the vector of motion $\dot{x}^p$ for population p has its tail at the current state x^p and its head at $m^p \sigma^p$, the representative of the mixed strategy $\sigma^p \in \Delta^p$ in the state space $X^p = m^p \Delta^p$.

The best response protocol is given by the multivalued map

$$\sigma^p(\pi^p) = M^p(\pi^p) \equiv \underset{y^p \in \Delta^p}{\mathrm{argmax}} \ (y^p)' \pi^p. \tag{6.2}$$

$M^p \colon \mathbf{R}^{n^p} \rightrightarrows \Delta^p$ is the *maximizer correspondence* for population p: the set $M^p(\pi^p)$ consists of those mixed strategies that only place mass on pure strategies optimal under

Best Response and Projection Dynamics

payoff vector π^p. Inserting this protocol into equation (6.1) yields the *best response dynamic*:

$$\dot{x}^p \in m^p M^p(F^p(x)) - x^p. \tag{BR}$$

One can also write (BR) as

$$\dot{x}^p \in m^p B^p(x) - x^p,$$

where $B^p = M^p \circ F^p$ is the *best response correspondence* for population p in game F.

Definition *The* best response dynamic *assigns each population game $F \in \mathcal{F}$ the set of solutions to the differential inclusion* (BR).

All the dynamics from chapter 5 are Lipschitz continuous, so the existence and uniqueness of their solutions is ensured by the Picard-Lindelöf theorem. Since the best response dynamic (BR) is a discontinuous differential inclusion, that theorem does not apply here. But while the map M^p is not a Lipschitz continuous function, it does exhibit other regularity properties: in particular, it is a convex-valued, upper-hemicontinuous correspondence. These properties impose enough structure on the dynamic (BR) to establish an existence result.

To state this result, call the Lipschitz continuous trajectory $\{x_t\}_{t \geq 0}$ a *Carathéodory solution* to the differential inclusion $\dot{x} \in V(x)$ if it satisfies $\dot{x}_t \in V(x_t)$ at all but a measure zero set of times in $[0, \infty)$.

Theorem 6.1.1 *Fix a continuous population game F. Then for each $\xi \in X$, there exists a trajectory $\{x_t\}_{t \geq 0}$ with $x_0 = \xi$ that is a Carathéodory solution to the differential inclusion* (BR).

It is important to note that while solutions to the best response dynamic exist, they need not be unique. As the following examples illustrate, multiple solution trajectories can emanate from a single initial condition. For a brief introduction to the theory of differential inclusions, see section 6.A.1.

In chapter 4, we justified our focus on deterministic dynamics by an appeal to a finite-horizon approximation theorem. This result, presented in chapter 10, shows that under certain regularity conditions, the stochastic evolutionary process $\{X_t^N\}$ generated by a game F and revision protocol ρ is well approximated by a solution to the mean dynamic (M) over any finite time horizon, as long as the population size is large enough. But because the revision protocol that generates the best response dynamic is discontinuous and multivalued, the finite-horizon approximation theorem from chapter 10 does not apply here. Indeed, since σ is multivalued, the Markov process $\{X_t^N\}$ is not even uniquely defined. Nevertheless, it is possible to prove versions of the finite-horizon approximation theorem that apply in the present setting (see the chapter notes).

6.1.2 Construction and Properties of Solution Trajectories

Because solutions to the best response dynamic need not be unique, they can be distinctly more complicated than solutions to Lipschitz continuous dynamics. But in another sense, solutions to the best response dynamic are rather simple.

Let $\{x_t\}$ be a solution to (BR), and suppose that at all times $t \in [0, T]$, population p's unique best response to state x_t is the pure strategy $i \in S^p$. Then during this time interval, evolution in population p is described by the affine differential equation

$$\dot{x}^p = m^p e_i^p - x^p.$$

In other words, the population state x^p moves directly toward vertex $v_i^p = m^p e_i^p$ of the set X^p, proceeding more slowly as the vertex is approached. It follows that throughout the interval $[0, T]$, the state $(x_t)^p$ lies on the line segment connecting $(x_0)^p$ and v_i^p; indeed, the previous equation can be solved to obtain an explicit formula for $(x_t)^p$:

$$(x_t)^p = (1 - e^{-t}) v_i^p + e^{-t}(x_0)^p \quad \text{for all } t \in [0, T].$$

Matters are more complicated at states that admit multiple best responses because at such states more than one future course of evolution is possible. Still, not every element of $B^p(x)$ need define a feasible direction of motion for population p: if $\{(x_t)^p\}$ is to head toward state $\hat{x}^p$ during a time interval of positive length, all pure strategies in the support of $\hat{x}^p$ must remain optimal throughout the interval.

Example 6.1.1: Standard Rock-Paper-Scissors Suppose a population of agents is randomly matched to play standard Rock-Paper-Scissors:

$$A = \begin{pmatrix} 0 & -l & w \\ w & 0 & -l \\ -l & w & 0 \end{pmatrix},$$

with $w = l$. The phase diagram for the best response dynamic in $F(x) = Ax$ is presented in figure 6.1. The upper, lower left, and lower right regions of the figure contain the states at which Paper, Scissors, and Rock are the unique best responses; in each of these regions, all solution trajectories head directly toward the appropriate vertex. When the boundary of a best response region is reached, multiple directions of motion are possible, at least in principle. But at all states other than the unique Nash equilibrium $x^* = (\frac{1}{3}, \frac{1}{3}, \frac{1}{3})$, the only direction of motion that can persist for a positive amount of time is the one heading toward the new best response. Therefore, the solution from each initial condition besides x^* is unique. (It is shown below that the solution from x^* is unique as well.)

Figure 6.1 appears to show that every solution trajectory converges to x^*. To prove this, note that along every solution trajectory $\{x_t\}$, whenever the best response to x_t is unique, we have

Best Response and Projection Dynamics

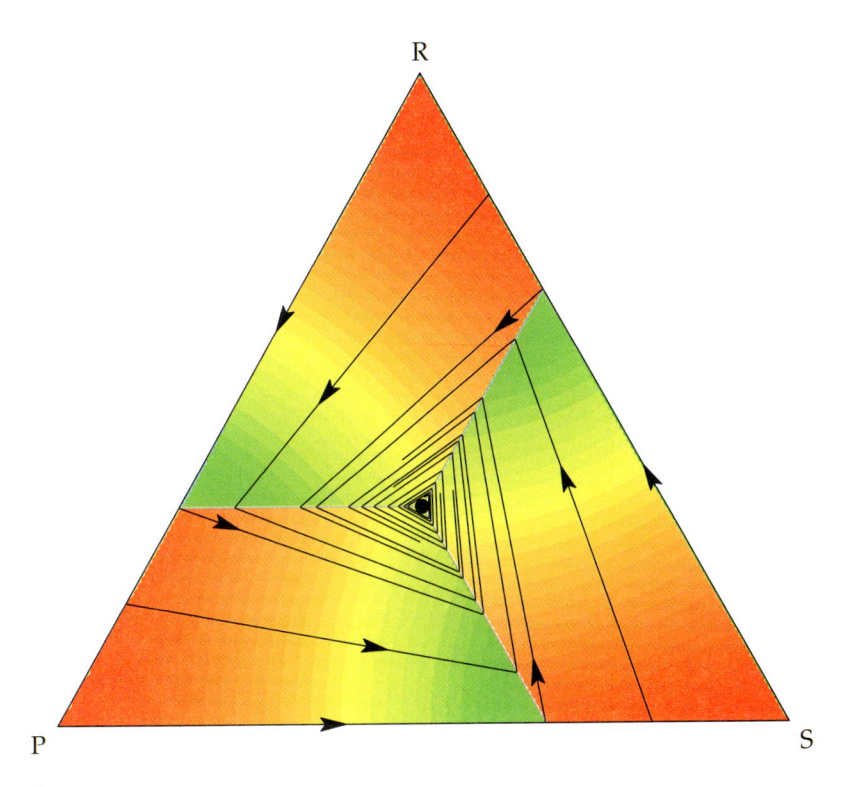

Figure 6.1
The best response dynamic in RPS.

$$\frac{d}{dt}\left(\max_{k \in S} F_k(x_t)\right) = -\max_{k \in S} F_k(x_t). \tag{6.3}$$

To see this, let x_t be a state at which there is a unique optimal strategy, say, Paper. At this state, $\dot{x}_t = e_P - x_t$. Since $F_P(x) = w(x_R - x_S)$, we can compute as follows:

$$\begin{aligned}\frac{d}{dt}F_P(x_t) &= \nabla F_P(x_t)'\dot{x}_t \\ &= w(e_R - e_S)'(e_P - x_t) \\ &= -w(e_R - e_S)'x_t \\ &= -F_P(x_t).\end{aligned}$$

It is clear from figure 6.1 that solutions with initial conditions other than x^* pass through states with multiple best responses at most a countable number of times. Equation (6.3) can therefore be integrated with respect to time. If $y_t = \max_{k \in S} F_k(x_t)$, then equation (6.3) says that $\frac{d}{dt}y_t = -y_t$. This implies that $y_t = e^{-t}y_0$, and hence that

$$\max_{k \in S} F_k(x_t) = e^{-t} \max_{k \in S} F_k(x_0). \tag{6.4}$$

In standard RPS, the maximum payoff function $\max_{k \in S} F_k$ is non-negative, equaling zero only at the Nash equilibrium x^*. This fact and equation (6.4) imply that if play begins away from x^*, then the maximal payoff falls over time, converging as t approaches infinity to its minimum value of 0; over this same time horizon, the state x_t converges to the Nash equilibrium x^*. It also follows that the unique solution starting from x^* is the stationary one, since a continuous trajectory leading from x^* to any other state would necessarily violate equation (6.4) during its initial segment. ◆

Example 6.1.2: Two-Strategy Coordination Suppose that agents are matched to play the two-strategy game with strategy set $S = \{U, D\}$ and payoff matrix

$$A = \begin{pmatrix} 1 & 0 \\ 0 & 2 \end{pmatrix}.$$

The resulting matching game $F(x) = Ax$ has three Nash equilibria, the two pure equilibria e_U and e_D and the mixed equilibrium $(x_U^*, x_D^*) = (\tfrac{2}{3}, \tfrac{1}{3})$.

To reduce the amount of notation, let $x = x_D$ represent the proportion of players choosing strategy D, so that the mixed Nash equilibrium becomes $x^* = \tfrac{1}{3}$. The best response dynamic for this game is described in terms of the state x as follows:

$$\dot{x} = \begin{cases} \{-x\} & \text{if } x < x^*, \\ [-\tfrac{1}{3}, \tfrac{2}{3}] & \text{if } x = x^*, \\ \{1-x\} & \text{if } x > x^*. \end{cases}$$

From every initial condition other than x^*, the dynamic admits a unique solution trajectory that converges to a pure equilibrium:

$$x_0 < x^* \Rightarrow x_t = e^{-t} x_0. \tag{6.5}$$

$$x_0 > x^* \Rightarrow x_t = e^{-t} x_0 + (1 - e^{-t}) = 1 - e^{-t}(1 - x_0). \tag{6.6}$$

But there are many solution trajectories starting from x^*: one solution is stationary; another proceeds to $x = 0$ according to equation (6.5), a third proceeds to $x = 1$ according to equation (6.6), and yet others follow the trajectories in (6.5) and (6.6) after some initial delay.

Notice that solutions (6.5) and (6.6) quickly leave the vicinity of x^*. This is unlike the behavior of Lipschitz continuous dynamics, under which solutions from all initial conditions are unique, and solutions that start near a stationary point initially move very slowly. ◆

Best Response and Projection Dynamics

Exercise 6.1.2: Two-Strategy Anticoordination Suppose players are matched to play the anticoordination game

$$A = \begin{pmatrix} -1 & 0 \\ 0 & -1 \end{pmatrix}.$$

Show that there is a unique solution to this dynamic from each initial condition x_0. Also show that each solution reaches the unique Nash equilibrium $x^* = \frac{1}{2}$ in finite time, and express this time as a function of the initial condition x_0. This is unlike the behavior of Lipschitz continuous dynamics, under which solutions can only reach rest points in the limit as the time t approaches infinity. ◇

Example 6.1.3: Three-Strategy Coordination Figure 6.2 presents the phase diagram for the best response dynamic generated by matching in the pure coordination game

$$A = \begin{pmatrix} 1 & 0 & 0 \\ 0 & 1 & 0 \\ 0 & 0 & 1 \end{pmatrix}.$$

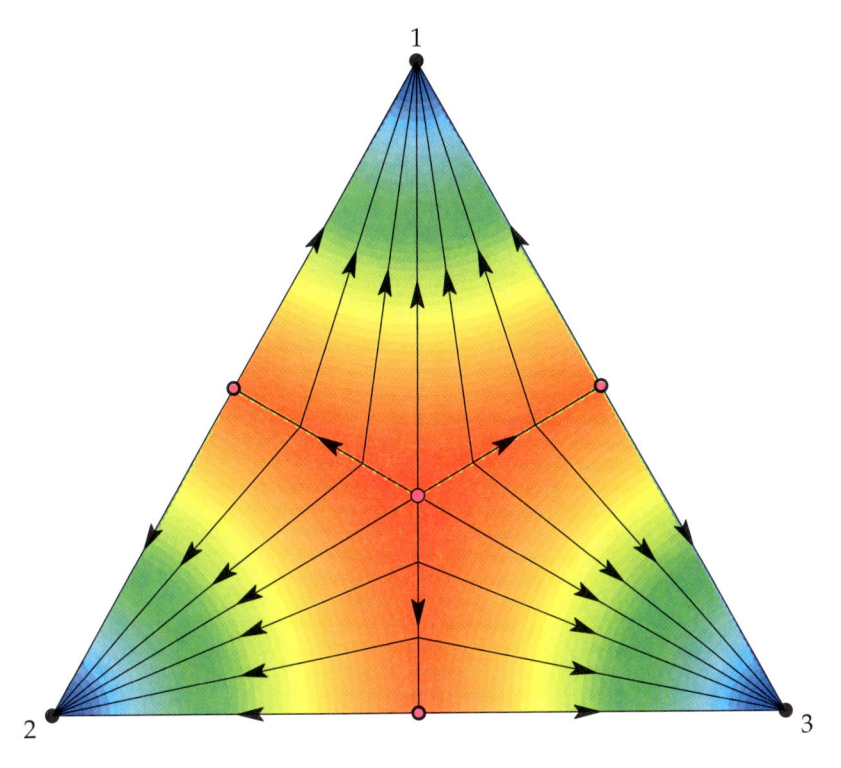

Figure 6.2
The best response dynamic in pure coordination.

The speed of motion is fastest near the mixed Nash equilibrium $x^* = (\frac{1}{3}, \frac{1}{3}, \frac{1}{3})$. As in example 6.1.2, solution trajectories are not unique. This time, whenever the state is on the Y-shaped set of boundaries between best response regions, it can leave this set and head into any adjoining basin of attraction. ◆

Exercise 6.1.3: Good and Bad RPS

i. Using an argument similar to that provided in example 6.1.1, show that in any good RPS game, the unique Nash equilibrium $x^* = (\frac{1}{3}, \frac{1}{3}, \frac{1}{3})$ is globally stable and is reached in finite time from every initial condition.

ii. Show that in any bad RPS game, solutions starting from almost all initial conditions converge to a limit cycle in the interior of the state space. (This limit cycle is a triangle whose vertices lie on the boundaries of the best response regions. In general, limit cycles of the best response dynamic are known as *Shapley polygons*.) In addition, argue that there are multiple solutions starting from the Nash equilibrium x^*: one is stationary, and others spiral outward toward the limit cycle. The latter solutions are not differentiable at $t = 0$. It is therefore possible for a solution to escape a Nash equilibrium without the solution beginning its motion in a well-defined direction. (*Hint:* Consider backward solution trajectories from initial conditions in the region bounded by the cycle.) ◇

Example 6.1.4: Zeeman's Game Consider the population game $F(x) = Ax$ generated by matching in the symmetric normal form game

$$A = \begin{pmatrix} 0 & 6 & -4 \\ -3 & 0 & 5 \\ -1 & 3 & 0 \end{pmatrix}$$

with strategy set $S = \{U, M, D\}$. The Nash equilibria of F are e_U, $x^* = (\frac{1}{3}, \frac{1}{3}, \frac{1}{3})$, and $y^* = (\frac{4}{5}, 0, \frac{1}{5})$. The best response dynamic for F is presented in figure 6.3. Solution trajectories from a majority of initial conditions are unique and converge to the pure equilibrium e_U. However, some initial conditions generate multiple solutions. Consider, for example, solutions starting at the interior Nash equilibrium x^*. There is a stationary solution at x^*, as well as solutions that head toward the vertex e_U, possibly after some delay. Other solutions head toward the Nash equilibrium y^*. Some of these converge to y^*; others leave segment x^*y^* before reaching y^*. Of those that leave, some head to e_U, and others head toward e_D and then return to x^*. If x^* is revisited, any of the behaviors just described can occur again. Therefore, there are solutions to (BR) that arrive at and depart from x^* in perpetuity. ◆

Example 6.1.5 While a strict equilibrium is locally stable under the dynamics studied so far, the set of initial conditions from which the equilibrium is reached may vary dramatically across dynamics. As an illustration, consider the population

Best Response and Projection Dynamics

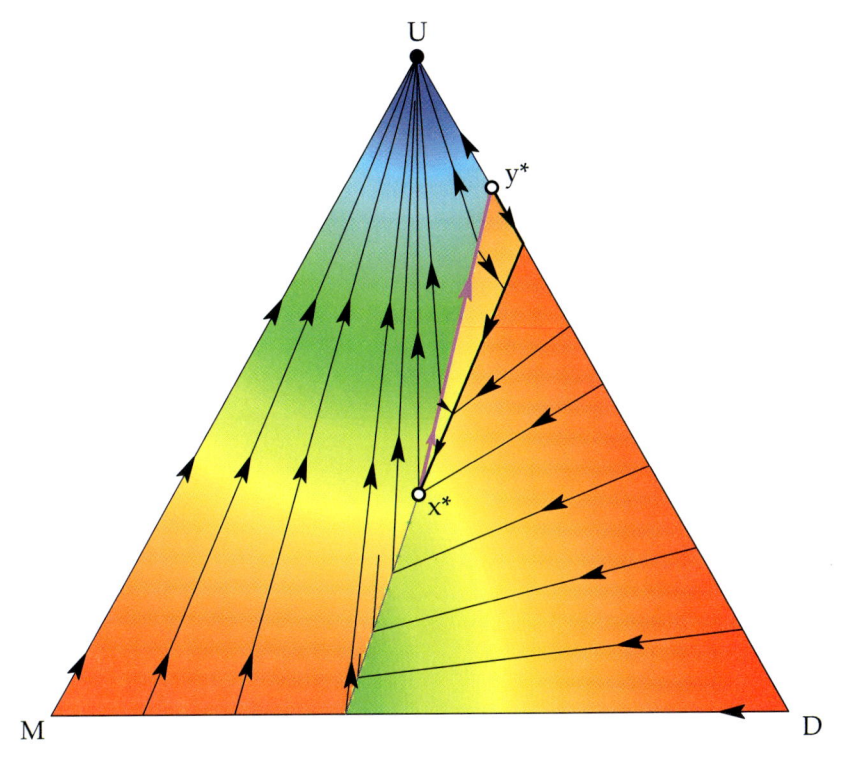

Figure 6.3
The best response dynamic in Zeeman's game.

game $F(x) = Ax$ generated by matching in the symmetric normal form game

$$A = \begin{pmatrix} 1 & -k & -\frac{1}{k} \\ 2-k^3 & 2 & 2 \\ 0 & 0 & 0 \end{pmatrix}.$$

If $k > 1$, this game has three Nash equilibria: the strict equilibria e_1 and e_2 and the mixed equilibrium $x^* = (\frac{1}{k+1}, 0, \frac{k}{k+1})$. The game has additional restricted equilibria at states e_3 and $y = (\frac{k+2}{k^3+k+1}, \frac{k^3-1}{k^3+k+1}, 0)$; these are rest points under any imitative dynamic (see section 5.4.6).

Suppose that $k = 5$, so that $x^* = (\frac{1}{6}, 0, \frac{5}{6})$ and $y = (\frac{7}{131}, \frac{124}{131}, 0) \approx (.0534, .9466, 0)$. Under the replicator dynamic (figure 6.4a), solutions from most initial conditions converge to the strict equilibrium e_1. Under the best response dynamic (figure 6.4b), solutions from most initial conditions head toward state e_3 before converging to the strict equilibrium e_2. In fact, one can show that as k grows large, the basins of e_1 under the replicator dynamic and of e_2 under the best response dynamic include nearly all initial conditions in the simplex (see the chapter notes).

(a) Replicator   (b) Best response

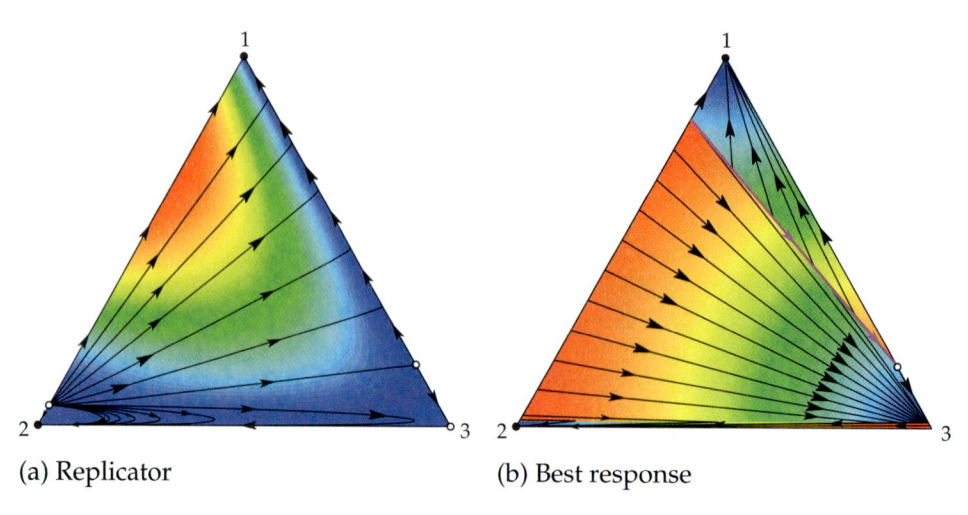

Figure 6.4
Unalike basins of attraction under imitative and optimizing dynamics.

The sources of the distinct behaviors of the two dynamics are not difficult to explain. At most states in the simplex—in particular, states that are not too close to boundaries e_1e_2 or e_2e_3—strategy 3 has a slightly higher payoff than strategy 1, and both these strategies have much higher payoffs than strategy 2: $F_3(x) > F_1(x) \gg F_2(x)$. Under the replicator dynamic, this payoff configuration implies that agents switch from strategy 2 to strategies 1 and 3 in such a way that the ratio of strategy 1 players to strategy 3 players remains nearly constant (see equation (7.39)). If the value of x_1 exceeds $x_1^* = \frac{1}{k+1}$ when virtually no strategy 2 players remain, then $F_1(x)$ will exceed $F_3(x)$, and the state will converge to equilibrium e_1.

Under the best response dynamic, the payoff ordering $F_3(x) > F_1(x) \gg F_2(x)$ implies that motion is directly toward vertex e_3; the large payoff difference between strategies 1 and 2 is of no consequence. When the number of strategy 1 players becomes small enough, strategy 2 becomes and then remains optimal, and the state converges to equilibrium e_2. ◆

6.1.3 Incentive Properties

Chapter 5 introduced two properties, positive correlation (PC) and Nash stationarity (NS), that link growth rates under evolutionary dynamics with payoffs in the underlying games.

$V_F^p(x) \neq \mathbf{0}$ implies that $V_F^p(x)'F^p(x) > 0$ for all $p \in \mathcal{P}$. (PC)

$V_F(x) = \mathbf{0}$ if and only if $x \in NE(F)$. (NS)

Best Response and Projection Dynamics

Both properties are designed for single-valued differential equations. We now establish that analogues of these two properties are satisfied by the differential inclusion (BR).

Theorem 6.1.4 *The best response dynamic satisfies*

$$(z^p)' F^p(x) = m^p \max_{j \in S^p} \hat{F}_j^p(x) \quad \text{for all } z^p \in V_F^p(x). \tag{6.7}$$

$$0 \in V_F(x) \quad \text{if and only if} \quad x \in NE(F). \tag{6.8}$$

Condition (6.7) asks that the correspondence $x \mapsto V_F^p(x)' F^p(x)$ be single-valued, always equaling the product of population p's mass and its maximal excess payoff. It follows that this map is Lipschitz continuous and non-negative, equaling zero if and only if all agents in population p are playing a best response (see lemma 5.5.3). Summing over populations shows that $V_F(x)' F(x) = \{0\}$ if and only if x is a Nash equilibrium of F.

Condition (6.8) requires that the differential inclusion $\dot{x} \in V_F(x)$ have a stationary solution at every Nash equilibrium but at no other states. As the examples show, this condition does not rule out the existence of additional solution trajectories that leave Nash equilibria.

Proof Property (6.8) is immediate. To prove property (6.7), fix $x \in X$, and let $z^p \in V_F^p(x)$. Then $z^p = m^p y^p - x^p$ for some $y^p \in M^p(F^p(x))$. Therefore,

$$(z^p)' F^p(x) = (m^p y^p - x^p)' F^p(x) = m^p \max_{j \in S^p} F_j^p(x) - m^p \bar{F}^p(x) = m^p \max_{j \in S^p} \hat{F}_j^p(x). \qquad \blacksquare$$

6.2 Perturbed Best Response Dynamics

The best response dynamic is a fundamental model of evolution in games; it provides an idealized description of the behavior of agents whose decisions condition on exact information about the current strategic environment. Of course, the flip side of exact information is discontinuity, a violation of desideratum (C) for revision protocols (see section 5.1).

We now introduce revision protocols under which agents choose best responses to payoffs that have been subjected to perturbations. The perturbations can represent actual payoff noise, but they can also represent errors in agents' perceptions of payoffs or in the agents' implementations of the best response rule. Regardless of how they are interpreted, the perturbations lead to revision protocols that are smooth functions of payoffs, and so to dynamics that can be analyzed using standard techniques.

The use of perturbed best response functions is not unique to evolutionary game theory. To mention one prominent example, researchers in experimental economics employ perturbed best response functions when attempting to rationalize experimental data. Consequently, the ideas developed in this section provide dynamic foundations for solution concepts in common use in experimental research (see the chapter notes).

6.2.1 Revision Protocols and Mean Dynamics

Perturbed best response protocols are exact target protocols defined in terms of *perturbed maximizer functions* $\tilde{M}^p \colon \mathbf{R}^{n^p} \to \mathrm{int}(\Delta^p)$:

$$\sigma^p(\pi^p) = \tilde{M}^p(\pi^p). \tag{6.9}$$

Unlike the maximizer correspondence M^p, the function $\tilde{M}^p$ is single-valued, continuous, and even differentiable. The mixed strategy $\tilde{M}^p(\pi^p) \in \mathrm{int}(\Delta^p)$ places most of its mass on the optimal pure strategies, but places positive mass on all pure strategies. Precise definitions of $\tilde{M}^p$ follow.

Example 6.2.1: Logit Choice When $p = 1$, the *logit choice function* with *noise level* $\eta > 0$ is written as

$$\tilde{M}_i(\pi) = \frac{\exp(\eta^{-1}\pi_i)}{\sum_{j \in S} \exp(\eta^{-1}\pi_j)}.$$

For any value of $\eta > 0$, each strategy receives positive probability under $\tilde{M}$ regardless of the payoff vector π. But if $\pi_i > \pi_j$ for all $j \neq i$, the probability with which strategy i is chosen approaches 1 as η approaches zero. Notice, too, that adding a constant vector to the payoff vector π has no effect on choice probabilities.

When there are just two strategies, the logit choice function reduces to

$$\tilde{M}_1(\pi) = \frac{\exp(\eta^{-1}(\pi_1 - \pi_2))}{\exp(\eta^{-1}(\pi_1 - \pi_2)) + 1} \quad \text{and} \quad \tilde{M}_1(\pi) + \tilde{M}_2(\pi) = 1.$$

In figure 6.5, we fix π_2 at 0, and graph as a function of π_1 the logit(η) choice probabilities $\tilde{M}_1(\pi)$ for $\eta = .25, .1$, and $.02$, as well as the optimal choice probabilities $M_1(\pi)$. Evidently, $\tilde{M}_1$ provides a smooth approximation of the discontinuous map M_1. While the function $\tilde{M}_1$ cannot converge uniformly to the correspondence M_1 as the noise level η goes to zero, one can show that the graph of $\tilde{M}_1$ converges uniformly in the Hausdorff metric (see the chapter notes) to the graph of M_1 as η approaches zero. ◆

The protocol (6.9) induces the *perturbed best response dynamic*

$$\dot{x}^p = m^p \tilde{M}^p(F^p(x)) - x^p \tag{6.10}$$

Best Response and Projection Dynamics

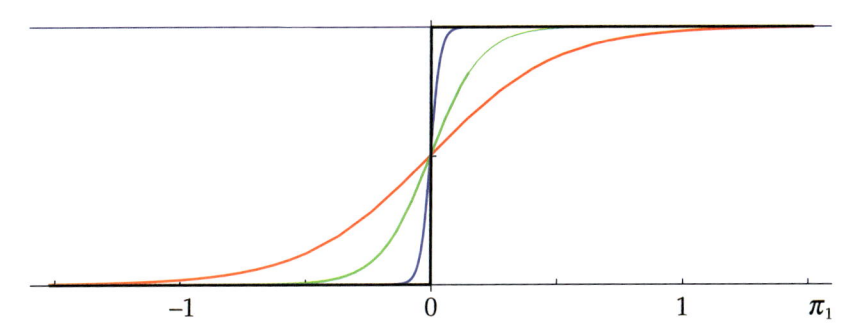

Figure 6.5
Logit choice probabilities $\tilde{M}_1(\pi_1, 0)$ for noise levels $\eta = .25$ (red), $\eta = .1$ (green), and $\eta = .02$ (blue), along with optimal choice probabilities $M_1(\pi_1, 0)$ (black).

as its mean dynamic. Equation (6.10) can also be written as

$$\dot{x}^p = m^p \tilde{B}^p(x) - x^p,$$

where the function $\tilde{B}^p = \tilde{M}^p \circ F^p$, which maps social states to mixed strategies, is the *perturbed best response function* for population p; it is a perturbed version of the best response correspondence $B^p = M^p \circ F^p$.

6.2.2 Perturbed Optimization: A Representation Theorem

We now consider two methods of defining perturbed maximizer functions. To simplify the notation, we focus on the single-population case.

The traditional method of defining $\tilde{M}$, a method with a long history in the theory of discrete choice, is based on *stochastic perturbations* of the payoffs to each *pure* strategy. In this construction, an agent chooses the best response to the vector of payoffs $\pi \in \mathbf{R}^n$, but only after the payoffs to her alternatives have been perturbed by some random vector ε.

$$\tilde{M}_i(\pi) = \mathbb{P}\left(i = \underset{j \in S}{\operatorname{argmax}} \, \pi_j + \varepsilon_j\right). \tag{6.11}$$

We require the random vector ε to be an *admissible stochastic perturbation*: it must admit a positive density on $\mathbf{R}^n$, and this density must be smooth enough that the function $\tilde{M}$ is continuously differentiable. For example, if the components ε_i are independent, standard results on convolutions imply that $\tilde{M}$ is C^1 whenever the densities of the components ε_i are bounded. In the discrete choice literature, the definition of $\tilde{M}$ via equation (6.11) is known as the *additive random utility model* (ARUM).

One can also define $\tilde{M}$ by introducing a *deterministic* perturbation of the payoffs to each *mixed* strategy. Call the function $v: \operatorname{int}(\Delta) \to \mathbf{R}$ an *admissible deterministic perturbation* if it is *differentiably strictly convex* and *steep near* bd(Δ). That is, v is admissible if its second derivative at y, $D^2 v(y) \in L_s^2(\mathbf{R}_0^n, \mathbf{R})$, is positive definite for all $y \in \text{int}(\Delta)$, and if $|\nabla v(y)|$ approaches infinity whenever y approaches bd(Δ). (Recall that $\mathbf{R}_0^n$ is an alternative notation for $T\Delta$, the tangent space of the simplex. For the definition of $L_s^2(\mathbf{R}_0^n, \mathbf{R})$, see section 3.B.3.) With an admissible v in hand, the function $\tilde{M}$ is defined by

$$\tilde{M}(\pi) = \underset{y \in \text{int}(\Delta)}{\text{argmax}} \left(y' \pi - v(y) \right). \tag{6.12}$$

One interpretation of the function v is that it represents a control cost that becomes large whenever an agent puts too little probability on any particular pure strategy. Because the base payoffs to each strategy are bounded, the steepness of v near bd(Δ) implies that it is never optimal for an agent to choose probabilities too close to zero.

Note that under either definition, choice probabilities under $\tilde{M}$ are unaffected by uniform shifts in the payoff vector π. The projection of $\mathbf{R}^n$ onto $\mathbf{R}_0^n$, $\Phi = I - \frac{1}{n}\mathbf{1}\mathbf{1}'$, employs just such a shift, so this property of $\tilde{M}$ can be expressed as follows:

$$\tilde{M}(\pi) = \tilde{M}(\Phi \pi) \quad \text{for all } \pi \in \mathbf{R}^n.$$

With this motivation, we define $\bar{M} \colon \mathbf{R}_0^n \to \text{int}(\Delta)$ to be the restriction of $\tilde{M}$ to the subspace $\mathbf{R}_0^n$.

The stochastic construction (6.11) is the traditional way of defining perturbed maximizer functions, and this construction has more intuitive appeal than the deterministic construction (6.12). But the latter construction is clearly more convenient for analysis. Under (6.11) choice probabilities must expressed as cumbersome multiple integrals, whereas under (6.12) they are obtained as interior maximizers of a strictly concave function.

Happily, we need not trade off intuitive appeal for convenience: every $\tilde{M}$ defined via equation (6.11) can be represented in form (6.12).

Theorem 6.2.1 *Let $\tilde{M}$ be a perturbed maximizer function defined in terms of an admissible stochastic perturbation ε via equation* (6.11). *Then $\tilde{M}$ satisfies equation* (6.12) *for some admissible deterministic perturbation v. In fact, $\bar{M} = \tilde{M}|_{\mathbf{R}_0^n}$ and ∇v are invertible, and $\bar{M} = (\nabla v)^{-1}$.*

Taking as given the initial statements in the theorem, it is easy to verify the last one. Suppose that $\tilde{M}$ (and hence $\bar{M}$) can be derived from the admissible deterministic perturbation v, that the gradient $\nabla v \colon \text{int}(\Delta) \to \mathbf{R}_0^n$ is invertible, and that the payoff vector π is in $\mathbf{R}_0^n$. Then $y^* = \bar{M}(\pi)$ satisfies

$$y^* = \underset{y \in \text{int}(\Delta)}{\text{argmax}} \left(y' \pi - v(y) \right).$$

Best Response and Projection Dynamics

This is a strictly concave maximization problem with an interior solution. Taking the first-order condition with respect to directions in $\mathbf{R}_0^n$ yields

$$\Phi(\pi - \nabla v(y^*)) = 0.$$

Since π and $\nabla v(y^*)$ are already in $\mathbf{R}_0^n$, the projection Φ does nothing, so rearranging yields

$$\tilde{M}(\pi) = y^* = (\nabla v)^{-1}(\pi).$$

In light of this argument, the main task in proving theorem 6.2.1 is to show that a function v with the desired properties exists. Accomplishing this requires the use of the Legendre transform, a classic tool from convex analysis. Appendix 6.B explains the basic properties of the Legendre transform. This device is used to prove the representation theorem in appendix 6.C, where some auxiliary results are also presented.

One such result is worth mentioning now. Theorem 6.2.1 says that every $\tilde{M}$ defined in terms of stochastic perturbations can be represented in terms of deterministic perturbations. Exercise 6.2.2 shows that the converse statement is false, and thus that the deterministic definition of $\tilde{M}$ is strictly more general than the stochastic one.

Exercise 6.2.2 Show that when $n \geq 4$, there is no stochastic perturbation of payoffs that yields the same choice probabilities as the admissible deterministic perturbation $v(y) = -\sum_{j \in S} \log y_j$. (*Hint:* Use theorem 6.C.6 in appendix 6.C.) ◇

6.2.3 Logit Choice and the Logit Dynamic

Example 6.2.1 introduced the best-known example of a perturbed maximizer function: the *logit choice function* with *noise level* $\eta > 0$.

$$\tilde{M}_i(\pi) = \frac{\exp(\eta^{-1} \pi_i)}{\sum_{j \in S} \exp(\eta^{-1} \pi_j)}. \tag{6.13}$$

This function generates as its mean dynamic the *logit dynamic* with *noise level* η:

$$\dot{x}_i^p = m^p \frac{\exp(\eta^{-1} F_i^p(x))}{\sum_{j \in S^p} \exp(\eta^{-1} F_j^p(x))} - x_i^p. \tag{L}$$

Rest points of logit dynamics are called *logit equilibria*.

Example 6.2.2 Figure 6.6 presents phase diagrams for 123 Coordination,

$$F(x) = Ax = \begin{pmatrix} 1 & 0 & 0 \\ 0 & 2 & 0 \\ 0 & 0 & 3 \end{pmatrix} \begin{pmatrix} x_1 \\ x_2 \\ x_3 \end{pmatrix} = \begin{pmatrix} x_1 \\ 2x_2 \\ 3x_3 \end{pmatrix},$$

(a) $\eta = .001$

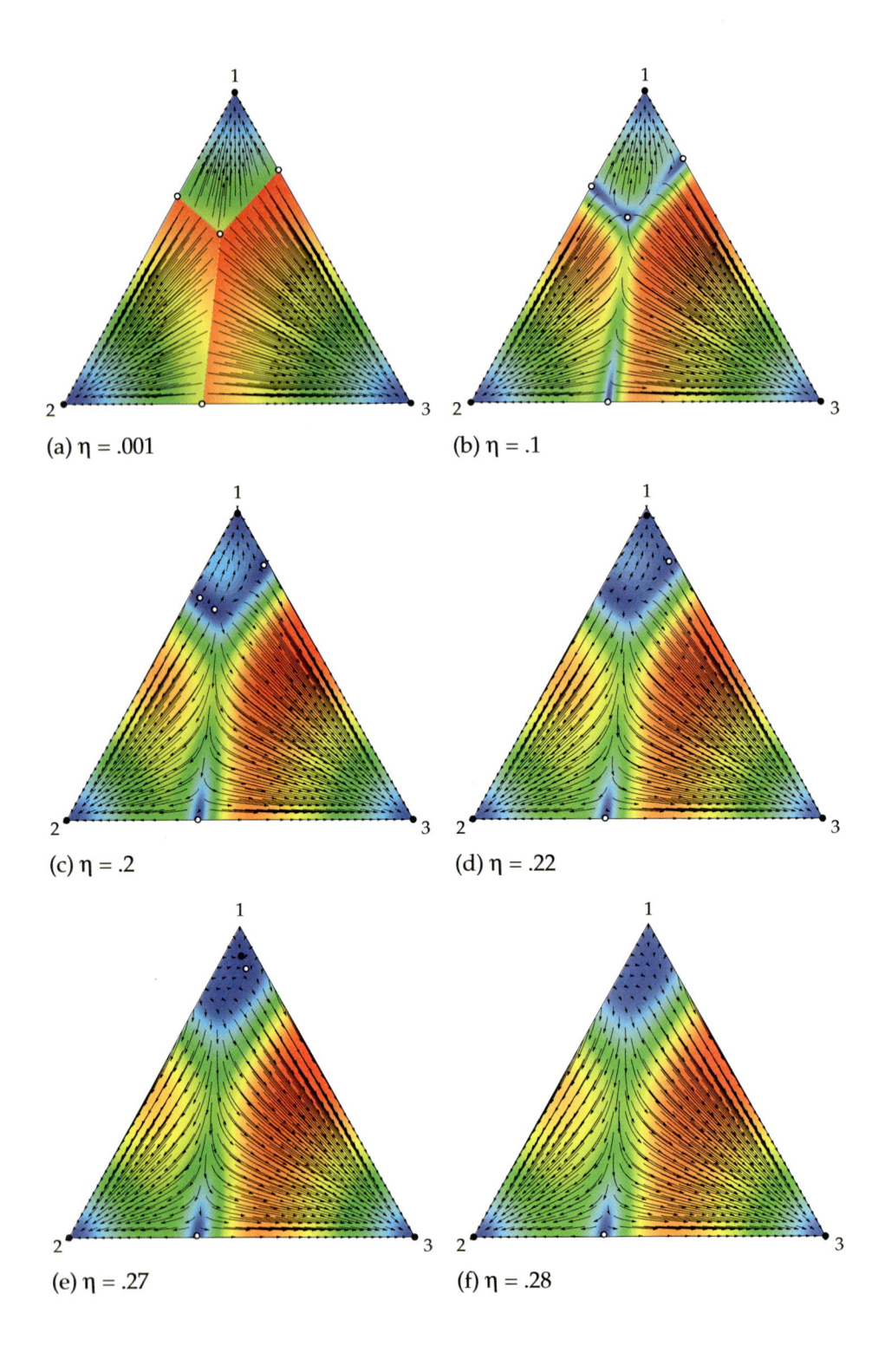

(b) $\eta = .1$

(c) $\eta = .2$

(d) $\eta = .22$

(e) $\eta = .27$

(f) $\eta = .28$

(g) η = .4

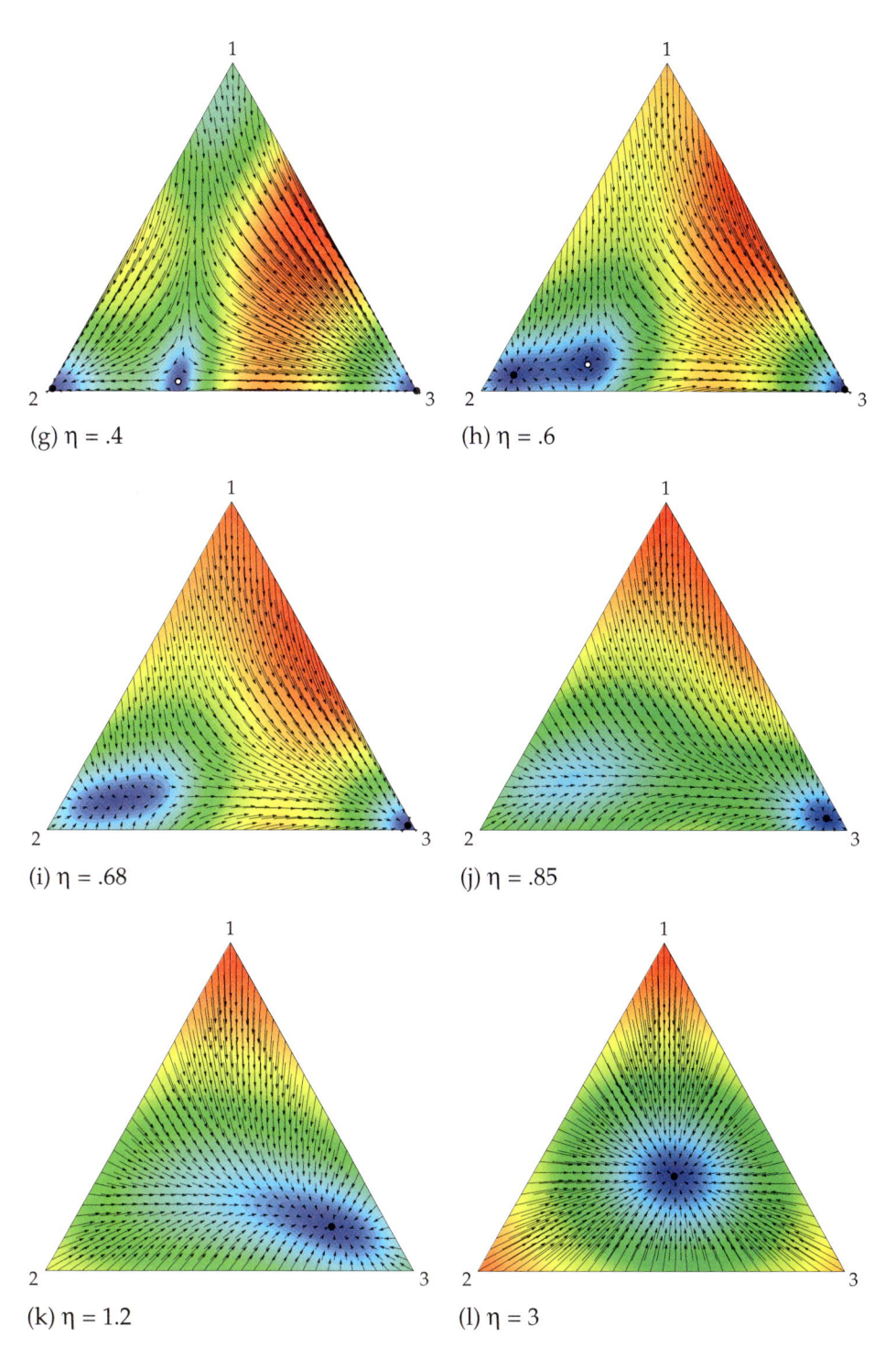

(h) η = .6

(i) η = .68

(j) η = .85

(k) η = 1.2

(l) η = 3

Figure 6.6
Logit dynamics in 123 Coordination.

under logit dynamics with a range of noise levels. As η passes from .01 to 1, the dynamics pass through four distinct regimes. At the lowest noise levels, the dynamics admit seven rest points, three stable and four unstable, corresponding to the seven Nash equilibria of F. When η reaches $\approx .22$, two of the unstable rest points annihilate one another, leaving five rest points in total. At $\eta \approx .28$, the stable rest point corresponding to Nash equilibrium e_1 and an unstable rest point eliminate one another, so that three rest points remain. Finally, when $\eta \approx .68$, the stable rest point corresponding to Nash equilibrium e_2 and an unstable rest point annihilate each other, leaving just a single stable rest point. As grows large η, the last rest point ultimately converges to the central state $(\frac{1}{3}, \frac{1}{3}, \frac{1}{3})$.

This example provides an illustration of a deep topological result called the *Poincaré-Hopf theorem*. In the present two-dimensional context, this theorem ensures that generically, the number of sinks plus the number of sources equals the number of saddles plus 1. ◆

Example 6.2.3: Stochastic Derivation of Logit Choice We can derive the logit choice function from stochastic perturbations that are i.i.d. with the *double exponential distribution*:

$$\mathbb{P}(\varepsilon_i \leq c) = \exp(-\exp(-\eta^{-1}c - \gamma)),$$

where $\gamma = \lim_{n \to \infty} (\sum_{k=1}^{n} \frac{1}{k} - \log n) \approx 0.5772$ is Euler's constant. For intuition, we mention without proof that $\mathbb{E}\varepsilon_i = 0$ and $\text{Var}(\varepsilon_i) = \frac{\eta^2 \pi^2}{6}$, so that $\text{SD}(\varepsilon_i) \approx 1.2826\eta$.

To see that these perturbations generate logit choice, note that the density of ε_i is $f(x) = \eta^{-1} \exp(-\eta^{-1}x - \gamma) \exp(-\exp(-\eta^{-1}x - \gamma))$. Using the substitutions $y = \exp(-\eta^{-1}x - \gamma)$ and $m_j = \exp(\eta^{-1}\pi_j)$, we compute as follows:

$$\mathbb{P}\left(i = \text{argmax}_{j \in S} \pi_j + \varepsilon_j\right) = \int_0^\infty f(x) \prod_{j \neq i} F(\pi_i + x - \pi_j)\, dx$$

$$= -\int_0^\infty \eta^{-1} y \exp(-y) \prod_{j \neq i} \exp\left(-y \frac{m_j}{m_i}\right) \frac{\eta}{y}\, dy$$

$$= -\int_0^\infty \exp\left(-y \sum_{j \in S} \frac{m_j}{m_i}\right) dy$$

$$= \frac{m_i}{\sum_{j \in S} m_j}$$

$$= \frac{\exp(\eta^{-1}\pi_i)}{\sum_{j \in S} \exp(\eta^{-1}\pi_j)}. \qquad ◆$$

Exercise 6.2.3: Deterministic Derivation of Logit Choice According to the representation theorem, it must also be possible to derive the logit choice function from an admissible deterministic perturbation. Show that this is accomplished using the (negated) entropy function $v(y) = \eta \sum_{j \in S} y_j \log y_j$. ◇

The next exercise gives explicit formulas for various functions from the proof of the representation theorem in the case of logit choice. Included is the derivative matrix $D\tilde{M}(\pi)$, a useful item in analyses of local stability (see chapter 8.) The exercise also shows how the entropy function v can be derived from the function $\tilde{M}$.

Exercise 6.2.4: Additional Results on Logit Choice

i. Show that $\tilde{\mu}(\pi) = \eta \log(\sum_{j \in S} \exp(\eta^{-1}\pi_j))$ is a potential function for $\tilde{M}$. (For the interpretation of this function, see observation 6.C.3 and theorem 6.C.4)

ii. Let $\bar{\mu}$ be the restriction of $\tilde{\mu}$ to $\mathbf{R}_0^n$, so that $\nabla\bar{\mu}(\pi) = \Phi\tilde{M}(\pi) = \tilde{M}(\pi) - \frac{1}{n}\mathbf{1} = \bar{M}(\pi) - \frac{1}{n}\mathbf{1}$. For $y \in \text{int}(\Delta)$, let $\hat{y} \equiv y - \frac{1}{n}\mathbf{1}$. Show that

$$(\nabla\bar{\mu})^{-1}(\hat{y}) = \bar{M}^{-1}(y) = \eta \begin{pmatrix} \log y_1 - \frac{1}{n}\sum_{j \in S}\log y_j \\ \vdots \\ \log y_n - \frac{1}{n}\sum_{j \in S}\log y_j \end{pmatrix}.$$

iii. Let $(C^*, \bar{\mu}^*)$ be the Legendre transform of $(\mathbf{R}_0^n, \bar{\mu})$, and define $v\colon \text{int}(\Delta) \to \mathbf{R}$ by $v(y) = \bar{\mu}^*(\hat{y})$. Show by direct computation that $v(y) = \eta \sum_{j \in S} y_j \log y_j$.

iv. Show that $\nabla v(y) = \bar{M}^{-1}(y)$. (*Hint:* Let $\tilde{v}$ be the natural extension of v to $\mathbf{R}_+^n$, and use the fact $\nabla v(y) = \Phi \nabla \tilde{v}(y)$.)

v. Show that $\nabla^2 v(y) = \eta\, \Phi\, \text{diag}([y^{-1}])\Phi$, where $[y^{-1}]_j = y_j^{-1}$ for all $j \in S$.

vi. Show that if $\pi \in \mathbf{R}_0^n$, then

$$D\tilde{M}(\pi) = \nabla^2 \tilde{\mu}(\pi) = \eta^{-1}\big(\text{diag}(\bar{M}(\pi)) - \bar{M}(\pi)\bar{M}(\pi)'\big) = \nabla^2\bar{\mu}(\pi) = D\bar{M}(\pi).$$

vii. Show that $\nabla^2 v(\bar{M}(\pi)) = (\nabla^2\bar{\mu}(\pi))^{-1}$ when these matrices are viewed as linear maps from $\mathbf{R}_0^n$ to $\mathbf{R}_0^n$. (*Hint:* Since both maps are of full rank on $\mathbf{R}_0^n$, it is enough to show that $\nabla^2\bar{\mu}(\pi)\nabla^2 v(\bar{M}(\pi)) = \Phi$, the orthogonal projection onto $\mathbf{R}_0^n$.) ◇

Exercise 6.2.5 Suppose that $\tilde{M}$ is a perturbed maximizer function derived from an admissible deterministic perturbation as in equation (6.12) (or from an admissible stochastic perturbation as in equation (6.11)). Show that if $\tilde{M}$ can be expressed as

$$\tilde{M}_i(\pi) = \frac{\alpha(\pi_i)}{\sum_{j \in S}\alpha(\pi_j)} \tag{6.14}$$

for some increasing differentiable function $\alpha\colon \mathbf{R} \to (0, \infty)$, then $\tilde{M}$ is the logit choice function with some noise level $\eta > 0$. (*Hint:* Combine equation (6.14) with the fact that the derivative matrix $D\tilde{M}(\pi)$ must be symmetric; see corollary 6.C.5 and theorem 6.C.6.) ◇

Exercise 6.2.6: The Variable-Rate Logit Dynamic The *variable-rate logit dynamic* with noise level $\eta > 0$ is defined by

$$\dot{x}_i^p = m^p \exp(\eta^{-1} F_i^p(x)) - x_i^p \sum_{j \in S^p} \exp(\eta^{-1} F_j^p(x)). \tag{6.15}$$

The previous exercise shows that the logit dynamic is the only perturbed best response dynamic that admits a modification of this sort.

i. Describe a simple revision protocol that generates this dynamic, and provide an interpretation.

ii. Show that if $p = 1$, then (6.15) is equivalent to the logit dynamic (L) up to a change in the speed at which solution trajectories are traversed. Explain why this is not the case when $p \geq 2$.

iii. Compare this dynamic with the excess payoff dynamics from chapter 5. Explain why those dynamics cannot be modified to resemble the logit dynamic (L). ◇

6.2.4 Perturbed Incentive Properties via Virtual Payoffs

Because they incorporate payoff disturbances, perturbed best response dynamics cannot satisfy positive correlation (PC) or Nash stationarity (NS). However, they do satisfy suitably perturbed versions of the two incentive properties. In light of the representation theorem, there is no loss of generality in focusing on dynamics generated by admissible deterministic perturbations $v = (v^1, \ldots, v^p)$.

The set of Nash equilibria of F can be described in terms of the best response correspondences B^p:

$NE(F) = \{x \in X \colon x^p \in m^p B^p(x) \text{ for all } p \in \mathcal{P}\}.$

In similar fashion, we define the set of *perturbed equilibria* of the pair (F, v) in terms of the perturbed best response functions $\tilde{B}^p$:

$PE(F, v) = \{x \in X \colon x^p = m^p \tilde{B}^p(x) \text{ for all } p \in \mathcal{P}\}.$

By definition, the rest points of the perturbed best response dynamic (6.10) are the perturbed equilibria of (F, v).

Best Response and Projection Dynamics

Observation 6.2.7 *All perturbed best response dynamics satisfy* perturbed stationarity:

$$V(x) = 0 \quad \text{if and only if} \quad x \in PE(F, v). \tag{6.16}$$

We can obtain an alternative characterization of perturbed equilibrium by introducing the notion of virtual payoffs. Define the *virtual payoffs* $\tilde{F}$: $\text{int}(X) \to \mathbf{R}^n$ for the pair (F, v) by

$$\tilde{F}^p(x) = F^p(x) - \nabla v^p(\tfrac{1}{m^p} x^p).$$

The virtual payoff function for population p is the difference between the population's true payoff function and the gradient of its deterministic perturbation.

For intuition, consider the single-population case. When x is far from the boundary of the simplex X, the perturbation v is relatively flat, so the virtual payoffs $\tilde{F}(x)$ are close to the true payoffs $F(x)$. But near the boundary of X, true and virtual payoffs are quite different. For example, when x_i is the only component of x that is close to zero, then for each alternative strategy $j \neq i$, moving inward in direction $e_i - e_j$ sharply decreases the value of v; thus, the directional derivative $\frac{\partial v}{\partial (e_i - e_j)}(x)$ is large in absolute value and negative. It follows that the difference $\tilde{F}_i(x) - \tilde{F}_j(x)$ between these strategies' virtual payoffs is large and positive. In other words, rare strategies are quite desirable in the virtual game $\tilde{F}$.

Individual agents do not use virtual payoffs to decide how to act. To obtain the maximized function in definition (6.12) from the virtual payoff function, one must replace the normalized population state $\frac{1}{m^p} x^p$ with the vector of choice probabilities y^p. But at perturbed equilibria, $\frac{1}{m^p} x^p$ and y^p agree. Therefore, perturbed equilibria of (F, v) correspond to Nash equilibria of the virtual game $\tilde{F}$.

Theorem 6.2.8 *Let $x \in X$ be a social state. Then $x \in PE(F, v)$ if and only if $\Phi \tilde{F}^p(x) = 0$ for all $p \in \mathcal{P}$.*

The equality $\Phi \tilde{F}^p(x) = 0$ means that $\tilde{F}^p(x)$ is a constant vector. Since uncommon strategies are quite desirable in the virtual game $\tilde{F}$, no state that includes an unused strategy can be a Nash equilibrium of $\tilde{F}$; thus, equality of all virtual payoffs in each population is the right definition of Nash equilibrium in $\tilde{F}$.

Theorem 6.2.8 follows immediately from perturbed stationarity (6.16) and lemma 6.2.9.

Lemma 6.2.9 *Let $x \in X$ be a social state. Then $V^p(x) = 0$ if and only if $\Phi \tilde{F}^p(x) = 0$.*

Proof Using the facts that $\tilde{M}^p(\pi^p) = \tilde{M}^p(\Phi \pi^p)$, that $\tilde{M}^p = (\nabla v^p)^{-1}$, and that the range of ∇v^p is $\mathbf{R}_0^{n^p}$ (so that $\nabla v^p = \Phi \circ \nabla v^p$), one obtains

$$V^p(x) = \mathbf{0} \Leftrightarrow m^p \tilde{M}^p(F^p(x)) = x^p$$

$$\Leftrightarrow \bar{M}^p(\Phi F^p(x)) = \tfrac{1}{m^p} x^p$$

$$\Leftrightarrow \Phi F^p(x) = \nabla v^p(\tfrac{1}{m^p} x^p)$$

$$\Leftrightarrow \Phi \tilde{F}^p(x) = \mathbf{0}. \qquad \blacksquare$$

Turning now to disequilibrium behavior, recall that positive correlation is defined in terms of inner products of growth rate vectors and payoff vectors:

$$V_F^p(x) \neq \mathbf{0} \quad \text{implies that} \quad V_F^p(x)' F^p(x) > 0 \quad \text{for all } p \in \mathcal{P}. \tag{PC}$$

In light of the preceding discussion, the natural analogue of property (PC) for perturbed best response dynamics replaces the true payoffs $F^p(x)$ with virtual payoffs $\tilde{F}^p(x)$. Doing so yields *virtual positive correlation*:

$$V^p(x) \neq \mathbf{0} \quad \text{implies that} \quad V^p(x)' \tilde{F}^p(x) > 0 \quad \text{for all } p \in \mathcal{P}. \tag{6.17}$$

All perturbed best response dynamics heed this property.

Theorem 6.2.10 *All perturbed best response dynamics satisfy virtual positive correlation* (6.17).

Proof Let $x \in X$ be a social state at which $V^p(x) \neq \mathbf{0}$. Then by definition,

$$y^p \equiv \tilde{M}^p(F^p(x)) = \bar{M}^p(\Phi F^p(x)) \neq \tfrac{1}{m^p} x^p. \tag{6.18}$$

Since $\nabla v^p = (\bar{M}^p)^{-1}$, the equality in expression (6.18) can be rewritten as $\nabla v^p(y^p) = \Phi F^p(x)$. Therefore, since $V^p(x) \in TX^p$,

$$V^p(x)' \tilde{F}^p(x) = \left(m^p \tilde{M}^p(F^p(x)) - x^p \right)' \Phi \tilde{F}^p(x)$$

$$= \left(m^p \bar{M}^p(\Phi F^p(x)) - x^p \right)' \left(\Phi F^p(x) - \nabla v^p(\tfrac{1}{m^p} x^p) \right)$$

$$= m^p \left(y^p - \tfrac{1}{m^p} x^p \right)' \left(\nabla v^p(y^p) - \nabla v^p(\tfrac{1}{m^p} x^p) \right) > 0,$$

where the final inequality follows from the fact that $y^p \neq \tfrac{1}{m^p} x^p$ and from the strict convexity of v^p. $\blacksquare$

6.3 The Projection Dynamic

6.3.1 Definition

Our main payoff monotonicity condition for evolutionary dynamics is positive correlation (PC). In geometric terms, (PC) requires that at each state where

Best Response and Projection Dynamics

population p is not at rest, the growth rate vector $V^p(x)$ must form an acute angle with the payoff vector $F^p(x)$. Put differently, (PC) demands that growth rate vectors not distort payoff vectors to too great a degree. Is there an evolutionary dynamic that minimizes this distortion?

If the vector field V is to define an evolutionary dynamic, each growth rate vector $V(x)$ must represent a feasible direction of motion, in the sense of lying in the tangent cone $TX(x)$. To minimize distortion, one can always take $V(x)$ to be the closest point in $TX(x)$ to the payoff vector $F(x)$.

Definition *The* projection dynamic *associates each population game $F \in \mathcal{F}$ with a differential equation*

$$\dot{x} = \Pi_{TX(x)}(F(x)), \tag{P}$$

where $\Pi_{TX(x)}$ is the closest point projection of $\mathbf{R}^n$ onto the tangent cone $TX(x)$.

It is easy to provide an explicit formula for (P) at social states in the interior of X. Since at such states $TX(x) = TX$, the closest point projection $\Pi_{TX(x)}$ is simply Φ, the orthogonal projection onto the subspace TX. In fact, whenever $x^p \in \text{int}(X^p)$, we have that

$$\dot{x}_i^p = (\Phi F^p(x))_i = F_i^p(x) - \frac{1}{n} \sum_{k \in S} F_k^p(x).$$

Thus, when x^p is an interior population state, the growth rate of strategy $i \in S^p$ is the difference between its payoff and the unweighted average of the payoffs to population p's strategies.

When x is a boundary state, the projection $\Pi_{TX(x)}$ does not reduce to an orthogonal projection, so providing an explicit formula for (P) becomes more complicated. Exercise 6.3.1 describes the possibilities in a three-strategy game, and exercise 6.3.2 provides an explicit formula for the general case.

Exercise 6.3.1 Let F be a three-strategy game. Give an explicit formula for $V(x) = \Pi_{TX(x)} F(x)$ when

i. $x \in \text{int}(X)$,

ii. $x_1 = 0$ but $x_2, x_3 > 0$,

iii. $x_1 = 1$. ◇

Exercise 6.3.2 Let F be an arbitrary single-population game. Show that the projection $\Pi_{TX(x)}(v)$ can be expressed as follows:

$$(\Pi_{TX(x)}(v))_i = \begin{cases} v_i - \frac{1}{\#S(v,x)} \sum_{j \in S(v,x)} v_j & \text{if } i \in S(v,x), \\ 0 & \text{otherwise.} \end{cases}$$

Here, the set $S(v, x) \subseteq S$ contains all strategies in support(x) along with any subset of $S -$ support(x) that maximizes the average $\frac{1}{\#S(v,x)} \sum_{j \in S(v,x)} v_j$. ◇

6.3.2 Solution Trajectories

The dynamic (P) is clearly discontinuous at the boundary of X, so the existence and uniqueness results for Lipschitz continuous differential equations do not apply. Nevertheless, the following result holds; it is an immediate consequence of theorem 6.A.4.

Theorem 6.3.3 *Fix a Lipschitz continuous population game F. Then for each $\xi \in X$, there exists a unique Carathéodory solution $\{x_t\}_{t \geq 0}$ to the projection dynamic (P) with $x_0 = \xi$. Moreover, solutions to (P) are Lipschitz continuous in their initial conditions: if $\{x_t\}_{t \geq 0}$ and $\{y_t\}_{t \geq 0}$ are solutions to (P), then $|y_t - x_t| \leq |y_0 - x_0| e^{Kt}$ for all $t \geq 0$, where K is the Lipschitz coefficient for F.*

Theorem 6.3.3 shows that the discontinuous differential equation (P) enjoys many of the properties of Lipschitz continuous differential equations. But there are important differences between the two types of dynamics. One difference is that solutions to (P) are solutions in the Carathéodory sense, and so can have kinks at a measure zero set of times. Other differences are more subtle. For instance, while the theorem ensures the uniqueness of the forward solution trajectory from each state $\xi \in X$, backward solutions need not be unique. It is therefore possible for distinct solution trajectories of the projection dynamic to merge with one another.

Example 6.3.1 Figure 6.7 presents phase diagrams for the projection dynamic in good RPS ($w = 2, l = 1$), standard RPS ($w = l = 1$), and bad RPS ($w = 1, l = 2$). In all three games, most solutions spiral around the Nash equilibrium $x^* = (\frac{1}{3}, \frac{1}{3}, \frac{1}{3})$.

In good RPS (figure 6.7a), all solutions converge to the Nash equilibrium. Solutions that begin close to a vertex hit and then travel along an edge of the simplex before heading into the interior of the simplex forever. Thus, there is a portion of each edge that is traversed by solutions starting from a positive measure set of initial conditions.

In standard RPS (figure 6.7b), all solutions enter closed orbits at a fixed distance from x^*. Solutions starting at distance $\frac{1}{\sqrt{6}}$ or greater from x^* (i.e., all solutions at least as far from x^* as the state $(0, \frac{1}{2}, \frac{1}{2})$) quickly enter the closed orbit at distance $\frac{1}{\sqrt{6}}$ from x^*; other solutions maintain their initial distance from x^* forever.

In bad RPS (figure 6.7c), all solutions other than the one starting at x^* enter the same closed orbit. This orbit alternates between segments through the interior of X and segments along the boundaries.

Best Response and Projection Dynamics   201

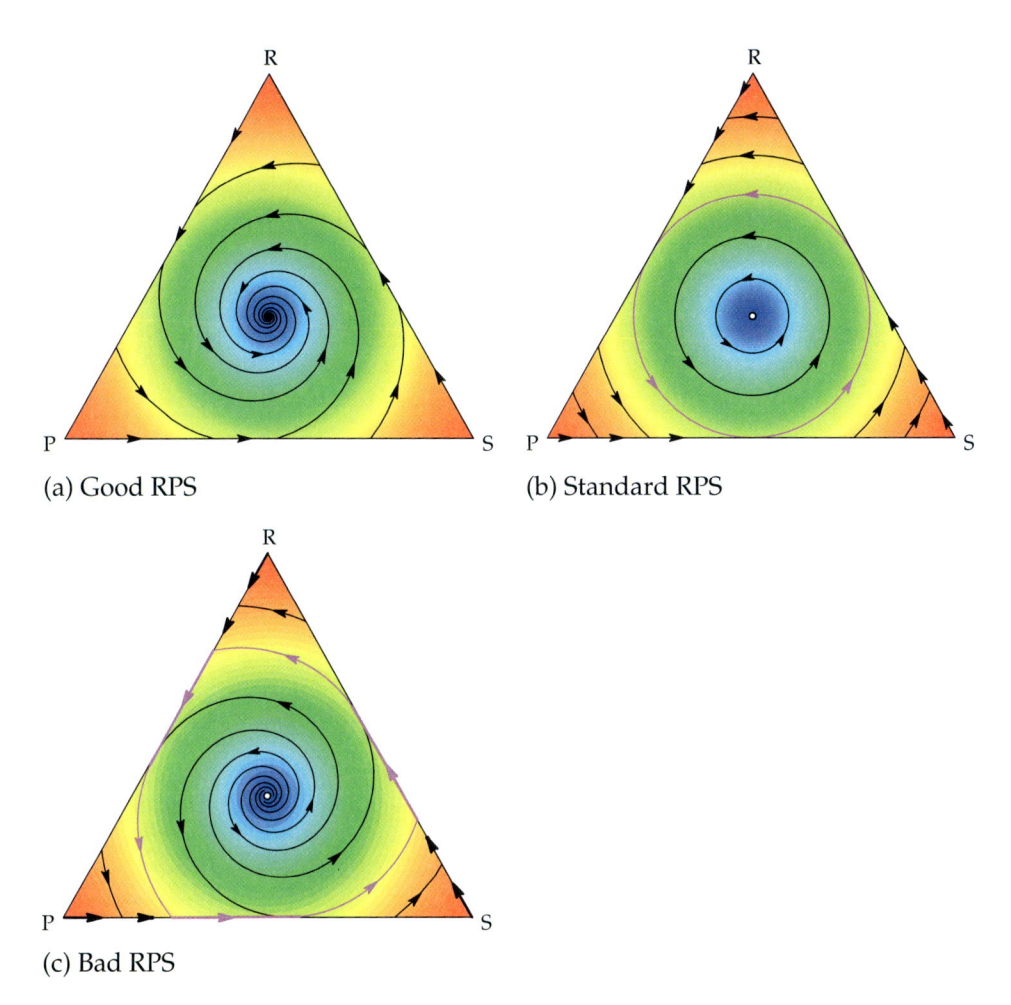

(a) Good RPS

(b) Standard RPS

(c) Bad RPS

Figure 6.7
The projection dynamic in three Rock-Paper-Scissors games.

Notice that in all three cases, solution trajectories starting in the interior of the state space can reach the boundary in finite time. This is impossible under any of the previous dynamics, including the best response dynamic. ◆

Exercise 6.3.4

i. Under what conditions is the dynamic (P) described by $\dot{x} = \Phi F(x)$ at all states $x \in X$ (i.e., not just at interior states)?

ii. Suppose that $F(x) = Ax$ is generated by matching in the symmetric normal form game A. What do the conditions from part (i) reduce to in this case? Note that under these conditions, $\dot x = \Phi A x$ is a linear differential equation; it is therefore possible to write down explicit formulas for the solution trajectories (see chapter 8). ◇

6.3.3 Incentive Properties

That solutions to the projection dynamic exist, are unique, and are continuous in their initial conditions is not obvious. But given this fact and the manner in which the dynamic is defined, it is not surprising that the dynamic satisfies both of our incentive properties. The proofs of these properties are simple applications of the Moreau decomposition theorem: given any closed convex cone $K \subseteq \mathbf{R}^n$ and any vector $\pi \in \mathbf{R}^n$, the projections $\Pi_K(\pi)$ and $\Pi_{K^\circ}(\pi)$ are the unique vectors satisfying $\Pi_K(\pi) \in K$, $\Pi_{K^\circ}(\pi) \in K^\circ$, and $\Pi_K(\pi) + \Pi_{K^\circ}(\pi) = \pi$ (see section 2.A.4).

Theorem 6.3.5 *The projection dynamic satisfies positive correlation* (PC) *and Nash stationarity* (NS).

Proof Using the Moreau decomposition theorem and the normal cone characterization of Nash equilibrium (see theorem 2.3.2), we find that

$$\Pi_{TX(x)}(F(x)) = \mathbf{0} \Leftrightarrow F(x) \in NX(x) \Leftrightarrow x \in NE(F),$$

establishing (NS). To prove (PC), again use the Moreau decomposition theorem:

$$V^p(x)' F^p(x) = \Pi_{TX^p(x^p)}(F^p(x))' \left(\Pi_{TX^p(x^p)}(F^p(x)) + \Pi_{NX^p(x^p)}(F^p(x)) \right)$$

$$= |\Pi_{TX^p(x^p)}(F(x^p))|^2$$

$$\geq 0.$$

The inequality binds if and only if $\Pi_{TX^p(x^p)}(F^p(x)) = V^p(x) = \mathbf{0}$. ∎

6.3.4 Revision Protocols and Connections with the Replicator Dynamic

To this point, the projection dynamic has been motivated entirely through geometric considerations. Can this dynamic be derived from a model of individual choice? This section describes revision protocols that generate the projection dynamic as their mean dynamics. These protocols can be used to argue that the projection dynamic models "revision driven by insecurity." The analysis reveals close connections between the projection dynamic and the replicator dynamic that will be developed further in the next chapter. We focus here on the single-population setting; the extension to multipopulation settings is straightforward.

At interior states the connections between the replicator and projection dynamics are especially strong. Chapter 4 introduced three revision protocols that generate the replicator dynamic as their mean dynamics:

Best Response and Projection Dynamics

$$\rho_{ij}(\pi, x) = x_j[\pi_j - \pi_i]_+. \tag{6.19}$$

$$\rho_{ij}(\pi, x) = x_j(K - \pi_i). \tag{6.20}$$

$$\rho_{ij}(\pi, x) = x_j(\pi_j + K). \tag{6.21}$$

The x_j term in each formula reflects the fact that these protocols are driven by imitation. For instance, to implement the first protocol, an agent whose clock rings picks an opponent from her population at random; she then imitates this opponent only if the opponent's payoff is higher, doing so with probability proportional to the payoff difference. The x_j term in these protocols endows their mean dynamic with a special functional form: the growth rate of each strategy is proportional to its prevalence in the population. For protocol (6.19), the derivation of the mean dynamic proceeds as follows:

$$\dot{x}_i = \sum_{j \in S} x_j \rho_{ji}(F(x), x) - x_i \sum_{j \in S} \rho_{ij}(F(x), x)$$

$$= \sum_{j \in S} x_j x_i [F_i(x) - F_j(x)]_+ - x_i \sum_{j \in S} x_j [F_j(x) - F_i(x)]_+$$

$$= x_i \sum_{j \in S} x_j (F_i(x) - F_j(x))$$

$$= x_i \left(F_i(x) - \sum_{j \in S} x_j F_j(x) \right).$$

To derive the projection dynamic on $\text{int}(X)$, we use analogues of these revision protocols, replacing x_j with $\frac{1}{nx_i}$:

$$\rho_{ij}(\pi, x) = \frac{[\pi_j - \pi_i]_+}{nx_i}. \tag{6.22}$$

$$\rho_{ij}(\pi, x) = \frac{K - \pi_i}{nx_i}. \tag{6.23}$$

$$\rho_{ij}(\pi, x) = \frac{\pi_j + K}{nx_i}. \tag{6.24}$$

While in each imitative protocol ρ_{ij} is *proportional* to the mass of agents playing the *candidate strategy j*, in the preceding protocols ρ_{ij} is *inversely proportional* to the mass of agents playing the *current strategy i*. One can therefore characterize the projection dynamic as capturing "revision driven by insecurity," because it describes the behavior of agents who are uncomfortable playing strategies not used by many others.

It is easy to verify that protocols (6.22), (6.23), and (6.24) all induce the projection dynamic on the interior of the state space. In the case of protocol (6.22), the calculation proceeds as follows:

$$\dot x_i = \sum_{j \in S} x_j \rho_{ji}(F(x), x) - x_i \sum_{j \in S} \rho_{ij}(F(x), x)$$

$$= \sum_{j \in S} x_j \frac{[F_i(x) - F_j(x)]_+}{nx_j} - x_i \sum_{j \in S} \frac{[F_j(x) - F_i(x)]_+}{nx_i}$$

$$= \frac{1}{n} \sum_{j \in S} (F_i(x) - F_j(x))$$

$$= F_i(x) - \frac{1}{n} \sum_{j \in S} F_j(x).$$

Because of the $\frac{1}{x_i}$ term in the revision protocol, this mean dynamic does not depend directly on the value of x_i, allowing the disappearance rates of rare strategies to stay bounded away from zero. In other words, it is because unpopular strategies can be abandoned quite rapidly that solutions to the projection dynamic can travel from the interior to the boundary of the state space in a finite amount of time.

Except in cases where the projection dynamic is defined by $\dot x = \Phi F(x)$ at all states (see exercise 6.3.4), the preceding revision protocols do not generate the projection dynamic on the boundary of X. Exercise 6.3.6 presents a revision protocol that achieves this goal, even while maintaining connections with the replicator dynamic.

Exercise 6.3.6 Consider the following two revision protocols

$$\rho_{ij}(\pi, x) = \begin{cases} [\hat\pi_i]_- \cdot \dfrac{x_j [\hat\pi_j]_+}{\sum_{k \in S} x_k [\hat\pi_k]_+} & \text{if } \sum_{k \in S} x_k [\hat\pi_k]_+ > 0, \\ 0 & \text{otherwise.} \end{cases} \qquad (6.25)$$

$$\rho_{ij}(\pi, x) = \begin{cases} \dfrac{[\tilde\pi_i^S]_-}{x_i} \cdot \dfrac{[\tilde\pi_j^S]_+}{\sum_{k \in S(\pi, x)} [\tilde\pi_k^S]_+} & \text{if } \sum_{k \in S(\pi, x)} x_i [\tilde\pi_k^S]_+ > 0, \\ 0 & \text{otherwise.} \end{cases} \qquad (6.26)$$

The set $S(\pi, x)$ in equation (6.26) is defined in exercise 6.3.2, and $\tilde\pi_i^S = \pi_i - \frac{1}{\#S(\pi, x)} \sum_{k \in S(\pi, x)} \pi_k$.

i. Provide an interpretation of protocol (6.25), and show that it generates the replicator dynamic as its mean dynamic.

Best Response and Projection Dynamics

ii. Provide an interpretation of protocol (6.26), and show that it generates the projection dynamic as its mean dynamic. ◇

6.A Appendix: Differential Inclusions

6.A.1 Basic Theory

A correspondence (i.e., a set-valued map) $V: \mathbf{R}^n \rightrightarrows \mathbf{R}^n$ defines a *differential inclusion* via

$$\dot{x} \in V(x). \tag{DI}$$

(DI) is a *good upper-hemicontinuous* (or *good UHC*) differential inclusion if V is

i. nonempty: $V(x) \neq \varnothing$ for all $x \in \mathbf{R}^n$;
ii. convex-valued: $V(x)$ is convex for all $x \in \mathbf{R}^n$;
iii. bounded: there exists a $K \in \mathbf{R}$ such that $\sup\{|y|: y \in V(x)\} \leq K$ for all $x \in \mathbf{R}^n$;
iv. upper-hemicontinuous: the *graph* of V, $\mathrm{gr}(V) = \{(x,y): y \in V(x)\}$, is closed.

While solutions to good UHC differential inclusions are neither as easily defined nor as well behaved as those of Lipschitz continuous differential equations, analogues of all the main properties of solutions to the latter can be established in the present setting.

The set of feasible directions of motion under (DI) changes abruptly at discontinuities of the correspondence V. The solution notion for (DI) must therefore admit trajectories with kinks; rather than requiring the relation (DI) to hold at every instant in time, it asks only that (DI) hold at almost all times. To formalize this notion, recall that the set $Z \subseteq \mathbf{R}$ has *measure zero* if for every $\varepsilon > 0$, there is a countable collection of open intervals of total length less than ε that covers Z. A property is said to hold for *almost all* $t \in [0,T]$ if it holds on subset of $[0,T]$ whose complement has measure zero. Finally, a trajectory $\{x_t\}_{t \in [0,T]}$, $T < \infty$, is a *Carathéodory solution* to (DI) if it is Lipschitz continuous and if $\dot{x}_t \in V(x_t)$ at almost all times $t \in [0,T]$. Since $\{x_t\}$ is Lipschitz continuous, its derivative $\dot{x}_t$ exists for almost all $t \in [0,T]$, and the fundamental theorem of calculus holds: $x_t - x_s = \int_s^t \dot{x}_u \, du$.

Observe that if $\{x_t\}$ is a Carathéodory solution to a continuous ODE $\dot{x} = V(x)$, it is also a solution to the ODE in the usual sense: $\dot{x}_t = V(x_t)$ at *all* times $t \in [0,T]$. The new concept does not introduce new solutions to standard differential equations, but it enables one to find solutions in settings where solutions of the old sort do not exist. In particular, we have the following existence result.

Theorem 6.A.1 *Let* (DI) *be a good UHC differential inclusion. Then for each* $\xi \in \mathbf{R}^n$ *there exists a Carathéodory solution* $\{x_t\}_{t \in [0,T]}$ *to* (DI) *with* $x_0 = \xi$.

The forward invariance result for ODEs extends to the current setting as follows.

Theorem 6.A.2 *Let $C \subseteq \mathbf{R}^n$ be a closed convex set, and let $V: C \Rightarrow \mathbf{R}^n$ satisfy the preceding conditions (i)-(iv). Suppose that $V(x) \subseteq TC(x)$ for all $x \in C$. Extend the domain of V to all of $\mathbf{R}^n$ by letting $V(y) = V(\Pi_C(y))$ for all $y \in \mathbf{R}^n - C$, and let this extension define the differential inclusion (DI) on $\mathbf{R}^n$. Then*

i. *(DI) is a good UHC differential inclusion;*
ii. *(DI) admits a forward Carathéodory solution $\{x_t\}_{t \in [0,T]}$ from each $x_0 \in \mathbf{R}^n$;*
iii. *C is forward invariant under (DI).*

The examples of best response dynamics in section 6.1 show that differential inclusions can admit multiple solution trajectories from a single initial condition, and hence that solutions need not be continuous in their initial conditions. However, the set of solutions to a differential inclusion still possesses considerable structure. To formalize this claim, let $C_{[0,T]}$ denote the space of continuous trajectories through $\mathbf{R}^n$ over the time interval $[0, T]$, equipped with the maximum norm:

$$C_{[0,T]} = \{x: [0,T] \to \mathbf{R}^n | x \text{ is continuous}\};$$

$$||x|| = \max_{t \in [0,T]} |x_t| \quad \text{for } x \in C_{[0,T]}.$$

Now recall two definitions from metric space topology. A set $\mathcal{A} \subseteq C_{[0,T]}$ is *connected* if it cannot be partitioned into two nonempty sets, each of which is disjoint from the closure of the other. The set $\mathcal{A}$ is *compact* if every sequence of elements of $\mathcal{A}$ admits a subsequence that converges to an element of $\mathcal{A}$.

Now let $S_{[0,T]}(V, \xi)$ be the set of solutions to (DI) with initial condition ξ:

$$S_{[0,T]}(V, \xi) = \{x \in C_{[0,T]}: x \text{ is a Carathéodory solution to (DI) with } x_0 = \xi\}.$$

Theorem 6.A.3 *Let (DI) be a good UHC differential inclusion. Then*

i. *for each $\xi \in \mathbf{R}^n$, $S_{[0,T]}(V, \xi)$ is connected and compact;*
ii. *the correspondence $S_{[0,T]}(V, \cdot): \mathbf{R}^n \to C_{[0,T]}$ is upper-hemicontinuous.*

Although an initial condition ξ may be the source of many solution trajectories of (DI), part (i) of the theorem shows that the set $S_{[0,T]}(V, \xi)$ of such trajectories has a simple structure: it is connected and compact. Given any continuous criterion $f: C_{[0,T]} \to \mathbf{R}$ (where continuity is defined with respect to the maximum norm on $C_{[0,T]}$) and any initial condition ξ, connectedness implies that the set of values $f(S_{[0,T]}(V, \xi))$ is an interval, and compactness implies that this set of values is compact. Thus, there is a solution that is optimal according to criterion f among those that start at ξ. Part (ii) of the theorem provides an analogue of continuity in initial conditions. It indicates that if a sequence of solution trajectories $\{x^k\}_{k=1}^{\infty}$ to (DI) (with

Best Response and Projection Dynamics 207

possibly differing initial conditions) converges to some trajectory $x \in C_{[0,T]}$, then x is also a solution to (DI).

6.A.2 Differential Equations Defined by Projections

Let $X \subseteq \mathbf{R}^n$ be a compact convex set, and let $F\colon X \to \mathbf{R}^n$ be Lipschitz continuous. Consider the differential equation

$$\dot{x} = \Pi_{TX(x)}(F(x)), \tag{P}$$

where $\Pi_{TX(x)}$ is the closest point projection onto the tangent cone $TX(x)$. This equation provides the closest approximation to the equation $\dot{x} = F(x)$ that is consistent with the forward invariance of X.

Since the right-hand side of (P) changes discontinuously at the boundary of X, the Picard-Lindelöf theorem does not apply here. Indeed, solutions to (P) have different properties than solutions of standard ODEs; for instance, solution trajectories from different initial conditions can merge after a finite amount of time has passed. But like solutions to standard ODEs, forward solutions to the dynamic (P) exist, are unique, and are Lipschitz continuous in their initial conditions.

Theorem 6.A.4 *Let F be Lipschitz continuous. Then for each $\xi \in X$, there exists a unique Carathéodory solution $\{x_t\}_{t\geq 0}$ to (P) with $x_0 = \xi$. Moreover, solutions are Lipschitz continuous in their initial conditions: $|y_t - x_t| \leq |y_0 - x_0| e^{Kt}$ for all $t \geq 0$, where K is the Lipschitz coefficient for F.*

The following sketches a proof of this result. Define the multivalued map $V\colon X \rightrightarrows \mathbf{R}^n$ by

$$V(x) = \bigcap_{\varepsilon > 0} \mathrm{cl}\left(\mathrm{conv}\left(\bigcup_{y \in X: |y-x| \leq \varepsilon} \Pi_{TX(y)}(F(y))\right)\right),$$

that is, $V(x)$ is the closed convex hull of all values of $\Pi_{TX(y)}(F(y))$ that obtain at points y arbitrarily close to x. It is easy to check that V is upper-hemicontinuous with closed convex values. Moreover, $V(x) \cap TX(x)$, the set of feasible directions of motion from x contained in $V(x)$, is always equal to $\{\Pi_{TX(x)}(F(x))\}$ and so in particular is nonempty. Because $V(x) \cap TX(x) \neq \emptyset$, an extension of theorem 6.A.2 called the *viability theorem* implies that for each $\xi \in X$, a solution $\{x_t\}_{t\geq 0}$ to $\dot{x} \in V(x)$ exists. But since $V(x) \cap TX(x) = \{\Pi_{TX(x)}(F(x))\}$, this solution must also solve the original equation (P). This establishes the existence of solutions to (P).

To prove uniqueness and continuity, let $\{x_t\}$ and $\{y_t\}$ be solutions to (P). Using the chain rule, the Moreau decomposition theorem, and the Lipschitz continuity of F, we obtain

$$\frac{d}{dt}|y_t - x_t|^2 = 2(y_t - x_t)'(\Pi_{TX(y_t)}(F(y_t)) - \Pi_{TX(x_t)}(F(x_t)))$$

$$= 2(y_t - x_t)'(F(y_t) - F(x_t)) - 2(y_t - x_t)'(\Pi_{NX(y_t)}(F(y_t)) - \Pi_{NX(x_t)}(F(x_t)))$$

$$= 2(y_t - x_t)'(F(y_t) - F(x_t)) + 2(x_t - y_t)'\Pi_{NX(y_t)}(F(y_t))$$

$$+ 2(y_t - x_t)'\Pi_{NX(x_t)}(F(x_t))$$

$$\leq 2(y_t - x_t)'(F(y_t) - F(x_t))$$

$$\leq 2K|y_t - x_t|^2,$$

and hence

$$|y_t - x_t|^2 \leq |y_0 - x_0|^2 + \int_0^t 2K|y_s - x_s|\, ds.$$

Gronwall's inequality then implies that

$$|y_t - x_t|^2 \leq |y_0 - x_0|^2 e^{2Kt}.$$

Taking square roots yields the inequality stated in the theorem.

6.B   Appendix: The Legendre Transform

The classical Legendre transform is the key tool for proving theorem 6.2.1, the representation theorem for the additive random utility model. This section introduces Legendre transforms of convex functions defined on open intervals and, more generally, on multidimensional convex domains.

6.B.1   Legendre Transforms of Functions on Open Intervals

Let $C = (a,b) \subseteq \mathbf{R}$ be an open interval, and let $f: C \to \mathbf{R}$ be a strictly convex, continuously differentiable function that becomes steep at the boundaries of C:

$$\lim_{x \downarrow a} f'(x) = -\infty \text{ if } a > -\infty \quad \text{and} \quad \lim_{x \uparrow b} f'(x) = \infty \text{ if } b < \infty.$$

The Legendre transform associates with the strictly convex function f a new strictly convex function f^*. Because $f: C \to \mathbf{R}$ is strictly convex, its derivative $f': C \to \mathbf{R}$ is increasing, and thus invertible. Its inverse is denoted $(f')^{-1}: C^* \to \mathbf{R}$, where the open interval C^* is the range of f'. Since $(f')^{-1}$ is itself increasing, its integral, denoted $f^*: C^* \to \mathbf{R}$, is strictly convex. With the right choice of the constant of integration K, the pair (C^*, f^*) is the Legendre transform of the pair (C,f). In summary:

Best Response and Projection Dynamics 209

$f: C \to \mathbf{R}$ is strictly convex $\qquad\qquad f^* \equiv \int (f')^{-1} + K$ is strictly convex

$\qquad\qquad\downarrow \qquad\qquad\qquad\qquad\qquad\qquad\qquad\uparrow$

$f': C \to C^*$ is increasing $\quad\longrightarrow\quad (f')^{-1}: C^* \to C$ is increasing

The cornerstone of this construction is the observation that the derivative of f^* is the inverse of the derivative of f. That is,

$$(f^*)' = (f')^{-1}. \qquad (6.27)$$

Or, in other words,

f^* has slope x at $y \Leftrightarrow f$ has slope y at x. $\qquad (6.28)$

Surprisingly, one can specify the function f^* in a simple, direct way. The *Legendre transform* (C^*, f^*) of the pair (C, f) is defined by

$$C^* = \mathrm{range}(f') \quad \text{and} \quad f^*(y) = \max_{x \in C} xy - f(x).$$

The first-order condition of the program at the right is $y = f'(x^*(y))$, or equivalently, $(f')^{-1}(y) = x^*(y)$. On the other hand, if we differentiate f^* with respect to y, the envelope theorem yields $(f^*)'(y) = x^*(y)$. Putting these equations together, we see that $(f^*)'(y) = (f')^{-1}(y)$, which is property (6.27).

Suppose that f'' exists and is positive. Then by differentiating both sides of the identity $(f^*)'(y) = (f')^{-1}(y)$, one obtains a simple relation between the second derivatives of f and f^*:

$$(f^*)''(y) = ((f')^{-1})'(y) = \frac{1}{f''(x)}, \quad \text{where } x = (f')^{-1}(y) = x^*(y).$$

In other words, to find $(f^*)''(y)$, evaluate f'' at the point $x \in C$ corresponding to $y \in C^*$, and then take the reciprocal.

Our initial discussion of the Legendre transform suggests that it is a *duality relation*: in other words, one can generate (C, f) from (C^*, f^*) using the same procedure through which (C^*, f^*) is generated from (C, f). To prove this, we begin with the simple observations that C^* is itself an open interval and that f^* is itself strictly convex and continuously differentiable. It is also easy to check that $|(f^*)'(y)|$ diverges whenever y approaches $\mathrm{bd}(C^*)$; in fact, this is just the contrapositive of the corresponding statement about f.

It is easy to verify that $(C^*)^* = C$:

$$(C^*)^* = \mathrm{range}((f^*)') = \mathrm{range}((f')^{-1}) = \mathrm{domain}(f') = C.$$

To show that $(f^*)^* = f$, we begin with the definition of $(f^*)^*$:

$$(f^*)^*(x) = \max_{y \in C^*} xy - f^*(y).$$

Taking the first-order condition yields $x = (f^*)'(y^*(x))$, and hence $y^*(x) = ((f^*)')^{-1}(x) = f'(x)$. Since $(f')^{-1}(y) = x^*(y)$, y^* and x^* are inverse functions. Therefore,

$$(f^*)^*(x) = x y^*(x) - f^*(y^*(x)) = x y^*(x) - (x^*(y^*(x)) y^*(x) - f(x^*(y^*(x)))) = f(x).$$

Putting this all together, we obtain the third characterization of the Legendre transform and of the implied bijection between C and C^*:

$$x \text{ maximizes } xy - f(x) \Leftrightarrow y \text{ maximizes } xy - f^*(y). \tag{6.29}$$

Example 6.B.1 If $C = \mathbf{R}$ and $f(x) = e^x$, then the Legendre transform of (C, f) is (C^*, f^*), where $C^* = (0, \infty)$ and $f^*(y) = y \log y - y$. ♦

Example 6.B.2 Suppose that $c \colon \mathbf{R} \to \mathbf{R}$ is a strictly convex cost function. (For convenience, we allow negative levels of output; the next example shows that this is without loss of generality if $c'(0) = 0$.) If output can be sold at price $p \in C^* = \text{range}(c')$, then maximized profit equals

$$\pi(p) = \max_{x \in \mathbf{R}} xp - c(x).$$

Thus, by definition, (C^*, π) is the Legendre transform of $(\mathbf{R}, c)$. The duality relation implies that if one starts instead with the maximized profit function $\pi \colon C^* \to \mathbf{R}$, one can recover the cost function c via the dual program

$$c(x) = \max_{p \in C^*} xp - \pi(p).$$
♦

Example 6.B.3 To obtain the class of examples easiest to visualize, suppose that the function $g \colon \mathbf{R} \to \mathbf{R}$ is continuous and increasing, and that it satisfies

$$\lim_{x \downarrow -\infty} g(x) = -\infty, \quad \lim_{x \uparrow \infty} g(x) = \infty \quad \text{and} \quad g(0) = 0.$$

Define $f(x) = \int_0^x g(s) \, ds$ on domain $\mathbf{R}$. Then the Legendre transform of $(\mathbf{R}, f)$ is $(\mathbf{R}, f^*)$, where $f^*(y) = \int_0^y g^{-1}(t) \, dt$. Evidently, $(f^*)' = g^{-1} = (f')^{-1}$. Indeed, figure 6.8 illustrates that x maximizes $xy - f(x)$ if and only if y maximizes $xy - f^*(y)$, and that f^* has slope x at y if and only if f has slope y at x. ♦

6.B.2 Legendre Transforms of Functions on Multidimensional Domains

Analogues of the previous results can be established in settings with multidimensional domains. Let Z be a linear subspace of $\mathbf{R}^n$. Call (C, f) a *Legendre pair* if $C \subseteq Z$ is (relatively) open and convex, and f is C^1, strictly convex, and steep near $\text{bd}(C)$, where f is *steep near* $\text{bd}(C)$ if $|\nabla f(x)| \to \infty$ whenever $x \to \text{bd}(C)$.

Best Response and Projection Dynamics

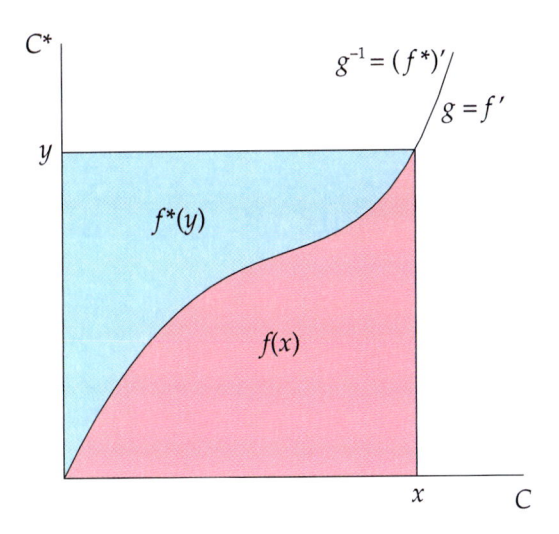

Figure 6.8
A Legendre transform.

The aim is to define a pair (C^*, f^*) that satisfies properties (6.30), (6.31), and (6.32):

$$\nabla f^* = (\nabla f)^{-1}. \tag{6.30}$$

f^* has slope x at $y \Leftrightarrow f$ has slope y at x. (6.31)

x maximizes $x'y - f(x) \Leftrightarrow y$ maximizes $x'y - f^*(y)$. (6.32)

As before, one can imagine obtaining f^* from f by differentiating, inverting, and then integrating, as illustrated in the following diagram:

$f : C \to \mathbf{R}$ is strictly convex $f^* \equiv \int (\nabla f)^{-1} + K$ is strictly convex

$\downarrow$ $\uparrow$

$\nabla f : C \to C^*$ is invertible $\longrightarrow$ $(\nabla f)^{-1} : C^* \to C$ is invertible

Since the domain of f is $C \subseteq Z$, the derivative of f, Df, is a map from C into $L(Z, \mathbf{R})$, the set of linear forms on Z. The gradient of f at x is the unique vector $\nabla f(x) \in Z$ that represents $Df(x)$; thus, ∇f is a map from C into Z.

The *Legendre transform* (C^*, f^*) of the pair (C, f) is defined by

$$C^* = \text{range}(\nabla f) \quad \text{and} \quad f^*(y) = \max_{x \in C} x'y - f(x).$$

The following theorem summarizes the Legendre transform's basic properties.

Theorem 6.B.1 *Suppose that (C,f) is a Legendre pair. Then*

i. (C^*, f^*) is a Legendre pair;
ii. $\nabla f \colon C \to C^*$ is bijective, and $(\nabla f)^{-1} = \nabla f^*$;
iii. $f(x) = \max_{y \in C^*} x'y - f^*(y)$;
iv. The maximizers x^* and y^* satisfy $x^*(y) = \nabla f^*(y) = (\nabla f)^{-1}(y)$ and $y^*(x) = \nabla f(x) = (\nabla f^*)^{-1}(x)$.

As in the one-dimensional case, the second derivatives of f^* can be related to the second derivatives of f. The second derivative $D^2 f$ is a map from C to $L_s^2(Z, \mathbf{R})$, the set of symmetric bilinear forms on $Z \times Z$. The Hessian of f at x, $\nabla^2 f(x) \in \mathbf{R}^{n \times n}$, is the unique representation of $D^2 f(x)$ by a symmetric matrix whose rows and columns are in Z. In fact, since the map $z \mapsto \nabla^2 f(x) z$ has range Z, the matrix $\nabla^2 f(x)$ can be viewed as a linear map from Z to Z. The following result relies on this observation.

Corollary 6.B.2 *If $D^2 f(x)$ exists and is positive definite for all $x \in C$, then $D^2 f^*(y)$ exists and is positive definite for all $y \in C^*$. In fact, $\nabla^2 f^*(y) = (\nabla^2 f(x))^{-1}$ as linear maps from Z to Z, where $x = (\nabla f)^{-1}(y)$.*

In the one-dimensional setting, the derivative f' is invertible because it is increasing. Both these properties also follow from the stronger assumption that $f''(x) > 0$ for all $x \in C$. In the multidimensional setting, it makes no sense to ask whether ∇f is increasing. But there is an analogue of the second derivative condition, namely, that the Hessian $\nabla^2 f(x)$ is positive definite on $Z \times Z$ for all $x \in C$. According to the *global inverse function theorem*, any function on a convex domain that is proper (i.e., preimages of compact sets are compact) and whose Jacobian determinant is everywhere nonvanishing is invertible; thus, the fact that $\nabla^2 f(x)$ is always positive definite implies that $(\nabla f)^{-1}$ exists. However, this deep result is not needed to prove theorem 6.B.1 or corollary 6.B.2.

6.C Appendix: Perturbed Optimization

6.C.1 Proof of the Representation Theorem

We now use the results on Legendre transforms from appendix 6.B to prove theorem 6.2.1. We defined the perturbed maximizer function $\tilde{M}$ using stochastic perturbations via

$$\tilde{M}_i(\pi) = \mathbb{P}\left(i = \underset{j \in S}{\operatorname{argmax}} \, \pi_j + \varepsilon_j\right). \tag{6.11}$$

Here, the random vector ε is an *admissible stochastic perturbation* if it has a positive density on $\mathbf{R}^n$ and if this density is sufficiently smooth that $\tilde{M}$ is C^1. We defined $\tilde{M}$ using deterministic perturbations via

Best Response and Projection Dynamics

$$\tilde{M}(\pi) = \underset{y \in \text{int}(\Delta)}{\text{argmax}} \, (y'\pi - v(y)). \tag{6.12}$$

Here, the function $v \colon \text{int}(\Delta) \to \mathbf{R}$ is an *admissible deterministic perturbation* if the Hessian matrix $\nabla^2 v(y)$ is positive definite on $\mathbf{R}_0^n \times \mathbf{R}_0^n$ for all $y \in \text{int}(\Delta)$, and if $|\nabla v(y)|$ approaches infinity whenever y approaches $\text{bd}(\Delta)$.

Theorem 6.2.1 *Let $\tilde{M}$ be a perturbed maximizer function defined in terms of an admissible stochastic perturbation ε via equation (6.11). Then $\tilde{M}$ satisfies equation (6.12) for some admissible deterministic perturbation v. In fact, $\bar{M} = \tilde{M}|_{\mathbf{R}_0^n}$ and ∇v are invertible, and $\bar{M} = (\nabla v)^{-1}$.*

Proof The probability that alternative i is chosen when the payoff vector is π is

$$\tilde{M}_i(\pi) = \mathbb{P}(\pi_i + \varepsilon_i \geq \pi_j + \varepsilon_j \text{ for all } j \in S)$$

$$= \mathbb{P}(\varepsilon_j \leq \pi_i + \varepsilon_i - \pi_j \text{ for all } j \in S)$$

$$= \int_{-\infty}^{\infty} \int_{-\infty}^{\pi_i + x_i - \pi_1} \cdots \int_{-\infty}^{\pi_i + x_i - \pi_{i-1}} \int_{-\infty}^{\pi_i + x_i - \pi_{i+1}} \cdots \int_{-\infty}^{\pi_i + x_i - \pi_n} f(x) \, dx_n \ldots dx_{i+1} \, dx_{i-1} \ldots dx_1 \, dx_i,$$

where f is the joint density function of the random perturbations ε. The following lemma lists some properties of the derivative of $\tilde{M}$. ∎

Lemma 6.C.1 *For all $\pi \in \mathbf{R}^n$,*

i. $D\tilde{M}(\pi)\mathbf{1} = \mathbf{0}$;

ii. $D\tilde{M}(\pi)$ is symmetric;

iii. $D\tilde{M}(\pi)$ has negative off-diagonal elements;

iv. $D\tilde{M}(\pi)$ is positive definite with respect to $\mathbf{R}_0^n \times \mathbf{R}_0^n$.

Proof Part (i) follows from differentiating the identity $\tilde{M}(\pi) = \tilde{M}(\Phi\pi)$. To establish parts (ii) and (iii), let i and $j > i$ be two distinct strategies. Then using the change of variable $\hat{x}_j = \pi_i + x_i - \pi_j$,

$$\frac{\partial \tilde{M}_i}{\partial \pi_j}(\pi) = -\int_{-\infty}^{\infty} \int_{-\infty}^{\pi_i + x_i - \pi_1} \cdots \int_{-\infty}^{\pi_i + x_i - \pi_{i-1}} \int_{-\infty}^{\pi_i + x_i - \pi_{i+1}} \cdots \int_{-\infty}^{\pi_i + x_i - \pi_{j-1}} \int_{-\infty}^{\pi_i + x_i - \pi_{j+1}} \cdots \int_{-\infty}^{\pi_i + x_i - \pi_n} f(x_1, \ldots, x_{j-1},$$
$$\pi_i + x_i - \pi_j, x_{j+1}, \ldots, x_n) \, dx_n \ldots dx_{j+1} \, dx_{j-1} \ldots dx_{i+1} \, dx_{i-1} \ldots dx_1 \, dx_i$$

$$= -\int_{-\infty}^{\infty} \int_{-\infty}^{\pi_j + \hat{x}_j - \pi_1} \cdots \int_{-\infty}^{\pi_j + \hat{x}_j - \pi_{i-1}} \int_{-\infty}^{\pi_j + \hat{x}_j - \pi_{i+1}} \cdots \int_{-\infty}^{\pi_j + \hat{x}_j - \pi_{j-1}} \int_{-\infty}^{\pi_j + \hat{x}_j - \pi_{j+1}} \cdots \int_{-\infty}^{\pi_j + \hat{x}_j - \pi_n} f(x_1, \ldots, x_{i-1},$$
$$\pi_j + \hat{x}_j - \pi_i, x_{i+1}, \ldots, x_n) \, dx_n \ldots dx_{j+1} \, dx_{j-1} \ldots dx_{i+1} \, dx_{i-1} \ldots dx_1 \, d\hat{x}_j$$

$$= \frac{\partial \tilde{M}_j}{\partial \pi_i}(\pi),$$

which implies claims (ii) and (iii). To establish claim (iv), let $z \in \mathbf{R}_0^n$. Then using claims (i), (ii), and (iii) in succession yields

$$z'D\tilde{M}(\pi)z = \sum_{i \in S}\sum_{j \in S} \frac{\partial \tilde{M}_i}{\partial \pi_j}(\pi) z_i z_j = \sum_{i \in S}\sum_{j \neq i} \frac{\partial \tilde{M}_i}{\partial \pi_j}(\pi) z_i z_j + \sum_{i \in S}\left(-\sum_{j \neq i} \frac{\partial \tilde{M}_i}{\partial \pi_j}(\pi)\right) z_i^2$$

$$= \sum_{i \in S}\sum_{j \neq i} \frac{\partial \tilde{M}_i}{\partial \pi_j}(\pi) \left(z_i z_j - z_i^2\right) = \sum_{i \in S}\sum_{j < i} \frac{\partial \tilde{M}_i}{\partial \pi_j}(\pi) \left(2 z_i z_j - z_i^2 - z_j^2\right)$$

$$= -\sum_{i \in S}\sum_{j < i} \frac{\partial \tilde{M}_i}{\partial \pi_j}(\pi) \left(z_i - z_j\right)^2 > 0. \qquad \blacksquare$$

Since the derivative matrix $D\tilde{M}(\pi)$ is symmetric, the vector field $\tilde{M}$ admits a potential function $\tilde{\mu} \colon \mathbf{R}^n \to \mathbf{R}$ (that is, a function satisfying $\nabla \tilde{\mu}(\pi) = \tilde{M}(\pi)$ for all $\pi \in \mathbf{R}^n$). Let $\bar{\mu} = \tilde{\mu}|_{\mathbf{R}_0^n}$ be the restriction of $\tilde{\mu}$ to $\mathbf{R}_0^n$. Then for all $\pi \in \mathbf{R}_0^n$, $\nabla \bar{\mu}(\pi) \in \mathbf{R}_0^n$ is given by

$$\nabla \bar{\mu}(\pi) = \Phi \nabla \tilde{\mu}(\pi) = \Phi \tilde{M}(\pi) = \tilde{M}(\pi) - \frac{1}{n}\mathbf{1} = \bar{M}(\pi) - \frac{1}{n}\mathbf{1},$$

where the third equality uses the fact that $\tilde{M}(\pi) \in \Delta$.

Since $\nabla^2 \bar{\mu}(\pi) = D\bar{M}(\pi)$ is positive definite with respect to $\mathbf{R}_0^n \times \mathbf{R}_0^n$, $\bar{\mu}$ is strictly convex; thus, since $\mathrm{bd}(\mathbf{R}_0^n)$ is empty, $(\mathbf{R}_0^n, \bar{\mu})$ is a Legendre pair. Let the pair $(C^*, \bar{\mu}^*)$ be the Legendre transform of $(\mathbf{R}_0^n, \bar{\mu})$, and define the function $v \colon (C^* + \frac{1}{n}\mathbf{1}) \to \mathbf{R}$ by $v(y) = \bar{\mu}^*(y - \frac{1}{n}\mathbf{1})$. Theorem 6.2.1 then follows immediately from lemma 6.C.2.

Lemma 6.C.2

i. $C^* + \frac{1}{n}\mathbf{1} = \mathrm{int}(\Delta)$.

ii. $\nabla v \colon \mathrm{int}(\Delta) \to \mathbf{R}_0^n$ is the inverse of $\bar{M} \colon \mathbf{R}_0^n \to \mathrm{int}(\Delta)$.

iii. v is an admissible deterministic perturbation.

iv. $\tilde{M}(\pi) = \mathrm{argmax}_{y \in \mathrm{int}(\Delta)} y'\pi - v(y)$ for all $\pi \in \mathbf{R}^n$.

Proof

i. The set $C^* = \mathrm{range}(\nabla \bar{\mu}) = \mathrm{range}(\bar{M}) - \frac{1}{n}\mathbf{1}$ is convex by theorem 6.B.1(i). Moreover, if the components $\pi_j, j \in J \subset S$ stay bounded while the remaining components approach infinity, then $\tilde{M}_j(\pi)$ approaches 0 for all $j \in J$, that is, $\tilde{M}(\pi)$ converges to a subface of the simplex Δ. Thus, $\mathrm{range}(\bar{M}) = \mathrm{range}(\tilde{M}) \subseteq \mathrm{int}(\Delta)$ contains points arbitrarily close to each corner of the simplex. Since $\mathrm{range}(\bar{M})$ is convex, it must equal $\mathrm{int}(\Delta)$.

Best Response and Projection Dynamics

ii. Let $y \in \text{int}(\Delta)$. Using theorem 6.B.1(ii), we obtain

$$\nabla v(y) = \nabla \bar{\mu}^*(y - \tfrac{1}{n}\mathbf{1}) = (\nabla \bar{\mu})^{-1}(y - \tfrac{1}{n}\mathbf{1}) = \tilde{M}^{-1}(y).$$

iii. $(C^*, \bar{\mu}^*)$ is a Legendre pair by theorem 6.B.1(i); thus, if y approaches $\text{bd}(\Delta) = \text{bd}(C^*) + \tfrac{1}{n}\mathbf{1}$, then $|\nabla v(y)| = |\nabla \bar{\mu}^*(y - \tfrac{1}{n}\mathbf{1})|$ diverges. In addition, since $\nabla^2 \bar{\mu}(\pi) = D\bar{M}(\pi)$ is positive definite with respect to $\mathbf{R}_0^n \times \mathbf{R}_0^n$ for all $\pi \in \mathbf{R}_0^n$, corollary 6.B.2 implies that $\nabla^2 v(y) = \nabla^2 \bar{\mu}^*(y - \tfrac{1}{n}\mathbf{1})$ is positive definite with respect to $\mathbf{R}_0^n \times \mathbf{R}_0^n$ for all $y \in \text{int}(\Delta)$.

iv. Since $\tilde{M}(\cdot) = \tilde{M}(\Phi(\cdot))$, it is enough to consider $\pi \in \mathbf{R}_0^n$. For such π,

$$\underset{y \in \text{int}(\Delta)}{\operatorname{argmax}}\, y'\pi - v(y) = \left(\underset{\hat{y} \in \text{int}(\Delta) - \tfrac{1}{n}\mathbf{1}}{\operatorname{argmax}}\, \hat{y}'\pi - \bar{\mu}^*(\hat{y}) \right) + \tfrac{1}{n}\mathbf{1}$$

$$= \nabla \bar{\mu}(\pi) + \tfrac{1}{n}\mathbf{1}$$

$$= \tilde{M}(\pi),$$

where the second equality follows from theorem 6.B.1(iv). ∎

This completes the proof of theorem 6.2.1. ∎

6.C.2 Additional Results

This section states without proof a few additional results on perturbed optimization. The first two of these concern the construction of the potential function $\tilde{\mu}$ of the perturbed maximizer function $\tilde{M}$. In fact, two constructions are available, one for each sort of perturbation.

If one defines $\tilde{M}$ in terms of an admissible deterministic perturbation v, then one can verify (using the envelope theorem or a direct calculation) that the *perturbed maximum function* associated with v is a potential function for $\tilde{M}$.

Observation 6.C.3 *The function $\tilde{\mu}: \mathbf{R}^n \to \mathbf{R}$ defined by*

$$\tilde{\mu}(\pi) = \max_{y \in \text{int}(\Delta)} y'\pi - v(y)$$

is a potential function for $\tilde{M}$ as defined in (6.12).

Alternatively, suppose $\tilde{M}$ is defined in terms of an admissible stochastic perturbation ε. In this case, the expectation of the maximal perturbed payoff is a potential function for $\tilde{M}$.

Theorem 6.C.4 *The function $\tilde{\mu}: \mathbf{R}^n \to \mathbf{R}$ defined by*

$$\tilde{\mu}(\pi) = \mathbb{E} \max_{j \in S} (\pi_j + \varepsilon_j)$$

is a potential function for $\tilde{M}$ as defined in (6.11).

The intuition behind this result is simple. If one marginally increases the value of π_i, the value of the maximum function $\max_j \pi_j + \varepsilon_j$ goes up at a unit rate at those values of ε where strategy i is optimal. The set of ε at which strategy i is optimal also changes, but the contribution of these points to the value of the maximum function is negligible. Building on these observations, one can show that

$$\frac{\partial \tilde{\mu}}{\partial \pi_i}(\pi) = \mathbb{E}\, 1_{\{i = \text{argmax}_j \pi_j + \varepsilon_j\}} = \mathbb{P}\left(i = \text{argmax}_j \pi_j + \varepsilon_j\right) = \tilde{M}_i(\pi).$$

Which functions are perturbed maximizer functions? The following characterization of the perturbed maximizer functions that can be derived from admissible deterministic perturbations follows from the proof of theorem 6.2.1.

Corollary 6.C.5 *A surjective function $\tilde{M}: \mathbf{R}^n \to \text{int}(\Delta)$ can be derived from an admissible deterministic perturbation if and only if for all $\pi \in \mathbf{R}^n$, $D\tilde{M}(\pi)$ is symmetric, positive definite on $\mathbf{R}_0^n$, and satisfies $D\tilde{M}(\pi)\mathbf{1} = \mathbf{0}$.*

The counterpart of this result for stochastic perturbations is known as the *Williams-Daly-Zachary theorem*.

Theorem 6.C.6 *A surjective function $\tilde{M}: \mathbf{R}^n \to \text{int}(\Delta)$ can be derived from an admissible stochastic perturbation if and only if for all $\pi \in \mathbf{R}^n$, $D\tilde{M}(\pi)$ is symmetric, positive definite on $\mathbf{R}_0^n$, and satisfies $D\tilde{M}(\pi)\mathbf{1} = \mathbf{0}$, and the partial derivatives of $\tilde{M}$ satisfy*

$$(-1)^k \frac{\partial^k \tilde{M}_{i_0}}{\partial \pi_{i_1} \cdots \partial \pi_{i_k}}(\pi) > 0$$

for each $k = 1, \ldots, n-1$ and each set of $k+1$ distinct indices $\{i_0, i_1, \ldots, i_k\} \subseteq S$.

To establish the necessity of the kth-order derivative conditions, one repeatedly differentiates the definition of $\tilde{M}$. The first-order derivative condition is derived in this way in the proof of theorem 6.2.1. These two results show that deterministic perturbations generate a strictly larger class of perturbed maximizer functions than stochastic perturbations; see exercise 6.2.2 for an explicit example.

Notes

Section 6.1
The best response dynamic was introduced by Gilboa and Matsui (1991) and further studied by Matsui (1992), Hofbauer (1995b), and Gaunersdorfer and Hofbauer (1995). Hofbauer (1995b) introduced the formulation of the best response dynamic as a differential inclusion. In the context of normal form games, the best response dynamic can be viewed as a continuous-time version of fictitious play, a process introduced by Brown (1949; 1951) as a method of computing equilibria. See Robinson (1951), Miyasawa (1961), and Shapley (1964) for other early work on this process; more recent references include Milgrom and Roberts (1991), Monderer and Shapley (1996a), Monderer and Sela (1997), Foster and Young (1998), Krishna and Sjöström (1998), and Berger (2005; 2007a; 2007b; 2008). A refinement

of the best response dynamic under which nonrobust best responses are not chosen was studied by Balkenborg, Hofbauer, and Kuzmics (2008). Zusai (2010) studies *tempered best response dynamics*, under which all revising agents choose best responses, but agents with low payoffs revise at faster rates than agents with high payoffs.

A complete analysis of best response dynamics in Rock-Paper-Scissors games (example 6.1.1 and exercise 6.1.3) can be found in Gaunersdorfer and Hofbauer (1995). Example 6.1.4 was introduced by Zeeman (1980), who showed that the interior Nash equilibrium of this game is not an ESS but is nevertheless asymptotically stable under the replicator dynamic (see example 8.5.1). The properties of the best response dynamic described in the example were explained by Hofbauer (1995b). Example 6.1.5 is due to Golman and Page (2009).

An approximation theorem for collections of Markov processes whose mean dynamics are differential inclusions was proved by Benaïm, Hofbauer, and Sorin (2005) in a setting in which the step size of the increments of the Markov processes shrinks over time. For results in the present constant step size setting, see Gorodeisky (2008; 2009) and Roth and Sandholm (2010).

Section 6.2

This section is based on Hofbauer and Sandholm (2002; 2007).

The perturbed best response dynamic first appeared in the work of Fudenberg and Kreps (1993), who used it to study the discrete-time stochastic process called stochastic fictitious play; see the chapter 12 notes for further references to work on this process. The logit dynamic first appeared in Fudenberg and Levine (1998). For the Hausdorff metric mentioned in example 6.2.1, see Ok (2007). For further references on logit models in game theory, see the chapter 11 notes. Other continuous approximations of exact best response dynamics include target projection dynamics (Tsakas and Voorneveld (2009)) and sampling best response dynamics (Oyama, Sandholm, and Tercieux (2010)).

In the experimental economics literature, perturbed equilibrium goes by the name of quantal response equilibrium, a term introduced by McKelvey and Palfrey (1995). Some authors use this term more narrowly to refer to logit equilibrium. For more on the use of these concepts in the experimental literature, see Goeree, Holt, and Palfrey (2008) and the references therein.

The properties of the derivative matrix $D\tilde{M}(\pi)$ have long been known in the discrete-choice literature; see McFadden (1981) or Anderson, de Palma, and Thisse (1992). The control cost interpretation of deterministic perturbations was suggested by van Damme (1991, ch. 4). That independent ε_i with bounded densities generate a continuously differentiable $\tilde{M}$ follows from standard results on convolutions; see Hewitt and Stromberg (1965, theorem 21.33).

An intuitive discussion of the Poincaré-Hopf theorem can be found in Hofbauer and Sigmund (1988, sec. 19); see Milnor (1965) for a formal treatment. See Ritzberger (1994), Demichelis and Germano (2000; 2002), and Demichelis and Ritzberger (2003) for intriguing uses of topological ideas to study the global properties of evolutionary game dynamics.

Section 6.3

Nagurney and Zhang (1996; 1997), building on work of Dupuis and Nagurney (1993), introduced the projection dynamic in the context of congestion games. Earlier, Friedman (1991) introduced an evolutionary dynamic that is equivalent to the projection dynamic on int(X), but that is different at states in bd(X). The presentation in this section follows Lahkar and Sandholm (2008) and Sandholm, Dokumacı, and Lahkar (2008). A related dynamic called the *target projection dynamic*, best viewed as a model of learning in normal form games, was introduced in Friesz et al. (1994), reintroduced and named in Sandholm (2005a), and provided with microfoundations and further analyzed in Tsakas and Voorneveld (2009).

Appendix 6.A

Smirnov (2002) provided a readable introduction to the theory of differential inclusions. A more comprehensive but less readable reference is Aubin and Cellina (1984).

The existence of solutions to differential inclusions defined by projections of multivalued maps was proved by Henry (1973); the approach described here follows Aubin and Cellina (1984, sec. 5.6). Restricting attention to differential equations defined by projections of Lipschitz continuous functions allows one to establish uniqueness and continuity results, a point noted, e.g., by Dupuis and Nagurney (1993).

Appendix 6.B
Formal treatments of the Legendre transform can be found in Rockafellar (1970) and Hiriart-Urruty and Lemaréchal (2001). Example 6.B.3 is borrowed from Roberts and Varberg (1973, sec. 15). For the global inverse function theorem, see Gordon (1972).

Appendix 6.C
Theorem 6.2.1 is due to Hofbauer and Sandholm (2002). For proofs of theorems 6.C.4 and 6.C.6, see McFadden (1981) or Anderson, de Palma, and Thisse (1992). The latter source is a good general reference on discrete choice theory.

III Convergence and Nonconvergence of Deterministic Dynamics

7 Global Convergence of Evolutionary Dynamics

The preceding chapters introduced a variety of classes of evolutionary dynamics and exhibited their basic properties. Links were established between the rest points of each dynamic and the Nash equilibria of the underlying game, and were shown to be are valid regardless of the nature of the game at hand. This connection is expressed in its strongest form by dynamics satisfying Nash stationarity (NS), under which rest points and Nash equilibria coincide.

Still, once one specifies an explicitly dynamic model of behavior, the most natural approach to prediction is not to focus immediately on equilibrium points, but to determine where the dynamic leads when set in motion from various initial conditions. If equilibrium occurs as the limiting state of this adjustment process, one can feel some confidence in predicting equilibrium play. If instead the dynamics lead to limit cycles or other more complicated limit sets, then those sets rather than the unstable rest points provide superior predictions of behavior.

In this chapter, we present conditions on games and dynamics under which behavior converges to equilibrium from all or nearly all initial population states. We reconsider the three classes of population games introduced in Chapter 3—potential games, stable games, and supermodular games—and derive conditions on evolutionary dynamics that ensure convergence in each class of games. We also establish convergence results for dominance solvable games, but these results are not robust to small changes in the dynamics for which they hold (see chapter 9).

The most common method for proving global convergence in a dynamical system is by constructing a *strict Lyapunov function*, a scalar-valued function that the dynamic ascends whenever it is not at rest. When the underlying game is a potential game, the game's potential function provides a natural candidate Lyapunov function for evolutionary dynamics. Section 7.1 verifies that potential functions serve as Lyapunov functions under any evolutionary dynamic that satisfies the basic monotonicity condition, positive correlation (PC). This fact is then used to prove global convergence in potential games under all of the evolutionary dynamics studied in chapters 5 and 6.

Unlike potential games, stable games do not come equipped with a scalar-valued function that is an obvious candidate Lyapunov function for evolutionary dynamics. But the structure of payoffs in these games—already reflected in the fact that their sets of Nash equilibria are convex—makes it natural to expect convergence results to hold.

In section 7.2, we develop approaches to constructing Lyapunov functions for stable games. Distance-like functions are found to serve as Lyapunov functions for the replicator and projection dynamics, allowing us to establish global convergence results for these dynamics in strictly stable games. For target dynamics, including excess payoff, best response, and perturbed best response dynamics, integrability of the revision protocol is the key to establishing convergence results. Section 7.2.2 argues that in the presence of payoff monotonicity, integrability of the protocol ensures that on average, the vector of motion deviates from the vector of payoffs in the direction of the equilibrium; given the geometry of equilibrium in stable games, this is enough to ensure convergence to equilibrium. All told, global convergence results are proved for all six fundamental dynamics.

Section 7.3 turns attention to supermodular games. The essential property of these games is the monotonicity of their best response correspondences, so it is not surprising that the convergence results address dynamics that respect this monotone structure. The section begins by considering the best response dynamic, and uses elementary methods to prove a convergence result for supermodular games generated by two-player normal form games that satisfy a diminishing-returns condition. Convergence results that demand less structure of the game are obtained using methods from the theory of cooperative differential equations, which are smooth differential equations under which increasing the value of one component of the state variable increases the growth rates of all other components. The smoothness requirement precludes applying these methods to the best response dynamic, but they can be used to study perturbed best response dynamics. We prove that after a natural change of coordinates, perturbed best response functions generated by stochastic perturbations of payoffs are monotone. This allows us to show that the corresponding perturbed best response dynamics converge to perturbed equilibrium from almost all initial conditions.

In Section 7.4, we study evolution in games with strictly dominated strategies. We find that under the best response dynamic and under imitative dynamics, strictly ꜓minated strategies are eliminated, as are strategies ruled out by iterative removal ᛫ictly dominated strategies. It follows that in games that are dominance solv- ᛫t is, in games where this iterative procedure leaves only one strategy for ᛫ation, the best response dynamic and all imitative dynamics converge

Global Convergence of Evolutionary Dynamics

to the dominance solution. These elimination results are *not* robust, however: we show in chapter 9 that under many small modifications of the dynamics covered by the elimination results, strictly dominated strategies can survive.

The definitions and tools from dynamical systems theory needed for the analyses are treated in the chapter appendices. Appendix 7.A introduces notions of stability, limit behavior, and recurrence for deterministic dynamics. Appendix 7.B presents stability and convergence results for dynamics that admit Lyapunov functions. Finally, Appendix 7.C introduces the theory of cooperative differential equations and monotone dynamical systems.

7.1 Potential Games

7.1.1 Potential Functions as Lyapunov Functions

In a potential game $F: X \to \mathbf{R}^n$, all information about incentives is captured by the potential function $f: X \to \mathbf{R}$, in that

$$\nabla f(x) = \Phi F(x) \quad \text{for all } x \in X. \tag{7.1}$$

In chapter 3, Nash equilibria of F were characterized as those states that satisfy the Kuhn-Tucker first-order conditions for maximizing f on X. As further step, one can use the potential function to describe disequilibrium adjustment. Lemma 7.1.1 shows that any evolutionary dynamic satisfying positive correlation,

$$V_F^p(x) \neq 0 \quad \text{implies that} \quad V_F^p(x)' F^p(x) > 0, \tag{PC}$$

must ascend the potential function f.

To state this result, we introduce the notion of a Lyapunov function. The C^1 function $L: X \to \mathbf{R}$ is an *(increasing) strict Lyapunov function* for the differential equation $\dot{x} = V_F(x)$ if $\dot{L}(x) \equiv \nabla L(x)' V_F(x) \geq 0$ for all $x \in X$, with equality only at rest points of V_F.

Lemma 7.1.1 *Let F be a potential game with potential function f. Suppose the evolutionary dynamic $\dot{x} = V_F(x)$ satisfies positive correlation (PC). Then f is a strict Lyapunov function for V_F.*

Proof Follows immediately from condition (PC) and the fact that

$$\dot{f}(x) = \nabla f(x)' \dot{x} = (\Phi F(x))' V_F(x) = \sum_{p \in \mathcal{P}} F^p(x)' V_F^p(x). \quad \blacksquare$$

The initial equality in this expression follows from an application of the chain rule (see section 3.A.4) to the composition $t \mapsto x_t \mapsto f(x_t)$. Versions of this argument are used often in the proofs that follow.

If a dynamic admits a strict Lyapunov function, all solution trajectories of the dynamic converge to sets of rest points. Combining this fact with lemma 7.1.1, one can prove a global convergence result for potential games. To state this result, we briefly present some definitions concerning limit behavior of deterministic trajectories; for more on these notions and their connections with Lyapunov functions, see appendices 7.A and 7.B.

The *ω-limit* of trajectory $\{x_t\}_{t \geq 0}$ is the set of all points that the trajectory approaches arbitrarily closely infinitely often:

$$\omega(\{x_t\}) = \left\{ y \in X \colon \text{there exists } \{t_k\}_{k=1}^{\infty} \text{ with } \lim_{k \to \infty} t_k = \infty \text{ such that } \lim_{k \to \infty} x_{t_k} = y \right\}.$$

For dynamics $\dot{x} = V_F(x)$ that admit a unique forward solution trajectory from each initial condition, $\omega(\xi)$ denotes the ω-limit set of the trajectory starting from state ξ, and

$$\Omega(V_F) = \bigcup_{\xi \in X} \omega(\xi)$$

denotes the set of all ω-limit points of all solution trajectories. The set $\Omega(V_F)$ (or its closure, when $\Omega(V_F)$ is not closed) provides a basic notion of recurrence for deterministic dynamics.

Theorem 7.1.2 *Let F be a potential game, and let $\dot{x} = V_F(x)$ be an evolutionary dynamic for F that admits a unique forward solution from each initial condition and that satisfies positive correlation* (PC). *Then $\Omega(V_F) = RP(V_F)$. In particular,*

i. If V_F is an imitative dynamic, then $\Omega(V_F) = RE(F)$, the set of restricted equilibria of F;

ii. If V_F is an excess payoff dynamic, a pairwise comparison dynamic, or the projection dynamic, then $\Omega(V_F) = NE(F)$.

Proof Immediate from lemma 7.1.1, theorem 7.B.3, and the characterizations of rest points from chapters 5 and 6. ∎

Example 7.1.1: 123 Coordination Figure 7.1 presents phase diagrams for the six fundamental dynamics in 123 coordination:

$$F(x) = Ax = \begin{pmatrix} 1 & 0 & 0 \\ 0 & 2 & 0 \\ 0 & 0 & 3 \end{pmatrix} \begin{pmatrix} x_1 \\ x_2 \\ x_3 \end{pmatrix} = \begin{pmatrix} x_1 \\ 2x_2 \\ 3x_3 \end{pmatrix}. \tag{7.2}$$

In the first five cases (a)–(e), the phase diagram is plotted atop the potential function

$$f(x) = \tfrac{1}{2} \left((x_1)^2 + 2(x_2)^2 + 3(x_3)^2 \right). \tag{7.3}$$

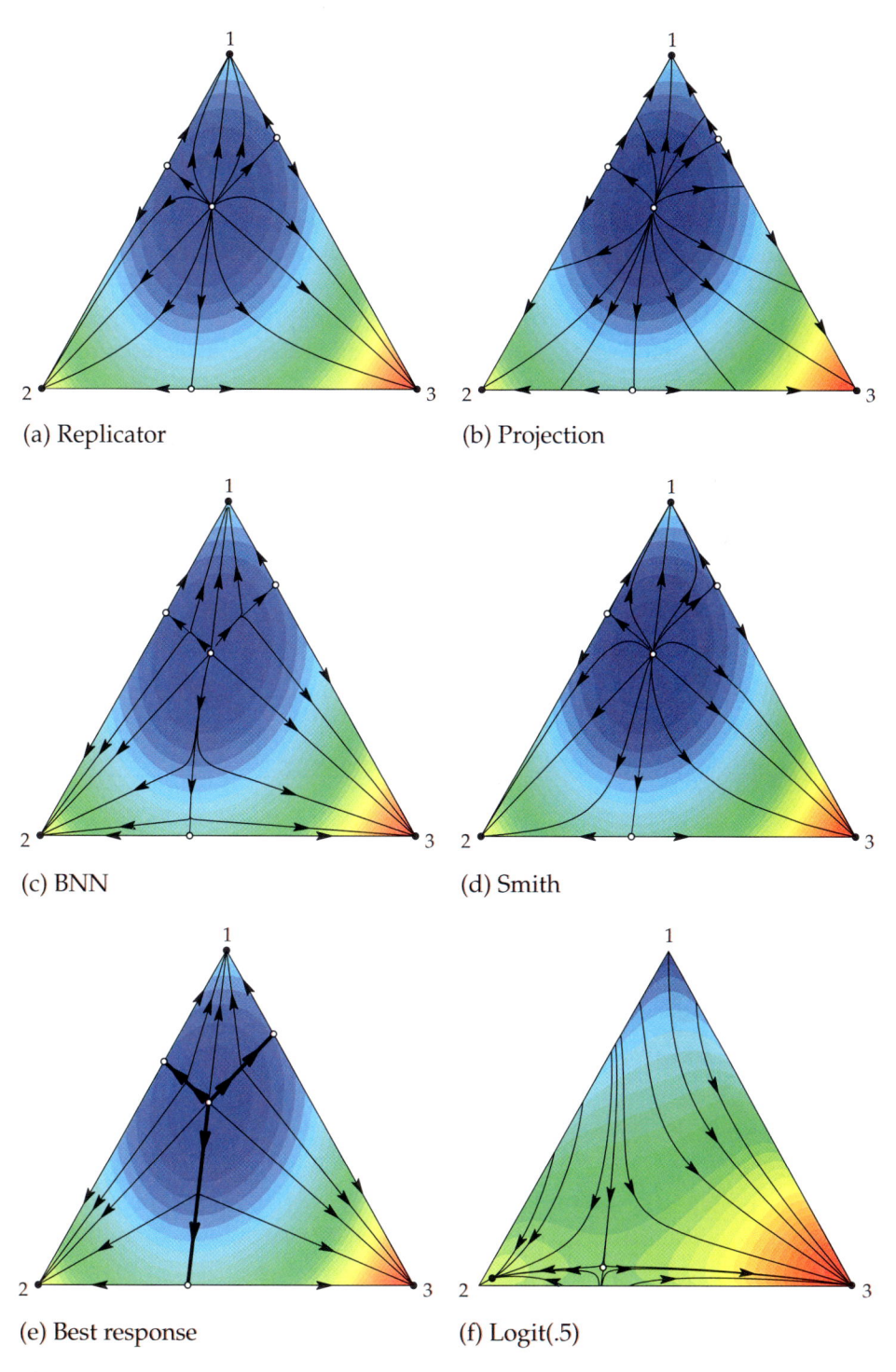

Figure 7.1
Six basic dynamics in 123 coordination. The contour plots are the potential function in (a)–(e), and the logit potential function in (f).

Of these, the first four cases (replicator, projection, BNN, Smith) are covered by theorem 7.1.2; evidently, every solution trajectory in diagrams (a)–(d) ascends the potential function, ultimately converging to one of the seven Nash equilibria of F.

It is worth noting that these equilibria are not all locally stable. The interior equilibrium is a *source*, with all nearby solution trajectories moving away from the equilibrium. The three equilibria with two-strategy supports are *saddles*; for each of these, one solution trajectory converges to the equilibrium and all other nearby trajectories eventually move away from the equilibrium. Only the three remaining equilibria—the three pure equilibria—are locally stable. For further discussion of local stability, see chapter 8. ◆

The convergence results for best response and perturbed best response dynamics require additional work. In the case of the best response dynamic

$$\dot{x}^p \in m^p M^p(F^p(x)) - x^p, \quad \text{where } M^p(\pi^p) = \operatorname*{argmax}_{i \in S^p} \pi_i^p, \tag{BR}$$

one must account for the fact that the dynamic is multivalued.

Theorem 7.1.3 *Let F be a potential game with potential function f, and let $\dot{x} \in V_F(x)$ be the best response dynamic for F. Then*

$$\frac{\partial f}{\partial z}(x) = \sum_{p \in \mathcal{P}} m^p \max_{j \in S^p} \hat{F}_j^p(x) \quad \text{for all } z \in V_F(x), x \in X.$$

Therefore, every solution trajectory $\{x_t\}$ of V_F satisfies $\omega(\{x_t\}) \subseteq NE(F)$.

Proof Recall from theorem 6.1.4 that the best response dynamic satisfies the following refinement of condition (PC):

$$(z^p)' F^p(x) = m^p \max_{j \in S^p} \hat{F}_j^p(x) \quad \text{for all } z^p \in V_F^p(x).$$

This condition immediately implies that

$$\frac{\partial f}{\partial z}(x) \equiv \nabla f(x)'z = (\Phi F(x))'z = \sum_{p \in \mathcal{P}} F^p(x)'z^p = \sum_{p \in \mathcal{P}} m^p \max_{j \in S^p} \hat{F}_j^p(x).$$

Thus, $\frac{\partial f}{\partial z}(x) \geq 0$ for all $x \in X$ and $z \in V_F(x)$, and lemma 5.5.3 implies that equality holds if and only if $x \in NE(F)$. The convergence result now follows from theorem 7.B.4. ∎

Example 7.1.2: 123 Coordination Revisited Figure 7.1e presents the phase diagram of the best response dynamic in 123 Coordination (7.2), again atop the potential function (7.3). As in example 6.1.3, there are multiple solutions starting from each initial condition on the Y-shaped set of boundaries between the best response

Global Convergence of Evolutionary Dynamics

regions. It is not hard to verify that each of these solutions converges to a Nash equilibrium. ◆

Finally, we consider perturbed best response dynamics, defining these dynamics via admissible deterministic perturbations v^p: $\text{int}(\Delta^p) \to \mathbf{R}$.

$$\dot{x}^p = m^p \tilde{M}^p(F(x)) - x^p, \quad \text{where } \tilde{M}^p(\pi^p) = \underset{y^p \in \text{int}(\Delta^p)}{\text{argmax}} \, (y^p)' \pi^p - v^p(y^p).$$

While these dynamics do not satisfy positive correlation (PC), theorem 6.2.10 showed that these dynamics do satisfy a perturbed analogue called virtual positive correlation:

$$V^p(x) \neq 0 \quad \text{implies that} \quad V^p(x)' \tilde{F}^p(x) > 0 \quad \text{for all } p \in \mathcal{P},$$

where the virtual payoffs $\tilde{F}$: $\text{int}(X) \to \mathbf{R}^n$ for the pair (F, v) are defined by

$$\tilde{F}^p(x) = F^p(x) - \nabla v^p(\tfrac{1}{m^p} x^p).$$

Accordingly, the Lyapunov function for a perturbed best response dynamic is not the potential function f, but a perturbed version thereof.

Theorem 7.1.4 *Let F be a potential game with potential function f, and let $\dot{x} = V_{F,v}(x)$ be the perturbed best response dynamic for F generated by the admissible deterministic perturbations $v = (v^1, \ldots, v^p)$. Define the perturbed potential function $\tilde{f}$: $\text{int}(X) \to \mathbf{R}$ by*

$$\tilde{f}(x) = f(x) - \sum_{p \in \mathcal{P}} m^p v^p(\tfrac{1}{m^p} x^p). \tag{7.4}$$

Then $\tilde{f}$ is a strict Lyapunov function for $V_{F,v}$, and so $\Omega(V_{F,v}) = PE(F, v)$.

Proof That $\tilde{f}$ is a strict Lyapunov function for $V_{F,v}$ follows immediately from virtual positive correlation and the fact that

$$\dot{\tilde{f}}(x) \equiv \nabla \tilde{f}(x)' \dot{x} = \sum_{p \in \mathcal{P}} \left(F^p(x) - \nabla v^p(\tfrac{1}{m^p} x^p) \right)' V^p_{F,v}(x) = \sum_{p \in \mathcal{P}} \tilde{F}^p(x)' V^p_{F,v}(x).$$

Since $PE(F, v) \equiv RP(V_{F,v})$, that $\Omega(V_{F,v}) = PE(F, v)$ follows from theorem 7.B.3. ∎

In the case of the logit(η) dynamic, the Lyapunov function from equation (7.4) takes the form

$$f^\eta(x) = f(x) - \eta \sum_{p \in \mathcal{P}} \sum_{i \in S} x_i^p \log(\tfrac{1}{m^p} x_i^p), \tag{7.5}$$

called the *logit potential function*. Theorem 7.1.4, combined with the results in chapter 10, shows that the logit potential function captures the *finite horizon behavior* of agents who play a potential game using the logit choice protocol. In chapter 12, the logit potential function is used to obtain a precise characterization of *infinite horizon behavior* in this setting.

Example 7.1.3: 123 Coordination Again Figure 7.1f presents the phase diagram for the logit(.5) dynamic in 123 Coordination (7.2). Here the contour plot is the logit potential function

$$f^\eta(x) = \tfrac{1}{2}\left((x_1)^2 + 2(x_2)^2 + (3(x_3)^2\right) - .5\sum_{i=1}^{3} x_i \log x_i.$$

Because the noise level is rather high, this phase diagram looks very different than the others; in particular, it includes only three rest points (two stable and one unstable) rather than seven. Nevertheless, every solution trajectory ascends the relevant Lyapunov function f^η, ultimately converging to a perturbed equilibrium. ◆

7.1.2 Gradient Systems for Potential Games

Lemma 7.1.1 shows that in potential games, any dynamic that satisfies condition (PC) must ascend the potential function f. Is there an evolutionary dynamic that ascends f in the fastest possible way?

A first answer to this question is suggested by figure 7.1b. In 123 Coordination, solution trajectories of the projection dynamic,

$$\dot{x} = \Pi_{TX(x)}(F(x)), \tag{P}$$

cross the level sets of the potential function orthogonally.

Observation 7.1.5 *Let $F: X \to \mathbf{R}^n$ be a potential game with potential function $f: X \to \mathbf{R}$. On int(X), the projection dynamic (P) is the gradient system for f:*

$$\dot{x} = \nabla f(x) \quad \text{on int}(X). \tag{7.6}$$

Surprisingly, there is an alternative answer to the question: it turns out that the replicator dynamic,

$$\dot{x}_i^p = x_i^p \hat{F}_i^p(x), \tag{R}$$

also defines a gradient system for the potential function f; however, this is only true after a clever change of variable. In addition to its inherent interest, this fact demonstrates a close connection between the replicator and projection dynamics; another connection is made in section 7.2.1.

We restrict the analysis to the single-population case. Define the set $\mathcal{X} = \{x \in \mathbf{R}_+^n : \sum_{i \in S} x_i^2 = 4\}$ to be the portion of the radius 2 sphere lying in the positive orthant.

Global Convergence of Evolutionary Dynamics 229

The change of variable is given by the *Akin transformation H*: $\text{int}(\mathbf{R}_+^n) \to \text{int}(\mathbf{R}_+^n)$, where $H_i(x) = 2\sqrt{x_i}$. Evidently, H is a homeomorphism that maps the interior of the simplex X onto the interior of the set $\mathcal{X}$. The transformation makes changes in component x_i look large when x_i itself is small.

Theorem 7.1.6 says that the replicator dynamic is a gradient dynamic on $\text{int}(X)$ after a change of variable that makes changes in the use of rare strategies look important relative to changes in the use of common ones. Intuitively, this reweighting accounts for the fact that under imitative dynamics, changes in the use of rare strategies are necessarily slow.

Theorem 7.1.6 *Let $F: X \to \mathbf{R}^n$ be a potential game with potential function $f: X \to \mathbf{R}$. Suppose one transports the replicator dynamic for F from $\text{int}(X)$ to $\text{int}(\mathcal{X})$ using the Akin transformation H. Then the resulting dynamic is the gradient system for the transported potential function $\phi = f \circ H^{-1}$.*

Proof Theorem 7.1.6 is proved in two steps. First, we derive the transported version of the replicator dynamic; then, we derive the gradient system for the transported version of the potential function, and show that it is the same dynamic on $\mathcal{X}$. The following notation simplifies the calculations: when $y \in \mathbf{R}_+^n$ and $a \in \mathbf{R}$, let $[y^a] \in \mathbf{R}^n$ be the vector whose ith component is $(y_i)^a$.

We can express the replicator dynamic on X as

$$\dot{x} = R(x) = \text{diag}(x)\left(F(x) - \mathbf{1}x'F(x)\right) = \left(\text{diag}(x) - xx'\right)F(x).$$

The transported version of this dynamic can be computed as

$$\dot{\chi} = \mathcal{R}(\chi) = DH(H^{-1}(\chi))R(H^{-1}(\chi)).$$

In other words, given a state $\chi \in \mathcal{X}$, we first find the corresponding state $x = H^{-1}(\chi) \in X$ and direction of motion $R(x)$. Since $R(x)$ represents a displacement from state x, we transport it to the tangent space of $\mathcal{X}$ by premultiplying it by $DH(x)$, the derivative of H evaluated at x.

Since $\chi = H(x) = 2[x^{1/2}]$, the derivative of H at x is given by

$$DH(x) = \text{diag}([x^{-1/2}]).$$

Using this fact, we derive a primitive expression for $\mathcal{R}(\chi)$ in terms of $x = H^{-1}(\chi) = \frac{1}{4}[\chi^2]$:

$$\dot{\chi} = \mathcal{R}(\chi)$$

$$= DH(x)R(x)$$

$$= \text{diag}([x^{-1/2}])(\text{diag}(x) - xx')F(x)$$

$$= \left(\text{diag}([x^{1/2}]) - [x^{1/2}]x'\right)F(x). \tag{7.7}$$

Now, we derive the gradient system on X generated by $\phi = f \circ H^{-1}$. To compute $\nabla \phi(x)$, we define an extension of ϕ to all of $\mathbf{R}^n_+$, compute its gradient, and then project the result onto the tangent space of X at x. The easiest way to proceed is to let $\tilde{f}: \text{int}(\mathbf{R}^n_+) \to \mathbf{R}$ be an arbitrary C^1 extension of f, and to define the extension $\tilde{\phi}: \text{int}(\mathbf{R}^n_+) \to \mathbf{R}$ by $\tilde{\phi} = \tilde{f} \circ H^{-1}$.

Since X is a portion of a sphere centered at the origin, the tangent space of X at x is the subspace $TX(x) = \{z \in \mathbf{R}^n : x'z = 0\}$. The orthogonal projection onto this set is represented by the $n \times n$ matrix

$$P_{TX(x)} = I - \frac{1}{x'x}xx' = I - \frac{1}{4}xx' = I - [x^{1/2}][x^{1/2}]'.$$

Also, since $\Phi \nabla \tilde{f}(x) = \nabla f(x) = \Phi F(x)$ by construction, it follows that $\nabla \tilde{f}(x) = F(x) + c(x)\mathbf{1}$ for some scalar-valued function $c: X \to \mathbf{R}$.

Using the chain rule (section 3.A.4), one obtains

$$\nabla \tilde{\phi}(x) = D(\tilde{f} \circ H^{-1})(x)' = (Df(H^{-1}(x))\, DH^{-1}(x))' = DH^{-1}(x)' \nabla \tilde{f}(x),$$

and applying the chain rule to the identity $H^{-1}(H(x)) \equiv x$ and rearranging yields

$$DH^{-1}(x) = DH(x)^{-1}.$$

Marshaling these observations, we find that the gradient system on X generated by ϕ is

$$\dot{x} = \nabla \phi(x)$$
$$= P_{TX(x)} \nabla \tilde{\phi}(x)$$
$$= P_{TX(x)} DH^{-1}(x)' \nabla \tilde{f}(x)$$
$$= P_{TX(x)} (DH(x)^{-1})' (F(x) + c(x)\mathbf{1})$$
$$= (I - [x^{1/2}][x^{1/2}]') \, \text{diag}([x^{1/2}]) \, (F(x) + c(x)\mathbf{1})$$
$$= (\text{diag}([x^{1/2}]) - [x^{1/2}]x')(F(x) + c(x)\mathbf{1})$$
$$= (\text{diag}([x^{1/2}]) - [x^{1/2}]x') F(x).$$

This agrees with equation (7.7), completing the proof of the theorem. ∎

Example 7.1.4: 123 Coordination Once More Figure 7.2 illustrates theorem 7.1.6 by presenting phase diagrams of the transported replicator dynamic $\dot{x} = \mathcal{R}(x)$ for 123 Coordination (see example 7.1.1). These phase diagrams on X are drawn atop contour plots of the transported potential function $\phi(x) = (f \circ H^{-1})(x) = \frac{1}{32}((x_1)^4 + 2(x_2)^4 + 3(x_3)^4)$. According to theorem 7.1.6, the solution trajectories of $\mathcal{R}$ should cross the level sets of ϕ orthogonally.

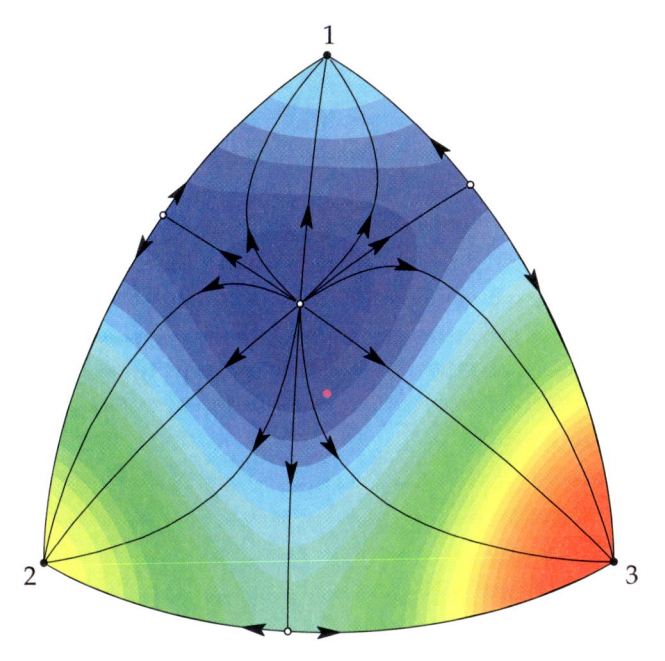

(a) Origin = $H(\frac{1}{3}, \frac{1}{3}, \frac{1}{3})$

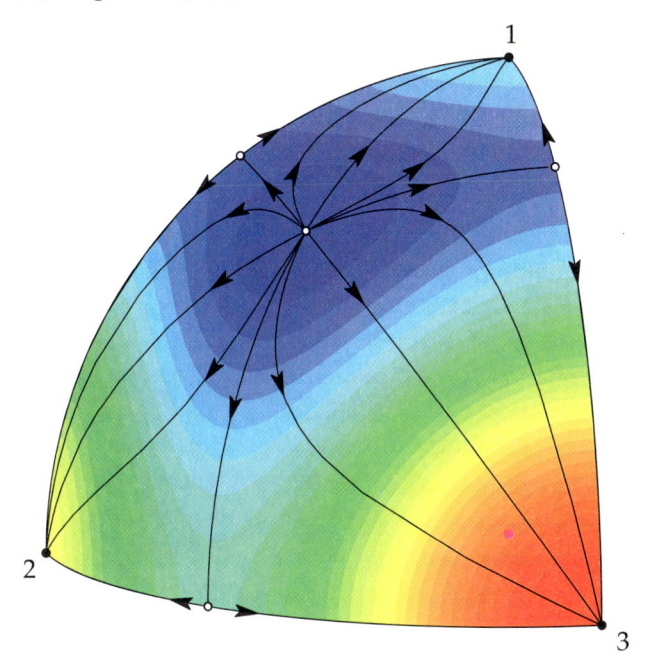

(b) Origin = $H(\frac{1}{7}, \frac{1}{7}, \frac{5}{7})$

Figure 7.2
The phase diagram of the transported replicator dynamic $\dot{x} = \mathcal{R}(x)$ for a coordination game. The pink dots represent the positions of the projection origins.

In figure 7.2 the crossings look orthogonal at the center of the figure, but not by the boundaries. This is an artifact of drawing a portion of the sphere in $\mathbf{R}^3$ by projecting it orthogonally onto a sheet of paper. (For exactly the same reason, latitude and longitude lines in an orthographic projection of the Earth only appear to cross at right angles in the center of the projection, not on the left and right sides.) To check whether the crossings near a given state $x \in X$ are truly orthogonal, we must minimize the distortion of angles near x by making x the origin of the projection, that is, the point where the sphere touches the sheet of paper. In the phase diagrams in figure 7.2 the projection origins are marked with pink dots; evidently, the crossings are orthogonal near these points. ◆

7.2 Stable Games

Recall that the population game F is stable if it satisfies

$$(y-x)'(F(y)-F(x)) \leq 0 \quad \text{for all } x, y \in X. \tag{7.8}$$

When F is C^1, this condition is equivalent to self-defeating externalities:

$$z'DF(x)z \leq 0 \quad \text{for all } z \in TX, x \in X. \tag{7.9}$$

The set of Nash equilibria of a stable game is convex, and most often a singleton.

In general, uniqueness of equilibrium is not enough to ensure convergence of evolutionary dynamics. There are many simple examples of games with a unique Nash equilibrium in which dynamics fail to converge (see chapter 9). Nevertheless, under many evolutionary dynamics, the structure provided by self-defeating externalities is enough to ensure convergence. While fewer dynamics converge here than in potential games, convergence does obtain under all six fundamental dynamics.

The convergence proofs for stable games again rely on the construction of Lyapunov functions, but here a distinct Lyapunov function must be constructed for each dynamic considered. It is natural to write these Lyapunov functions so that their values fall over time. Thus, a C^1 function L is a (*decreasing*) *strict Lyapunov function* for the dynamic $\dot{x} = V_F(x)$ if $\dot{L}(x) \leq 0$ for all $x \in X$, with equality only at rest points of V_F. Apart from those for perturbed best response dynamics, the Lyapunov functions are also non-negative, with zeros coinciding with the Nash equilibria of the underlying game F.

7.2.1 The Projection and Replicator Dynamics in Strictly Stable Games

To obtain convergence results for the projection and replicator dynamics, we must restrict attention to *strictly stable games*, that is, games in which condition (7.8) holds strictly for all $x, y \in X$. The Lyapunov functions for these dynamics are based on explicit notions of "distance" from the game's unique Nash equilibrium x^*.

Global Convergence of Evolutionary Dynamics

Theorem 7.2.1 shows that under the projection dynamic, x^* is *globally asymptotically stable*: all solution trajectories converge to x^*, and solutions that start near x^* never move too far away from x^* (see section 7.A.2).

Theorem 7.2.1 *Let F be a strictly stable game with unique Nash equilibrium x^*, and let $\dot{x} = V_F(x)$ be the projection dynamic for F. Let the function $E_{x^*}: X \to \mathbf{R}_+$, defined by*

$$E_{x^*}(x) = |x - x^*|^2,$$

represent squared Euclidean distance from x^*. Then E_{x^*} is a strict Lyapunov function for V_F, and so x^* is globally asymptotically stable under V_F.

Proof Since F is a strictly stable game, its unique Nash equilibrium x^* is also its unique globally evolutionarily stable state (GESS):

$$(x - x^*)'F(x) < 0 \quad \text{for all } x \in X - \{x^*\}.$$

This fact and the Moreau decomposition theorem imply that

$$\begin{aligned}
\dot{E}_{x^*}(x) &= \nabla E_{x^*}(x)'\dot{x} \\
&= 2(x - x^*)'\Pi_{TX(x)}(F(x)) \\
&= 2(x - x^*)'F(x) + 2(x^* - x)'\Pi_{NX(x)}(F(x)) \\
&\leq 2(x^* - x)'\Pi_{NX(x)}(F(x)) \\
&\leq 0,
\end{aligned}$$

where the penultimate inequality is strict whenever $x \neq x^*$. Global asymptotic stability of $NE(F)$ then follows from corollary 7.B.6. ∎

Exercise 7.2.2 Let F be a stable game, and let x^* be a Nash equilibrium of F.

i. Show that x^* is Lyapunov stable under (P).

ii. Suppose that F is a null stable game (i.e., that $(y - x)'(F(y) - F(x)) = 0$ for all $x, y \in X$). Show that if $x^* \in \text{int}(X)$, then E_{x^*} defines a *constant of motion* for (P) on $\text{int}(X)$: the value of E_{x^*} is constant along interior portions of solution trajectories of (P). ◇

Exercise 7.2.3 Show that if F is a C^1 stable game, then the squared speed of motion $L(x) = |\Phi F(x)|^2$ is a Lyapunov function for (P) on $\text{int}(X)$. Show that if F is null stable, then L defines a constant of motion for (P) on $\text{int}(X)$. (Notice that unlike that of E_{x^*}, the definition of L does not directly incorporate the Nash equilibrium x^*.) ◇

Under the replicator dynamic (R), as under any imitative dynamic, strategies that are initially unused remain unused for all time. Therefore, if state x places no mass on a strategy in the support of the Nash equilibrium x^*, the solution to (R) starting from x cannot converge to x^*. Thus, in stating the convergence result for the replicator dynamic, one needs to carefully specify the set of states from which convergence to equilibrium occurs.

With this motivation, let $S^p(x^p) = \{i \in S^p : x_i^p > 0\}$ denote the support of x^p. Then $X_{y^p}^p = \{x^p \in X^p : S^p(y^p) \subseteq S^p(x^p)\}$ is the set of states in X^p whose supports contain the support of y^p, and $X_y = \prod_{p \in \mathcal{P}} X_{y^p}^p$ is the set of states in X whose supports contain the support of y. To construct the Lyapunov function, define the function $h_{y^p}^p : X_{y^p}^p \to \mathbf{R}$ by

$$h_{y^p}^p(x^p) = \sum_{i \in S^p(y^p)} y_i^p \log \frac{y_i^p}{x_i^p}.$$

If population p is of unit mass, so that y^p and x^p are probability distributions, $h_{y^p}^p(x^p)$ is known as the *relative entropy* of y^p given x^p.

Theorem 7.2.4 *Let F be a strictly stable game with unique Nash equilibrium x^*, and let $\dot{x} = V_F(x)$ be the replicator dynamic for F. Define the function $H_{x^*} : X_{x^*} \to \mathbf{R}_+$ by*

$$H_{x^*}(x) = \sum_{p \in \mathcal{P}} h_{(x^*)^p}^p(x^p).$$

Then $H_{x^*}^{-1}(0) = \{x^*\}$, and $H_{x^*}(x)$ approaches infinity whenever x approaches $X - X_{x^*}$. Moreover, $\dot{H}_{x^*}(x) \leq 0$, with equality only when $x = x^*$. Therefore, x^* is globally asymptotically stable with respect to X_{x^*}.

The proofs of this theorem and a number of those to follow are given for the single-population case ($p = 1$); extensions to the multipopulations case are straightforward.

Proof ($p = 1$) To see that H_{x^*} is non-negative with $H_{x^*}^{-1}(0) = \{x^*\}$, observe that by Jensen's inequality,

$$-H_{x^*}(x) = \sum_{i \in S(x^*)} x_i^* \log \frac{x_i}{x_i^*} \leq \log \left(\sum_{i \in S(x^*)} x_i^* \cdot \frac{x_i}{x_i^*} \right) = \log \left(\sum_{i \in S(x^*)} x_i \right) \leq \log 1 = 0,$$

with equality if and only if $x = x^*$. The second claim is immediate. For the third claim, note that since F is strictly stable, x^* is a GESS, so for all $x \in X_{x^*}$,

Global Convergence of Evolutionary Dynamics

$$\dot{H}_{x^*}(x) = \nabla H_{x^*}(x)' \dot{x}$$

$$= -\sum_{i \in S(x^*)} \frac{x_i^*}{x_i} \cdot x_i \hat{F}_i(x)$$

$$= -\sum_{i \in S} x_i^* \hat{F}_i(x)$$

$$= -(x^*)'\big(F(x) - \mathbf{1}\, x'F(x)\big)$$

$$= -(x^* - x)'F(x)$$

$$\leq 0,$$

where the inequality binds precisely when $x = x^*$. The conclusions about stability then follow from theorems 7.B.2 and 7.B.3. ∎

Exercise 7.2.5 Let F be a stable game, and let x^* be a Nash equilibrium of F.

i. Show that x^* is Lyapunov stable under (R).

ii. Show that if F is a null stable game and $x^* \in \text{int}(X)$, then H_{x^*} defines a constant of motion for (R) on $\text{int}(X)$. ◇

7.2.2 Integrable Target Dynamics

Of the six fundamental dynamics, three—the BNN, best response, and logit dynamics—can be expressed as target dynamics of the form

$$\tau^p(\pi^p, x^p) = \tau^p(\hat{\pi}^p),$$

under which conditional switch rates only depend on on the vector of excess payoffs $\hat{\pi}^p = \pi^p - \frac{1}{m^p}\mathbf{1}(x^p)'\pi^p$. This is clearly true of the BNN dynamic. For the other two cases, note that shifting all components of the payoff vector by the same constant has no effect on either exact or perturbed best responses: in particular, the definitions (6.2) and (6.12) of the maximizer correspondence $M^p: \mathbf{R}^{n^p} \rightrightarrows \Delta^p$ and the perturbed maximizer function $\tilde{M}^p: \mathbf{R}^{n^p} \to \Delta^p$ satisfy $M^p(\hat{\pi}^p) = M^p(\pi^p)$ and $\tilde{M}^p(\hat{\pi}^p) = \tilde{M}^p(\pi^p)$.

We now show that these three dynamics converge to equilibrium in all stable games, as do all close enough relatives of these dynamics. Unlike in the context of potential games, monotonicity properties alone are not enough to ensure that a dynamic converges; in addition, integrability of the revision protocol plays a key role in establishing convergence results.

The following example illustrates that monotonicity properties alone do not ensure convergence of target dynamics in stable games.

Example 7.2.1: Cycling in Good RPS   Fix $\varepsilon > 0$, and let $g^\varepsilon \colon \mathbf{R} \to \mathbf{R}$ be a continuous decreasing function that equals 1 on $(-\infty, 0]$, equals ε^2 on $[\varepsilon, \infty)$, and is linear on $[0, \varepsilon]$. Then define the revision protocol τ for Rock-Paper-Scissors games by

$$\begin{pmatrix} \tau_R(\hat{\pi}) \\ \tau_P(\hat{\pi}) \\ \tau_S(\hat{\pi}) \end{pmatrix} = \begin{pmatrix} [\hat{\pi}_R]_+ g^\varepsilon(\hat{\pi}_S) \\ [\hat{\pi}_P]_+ g^\varepsilon(\hat{\pi}_R) \\ [\hat{\pi}_S]_+ g^\varepsilon(\hat{\pi}_P) \end{pmatrix}. \tag{7.10}$$

Under this protocol, the weight placed on a strategy is proportional to the positive part of the strategy's excess payoff, as in the protocol for the BNN dynamic; however, this weight is only of order ε^2 if the strategy it beats in RPS has an excess payoff greater than ε.

It is easy to verify that protocol (7.10) satisfies acuteness (5.22):

$$\tau(\hat{\pi})'\hat{\pi} = [\hat{\pi}_R]_+^2 g^\varepsilon(\hat{\pi}_S) + [\hat{\pi}_P]_+^2 g^\varepsilon(\hat{\pi}_R) + [\hat{\pi}_S]_+^2 g^\varepsilon(\hat{\pi}_P),$$

which is positive when $\hat{\pi} \in \text{int}(\mathbf{R}_*^n)$. Thus, the target dynamic induced by τ is an excess payoff dynamic. Figure 7.3 presents a phase diagram for this dynamic in the good RPS game

$$F(x) = Ax = \begin{pmatrix} 0 & -2 & 3 \\ 3 & 0 & -2 \\ -2 & 3 & 0 \end{pmatrix} \begin{pmatrix} x_R \\ x_P \\ x_S \end{pmatrix}.$$

Evidently, solutions from many initial conditions lead to a limit cycle.   ◆

To explain why cycling occurs in this example, we review some ideas about the geometry of stable games and target dynamics. By theorem 3.3.10, every Nash equilibrium x^* of a stable game is a globally neutrally stable state (GNSS). Geometrically, this means that at every nonequilibrium state x, the projected payoff vector $\Phi F(x)$ forms an acute or right angle with the line segment from x back to x^* (figures 3.6, 3.8, and 3.9). Meanwhile, our monotonicity condition for dynamics, positive correlation (PC), requires that away from equilibrium, each vector of motion $V_F(x)$ forms an acute angle with the projected payoff vector $\Phi F(x)$ (figures 5.1 and 5.2). Combining these observations, we conclude that if the law of motion $\dot{x} = V_F(x)$ tends to deviate from the projected payoffs ΦF in outward directions, that is, in directions heading away from equilibrium, then cycling will occur (compare figure 3.9 with figure 7.3). On the other hand, if the deviations of V_F from ΦF tend to be inward, then solutions should converge to equilibrium.

By this logic, one should be able to guarantee convergence of target dynamics in stable games by ensuring that the deviations of V_F from ΦF are toward the equilibrium, at least in some average sense. To accomplish this, we introduce an additional condition for revision protocols: *integrability*.

Global Convergence of Evolutionary Dynamics

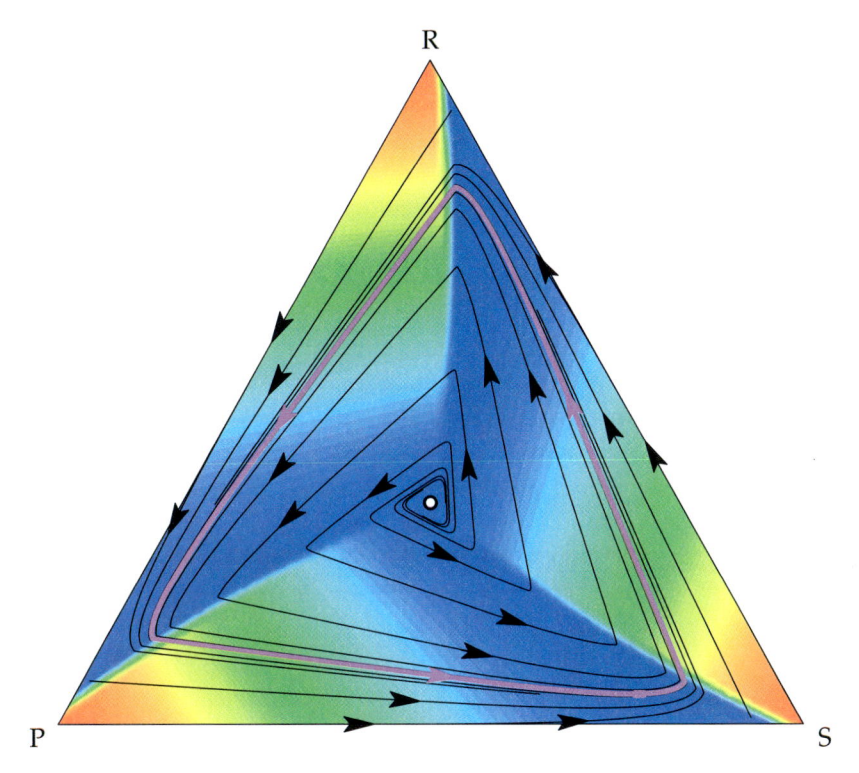

Figure 7.3
An excess payoff dynamic in good RPS ($w = 3, l = 2$).

There exists a C^1 function $\gamma^p \colon \mathbf{R}^{n^p} \to \mathbf{R}$ such that $\tau^p \equiv \nabla \gamma^p$. (7.11)

We call the functions γ^p in this condition *revision potentials*.

To give this condition a behavioral interpretation, it is useful to compare it to *separability*:

$$\tau_i^p(\hat{\pi}^p) \text{ is independent of } \hat{\pi}_{-i}^p. \tag{7.12}$$

The latter condition is stronger than the former: if τ^p satisfies (7.12), then it satisfies (7.11) with

$$\gamma^p(\hat{\pi}^p) = \sum_{i \in S^p} \int_0^{\hat{\pi}_i^p} \tau_i^p(s)\, ds. \tag{7.13}$$

In example 7.2.1, the protocol (7.10) that generated cycling has the following noteworthy feature: the weights agents place on each strategy depend systematically on the payoffs of the next strategy in the best response cycle. Building on this motivation, one can obtain a game-theoretic interpretation of integrability. Roughly speaking, integrability (7.11) is equivalent to a requirement that in expectation, learning the weight placed on strategy j does not convey information about other strategies' excess payoffs. It thus generalizes separability (7.12), which requires that learning the weight placed on strategy j conveys no information at all about other strategies' excess payoffs (see the chapter notes).

Before turning to convergence theorems, we address a missing step in the motivating argument: how does integrability ensure that the law of motion V_F tends to deviate from the projected payoffs ΦF in the direction of equilibrium? To make this link, recall a characterization of integrablility from section 3.A.9: the map $\tau: \mathbf{R}^n \to \mathbf{R}^n$ is integrable if and only if its line integral over any piecewise smooth closed curve $C \subset \mathbf{R}^n$ evaluates to zero:

$$\oint_C \tau(\hat{\pi}) \cdot d\hat{\pi} = 0. \tag{7.14}$$

Example 7.2.2 Let the population game F be generated by matching in standard RPS:

$$F(x) = Ax = \begin{pmatrix} 0 & -1 & 1 \\ 1 & 0 & -1 \\ -1 & 1 & 0 \end{pmatrix} \begin{pmatrix} x_R \\ x_P \\ x_S \end{pmatrix}.$$

The unique Nash equilibrium of F is the GNSS $x^* = (\frac{1}{3}, \frac{1}{3}, \frac{1}{3})$. Game F has the convenient property that at each state $x \in X$, the payoff vector $F(x)$, the projected payoff vector $\Phi F(x)$, and the excess payoff vector $\hat{F}(x)$ are all the same, a fact that simplifies the notation in the following argument.

Since F is null stable, at each state $x \neq x^*$ the payoff vector $F(x)$ is orthogonal to the vector $x^* - x$. In figure 3.9 these payoff vectors point counterclockwise relative to x^*. Since positive correlation (PC) requires that the direction of motion $V_F(x)$ form an acute angle with $F(x)$, dynamics satisfying (PC) also travel counterclockwise around the equilibrium.

To address whether the deviations of V_F from F tend to be inward or outward, let $C \subset X$ be a circle of radius $c \in (0, \frac{1}{\sqrt{6}}]$ centered at the equilibrium x^*. This circle is parameterized by the function $\xi: [0, 2\pi] \to X$, where

$$\xi_\alpha = \frac{c}{\sqrt{6}} \begin{pmatrix} -2\sin\alpha \\ \sqrt{3}\cos\alpha + \sin\alpha \\ -\sqrt{3}\cos\alpha + \sin\alpha \end{pmatrix} + x^*. \tag{7.15}$$

Here α is the counterclockwise angle between the vector $\xi_\alpha - x^*$ and a rightward horizontal vector (see figure 7.4).

Global Convergence of Evolutionary Dynamics

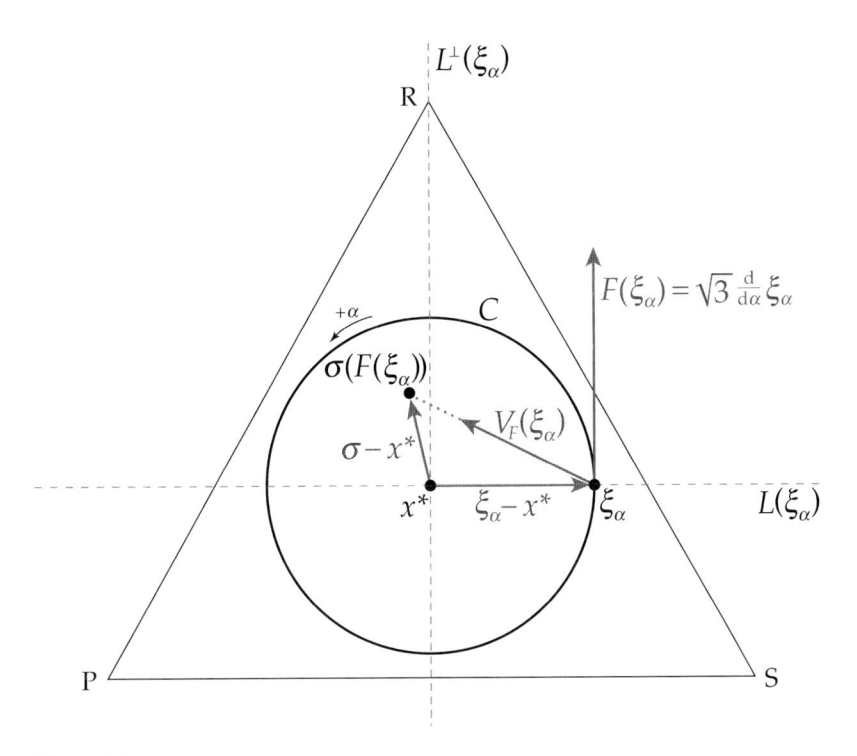

Figure 7.4
Integrability and inward motion of target dynamics in standard RPS.

Since state ξ_α lies on the circle C, the vector $x^* - \xi_\alpha$ can be drawn as a radius of C; thus, the payoff vector $\pi_\alpha \equiv F(\xi_\alpha)$, which is orthogonal to $x^* - \xi_\alpha$, must be tangent to C at ξ_α, as shown in figure 7.4. This observation is easy to verify analytically:

$$\pi_\alpha = F(\xi_\alpha) = \frac{c}{\sqrt{6}} \begin{pmatrix} -2\sqrt{3}\cos\alpha \\ -3\sin\alpha + \sqrt{3}\cos\alpha \\ 3\sin\alpha + \sqrt{3}\cos\alpha \end{pmatrix} = \sqrt{3}\frac{\mathrm{d}}{\mathrm{d}\alpha}\xi_\alpha. \qquad (7.16)$$

If we differentiate both sides of identity (7.16) with respect to the angle α, and note that $\frac{\mathrm{d}^2}{(\mathrm{d}\alpha)^2}\xi_\alpha = -(\xi_\alpha - x^*)$, we can link the rate of change of the payoff vector $\pi_\alpha = F(\xi_\alpha)$ to the displacement of state ξ_α from x^*:

$$\frac{\mathrm{d}}{\mathrm{d}\alpha}\pi_\alpha = \sqrt{3}\frac{\mathrm{d}^2}{(\mathrm{d}\alpha)^2}\xi_\alpha = -\sqrt{3}(\xi_\alpha - x^*). \qquad (7.17)$$

Now introduce an acute, integrable revision protocol τ. By combining integrability condition (7.14) with equation (7.17), we obtain

$$0 = \oint_C \tau(\pi) \cdot d\pi \equiv \int_0^{2\pi} \tau(\pi_\alpha)' \left(\frac{d}{d\alpha} \pi_\alpha\right) d\alpha = -\sqrt{3} \int_0^{2\pi} \tau(\pi_\alpha)' (\xi_\alpha - x^*) \, d\alpha. \qquad (7.18)$$

Write $\lambda(\pi) = \sum_{i \in S} \tau_i(\pi)$ and $\sigma_i(\pi) = \frac{\tau_i(\pi)}{\lambda(\pi)}$ to express the dynamic in target form. Then because $\xi_\alpha - x^* \in TX$ is orthogonal to $x^* = \frac{1}{3}\mathbf{1}$, we can conclude from equation (7.18) that

$$\int_0^{2\pi} \lambda(F(\xi_\alpha))(\sigma(F(\xi_\alpha)) - x^*)'(\xi_\alpha - x^*) \, d\alpha = 0. \qquad (7.19)$$

Equation (7.19) is a form of the requirement described at the start of this section; it asks that at states on the circle C, the vector of motion under the target dynamic

$$\dot{x} = V_F(x) = \lambda(F(x)) \left(\sigma(F(x)) - x\right) \qquad (7.20)$$

typically deviate from the payoff vector $F(x)$ in an inward direction, that is, in the direction of the equilibrium x^*.

To reach this interpretation of equation (7.19), note first that if the target state $\sigma(F(\xi_\alpha))$ lies on or even near line $L^\perp(\xi_\alpha)$, then motion from ξ_α toward $\sigma(F(\xi_\alpha))$ is initially inward, as shown in figure 7.4. (Of course, target state $\sigma(F(\xi_\alpha))$ lies above $L(\xi_\alpha)$ by virtue of positive correlation (PC).) Now, the integrand in (7.19) contains the inner product of the vectors $\sigma(F(\xi_\alpha)) - x^*$ and $\xi_\alpha - x^*$. This inner product is zero precisely when the two vectors are orthogonal, or equivalently, when target state $\sigma(F(\xi_\alpha))$ lies on $L^\perp(\xi_\alpha)$. Equation (7.19) does not require the two vectors to be orthogonal, but it asks that this be true on average, where the average is taken over states $\xi_\alpha \in C$ and weighted by the rates $\lambda(F(\xi_\alpha))$ at which ξ_α approaches $\sigma(F(\xi_\alpha))$. Thus, in the presence of acuteness, integrability implies that on average, the dynamic (7.20) tends to point inward, toward the equilibrium x^*. ◆

The foregoing arguments suggest that together, monotonicity and integrability are enough to ensure global convergence of target dynamics in stable games. This intuition can be developed into formal results by constructing suitable Lyapunov functions.

As a point of comparison, recall from section 7.1.1 that in the case of dynamics for potential games, monotonicity conditions alone are sufficient to prove global convergence results because the game's potential function serves as a Lyapunov function for any dynamic satisfying positive correlation (PC). Unlike potential games, stable games do not come equipped with candidate Lyapunov functions. But if the revision protocol that agents follow is integrable, then the revision potential of this protocol provides a building block for constructing a suitable Lyapunov function. Evidently, this Lyapunov function will vary with the dynamic under study, even when the game under consideration is fixed.

Global Convergence of Evolutionary Dynamics

The first result concerns *integrable excess payoff dynamics*, that is, excess payoff dynamics whose protocols τ^p are Lipschitz continuous, acute (5.22), and integrable (7.11). The prototype for this class is the BNN dynamic. Its protocol $\tau_i^p(\hat{\pi}^p) = [\hat{\pi}_i^p]_+$ is not only acute and integrable but also separable (7.12), and so admits potential function $\gamma^p(\hat{\pi}^p) = \frac{1}{2}\sum_{i \in S^p}[\hat{\pi}_i^p]_+^2$ (see equation (7.13)).

Theorem 7.2.6 *Let F be a C^1 stable game, and let $\dot{x} = V_F(x)$ be the integrable excess payoff dynamic for F based on revision protocols τ^p with revision potentials γ^p. Define the C^1 function $\Gamma \colon X \to \mathbf{R}$ by*

$$\Gamma(x) = \sum_{p \in \mathcal{P}} m^p \gamma^p(\hat{F}^p(x)).$$

Then Γ is a strict Lyapunov function for V_F, and NE(F) is globally attracting. In addition, if F admits a unique Nash equilibrium, or if the protocols τ^p also satisfy separability (7.12), then the functions γ^p can be chosen in such a way that Γ is non-negative with $\Gamma^{-1}(0) = NE(F)$, implying that NE(F) is globally asymptotically stable.

For future reference, observe that the value of the Lyapunov function Γ at state x is the (m^p-weighted) sum of the values of the revision potentials γ^p evaluated at the excess payoff vectors $\hat{F}^p(x)$.

The conditions introduced in the last sentence of the theorem are needed to ensure that the Lyapunov function Γ is constant on the set *NE(F)* of Nash equilibria. Were this not the case, the set *NE(F)* could be globally attracting without being Lyapunov stable (see example 7.B.1).

The proofs of theorem 7.2.6 and subsequent theorems make heavy use of multivariate product and chain rules (reviewed in section 3.A.4). The proofs all focus on the single-population case.

Proof of theorem 7.2.6 ($p=1$) Recall that the excess payoff vector $\hat{F}(x)$ is equal to $F(x) - \mathbf{1}\bar{F}(x)$, where $\bar{F}(x) = x'F(x)$ is the population's average payoff. By the product rule, the derivative of $\bar{F}$ is

$$D\bar{F}(x) = x'DF(x) + F(x)'.$$

Therefore, the derivative matrix for the excess payoff function $\hat{F}(x) = F(x) - \mathbf{1}\bar{F}(x)$ is

$$\begin{aligned}
D\hat{F}(x) &= D(F(x) - \mathbf{1}\bar{F}(x))\\
&= DF(x) - \mathbf{1}D\bar{F}(x)\\
&= DF(x) - \mathbf{1}(x'DF(x) + F(x)').
\end{aligned} \qquad (7.21)$$

Using (7.21) and the chain rule, we can compute the time derivative of Γ:

$$\dot\Gamma(x) = \nabla\Gamma(x)'\dot x$$
$$= \nabla\gamma(\hat F(x))'D\hat F(x)\dot x$$
$$= \tau(\hat F(x))'\left(DF(x) - \mathbf{1}\left(x'DF(x) + F(x)'\right)\right)\dot x$$
$$= \left(\tau(\hat F(x)) - \tau(\hat F(x))'\mathbf{1}x\right)'DF(x)\dot x - \tau(\hat F(x))'\mathbf{1}F(x)'\dot x$$
$$= \dot x'DF(x)\dot x - (\tau(\hat F(x))'\mathbf{1})(F(x)'\dot x)$$
$$\leq 0,$$

where the inequality follows from the facts that F is stable and V_F satisfies positive correlation (PC).

We now show that this inequality binds precisely on the set $NE(F)$. First, note that if $x \in RP(V_F)$ (i.e., if $\dot x = \mathbf{0}$), then $\dot\Gamma(x) = 0$. On the other hand, if $x \notin RP(V_F)$, then $\tau(\hat F(x))'\mathbf{1} > 0$ and $F(x)'\dot x > 0$ (by condition (PC)), implying that $\dot\Gamma(x) < 0$. Since $NE(F) = RP(V_F)$, the claim is proved. That $NE(F)$ is globally attracting then follows from theorem 7.B.3.

If F admits a unique Nash equilibrium x^*, then the foregoing argument implies that x^* is the unique minimizer of Γ. Since the value of Γ is nonincreasing over time, a solution starting from a state x with $\Gamma(x) < \Gamma(x^*)$ could not converge to x^*, contradicting that x^* is globally attracting. Thus, after normalizing by an additive constant, we find that Γ is non-negative with $\Gamma^{-1}(0) = \{x^*\}$, so the global asymptotic stability of x^* follows from corollary 7.B.6.

If instead τ satisfies separability (7.12), the revision potential γ is defined as in equation (7.13). It then follows from exercise 5.5.6 that Γ is non-negative, with $\Gamma(x) = 0$ if and only if $\hat F(x) \in \mathrm{bd}(\mathbf{R}_*^n)$. Thus, lemma 5.5.3 implies that $\Gamma(x) = 0$ if and only if $x \in NE(F)$, and so the global asymptotic stability of $NE(F)$ again follows from corollary 7.B.6. ∎

Next, consider the best response dynamic, here expressed by applying the maximizer correspondence

$$M^p(\hat\pi^p) = \underset{y^p \in \Delta^p}{\mathrm{argmax}}\ (y^p)'\hat\pi^p$$

to the vector of excess payoffs, yielding the exact target dynamic

$$\dot x^p \in m^p M^p(\hat F^p(x)) - x^p. \tag{BR}$$

Following the previous logic, one can assess the possibilities for convergence in stable games by checking monotonicity and integrability. Monotonicity was

Global Convergence of Evolutionary Dynamics

established in theorem 6.1.4, which showed that (BR) satisfies an analogue of positive correlation (PC) appropriate for differential inclusions. For integrability, one can argue that the protocol M^p, despite being multivalued, is integrable in a suitably defined sense, with its "potential function" being given by the *maximum function*

$$\mu^p(\pi^p) = \max_{y^p \in \Delta^p} (y^p)' \pi^p = \max_{i \in S^p} \pi_i^p.$$

Note that if the payoff vector π^p, and hence the excess payoff vector $\hat{\pi}^p$, have a unique maximizing component $i \in S^p$, then the gradient of μ^p at $\hat{\pi}^p$ is the standard basis vector e_i^p. But this vector corresponds to the unique mixed best response to $\hat{\pi}^p$, and so

$$\nabla \mu^p(\hat{\pi}^p) = e_i^p = M^p(\hat{\pi}^p).$$

One can account for multiple optimal components using a broader notion of differentiation: for all $\hat{\pi}^p \in \mathbf{R}^n$, $M^p(\hat{\pi}^p)$ is the subdifferential of the convex function μ^p at $\hat{\pi}^p$ (see the chapter notes).

With monotonicity and integrability verified, we again construct the candidate Lyapunov function by plugging the excess payoff vectors into the revision potentials μ^p. The resulting function G is very simple; it measures the difference between the payoffs agents could obtain by choosing optimal strategies and their actual aggregate payoffs.

Theorem 7.2.7 *Let F be a C^1 stable game, and let $\dot{x} \in V_F(x)$ be the best response dynamic for F. Define the Lipschitz continuous function $G: X \to \mathbf{R}_+$ by*

$$G(x) = \max_{y \in X} (y - x)' F(x) = \sum_{p \in \mathcal{P}} m^p \max_{i \in S^p} \hat{F}_i^p(x).$$

Then $G^{-1}(0) = NE(F)$. Moreover, if $\{x_t\}_{t \geq 0}$ is a solution to V_F, then $\dot{G}(x_t) \leq -G(x_t)$ for almost all $t \geq 0$, and so NE(F) is globally asymptotically stable under V_F.

Proof ($p = 1$) That $G^{-1}(0) = NE(F)$ follows from lemma 5.5.3. To prove the second claim, let $\{x_t\}_{t \geq 0}$ be a solution to V_F, and let $S^*(t) \subseteq S$ be the set of pure best responses to state x_t. Since $\{x_t\}_{t \geq 0}$ is Lipschitz continuous, the map $t \mapsto \hat{F}_i(x_t)$ is also Lipschitz continuous for each strategy $i \in S$. Thus, since $G(x) = \max_{y \in X} (y - x)' F(x) = \max_{i \in S} \hat{F}_i(x)$, it follows from Danskin's envelope theorem (see the chapter notes) that the map $t \mapsto G(x_t)$ is Lipschitz continuous, and that at almost all $t \in [0, \infty)$,

$$\dot{G}(x_t) \equiv \tfrac{d}{dt} \max_{i \in S} \hat{F}_i(x_t) = \tfrac{d}{dt} \hat{F}_{i^*}(x_t) \quad \text{for all } i^* \in S^*(t). \tag{7.22}$$

Applying equation (7.21), we find that for t satisfying equation (7.22) and at which $\dot{x}_t$ exists,

$$\dot{G}(x_t) = \frac{d}{dt}\hat{F}_{i*}(x_t) \quad \text{for all } i^* \in S^*(t)$$

$$= \left(e'_{i*}DF(x_t) - x'_t DF(x_t) - F(x_t)'\right)\dot{x}_t \quad \text{for all } i^* \in S^*(t)$$

$$= (y^* - x_t)'DF(x_t)\dot{x}_t - F(x_t)'\dot{x}_t \quad \text{for all } y^* \in \operatorname{argmax}_{y \in \Delta} y'\hat{F}(x_t)$$

$$= \dot{x}'_t DF(x_t)\dot{x}_t - F(x_t)'\dot{x}_t$$

$$\leq -F(x_t)'\dot{x}_t$$

$$= -\max_{y \in X} F(x_t)'(y - x_t)$$

$$= -G(x_t),$$

where the inequality follows from the fact that F is a stable game. (Note that the equality of the third to last and last expressions is also implied by theorem 6.1.4.) The global asymptotic stability of $NE(F)$ then follows from theorems 7.B.2 and 7.B.5. ∎

Finally, consider convergence under perturbed best response dynamics. These are exact target dynamics of the form

$$\dot{x}^p = m^p \tilde{M}^p(\hat{F}^p(x)) - x^p;$$

here, the target protocol is the perturbed maximizer function

$$\tilde{M}^p(\hat{\pi}^p) = \operatorname*{argmax}_{y^p \in \operatorname{int}(\Delta^p)} (y^p)'\hat{\pi}^p - v^p(y^p),$$

where $v^p \colon \operatorname{int}(\Delta^p) \to \mathbf{R}$ is an admissible deterministic perturbation (see section 6.2.2).

Once again, we verify the two conditions that underlie convergence. Theorem 6.2.10 showed that all perturbed best response dynamics satisfy *virtual positive correlation* (6.17), establishing the required monotonicity. As for integrability, observation 6.C.3 showed that the protocol $\tilde{M}^p$ is integrable; its revision potential,

$$\tilde{\mu}^p(\pi^p) = \max_{y^p \in \operatorname{int}(\Delta^p)} (y^p)'\pi^p - v^p(y^p), \tag{7.23}$$

is the *perturbed maximum function* induced by v^p. Now, mimicking theorem 7.2.6, we construct our Lyapunov function by composing the revision potentials $\tilde{\mu}^p$ with the excess payoff functions $\hat{F}^p$.

Theorem 7.2.8 *Let F be a C^1 stable game, and let $\dot{x} = V_{Fv}(x)$ be the perturbed best response dynamic for F generated by the admissible deterministic perturbations v. Define the function $\tilde{G}\colon \operatorname{int}(X) \to \mathbf{R}_+$ by*

$$\tilde{G}(x) = \sum_{p \in \mathcal{P}} m^p \left(\tilde{\mu}^p(\hat{F}^p(x)) + v^p(\tfrac{1}{m^p}x^p)\right).$$

Global Convergence of Evolutionary Dynamics   245

Then $G^{-1}(0) = PE(F, v)$, and this set is a singleton. Moreover, $\tilde{G}$ is a strict Lyapunov function for $V_{F,v}$, and so $PE(F, v)$ is globally asymptotically stable under $V_{F,v}$.

Proof ($p = 1$)   As in section 6.2, let $\tilde{F}(x) = F(x) - \nabla v(x)$ be the virtual payoff function generated by (F, v). Then

$$x \in PE(F,v) \Leftrightarrow \Phi\tilde{F}(x) = \mathbf{0} \Leftrightarrow x = \underset{y \in \text{int}(\Delta)}{\operatorname{argmax}} \left(y'F(x) - v(y) \right) \Leftrightarrow \tilde{G}(x) = 0.$$

To prove that $\tilde{G}$ is a strict Lyapunov function, recall from observation 6.C.3 that the perturbed maximum function $\tilde{\mu}$ defined in equation (7.23) is a potential function for the perturbed maximizer function $\tilde{M}$: that is, $\nabla\tilde{\mu} \equiv \tilde{M}$. Therefore, since F is stable, virtual positive correlation (6.17) implies that

$$\dot{\tilde{G}}(x) = \frac{d}{dt}\left(\tilde{\mu}(\hat{F}(x)) + v(x) \right)$$

$$= \frac{d}{dt}\left(\tilde{\mu}(F(x)) - (x'F(x) - v(x)) \right)$$

$$= \tilde{M}(F(x))'DF(x)\dot{x} - \left(x'DF(x)\dot{x} + \dot{x}'F(x) - \dot{x}'\nabla v(x) \right)$$

$$= (\tilde{M}(F(x)) - x)'DF(x)\dot{x} - \dot{x}'(F(x) - \nabla v(x))$$

$$= \dot{x}'DF(x)\dot{x} - \dot{x}'\tilde{F}(x)$$

$$\leq 0,$$

with equality if and only if x is a rest point. But $RP(V_{F,v}) = PE(F, v)$ by definition, so Corollary 7.B.6 implies that $PE(F, v)$ is globally asymptotically stable.

Finally, we prove that $PE(F, v)$ is a singleton. Let

$$\phi_{x,h}(t) = h'\tilde{F}(x + th)$$

for all $x \in X$, $h \in TX - \{\mathbf{0}\}$, and $t \in \mathbf{R}$ such that $x + th \in \text{int}(X)$. Since F is stable and $D^2 v(x + th)$ is positive definite with respect to $TX \times TX$, it follows that

$$\phi'_{x,h}(t) = h'D\tilde{F}(x+th)h = h'DF(x+th)h - h'D^2 v(x+th)h < 0, \tag{7.24}$$

and so $\phi_{x,h}(t)$ is decreasing in t. Moreover,

$$x \in PE(F,v) \Leftrightarrow \tilde{F}(x) \text{ is a constant vector} \Leftrightarrow \phi_{x,h}(0) = 0 \text{ for all } h \in TX - \{\mathbf{0}\}. \tag{7.25}$$

Now let $x \in PE(F, v)$ and $y \in X - \{x\}$. Then $y = x + t_y h_y$ for some $t_y > 0$ and $h_y \in TX - \{\mathbf{0}\}$. Statements (7.24) and (7.25) imply that

$$\phi_{y,h_y}(0) = h'_y \tilde{F}(y) = h'_y \tilde{F}(x + t_y h_y) = \phi_{x,h_y}(t_y) < \phi_{x,h_y}(0) = 0.$$

Therefore, statement (7.25) implies that $y \notin PE(F, v)$ and hence that $PE(F, v) = \{x\}$. ∎

7.2.3 Impartial Pairwise Comparison Dynamics

In section 5.6, we defined pairwise comparison dynamics using Lipschitz continuous revision protocols ρ^p that only condition on payoffs and that are sign-preserving:

$$\text{sgn}(\rho_{ij}^p(\pi^p)) = \text{sgn}([\pi_j^p - \pi_i^p]_+) \quad \text{for all } i,j \in S^p \text{ and } p \in \mathcal{P}.$$

To obtain a general convergence result for stable games, an additional condition is needed, namely, *impartiality*:

$$\rho_{ij}^p(\pi^p) = \phi_j^p(\pi_j^p - \pi_i^p) \quad \text{for some functions } \phi_j^p \colon \mathbf{R} \to \mathbf{R}_+. \tag{7.26}$$

Combining this restriction with mean dynamic equation (M), we see that impartial pairwise comparison dynamics take the form

$$\dot{x}_i^p = \sum_{j \in S^p} x_j^p \phi_i^p(F_i^p(x) - F_j^p(x)) - x_i^p \sum_{j \in S^p} \phi_j^p(F_j^p(x) - F_i^p(x)).$$

Under impartiality (7.26), the function of the payoff difference $\pi_j^p - \pi_i^p$ that describes the conditional switch rate from i to j does not depend on an agent's current strategy i. This restriction introduces at least a superficial connection with the target dynamics studied in section 7.2.2, as both restrict the dependence of agents' decisions on their current choices of strategy.

Theorem 7.2.9 shows that together, sign preservation and impartiality ensure global convergence to Nash equilibrium in stable games.

Theorem 7.2.9 *Let F be a C^1 stable game, and let $\dot{x} = V_F(x)$ be an impartial pairwise comparison dynamic for F. Define the Lipschitz continuous function $\Psi \colon X \to \mathbf{R}_+$ by*

$$\Psi(x) = \sum_{p \in \mathcal{P}} \sum_{i \in S^p} \sum_{j \in S^p} x_i^p \psi_j^p (F_j^p(x) - F_i^p(x)), \quad \text{where } \psi_k^p(d) = \int_0^d \phi_k^p(s) \, ds$$

is the definite integral of ϕ_k^p. Then $\Psi^{-1}(0) = NE(F)$. Moreover, $\dot{\Psi}(x) \leq 0$ for all $x \in X$, with equality if and only if $x \in NE(F)$, and so $NE(F)$ is globally asymptotically stable.

To understand the role played by impartiality (7.26), recall the general formula for the mean dynamic:

$$\dot{x}_i^p = \sum_{j \in S^p} x_j^p \rho_{ji}^p(F^p(x), x^p) - x_i^p \sum_{j \in S^p} \rho_{ij}^p(F^p(x), x^p). \tag{M}$$

According to the second term of this expression, the rate of outflow from strategy i is $x_i^p \sum_{k \in S^p} \rho_{ik}^p$; thus, the *percentage* rate of outflow from i, $\sum_{k \in S^p} \rho_{ik}^p$, varies with i. It follows that strategies with high payoffs can nevertheless have high percentage outflow rates; even if $\pi_i^p > \pi_j^p$, one can still have $\rho_{ik}^p > \rho_{jk}^p$ for $k \neq i, j$.

Global Convergence of Evolutionary Dynamics

Having good strategies lose players more quickly than bad strategies is an obvious impediment to convergence to Nash equilibrium.

Impartiality (7.26) places controls on these percentage outflow rates. If the conditional switch rates ϕ_j^p are monotone in payoffs, then condition (7.26) ensures that better strategies have lower percentage outflow rates. If the conditional switch rates are not monotone, but merely sign-preserving, condition (7.26) still implies that the *integrated* conditional switch rates ψ_k^p are ordered by payoffs. According to the following analysis, this control is enough to ensure convergence of pairwise comparison dynamics to Nash equilibrium in stable games.

Proof ($p = 1$) The first claim is proved as follows:

$$\Psi(x) = 0 \Leftrightarrow [x_i = 0 \text{ or } \psi_j(F_j(x) - F_i(x)) = 0] \quad \text{for all } i,j \in S$$

$$\Leftrightarrow [x_i = 0 \text{ or } F_i(x) \geq F_j(x)] \quad \text{for all } i,j \in S$$

$$\Leftrightarrow [x_i = 0 \text{ or } F_i(x) \geq \max_{j \in S} F_j(x)] \quad \text{for all } i,j \in S$$

$$\Leftrightarrow x \in NE(F).$$

To begin the proof of the second claim, compute the partial derivatives of Ψ:

$$\frac{\partial \Psi}{\partial x_l}(x) = \sum_{i \in S} \sum_{j \in S} x_i \rho_{ij} \left(\frac{\partial F_j}{\partial x_l}(x) - \frac{\partial F_i}{\partial x_l}(x) \right) + \sum_{k \in S} \psi_k (F_k(x) - F_l(x))$$

$$= \sum_{i \in S} \sum_{j \in S} (x_i \rho_{ij} - x_j \rho_{ji}) \frac{\partial F_j}{\partial x_l}(x) + \sum_{k \in S} \psi_k (F_k(x) - F_l(x))$$

$$= \sum_{j \in S} \dot{x}_j \frac{\partial F_j}{\partial x_l}(x) + \sum_{k \in S} \psi_k (F_k(x) - F_l(x)).$$

Using this expression, find the rate of change of Ψ over time along solutions to (M):

$$\dot{\Psi}(x) = \nabla \Psi(x)' \dot{x}$$

$$= \dot{x}' DF(x) \dot{x} + \sum_{i \in S} \dot{x}_i \sum_{k \in S} \psi_k (F_k - F_i)$$

$$= \dot{x}' DF(x) \dot{x} + \sum_{i \in S} \sum_{j \in S} (x_j \rho_{ji} - x_i \rho_{ij}) \sum_{k \in S} \psi_k (F_k - F_i)$$

$$= \dot{x}' DF(x) \dot{x} + \sum_{i \in S} \sum_{j \in S} \left(x_j \rho_{ji} \sum_{k \in S} (\psi_k (F_k - F_i) - \psi_k (F_k - F_j)) \right).$$

To evaluate the summation, first observe that if $F_i(x) > F_j(x)$, then $\rho_{ji}(F(x)) \equiv \phi_i(F_i(x) - F_j(x)) > 0$ and $F_k(x) - F_i(x) < F_k(x) - F_j(x)$; since each ψ_k is nondecreasing, it follows that $\psi_k(F_k - F_i) - \psi_k(F_k - F_j) \le 0$. In fact, when $k = i$, the comparison between payoff differences becomes $0 < F_i(x) - F_j(x)$; since each ψ_i is increasing on $[0, \infty)$, it follows that $\psi_i(0) - \psi_i(F_i - F_j) < 0$. One can therefore conclude that if $F_i(x) > F_j(x)$, then $\rho_{ji}(F(x)) > 0$ and $\sum_{k \in S} (\psi_k(F_k - F_i) - \psi_k(F_k - F_j)) < 0$. On the other hand, if $F_j(x) \ge F_i(x)$, it follows immediately that $\rho_{ji}(F(x)) = 0$. And, of course, $\dot{x}' DF(x) \dot{x} \le 0$, since F is stable.

Marshaling these facts, we find that $\dot{\Psi}(x) \le 0$, and that

$$\dot{\Psi}(x) = 0 \quad \text{if and only if} \quad x_j \rho_{ji}(F(x)) = 0 \quad \text{for all } i, j \in S. \tag{7.27}$$

Lemma 5.6.4 shows that the second condition in (7.27) defines the set $RP(V_F)$, which is equal to $NE(F)$ by theorem 5.6.2; this proves the second claim. Finally, the global asymptotic stability of $NE(F)$ follows from corollary 7.B.6. ∎

Exercise 7.2.10 Construct a pairwise comparison dynamic that generates cycling in the good RPS game from example 7.2.1. ◇

7.2.4 Summary

Table 7.1 summarizes the results in this section by presenting the Lyapunov functions for single-population stable games for the six fundamental evolutionary dynamics. The Lyapunov functions are divided into three classes: those based on an explicit notion of "distance" from equilibrium, those based on revision potentials for target protocols, and the Lyapunov function for the Smith dynamic, which stands alone.

Table 7.1
Lyapunov functions for the Six Fundamental Dynamics in Stable Games

Dynamic	Formula	Lyapunov Function
Projection	$\dot{x} = \Pi_{TX(x)}(F(x))$	$E_{x^*}(x) = \lvert x - x^* \rvert^2$
Replicator	$\dot{x}_i = x_i \hat{F}_i(x)$	$H_{x^*}(x) = \sum_{i \in S(x^*)} x_i^* \log \frac{x_i^*}{x_i}$
Best response	$\dot{x} \in M(\hat{F}(x)) - x$	$G(x) = \mu(\hat{F}(x))$
Logit	$\dot{x} = \tilde{M}(\hat{F}(x)) - x$	$\tilde{G}(x) = \tilde{\mu}(\hat{F}(x)) + v(x)$
BNN	$\dot{x}_i = [\hat{F}_i(x)]_+ - x_i \sum_{j \in S}[\hat{F}_j(x)]_+$	$\Gamma(x) = \frac{1}{2} \sum_{i \in S}[\hat{F}_i(x)]_+^2$
Smith	$\dot{x}_i = \sum_{j \in S} x_j [F_i(x) - F_j(x)]_+ - x_i \sum_{j \in S}[F_j(x) - F_i(x)]_+$	$\Psi(x) = \frac{1}{2} \sum_{i \in S} \sum_{j \in S} x_i [F_j(x) - F_i(x)]_+^2$

Example 7.2.3: Matching Pennies Figure 7.5 presents phase diagrams of the six fundamental dynamics in two-population Matching Pennies:

$$\begin{pmatrix} F_H^1(x) \\ F_T^1(x) \\ F_h^2(x) \\ F_t^2(x) \end{pmatrix} = \begin{pmatrix} 0 & 0 & 1 & -1 \\ 0 & 0 & -1 & 1 \\ -1 & 1 & 0 & 0 \\ 1 & -1 & 0 & 0 \end{pmatrix} \begin{pmatrix} x_H^1 \\ x_T^1 \\ x_h^2 \\ x_t^2 \end{pmatrix} = \begin{pmatrix} x_h^2 - x_t^2 \\ x_t^2 - x_h^2 \\ x_T^1 - x_H^1 \\ x_H^1 - x_T^1 \end{pmatrix}.$$

Each phase diagram is drawn atop a contour plot of the relevant Lyapunov function. Since Matching Pennies is a zero-sum game, F is null stable; thus, the Lyapunov functions for the replicator and projection dynamics define constants of motion for these dynamics, with solution trajectories cycling along level curves. In the remaining cases, all solutions converge to the unique Nash equilibrium, $x^* = ((\frac{1}{2}, \frac{1}{2}), (\frac{1}{2}, \frac{1}{2}))$. ◆

7.3 Supermodular Games

In a supermodular game, higher choices by one's opponents make one's own higher strategies look relatively more desirable. In section 3.4, this property was used to show that the best response correspondences of supermodular games are monotone in the stochastic dominance order; that implied in turn that these games admit minimal and maximal Nash equilibria.

Given this monotone structure on best response correspondences, it is natural to look for convergence results for supermodular games under the best response dynamic (BR). Section 7.3.1 uses elementary methods to establish a global convergence result for (BR) under some strong additional assumptions on the underlying game: in particular, it must be derived from a two-player normal form game that satisfies both supermodularity and diminishing returns conditions.

To prove more general convergence results, we appeal to the theory of cooperative differential equations. These are smooth differential equations under which increasing the value of any component of the state variable increases the growth rates of all other components. Under some mild regularity conditions, almost all solutions of these equations converge to rest points.

Because of the smoothness requirement, these techniques cannot be applied to the best response dynamic itself. Fortunately, the needed monotonicity carries over from exact best responses to perturbed best responses, although only those that can be generated from *stochastic* perturbations of payoffs. In section 7.3.2, we use this idea to prove almost global convergence of stochastically perturbed best response dynamics in supermodular games.

(a) Replicator

(b) Projection

(c) Brown–von Neumann–Nash

(d) Smith

(e) Best response

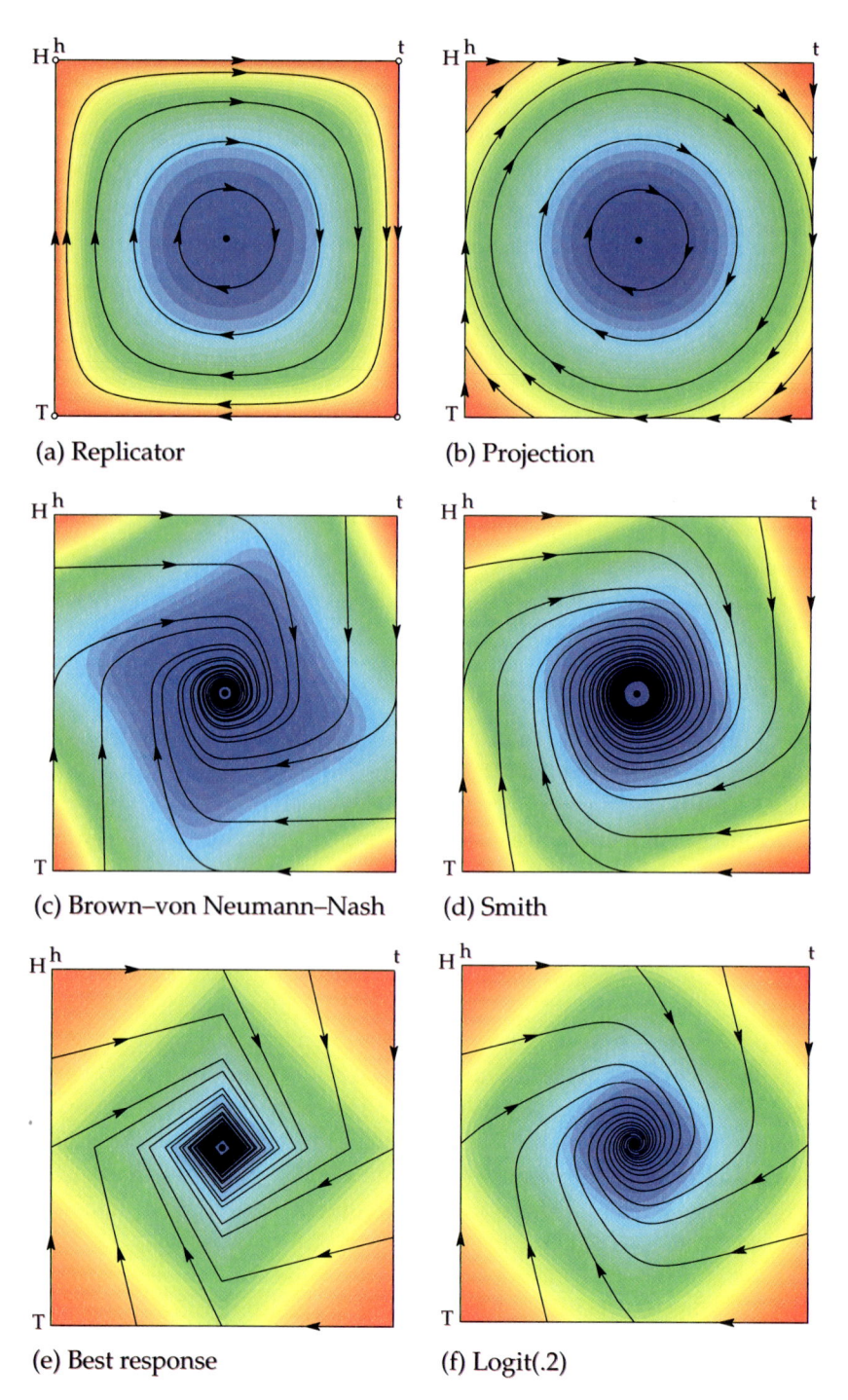

(f) Logit(.2)

Figure 7.5
Six basic dynamics in Matching Pennies. The contour plots are the corresponding Lyapunov functions.

7.3.1 The Best Response Dynamic in Two-Player Normal Form Games

Let $U = (U^1, U^2)$ be a two-player normal form game, and let F be the population game obtained when members of two populations are matched to play U (see example 2.2.2). Then the best response dynamic (BR) for F takes the form

$$\dot{x}^1 \in B^1(x) - x^1 = M^1(F^1(x)) - x^1 = M^1(U^1 x^2) - x^1;$$
$$\dot{x}^2 \in B^2(x) - x^2 = M^2(F^2(x)) - x^2 = M^2((U^2)' x^1) - x^2. \quad \text{(BR)}$$

The convergence result for supermodular games concerns simple solutions of this dynamic. A solution $\{x_t\}_{t \geq 0}$ of (BR) is *simple* if the set of times at which it is not differentiable has no accumulation point, and if at other times, all elements of the sets of target states $B^p(x_t)$ are pure (i.e., vertices of X^p).

Exercise 7.3.1

i. Provide an example of a 2×2 game with a Nash equilibrium x^* such that no solution to (BR) starting from x^* is simple.

ii. Show that there exists a simple solution to (BR) from every initial condition in game $U = (U^1, U^2)$ if for all nonempty sets $\hat{S}^1 \subseteq S^1$ and $\hat{S}^2 \subseteq S^2$, the game in which players are restricted to strategies in $\hat{S}^1$ and $\hat{S}^2$ admits a pure Nash equilibrium. (Theorem 3.4.9 implies that U has this property if it is supermodular.) ◇

If $\{x_t\}_{t \geq 0}$ is a simple solution trajectory of (BR), one can list the sequence of times $\{t_k\}$ at which the solution is not differentiable (i.e., at which the target state for at least one population changes). During each open interval of times $I_k = (t_{k-1}, t_k)$, the pure strategies $i_k \in S^1$ and $j_k \in S^2$ selected by revising agents are fixed; by continuity, these strategies are optimal not only at times in (t_{k-1}, t_k), but also at the initial and terminal times t_{k-1} and t_k. We call strategies i_k and j_k the *interval k selections* for populations 1 and 2.

The following lemma shows that i_{k+1} must perform at least as well as i_k against both j_k and j_{k+1}, and that the analogous comparisons between the payoffs of j_k and j_{k+1} also hold.

Lemma 7.3.2 *Suppose that revising agents select strategies $i = i_k$ and $j = j_k$ during interval I_k, and strategies $i' = i_{k+1}$ and $j' = j_{k+1}$ during interval I_{k+1}. Then*

i. $U^1_{i'j} \geq U^1_{ij}$ and $U^2_{ij'} \geq U^2_{ij}$;

ii. $U^1_{i'j'} \geq U^1_{ij'}$ and $U^2_{i'j'} \geq U^2_{i'j}$.

Exercise 7.3.3 Prove lemma 7.3.2. (*Hint:* Notice that $x^2_{t_k}$ is a convex combination of $x^2_{t_{k-1}}$ and the vertex v^2_j, and that $x^2_{t_{k+1}}$ is a convex combination of $x^2_{t_k}$ and v^2_j. For part (ii), use the facts that strategies i and i' are both optimal at time t_k, and that strategy i' is optimal at time t_{k+1}.) ◇

Now, recall from exercise 3.4.4 that $U = (U^1, U^2)$ is supermodular if

$$U^1_{i+1,j+1} - U^1_{i,j+1} \geq U^1_{i+1,j} - U^1_{i,j} \text{ and } U^2_{i+1,j+1} - U^2_{i+1,j} \geq U^2_{i,j+1} - U^2_{i,j}$$
$$\text{for all } i < n^1, j < n^2. \tag{7.28}$$

(When (7.28) holds, the population game F induced by U is supermodular as well.) If the inequalities in (7.28) always hold strictly, U is *strictly supermodular*.

The convergence result requires two additional conditions on U. The game U exhibits *strictly diminishing returns* if for each fixed strategy of the opponent, the benefit a player obtains by increasing his strategy is decreasing, in other words, if payoffs are "concave in own strategy":

$$U^1_{i+2,j} - U^1_{i+1,j} < U^1_{i+1,j} - U^1_{i,j} \quad \text{for all } i \leq n^1 - 2, j \in S^2;$$
$$U^2_{i,j+2} - U^2_{i,j+1} < U^2_{i,j+1} - U^2_{i,j} \quad \text{for all } i \in S^1, j \leq n^2 - 2.$$

Finally, U is *nondegenerate* if for each fixed pure strategy of the opponent, a player is not indifferent among any of his pure strategies.

Theorem 7.3.4 *Suppose that F is generated by matching in a two-player normal form game U that is strictly supermodular, exhibits strictly diminishing returns, and is nondegenerate. Then every simple solution trajectory of the best response dynamic* (BR) *converges to a pure Nash equilibrium.*

Proof Suppose that the sequence of times $\{t_k\}$ is finite, with final element t_K. Let i^* and j^* be the selections made by revising agents after time t_K. Then the pure state $x^* = (v^1_{i^*}, v^2_{j^*})$ is in $B(x_t)$ for all $t \geq t_K$, and $\{x_t\}$ converges to x^*. Since payoffs are continuous, it follows that $x^* \in B(x^*)$, and so that x^* is a Nash equilibrium. To complete the proof of the theorem, we establish by contradiction that the sequence of times $\{t_k\}$ cannot be infinite.

Note that at time t_k, agents in each population p are indifferent between their interval k and interval $k+1$ selections. Moreover, since U exhibits strictly decreasing returns, it is easy to verify that whenever such an indifference occurs, it must be between two consecutive strategies in S^p. Putting these observations together, we find that each transition in the sequence $\{(i_k, j_k)\}$ is of length 1, in the sense that

$$|i_{k+1} - i_k| \leq 1 \quad \text{and} \quad |j_{k+1} - j_k| \leq 1 \quad \text{for all } k.$$

There is an *improvement step* from $(i,j) \in S$ to $(i', j') \in S$, denoted $(i,j) \nearrow (i', j')$, either if $U^1_{i'j} > U^1_{ij}$ and $j' = j$, or if $i' = i$ and $U^2_{ij'} > U^2_{ij}$. Lemma 7.3.2(i) and the fact that U is nondegenerate imply that $(i_k, j_k) \nearrow (i_{k+1}, j_{k+1})$ if either $i_k = i_{k+1}$ or $j_k = j_{k+1}$.

Moreover, applying both parts of the lemma, we find that if $i_k \neq i_{k+1}$ and $j_k \neq j_{k+1}$, then $(i_k, j_k) \nearrow (i_{k+1}, j_k) \nearrow (i_{k+1}, j_{k+1})$ and $(i_k, j_k) \nearrow (i_k, j_{k+1}) \nearrow (i_{k+1}, j_{k+1})$.

Now suppose that the sequence $\{t_k\}$ is infinite. Then since S is finite, there must be a strategy profile that is the interval k selection for more than one k. In this case, the arguments in the previous two paragraphs imply that there is a length 1 improvement cycle, that is, a sequence of length 1 improvement steps beginning and ending with the same strategy profile.

Evidently, this cycle must contain an improvement step of the form $(\tilde{i}, \tilde{j}) \nearrow (\tilde{i}, \tilde{j}+1)$ for some $(\tilde{i}, \tilde{j}) \in S$. Strict supermodularity of U then implies that

$$(i, \tilde{j}) \nearrow (i, \tilde{j}+1) \quad \text{for all } i \geq \tilde{i}. \tag{7.29}$$

It follows that for the sequence of length 1 improvement steps to return to $(\tilde{i}, \tilde{j})$, there must be an improvement step of the form $(\tilde{i}, \hat{j}) \nearrow (\tilde{i}-1, \hat{j})$ for some $\hat{j} > \tilde{j}$ (figure 7.6). This time, strict supermodularity of U implies that

$$(\tilde{i}, j) \nearrow (\tilde{i}-1, j) \quad \text{for all } j \leq \hat{j}. \tag{7.30}$$

From (7.29) and (7.30), it follows that no cycle of length 1 improvement steps containing $(\tilde{i}, \tilde{j}) \nearrow (\tilde{i}, \tilde{j}+1)$ can reach any strategy profile (i, j) with $i \geq \tilde{i}$ and $j \leq \hat{j}$. In particular, the cycle cannot return to $(\tilde{i}, \tilde{j})$, which is a contradiction. This completes the proof of the theorem. ∎

7.3.2 Stochastically Perturbed Best Response Dynamics

Theorem 7.3.4 was proved using elementary techniques, but the theorem was not as general as one might hope. It restricted attention to two-player normal form games, and required not only the assumption of supermodularity but also that of diminishing returns. In order to obtain a more general convergence result, one must turn from exact best response dynamics to perturbed best response dynamics.

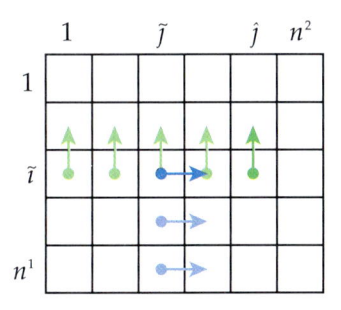

Figure 7.6
The proof of theorem 7.3.4.

Doing so makes available a powerful set of techniques for smooth dynamics with a monotone structure: the theory of cooperative differential equations.

Recall the transformations used to discuss the stochastic dominance order. In section 3.4, we defined the matrices $\Sigma \in \mathbf{R}^{(n^p-1) \times n^p}$, $\tilde{\Sigma} \in \mathbf{R}^{n^p \times (n^p-1)}$, and $\Omega \in \mathbf{R}^{n^p \times n^p}$ by

$$\Sigma = \begin{pmatrix} 0 & 1 & \cdots & 1 \\ \vdots & \ddots & \ddots & \vdots \\ 0 & \cdots & 0 & 1 \end{pmatrix}, \quad \tilde{\Sigma} = \begin{pmatrix} -1 & 0 & \cdots & 0 \\ 1 & -1 & \ddots & \vdots \\ 0 & 1 & \ddots & 0 \\ \vdots & \ddots & \ddots & -1 \\ 0 & \ddots & 0 & 1 \end{pmatrix}, \quad \Omega = \begin{pmatrix} 1 & 1 & \cdots & \cdots & 1 \\ 0 & 0 & \cdots & \cdots & 0 \\ 0 & 0 & \ddots & & \vdots \\ \vdots & \vdots & & \ddots & \vdots \\ 0 & 0 & \cdots & \cdots & 0 \end{pmatrix}.$$

Then $y^p \in X^p$ stochastically dominates $x^p \in X^p$ if and only if $\Sigma y^p \geq \Sigma x^p$, and

$$\tilde{\Sigma}\Sigma = I - \Omega. \tag{7.31}$$

Since Ω is the null operator on TX^p, equation (7.31) describes a sense in which the stochastic dominance operator Σ is inverted by the difference operator $\tilde{\Sigma}$.

Applying the change of coordinates Σ to the set X^p yields the set of transformed population states

$$\chi^p \equiv \Sigma X^p = \left\{ \chi^p \in \mathbf{R}^{n^p-1} : m^p \geq \chi_1^p \geq \cdots \geq \chi_{n^p-1}^p \geq 0 \right\}.$$

By postmultiplying both sides of (7.31) by x^p and letting $\underline{x}^p = (m^p, 0, \ldots, 0)$ denote the minimal state in X^p, the inverse of the map $\Sigma : X^p \to \chi^p$ can be described as follows:

$$\chi^p = \Sigma x^p \Leftrightarrow x^p = \tilde{\Sigma}\chi^p + \underline{x}^p. \tag{7.32}$$

To work with full social states $x \in X$, introduce the block diagonal matrices $\boldsymbol{\Sigma} = \text{diag}(\Sigma, \ldots, \Sigma)$ and $\tilde{\boldsymbol{\Sigma}} = \text{diag}(\tilde{\Sigma}, \ldots, \tilde{\Sigma})$, and let $\mathcal{X} \equiv \boldsymbol{\Sigma}X = \prod_{p \in \mathcal{P}} \chi^p$. If $\underline{x} = (\underline{x}^1, \ldots, \underline{x}^p)$ is the minimal state in X, then the inverse of the map $\boldsymbol{\Sigma} : X \to \mathcal{X}$ is described by

$$\chi = \boldsymbol{\Sigma}x \Leftrightarrow x = \tilde{\boldsymbol{\Sigma}}\chi + \underline{x}. \tag{7.33}$$

To simplify the discussion, assume for convenience that each population is of mass 1. Then the stochastically perturbed best response dynamic takes the form

$$\dot{x}^p = \tilde{M}^p(F^p(x)) - x^p, \tag{7.34}$$

where

$$\tilde{M}_i^p(\pi^p) = \mathbb{P}\left(i = \text{argmax}_{j \in S^p} \pi_j^p + \varepsilon_j^p\right)$$

for some admissible stochastic perturbations $\varepsilon = (\varepsilon^1, \ldots, \varepsilon^p)$. Rather than study this dynamic directly, we apply the change of variable (7.33) to obtain a new dynamic on the set $\mathcal{X}$:

$$\dot{\chi}^p = \Sigma \tilde{M}^p(F^p(\tilde{\Sigma}\chi + \underline{x})) - \chi^p. \tag{7.35}$$

Given the current state $\chi \in \mathcal{X}$, the inverse transformation $\chi \mapsto x \equiv \tilde{\Sigma}\chi + \underline{x}$ yields the input for the payoff function F^p, and the original transformation $\tilde{M}^p(F^p(x)) \mapsto \Sigma \tilde{M}^p(F^p(x))$ is used to convert the perturbed best response into an element of $\mathcal{X}^p$. The next observation verifies the relation between solutions to the transformed dynamic (7.35) and solutions to the original dynamic (7.34).

Observation 7.3.5 *The equations (7.34) and (7.35) are affinely conjugate:* $\{x_t\} = \{\tilde{\Sigma}\chi_t + \underline{x}\}$ *solves (7.34) if and only if* $\{\chi_t\} = \{\Sigma x_t\}$ *solves (7.35).*

Write the dynamic (7.35) as $\dot{\chi} = \mathcal{V}(\chi)$, The next task is to show that if F is a supermodular game, then (7.35) is a *cooperative differential equation*:

$$\frac{\partial \mathcal{V}_i^p}{\partial \chi_j^q}(\chi) \geq 0 \quad \text{for all } \chi \in \mathcal{X} \text{ when } (i, p) \neq (j, q).$$

If this inequality is always satisfied strictly, then (7.35) is *strongly cooperative*. As explained in appendix 7.C, strongly cooperative differential equations converge to rest points from almost all initial conditions. Thus, if one can prove that equation (7.35) is strongly cooperative, one can conclude that almost all solutions of the original dynamic (7.34) converge to perturbed equilibria.

To prove that (7.35) is strongly cooperative, we marshal our facts about supermodular games and stochastically perturbed best responses.

Recall from chapter 3 that if the population game F is C^1, then F is a *supermodular* if and only if

$$\tilde{\Sigma}' DF(x) \tilde{\Sigma} \geq \mathbf{0} \quad \text{for all } x \in X.$$

Our result requires an additional nondegeneracy condition: we call F is *irreducible* if each column of $\tilde{\Sigma}' DF(x) \tilde{\Sigma}$ contains a positive element.

Next, recall from lemma 6.C.1 the basic properties of $D\tilde{M}(\pi)$, the derivative matrix of the stochastically perturbed best response function $\tilde{M}$.

Lemma 7.3.6 *Fix $\pi \in \mathbf{R}^n$, and suppose that the perturbed best response function $\tilde{M}$ is derived from admissible stochastic payoff perturbations. Then the derivative matrix $D\tilde{M}(\pi)$ is symmetric, has negative off-diagonal elements, and satisfies $D\tilde{M}(\pi)\mathbf{1} = \mathbf{0}$.*

Combining these facts yields the desired result.

Theorem 7.3.7 *Let F be a C^1 irreducible supermodular game, and let (7.34) be a stochastically perturbed best response dynamic for F. Then the transformed dynamic (7.35) is strongly cooperative.*

Proof ($p = 1$) Write the dynamic (7.35) as $\dot{\chi} = \mathcal{V}(\chi)$. Then

$$D\mathcal{V}(\chi) = D(\Sigma \tilde{M}(F(\tilde{\Sigma}\chi + \underline{x}))) - I. \tag{7.36}$$

Since all off-diagonal elements of I equal zero, it is enough to show that the first term on the right-hand side of (7.36) has all positive components.

Let $x = \tilde{\Sigma}\chi + \underline{x}$ and $\pi = F(x)$. Using the facts that $\tilde{\Sigma}\Sigma = I - \Omega$ and $D\tilde{M}(\pi)\mathbf{1} = \mathbf{0}$, we express the first term of the right-hand side of (7.36) as follows:

$$D(\Sigma \tilde{M}(F(\tilde{\Sigma}\chi + \underline{x}))) = \Sigma\, D\tilde{M}(\pi)\, DF(x)\, \tilde{\Sigma}$$

$$= \Sigma\, D\tilde{M}(\pi)\, (\Sigma'\tilde{\Sigma}' + \Omega')\, DF(x)\, \tilde{\Sigma}$$

$$= (\Sigma D\tilde{M}(\pi)\Sigma')(\tilde{\Sigma}'DF(x)\tilde{\Sigma}).$$

Lemma 7.3.6 and the fact that

$$(\Sigma D\tilde{M}(\pi)\Sigma')_{ij} = \sum_{k>i}\sum_{l>j} D\tilde{M}(\pi)_{kl}$$

imply that every component of $\Sigma D\tilde{M}(\pi)\Sigma'$ is positive (see exercise 7.3.8). Since F is supermodular and irreducible, $\tilde{\Sigma}'DF(x)\tilde{\Sigma}$ is non-negative, with each column containing a positive element. Thus, the product of these two matrices has all positive elements. This completes the proof of the theorem. ∎

Exercise 7.3.8

i. Prove that every component of $\Sigma D\tilde{M}(\pi)\Sigma'$ is positive.

ii. Explain why theorem 7.3.7 need not hold when $\tilde{M}$ is generated by deterministic perturbations. ◇

Observation 7.3.5, theorem 7.3.7, and theorems 7.C.1, 7.C.2, and 7.C.3 immediately imply the following "almost global" convergence result. In part (i) of theorem 7.3.9, $\underline{x} = (\underline{x}^1, \ldots, \underline{x}^p)$ is the minimal state in X; similarly, $\bar{x}^p = (0, \ldots, m^p)$ is the maximal state in X^p, and $\bar{x} = (\bar{x}^1, \ldots, \bar{x}^p)$ is the maximal state in X.

Theorem 7.3.9 *Let F be a C^1 irreducible supermodular game, and let $\dot{x} = V_{F,\varepsilon}(x)$ be a stochastically perturbed best response dynamic for F. Then*

i. *states $\underline{x}^* \equiv \omega(\underline{x})$ and $\bar{x}^* \equiv \omega(\bar{x})$ exist and are the minimal and maximal elements of $PE(F, \varepsilon)$; moreover, $[\underline{x}^*, \bar{x}^*]$ contains all ω-limit points of $V_{F,\varepsilon}$ and is globally asymptotically stable;*

Global Convergence of Evolutionary Dynamics

ii. solutions to $\dot{x} = V_{F,\varepsilon}(x)$ from an open, dense, full measure set of initial conditions in X converge to states in $PE(F, \varepsilon)$.

The following example shows that the conclusion of theorem 7.3.9 cannot be extended from convergence from almost all initial conditions to convergence from all initial conditions.

Example 7.3.1 Let U be a normal form game with $p \geq 5$ players and two strategies per player. Each player p in U obtains a payoff of 1 if she chooses the same strategy as player $p+1$ (with the convention that $p+1 = 1$) and obtains a payoff of 0 otherwise. U has three Nash equilibria: two strict equilibria in which all players coordinate on the same strategy and the mixed equilibrium $x^* = ((\frac{1}{2}, \frac{1}{2}), \ldots, (\frac{1}{2}, \frac{1}{2}))$. If F is the p population game generated by matching in U, it can be shown that F is supermodular and irreducible (see exercise 7.3.10(i)).

Now introduce random perturbations $\varepsilon^p = (\varepsilon_1^p, \varepsilon_2^p)$ to each player's payoffs. These perturbations are such that the differences $\varepsilon_2^p - \varepsilon_1^p$ admit a common density g that is symmetric about 0, is decreasing on $\mathbf{R}_+$, and satisfies $g(0) > \frac{1}{2}$. It can be shown that the resulting perturbed best response dynamic (7.34) possesses exactly three rest points: the mixed equilibrium x^* and two stable symmetric rest points that approximate the two pure Nash equilibria (see exercise 7.3.10(ii)).

One can show that the rest point x^* is unstable under (7.34). It then follows from theorem 7.3.9 that the two stable rest points of (7.34) attract almost all initial conditions in X, and that the basins of attraction for these rest points are separated by a $p-1$ dimensional invariant manifold $\mathcal{M}$ that contains x^*. Furthermore, one can show that when $p \geq 5$, the rest point x^* is unstable with respect to the manifold $\mathcal{M}$. Thus, solutions from all states in $\mathcal{M} - \{x^*\}$ fail to converge to a rest point. ◆

The details of these last arguments require techniques for determining the local stability of rest points. This is the topic of chapter 8.

Exercise 7.3.10

i. Prove that the game F introduced in example 7.3.1 is supermodular and irreducible.

ii. Prove that under the assumption on payoff perturbations stated in the example, there are exactly three perturbed equilibria, all of which are symmetric. ◇

7.4 Dominance Solvable Games

The elimination of strictly dominated strategies is the mildest requirement employed in standard game-theoretic analyses, and so it seems natural to expect evolutionary dynamics to obey this dictum. This section provides some positive results on the elimination of dominated strategies. Under the best response dynamic, any strictly dominated strategy must vanish in the limit; the same is true under any imitative dynamic as long as the focus is on interior initial conditions. Arguing inductively, one can show that any strategy that does not survive iterated elimination of strictly dominated strategies vanishes as well. In particular, if a game is dominance solvable, that is, if iteratively removing dominated strategies leaves only one strategy for each population, then best response and imitative dynamics select this strategy.

These results may seem unsurprising. However, we argue in Chapter 9 that they are actually borderline cases: under typical evolutionary dynamics, strictly dominated strategies can survive in perpetuity.

7.4.1 Dominated and Iteratively Dominated Strategies

Let F be a population game. Strategy $i \in S^p$ is *strictly dominated* if there exists a strategy $j \in S^p$ such that $F_j(x) > F_i(x)$ for all $x \in X$, that is, if there is a strategy j that outperforms strategy i regardless of the population state. Similarly, if $\hat{S}^p$ is a nonempty subset of S^p and $\hat{S} = \prod_{p \in \mathcal{P}} \hat{S}^p$, then $i \in S^p$ is *strictly dominated relative to* $\hat{S}$, denoted $i \in \mathcal{D}^p(\hat{S})$, if there exists a strategy $j \in \hat{S}^p$ such that $F_j(x) > F_i(x)$ for all $x \in X$ that satisfy support$(x^p) \subseteq \hat{S}^p$ for all $p \in \mathcal{P}$.

These definitions can be used to introduce the notion of iterative dominance. Set $S_0 = S$. Then $\mathcal{D}^p(S_0)$ is the set of strictly dominated strategies for population p, and $S_1^p = S_0^p - \mathcal{D}^p(S_0)$ is the set of strategies that are not strictly dominated. Proceeding inductively, define $\mathcal{D}^p(S_k)$ to be the set of strategies that are eliminated during the $(k+1)$st round of removal of iteratively dominated strategies, and let $S_{k+1}^p = S_k^p - \mathcal{D}^p(S_k)$ be the set of strategies that survive $k+1$ rounds of removal of such strategies.

Since the number of strategies is finite, this iterative procedure must converge, leaving some nonempty sets $S_*^1, \ldots, S_*^p$. Strategies in these sets are said to *survive iterative removal of strictly dominated strategies*. If each of these sets is a singleton, then the game F is said to be *dominance solvable*. In this case, the pure social state at which each agent plays her population's sole surviving strategy is the game's unique Nash equilibrium; this state is the *dominance solution* of F.

7.4.2 The Best Response Dynamic

Under the best response dynamic, revising agents always switch to optimal strategies. Since strictly dominated strategies are never optimal, such strategies cannot persist.

Observation 7.4.1 *Let $\{x_t\}$ be a solution trajectory of (BR) for population game F, in which strategy $i \in S^p$ is strictly dominated. Then $\lim_{t \to \infty} (x_t)_i^p = 0$.*

Indeed, since i is never a best response, we have that $(\dot{x}_t)_i^p \equiv -(x_t)_i^p$, and hence that $(x_t)_i^p = (x_0)_i^p \, \mathrm{e}^{-t}$: the mass playing the dominated strategy converges to zero exponentially quickly.

Introducing an inductive argument yields the following result.

Theorem 7.4.2 *Let $\{x_t\}$ be a solution trajectory of* (BR) *for population game F, in which strategy $i \in S^p$ does not survive iterative elimination of strictly dominated strategies. Then $\lim_{t \to \infty} (x_t)_i^p = 0$. In particular, if F is dominance solvable, then all solutions of* (BR) *converge to the dominance solution.*

Proof Observation 7.4.1 provides the basis for this induction: if $i \notin S_1^p$, then $\lim_{t \to \infty} (x_t)_i^p = 0$. As the inductive hypothesis, suppose that this same equality holds for all $i \notin S_k^p$. Now let $j \in S_k^p - S_{k+1}^p$. Then by definition, there exists a $j' \in S_{k+1}^p$ such that $F_{j'}^p(x) > F_j^p(x)$ whenever $x \in X_k$, where $X_k = \{x \in X \colon x_i^p > 0 \Rightarrow i \in S_k^p\}$ is the set of social states in which all agents in each population p choose strategies in S_k^p. Since X_k is compact and F is continuous, it follows that for some $c > 0$, we have that $F_{j'}^p(x) > F_j^p(x) + c$ whenever $x \in X_k$, and so that for some $\varepsilon > 0$, we have that $F_{j'}^p(x) > F_j^p(x)$ whenever $x \in X_{k,\varepsilon} = \{x \in X \colon x_i^p > \varepsilon \Rightarrow i \in S_k^p\}$. By the inductive hypothesis, there exists a $T > 0$ such that $x_t \in X_{k,\varepsilon}$ for all $t \geq T$. Thus, for such t, j is not a best response to x_t. This implies that $(\dot{x}_t)_j^p = -(x_t)_j^p$ for $t \geq T$ and hence that $(x_t)_j^p = (x_T)_j^p \, \mathrm{e}^{T-t}$, which converges to 0 as t approaches infinity. ∎

Exercise 7.4.3 Show that under (BR), the time until convergence to the set $X_{*,\varepsilon} = \{x \in X \colon x_i^p > \varepsilon \Rightarrow i \in S_*^p\}$ is uniform over initial conditions in X. In other words, show that there is a $T < \infty$ such that all solutions to (BR) from all initial conditions in X enter $X_{*,\varepsilon}$ by time T. ◇

7.4.3 Imitative Dynamics

Analogous results exist for imitative dynamics. Since these dynamics leave the boundary of the state space invariant, the elimination results can only hold for solutions starting from interior initial conditions.

Theorem 7.4.4 *Let $\{x_t\}$ be an interior solution trajectory of an imitative dynamic for population game F, in which strategy $i \in S^p$ is strictly dominated. Then $\lim_{t \to \infty} (x_t)_i^p = 0$.*

Proof ($p = 1$) Observation 5.4.8 indicates that all imitative dynamics $\dot{x} = V_F(x)$ exhibit monotone percentage growth rates (5.18): they can be expressed as

$$\dot{x}_i = x_i G_i(x), \tag{7.37}$$

where the continuous function $G \colon X \to \mathbf{R}^n$ satisfies

$$G_k(x) \leq G_l(x) \quad \text{if and only if} \quad F_k(x) \leq F_l(x) \quad \text{for all } x \in \mathrm{int}(X). \tag{7.38}$$

Now suppose strategy i is strictly dominated by strategy $j \in S$. Since X is compact and F is continuous, one can find a $c > 0$ such that $F_j(x) - F_i(x) > c$ for all $x \in X$. Since G is continuous as well, equation (7.38) implies that for some $C > 0$, one has $G_j(x) - G_i(x) > C$ for all $x \in X$.

Now write $r = x_i/x_j$. Equation (7.37) and the quotient rule imply that

$$\frac{d}{dt} r = \frac{d}{dt} \frac{x_i}{x_j} = \frac{\dot{x}_i x_j - \dot{x}_j x_i}{(x_j)^2} = \frac{x_i G_i(x) x_j - x_j G_j(x) x_i}{(x_j)^2} = r\left(G_i(x) - G_j(x)\right). \tag{7.39}$$

Thus, along every interior solution trajectory $\{x_t\}$,

$$r_t = r_0 + \int_0^t r_s \left(G_i(x) - G_j(x)\right) ds \leq r_0 - C \int_0^t r_s \, ds.$$

Grönwall's inequality (lemma 4.A.4) then implies that $r_t \leq r_0 \exp(-Ct)$, and hence that r_t vanishes as t approaches infinity. Since $(x_t)_j$ is bounded above by 1, $(x_t)_i$ must approach 0 as t approaches infinity. ∎

An argument similar to the one used to prove theorem 7.4.2 can be used to prove that iteratively dominated strategies are eliminated by imitative dynamics.

Theorem 7.4.5 *Let $\{x_t\}$ be an interior solution trajectory of an imitative dynamic for population game F, in which strategy $i \in S^p$ does not survive iterative elimination of strictly dominated strategies. Then $\lim_{t \to \infty} (x_t)_i^p = 0$. In particular, if F is dominance solvable, then all interior solutions of any imitative dynamic converge to the dominance solution.*

Exercise 7.4.6

i. Prove theorem 7.4.5.

ii. Is the time until convergence to $X_{*,\varepsilon} = \{x \in X : x_i^p > \varepsilon \Rightarrow i \in S_*^p\}$ uniform over initial conditions in $\text{int}(X)$? Explain. ◇

7.A Appendix: Limit and Stability Notions for Deterministic Dynamics

This appendix considers differential equations and differential inclusions that are forward invariant on the compact set $X \subset \mathbf{R}^n$.

$\dot{x} = V(x)$, a unique forward solution exists from each $\xi \in X$. (D)

$\dot{x} \in V(x)$, V is nonempty, convex-valued, bounded, and upper-hemicontinuous. (DI)

When V is discontinuous, solutions are allowed to be of the Carathéodory type, that is, to satisfy $\dot{x}_t = V(x_t)$ (or $\dot{x}_t \in V(x_t)$) at almost all $t \in [0, \infty)$.

7.A.1 ω-Limits and Notions of Recurrence

Let $\{x_t\} = \{x_t\}_{t \geq 0}$ be a solution trajectory to (D) or (DI). The *ω-limit* of $\{x_t\}$ is the set of all points that the trajectory approaches arbitrarily closely infinitely often:

$$\omega(\{x_t\}) = \left\{ y \in X \colon \text{there exists } \{t_k\}_{k=1}^\infty \text{ with } \lim_{k \to \infty} t_k = \infty \text{ such that } \lim_{k \to \infty} x_{t_k} = y \right\}.$$

If $\{x_t\}$ is the unique solution to (D) with initial condition $x_0 = \xi$, we write $\omega(\xi)$ in place of $\omega(\{x_t\})$. The following proposition lists some basic properties of ω-limit sets for this case. Recall from section 4.A.2 that $A \subseteq X$ is an invariant set under (D) if for each $\chi \in A$, the solution trajectory $\{y_t\}_{t \in (-\infty, \infty)}$ with $y_0 = \chi$ exists and is contained in A.

Proposition 7.A.1 *Let $\{x_t\}$ be the solution to* (D) *from initial condition ξ. Then*

i. $\omega(\xi)$ *is non-empty and connected;*
ii. $\omega(\xi)$ *is closed, in fact,* $\omega(\xi) = \bigcap_{t \geq 0} \mathrm{cl}(\{x_s : s \geq t\});$
iii. $\omega(\xi)$ *is invariant under* (D).

The properties of limit sets and the definition of invariance for the differential inclusion (DI) are more subtle; see the chapter notes for references.

Focusing again on the differential equation (D), define the set

$$\Omega = \bigcup_{\xi \in X} \omega(\xi).$$

The set Ω contains all points that are approached arbitrarily closely infinitely often by some solution of (D). Among other things, Ω contains all rest points, periodic orbits, and chaotic attractors of (D). Since Ω need not be closed, its closure $\bar\Omega = \mathrm{cl}(\Omega)$ is used to define a standard notion of recurrence for differential equations.

Example 7.A.1 To see that Ω need not be closed, consider the replicator dynamic in standard Rock-Paper-Scissors (figure 5.3a). The unique Nash equilibrium $x^* = (\frac{1}{3}, \frac{1}{3}, \frac{1}{3})$ is a rest point, and solution trajectories from all other interior initial conditions form closed orbits around x^*. The vertices e_R, e_P, and e_S are also rest points, and each trajectory starting from a boundary point that is not a vertex converges to a vertex. Thus, $\Omega = \mathrm{int}(X) \cup \{e_R, e_P, e_S\}$, but $\bar\Omega = X$. ◆

Many other notions of recurrence besides $\bar\Omega$ are available. To obtain a more demanding notion of recurrence for (D), call the state ξ *recurrent*, denoted $\xi \in \mathcal{R}$, if the solution to (D) from ξ returns arbitrarily close to ξ infinitely often, in other words, if $\xi \in \omega(\xi)$. The *Birkhoff center* of (D) is the closure $\mathrm{cl}(\mathcal{R})$ of the set of recurrent points of (D).

More inclusive notions of recurrence can be obtained by allowing occasional short jumps between nearby solution trajectories. Given a differential equation (D) with flow ϕ, an *ε-chain* of length T from x to y is a sequence of states $x = x_0, x_1, \ldots, x_k = y$ such that for some sequence of times $t_1, \ldots, t_n \geq 1$ satisfying $\sum_{j=1}^{k} t_i = T$, we have $\left| \phi_{t_i}(x_{i-1}) - x_j \right| < \varepsilon$ for all $i \in \{1, \ldots, k\}$. State x is said to be *chain recurrent*, denoted $x \in C\mathcal{R}$, if for all $\varepsilon > 0$ there is an ε-chain from x to itself.

The primacy of the notion of chain recurrence is captured by theorem 9.B.4, known as the *fundamental theorem of dynamical systems*: if ϕ is a smooth flow on a compact set X, then X can be decomposed into two sets: a set on which the flow admits a Lyapunov function and the set $C\mathcal{R}$ of chain recurrent points. Chain recurrence also plays a basic role in characterizing long-run behavior in models of learning in games (see the chapter notes).

7.A.2 Stability of Sets of States

Let $A \subseteq X$ be a closed set, and call $O \subseteq X$ a *neighborhood* of A if it is open relative to X and contains A. Then A is *Lyapunov stable* under (D) (or (DI)) if for every neighborhood O of A there exists a neighborhood O' of A such that every solution $\{x_t\}$ that starts in O' is contained in O, that is, $x_0 \in O'$ implies that $x_t \in O$ for all $t \geq 0$. A is *attracting* if there is a neighborhood Y of A such that every solution that starts in Y converges to A, that is, $x_0 \in Y$ implies that $\omega(\{x_t\}) \subseteq A$. A is *globally attracting* if it is attracting with $Y = X$. Finally, the set A is *asymptotically stable* if it is Lyapunov stable and attracting, and it is *globally asymptotically stable* if it is Lyapunov stable and globally attracting.

Example 7.A.2 Attracting sets need not be asymptotically stable. A counterexample is provided by a flow on the unit circle that moves clockwise except at a single point. The fact that the domain is the unit circle is unimportant, as one can embed this flow as a limit cycle in a flow on the plane. ◆

Example 7.A.3 Invariance is not included in the definition of asymptotic stability. Thus, under the dynamic $\dot{x} = -x$ on $\mathbf{R}$, any closed interval containing the origin is asymptotically stable. ◆

7.B Appendix: Stability Analysis via Lyapunov Functions

Let $Y \subseteq X$. The function $L: Y \to \mathbf{R}$ is a *Lyapunov function* for (D) or (DI) if its value changes monotonically along every solution trajectory. The following results are stated for the case in which the value of L decreases along solution trajectories; of course, the analogues of these results hold for the opposite case.

The following lemma proves useful in a number of analyses to follow.

Global Convergence of Evolutionary Dynamics

Lemma 7.B.1 *Suppose that the function $L: Y \to \mathbf{R}$ and the trajectory $\{x_t\}_{t \geq 0}$ are Lipschitz continuous.*

i. If $\dot{L}(x_t) \leq 0$ for almost all $t \geq 0$, then the map $t \mapsto L(x_t)$ is nonincreasing.

ii. If in addition $\dot{L}(x_s) < 0$, then $L(x_t) < L(x_s)$ for all $t > s$.

Proof The composition $t \mapsto L(x_t)$ is Lipschitz continuous, and therefore absolutely continuous. It thus follows from the fundamental theorem of calculus that when $t > s$,

$$L(x_t) - L(x_s) = \int_s^t \dot{L}(x_u)\, du \leq 0,$$

where the inequality is strict if $\dot{L}(x_s) < 0$. ∎

7.B.1 Lyapunov Stable Sets

The basic theorem on Lyapunov stability applies both to differential equations (D) and differential inclusions (DI).

Theorem 7.B.2 (Lyapunov Stability) *Let $A \subseteq X$ be closed, and let $Y \subseteq X$ be a neighborhood of A. Let $L: Y \to \mathbf{R}_+$ be Lipschitz continuous with $L^{-1}(0) = A$. If each solution $\{x_t\}$ of (D) (or (DI)) satisfies $\dot{L}(x_t) \leq 0$ for almost all $t \geq 0$, then A is Lyapunov stable under (D) (or (DI)).*

Proof Let O be a neighborhood of A such that $\mathrm{cl}(O) \subset Y$. Let $c = \min_{x \in \mathrm{bd}(O)} L(x)$, so that $c > 0$. Finally, let $O' = \{x \in O: L(x) < c\}$. Lemma 7.B.1 implies that solution trajectories that start in O' do not leave O, and hence that A is Lyapunov stable. ∎

Example 7.B.1 The requirement that the function L be constant on A cannot be dispensed with. Consider a flow on the unit circle $C = \{x \in \mathbf{R}^2: (x_1)^2 + (x_2)^2 = 1\}$ that moves clockwise at states x with $x_1 > 0$ and is at rest at states on the semicircle $A = \{x \in C: x_1 \leq 0\}$. Let $L(x) = x_2$; then $\dot{L}(x) \leq 0$ for all $x \in C$ and A is attracting (see theorem 7.B.3), but A is not Lyapunov stable.

This example can be extended so that the flow is defined on the unit disk $D = \{x \in \mathbf{R}^2: (x_1)^2 + (x_2)^2 \leq 1\}$. Suppose that when $x_1 > 0$, the flow travels clockwise along the circles centered at the origin, and that the half disk $A' = \{x \in D: x_1 \leq 0\}$ consists entirely of rest points. Then $L(x) = x_2$ satisfies $\dot{L}(x) \leq 0$ for all $x \in D$, and A' is attracting, but A' is not Lyapunov stable. ◆

7.B.2 ω-Limits and Attracting Sets

This section uses Lyapunov functions to characterize ω-limits of solution trajectories that begin in the Lyapunov function's domain. The analyses here immediately yield sufficient conditions for a set to be attracting. To state the results, we call the (relatively) open set $Y \subset X$ *inescapable* if for each solution trajectory $\{x_t\}_{t \geq 0}$ with $x_0 \in Y$, we have that $\text{cl}(\{x_t\}) \cap \text{bd}(Y) = \emptyset$.

The first result focuses on the differential equation (D).

Theorem 7.B.3 *Let $Y \subset X$ be relatively open and inescapable under (D). Let $L: Y \to \mathbf{R}$ be C^1, and suppose that $\dot{L}(x) \equiv \nabla L(x)'V(x) \leq 0$ for all $x \in Y$. Then $\omega(x_0) \subseteq \{x \in Y: \dot{L}(x) = 0\}$ for all $x_0 \in Y$. Thus, if $\dot{L}(x) = 0$ implies that $V(x) = \mathbf{0}$, then $\omega(x_0) \subseteq RP(V) \cap Y$.*

Proof Let $\{x_t\}$ be the solution to (D) with initial condition $x_0 = \xi \in Y$, let $\chi \in \omega(\xi)$, and let $\{y_t\}$ be the solution to (D) with $y_0 = \chi$. Since Y is inescapable, the closures of trajectories $\{x_t\}$ and $\{y_t\}$ are contained in Y.

Suppose by way of contradiction that $\dot{L}(\chi) \neq 0$. Since $\chi \in \omega(\xi)$, we can find a divergent sequence of times $\{t_k\}_{k=1}^\infty$ such that $\lim_{k \to \infty} x_{t_k} = \chi = y_0$. Since solutions to (D) are unique, and hence continuous in their initial conditions, we have

$$\lim_{k \to \infty} x_{t_k+1} = y_1, \quad \text{and hence} \quad \lim_{k \to \infty} L(x_{t_k+1}) = L(y_1). \tag{7.40}$$

But since $y_0 = \chi \in \omega(\xi)$ and $\dot{L}(\chi) \neq 0$, applying lemma 7.B.1 to both $\{x_t\}$ and $\{y_t\}$ yields

$$L(x_t) \geq L(\chi) > L(y_1)$$

for all $t \geq 0$, contradicting the second limit in (7.40). This proves the first claim of the theorem, and the second claim follows immediately from the first. ∎

Theorem 7.B.4 is an analogue of theorem 7.B.3 for upper-hemicontinous differential inclusions. Where the proof of theorem 7.B.3 relied on the continuity of solutions to (D) in their initial conditions, the proof of theorem 7.B.4 takes advantage of the upper-hemicontinuity of the map from initial conditions ξ to solutions of (DI) starting from ξ.

Theorem 7.B.4 *Let $Y \subset X$ be relatively open and inescapable under (DI). Let $L: Y \to \mathbf{R}$ be C^1 and satisfy (i) $\frac{\partial L}{\partial v}(x) \equiv \nabla L(x)'v \leq 0$ for all $v \in V(x)$ and $x \in Y$, and (ii) $[\mathbf{0} \notin V(x)$ implies that $\frac{\partial L}{\partial v}(x) < 0]$ for all $v \in V(x)$ and $x \in Y$. Then for all solutions $\{x_t\}$ of (DI) with $x_0 \in Y$, we have that $\omega(\{x_t\}) \subseteq \{x \in Y: \mathbf{0} \in V(x)\}$.*

Proof Suppose that $\chi \in \omega(\{x_t\})$ but that $\mathbf{0} \notin V(\chi)$. Then $\frac{\partial L}{\partial v}(\chi) < 0$ for all $v \in V(\chi)$. Thus, since $V(\chi)$ is compact by assumption, there exists a $b > 0$ such that $\frac{\partial L}{\partial v}(\chi) < -b$ for all $v \in V(\chi)$. Because V is upper-hemicontinuous and L is C^1, it follows that $\frac{\partial L}{\partial \hat{v}}(\hat{\chi}) < -\frac{b}{2}$ for all $\hat{v} \in V(\hat{\chi})$ and all $\hat{\chi}$ sufficiently close to χ. So since V is bounded, there is a time $u \in (0, 1]$ such that all solutions $\{y_t\}$ of (DI) with $y_0 = \chi$ satisfy

$$L(y_t) \leq L(y_s) \leq L(\chi) - \frac{bs}{2} \quad \text{for all } s \in [0, u] \text{ and } t > s. \tag{7.41}$$

Global Convergence of Evolutionary Dynamics 265

Now let $\{t_k\}_{k=1}^{\infty}$ be a divergent sequence of times such that $\lim_{k \to \infty} x_{t_k} = \chi$, and for each k, define the trajectory $\{x_t^k\}_{t \geq 0}$ by $x_t^k = x_{t+t_k}$. Since the set of continuous trajectories $C_{[0,T]}(X)$ is compact in the sup norm topology, the sequence of trajectories $\{\{x_t^k\}\}_{k=1}^{\infty}$ has a convergent subsequence, which without loss of generality is taken to be $\{\{x_t^k\}\}_{k=1}^{\infty}$ itself. Call the limit of this subsequence $\{\hat{y}_t\}$. Evidently, $\hat{y}_0 = \chi$.

Given the conditions on the correspondence V, the set-valued map

$$\hat{\chi} \mapsto \{\{x_t\}: \{x_t\} \text{ is a solution to (DI) with } x_0 = \hat{\chi}\}$$

is upper-hemicontinuous with respect to the sup norm topology on $C_{[0,T]}(X)$ (see appendix 6.A). It follows that $\{\hat{y}_t\}$ is a solution to (DI). Thus

$$\lim_{k \to \infty} x_{t_k+1} = \hat{y}_1, \quad \text{and hence} \quad \lim_{k \to \infty} L(x_{t_k+1}) = L(\hat{y}_1). \tag{7.42}$$

But lemma 7.B.1 and inequality (7.41) imply that

$$L(x_t) \geq L(\chi) > L(\hat{y}_1)$$

for all $t \geq 0$, contradicting the second limit in (7.42). ∎

Theorem 7.B.5 is a simple convergence result for differential inclusions. Here the Lyapunov function need only be Lipschitz continuous (rather than C^1), but the condition on the rate of decrease of this function is stronger than in the previous results.

Theorem 7.B.5 *Let $Y \subset X$ be relatively open and inescapable under* (DI), *and let $L: Y \to \mathbf{R}_+$ be Lipschitz continuous. Suppose that along each solution $\{x_t\}$ of* (DI) *with $x_0 \in Y$, we have that $\dot{L}(x_t) \leq -L(x_t)$ for almost all $t \geq 0$. Then $\omega(\{x_t\}) \subset \{x \in Y: L(x) = 0\}$.*

Proof   Observe that

$$L(x_t) = L(x_0) + \int_0^t \dot{L}(x_u)\, du \leq L(x_0) + \int_0^t (-L(x_u))\, du = L(x_0)\, e^{-t},$$

where the final equality follows from the fact that $\alpha_0 + \int_0^t (-\alpha_u)\, du$ is the value at time t of the solution to the linear ODE $\dot{\alpha}_t = -\alpha_t$ with initial condition $\alpha_0 \in \mathbf{R}$. It follows immediately that $\lim_{t \to \infty} L(x_t) = 0$. ∎

7.B.3 Asymptotically Stable and Globally Asymptotically Stable Sets

Combining theorem 7.B.2 with theorem 7.B.3, 7.B.4, or 7.B.5 yields asymptotic stability and global asymptotic stability results for deterministic dynamics. Corollary 7.B.6 offers such a result for the differential equation (D).

Corollary 7.B.6 *Let $A \subseteq X$ be closed, and let $Y \subseteq X$ be a neighborhood of A. Let $L: Y \to \mathbf{R}_+$ be C^1 with $L^{-1}(0) = A$. If $\dot{L}(x) \equiv \nabla L(x)' V(x) < 0$ for all $x \in Y - A$, then A*

is asymptotically stable under (D). If in addition $Y = X$, then A is globally asymptotically stable under (D).

7.C Appendix: Cooperative Differential Equations

Cooperative differential equations are defined by the property that increases in the value of one component of the state variable increase the growth rates of all other components. Their solutions have appealing monotonicity and convergence properties.

Let $\leq$ denote the standard partial order on $\mathbf{R}^n$, that is, $x \leq y$ if and only if $x_i \leq y_i$ for all $i \in \{1,\ldots,n\}$. We write $x < y$ when $x \leq y$ and $x \neq y$, so that $x_j < y_j$ for some j. Finally, we write $x \ll y$ when $x_i < y_i$ for all $i \in \{1,\ldots,n\}$. A vector or a matrix is *strongly positive* if all its components are positive; thus, $x \in \mathbf{R}^n$ is strongly positive if $x \gg 0$.

Let $X \subset \mathbf{R}^n$ be a compact convex set that possesses a minimal and a maximal element with respect to the partial order $\leq$. Let $V: X \to \mathbf{R}^n$ be a C^1 vector field with $V(x) \in TX(x)$ for all $x \in X$, so that the differential equation

$$\dot{x} = V(x) \tag{7.43}$$

is forward invariant on X. The differential equation (7.43) is *cooperative* if

$$\frac{\partial V_i}{\partial x_j}(x) \geq 0 \quad \text{for all } i \neq j, x \in X. \tag{7.44}$$

Equation (7.43) is *irreducible* if for every $x \in X$ and every nonempty proper subset I of the index set $\{1,\ldots,n\}$, there exist indices $i \in I$ and $j \in \{1,\ldots,n\} - I$ such that $\frac{\partial V_i}{\partial x_j}(x) \neq 0$. An obvious sufficient condition for (7.43) to be irreducible is that it be *strongly cooperative*, meaning that the inequality in condition (7.44) is strict for all $i \neq j$ and $x \in X$.

In section 4.A.3, we showed how to represent all solutions to the dynamic (7.43) simultaneously via the *semiflow* $\phi: \mathbf{R}_+ \times X \to X$, defined by $\phi_t(\xi) = x_t$, where $\{x_t\}_{t \geq 0}$ is the solution to (7.43) with initial condition $x_0 = \xi$. The semiflow ϕ is *monotone* if $x \leq y$ implies that $\phi_t(x) \leq \phi_t(y)$ for all $t \geq 0$, that is, weakly ordered initial conditions induce weakly ordered solution trajectories. If in addition $x < y$ implies that $\phi_t(x) \ll \phi_t(y)$ for all $t > 0$, then ϕ is *strongly monotone*.

Theorem 7.C.1 says us that cooperative irreducible differential equations generate strongly monotone semiflows.

Theorem 7.C.1 *Suppose that $\dot{x} = V(x)$ is cooperative and irreducible. Then*

i. *for all $t > 0$, the derivative matrix of its semiflow ϕ is strongly positive: $D\phi_t(x) \gg 0$;*

ii. *the semiflow ϕ is strongly monotone.*

Global Convergence of Evolutionary Dynamics

For the intuition behind this theorem, let $\{x_t\}$ and $\{y_t\}$ be solutions to (7.43) with $x_0 < y_0$. Suppose that at some time $t > 0$, we have that $x_t \leq y_t$ and $(x_t)_i = (y_t)_i$. If we could show that $V_i(x_t) \leq V_i(y_t)$, then it seems reasonable to expect that $(x_{t+\varepsilon})_i$ would not be able to surpass $(y_{t+\varepsilon})_i$. But since x_t and y_t only differ in components other than i, the vector $z = y_t - x_t \geq \mathbf{0}$ has $z_i = 0$, and so

$$V_i(y_t) - V_i(x_t) = \int_0^1 \nabla V_i(x_t + \alpha z)' z \, d\alpha = \int_0^1 \sum_{j \neq i} \frac{\partial V_i}{\partial x_j}(x_t + \alpha z) z_j \, d\alpha.$$

The final expression is non-negative as long as $\frac{\partial V_i}{\partial x_j} \geq 0$ whenever $j \neq i$.

The next theorem sets out the basic properties of strongly monotone semiflows on X. To state this result, let $C(\phi) = \{x \in X : \omega(x) = \{x^*\} \text{ for some } x^* \in RP(\phi)\}$ denote the set of initial conditions from which the semiflow ϕ converges to a rest point. Also, let $\Omega(\phi) = \bigcup_{x \in X} \omega(x)$ be the set of ω-limit points under ϕ.

Theorem 7.C.2 *Suppose that the semiflow ϕ on X is strongly monotone. Then the following hold:*

i. (Convergence criteria) *If $\phi_T(x) \geq x$ for some $T > 0$, then $\omega(x)$ is periodic with period T. If $\phi_t(x) \geq x$ over some nonempty open interval of times, then $x \in C(\phi)$.*

ii. (Unordered ω-limit sets) *If $x, y \in \omega(z)$, then $x \not> y$ and $y \not> x$.*

iii. (Minimal and maximal rest points) *Let $\underline{x} = \min X$ and $\bar{x} = \max X$. Then $\underline{x}^* = \min RP(\phi)$ and $\bar{x}^* = \max RP(\phi)$ exist; in fact, $\omega(\underline{x}) = \underline{x}^*$ and $\omega(\bar{x}) = \bar{x}^*$. Moreover, $[\underline{x}^*, \bar{x}^*]$ contains $\Omega(\phi)$ and is globally asymptotically stable.*

Proof

i. If $\phi_T(x) \geq x$, then $\phi_{(n+1)T}(x) \geq \phi_{nT}(x)$ for all positive integers n, so monotonicity and the compactness of X imply that $\lim_{n \to \infty} \phi_{nT}(x) = y$ for some $y \in X$. By the continuity and group properties of the flow,

$$\phi_{t+T}(y) = \phi_{t+T}\left(\lim_{n \to \infty} \phi_{nT}(x)\right) = \lim_{n \to \infty} \phi_{t+(n+1)T}(x) = \lim_{n \to \infty} \phi_t(\phi_{(n+1)T}(x)) = \phi_t(y),$$

so the flow from y is T-periodic. A continuity argument shows that the orbit from y is none other than $\omega(x)$. The proof of the second claim is omitted.

ii. Suppose that $x, y \in \omega(z)$ and that $x < y$. Since ϕ is strongly monotone, and by the continuity of $\phi_t(\xi)$ in ξ, there are neighborhoods $N_x, N_y \subset X$ of x and y and a time $T > 0$ such that $\phi_T(N_x) \ll \phi_T(N_y)$. Choose $\tau_y > \tau_x > 0$ such that $\phi_{\tau_x}(z) \in N_x$ and $\phi_{\tau_y}(z) \in N_y$. Then for all t close enough to τ_y,

$$\phi_{\tau_x + T}(z) \ll \phi_{t+T}(z) = \phi_{t - \tau_x}(\phi_{\tau_x + T}(z)).$$

Therefore, part (i) implies that $\omega(z)$ is a singleton, a contradiction.

iii. Since $\underline{x}$ and $\bar{x}$ are the minimal and maximal points in X, part (i) implies that $\omega(\underline{x}) = \underline{x}^*$ and $\omega(\bar{x}) = \bar{x}^*$ for some $\underline{x}^*, \bar{x}^* \in RP(\phi)$. Hence, if $x \in X \subseteq [\underline{x}, \bar{x}]$, then $\phi_t(\underline{x}) \leq \phi_t(x) \leq \phi_t(\bar{x})$ for all $t \geq 0$, so taking limits yields $\underline{x}^* \leq \omega(x) \leq \bar{x}^*$; thus, $\Omega(\phi) \subseteq [\underline{x}^*, \bar{x}^*]$. Finally, if $[\underline{x}^*, \bar{x}^*] \subseteq [y, z] \subseteq X$, then $x \in [y, z]$ implies that $\phi_t(x) \in [\phi_t(y), \phi_t(z)] \subseteq [y, z]$, so $[\underline{x}^*, \bar{x}^*]$ is Lyapunov stable, and hence globally asymptotically stable by the previous argument. ∎

If the derivative matrices of the semiflow are strongly positive, one can obtain even stronger results, including the convergence of solution trajectories from generic initial conditions to rest points.

Theorem 7.C.3 *Suppose that the semiflow ϕ on X is strongly monotone and that its derivative matrices $D\phi_t(x)$ are strongly positive for all $t > 0$. Then the following hold:*

i. (Limit set dichotomy) *If $x < y$, then either $\omega(x) < \omega(y)$, or $\omega(x) = \omega(y) = \{x^*\}$ for some $x^* \in RP(\phi)$.*

ii. (Generic convergence to equilibrium) *$C(\phi)$ is an open, dense, full measure subset of X.*

Notes

Section 7.1
The results in Section 7.1.1 were proved for symmetric normal form games in Hofbauer (2000), the seminal reference on Lyapunov functions for evolutionary dynamics. Global convergence in all potential games of dynamics satisfying positive correlation was proved in Sandholm (2001a), building on earlier work of Hofbauer and Sigmund (1988) and Monderer and Shapley (1996b). Convergence of perturbed best response dynamics in potential games was proved by Hofbauer and Sandholm (2007).

Shahshahani (1979), building on the early work of Kimura (1958), showed that the replicator dynamic for a potential game is a gradient dynamic after a "change in geometry," that is, after the introduction of an appropriate Riemannian metric on int(X). Subsequently, Akin (1979; 1990) proved that Shahshahani's (1979) result can also be represented using the change of variable presented in theorem 7.1.6. The direct proof offered in the text is from Sandholm, Dokumacı, and Lahkar (2008).

Section 7.2
Theorem 7.2.1 is due to Nagurney and Zhang (1997); the proof in the text is from Sandholm, Dokumacı, and Lahkar (2008). Theorem 7.2.4 was first proved for normal form games with an interior ESS by Hofbauer, Schuster, and Sigmund (1979) and Zeeman (1980). Akin (1990, theorem 6.4) and Aubin (1991, sec. 1.4) extended this result to nonlinear single-population games, and Cressman, Garay, and Hofbauer (2001) extended it to linear multipopulation games.

Section 7.2.2 follows Hofbauer and Sandholm (2007; 2009). These papers took inspiration from Hart and Mas-Colell (2001), who pointed out the role of integrability in models of regret-based learning in repeated normal form games. Hofbauer (2000) proved the convergence of the BNN, best response, and perturbed best response dynamics in normal form games with an interior ESS. A proof of the existence of a cycle in example 7.2.1 can be found in Hofbauer and Sandholm (2009); this reference also contains a statement and proof of the version of Danskin's envelope theorem cited in the text. The probabilistic characterization of integrability alluded to the text was presented in Sandholm (2006).

Global Convergence of Evolutionary Dynamics 269

For subdifferentials of convex functions, see Hiriart-Urruty and Lemaréchal (2001); their example D.3.4 is especially relevant to the discussion in the text.

Smith (1984) proved Theorem 7.2.9 for his dynamic; the general result presented in the text is due to Hofbauer and Sandholm (2009).

Kojima and Takahashi (2007) considered a class of normal form games called anti-coordination games, in which at each state x, the worst response to x is always in the support of x. They proved (see also Hofbauer 1995b) that such games must have a unique equilibrium, that this equilibrium is interior, and that it is globally asymptotically stable under the best response dynamic. However, also they presented an example (due to Hofbauer) showing that neither the replicator dynamic nor the logit dynamic need converge in these games, the latter even at arbitrarily low noise levels.

Section 7.3
Section 7.3.1 follows Berger (2007b). Exercise 7.3.1b is due to Hofbauer (1995b), and lemma 7.3.2(i) is due to Monderer and Sela (1997). It is worth noting that theorem 7.3.4 extends immediately to ordinal supermodular games (also known as quasi-supermodular games; see Milgrom and Shannon 1994). Moreover, since ordinal potential games (Monderer and Shapley 1996b) are defined by the absence of cycles of improvement steps, a portion of the proof of theorem 7.3.4 establishes the convergence of simple solutions of (BR) in nondegenerate ordinal potential games.

Section 7.3.2 follows Hofbauer and Sandholm (2002; 2007).

Section 7.4
Akin (1980) showed that starting from any interior population state, the replicator dynamic eliminates strategies that are strictly dominated by a pure strategy. Versions of theorems 7.4.4 and 7.4.5 can be found in Nachbar (1990) and Samuelson and Zhang (1992); see also Hofbauer and Weibull (1996).

Appendix 7.A
For properties of ω-limit sets of differential equations, see Robinson (1995); for ω-limit sets of differential inclusions, see Benaïm, Hofbauer, and Sorin (2005). For applications of chain recurrence in the theory of learning in games, see Benaïm and Hirsch (1999a), Hofbauer and Sandholm (2002), and Benaïm, Hofbauer, and Sorin (2005; 2006). The fundamental theorem of dynamical systems is due to Conley (1978); see Robinson (1995) for a textbook treatment. Other good general references on notions of recurrence for differential equations include Nemytskii and Stepanov (1960), Akin (1993), and Benaïm (1998; 1999).

Appendix 7.B
The standard reference on Lyapunov functions for flows is Bhatia and Szegő (1970).

Appendix 7.C
The standard reference on cooperative differential equations and monotone dynamical systems is Smith (1995). Theorems 7.C.1, 7.C.2(i), 7.C.2(ii), and 7.C.3(i) in the text are Smith's (1995) theorems 4.1.1, 1.2.1, 1.2.3, and 2.4.5, respectively. Theorem 7.C.3(ii) combines theorem 2.4.7 of Smith (1995) with theorem 1.1 of Hirsch (1988), the latter after a reversal of time.

8 Local Stability under Evolutionary Dynamics

Chapter 7 analyzed classes of games in which evolutionary dynamics converge to equilibrium from all or most initial conditions. Although games from many applications lie in these classes, at least as many interesting games do not.

In cases where global convergence results are not available, one can turn instead to analyses of local stability. If a society somehow finds itself playing a particular equilibrium, how can one tell whether this equilibrium will persist in the face of occasional small disturbances in behavior? This chapter introduces a refinement of Nash equilibrium—the notion of an *evolutionarily stable state* (ESS)—that captures the robustness of the equilibrium to invasion by small groups with different aggregate behaviors. The main results in this chapter show that states satisfying a version of this concept called *regular Taylor ESS* are locally stable under many evolutionary dynamics.

Games with an ESS share some structural properties with stable games, at least in the neighborhood of the ESS. Through this connection, section 8.4 shows how to establish local stability of ESS under some dynamics by the use of local Lyapunov functions. The results build on the analyses from section 7.2 of Lyapunov functions for stable games.

The other leading approach to local stability analysis is linearization. Given a rest point of a nonlinear (but smooth) dynamic, one can approximate the behavior of the dynamic in a neighborhood of the rest point by studying an appropriate linear dynamic, namely, the one defined by the derivative matrix of the nonlinear dynamic evaluated at the rest point in question. In sections 8.5 and 8.6, we use linearization to study the two families of smooth dynamics introduced in chapters 5 and 6: imitative dynamics and perturbed best response dynamics. Surprisingly, this analysis leads to a deep and powerful connection between the replicator and logit dynamics, one that seems difficult to reach by other means.

It is worth noting that linearization is also very useful for establishing *instability* results. For this reason, the techniques developed in this chapter are very important for the analyses of nonconvergent dynamics in chapter 9.

The first two sections of this chapter formally establish some results that were hinted at earlier. Section 8.1 indicates two senses in which a non-Nash rest point of an imitative dynamic cannot be stable. Section 8.2 shows that under most dynamics, a Nash equilibrium of a potential game is locally stable if and only if it is a local maximizer of potential.

The linearization techniques used in sections 8.5 and 8.6 (and in chapter 9) require a working knowledge of matrix analysis and linear differential equations. These topics are reviewed in detail in appendices 8.A and 8.B. The main theorems of linearization theory are presented in appendix 8.C.

8.1 Non-Nash Rest Points of Imitative Dynamics

Chapters 5 and 6 showed that under five of the six classes of evolutionary dynamics studied in this book, rest points are identical to Nash equilibria (or to perturbed versions thereof). The lone exception is imitative dynamics; theorem 5.4.13 showed that the rest points of these dynamics are the restricted equilibria, a set that includes not only the Nash equilibria but also any state that would be a Nash equilibrium if the strategies unused at that state were removed from the game. Theorem 5.7.1 established one sense in which these extra rest points are fragile: by combining a small amount of a "better behaved" dynamic with an imitative dynamic, one obtains a new dynamic that satisfies Nash stationarity. But as mentioned in section 5.4.6, this fragility can be expressed more directly: non-Nash rest points of imitative dynamics cannot be locally stable and so are not plausible predictions of play.

Now this last claim can be established formally. Recall from observation 5.4.8 that imitative dynamics exhibit *monotone percentage growth rates*: they can be expressed in the form

$$\dot{x}_i^p = x_i^p G_i^p(x), \tag{8.1}$$

with the percentage growth rates $G_i^p(x)$ ordered by payoffs $F_i^p(x)$ as in equation (5.18). This fact drives the instability result.

Theorem 8.1.1 *Let V_F be an imitative dynamic for population game F, and let $\hat{x}$ be a non-Nash rest point of V_F. Then $\hat{x}$ is not Lyapunov stable under V_F, and no interior solution trajectory of V_F converges to $\hat{x}$.*

Proof ($p = 1$) Since $\hat{x}$ is a restricted equilibrium that is not a Nash equilibrium, each strategy j in the support of $\hat{x}$ satisfies $F_j(\hat{x}) = \bar{F}(\hat{x})$, and any best response i to $\hat{x}$ is an unused strategy that satisfies $F_i(\hat{x}) > \bar{F}(\hat{x})$. Also, since $\hat{x}$ is a rest point of V_F, equation (8.1) implies that each j in the support of $\hat{x}$ has $G_j(\hat{x}) = 0$. Thus, monotonicity of percentage growth rates implies that $G_i(\hat{x}) > G_j(\hat{x}) = 0$, and so the continuity of G_i implies $G_i(x) \geq k > 0$ on some small neighborhood O of $\hat{x}$.

Local Stability under Evolutionary Dynamics

Let $\{x_t\}$ be an interior solution trajectory of V_F (see theorem 5.4.7). Then if $x_s \in O$ for all $s \in (t, u)$, it follows that

$$\log((x_u)_i) - \log((x_t)_i) = \int_t^u \left(\frac{d}{ds} \log((x_s)_i)\right) ds = \int_t^u \frac{(\dot{x}_s)_i}{(x_s)_i} ds = \int_t^u G_i(x_s) ds \geq k(u - t).$$

Rearranging and exponentiating yields

$$(x_u)_i \geq (x_t)_i \exp(k(u - t)).$$

Thus, during intervals that x_s is in O, $(x_s)_i$ is increasing. This immediately implies that if O is small, there is no neighborhood O' of $\hat{x}$ such that solutions starting in O' stay in O, and so $\hat{x}$ is not Lyapunov stable. Also, since $(x_t)_i$ cannot decrease inside $O \cap \text{int}(X)$, no interior solution trajectory can converge to $\hat{x}$. ∎

8.2 Local Stability in Potential Games

In potential games, the potential function serves as a strict Lyapunov function for any evolutionary dynamic satisfying positive correlation (PC); solution trajectories of such dynamics ascend the potential function and converge to connected sets of rest points (see section 7.1). For dynamics that also satisfy Nash stationarity (NS), these sets consist entirely of Nash equilibria.

That the potential function is a strict Lyapunov function has important implications for local stability of sets of rest points. Call $A \subseteq X$ a *local maximizer set* of the potential function $f: X \to \mathbf{R}$ if it is connected, if f is constant on A, and if there exists a neighborhood O of A such that $f(x) > f(y)$ for all $x \in A$ and all $y \in O - A$. Theorem 3.1.3 implies that such a set consists entirely of Nash equilibria. The set $A \subseteq NE(F)$ is *isolated* if there is a neighborhood of A that does not contain any Nash equilibria other than those in A.

If the value of f is nondecreasing along solutions of a dynamic, then these solutions cannot escape from a neighborhood of a local maximizer set. If the value of f is increasing in this neighborhood, then solutions in the neighborhood should converge to the set. This is the content of the following theorem.

Theorem 8.2.1 *Let F be a potential game with potential function f, let V_F be an evolutionary dynamic for F, and suppose that $A \subseteq NE(F)$ is a local maximizer set of f.*

i. If V_F satisfies positive correlation (PC), then A is Lyapunov stable under V_F.

ii. If in addition V_F satisfies Nash stationarity (NS) and A is isolated, then A is an asymptotically stable set under V_F.

Proof Part (i) of the theorem follows immediately from lemma 7.1.1 and theorem 7.B.2. To prove part (ii), note that (NS), (PC), and the fact that A is isolated imply that there is a neighborhood O of A such that $\dot f(x) = \nabla f(x)'V_F(x) > 0$ for all $x \in O - A$. Corollary 7.B.6 then implies that A is asymptotically stable. ∎

For dynamics satisfying (PC) and (NS), being an isolated local maximizer set is not only a sufficient condition for being asymptotically stable; it is also necessary.

Theorem 8.2.2 *Let F be a potential game with potential function f, and let V_F be an evolutionary dynamic for F that satisfies (PC) and (NS). Suppose that $A \subseteq NE(F)$ is a smoothly connected asymptotically stable set under V_F. Then A is an isolated local maximizer set of f.*

Proof Since A is a smoothly connected set of Nash equilibria, exercise 3.1.9 implies that f takes some fixed value c throughout A. Now let ξ be an initial condition in $O - A$, where O is the basin of attraction of A. Then $\omega(\xi) \subseteq A$. But since f is a strict Lyapunov function for V_F, it follows that $f(\xi) < c$. Since $\xi \in O - A$ was arbitrary, A is an isolated local maximizer set. ∎

Theorems 8.2.1 and 8.2.2 allow us to characterize locally stable rest points for dynamics satisfying positive correlation (PC). Since the best response and perturbed best response dynamics do not satisfy this condition, the former because of lack of smoothness and the latter because of the perturbations, theorems 8.2.1 and 8.2.2 do not apply.

In the case of the best response dynamic, theorem 6.1.4 establishes analogues of (NS) and (PC), which in turn imply that solution trajectories ascend the potential function and converge to Nash equilibrium (see theorem 7.1.3). These results and the previous arguments yield the following theorem.

Theorem 8.2.3 *Let F be a potential game with potential function f, let V_F be the best response dynamic for F, and let $A \subseteq NE(F)$ be smoothly connected. Then A is an isolated local maximizer set of f if and only if A is asymptotically stable under V_F.*

In the case of perturbed best response dynamics, the roles of conditions (PC) and (NS) are played by virtual positive correlation and perturbed stationarity (see theorem 6.2.10 and observation 6.2.7). These in turn ensure that the dynamics ascend the perturbed potential function

$$\tilde f(x) = f(x) - \sum_{p \in \mathcal{P}} m^p v^p(\tfrac{1}{m^p}x^p)$$

(see theorem 7.1.4). Substituting these results into the foregoing arguments yields the following theorem.

Theorem 8.2.4 *Let F be a potential game with potential function f, let $V_{F,v}$ be the perturbed best response dynamic for F generated by the admissible deterministic perturbations $v = (v^1, \ldots, v^p)$, and let $A \subseteq PE(F,v)$ be smoothly connected. Then A is an isolated local maximizer set of $\tilde{f}$ if and only if A is asymptotically stable under $V_{F,v}$.*

8.3 Evolutionarily Stable States

In the remainder of this chapter, we introduce the notion of an *evolutionarily stable state* and show that it provides a sufficient condition for local stability under a wide range of evolutionary dynamics, including all the dynamics that were shown to be globally convergent in stable games in chapter 7.

The birth of evolutionary game theory can be dated to the definition of an *evolutionarily stable strategy* in single-population matching environments by Maynard Smith and Price (1973). In introducing this concept, those authors envisioned a model of evolution quite different from the dynamic models considered in this book. They focused on monomorphic populations—populations whose members all choose the same strategy—but allowed this common strategy to be a mixed strategy. Their notion of an evolutionarily stable strategy was meant to capture the capacity of a monomorphic population to resist invasion by a monomorphic mutant group whose members play some alternative mixed strategy.

Clearly, Maynard Smith and Price's model is different from the polymorphic population, pure strategist model studied in this book. Even so, their formal definition of an evolutionarily stable strategy remains coherent in this setting; indeed, it is adopted as the definition of an evolutionarily stable state, allowing use of the acronym ESS without regard to context.

The interpretation of ESS in the polymorphic population setting is somewhat strained because it relies on comparisons between the aggregate payoffs of the incumbent and invading populations rather than on direct comparisons of the payoffs to different strategies. Still, the fact that the ESS condition is sufficient for local stability under many population dynamics amply justifies its use.

Even for single-population settings, the literature offers many alternative definitions of ESS and related concepts. The differences between these definitions are rather subtle, and in normal form environments all the concepts considered here are equivalent. But for multipopulation settings, there are two quite distinct definitions of ESS. One is most natural for studying monomorphic models à la Maynard Smith and Price, while the other is most natural for the polymorphic models considered here. It is a definition of the latter type, which we dub *regular Taylor ESS*, that provides the sufficient condition for stability for multipopulation dynamics.

8.3.1 Single-Population Games

In the context of single-population games, $x \in X$ is an *evolutionarily stable state* (ESS) of F if

There is a neighborhood O of x such that $(y - x)'F(y) < 0$ for all $y \in O - \{x\}$. (8.2)

Two equivalent characterizations of ESS are provided in theorems 8.3.1 and 8.3.5. The conditions from theorem 8.3.5 are the closest to the original definition of ESS (see the chapter notes), but definition (8.2) is the most concise.

Definition (8.2) can be interpreted using the notion of invasion (see section 3.3.3). Fix $x \in X$, and let $y \in O$ be a population state near x. Condition (8.2) requires that if there is an incumbent population whose aggregate behavior is described by y, and an infinitesimal group of invaders whose aggregate behavior is described by x, then the average payoff of the invaders must exceed the average payoff in the incumbent population.

While it is appealingly simple, it is not immediately clear why definition (8.2) should be viewed as a stability condition for x. It considers invasions of other states y by x, whereas one would expect a stability condition for x to address invasions of x by other states. In fact, (8.2) is equivalent to a condition that is somewhat more cumbersome but is stated in terms of invasions of x by other states.

This new condition is stated in terms of inequalities of the form

$$(y - x)'F(\varepsilon y + (1 - \varepsilon)x) < 0. \tag{8.3}$$

Suppose that an incumbent population with aggregate behavior x is invaded by group with aggregate behavior y, with the invaders making up an ε share of the postentry population. Inequality (8.3) requires that the average payoffs of the incumbents exceed the average payoffs of the invaders.

Now, consider the following requirement on the population state x:

There is an $\bar{\varepsilon} > 0$ such that (8.3) holds for all $y \in X - \{x\}$ and $\varepsilon \in (0, \bar{\varepsilon})$. (8.4)

Condition (8.4) says that x admits a *uniform invasion barrier*: as long as the proportion of invaders in the postentry population is less than $\bar{\varepsilon}$, the incumbents will receive higher payoffs than the invaders in aggregate. If the *invasion barrier* of x against y is defined by

$$b_x(y) = \inf(\{\varepsilon \in (0, 1) : (y - x)'F(\varepsilon y + (1 - \varepsilon)x) \geq 0\} \cup \{1\}),$$

then condition (8.4) says that $b_x(y) \geq \bar{\varepsilon} > 0$ for all $y \in X - \{x\}$.

Theorem 8.3.1 shows that ESSs are characterized by the existence of a uniform invasion barrier.

Theorem 8.3.1 *State $x \in X$ is an ESS if and only if condition (8.4) holds.*

Local Stability under Evolutionary Dynamics

Exercise 8.3.2 Prove theorem 8.3.1 via the following three steps.

i. Show that if condition (8.4) holds, then there is a $\delta > 0$ such that the set $U = \{(1-\lambda)x + \lambda y\colon y \in X, \lambda \in [0, b_x(y))\}$ contains a δ-neighborhood of x. (*Hint:* Start by representing each point in $X - \{x\}$ as a convex combination of x and a point in the set $C = \{y \in X\colon y_i = 0 \text{ for some } i \in \text{support}(x)\}$.)

ii. Use part (i) to show that condition (8.4) is equivalent to the following condition:

There is a neighborhood O of x such that (8.3) holds
$$\text{for all } y \in O - \{x\} \text{ and } \varepsilon \in (0, 1). \tag{8.5}$$

iii. Show that x is an ESS if and only if condition (8.5) holds. ◇

Exercise 8.3.3 Consider the following variant of condition (8.4):

For each $y \in X - \{x\}$, there is an $\bar{\varepsilon} > 0$ such that (8.3) holds for all $\varepsilon \in (0, \bar{\varepsilon})$. (8.6)

This condition requires a positive invasion barrier $b_x(y)$ for each $y \in X - \{x\}$ but does not require uniformity; invasion barriers need not be bounded away from 0.

i. Show that if $F(x) = Ax$ is linear, then condition (8.6) is equivalent to condition (8.4) and so characterizes ESS in these games. (*Hint:* Use the fact that

$$b_x(y) = \begin{cases} \min\left\{\frac{(x-y)'Ax}{(x-y)'A(x-y)}, 1\right\} & \text{if } (y-x)'Ax < 0 \text{ and } (y-x)'Ay > 0, \\ 0 & \text{otherwise,} \end{cases}$$

along with the hint from exercise 8.3.2(i) and a compactness argument.)

ii. Construct a three-strategy game with a state x^* that satisfies condition (8.6) but that is not an ESS. (*Hint:* Let $x^* = (0, \frac{1}{2}, \frac{1}{2})$, and let D_1 and D_2 be closed disks in $X \subset \mathbf{R}^3$ that are tangent to $\text{bd}(X)$ at x^* and whose radii are r_1 and $r_2 > r_1$. Introduce a payoff function of the form $F(x) = -c(x)(x - x^*)$, where $c(x)$ is positive on $\text{int}(D_1) \cup (X - D_2)$ and negative on $\text{int}(D_2) - D_1$. Then use proposition 8.3.4.) ◇

What is the relation between ESS and Nash equilibrium? As a first step, one can show that the former is a refinement of the latter.

Proposition 8.3.4 *Every ESS is an isolated Nash equilibrium.*

Proof Let x be an ESS of F, let O be the neighborhood posited in condition (8.2), and let $y \in X - \{x\}$. Then for all small enough $\varepsilon > 0$, $x_\varepsilon = \varepsilon y + (1 - \varepsilon)x$ is in O, and so satisfies $(x - x_\varepsilon)'F(x_\varepsilon) > 0$. Simplifying and dividing by ε yields $(x - y)'F(x_\varepsilon) > 0$, so taking ε to zero yields $(y - x)'F(x) \leq 0$. That is, x is a Nash equilibrium. To see that x is isolated, note that if $w \in O - \{x\}$ were a Nash equilibrium, we would have $(w - x)'F(w) \geq 0$, contradicting that x satisfies (8.2). ■

The converse of proposition 8.3.4 is false. The mixed equilibrium of a two-strategy coordination game provides a simple counterexample.

Theorem 8.3.5 shows precisely what restrictions ESS adds to those already imposed by Nash equilibrium.

Theorem 8.3.5 *Suppose that F is Lipschitz continuous. Then state x is an ESS if and only if the following hold:*

x is a Nash equilibrium: $(y-x)'F(x) \leq 0$ *for all* $y \in X$. (8.7)

There is a neighborhood O of x such that

for all $y \in O - \{x\}, (y-x)'F(x) = 0$ *implies that* $(y-x)'F(y) < 0$. (8.8)

According to the theorem, an ESS x is a Nash equilibrium that satisfies the following additional property: if a state y near x is an alternative best response to x, then an infinitesimal group of invaders whose aggregate behavior is described by x can invade an incumbent population playing y.

Exercise 8.3.6 Show that if $F(x) = Ax$ is linear, then condition (8.8) is equivalent to the global condition

For all $y \in X - \{x\}, (y-x)'F(x) = 0$ implies that $(y-x)'F(y) < 0$. ◇ (8.9)

Proof of theorem 8.3.5 That condition (8.2) implies conditions (8.7) and (8.8) follows easily from proposition 8.3.4. The converse is immediate if $x \in \text{int}(X)$, but in general the proof of the converse requires a delicate argument.

Suppose that $x \in X$ satisfies conditions (8.7) and (8.8). Let $S^* = \text{argmax}_{i \in S} F_i(x)$ be the set of pure best responses to x, let $S^0 = S - S^*$, let $X^* = \{v^* \in X: \text{support}(v^*) \subseteq S^*\}$ be the set of mixed best responses to x, and let $X^0 = \{v^0 \in X: \text{support}(v^0) \subseteq S^0\}$ be the set of states at which all best responses to x are unused. Since x is a Nash equilibrium, $\text{support}(x) \subseteq S^*$ and $x \in X^*$. Moreover, each $y \in X$ can be represented as a convex combination of the form

$$y = (1-\lambda)y^* + \lambda y^0,$$

where $y^* \in X^*$, $y^0 \in X^0$, and $\lambda = \sum_{j \in S^0} y_j \in [0,1]$. Evidently, $y^* = y$ when $\lambda = 0$, and $y^0 = y$ when $\lambda = 1$; in all other cases, y uniquely determines both y^* and y^0.

The aim is to show that for some neighborhood U of x, $(y-x)'F(y) < 0$ for all $y \in U - \{x\}$. Begin with the following decomposition:

$$\begin{aligned}(y-x)'F(y) &= ((1-\lambda)y^* + \lambda y^0 - x)'F(y) \\ &= \lambda(y^0 - x)'F(y) + (1-\lambda)(y^* - x)'(F(y) - F(y^*)) \\ &\quad + (1-\lambda)(y^* - x)'F(y^*) \\ &\equiv T_1(y) + T_2(y) + T_3(y).\end{aligned}$$ (8.10)

Local Stability under Evolutionary Dynamics

To prove the theorem, it is enough to establish these two claims:

$T_1(y) + T_2(y) \leq 0$ when $y \in U$, and $T_1(y) + T_2(y) < 0$ when $y \in U - X^*$; (8.11)

$T_3(y) \leq 0$ when $y \in U$, and $T_3(y) < 0$ when $y \in U \cap X^* - \{x\}$. (8.12)

To accomplish this, let $\|v\| = \sum_{i=1}^n |v_i|$ denote the L^1 norm of $v \in \mathbf{R}^n$, and let K be the Lipschitz constant for F with respect to this norm. Also, let O be the neighborhood from condition (8.8), and choose $r > 0$ so that O contains a ball of radius r centered at x.

Since $x \in X^*$ and $y^0 \in X^0$, we have that $(y^0 - x)'F(x) < 0$. Therefore, since F is continuous, we can choose a neighborhood U' of x and a positive constant ε such that

$$\lambda(y^0 - x)'F(y) < -\lambda\varepsilon \quad \text{for all } y \in U'. \tag{8.13}$$

Moreover, we can choose a neighborhood $U \subseteq U'$ of x such that

$$\|y - x\| < \min\{\tfrac{\varepsilon}{20K}, \tfrac{r}{5}, \tfrac{1}{2}\} \quad \text{when } y \in U. \tag{8.14}$$

Suppose that $\|y - x\| \leq \tfrac{1}{2}$. Since support$(x) \cap S^0 = \emptyset$, we have that

$$\lambda = \sum_{j \in S^0} |y_j| = \sum_{j \in S^0} |y_j - x_j| \leq \sum_{i \in S^*} |y_i - x_i| + \sum_{j \in S^0} |y_j - x_j| = \|y - x\| \leq \tfrac{1}{2},$$

and so that $\tfrac{1}{1-\lambda} \leq 2$. Since $\|v - y\| \leq 2$ for any $v \in X$, it follows that

$$\|y^* - x\| = \|\tfrac{1}{1-\lambda}(y - \lambda y^0) - x\|$$
$$\leq \|y - x\| + \tfrac{\lambda}{1-\lambda}\|y^0 - y\|$$
$$\leq \|y - x\| + 4\lambda$$
$$\leq 5\|y - x\|.$$

Equation (8.14) therefore yields

$$\|y^* - x\| < \min\{\tfrac{\varepsilon}{4K}, r\} \quad \text{when } y \in U. \tag{8.15}$$

Now suppose that $y \in U$. Applying the first bound in (8.15), we have

$$(1 - \lambda)(y^* - x)'(F(y) - F(y^*)) \leq \|y^* - x\| K \|y - y^*\|$$
$$= \|y^* - x\| K \|\lambda(y^0 - y^*)\|$$
$$= 2\lambda K \|y^* - x\|$$
$$\leq \tfrac{1}{2}\lambda\varepsilon.$$

Since $\lambda > 0$ when $y \notin X^*$, combining this bound with (8.13) yields claim (8.11).

The second bound in (8.15) reveals that $y^* \in O$. Since $y^* \in X^*$ as well, we have that $(y^* - x)'F(x) = 0$, so condition (8.8) implies that

$$(y^* - x)'F(y^*) \leq 0, \quad \text{with equality if and only if } y^* = x.$$

Since y^* is distinct from x whenever $y \in X^* - \{x\}$, we have claim (8.12). This completes the proof of the theorem. ∎

8.3.2 Multipopulation Games

There are two rather different ways of extending the definition of ESS from a single-population setting to a multipopulation setting. If F is a game played by $p \geq 1$ populations, we call $x \in X$ a *Taylor ESS* of F if

There is a neighborhood O of x such that $(y - x)'F(y) < 0$ for all $y \in O - \{x\}$. (8.16)

(The text of this condition is identical to that in (8.2); the only difference is that F may now be a multipopulation game.) We call x a *Cressman ESS* of F if

There is a neighborhood O of x such that for all $y \in O - \{x\}$, there is a $p \in \mathcal{P}$
such that $(y^p - x^p)'F^p(y) < 0$. (8.17)

Condition (8.17) is identical to condition (8.16) in single-population settings. But in multipopulation settings, it is weaker. Both conditions consider invasions of a collection of incumbent populations $y = (y^1, \ldots, y^p) \in O - \{x\}$ by a collection of invading populations $x = (x^1, \ldots, x^p)$. For x to be a Taylor ESS, the aggregate payoff of the invading populations must exceed the aggregate payoff of the incumbent populations. But for x to be a Cressman ESS, it is enough that one of the invading populations x^p earn a higher average payoff than the corresponding incumbent population y^p.

For the evolutionary setting studied by Maynard Smith and Price—monomorphic populations of mixed strategists—the appropriate extension of the ESS concept to multiple populations is Cressman ESS (see the chapter notes for an extended discussion.) But to understand the dynamics of behavior in polymorphic populations of pure strategists, Taylor ESS turns out to be the more useful condition. Because of this, we will write "ESS" in place of *Taylor ESS* in some of the discussions below.

Exercise 8.3.7 Let $F = (F^1, F^2)$ be a population game, and let $\hat{F} = (F^1, 2F^2)$ be the game obtained by doubling the payoffs of population 2's strategies. Show that F and $\hat{F}$ have the same Nash equilibria and Cressman ESSs but that their Taylor ESSs may differ. ◇

Local Stability under Evolutionary Dynamics

Exercise 8.3.8 Suppose that F has no own-population interactions: $F^p(x)$ is independent of x^p for all $p \in \mathcal{P}$. Show that if x^* is a Cressman ESS of F, then it is a pure social state: $(x^*)^p = m^p e_i^p$ for some $i \in S^p$ and $p \in \mathcal{P}$. Of course, this implies that any Taylor ESS is a pure social state as well. See proposition 3.3.6 for a closely related result in the context of stable games. (*Hint*: If x^p is not pure, consider an invasion by $y = (y^p, x^{-p})$, where y^p is an alternative best response to x.) ◇

8.3.3 Regular Taylor ESS

While section 8.3.2 focused on the differences between Taylor ESS and Cressman ESS, both of these concepts admit characterizations corresponding to those of single-population ESS. For example, theorem 8.3.5 has the following analogue for Taylor ESS.

Corollary 8.3.9 *Suppose that F is Lipschitz continuous. Then x is a Taylor ESS if and only if*

x is a Nash equilibrium: $(y - x)'F(x) \leq 0$ for all $y \in X$.   (8.18)

There is a neighborhood O of x such that
  for all $y \in O - \{x\}$, $(y - x)'F(x) = 0$ implies that $(y - x)'F(y) < 0$.   (8.19)

The text of these conditions is identical to that in conditions (8.7) and (8.8), but F is now allowed to be a multipopulation game.

Some local stability results require a slight strengthening of these conditions. To strengthen the Nash equilibrium condition (8.18), we suppose that x is a *quasistrict equilibrium*; within each population, all strategies in use earn the same payoff, a payoff that is strictly greater than that of each unused strategy. (This is a generalization of *strict equilibrium*, which in addition requires x to be a pure state.) To strengthen (8.19), we replace the inequality in this condition with a differential version. All told, we call $x \in X$ a *regular Taylor ESS* if

x is a quasistrict equilibrium: $F_i^p(x) = \bar{F}^p(x) > F_j^p(x)$ when $x_i^p > 0, x_j^p = 0$;   (8.20)

For all $y \in X - \{x\}$, $(y - x)'F(x) = 0$ implies that $(y - x)'DF(x)(y - x) < 0$.   (8.21)

When $p = 1$, we call a state x satisfying (8.20) and (8.21) a *regular ESS* for short.

Exercise 8.3.10

i. Confirm that every regular Taylor ESS is a Taylor ESS.

ii. Show that condition (8.21) does not change if the implication is only checked for $y \neq x$ in a neighborhood of x, as in condition (8.19).

iii. Show that if F is linear, then condition (8.21) is equivalent to condition (8.19). ◇

It is useful to have a more concise characterization of regular Taylor ESS. For any set of strategies $I \subset \bigcup_{p \in \mathcal{P}} S^p$, let $\mathbf{R}_I^n = \{y \in \mathbf{R}^n : y_j^p = 0 \text{ whenever } j \notin I\}$ denote the set of vectors in $\mathbf{R}^n$ whose components corresponding to strategies outside I equal zero. Also, let $S(x) \subseteq \bigcup_{p \in \mathcal{P}} S^p$ denote the support of state x. Then it is easy to verify this observation.

Observation 8.3.11 *State x is a regular Taylor ESS if and only if it is a quasistrict equilibrium that satisfies*

$$z'DF(x)z < 0 \quad \text{for all nonzero } z \in TX \cap \mathbf{R}_{S(x)}^n. \tag{8.22}$$

Condition (8.22) resembles the derivative condition associated with strictly stable games. However, the condition need only hold at the equilibrium, and negative definiteness is only required to hold in directions that move along the face of X on which the equilibrium lies.

8.4 Local Stability via Lyapunov Functions

In this remainder of this chapter, we argue that any regular Taylor ESS x^* is locally stable under many evolutionary dynamics. The approach in this section is to construct a *strict local Lyapunov function* for each dynamic in question, that is, a non-negative function defined in a neighborhood of x^* that vanishes precisely at x^* and whose value decreases along every solution of the dynamic other than the stationary one at x^*. The results presented in appendix 7.B show that the existence of such a function ensures the asymptotic stability of x^*.

The similarity between the definitions of regular ESS and of stable games—in particular, the negative semidefiniteness conditions that play a central role in both contexts—suggests the Lyapunov functions for stable games from section 7.2 as the natural starting points for the stability analyses of ESSs. In some cases—under the projection and replicator dynamics, and whenever the ESS is interior—one can use the Lyapunov functions from section 7.2 without amendment. But more generally, these functions must be modified in order to make them local Lyapunov functions for ESSs.

8.4.1 The Replicator and Projection Dynamics

The analysis is simplest in the cases of the replicator and projection dynamics. Section 7.2 established global convergence of these dynamics in every strictly stable game by showing that measures of "distance" from the game's unique Nash equilibrium served as global Lyapunov functions. The proofs of these convergence results relied on nothing about the payoff structure of the game apart from the fact that the game's unique Nash equilibrium is also a globally evolutionarily stable state (GESS).

Local Stability under Evolutionary Dynamics

This observation suggests that if state x^* is a Taylor ESS of an arbitrary population game, the same distance functions will serve as *local* Lyapunov functions for x^* under the two dynamics. This logic is confirmed in the following theorem.

Theorem 8.4.1 *Let x^* be a Taylor ESS of F. Then x^* is asymptotically stable under*

i. *the replicator dynamic for F; and*

ii. *the projection dynamic for F.*

Exercise 8.4.2 Prove theorem 8.4.1 by showing that the functions H_{x^*} and E_{x^*} from theorems 7.2.4 and 7.2.1 define strict local Lyapunov functions for the two dynamics. ◇

8.4.2 Target and Pairwise Comparison Dynamics: Interior ESS

The proofs of convergence for other classes of dynamics in section 7.2 relied directly on the negative semidefiniteness condition (3.16) that characterizes stable games. If a game admits an interior ESS that satisfies the strict inequalities in (8.22), then condition (3.16) holds in a neighborhood of the ESS. This again permits use of the Lyapunov functions from section 7.2 without amendment to prove local stability results.

Theorem 8.4.3 *Let $x^* \in \text{int}(X)$ be a regular Taylor ESS of F. Then x^* is asymptotically stable under*

i. *any separable excess payoff dynamic for F,*

ii. *the best response dynamic for F,*

iii. *any impartial pairwise comparison dynamic for F.*

Exercise 8.4.4 Prove theorem 8.4.3 by showing that the functions Γ, G, and Ψ from theorems 7.2.6, 7.2.7, and 7.2.9 define strict local Lyapunov functions for an ESS x^* under the three varieties of dynamics. ◇

Rest points of perturbed best response dynamics generally do not coincide with Nash equilibria, and hence with ESSs. Nevertheless, the next exercise indicates that an appropriate negative definiteness condition is still enough to ensure local stability.

Exercise 8.4.5 Let $\tilde{x}$ be a perturbed equilibrium of (F, v) for some admissible deterministic perturbations $v = (v^1, \ldots, v^p)$, and suppose that $z'DF(\tilde{x})z < 0$ for all nonzero $z \in TX$. Show that $\tilde{x}$ is isolated in the set of perturbed equilibria, and that the function $\tilde{G}$ from theorem 7.2.8 defines a strict local Lyapunov function for $\tilde{x}$. (*Hint:* To show that $\tilde{x}$ is isolated, use the argument at the end of the proof of theorem 7.2.8.) ◇

For consistency with the previous results, it is natural to try to prove stability results for perturbed best response dynamics for games with an interior ESS. To do so, one assumes that the size of the perturbations is small, in the hope that there will be a perturbed equilibrium that is close to the ESS. Since the logit dynamic is parameterized by a noise level η, it provides a natural setting for the desired result.

Theorem 8.4.6 *Let $x^* \in \text{int}(X)$ be a regular Taylor ESS of F. Then for some neighborhood O of x^* and each small enough $\eta > 0$, there is a unique logit(η) equilibrium $\tilde{x}^\eta$ in O, and this equilibrium is asymptotically stable under the logit(η) dynamic. Finally, $\tilde{x}^\eta$ varies continuously in η, and $\lim_{\eta \to 0} \tilde{x}^\eta = x^*$.*

Proof ($p = 1$) Theorem 7.2.8 and exercises 6.2.3 and 6.2.4 show that for $\eta > 0$, the function

$$\tilde{G}^\eta(x) = \eta \log \left(\sum_{j \in S} \exp(\eta^{-1} \hat{F}_j(x)) \right) + \eta \sum_{j \in S} x_j \log x_j$$

(with $0 \log 0 \equiv 0$) is a Lyapunov function for the logit(η) dynamic when F is a stable game. If one defines

$$\tilde{G}^0(x) \equiv G(x) = \max_{j \in S} \hat{F}_j(x)$$

to be the Lyapunov function for the best response dynamic in stable games, then $\tilde{G}^\eta(x)$ is continuous in (x, η) on $X \times [0, \infty)$,

By exercise 8.4.4, G defines a strict local Lyapunov function for the best response dynamic at the interior ESS x^*. In particular, x^* is a local minimizer of G: there is an open, convex neighborhood $O \subset X$ of x^* such that $G(x) > G(x^*)$ for all $x \in O - \{x^*\}$. Moreover, since F is C^1 and satisfies $z'DF(x^*)z < 0$ for all nonzero $z \in TX$, one can choose O in such a way that $z'DF(x)z < 0$ for all nonzero $z \in TX$ and $x \in O$.

Because $\tilde{G}^\eta(x)$ is continuous in (x, η), the theorem of the maximum (see the chapter notes) implies that the map

$$\eta \mapsto \tilde{\beta}(\eta) \equiv \underset{x \in \text{cl}(O)}{\text{argmin}} \, \tilde{G}^\eta(x)$$

is upper-hemicontinuous on $[0, \infty)$. Thus, since $\tilde{\beta}(0) = \{x^*\} \subset O$ (in particular, since $x^* \notin \text{bd}(O)$), there is an $\hat{\eta} > 0$ such that $\tilde{\beta}(\eta) \subset O$ for all $\eta < \hat{\eta}$. This implies that each $\tilde{x}^\eta \in \tilde{\beta}(\eta)$ is a local minimizer of $\tilde{G}^\eta$ with respect to $\text{cl}(O)$, and so with respect to the full state space X.

Exercise 8.4.5 implies that the value of $\tilde{G}^\eta$ is decreasing along solutions to the logit(η) dynamic in the set O, implying that each local minimizer $\tilde{x}^\eta$ is a rest point

Local Stability under Evolutionary Dynamics

of this dynamic; indeed, $\tilde{x}^\eta$ must be an asymptotically stable rest point. Finally, since O is convex, the last paragraph of the proof of theorem 7.2.8 shows that when $\eta < \hat{\eta}$, $\tilde{\beta}(\eta) \subset O$ is a singleton. This completes the proof of the theorem. ∎

8.4.3 Target and Pairwise Comparison Dynamics: Boundary ESS

It remains to prove local stability results for boundary ESSs for the dynamics considered in theorem 8.4.3.

Theorem 8.4.7 *Let x^* be a regular Taylor ESS of F. Then x^* is asymptotically stable under*

i. *any separable excess payoff dynamic for F,*

ii. *the best response dynamic for F,*

iii. *any impartial pairwise comparison dynamic for F.*

To prove theorem 8.4.7, we show that suitably modified versions of the Lyapunov functions for stable games serve as local Lyapunov functions here. Letting $S^p(x^*) = \text{support}((x^*)^p)$ and $C > 0$, we augment the functions Γ, G, and Ψ from section 7.2 by the function

$$\Upsilon_{x^*}(x) = C \sum_{p \in \mathcal{P}} \sum_{j \notin S^p(x^*)} x_j^p, \tag{8.23}$$

which is proportional to the number of agents using strategies outside the support of x^*.

For intuition, let F be a single-population game, and suppose that $x^* \notin \text{int}(X)$ is a regular ESS of F in which at least one pure strategy is unused. Because x^* is a quasistrict equilibrium, all unused strategies earn strictly lower payoffs than strategies in the support of x^*; because payoffs are continuous, this is true not only at x^* itself, but also at states near x^*. Under any dynamic that respects these payoff differences, solutions from initial conditions near x^* should converge to $X_{x^*} = \{x \in X: S(x) = S(x^*)\}$, the face of X that contains x^*. If x^* is a pure state (i.e., a vertex of X), and thus a strict equilibrium, then X_{x^*} is simply the singleton $\{x^*\}$, and the foregoing argument suffices to prove local stability (see exercise 8.4.9).

Now assume that x^* is neither in the interior nor at a vertex of X, and focus on the behavior of the dynamic on face X_{x^*} in the vicinity of x^*. One way to do so is to consider a restricted game in which only the strategies in the support of x^* are available. Observation 8.3.11 says that this restricted game resembles a stable game, at least in a neighborhood of x^*. It then follows from theorem 8.4.3 that under the dynamic for the original game, solutions from initial conditions that are on face X_{x^*} and near x^* must converge to x^*.

To prove theorem 8.4.7, we need to construct local Lyapunov functions whose values decrease not only along solutions on face X_{x^*}, but also along solutions in the interior of X starting near x^*. To do so, we augment the Lyapunov functions for stable games, Γ, G, and Ψ, by the function Υ_{x^*} defined in (8.23), which captures the mass placed on strategies outside the support of x^*. For instance, in the case of impartial pairwise comparison dynamics, we replace the original Lyapunov function Ψ with the function

$$\Psi_{x^*}(x) = \Psi(x) + \Upsilon_{x^*}(x) = \Psi(x) + C \sum_{j \notin S(x^*)} x_j. \tag{8.24}$$

When the current state x is in the interior of X, the value of Ψ need not decrease. But if x is close to x^*, then the value of Υ_{x^*} does decrease, as agents playing strategies outside of $S(x^*)$ switch to strategies in $S(x^*)$, although as the state approaches the boundary of X, the rate of decrease of Υ_{x^*} approaches zero. To prove the theorem, we must show that if the constant $C > 0$ is large enough, then the value of $C \Upsilon_{x^*}$ always falls fast enough to compensate for any growth in the value of Ψ, so that, all told, the value of Ψ_{x^*} falls (see lemma 8.4.8 and exercise 8.4.11).

A detailed proof of theorem 8.4.7 follows for the case of impartial pairwise comparison dynamics. The proofs of the other two cases are left as exercises.

Proof of theorem 8.4.7(iii) (p = 1) Let $\dot{x} = V_F(x)$ be an impartial pairwise comparison dynamic for F. Let $\Psi_{x^*} \colon X \to \mathbf{R}$ be the C^1 function defined in equation (8.24), where Ψ is defined in theorem 7.2.9; the constant $C > 0$ is determined below.

Since V_F is an impartial pairwise comparison dynamic, theorem 7.2.9 shows that the function Ψ is non-negative, with $\Psi(x) = 0$ if and only if $x \in NE(F)$. It follows that Ψ_{x^*}, too, is non-negative, with $\Psi_{x^*}(x) = 0$ if and only if x is a Nash equilibrium of F with support$(x) \subseteq$ support(x^*). Thus, since x^* is an ESS, it is isolated in the set of Nash equilibria (see proposition 8.3.4), so there is a neighborhood O of x^* on which x^* is the unique zero of Ψ_{x^*}. If we can show that there is also a neighborhood O' of x^* such that $\dot{\Psi}_{x^*}(x) < 0$ for all $x \in O' - \{x^*\}$, then Ψ_{x^*} is a strict local Lyapunov function for x^*, so the conclusion of the theorem will follow from corollary 7.B.6.

To reduce the amount of notation, let $\mathbf{1}^0 \in \mathbf{R}^n$ be the vector whose jth component equals 0 if $j \in$ support(x^*) and equals 1 otherwise, so that $(\mathbf{1}^0)'x$ represents the mass of agents who use strategies outside the support of x^* at state x. Then $\Psi_{x^*}(x) = \Psi(x) + C (\mathbf{1}^0)'x$, and so the time derivative of Ψ_{x^*} is

$$\dot{\Psi}_{x^*}(x) = \dot{\Psi}(x) + C (\mathbf{1}^0)' \dot{x}.$$

Now, the proof of theorem 7.2.9 shows that the time derivative of Ψ satisfies

$$\dot{\Psi}(x) \leq \dot{x}' DF(x) \dot{x},$$

Local Stability under Evolutionary Dynamics

with equality holding precisely at the Nash equilibria of V_F. To finish the proof, it is enough to show that

$$\dot{x}'DF(x)\dot{x} + C(\mathbf{1}^0)'\dot{x} \leq 0 \quad \text{for all } x \in O' - \{x^*\}.$$

This follows directly from the following lemma, choosing $C \geq M/N$.

Lemma 8.4.8 *Let $\dot{x} = V_F(x)$ be a pairwise comparison dynamic for F, and let x^* be a regular ESS of F. Then there is a neighborhood O' of x^* and constants $M, N > 0$ such that for all $x \in O'$,*

i. $\dot{x}'DF(x)\dot{x} \leq M(\mathbf{1}^0)'x;$

ii. $(\mathbf{1}^0)'\dot{x} \leq -N(\mathbf{1}^0)'x.$

Proof Suppose without loss of generality that $S(x^*) = \text{support}(x^*)$ is given by $\{1, \ldots, n^*\}$. Then, to complement $\mathbf{1}^0 \in \mathbf{R}^n$, let $\mathbf{1}^* \in \mathbf{R}^n$ be the vector whose first n^* components equal 1 and whose remaining components equal 0, so that $\mathbf{1} = \mathbf{1}^* + \mathbf{1}^0$. Next, decompose the identity matrix I as $I^* + I^0$, where $I^* = \text{diag}(\mathbf{1}^*)$ and $I^0 = \text{diag}(\mathbf{1}^0)$, and finally, decompose I^* as $\Phi^* + \Xi^*$, where $\Xi^* = \frac{1}{n^*}\mathbf{1}^*(\mathbf{1}^*)'$ and $\Phi^* = I^* - \Xi^*$. Notice that Φ^* is the orthogonal projection of $\mathbf{R}^n$ onto $\mathbf{R}^n_0 \cap \mathbf{R}^n_{S(x^*)}$, where $\mathbf{R}^n_0 = \{z \in \mathbf{R}^n : \mathbf{1}'z = 0\}$ and $\mathbf{R}^n_{S(x^*)} = \{z \in \mathbf{R}^n : z_j = 0 \text{ whenever } j \notin S(x^*)\}$, and that $I = \Phi^* + \Xi^* + I^0$.

Using this decomposition of the identity matrix, we can write

$$\dot{x}'DF(x)\dot{x} = ((\Phi^* + \Xi^* + I^0)\dot{x})'DF(x)((\Phi^* + \Xi^* + I^0)\dot{x})$$
$$= (\Phi^*\dot{x})'DF(x)(\Phi^*\dot{x}) + ((\Xi^* + I^0)\dot{x})'DF(x)\dot{x} + (\Phi^*\dot{x})'DF(x)((\Xi^* + I^0)\dot{x}). \tag{8.25}$$

Since x^* is a regular ESS, $z'DF(x^*)z < 0$ for all nonzero $z \in TX \cap \mathbf{R}^n_{S(x^*)}$. Thus, since $DF(x)$ is continuous in x, there is a neighborhood $\hat{O}$ of x^* on which the first term of (8.25) is nonpositive.

Turning to the second term, note that since $\mathbf{1}'\dot{x} = 0$ and $(\mathbf{1}^0)' = \mathbf{1}'I^0$, we have

$$(\Xi^* + I^0)\dot{x} = (\tfrac{1}{n^*}\mathbf{1}^*(\mathbf{1}^*)' + I^0)\dot{x} = (-\tfrac{1}{n^*}\mathbf{1}^*(\mathbf{1}^0)' + I^0)\dot{x} = ((I - \tfrac{1}{n^*}\mathbf{1}^*\mathbf{1}')I^0)\dot{x}.$$

Let $\|A\|$ denote the spectral norm of the matrix A (see section 8.A.6). Then applying spectral norm inequalities and the Cauchy-Schwarz inequality, we have

$$((\Xi^* + I^0)\dot{x})'DF(x)\dot{x} = ((I - \tfrac{1}{n^*}\mathbf{1}^*\mathbf{1}')I^0\dot{x})'DF(x)\dot{x} \leq |I^0\dot{x}| \, \|I - \tfrac{1}{n^*}\mathbf{1}(\mathbf{1}^*)'\| \, \|DF(x)\| \, |\dot{x}|. \tag{8.26}$$

Since $DF(x)$, $V_F(x)$, and $\rho_{ij}(F(x), x)$ are continuous in x on the compact set X, we can find constants K and R such that

$$\left\|I - \tfrac{1}{n^*}\mathbf{1}(\mathbf{1}^*)'\right\| \, \|DF(x)\| \, |\dot{x}| \le K \quad \text{and} \quad \max_{i,j \in S} \rho_{ij}(F(x),x) \le R \quad \text{for all } x \in X. \qquad (8.27)$$

Now, since x^* is a quasistrict equilibrium, $F_i(x^*) = \bar{F}(x^*) > F_j(x^*)$ for all $i \in \text{support}(x^*) = \{1,\dots,n^*\}$ and all $j \notin \text{support}(x^*)$. Thus, since the pairwise comparison dynamic satisfies sign preservation (5.25), we have $\rho_{ij}(F(x^*),x^*) = 0$ for such i and j, and because F is continuous, there is a neighborhood $O' \subseteq \hat{O}$ of x^* on which for such i and j we have $F_i(x) > F_j(x)$, and hence $\rho_{ij}(F(x),x) = 0$. From this argument and the bound on ρ_{ij} in (8.27), it follows that for $x \in O'$,

$$|I^0 \dot{x}| = \sqrt{\sum_{j>n^*} |\dot{x}_j|^2}$$

$$\le \sum_{j>n^*} |\dot{x}_j|$$

$$= \sum_{j>n^*} \left| \sum_{k \in S} x_k \rho_{kj}(F(x),x) - x_j \sum_{k \in S} \rho_{jk}(F(x),x) \right|$$

$$\le \sum_{j>n^*} \left(\sum_{k \in S} x_k \rho_{kj}(F(x),x) + x_j \sum_{k \in S} \rho_{jk}(F(x),x) \right)$$

$$= \sum_{j>n^*} \sum_{k>n^*} x_k \rho_{kj}(F(x),x) + \sum_{j>n^*} x_j \sum_{k \in S} \rho_{jk}(F(x),x)$$

$$\le 2Rn \sum_{j>n^*} x_j$$

$$= 2Rn \, (\mathbf{1}^0)'x.$$

Thus, at all $x \in O'$,

$$((\Xi^* + I^0)\dot{x})'DF(x)\dot{x} \le 2KRn \, (\mathbf{1}^0)'x.$$

Essentially the same argument provides a similar bound on the third term of (8.25), completing the proof of part (i) of the lemma.

To prove part (ii) of the lemma, follow the line of argument after equation (8.27) and note that since x^* is quasistrict and since the pairwise comparison dynamic satisfies sign preservation, $\rho_{ji}(F(x^*),x^*) > 0$ and $\rho_{ij}(F(x^*),x^*) = 0$ whenever $i \in \text{support}(x^*) = \{1,\dots,n^*\}$ and $j \notin \text{support}(x^*)$. So, since F and ρ are continuous, sign preservation implies that there is a neighborhood O' of x^* and an $r > 0$ such that $\rho_{ji}(F(x),x) > r$ and $\rho_{ij}(F(x),x) = 0$ for all $i \le n^*, j > n^*$, and $x \in O'$. Applying this observation, and then canceling like terms when both j and k are greater than n^* in the following sums, we have that for all $x \in O'$,

Local Stability under Evolutionary Dynamics

$$(\mathbf{1}^0)'\dot{x} = \sum_{j>n^*} \dot{x}_j$$

$$= \sum_{j>n^*} \left(\sum_{k \in S} x_k \rho_{kj}(F(x), x) - x_j \sum_{k \in S} \rho_{jk}(F(x), x) \right)$$

$$= \sum_{j>n^*} \left(\sum_{k>n^*} x_k \rho_{kj}(F(x), x) - x_j \sum_{k \in S} \rho_{jk}(F(x), x) \right)$$

$$= - \sum_{j>n^*} x_j \sum_{i \leq n^*} \rho_{ji}(F(x), x)$$

$$\leq -r\, n^* (\mathbf{1}^0)' x.$$

This completes the proof of the lemma, and thus the proof of Theorem 8.4.7. ∎

Exercise 8.4.9 Let e_i be a strict equilibrium of the single-population game F: $F_i(e_i) > F_j(e_i)$ for all $j \neq i$. Show that x^* is asymptotically stable under

i. any excess payoff dynamic for F,

ii. the best response dynamic for F,

iii. any pairwise comparison dynamic for F.

Note that statements (i) and (iii) are not implied by theorem 8.4.7 because the excess payoff dynamic in (i) is not assumed to be separable, and the pairwise comparison dynamic in (iii) is not assumed to be impartial. (*Hint:* In all cases, show that the function Υ_{e_i} defined in (8.23) is a strict local Lyapunov function.) ◇

Exercise 8.4.10 Prove theorem 8.4.7(ii) (for $p = 1$) by showing that under the best response dynamic, the function

$$G_{x^*}(x) = G(x) + \Upsilon_{x^*}(x) = \max_{y \in X} (y - x)' F(x) + C \sum_{j \notin S(x^*)} x_j$$

is a strict local Lyapunov function for any regular ESS x^*. (*Hint:* The proof is nearly the same as the one just given, but it builds on the proof of theorem 7.2.7 instead of the proof of theorem 7.2.9, and uses theorems 7.B.2 and 7.B.5 in place of corollary 7.B.6.) ◇

Exercise 8.4.11 Prove theorem 8.4.7(i) (for $p = 1$) by showing that under the separable excess payoff dynamic with revision protocol τ, the function

$$\Gamma_{x^*}(x) = \Gamma(x) + \Upsilon_{x^*}(x) = \sum_{i \in S} \int_0^{\hat{F}_i(x)} \tau_i(s)\, ds + C \sum_{j \notin S(x^*)} x_j$$

is a strict local Lyapunov function for any regular ESS x^*. (*Hint:* Establish this variant of lemma 8.4.8: under the excess payoff dynamic generated by τ, there is a neighborhood O' of x^* such that

i. $\dot{x}'DF(x)\dot{x} \leq K T(x)(\mathbf{1}^0)'x$ and
ii. $(\mathbf{1}^0)'\dot{x} = -T(x)(\mathbf{1}^0)'x$,

for all $x \in O'$, where $T(x) = \sum_{i \in S} \tau_i(\hat{F}_i(x))$.) $\diamond$

8.5 Linearization of Imitative Dynamics

In this section and the next, we study the stability of rest points of evolutionary dynamics using linearization. This technique requires the dynamic to be smooth, at least near the rest point, and it can be inconclusive in borderline cases. But, more optimistically, it does not require the guesswork needed to find Lyapunov functions. Furthermore, instead of establishing just asymptotic stability, a rest point found stable via linearization (i.e., one that is *linearly stable*) must attract solutions from all nearby initial conditions at an exponential rate (see appendix 8.C). Linearization is also useful for proving that a rest point is unstable, a fact used repeatedly in studying nonconvergence (see chapter 9). Finally, linearization techniques can be used to prove local stability results for imitative dynamics other than the replicator dynamic, for which no Lyapunov functions have been proposed.

The appendices explain the techniques from matrix analysis (appendix 8.A), linear differential equation theory (appendix 8.B), and linearization theory (appendix 8.C) needed here and in chapter 9. In both places, we avoid the use of affine calculus by assuming that payoffs are defined on the positive orthant (see section 3.A.7). Reviewing the multivariate product and chain rules (see section 3.A.4) may be helpful for following the arguments to come.

We begin the analysis with some general background on linearization of evolutionary dynamics. Recall that a single-population dynamic

$$\dot{x} = V(x) \tag{D}$$

describes the evolution of the population state through the simplex X. In evaluating the stability of the rest point x^* using linearization, we rely on the fact that near x^*, the dynamic (D) can typically be well approximated by the linear dynamic

$$\dot{z} = DV(x^*)z. \tag{L}$$

We are interested here in how (D) behaves on the simplex, and thus in how (L) behaves on the tangent space TX. Indeed, it is because (D) defines a dynamic on X that it makes sense to think of (L) as a dynamic on TX. At each state $x \in X$,

Local Stability under Evolutionary Dynamics

$V(x) \in TX$ describes the current direction of motion through the simplex. It follows that the derivative $DV(x)$ must map any tangent vector z into TX, as one can verify by writing

$$V(x+z) = V(x) + DV(x)z + o(|z|)$$

and noting that $V(x)$ and $V(x+z)$ are both in TX. Thus, in (L), $\dot{y}$ lies in TX whenever y lies in TX, implying that TX is invariant under (L).

Keeping this argument in mind is important when using linearization to study stability under the dynamic (D). Rather than looking at all the eigenvalues of $DV(x^*)$, one should consider only those associated with the restricted linear map $DV(x^*)\colon TX \to TX$, which sends each tangent vector $z \in TX$ to a new tangent vector $DV(x^*)z \in TX$. The scalar $\lambda = a + ib$ is an eigenvalue of this restricted map if $DV(x^*)z = \lambda z$ for some vector z whose real and imaginary parts are both in TX. If all eigenvalues of this restricted map have negative real part, then the rest point x^* is linearly stable under (D) (see corollary 8.C.2).

Hines's lemma, stated next and proved in section 8.A.7, is often the key to making these determinations. In stating this result, we let $\mathbf{R}_0^n = \{z \in \mathbf{R}^n : \mathbf{1}'z = 0\}$ denote the tangent space of the simplex. In the single-population case, TX and $\mathbf{R}_0^n$ are the same, but it is useful to separate these two notations in multipopulation cases, where $TX = \prod_{p \in \mathcal{P}} \mathbf{R}_0^{n^p}$.

Lemma 8.5.1 *Suppose that $Q \in \mathbf{R}^{n \times n}$ is symmetric, satisfies $Q\mathbf{1} = \mathbf{0}$, and is positive definite with respect to $\mathbf{R}_0^n$, and that $A \in \mathbf{R}^{n \times n}$ is negative definite with respect to $\mathbf{R}_0^n$. Then each eigenvalue of the linear map $QA\colon \mathbf{R}_0^n \to \mathbf{R}_0^n$ has negative real part.*

8.5.1 The Replicator Dynamic

To show that any regular Taylor ESS x^* is linearly stable under the replicator dynamic, we first focus on the case in which x^* is interior.

Theorem 8.5.2 *Let $x^* \in \mathrm{int}(X)$ be a regular Taylor ESS of F. Then x^* is linearly stable under the replicator dynamic.*

Proof ($p = 1$) The single-population replicator dynamic is given by

$$\dot{x}_i = V_i(x) = x_i \hat{F}_i(x). \tag{R}$$

To compute $DV(x)$, recall from equation (7.21) that the derivative of the excess payoff function $\hat{F}(x) = F(x) - \mathbf{1}\bar{F}(x)$ is given by

$$D\hat{F}(x) = DF(x) - \mathbf{1}(x'DF(x) + F(x)') = (I - \mathbf{1}x')DF(x) - \mathbf{1}F(x)'.$$

Then applying the product rule for componentwise products (see section 3.A.4), we have

$$DV(x) = D(\text{diag}(x)\hat{F}(x))$$
$$= \text{diag}(x)D\hat{F}(x) + \text{diag}(\hat{F}(x))$$
$$= \text{diag}(x)((I - 1x')DF(x) - 1F(x)') + \text{diag}(\hat{F}(x))$$
$$= Q(x)DF(x) - xF(x)' + \text{diag}(\hat{F}(x)), \tag{8.28}$$

where $Q(x) = \text{diag}(x) - xx'$.

Since x^* is an interior Nash equilibrium, $F(x^*)$ is a constant vector, implying that $F(x^*)'\Phi = 0'$ and that $\hat{F}(x^*) = 0$. Thus, equation (8.28) becomes

$$DV(x^*)\Phi = Q(x^*)DF(x^*)\Phi. \tag{8.29}$$

Since the matrices $Q(x^*)$ and $DF(x^*)\Phi$ satisfy the conditions of Hines's lemma, the eigenvalues of $DV(x^*)\Phi$ (and hence of $DV(x^*)$) corresponding to directions in $\mathbf{R}_0^n$ have negative real part. This completes the proof of the theorem. ∎

Exercise 8.5.3 Let x^* be an interior Nash equilibrium of F that satisfies $z'DF(x^*)z > 0$ for all nonzero $z \in TX$. Show that x^* is a source under the replicator dynamic; that is, all relevant eigenvalues of $DV(x^*)$ have positive real parts implying that all solutions of the replicator dynamic that start near x^* are repelled. (*Hint:* See the discussion in section 8.A.7.) Also, construct a game with an equilibrium that satisfies the conditions of this result. ◇

Exercise 8.5.4 Show that if $x^* \in \text{int}(X)$ is a regular Taylor ESS, then x^* is linearly stable under the projection dynamic. ◇

The following example highlights the fact that being a regular ESS is only a sufficient condition for an interior equilibrium to be locally stable under the replicator dynamic, not a necessary condition.

Example 8.5.1: Zeeman's Game Revisited Example 6.1.4 introduced the single-population game $F(x) = Ax$ generated by matching in the symmetric normal form game

$$A = \begin{pmatrix} 0 & 6 & -4 \\ -3 & 0 & 5 \\ -1 & 3 & 0 \end{pmatrix}.$$

This game admits Nash equilibria at states $x^* = (\frac{1}{3}, \frac{1}{3}, \frac{1}{3})$, $(\frac{4}{5}, 0, \frac{1}{5})$, and e_1; the replicator dynamic has rest points at these states as well as at the restricted equilibria $(0, \frac{5}{8}, \frac{3}{8})$, e_2, and e_3. Figure 8.1 shows that the behavior of the dynamic near the non-Nash rest points is consistent with theorem 8.1.1.

Local Stability under Evolutionary Dynamics

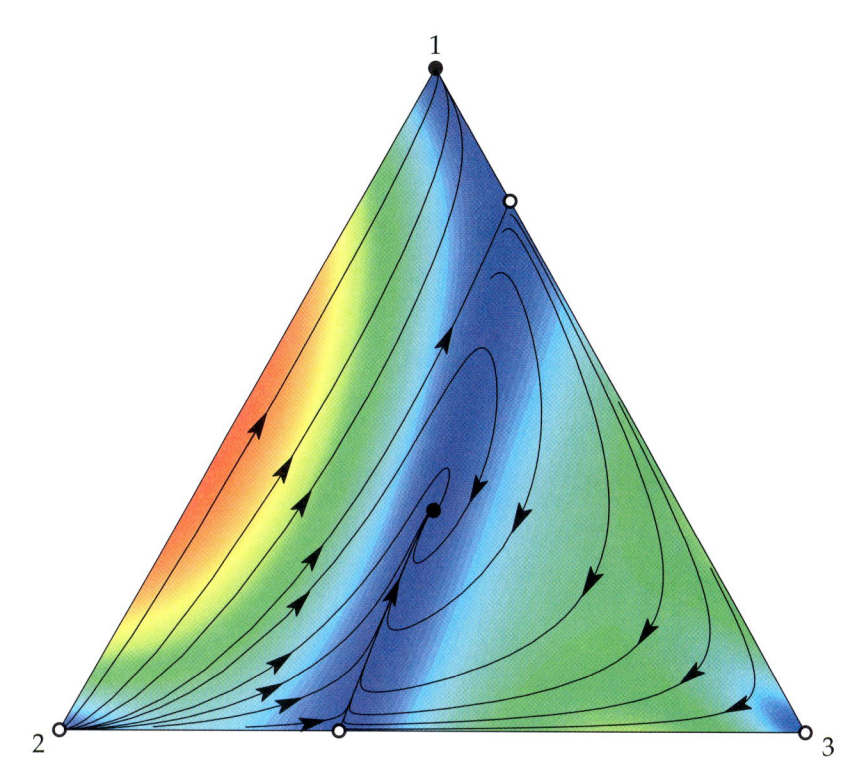

Figure 8.1
The replicator dynamic in Zeeman's game.

Since F is not a stable game (why not?), theorem 8.5.2 does not reveal whether x^* is stable. But this can be checked directly. Following the proof of theorem 8.5.2, compute

$$DV(x^*)\Phi = Q(x^*)DF(x^*)\Phi = Q(x^*)A\Phi = \frac{1}{9}\begin{pmatrix} 4 & 9 & -13 \\ -5 & -9 & 14 \\ 1 & 0 & -1 \end{pmatrix}.$$

In addition to the irrelevant eigenvalue of 0 corresponding to eigenvector **1**, this matrix has pair of complex eigenvalues, $-\frac{1}{3} \pm i\frac{\sqrt{2}}{3}$, corresponding to eigenvectors $(-2 \pm i(3\sqrt{2}), 1 \mp i(3\sqrt{2}), 1)$ whose real and complex parts lie in $\mathbf{R}_0^n$. Since the real parts of the relevant eigenvalues are both $-\frac{1}{3}$, the Nash equilibrium x^* is linearly stable under the replicator dynamic. ◆

The following theorem establishes the stability of all regular Taylor ESSs.

Theorem 8.5.5 *Let x^* be a regular Taylor ESS of F. Then x^* is linearly stable under the replicator dynamic.*

Proof ($p = 1$) Suppose without loss of generality that the support of x^* is $\{1, \ldots, n^*\}$, so that the number of unused strategies at x^* is $n^0 = n - n^*$. For any matrix $M \in \mathbf{R}^{n \times n}$, let $M^{++} \in \mathbf{R}^{n^* \times n^*}$ denote the upper left $n^* \times n^*$ block of M, and define the blocks $M^{+0} \in \mathbf{R}^{n^* \times n^0}$, $M^{0+} \in \mathbf{R}^{n^0 \times n^*}$, and $M^{00} \in \mathbf{R}^{n^0 \times n^0}$ similarly. Also, for each vector $v \in \mathbf{R}^n$, let $v^+ \in \mathbf{R}^{n^*}$ and $v^0 \in \mathbf{R}^{n^0}$ denote the upper and lower "blocks" of v.

Recall the expression (8.28) for the derivative matrix of the replicator dynamic:

$$DV(x) = Q(x)DF(x) - x F(x)' + \text{diag}(\hat{F}(x)),$$

where $Q(x) = \text{diag}(x) - xx'$. Now, observe that $x_j^* = 0$ for all $j > n^*$, that $\hat{F}_i(x^*) = 0$ for all $i \leq n^*$, and since x^* is quasistrict, that $\hat{F}_j(x^*) < 0$ for all $j > n^*$ (see the proof of lemma 5.5.3). Therefore, writing $Q = Q(x^*)$, $D = DF(x^*)$, $\pi = F(x^*)$, and $\hat{\pi} = \hat{F}(x^*)$, one can express $DV(x^*)$ in the block diagonal form

$$DV(x^*) = \begin{pmatrix} Q^{++}D^{++} - (x^*)^+(\pi^+)' & Q^{++}D^{+0} - (x^*)^+(\pi^0)' \\ 0 & \text{diag}(\hat{\pi}^0) \end{pmatrix}. \tag{8.30}$$

To complete the proof of the theorem, it is enough to show that if $v + iw$ with $v, w \in \mathbf{R}_0^n$ is an eigenvector of $DV(x^*)$ with eigenvalue $a + ib$, then $a < 0$.

We split the analysis into two cases. Suppose first that $(v + iw)^0 = \mathbf{0}$ (i.e., that $v_j = w_j = 0$ whenever $j > n^*$). Then it is easy to see that $(v + iw)^+$ must be an eigenvector of $DV(x^*)^{++} = Q^{++}D^{++} - (x^*)^+(\pi^+)'$. Now, because x^* is a Nash equilibrium with support $\{1, \ldots, n^*\}$, π^+ is a constant vector, and since $v, w \in \mathbf{R}_0^n$ and $(v + iw)^0 = \mathbf{0}$, the components of $(v + iw)^+$ sum to zero. Together, these observations imply that $(x^*)^+(\pi^+)'(v + iw)^+ = 0$. Finally, $Q^{++} \in \mathbf{R}^{n^* \times n^*}$ and $D^{++} \in \mathbf{R}^{n^* \times n^*}$ satisfy the conditions of Hines's lemma, the latter by requirement (8.22) for regular ESSs, and so this lemma allows us to conclude that $a < 0$.

Now suppose that $(v + iw)^0 \neq \mathbf{0}$, so that $v_j + iw_j \neq 0$ for some $j > n^*$. Then, since the lower right block of $DV(x^*)$ is the diagonal matrix $\text{diag}(\hat{\pi}^0)$, the jth component of the eigenvector equation for $DV(x^*)$ is $\hat{\pi}_j(v_j + iw_j) = (a + ib)(v_j + iw_j)$, implying that $a = \hat{\pi}_j$ (and also that $b = w_j = 0$). But as noted above, the fact that x^* is a quasistrict equilibrium implies that $\hat{\pi}_j < 0$, and so that $a < 0$. This completes the proof of the theorem. ∎

Exercise 8.5.6 Suppose that $x^* = e_i$ is a strict equilibrium of F. Show that for each $j \neq i$, the vector $e_j - e_i$ is an eigenvector of $DV(x^*)$ with eigenvalue $F_j(x^*) - F_i(x^*)$. ◊

Exercise 8.5.7 Suppose that x^* is a quasistrict Nash equilibrium of F. The proof of theorem 8.5.5 showed that for each unused strategy j, the excess payoff $\hat{F}_j(x^*)$ is an

Local Stability under Evolutionary Dynamics

eigenvalue of $DV(x^*)$ corresponding to an eigenvector in TX. Assume that $\hat{F}_j(x^*)$ is not an eigenvalue of $DV(x^*)$ corresponding to an eigenvector in $TX \cap \mathbf{R}^n_{S(x^*)}$. Show that

$$\begin{pmatrix} \zeta + \frac{1}{n^*}\mathbf{1} \\ -\iota_j \end{pmatrix} \in TX$$

is an eigenvector of $DV(x^*)$ corresponding to eigenvalue $\hat{F}_j(x^*)$, where ι_j is the appropriate standard basis vector in $\mathbf{R}^{n^0}$, and where ζ is the unique vector in $\mathbf{R}^{n^*}$ satisfying $\mathbf{1}'\zeta = 0$ and

$$(Q^{++}D^{++} - \hat{\pi}_j I)\zeta = \hat{\pi}_j(\tfrac{1}{n^*}\mathbf{1} - (x^*)^+) + Q^{++}(D^{+0}\iota_j - \tfrac{1}{n^*}D^{++}\mathbf{1}).$$

Why is there exactly one vector that satisfies these conditions? What goes wrong if the restriction on $\hat{F}_j(x^*)$ does not hold? ◇

8.5.2 General Imitative Dynamics

Theorem 8.5.5 established the local stability of all regular Taylor ESSs under the replicator dynamic. Theorem 8.5.8 parlays the previous analysis into a local stability result for all imitative dynamics.

Theorem 8.5.8 *Assume that x^* is a hyperbolic rest point of both the replicator dynamic (R) and a given imitative dynamic (5.6). Then x^* is linearly stable under (R) if and only if it is linearly stable under (5.6). Thus, if x^* is a regular Taylor ESS that satisfies the hyperbolicity assumptions, it is linearly stable under (5.6).*

Although the proof of this result requires a somewhat involved argument, the key step is presented in lemma 8.5.9, which shows that at interior equilibria, the linearization of any monotone percentage growth rate function G is a multiple of the linearization of the payoff function F.

Proof of theorem 8.5.8 ($p = 1$) We only consider the case in which x^* is interior; for boundary cases, see exercise 8.5.11.

Recall from observation 5.4.8 that any imitative dynamic (5.6) has monotone percentage growth rates: we can express the dynamic as

$$\dot{x}_i = x_i G_i(x), \tag{8.31}$$

where

$$G_i(x) \geq G_j(x) \quad \text{if and only if} \quad F_i(x) \geq F_j(x). \tag{8.32}$$

Lemma 8.5.9 shows that property (8.32) imposes a remarkable amount of structure on the derivative matrix of the percentage growth rate function G at the equilibrium x^*.

Lemma 8.5.9 *Let x^* be an interior Nash equilibrium, and suppose that $\Phi DF(x^*)$ and $\Phi DG(x^*)$ define invertible maps from TX to itself. Then $\Phi DG(x^*)\Phi = c\,\Phi DF(x^*)\Phi$ for some $c > 0$.*

Proof Since x^* is a Nash equilibrium, and hence a rest point of (8.31), $\Phi F(x^*) = \Phi G(x^*) = \mathbf{0}$. It follows that

$$\Phi F(x^* + \varepsilon z) = \varepsilon \Phi DF(x^*)z + o(\varepsilon) \quad \text{and} \quad \Phi G(x^* + \varepsilon z) = \varepsilon \Phi DG(x^*)z + o(\varepsilon) \quad (8.33)$$

for all $z \in TX$. Since we can rewrite condition (8.32) as

$$(e_i - e_j)'G(x) \geq 0 \quad \text{if and only if} \quad (e_i - e_j)'F(x) \geq 0,$$

and since $e_i - e_j \in TX$, equation (8.33) implies that for all $i, j \in S$ and $z \in TX$,

$$(e_i - e_j)'\Phi DG(x^*)z \geq 0 \quad \text{if and only if} \quad (e_i - e_j)'\Phi DF(x^*)z \geq 0. \quad (8.34)$$

(This observation is trivial when $z = \mathbf{0}$, and when $z \neq \mathbf{0}$ it follows from the fact that the linear terms dominate in (8.33) when ε is small.) By proposition 3.B.4, condition (8.34) is equivalent to the requirement that for all $i, j \in S$, there is a $c_{ij} > 0$ such that

$$(e_i - e_j)'\Phi DG(x^*)\Phi = c_{ij}(e_i - e_j)'\Phi DF(x^*)\Phi. \quad (8.35)$$

Now write $g_{ij} = (e_i - e_j)'\Phi DG(x^*)\Phi$ and $f_{ij} = (e_i - e_j)'\Phi DF(x^*)\Phi$. Since by assumption $\Phi DF(x^*)\Phi$ is an invertible map from TX to itself, so is its transpose (see exercise 8.5.10). Therefore, when i, j, and k are distinct, the unique decomposition of f_{ik} as a linear combination of f_{ij} and f_{jk} is as $f_{ij} + f_{jk}$. But equation (8.35) reveals that

$$c_{ij}f_{ij} + c_{jk}f_{jk} = g_{ij} + g_{jk} = g_{ik} = c_{ik}f_{ik},$$

and so $c_{ij} = c_{jk} = c_{ik}$. This and the fact that $c_{ij} = c_{ji}$ imply that c_{ij} is independent of i and j. So, since vectors of the form $e_i - e_j$ span TX, we conclude from equation (8.35) that $\Phi DG(x^*)\Phi = c\,\Phi DF(x^*)\Phi$, where c is the common value of the constants c_{ij}. This completes the proof of the lemma. ∎

We proceed with the proof of theorem 8.5.8. Let $V(x) = \text{diag}(x)\hat{F}(x)$ and $W(x) = \text{diag}(x)G(x)$ denote the replicator dynamic (R) and the dynamic (8.31), respectively. Since $W(x) \in TX$, we have that $\mathbf{1}'W(x) = x'G(x) = 0$, and hence that $\hat{G}(x) \equiv G(x) - \mathbf{1}x'G(x) = G(x)$. Thus (8.31) can be rewritten as $W(x) = \text{diag}(x)\hat{G}(x)$.

Now, repeating calculation (8.28) reveals that

$$DW(x) = Q(x)DG(x) - x\,G(x)' + \text{diag}(\hat{G}(x)).$$

Since x^* is an interior rest point of W, $G(x^*)$ is a constant vector, and so

$$DW(x^*)\Phi = Q(x^*)DG(x^*)\Phi = Q(x^*)\Phi DG(x^*)\Phi,$$

Local Stability under Evolutionary Dynamics

where the second equality follows from the fact that $Q(x^*)\mathbf{1} = \mathbf{0}$. Similar reasoning for the replicator dynamic V shows that

$$DV(x^*)\Phi = Q(x^*)\Phi DF(x^*)\Phi.$$

Lemma 8.5.9 says that $\Phi DG(x^*)\Phi = c\Phi DF(x^*)\Phi$ for some $c > 0$. We therefore conclude from the previous two equations that if x^* is a hyperbolic rest point under V and W, its stability properties under the two dynamics are the same. ∎

Exercise 8.5.10 Suppose that $A \in \mathbf{R}^{n \times n}$ defines an invertible map from $\mathbf{R}_0^n$ to itself and maps the vector $\mathbf{1}$ to the origin. Show that A' must also have these properties. (*Hint:* Use the fundamental theorem of linear algebra (8.42).) ◇

Exercise 8.5.11 Extend the proof of theorem 8.5.8 to the case of boundary equilibria. (*Hint:* Combine lemma 8.5.9 with the proof of theorem 8.5.5.) ◇

8.6 Linearization of Perturbed Best Response Dynamics

Linearization is also a useful tool for studying perturbed best response dynamics, the other main class of differentiable evolutionary dynamics.

8.6.1 Deterministically Perturbed Best Response Dynamics

Perturbed best response dynamics can be defined in terms of either stochastic or deterministic payoff perturbations (see chapter 6). But theorem 6.2.1 showed that there is no loss of generality in focusing on the latter case, as is done here.

Our first result shows that a negative definiteness condition on the payoff derivative is a sufficient condition for stability. This conclusion is similar to that from exercise 8.4.5, but the analysis is much simpler, and establishes not only asymptotic stability, but also linear stability.

Theorem 8.6.1 *Consider the perturbed best response dynamic for the pair (F, v), and let $\tilde{x}$ be a perturbed equilibrium of this pair. If $DF(\tilde{x})$ is negative definite with respect to TX, then $\tilde{x}$ is linearly stable.*

Proof ($p = 1$) In the single-population case, the stochastically perturbed best response dynamic takes the form

$$\dot{x} = \tilde{M}(F(x)) - x, \tag{8.36}$$

where the perturbed maximizer function $\tilde{M}$ is defined in equation (6.12). By the chain rule, the derivative of law of motion (8.36) is

$$DV(x) = D\tilde{M}(F(x))DF(x) - I. \tag{8.37}$$

To determine the eigenvalues of the product $D\tilde{M}(F(x))DF(x)$, recall the properties of the derivative matrix $D\tilde{M}(\pi)$ from corollary 6.C.5: it is symmetric, positive definite on $\mathbf{R}_0^n$, and satisfies $D\tilde{M}(\pi)\mathbf{1} = \mathbf{0}$. Since $DF(\tilde{x})$ is negative definite with respect to $\mathbf{R}_0^n$ by assumption, Hines's lemma implies that the eigenvalues of $D\tilde{M}(F(\tilde{x}))DF(\tilde{x})$ (as a map from $\mathbf{R}_0^n$ to itself) have negative real part. Subtracting the identity matrix I from the matrix product reduces each of these eigenvalues by 1, so the theorem is proved. ∎

Exercise 8.6.2 Show that the conclusion of the theorem continues to hold if $DF(x)$ is only negative semidefinite with respect to TX. (*Hint:* See the discussion in section 8.A.7.) ◇

Exercise 8.6.3 Let $\tilde{x}$ be a perturbed equilibrium for (F, v). Let $\bar{\lambda}$ be the largest eigenvalue of $D\tilde{M}(F(\tilde{x}))$, and let $\bar{s}$ be the largest singular value of $\Phi DF(\tilde{x})\Phi$ (see section 8.A.6). Show that if $\bar{\lambda}\bar{s} < 1$, then $\tilde{x}$ is linearly stable: that is, $\tilde{x}$ is stable whenever choice probabilities are not too sensitive to changes in payoffs, or payoffs are not too sensitive to changes in the state. ◇

8.6.2 The Logit Dynamic

With the additional structure provided by logit choice, the local stability analysis can be developed further. First, building on theorem 8.4.6, one can conclude that any regular interior ESS must have a linearly stable logit(η) equilibrium nearby whenever the noise level η is sufficiently small.

Corollary 8.6.4 *Let $x^* \in \text{int}(X)$ be a regular Taylor ESS of F. Then for some neighborhood O of x^* and all $\eta > 0$ less than some $\hat{\eta} > 0$, there is a unique and linearly stable logit(η) equilibrium $\tilde{x}^\eta$ in O.*

Proof ($p = 1$) Theorem 8.4.6 says that for η small enough, the equilibrium $\tilde{x}^\eta$ exists and is unique, and that $\lim_{\eta \to 0} \tilde{x}^\eta = x^*$. Since x^* is a regular interior ESS, $DF(x^*)$ is negative definite with respect to TX, so by continuity, $DF(\tilde{x}^\eta)$ is negative definite with respect to TX for all η close enough to 0. The result therefore follows from theorem 8.6.1. ∎

The derivative matrix for the logit dynamic takes an especially appealing form. Recall from exercise 6.2.4 that the derivative matrix of the logit(η) choice function is

$$D\tilde{M}^\eta(\pi) = \eta^{-1}\left(\text{diag}(\tilde{M}^\eta(\pi)) - \tilde{M}^\eta(\pi)\tilde{M}^\eta(\pi)'\right) = \eta^{-1}Q(\tilde{M}^\eta(\pi)). \tag{8.38}$$

Now by definition, the logit equilibrium $\tilde{x}^\eta$ satisfies $\tilde{M}^\eta(F(\tilde{x}^\eta)) = \tilde{x}^\eta$. Substituting this fact into equations (8.37) and (8.38) yields

$$DV^\eta(\tilde{x}^\eta) = \eta^{-1}Q(\tilde{x}^\eta)DF(\tilde{x}^\eta) - I. \tag{8.39}$$

Local Stability under Evolutionary Dynamics

To see the importance of this equation, recall from equation (8.29) that at interior rest points, the derivative matrix for the replicator dynamic satisfies

$$DV(x^*)\Phi = Q(x^*)DF(x^*)\Phi. \tag{8.40}$$

Together, equations (8.39) and (8.40) show that when evaluated at their respective rest points and in the relevant tangent directions, the linearizations of the replicator and logit dynamics at their interior rest points differ only by a positive affine transformation.

Example 8.6.1 To obtain the cleanest connections between the two dynamics, consider a game that admits a Nash equilibrium $x^* = \frac{1}{n}\mathbf{1}$ at the barycenter of the simplex. Then by symmetry, $\tilde{x}^\eta = x^*$ is also a logit(η) equilibrium for every $\eta > 0$. By the previous logic, λ is a relevant eigenvalue of (8.40) if and only if $\eta^{-1}\lambda - 1$ is a relevant eigenvalue of (8.39). It follows that if x^* is linearly stable under the replicator dynamic, then it is also linearly stable under the logit(η) dynamic for any $\eta > 0$. ◆

The foregoing discussion shows how analyses of local stability under the replicator and logit dynamics can be linked. Pushing these arguments further, one can use equations (8.39) and (8.40) to connect the long-run behaviors of the replicator and best response dynamics starting from arbitrary initial conditions (see the chapter notes for further discussion).

8.A Appendix: Matrix Analysis

This appendix reviews some basic ideas from matrix analysis, laying the groundwork for the discussion of linear differential equations in appendix 8.B and of local linearization of nonlinear differential equations in appendix 8.C. The techniques presented here are also needed to perform the explicit calculations that arise when using linearization to analyze evolutionary dynamics.

8.A.1 Rank and Invertibility

Most of this section focuses on square matrices, but it begins with matrices $A \in \mathbf{R}^{m \times n}$ of arbitrary dimensions. The *rank* of A is the number of linearly independent columns of A, or equivalently, the dimension of its *range*, range$(A) = \{y \in \mathbf{R}^m : Ax = y \text{ for some } x \in \mathbf{R}^n\}$. The *nullspace* (or *kernel*) of A, nullspace$(A) = \{x \in \mathbf{R}^n : Ax = \mathbf{0}\}$ is the set of vectors in that the matrix maps to the origin, and the dimension of this set is called the *nullity* of A. The rank and nullity of a matrix must sum to its number of columns:

$$\dim(\text{nullspace}(A)) + \dim(\text{range}(A)) = n;$$

$$\dim(\text{nullspace}(A')) + \dim(\text{range}(A')) = m. \tag{8.41}$$

The foregoing definitions identify the matrices A and A' with the linear maps $x \in \mathbf{R}^n \mapsto Ax \in \mathbf{R}^m$ and $y \in \mathbf{R}^m \mapsto A'y \in \mathbf{R}^n$. This identification is used implicitly in many of the discussions to follow.

Section 3.B.2 introduced the *fundamental theorem of linear algebra*:

$$\text{range}(A) = (\text{nullspace}(A'))^\perp. \tag{8.42}$$

To derive a key implication of (8.42) for the ranks of matrices, first recall that any subspace $V \subseteq \mathbf{R}^m$ satisfies $\dim(V) + \dim(V^\perp) = m$. Letting $V = \text{nullspace}(A')$ and then combining the result with equation (8.41) yields

$$\dim(\text{range}(A')) = \dim((\text{nullspace}(A'))^\perp).$$

Therefore, (8.42) yields

$$\dim(\text{range}(A')) = \dim(\text{range}(A)),$$

that is, every matrix has the same rank as its transpose.

From this point forward, we suppose that $A \in \mathbf{R}^{n \times n}$ is a square matrix. The matrix A is *invertible* if it admits an *inverse matrix* A^{-1}, that is, a matrix satisfying $A^{-1}A = I$. Such a matrix also satisfies $AA^{-1} = I$, and when an inverse matrix exists, it is unique. Invertible matrices can be characterized in a variety of ways. For instance, a matrix is invertible if and only if it has *full rank* (i.e., if $A \in \mathbf{R}^{n \times n}$ has rank n); alternatively, a matrix is invertible if and only if its determinant is nonzero.

8.A.2 Eigenvectors and Eigenvalues

Let $A \in \mathbf{R}^{n \times n}$, and suppose that

$$Ax = \lambda x \tag{8.43}$$

for some complex scalar $\lambda \in \mathbf{C}$ and some nonzero complex vector $x \in \mathbf{C}^n$. Then λ is an *eigenvalue* of A, and x is an *eigenvector* of A associated with λ; sometimes, the pair (λ, x) is referred to as an *eigenpair*.

The eigenvector equation (8.43) can be rewritten as $(\lambda I - A)x = \mathbf{0}$. This equation can only be satisfied by a nonzero vector if $(\lambda I - A)$ is not invertible, or equivalently, if $\det(\lambda I - A) = 0$. It follows that λ is an eigenvalue of A if and only if λ is a root of the *characteristic polynomial* $\det(tI - A)$.

Since $\det(tI - A)$ is a polynomial of degree n in t, the fundamental theorem of algebra ensures that it has n complex roots:

$$\det(tI - A) = (t - \lambda_1)(t - \lambda_2) \ldots (t - \lambda_n). \tag{8.44}$$

To be sure of obtaining n roots, one must count multiplicities: if the values of λ_i in (8.44) are not all distinct, the repeated values must be tallied each time they appear.

Evidently, each λ_i in (8.44) is an eigenvalue of A; if the value λ is repeated k times in (8.44), then λ is an eigenvalue of A of (*algebraic*) *multiplicity k*.

The sum and the product of the eigenvalues of A can be described very simply:

$$\sum_{i=1}^{n} \lambda_i = \operatorname{tr}(A); \quad \prod_{i=1}^{n} \lambda_i = \det(A).$$

(Here, the *trace* $\operatorname{tr}(A)$ of the matrix A is the sum of its diagonal elements.) To remember these formulas, notice that they are trivially true if A is a diagonal matrix, since in this case the eigenvalues of A are its diagonal entries.

Each eigenvalue of A corresponds to at least one eigenvector of A, and if an eigenvalue λ is of algebraic multiplicity k, then there can be as many as k linearly independent eigenvectors of A corresponding to this eigenvalue. This number of linearly independent eigenvectors is called the *geometric multiplicity* of λ. The collection of all eigenvectors corresponding to λ, the *eigenspace* of λ, is a subspace of $\mathbf{C}^n$ of dimension equal to the geometric multiplicity of λ.

Example 8.A.1 Let $a, b \in \mathbf{R}$ be nonzero, and consider these three 2×2 matrices:

$$A = \begin{pmatrix} a & 0 \\ 0 & a \end{pmatrix}; \quad B = \begin{pmatrix} a & b \\ 0 & a \end{pmatrix}; \quad C = \begin{pmatrix} a & b \\ -b & a \end{pmatrix}.$$

The matrix A has just one eigenvalue, a, which therefore has algebraic multiplicity 2. It also has geometric multiplicity 2 because its eigenspace is all of $\mathbf{C}^2 = \operatorname{span}(\{e_1, e_2\})$. (This description of $\mathbf{C}^2$ relies on allowing complex scalars when taking linear combinations of e_1 and e_2.)

The matrix B also has a lone eigenvalue of a of algebraic multiplicity 2. But here the geometric multiplicity of a is just 1, since its eigenspace is $\operatorname{span}(\{e_1\})$.

The matrix C has no real eigenvalues or eigenvectors; however, it has complex eigenvalues $a \pm i b \in \mathbf{C}$ corresponding to the complex eigenvectors $e_1 \pm i e_2 \in \mathbf{C}^2$.

We note for future reference the geometry of the linear map $x \mapsto Cx$. By writing $r = \sqrt{a^2 + b^2}$ and $\theta = \cos^{-1}\left(\frac{a}{r}\right)$, we can express the matrix C as

$$C = r \begin{pmatrix} \cos\theta & \sin\theta \\ -\sin\theta & \cos\theta \end{pmatrix}.$$

Computing Cx for various values of x (try $x = e_1$ and $x = e_2$) reveals that the map $x \mapsto Cx$ first rotates the vector x around the origin clockwise by an angle of θ and then rescales the result by a factor of r. ◆

8.A.3 Similarity, (Block) Diagonalization, and the Spectral Theorem

The matrix $A \in \mathbf{R}^{n \times n}$ is *similar* to matrix $B \in \mathbf{R}^{n \times n}$ if there exists an invertible matrix $S \in \mathbf{C}^{n \times n}$, called a *similarity matrix*, such that

$$B = S^{-1}AS.$$

When A is similar to B, the linear transformations $x \mapsto Ax$ and $y \mapsto By$ are equivalent up to a linear change of variable. Similarity defines an equivalence relation on the set of $n \times n$ matrices, and matrices that are similar have the same characteristic polynomial and the same eigenvalues, counting either algebraic or geometric multiplicities.

If A is similar to a diagonal matrix D, that is, if A is *diagonalizable*, then the eigenvalues of A are simply the diagonal elements of D. In this definition the similarity matrix is allowed to be complex; if the similarity can be achieved via a real similarity matrix $S \in \mathbf{R}^{n \times n}$, then the diagonal matrix D is also real, and A is *real diagonalizable*.

It follows easily from these definitions that a matrix A is diagonalizable if and only if the sum of the geometric multiplicities of the eigenvalues of A is n. Equivalently, A is diagonalizable if and only if each of its eigenvalues has equal algebraic and geometric multiplicities. It is simple to verify that in this case, a similarity matrix S can be constructed by choosing n linearly independent eigenvectors of A to be its columns.

It is especially convenient when similarity can be achieved using a similarity matrix that is itself of a simple form. The most important instance occurs when this matrix is an *orthogonal matrix*, meaning that its columns form an *orthonormal basis* for $\mathbf{R}^n$: each column is of length 1, and distinct columns are orthogonal. (It would make more sense to call such a matrix an orthonormal matrix, but the term "orthogonal matrix" is traditional.)

Orthogonal matrices can be characterized in a variety of ways.

Theorem 8.A.1 *The following are equivalent:*

i. R *is an orthogonal matrix.*

ii. $RR' = I$.

iii. $R' = R^{-1}$.

iv. The map $x \mapsto Rx$ *preserves lengths:* $|Rx| = |x|$ *for all* $x \in \mathbf{R}^n$.

v. The map $x \mapsto Rx$ *preserves inner products:* $(Rx)'(Ry) = x'y$ *for all* $x, y \in \mathbf{R}^n$.

vi. The map $x \mapsto Rx$ *is a composition of rotations and reflections.*

The last three items are summarized by saying that the linear transformation $x \mapsto Rx$ defined by an orthogonal matrix R is a *Euclidean isometry*.

Local Stability under Evolutionary Dynamics

Showing that a matrix is similar to a diagonal matrix is quite useful, but showing similarity to a block diagonal matrix often serves just as well. We focus on block diagonal matrices with diagonal blocks of these two types:

$$J_1 = (\lambda); \qquad J_2 = \begin{pmatrix} a & b \\ -b & a \end{pmatrix}.$$

For reasons that will become clear in section 8.A.5, block diagonal matrices of this form are called *simple Jordan matrices*. Calculations with simple Jordan matrices are often little more difficult than those with diagonal matrices; for instance, multiplying such a matrix by itself retains its block diagonal structure.

To combine these ideas, call the matrix $A \in \mathbf{R}^{n \times n}$ *normal* if it commutes with itself, that is, if $A'A = AA'$.

Theorem 8.A.2 (The Spectral Theorem for Real Normal Matrices) *The matrix $A \in \mathbf{R}^{n \times n}$ is normal if and only if it is similar via an orthogonal matrix R to a simple Jordan matrix $B = R^{-1}AR$. The matrix B is unique up to the ordering of the diagonal blocks.*

The spectral decomposition of A provides a full account of the eigenvalues and eigenvectors of A. Each J_1 block (λ) contains a real eigenvalue of A, and the two complex numbers $a \pm i b$ derived from each J_2 block are complex eigenvalues of A. Moreover, columns of the orthogonal similarity matrix R either are real eigenvectors of A or real and imaginary parts of complex eigenvectors of A.

The spectral theorem says that if A is normal, the behavior of the linear map $x \mapsto Ax = RBR^{-1}x$ can be decomposed into three simple steps. First, one applies the orthogonal transformation $R^{-1} = R'$ to x, obtaining $y = R'x$. Second, one applies the block diagonal matrix B to y; each J_1 block rescales a component of y, and each J_2 block rotates and rescales a pair of components of y (see example 8.A.1). Third, one applies R to $BR'x$ to undo the initial orthogonal transformation.

Additional restrictions on the J_1 and J_2 blocks yield characterizations of important subclasses of the normal matrices.

Corollary 8.A.3

i. The matrix $A \in \mathbf{R}^{n \times n}$ is symmetric ($A' = A$) if and only if it is similar via an orthogonal matrix R to a simple Jordan matrix containing only J_1 blocks. Thus, the symmetric matrices are the normal matrices with real eigenvalues.

ii. The matrix $A \in \mathbf{R}^{n \times n}$ is skew-symmetric ($A' = -A$) if and only if it is similar via an orthogonal matrix R to a simple Jordan matrix whose J_1 blocks all have $\lambda = 0$ and whose J_2 blocks all have $a = 0$. Thus, the skew-symmetric matrices are the normal matrices with purely imaginary eigenvalues.

iii. The matrix $A \in \mathbf{R}^{n \times n}$ is orthogonal ($A' = A^{-1}$) if and only if it is similar via an orthogonal matrix R to a simple Jordan matrix whose J_1 blocks all have $\lambda^2 = 1$ and whose J_2 blocks all have $a^2 + b^2 = 1$. Thus, the orthogonal matrices are the normal matrices whose eigenvalues have modulus 1.

8.A.4 Symmetric Matrices

Which matrices are real diagonalizable by an orthogonal matrix? The *spectral theorem for symmetric matrices* says that A is real diagonalizable by an orthogonal matrix if and only if it is symmetric. (This is just a restatement of corollary 8.A.3(i).) Among other things, the spectral theorem implies that the eigenvalues of a symmetric matrix are real.

A matrix A is often associated with the linear transformation $x \mapsto Ax$, but a symmetric matrix is also naturally associated with a quadratic form, $x \mapsto x'Ax$. In fact, the eigenvalues of a symmetric matrix can be characterized in terms of its quadratic form. The *Rayleigh-Ritz theorem* provides simple descriptions of $\bar{\lambda}$ and $\underline{\lambda}$, the maximal and minimal eigenvalues of A:

$$\bar{\lambda} = \max_{x \in \mathbf{R}^n : |x| = 1} x'Ax; \qquad \underline{\lambda} = \min_{x \in \mathbf{R}^n : |x| = 1} x'Ax.$$

The *Courant-Fischer theorem* shows how the remaining eigenvalues of A can be expressed in terms of a related sequence of minmax problems.

The matrices $A, B \in \mathbf{R}^{n \times n}$ are *congruent* if there is an invertible matrix $Q \in \mathbf{R}^{n \times n}$ such that

$$B = QAQ'.$$

Congruence plays the same role for quadratic forms as similarity does for linear transformations. If two symmetric matrices are congruent, they define the same quadratic form up to a linear change of variable. Like similarity, congruence defines an equivalence relation on the set of $n \times n$ matrices. Note that two symmetric matrices that are similar by an orthogonal matrix Q are also congruent, since in this case $Q' = Q^{-1}$.

The eigenvalues of congruent symmetric matrices are closely linked. Define the *inertia* of a symmetric matrix to be the ordered triple consisting of the numbers of positive, negative, and zero eigenvalues of the matrix. *Sylvester's law of inertia* states that congruent symmetric matrices have the same inertia. *Ostrowski's theorem* provides a quantitative extension of this result: if the eigenvalues of A and the eigenvalues of B are listed in increasing order, then the ratios between pairs of corresponding eigenvalues are bounded by the minimal and maximal eigenvalues of $Q'Q$.

8.A.5 The Real Jordan Canonical Form

How can one tell if two matrices are similar? If the matrices are diagonalizable, then one can check for similarity by diagonalizing the two matrices and seeing whether the same diagonal matrix is obtained in each case. To apply this logic beyond the diagonalizable case, one would need to find a simple class of matrices with the property that every matrix is similar to a unique representative from this class. Such a class of matrices would also provide a powerful computational aid, since calculations involving arbitrary matrices could be reduced by similarity to calculations with these simple matrices.

With this motivation, define a *real Jordan matrix* to be a block diagonal matrix whose diagonal blocks, known as *Jordan blocks*, are of these four types:

$$J_1 = (\lambda); \quad J_2 = \begin{pmatrix} a & b \\ -b & a \end{pmatrix};$$

$$J_3 = \begin{pmatrix} \lambda & 1 & 0 & 0 & 0 \\ 0 & \lambda & 1 & 0 & 0 \\ \vdots & \ddots & \ddots & \ddots & \vdots \\ 0 & 0 & 0 & \lambda & 1 \\ 0 & 0 & 0 & 0 & \lambda \end{pmatrix}; \quad J_4 = \begin{pmatrix} J_2 & I & 0 & 0 & 0 \\ 0 & J_2 & I & 0 & 0 \\ \vdots & \ddots & \ddots & \ddots & \vdots \\ 0 & 0 & 0 & J_2 & I \\ 0 & 0 & 0 & 0 & J_2 \end{pmatrix}.$$

Theorem 8.A.4 *Every matrix $A \in \mathbf{R}^{n \times n}$ is similar via a real similarity matrix S to a real Jordan matrix $J = S^{-1}AS$. The latter matrix is unique up to the ordering of the Jordan blocks.*

The real Jordan matrix in the statement of the theorem is called the *real Jordan canonical form* of A.

The blocks in the real Jordan form of A provide detailed information about the eigenvalues of A. Each J_1 block corresponds to a real eigenvalue λ; each J_2 block corresponds to a pair of complex eigenvalues $a \pm i b$; each J_3 block corresponds to a real eigenvalue with less than full geometric multiplicity; and each J_4 block corresponds to a pair of complex eigenvalues with less than full geometric multiplicities. (We can say more if each Jordan block represents a distinct eigenvalue: then each eigenvalue has geometric multiplicity 1; the J_1 and J_2 blocks correspond to eigenvalues whose algebraic multiplicities are also 1; and the J_3 and J_4 blocks correspond to eigenvalues with higher algebraic multiplicities, with these multiplicities given by the number of appearances of λ (in a J_3 block) or of J_2 blocks (in a J_4 block).)

Example 8.A.2 Suppose that $A \in \mathbf{R}^{2 \times 2}$ has complex eigenvalues $a \pm i b$ with complex eigenvectors $v \pm i w$. Then $A(v + i w) = (a + i b)(v + i w)$. Equating the real and imaginary parts of this equation yields

$$A \begin{pmatrix} v & w \end{pmatrix} = \begin{pmatrix} v & w \end{pmatrix} \begin{pmatrix} a & b \\ -b & a \end{pmatrix}.$$

Premultiplying by $(v\ w)^{-1}$ reveals that the real Jordan form of A is a single J_2 block. ◆

Example 8.A.3 Suppose that $A \in \mathbf{R}^{2 \times 2}$ has a lone eigenvalue, $\lambda \in \mathbf{R}$, which is of algebraic multiplicity 2 but geometric multiplicity 1. Let $x \in \mathbf{R}^2$ be an eigenvector of A, so that $(A - \lambda I)x = 0$. It can be shown that there exists a vector y that is linearly independent of x and that satisfies $(A - \lambda I)y = x$. (Such a vector, and, more generally, vectors that satisfy higher iterates of this equation, are called *generalized eigenvectors* of A.) Rewriting the two previous equations yields

$$A \begin{pmatrix} x & y \end{pmatrix} = \begin{pmatrix} \lambda x & x + \lambda y \end{pmatrix} = \begin{pmatrix} x & y \end{pmatrix} \begin{pmatrix} \lambda & 1 \\ 0 & \lambda \end{pmatrix}.$$

Premultiplying the first and last expressions by $(x\ y)^{-1}$ shows that A has a real Jordan form consisting of a single J_3 block. ◆

8.A.6 The Spectral Norm and Singular Values

It is often useful to be able to place bounds on the amount of expansion generated by a linear map $x \mapsto Ax$ or by a composite linear map $x \mapsto Bx \mapsto ABx$. One can obtain such bounds by introducing the *spectral norm* of a matrix $A \in \mathbf{R}^{n \times n}$, defined by

$$\|A\| = \max_{x:\,|x|=1} |Ax|.$$

(As always in this book, $|x|$ denotes the Euclidean norm of the vector x.) It is not difficult to check that the spectral norm is submultiplicative, in the following two senses:

$$|Ax| \leq \|A\|\,|x| \quad \text{and} \quad \|AB\| \leq \|A\|\,\|B\|.$$

These inequalities often work hand in hand with the *Cauchy-Schwarz inequality*, which expresses the submultiplicativity of inner products of vectors:

$$|x'y| \leq |x|\,|y|.$$

To compute the spectral norm of a matrix, it is best to describe it in a different way. Note that the product $A'A$ generated by any matrix A is symmetric. This product therefore has n real eigenvalues (see section 8.A.4), and it can be shown that these eigenvalues are non-negative. The square roots of the eigenvalues of $A'A$ are called the *singular values* of A.

One can show that the spectral norm of A equals the largest singular value of A:

$$\|A\| = \max\left\{\sqrt{\lambda} : \lambda \text{ is an eigenvalue of } A'A\right\}.$$

It makes no difference here if we replace $A'A$ with AA', since for any $A, B \in \mathbf{R}^{n \times n}$, AB and BA have the same eigenvalues.

The notion of a singular value also underpins the *singular value decomposition*.

Theorem 8.A.5 *Every matrix $A \in \mathbf{R}^{n \times n}$ can be expressed as $A = V\Sigma W'$, where V and W are orthogonal matrices, and where Σ is a diagonal matrix whose diagonal entries are the singular values of A.*

In this decomposition, the columns of V are eigenvectors of AA', and the columns of W are eigenvectors of $A'A$.

8.A.7 Hines's Lemma

This section presents the proof of *Hines's lemma* (lemma 8.5.1), introduced in section 8.5.

Lemma 8.5.1. *Suppose that $Q \in \mathbf{R}^{n \times n}$ is symmetric, satisfies $Q\mathbf{1} = \mathbf{0}$, and is positive definite with respect to $\mathbf{R}_0^n$, and that $A \in \mathbf{R}^{n \times n}$ is negative definite with respect to $\mathbf{R}_0^n$. Then each eigenvalue of the linear map $QA: \mathbf{R}_0^n \to \mathbf{R}_0^n$ has negative real part.*

If one ignores the complications caused by our dynamics' being restricted to the simplex, lemma 8.5.1 reduces to the following.

Lemma 8.A.6 *If Q is symmetric positive definite and A is negative definite, then the eigenvalues of QA have negative real parts.*

The proof of lemma 8.A.6 is a simpler version of the proof of Hines's lemma. The argument that follows can also be used when other definiteness conditions are imposed on A. In particular, if A is only negative semidefinite with respect to $\mathbf{R}_0^n$, then the relevant eigenvalues of QA have nonpositive real parts, and if A is positive definite with respect to $\mathbf{R}_0^n$, the relevant eigenvalues of QA have positive real parts.

Proof of lemma 8.5.1 Since Q is positive definite with respect to $\mathbf{R}_0^n$, since $Q\mathbf{1} = \mathbf{0}$, and since $\mathbf{R}^n = \mathbf{R}_0^n \oplus \text{span}(\{\mathbf{1}\})$, we have that $\text{nullspace}(Q) = \text{span}(\{\mathbf{1}\})$. Thus, because Q is symmetric, the fundamental theorem of linear algebra (8.42) implies that

$$\text{range}(Q) = (\text{nullspace}(Q'))^\perp = (\text{nullspace}(Q))^\perp = (\text{span}(\{\mathbf{1}\}))^\perp = \mathbf{R}_0^n.$$

In other words, Q maps $\mathbf{R}_0^n$ onto itself, and so is invertible on this space.

Now, suppose that

$$QA(v + iw) = (a + ib)(v + iw) \tag{8.45}$$

for some $v, w \in \mathbf{R}_0^n$ with $v + iw \neq \mathbf{0}$ and some a, b in $\mathbf{R}$. Since Q is invertible on $\mathbf{R}_0^n$, there exist $y, z \in \mathbf{R}_0^n$, at least one of which is not $\mathbf{0}$, such that $Qy = v$ and $Qz = w$. Equation (8.45) can therefore be rewritten as

$$QA(v + iw) = (a + ib)Q(y + iz).$$

Since Q is invertible on $\mathbf{R}_0^n$, the previous equality implies that

$$A(v + iw) = (a + ib)(y + iz).$$

Premultiplying by $(v - iw)' = (Q(y - iz))'$ yields

$$(v - iw)'A(v + iw) = (a + ib)(y - iz)'Q(y + iz).$$

Equating the real parts of each side then yields

$$v'Av + w'Aw = a(y'Qy + z'Qz).$$

Since Q is positive definite with respect to $\mathbf{R}_0^n$, and since A is negative definite with respect to $\mathbf{R}_0^n$, we conclude that $a < 0$. ∎

8.B   Appendix: Linear Differential Equations

The simplest ordinary differential equations on $\mathbf{R}^n$ are *linear differential equations*:

$$\dot{x} = Ax, \tag{L}$$

where $A \in \mathbf{R}^{n \times n}$. Although our main interest in this book is in nonlinear differential equations, linear differential equations are still very important to us: as explained in appendix 8.C, the behavior of a nonlinear equation in the neighborhood of a rest point is often well approximated by the behavior of a linear equation in a neighborhood of the origin.

8.B.1   Examples

Example 8.B.1: Linear Dynamics on the Line   In the one-dimensional case, equation (L) becomes $\dot{x} = ax$. The solutions to this equation from initial condition $x_0 = \xi$ were described in example 4.A.1; they are of the form $x_t = \xi \exp(at)$. Thus, if $a \neq 0$, the equation has its unique rest point at the origin. If $a > 0$, all solutions other than the stationary one move away from the origin, whereas if $a < 0$, all solutions converge to the origin.   ◆

One can apply a linear change of variable to (L) to reduce it to a simpler form. In particular, if $B = SAS^{-1}$ is similar to A, let $y = Sx$; then since $\dot{y} = S\dot{x}$, (L) can be rewritten as $S^{-1}\dot{y} = AS^{-1}y$, and hence as $\dot{y} = By$. It follows from this observation and from theorem 8.A.4 that to understand linear differential equations, it

Local Stability under Evolutionary Dynamics

is enough to understand linear differential equations defined by real Jordan matrices.

Example 8.B.2: Linear Dynamics on the Plane There are three generic types of 2×2 matrices: diagonalizable matrices with two real eigenvalues, diagonalizable matrices with two complex eigenvalues, and nondiagonalizable matrices with a single real eigenvalue. The corresponding real Jordan forms are a diagonal matrix (which contains two J_1 blocks), a J_2 matrix, and a J_3 matrix, respectively. We therefore consider linear differential equations based on these three types of real Jordan matrices.

When A is diagonal, the linear equation (L) and its solution from initial condition $x_0 = \xi$ are of the following form:

$$\dot{x} = Ax = \begin{pmatrix} \lambda & 0 \\ 0 & \mu \end{pmatrix} \begin{pmatrix} x_1 \\ x_2 \end{pmatrix}; \qquad x_t = \begin{pmatrix} \xi_1 e^{\lambda t} \\ \xi_2 e^{\mu t} \end{pmatrix}.$$

The phase diagrams in figure 8.2 show that the behavior of this dynamic depends on the values of the eigenvalues λ and μ: if both are negative, the origin is a *stable node*, if their signs differ, the origin is a *saddle*, and if both are positive, the origin is an *unstable node*.

Now suppose that A is the real Jordan form of a matrix with complex eigenvalues $a \pm ib$. Then

$$\dot{x} = Ax = \begin{pmatrix} a & b \\ -b & a \end{pmatrix} \begin{pmatrix} x_1 \\ x_2 \end{pmatrix}; \qquad x_t = \begin{pmatrix} \xi_1 e^{at} \cos bt + \xi_2 e^{at} \sin bt \\ -\xi_1 e^{at} \sin bt + \xi_2 e^{at} \cos bt \end{pmatrix}.$$

Phase diagrams for this equation are presented in figure 8.3. Evidently, the stability of the origin is determined by the real part of the eigenvalues: if $a < 0$, the origin is a *stable spiral*, while if $a > 0$, the origin is an *unstable spiral*. In the nongeneric

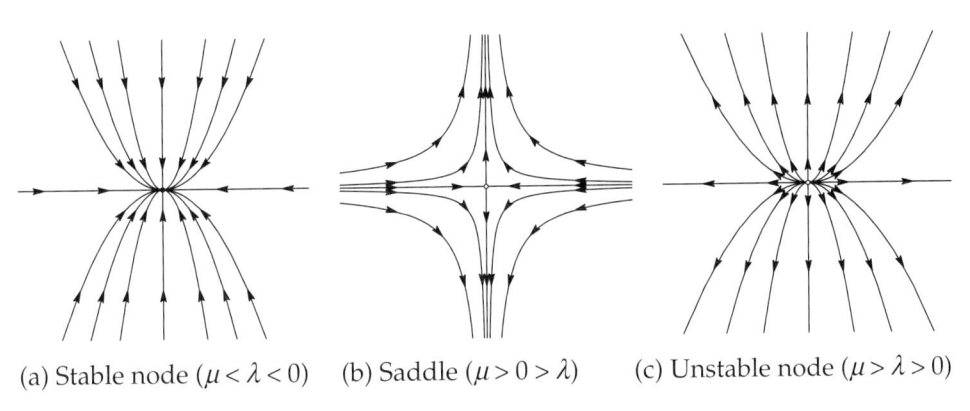

(a) Stable node ($\mu < \lambda < 0$)   (b) Saddle ($\mu > 0 > \lambda$)   (c) Unstable node ($\mu > \lambda > 0$)

Figure 8.2
Linear dynamics on the plane: two real eigenvalues λ, μ.

(a) Stable spiral ($a < 0$) **(b)** Center ($a = 0$) **(c)** Unstable spiral ($a > 0$)

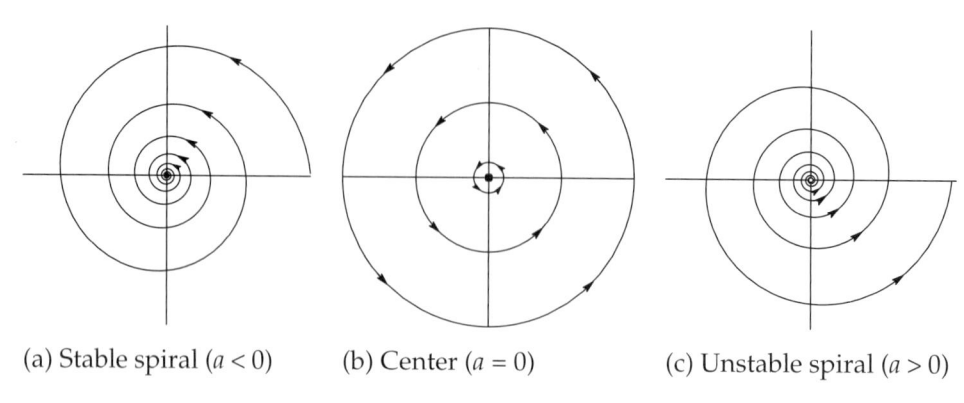

Figure 8.3
Linear dynamics on the plane: complex eigenvalues $a \pm ib, b < 0$.

case where $a = 0$, the origin is a *center*, with each solution following a closed orbit around the origin. The value of b determines the orientation of the cycles. The diagrams in figure 8.3 use $b < 0$, which causes solutions to cycle counterclockwise; with $b > 0$, these orientations would be reversed.

Finally, suppose that A is the real Jordan form of a nondiagonalizable matrix with lone eigenvalue λ. Then

$$\dot{x} = Ax = \begin{pmatrix} \lambda & 1 \\ 0 & \lambda \end{pmatrix} \begin{pmatrix} x_1 \\ x_2 \end{pmatrix}; \qquad x_t = \begin{pmatrix} \xi_1 e^{\lambda t} + \xi_2 t e^{\lambda t} \\ \xi_1 e^{\lambda t} \end{pmatrix}.$$

The phase diagrams in figure 8.4 reveal the origin to be an *improper* (or *degenerate*) *node*. It is stable if the eigenvalue λ is negative and unstable if λ is positive. ◆

8.B.2 Solutions

The Picard-Lindelöf theorem (theorem 4.A.1) implies that for any matrix $A \in \mathbf{R}^{n \times n}$ there is a unique solution to the linear equation (L) starting from each initial condition $\xi \in \mathbf{R}^n$. While solutions of nonlinear differential equations generally cannot be expressed in closed form, the solutions to linear equations can always be described explicitly. In the planar case, example 8.B.2 provided explicit formulas when A is a Jordan matrix, and the solutions for other matrices can be obtained through a change of variable. Similar logic can be employed in the general case, yielding the following result.

Theorem 8.B.1 *Let $\{x_t\}_{t \in (-\infty, \infty)}$ be the solution to (L) from initial condition x_0. Then each coordinate of x_t is a linear combination of terms of the form $t^k e^{at} \cos(bt)$ and $t^k e^{at} \sin(bt)$, where $a + ib \in \mathbf{C}$ is an eigenvalue of A and $k \in \mathbf{Z}_+$ is less than the algebraic multiplicity of this eigenvalue.*

Local Stability under Evolutionary Dynamics

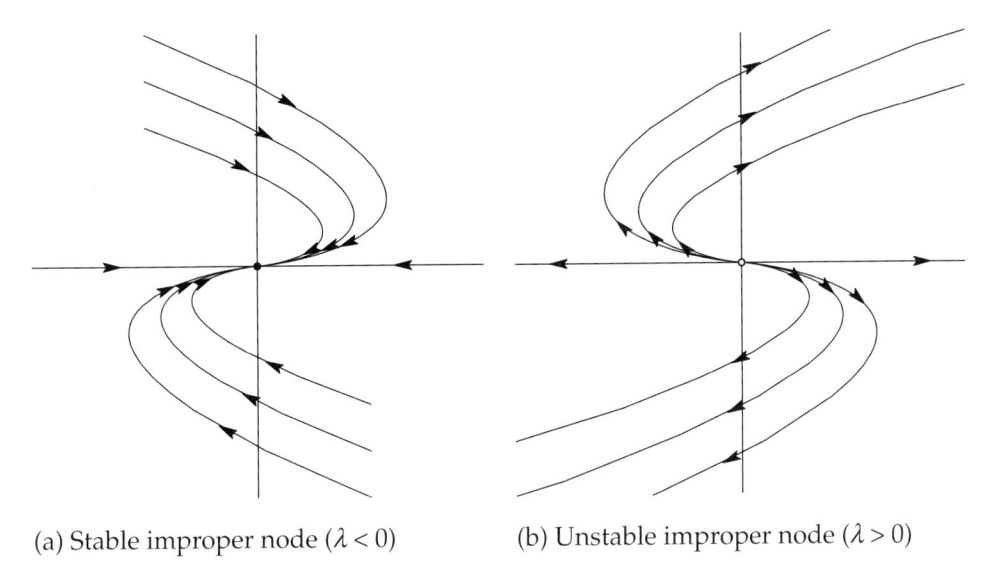

(a) Stable improper node ($\lambda < 0$) (b) Unstable improper node ($\lambda > 0$)

Figure 8.4
Linear dynamics on the plane: A not diagonalizable, one real eigenvalue λ.

For purposes of analysis, it is often convenient to express solutions of the linear equation (L) in terms of *matrix exponentials*. Given a matrix $A \in \mathbf{R}^{n \times n}$, we define $e^A \in \mathbf{R}^{n \times n}$ by applying the series definition of the exponential function to the matrix A, that is,

$$e^A = \sum_{k=0}^{\infty} \frac{A^k}{k!}, \tag{8.46}$$

where A^k denotes the kth power of A and $A^0 \equiv I$ is the identity matrix.

Recall that the *flow* $\phi \colon (-\infty, \infty) \times \mathbf{R}^n \to \mathbf{R}^n$ generated by (L) is defined by $\phi_t(\xi) = x_t$, where $\{x_t\}_{t \in (-\infty, \infty)}$ is the solution to (L) with initial condition $x_0 = \xi$. Theorem 8.B.2 provides a concise expression for solutions to (L) in terms of matrix exponentials.

Theorem 8.B.2 *The flow of* (L) *is* $\phi_t(\xi) = e^{At}\xi$.

A benefit of representing solutions to (L) in this way is that properties established for matrix exponentials can be given immediate interpretations in terms of solutions to (L). For examples, consider these properties.

Proposition 8.B.3

i. If A and B commute, then $e^{A+B} = e^B e^A$.

ii. If $B = S^{-1}AS$, then $e^B = S^{-1}e^A S$.

iii. $e^{(A')} = (e^A)'$.

Applying part (i) of the proposition to matrices As and At yields the group property of the flow of (L): $\phi_{s+t}(\xi) = \phi_t(\phi_s(\xi))$. Part (ii) shows that linear flows generated by similar matrices are linearly conjugate (i.e., they are equivalent up to a linear change of variables), as discussed earlier. Applying parts (iii) and (i) to At when A is skew-symmetric shows that in this case, e^{At} is an orthogonal matrix; thus, for each fixed time t, the map $\xi \mapsto \phi_t(\xi)$ is a Euclidean isometry (see figure 8.3(b)).

8.B.3 Stability and Hyperbolicity

Theorem 8.B.1 shows that in generic cases, the stability of the origin under the linear equation (L) is determined by the eigenvalues $\{a_1 + i b_1, \ldots, a_n + i b_n\}$ of A, or more precisely, by the real parts a_i of these eigenvalues. If each a_i is negative, then all solutions to (L) converge to the origin; in this case, the origin is called a *sink*, and the flow $\phi_t(x) = e^{At}x$ is called a *contraction*. If instead each a_i is positive, then all solutions besides the stationary solution at the origin move away from the origin; in this case, the origin is called a *source*, and the flow of (L) is called an *expansion*.

When the origin is a sink, solutions to (L) converge to the origin at an exponential rate. Define a norm on $\mathbf{R}^n$ by $\|x\|_S = |S^{-1}x|$, where S is the similarity matrix from the Jordan decomposition $J = S^{-1}AS$ of A. Then for any $a > 0$ satisfying $a < |a_i|$ for all $i \in \{1, \ldots, n\}$, the flow ϕ of (L) satisfies

0 is a sink $\Leftrightarrow$ $\|\phi_t(\xi)\|_S \leq e^{-at} \|\xi\|_S$ for all $t \geq 0$, $\xi \in \mathbf{R}^n$.

A similar statement in terms of the Euclidean norm holds if one introduces an appropriate multiplicative constant $C = C(a) \geq 1$:

0 is a sink $\Leftrightarrow$ $|\phi_t(\xi)| \leq Ce^{-at} |\xi|$ for all $t \geq 0$, $\xi \in \mathbf{R}^n$. (8.47)

If the origin is the source, analogous statements hold if time is run backward. For instance,

0 is a source $\Leftrightarrow$ $|\phi_t(\xi)| \leq Ce^{-a|t|} |\xi|$ for all $t \leq 0$, $\xi \in \mathbf{R}^n$. (8.48)

More generally, the flow of (L) may be contracting in some directions and expanding in others. In the generic case in which each real part a_i of an eigenvalue of A is nonzero, the differential equation $\dot{x} = Ax$, its rest point at the origin, and its flow $\phi_t(x) = e^{At}x$ are all said to be *hyperbolic*. Hyperbolic linear flows come in three varieties: contractions (if all a_i are negative, as in (8.47)), expansions (if all a_i are positive, as in (8.48)), and saddles (if there is at least one a_i of each sign). If a linear flow is hyperbolic, then the origin is globally asymptotically stable if it is a sink, and it is unstable otherwise.

If the flow of (L) is hyperbolic, then A has k eigenvalues with negative real parts (counting algebraic multiplicities) and $n - k$ eigenvalues with positive real parts. In this case, one can view $\mathbf{R}^n = E^s \oplus E^u$ as the direct sum of subspaces of dimensions $\dim(E^s) = k$ and $\dim(E^u) = n - k$, where the *stable subspace* E^s contains all solutions of (L) that converge to the origin at an exponential rate (as in (8.47)), and the *unstable subspace* E^u contains all solutions of (L) that converge to the origin at an exponential rate if time is run backward (as in (8.48)).

If A is real diagonalizable, then it follows easily from theorem 8.B.1 that E^s and E^u are the spans of the eigenvectors of A corresponding to the eigenvalues of A with negative and positive real parts, respectively. More generally, E^s and E^u can be computed by way of the real Jordan form $J = S^{-1}AS$ of A. Arrange S and J so that the Jordan blocks of J corresponding to eigenvalues of A with negative real parts appear in the first k rows and columns, while the blocks corresponding to eigenvalues with positive real parts appear in the remaining $n - k$ rows and columns. Then E^s is the span of the first k columns of the similarity matrix S, and E^u is the span of the remaining $n - k$ columns of S. (The columns of S are the real and imaginary parts of the so-called *generalized eigenvectors* of A; see example 8.A.3.)

8.C Appendix: Linearization of Nonlinear Differential Equations

Virtually all the differential equations studied in this book are nonlinear. Nevertheless, when studying the behavior of nonlinear equations in the neighborhood of a rest point, the theory of linear equations takes on a central role.

Consider the C^1 differential equation

$$\dot{x} = V(x) \tag{D}$$

with rest point x^*. By the definition of the derivative, one can approximate the value of V in the neighborhood of x^* via

$$V(y) = 0 + DV(x^*)(y - x^*) + o(|y - x^*|).$$

This suggests that the behavior of the dynamic (D) near x^* can be approximated by the behavior near the origin of the linear equation

$$\dot{y} = DV(x^*)y. \tag{L}$$

Making this idea precise requires some new definitions. Let X and Y be subsets of $\mathbf{R}^n$. The function $h\colon X \to Y$ is called a *homeomorphism* if it is bijective (i.e., one-to-one and onto) and continuous with a continuous inverse.

Now let $I \subseteq \mathbf{R}$ be an interval containing 0, and let $\phi\colon I \times X \to X$ and $\psi\colon I \times Y \to Y$ be two flows. Then ϕ and ψ are *topologically conjugate* on X and Y if there is a homeomorphism $h: X \to Y$ such that $\phi_t(x_0) = h^{-1} \circ \psi_t \circ h(x_0)$ for all times $t \in I$. In other words, ϕ and ψ are topologically conjugate if there is a continuous map with continuous inverse that sends trajectories of ϕ to trajectories of ψ (and vice versa), preserving the rate of passage of time. Therefore, to find $\phi_t(x_0)$, the position at time t under flow ϕ when the initial state is $x_0 \in X$, one can apply $h: X \to Y$ to x_0 to obtain the transformed initial condition $y_0 = h(x_0) \in Y$, then run the flow ψ from y_0 for t time units, and finally apply h^{-1} to the result. We summarize this construction in the diagram below:

$$\begin{array}{ccc} x_0 & \xrightarrow{h} & h(x_0) \\ \phi_t \downarrow & & \downarrow \psi_t \\ \phi_t(x_0) & \xleftarrow{h^{-1}} & \psi_t(h(x_0)) \end{array}$$

The use of linearization to study the behavior of nonlinear differential equations around fixed points is justified by the *Hartman-Grobman theorem*.

Theorem 8.C.1 (The Hartman-Grobman Theorem) *Let ϕ and ψ be the flows of the C^1 equation (D) and the linear equation (L), where x^* is a hyperbolic rest point of (D). Then there exist neighborhoods O_{x^*} of x^* and O_0 of the origin $\mathbf{0}$ on which ϕ and ψ are topologically conjugate.*

Combining the Hartman-Grobman theorem with our analysis in section 8.B.3 provides a simple characterization of the stability of hyperbolic rest points of (D).

Corollary 8.C.2 *Let x^* be a hyperbolic rest point of (D). Then x^* is asymptotically stable if all eigenvalues of $DV(x^*)$ have negative real parts, and x^* is unstable otherwise.*

By virtue of these results, we call x^* *linearly stable* if the eigenvalues of $DV(x^*)$ all have negative real part. Although the Hartman-Grobman theorem implies that a linearly stable rest point is asymptotically stable, it can be shown further that solutions starting near a linearly stable rest point converge to it at an exponential rate, as in equation (8.47).

The rest point x^* is *linearly unstable* if $DV(x^*)$ has at least one eigenvalue with positive real part. (x^* is not required to be hyperbolic.) It can be shown that as long as one eigenvalue of $DV(x^*)$ has positive real part, most solutions of (D) will move away from x^* at an exponential rate.

While the topological conjugacy established in theorem 8.C.1 is sufficient for local stability analysis, topological conjugacy need not preserve the *geometry* of a flow. The following result for linear equations makes this point clear.

Theorem 8.C.3 *Let $\dot x = Ax$ and $\dot y = By$ be hyperbolic linear differential equations on $\mathbf{R}^n$ with flows ϕ and ψ. If A and B have the same numbers of eigenvalues with negative real part (counting algebraic multiplicities), then ϕ and ψ are topologically conjugate throughout $\mathbf{R}^n$.*

In example 8.B.2, the phase diagrams of stable nodes (figure 8.2a), stable spirals (figure 8.3a), and stable improper nodes (figure 8.4a) have very different appearances. Nevertheless, theorem 8.C.3 reveals that the flows described in these figures are topologically conjugate, that is, they can be continuously transformed into one another. To ensure that the geometry of phase diagrams is preserved, one needs not only topological conjugacy but also *differentiable conjugacy*—that is, conjugacy under a *diffeomorphism* (a differentiable transformation with differentiable inverse). As it turns out, it is possible to establish a local differentiable conjugacy between (D) near x^* and (L) near $\mathbf{0}$ if V is sufficiently smooth, and if the eigenvalues of $DV(x^*)$ are distinct and satisfy a mild nonresonance condition (see the chapter notes).

Much additional information about the flow of (D) can be surmised from the derivative matrix $DV(x^*)$ at a hyperbolic rest point x^*. Suppose that $DV(x^*)$ has k eigenvalues with negative real part and $n - k$ eigenvalues with positive real part, counting algebraic multiplicities. The *stable manifold theorem* says that within some neighborhood of x^*, there is k dimensional *local stable manifold* M^s_{loc} on which solutions converge to x^* at an exponential rate (as in (8.47)), and an $n-k$ dimensional *local unstable manifold* M^u_{loc} on which solutions converge to x^* at an exponential rate if time is run backward (as in (8.48)).

Moreover, both of these manifolds can be extended globally: the k dimensional (*global*) *stable manifold* M^s includes all solutions of (D) that converge to x^*, and the $n-k$ dimensional (*global*) *unstable manifold* M^u includes all solutions that converge to x^* as time runs backward. Among other implications of the existence of these manifolds, it follows that if x^* is hyperbolic and unstable, then the set M^s of states from which solutions converge to x^* is of measure zero, while the complement of this set is open, dense, and of full measure.

Notes

Section 8.1
Theorem 8.1.1 was established by Bomze (1986) for the replicator dynamic and by Nachbar (1990) for general imitative dynamics; see also Weibull (1995).

Section 8.2
This section follows Sandholm (2001a). Bomze (2002) provided an exhaustive treatment of local stability under the replicator dynamic for single-population linear potential games (which are generated by matching in common interest games), and the connections between this stability analysis and quadratic programming.

Section 8.3
The notion of an evolutionarily stable strategy was introduced by Maynard Smith and Price (1973). The distinction between evolutionarily stable strategies and evolutionarily stable states was emphasized by Thomas (1984). General references on ESS theory include the survey of Hines (1987) and the monographs of Bomze and Pötscher (1989) and Cressman (1992).

Most early work on evolutionarily stable strategies considers single populations matched to play symmetric normal form games. The original ESS definition of Maynard Smith and Price (1973) (see also Maynard Smith 1974) is via conditions (8.7) and (8.9). The characterizations of ESS in terms of invasion barriers (8.6) and invasion of nearby states (8.2) in this linear setting are due to Taylor and Jonker (1978) and Hofbauer, Schuster, and Sigmund (1979), respectively. That invasion barriers are uniform in this setting (exercise 8.3.3(ii)) was pointed out explicitly by Vickers and Cannings (1987); see also Bomze (1986), Zeeman (1980), and Hofbauer and Sigmund (1988).

Regarding single-population games with nonlinear payoffs, theorem 8.3.5 was announced in Pohley and Thomas (1983), where a state satisfying condition (8.2) is called a local ESS. The theorem was proved in Thomas (1985), and the proof in the text is a streamlined version of Thomas's (1985) proof. Theorem 8.3.1 is due to Bomze (1991), who called a state satisfying ESS condition (8.2) strongly uninvadable and a state satisfying the uniform invasion barrier condition (8.4) uninvadable; see also Bomze and Weibull (1995). Exercise 8.3.3b is from Bomze and Pötscher (1989, example 18).

Definition (8.16) of Taylor ESS is introduced by Taylor (1979); also see Schuster et al. (1981c). Exercise 8.3.8 is essentially due to Selten (1980); see also van Damme (1991) and Swinkels (1992).

The definition (8.17) of Cressman ESS is due to Cressman (1992; 1995; 1996b; 2006) and Cressman, Garay, and Hofbauer (2001), who referred to it as *monomorphic ESS* and *p-species ESS*. To show that this definition is the heir of the single-population ESS of Maynard Smith and Price (1973), these papers studied a collection of p-dimensional replicator systems, with one system for each strategy profile $y = (y^1, \ldots, y^p)$ other than the candidate for stability, $x = (x^1, \ldots, x^p)$. The pth component of the state variable in the p-dimensional system describes the fraction of the pth species using mixed strategy y^p; the remainder of the species uses the incumbent mixed strategy x^p. Results in Cressman, Garay, and Hofbauer (2001) and Cressman (2006) imply that the origin (i.e., the state at which all members of each species p choose mixed strategy x^p) is asymptotically stable in each such system if and only if x satisfies condition (8.17). (To see this, use equations (1) and (6) in Cressman, Garay, and Hofbauer (2001) to show that the B-matrix conditions appearing in theorems 3 and 5 of that paper are equivalent to condition (8.17) here.) Interestingly, Cressman (1992) showed that in two-population linear games, any Cressman ESS is asymptotically stable under the replicator dynamic, but that this is not true in games played by more than two populations.

The notion of regular ESS was introduced in a single-population setting by Taylor and Jonker (1978), who proved that a regular ESS is asympotically stable under the replicator dynamic. Taylor (1979) extended this notion to the multipopulation case and observed that the stability result for the replicator dynamic extends to this setting.

Thomas (1985), Swinkels (1992), Balkenborg and Schlag (2001; 2007), and Cressman (2003) considered set-valued generalizations of the ESS concept, which are particularly useful in the context of matching in extensive form games.

Section 8.4
Theorem 8.4.1(i) on the local stability of ESS under the replicator dynamic is one of the earliest results on evolutionary game dynamics; see Taylor and Jonker (1978), Taylor (1979), Hofbauer, Schuster, and Sigmund (1979), Zeeman (1980), Schuster et al. (1981c), and Hofbauer and Sigmund (1988). Theorem 8.4.1(ii) follows easily from results of Nagurney and Zhang (1997); see also Sandholm, Dokumacı, and Lahkar (2008). The results in section 8.4.2 are extensions of results from Hofbauer and Sandholm (2009). For the theorem of the maximum, see Ok (2007). Theorem 8.4.7 is due to Sandholm (2010b). Hofbauer (1995b) established the asymptotic stability of ESS under the best response dynamic in a single-population normal form context using a construction different from the one presented here.

Local Stability under Evolutionary Dynamics

Section 8.5
Lemma 8.5.1 is due to Hines (1980); see also Hofbauer and Sigmund (1988), Hopkins (1999), and Sandholm (2007a). Versions of theorems 8.5.2 and 8.5.5 can be found in Taylor and Jonker (1978), Taylor (1979), Hines (1980), and Cressman (1992; 1997). Example 8.5.1 is taken from Zeeman (1980). Theorem 8.5.8 is due to Cressman (1997).

Section 8.6
Linearization of perturbed best response dynamics was studied by Hopkins (1999; 2002), Hofbauer (2000), Hofbauer and Sandholm (2002; 2007), Hofbauer and Hopkins (2005), and Sandholm (2007a). Exercise 8.6.3 was used in Sandholm (2007a) to show that Nash equilibria of normal form games can always be purified (in the sense of Harsanyi 1973) in an evolutionarily stable fashion through an appropriate choice of payoff noise. See Ellison and Fudenberg (2000) and Ely and Sandholm (2005) for related results. Example 8.6.1 is due to Hopkins (1999). Hopkins (2002) used this result to show that solutions of the replicator dynamic closely approximate the evolution of choice probabilities under stochastic fictitious play. Hofbauer, Sorin, and Viossat (2009) used similar ideas to establish an exact relation between the long-run time-averaged behavior of the replicator dynamic and the long-run behavior of the best response dynamic.

Appendix 8.A
Horn and Johnson (1985) is an outstanding general reference on matrix analysis. Many of the results described in the present text can also be found in Hirsch and Smale (1974).

Appendix 8.B
See Hirsch and Smale (1974) and Robinson (1995) for thorough treatments of linear differential equations at the undergraduate and graduate levels, respectively.

Appendix 8.C
Robinson (1995) is an excellent reference on dynamical systems in general and on linearization in particular. For more on differentiable conjugacy around rest points, see Hartman (1964).

9 Nonconvergence of Evolutionary Dynamics

The analysis of global behavior of evolutionary dynamics in chapter 7 focused on combinations of games and dynamics generating global or almost global convergence to equilibrium. The analysis there demonstrated that global payoff structures—in particular, the structure captured in the definitions of potential, stable, and supermodular games—make compelling evolutionary justifications of the Nash prediction possible. On the other hand, when one moves beyond these classes of well-behaved games, it is not clear how often convergence will occur. This chapter investigates nonconvergence of evolutionary dynamics for games, describing a variety of environments in which cycling or chaos offer the best predictions of long-run behavior.

Section 9.1 studies conservative properties of evolutionary dynamics, with a focus on the existence of constants of motion and the preservation of volume under the replicator and projection dynamics. Section 9.2 offers a variety of examples of nonconvergence, including games in which no reasonable evolutionary dynamic converges to equilibrium, thus demonstrating that no evolutionary dynamic can provide a blanket justification for the prediction of Nash equilibrium play. Section 9.3 presents examples of chaotic evolutionary dynamics, that is, dynamics exhibiting complicated attracting sets and sensitive dependence on initial conditions.

The possibility of nonconvergence has surprising implications for evolutionary support of traditional solution concepts. Under dynamics that satisfy Nash stationarity (NS), solution trajectories that converge necessarily converge to Nash equilibria. But since no reasonable evolutionary dynamic converges in all games, general support for standard solution concepts is not assured.

Since the Nash prediction is not always supported by an evolutionary analysis, it is natural to turn to a less demanding condition, namely, the elimination of strategies that are strictly dominated by a pure strategy. This requirement is the mildest employed in standard game-theoretic analyses, so it is natural to seek support for this requirement via an evolutionary approach.

Section 9.4 presents the striking finding that evolutionary dynamics satisfying four mild conditions—continuity, Nash stationarity, positive correlation, and innovation—do not eliminate strictly dominated strategies in all games. Moreover, although imitative dynamics and the best response dynamic were shown in chapter 7 to eliminate strictly dominated strategies, we show here that small perturbations of these dynamics do not. This analysis demonstrates that evolutionary dynamics provide surprisingly little support for a basic rationality criterion.

The chapter appendices provide the mathematical background necessary for the analysis. Appendix 9.A describes some classical theorems on nonconvergence. Appendix 9.B introduces the notion of an attractor of a dynamic, and establishes the continuity properties of attractors that underlie the analysis of dominated strategies.

9.1 Conservative Properties of Evolutionary Dynamics

It is often impossible to provide precise descriptions of long-run behavior under nonconvergent dynamics. An important exception occurs in cases where the dynamics lead certain quantities to be preserved. We argue now that in certain strategic environments, the replicator and projection dynamics exhibit noteworthy conservative properties.

9.1.1 Constants of Motion in Null Stable Games

Section 7.2.1 introduced *null stable* population games, which are defined by the requirement that

$$(y-x)'(F(y)-F(x)) = 0 \quad \text{for all } x, y \in X$$

and which include zero-sum games (example 3.3.3) and multi-zero-sum games (exercise 3.3.5) as special cases.

Exercise 7.2.2 showed that if x^* is an interior Nash equilibrium of a null stable game $F: X \to \mathbf{R}^n$, then the value of the function

$$E_{x^*}(x) = |x - x^*|^2$$

is preserved along interior segments of solution trajectories of the projection dynamic. Thus, as these segments are traversed, Euclidean distance from the equilibrium x^* is fixed. Similar conclusions hold for interior solutions of the replicator dynamic. Exercise 7.2.5 showed that such solutions preserve the value of the function

$$H_{x^*}(x) = \sum_{p \in \mathcal{P}} h^p_{(x^*)^p}(x^p), \quad \text{where } h^p_{y^p}(x^p) = \sum_{i \in S^p(y^p)} y^p_i \log \frac{y^p_i}{x^p_i}$$

is a relative entropy function.

Nonconvergence of Evolutionary Dynamics

When x^* is interior, the level sets of E_{x^*} and H_{x^*} foliate from x^* like the layers of an onion. Each solution trajectory is limited to one of these layers, a manifold whose dimension is one less than that of X.

Example 9.1.1 Figure 5.3 presented phase diagrams of the six basic evolutionary dynamics for standard Rock-Paper-Scissors,

$$F(x) = \begin{pmatrix} F_R(x) \\ F_P(x) \\ F_S(x) \end{pmatrix} = \begin{pmatrix} 0 & -1 & 1 \\ 1 & 0 & -1 \\ -1 & 1 & 0 \end{pmatrix} \begin{pmatrix} x_R \\ x_P \\ x_S \end{pmatrix} = \begin{pmatrix} x_S - x_P \\ x_R - x_S \\ x_P - x_R \end{pmatrix},$$

a zero-sum game with unique Nash equilibrium $x^* = (\frac{1}{3}, \frac{1}{3}, \frac{1}{3})$. Figures 5.3a and 5.3b showed that interior solutions of the replicator and projection dynamics form closed orbits around x^*. These orbits describe the level sets of the functions E_{x^*} and H_{x^*}. Note that an affine transformation of H_{x^*} yields a simpler constant of motion for the replicator dynamic in this game, $\mathcal{H}(x) = -\sum_{i \in S} \log x_i$. ◆

When $\dim(X) > 2$, the level sets of E_{x^*} and H_{x^*} need not pin down the locations of interior solutions of (P) and (R). But if the null stable game F has multiple Nash equilibria, then there are multiple collections of level sets, and intersections of these sets do determine the positions of interior solutions.

Example 9.1.2 Consider the population game F generated by matching in the symmetric zero-sum game A:

$$F(x) = Ax = \begin{pmatrix} 0 & -1 & 0 & 1 \\ 1 & 0 & -1 & 0 \\ 0 & 1 & 0 & -1 \\ -1 & 0 & 1 & 0 \end{pmatrix} \begin{pmatrix} x_1 \\ x_2 \\ x_3 \\ x_4 \end{pmatrix} = \begin{pmatrix} x_4 - x_2 \\ x_1 - x_3 \\ x_2 - x_4 \\ x_3 - x_1 \end{pmatrix}. \tag{9.1}$$

The Nash equilibria of F are the points on line segment NE connecting states $(\frac{1}{2}, 0, \frac{1}{2}, 0)$ and $(0, \frac{1}{2}, 0, \frac{1}{2})$.

The arguments above show that interior solutions to the projection dynamic maintain a constant distance from every Nash equilibrium of F. This is illustrated in figure 9.1, which presents solutions on the sphere inscribed in the pyramid X; this is the level set on which E_{x^*} takes the value $\frac{\sqrt{3}}{12}$, where $x^* = (\frac{1}{4}, \frac{1}{4}, \frac{1}{4}, \frac{1}{4})$. Each solution drawn in the figure is a circular closed orbit orthogonal to line segment NE.

Figure 9.2 presents solution trajectories of the replicator dynamic for game F. Diagrams 9.2a and 9.2b show solutions on level sets of H_{x^*} where $x^* = (\frac{1}{4}, \frac{1}{4}, \frac{1}{4}, \frac{1}{4})$; the first (smaller) level set is nearly spherical, and the second approximates the shape of the pyramid X. Diagrams 9.2c and 9.2d present solutions on level sets of H_{x^*} with $x^* = (\frac{3}{8}, \frac{1}{8}, \frac{3}{8}, \frac{1}{8})$ and $x^* = (\frac{1}{8}, \frac{3}{8}, \frac{1}{8}, \frac{3}{8})$. As noted above, the intersection of the two level sets is a closed curve describing a single orbit of the dynamic. ◆

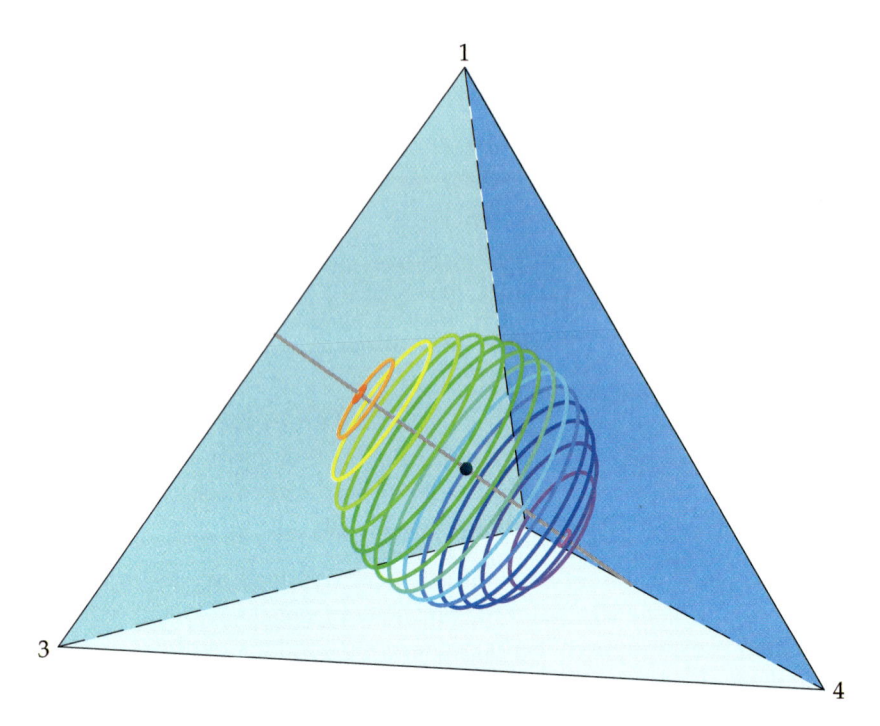

Figure 9.1
Solutions of the projection dynamic on level set $E_{x^*}(x) = \frac{\sqrt{3}}{12}$, $x^* = (\frac{1}{4}, \frac{1}{4}, \frac{1}{4}, \frac{1}{4})$.

Example 9.3.2 in section 9.3 shows that even in zero-sum games, very complicated dynamics can arise within the level sets of H_{x^*}.

Exercise 9.1.1

i. Suppose that $A \in \mathbf{R}^{n \times n}$ is skew-symmetric. Show that the eigenvalues of A all have zero real part, and so that the number of nonzero eigenvalues is even.

ii. Suppose that $A \in \mathbf{R}^{n \times n}$ is a symmetric zero-sum game that admits an interior Nash equilibrium x^*. Show that if n is even, then x^* is contained in a line segment consisting entirely of Nash equilibria. (*Hint:* Consider the matrix $\Phi A \Phi$.) ◇

The previous analysis shows that in zero-sum games, typical solutions of the replicator dynamic do not converge. The next exercise shows that the *time averages* of these solutions do converge, and that the limits of the time averages are Nash equilibria.

Exercise 9.1.2: Convergence of Time Averages under the Replicator Dynamic
Let $F(x) = Ax$ be the population game generated by matching in the symmetric normal form game $A \in \mathbf{R}^{n \times n}$, and let $\dot{x} = V_F(x)$ be the replicator dynamic for this game. Suppose that $\{x_t\}_{t \geq 0}$ is a solution to V_F that is bounded away from bd(X)

Nonconvergence of Evolutionary Dynamics

(a) $x^* = (\frac{1}{4}, \frac{1}{4}, \frac{1}{4}, \frac{1}{4})$, $H_{x^*}(x) = .02$

(b) $x^* = (\frac{1}{4}, \frac{1}{4}, \frac{1}{4}, \frac{1}{4})$, $H_{x^*}(x) = .58$

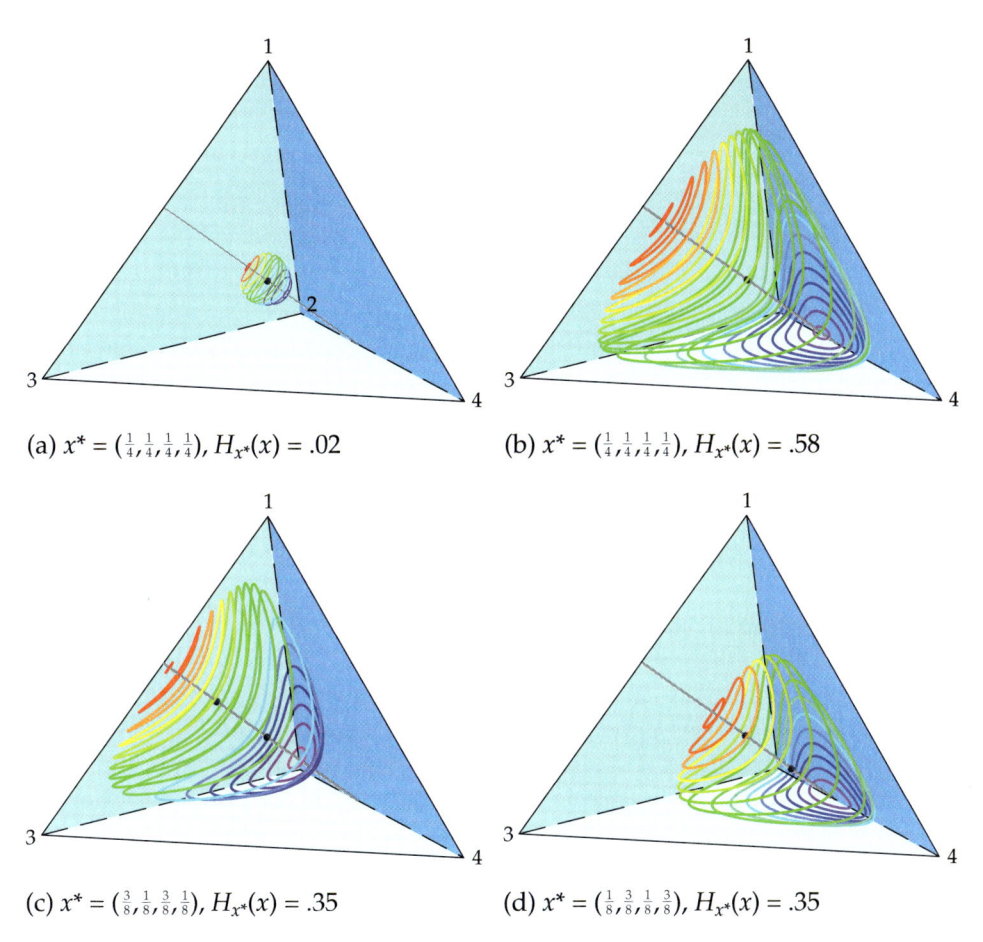

(c) $x^* = (\frac{3}{8}, \frac{1}{8}, \frac{3}{8}, \frac{1}{8})$, $H_{x^*}(x) = .35$

(d) $x^* = (\frac{1}{8}, \frac{3}{8}, \frac{1}{8}, \frac{3}{8})$, $H_{x^*}(x) = .35$

Figure 9.2
Solutions of the replicator dynamic on level sets of H_{x^*}.

(i.e., that there is an $\varepsilon > 0$ such that $(x_t)_i \geq \varepsilon$ for all $t \geq 0$ and $i \in S$). Let

$$\bar{x}_t = \frac{1}{t} \int_0^t x_s \, ds$$

be the average value of the state over the time interval $[0, t]$. Following the steps below, prove that $\{\bar{x}_t\}_{t \geq 0}$ converges to the set of (interior) Nash equilibria of F as t approaches infinity:

$$\lim_{t \to \infty} \min_{x^* \in NE(F)} |\bar{x}_t - x^*| = 0. \tag{9.2}$$

In particular, if F has a unique interior Nash equilibrium x^*, then $\{\bar{x}_t\}$ converges to x^*.

i. Define $y_t \in \mathbf{R}^n$ by $(y_t)_i = \log(x_t)_i$. Compute $\frac{d}{dt} y_t$.

ii. Show that

$$\frac{1}{t}(y_t - y_0) = \frac{1}{t}\int_0^t (Ax_s - \mathbf{1}x_s' Ax_s)\, ds.$$

iii. Let $\tilde{x}^*$ be an ω-limit point of the trajectory $\{\tilde{x}_t\}$. Show that $A\tilde{x}^*$ is a constant vector and hence that $\tilde{x}^*$ is a Nash equilibrium. (*Hint:* Use the fact that the trajectory $\{y_t\}$ is constrained to a compact set.)

iv. Conclude that (9.2) holds. (*Hint:* Use the fact that the trajectory $\{\tilde{x}_t\}$ is constrained to a compact set.) ◇

Exercise 9.1.3 Prove that the conclusion of exercise 9.1.2 continues to hold in a two-population matching setting. ◇

Exercise 9.1.4 Explain why the argument in exercise 9.1.2 does not allow its conclusion to be extended to matching in $p \geq 3$ populations. ◇

9.1.2 Preservation of Volume

Let $\dot{x} = V(x)$ be a differential equation on X with flow $\phi\colon \mathbf{R} \times X \to X$, and let μ denote Lebesgue measure on X. The differential equation is said to be *volume-preserving* (or *incompressible*) on $Y \subseteq X$ if for any measurable set $A \subseteq Y$, we have $\mu(\phi_t(A)) = \mu(A)$ for all $t \in \mathbf{R}$. Preservation of volume has strong implications for local stability of rest points; since an asymptotically stable rest point must draw in all nearby initial conditions, no such rest points can exist in regions where volume is preserved (see theorem 9.A.4).

In single-population zero-sum games, the replicator dynamic is volume-preserving after a well-chosen change in speed. Compared to the standard replicator dynamic, the *speed-adjusted replicator dynamic* on $\text{int}(X)$,

$$\dot{x}_i^p = q(x)\, x_i^p \hat{F}_i^p(x), \quad \text{where } q(x) = \prod_{r \in \mathcal{P}} \prod_{j \in S} \frac{1}{x_j^r}, \tag{9.3}$$

moves relatively faster at states closer to the boundary of the simplex, with speeds approaching infinity as the boundary is approached. The solution trajectories of (9.3) have the same locations as those of the standard replicator dynamic (see exercise 5.4.3), so the implications of volume preservation for stability of rest points extend immediately to the latter dynamic.

Theorem 9.1.5 *Let $F(x) = Ax$ be generated by matching in the symmetric zero-sum game $A = -A' \in \mathbf{R}^{n \times n}$. Then the dynamic (9.3) for F is volume-preserving on $\text{int}(X)$. Therefore, no interior Nash equilibrium of F is asymptotically stable under the replicator dynamic.*

Nonconvergence of Evolutionary Dynamics

The proof of theorem 9.1.5 is based on *Liouville's theorem*, which says that the rate at which the dynamic $\dot{x} = V(x)$ expands or contracts volume near state x is given by the *divergence* $\operatorname{div} V(x) \equiv \operatorname{tr}(DV(x))$. More precisely, Liouville's theorem states that

$$\frac{d}{dt}\mu(\phi_t(A)) = \int_{\phi_t(A)} \operatorname{div} V(x)\, d\mu(x).$$

for each Lebesgue measurable set A. Thus, if $\operatorname{div} V \equiv 0$, so that V is *divergence-free*, then the flow ϕ is volume-preserving (see section 9.A.1).

Proof The replicator dynamic is described by the vector field $R\colon X \to TX$, where

$$R(x) = \operatorname{diag}(x)(F(x) - \mathbf{1}x'F(x)).$$

Since $F(x) = Ax$, and since $x'Ax \equiv 0$ (because A is symmetric zero-sum), the previous expression can be written as

$$R(x) = \operatorname{diag}(x)Ax. \tag{9.4}$$

The dynamic (9.3) can be expressed as

$$V(x) = q(x)R(x),$$

where q is the function from $\operatorname{int}(X)$ to $\mathbf{R}_+$ defined in equation (9.3). If we can show that V is divergence-free on $\operatorname{int}(X)$, then the result will follow from Liouville's theorem.

To compute $DV(x)$, let $\hat{q}\colon \operatorname{int}(\mathbf{R}^n_+) \to \mathbf{R}_+$ and $\hat{R}\colon \mathbf{R}^n \to \mathbf{R}^n$ be the natural extensions of q and R, so that $\nabla q(x) = \Phi \nabla \hat{q}(x)$ and $DR(x) = D\hat{R}(x)\Phi$. Then the chain rule implies that

$$DV(x) = q(x)DR(x) + R(x)\nabla q(x)' = \left(q(x)D\hat{R}(x) + R(x)\nabla \hat{q}(x)'\right)\Phi. \tag{9.5}$$

To evaluate this expression, write $[x^{-1}] = (\frac{1}{x_1}, \ldots, \frac{1}{x_n})$, and compute from equations (9.3) and (9.4) that

$$\nabla \hat{q}(x) = -\hat{q}(x)[x^{-1}] \quad \text{and} \quad D\hat{R}(x) = \operatorname{diag}(x)A + \operatorname{diag}(Ax).$$

Substituting into equation (9.5) yields

$$DV(x) = q(x)\left((\operatorname{diag}(x)A + \operatorname{diag}(Ax) - \operatorname{diag}(x)Ax[x^{-1}]'\right)\Phi$$
$$= q(x)\Big[(\operatorname{diag}(x)A + \operatorname{diag}(Ax) - \operatorname{diag}(x)Ax[x^{-1}]')$$
$$\quad - \tfrac{1}{n}\left(\operatorname{diag}(x)A + \operatorname{diag}(Ax) - \operatorname{diag}(x)Ax[x^{-1}]'\right)\mathbf{11}'\Big].$$

Therefore,

$$\operatorname{div} V(x) = q(x) \left[\sum_{i \in S} x_i A_{ii} + \sum_{i \in S} (Ax)_i - \sum_{i \in S} x_i (Ax)_i \frac{1}{x_i} \right.$$

$$\left. - \frac{1}{n} \sum_{i \in S} x_i \sum_{j \in S} A_{ij} - \frac{1}{n} \sum_{i \in S} \sum_{j \in S} A_{ij} x_j + \frac{1}{n} \sum_{i \in S} \sum_{j \in S} x_i A_{ij} x_j \sum_{k \in S} \frac{1}{x_k} \right].$$

The first term in the brackets equals 0 since $A_{ii} = 0$; the second and third terms cancel; the fourth and fifth terms cancel since $A_{ij} = -A_{ji}$; and the sixth term is 0 since $x'Ax = 0$. Therefore, $\operatorname{div} V(x) = 0$ on $\operatorname{int}(X)$, and hence the flow of (9.3) is volume-preserving. The conclusion about asymptotic stability follows from theorem 9.A.4. ∎

Under single-population matching, volume preservation under the replicator dynamic is only assured in zero-sum games. Remarkably, moving to multipopulation matching ensures volume preservation regardless of the payoffs in the underlying normal form game.

Suppose the population game F is generated by matching of members of $p \geq 2$ populations to play a p-player normal form game. Since each agent's opponents in a match will be members of the other populations, the agent's payoffs do not depend on his own population's state: $F^p(x) \equiv F^p(x^{-p})$. Theorem 9.1.6 shows that this last condition is sufficient to prove that the flow of the replicator dynamic for F is volume-preserving.

Theorem 9.1.6 *Let F be a game played by $p \geq 2$ populations that satisfies $F^p(x) \equiv F^p(x^{-p})$. Then the dynamic (9.3) for F is volume-preserving on $\operatorname{int}(X)$. Therefore, no interior Nash equilibrium of F is asymptotically stable under the replicator dynamic.*

Exercise 9.1.7 Prove theorem 9.1.6. To simplify the notation, assume that each population is of unit mass. (*Hint:* To prove that the vector field V from equation (9.3) is divergence-free, start by showing that the derivative matrix of V^p at x with respect to directions in TX^p is the $n^p \times n^p$ matrix

$$D_{TX^p} V^p(x) = q(x) \left(\operatorname{diag}(\pi^p) - \bar{\pi}^p I - x^p (\pi^p)' - \operatorname{diag}(x^p) \pi^p [(x^p)^{-1}]' + \bar{\pi}^p x^p [(x^p)^{-1}]' \right) \Phi,$$

where $\pi^p = F^p(x^{-p})$ and $\bar{\pi}^p = \bar{F}^p(x^{-p}) = (x^p)' \pi^p$.) ◇

Analogues of theorems 9.1.5 and 9.1.6 can be established for projection dynamics via much simpler calculations and without introducing a change in speed.

Exercise 9.1.8 Let $F(x) = Ax$ be generated by matching in the symmetric zero-sum game $A = -A' \in \mathbf{R}^{n \times n}$. Show that the projection dynamic for F is volume-preserving on the set of states whose forward solutions are contained in $\operatorname{int}(X)$. ◇

Exercise 9.1.9 Let F be a game played by $p \geq 2$ unit-mass populations that satisfies $F^p(x) \equiv F^p(x^{-p})$. Show that the projection dynamic for F is volume-preserving on the set of states whose forward solutions are contained in $\text{int}(X)$. ◇

9.2 Games with Nonconvergent Evolutionary Dynamics

This section introduces examples of games for which many evolutionary dynamics fail to converge to equilibrium.

9.2.1 Circulant Games

The matrix $A \in \mathbf{R}^{n \times n}$ is called a *circulant matrix* if it is of the form

$$A = \begin{pmatrix} a_0 & a_1 & \cdots & a_{n-2} & a_{n-1} \\ a_{n-1} & a_0 & a_1 & \cdots & a_{n-2} \\ \ddots & \ddots & \ddots & \ddots & \ddots \\ a_2 & \cdots & a_{n-1} & a_0 & a_1 \\ a_1 & a_2 & \cdots & a_{n-1} & a_0 \end{pmatrix}.$$

When A is viewed as the payoff matrix for a symmetric normal form game, A is a *circulant game*. Such games always include the barycenter $x^* = \frac{1}{n}\mathbf{1}$ among their Nash equilibria. Note that Rock-Paper-Scissors games are circulant games with $n = 3$, $a_0 = 0$, $a_1 = -l$, and $a_2 = w$. Most of the specific games considered here will also have diagonal payoffs equal to 0.

The symmetric structure of circulant games makes them simple to analyze. In doing so, it is convenient to refer to strategies modulo n.

Exercise 9.2.1 Verify that the eigenvalue/eigenvector pairs of the circulant matrix A are

$$(\lambda_k, v_k) = \left(\sum_{j=0}^{n-1} a_j \iota_n^{jk}, (1, \iota_n^k, \ldots, \iota_n^{(n-1)k}) \right), \qquad k = 0, \ldots, n-1, \tag{9.6}$$

where $\iota_n = \exp(\frac{2\pi i}{n}) = \cos(\frac{2\pi}{n}) + i\sin(\frac{2\pi}{n})$ is the nth root of unity. ◇

Exercise 9.2.2 Let $F(x) = Ax$ be generated by matching in the circulant game A, and let $\dot{x} = R(x) = \text{diag}(x)(Ax - \mathbf{1}x'Ax)$ be the replicator dynamic for F. Show that the derivative matrix of R at the Nash equilibrium $x^* = \frac{1}{n}\mathbf{1}$ is the circulant matrix

$$DR(x^*) = \frac{1}{n}(A - 2\,\mathbf{1}\mathbf{1}'\bar{a}),$$

where $\bar{a} = \frac{1}{n}\mathbf{1}'a$ is the average of the components of the vector $a = (a_0, a_1, \ldots, a_{n-1})$. It then follows from the previous exercise that the eigenvalue/eigenvector pairs

(λ_k, v_k) of $DR(x^*)$ are given by

$$(\lambda_k, v_k) = \left(\frac{1}{n} \sum_{j=0}^{n-1} (a_j - 2\bar{a}) \iota_n^{jk}, \, (1, \iota_n^k, \ldots, \iota_n^{(n-1)k}) \right), \qquad k = 0, \ldots, n-1. \qquad \diamond \quad (9.7)$$

Example 9.2.1: The Hypercycle System Suppose that $a_0 = \ldots = a_{n-2} = 0$ and that $a_{n-1} = 1$, so that each strategy yields a positive payoff only against the strategy that precedes it (modulo n). In this case, $x^* = \frac{1}{n}\mathbf{1}$ is the unique Nash equilibrium of F, and the replicator dynamic for A is known as the *hypercycle system*.

We evaluate the local stability of the rest point x^* by considering the eigenvalues of $DR(x^*)$. Substitution into equations (9.6) and (9.7) shows that the eigenvector/eigenvalue pairs are of the form

$$(\lambda_k, v_k) = \left(\frac{1}{n} \iota_n^{(n-1)k} - \frac{2}{n^2} \sum_{j=0}^{n-1} \iota_n^{jk}, \, (1, \iota_n^k, \ldots, \iota_n^{(n-1)k}) \right), \qquad k = 0, \ldots, n-1.$$

Eigenvalue $\lambda_0 = \frac{1}{n} - \frac{2}{n} = -\frac{1}{n}$ corresponds to eigenvector $v_0 = \mathbf{1}$ and so has no bearing on the stability analysis. For $k \geq 1$, the sum in the formula for λ_k vanishes (why?), leaving $\lambda_k = \frac{1}{n}\iota_n^{(n-1)k} = \frac{1}{n}\iota_n^{-k}$. The stability of x^* therefore depends on whether any λ_k with $k > 0$ has positive real part. As figure 9.3 illustrates, the largest real part of a relevant eigenvalue is negative when $n \leq 3$, zero when $n = 4$, and positive when $n \geq 5$. It follows that x^* is asymptotically stable when $n \leq 3$ but unstable when $n \geq 5$. Exercise 9.2.3 shows that the local stability results can be extended to global stability results, and that global stability can also be proved when $n = 4$. When $n \geq 5$, it is possible to show that the boundary of X is repelling, as it is in the

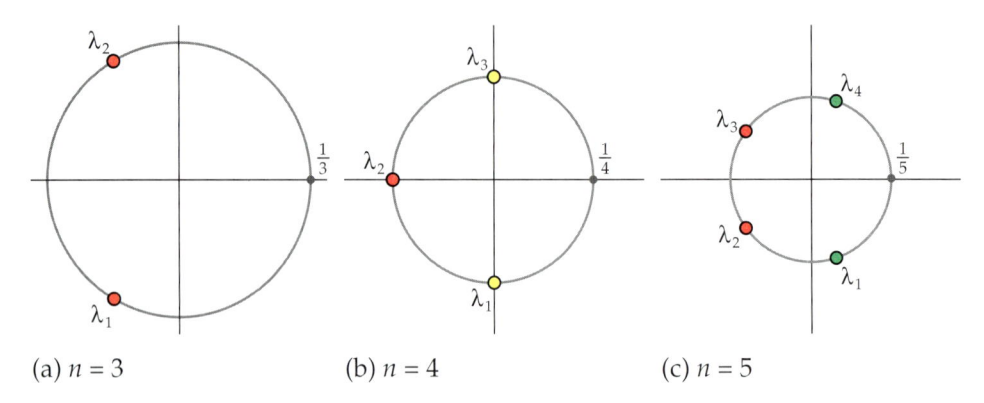

(a) $n = 3$ (b) $n = 4$ (c) $n = 5$

Figure 9.3
Eigenvalues of the hypercycle system.

lower-dimensional cases, and that the dynamic admits a stable periodic orbit (see the chapter notes). ◆

Exercise 9.2.3 Consider the function $\mathcal{H}\colon \mathrm{int}(X) \to \mathbf{R}$ defined by $\mathcal{H}(x) = -\sum_{i \in S} \log x_i$ (see example 9.1.1).

i. Show that under the hypercycle equation with $n = 2$ or 3, $\mathcal{H}$ is a strict Lyapunov function on $\mathrm{int}(X)$, and hence that x^* is globally asymptotically stable with respect to $\mathrm{int}(X)$.

ii. Show that under the hypercycle equation with $n = 4$ we have $\dot{\mathcal{H}}(x) \leq 0$ on $\mathrm{int}(X)$, with equality if and only if x lies in $Y = \{y \in \mathrm{int}(X): y_1 + y_3 = y_2 + y_4\}$. Show that the sole invariant subset of Y is $\{x^*\}$. Then use theorems 7.B.2 and 7.B.3 and proposition 7.A.1(iii) to conclude that x^* is globally asymptotically stable with respect to $\mathrm{int}(X)$. ◇

Example 9.2.2: Monocyclic Games A circulant game A is *monocyclic* if $a_0 = 0$, $a_1, \ldots, a_{n-2} \leq 0$, and $a_{n-1} > 0$. Let $\bar{a} = \frac{1}{n}\sum_i a_i$. Assume that $\bar{a} < 0$; then the Nash equilibrium $x^* = \frac{1}{n}\mathbf{1}$, which yields a payoff of $\bar{a}$ for each strategy, is the unique interior Nash equilibrium of $F(x) = Ax$. More important, there is an open, dense, full measure set of initial conditions from which the best response dynamic for $F(x) = Ax$ converges to a limit cycle; this limit cycle, known as a *Shapley polygon*, is contained in the set where $M(x) = \max_{i \in S} F_i(x)$ equals 0.

Here is a sketch of the proof. Consider a solution trajectory $\{x_t\}$ of the best response dynamic that lies in set $B_1 = \{x \in X: \mathrm{argmax}_{i \in S} F_i(x) = \{1\}\}$ during time interval $[0, T)$. For any $t \in [0, T)$, we have

$$x_t = e^{-t}x_0 + (1 - e^{-t})e_1.$$

Since the diagonal elements of A all equal zero, it follows that

$$M(x_t) = F_1(x_t) = e^{-t}F_1(x_0) = e^{-t}M(x_0). \tag{9.8}$$

For $j \notin \{1, 2\}$ we have

$$F_j(x_t) = e^{-t}F_j(x_0) + (1 - e^{-t})A_{j1} \leq e^{-t}F_j(x_0) < e^{-t}F_1(x_0) = F_1(x_t). \tag{9.9}$$

Equations (9.8) and (9.9) and the fact that

$$F_1(e_1) = 0 < a_{n-1} = F_2(e_1)$$

imply that a solution starting in region B_1 must hit the set $B_{12} = \{x \in X: \mathrm{argmax}_{i \in S} F_i(x) = \{1, 2\}\}$, and then immediately enter region $B_2 = \{x \in X: \mathrm{argmax}_{i \in S} F_i(x) = \{2\}\}$.

Repeating the foregoing argument shows that the trajectory next enters best response regions $B_3, B_4, \ldots, B_0$ in succession before returning to region B_1. Therefore, if we denote by B the set of states at which there are at most two best responses, then B is forward invariant under the best response dynamic. Moreover, equation (9.8) implies that the maximal payoff $M(x_t)$ approaches 0 along all solution trajectories in B.

In light of this discussion, we can define the *return map* $r: B_{12} \to B_{12}$, where $r(x)$ is the position at which a solution starting at $x \in B_{12}$ first returns to B_{12}. All fixed points of r lie in $M^{-1}(0)$. In fact, it can be shown that r is a contraction on $M^{-1}(0)$ for an appropriate choice of metric, and so that r has a unique fixed point (see the chapter notes). We therefore conclude that any solution trajectory starting in the open, dense, full measure set B converges to the closed orbit that passes through the unique fixed point of the return map r. ◆

9.2.2 Continuation of Attractors for Parameterized Games

The games we construct in the coming examples generate nonconvergent behavior for large classes of evolutionary dynamics. Recall the general formulation of evolutionary dynamics from chapter 4: each revision protocol ρ defined a map from population games F to differential equations $\dot{x} = V_F(x)$ via

$$\dot{x}_i^p = (V_F)_i^p(x) = \sum_{j \in S^p} x_j^p \rho_{ji}^p(F^p(x), x^p) - x_i^p \sum_{j \in S^p} \rho_{ij}^p(F^p(x), x^p). \tag{9.10}$$

Chapter 5 introduced the following desiderata for ρ and V.

Continuity: ρ^p is Lipschitz continuous.   (C)

Nash stationarity: $V_F(x) = \mathbf{0}$ if and only if $x \in NE(F)$.   (NS)

Positive correlation: $V_F^p(x) \neq \mathbf{0}$ implies that $V_F^p(x)'F^p(x) > 0$.   (PC)

Under continuity condition (C), any Lipschitz continuous population game F will generate a Lipschitz continuous differential equation (9.10), an equation that admits unique solutions from every initial condition in X. But a distinct consequence of condition (C)—one involving comparisons of dynamics across games—is equally important now.

Consider a collection of population games $\{F^\varepsilon\}_{\varepsilon \in (-\bar\varepsilon, \bar\varepsilon)}$ with identical strategy sets whose payoffs vary continuously in ε. Under condition (C), the law of motion $\dot{x} = V_{F^\varepsilon}(x)$ varies continuously in ε. Moreover, if $\phi^\varepsilon: \mathbf{R}_+ \times X \to X$ denotes the semiflow under V_{F^ε}, then the map $(\varepsilon, t, x) \mapsto \phi_t^\varepsilon(x)$ is continuous as well. This fact is important for understanding how evolution under $V_{(\cdot)}$ changes as we vary the underlying game. To capture the effects on long-run behavior under $V_{(\cdot)}$, we must introduce the notion of an attractor. The introduction here is brief; additional details can be found in appendix 9.B.

Nonconvergence of Evolutionary Dynamics   331

A set $\mathcal{A} \subseteq X$ is an *attractor* of the flow ϕ if it is nonempty, compact, and invariant under ϕ, and if there is a neighborhood U of $\mathcal{A}$ such that

$$\limsup_{t \to \infty} \operatorname{dist}(\phi_t(x), \mathcal{A}) = 0, \qquad (9.11)$$
$$_{x \in U}$$

where $\operatorname{dist}(y, z) = \min_{z \in Z} |y - z|$. The set $B(\mathcal{A}) = \{x \in X : \omega(x) \subseteq \mathcal{A}\}$ is called the *basin* of $\mathcal{A}$. Put differently, attractors are asymptotically stable sets that are also invariant under the flow.

A key property of attractors for the current context is known as *continuation*. Fix an attractor $\mathcal{A} = \mathcal{A}^0$ of the flow ϕ^0. Then as ε varies continuously from 0, there exist attractors $\mathcal{A}^\varepsilon$ of the flows ϕ^ε that vary upper-hemicontinuously from $\mathcal{A}$; their basins $B(\mathcal{A}^\varepsilon)$ vary lower-hemicontinuously from $B(\mathcal{A})$. Thus, after a slight change in the parameter ε, the attractors that exist under ϕ^0 continue to exist, and they do not explode.

Exercise 9.2.4 An attractor defined via equation (9.11) is required to attract solutions from all nearby states uniformly in time. To understand the role of uniformity in this definition, let ϕ be a flow on the unit circle that moves clockwise except at the topmost point x^* (see example 7.A.2). Explain why $\{x^*\}$ is not an attractor under this flow. ◇

As a first application of these ideas, consider the 4×4 circulant game

$$F^\varepsilon(x) = A^\varepsilon x = \begin{pmatrix} 0 & 0 & -1 & \varepsilon \\ \varepsilon & 0 & 0 & -1 \\ -1 & \varepsilon & 0 & 0 \\ 0 & -1 & \varepsilon & 0 \end{pmatrix} \begin{pmatrix} x_1 \\ x_2 \\ x_3 \\ x_4 \end{pmatrix}. \qquad (9.12)$$

When $\varepsilon = 0$, the payoff matrix $A^\varepsilon = A^0$ is symmetric, so F^0 is a potential game with potential function $f(x) = \frac{1}{2}x'A^0 x = -x_1 x_3 - x_2 x_4$. The function f attains its minimum of $-\frac{1}{4}$ at states $v = (\frac{1}{2}, 0, \frac{1}{2}, 0)$ and $w = (0, \frac{1}{2}, 0, \frac{1}{2})$, has a saddle point with value $-\frac{1}{8}$ at the Nash equilibrium $x^* = (\frac{1}{4}, \frac{1}{4}, \frac{1}{4}, \frac{1}{4})$, and attains its maximum of 0 along the closed path of Nash equilibria γ consisting of edges $\overline{e_1 e_2}$, $\overline{e_2 e_3}$, $\overline{e_3 e_4}$, and $\overline{e_4 e_1}$. It follows from results in section 7.1 that if $\dot{x} = V_{F^0}(x)$ satisfies (NS) and (PC), then all solutions whose initial conditions ξ satisfy $f(\xi) > -\frac{1}{8}$ converge to γ. (In fact, if x^* is a hyperbolic rest point of V_{F^ε}, then the stable manifold theorem (see appendix 8.C) tells us that the set of initial conditions from which solutions converge to x^* is a manifold of dimension at most 2 and hence has measure zero.) The phase diagram for the Smith dynamic in game F^0 is presented in figure 9.4a.

Now suppose that $\varepsilon > 0$. If the revision protocol satisfies continuity (C), then the attractor γ of V_{F^0} continues to an attractor γ^ε of V_{F^ε}; γ^ε is contained in a neighborhood of γ, and its basin approximates that of γ (figure 9.4b). At the same

(a) $\varepsilon = 0$

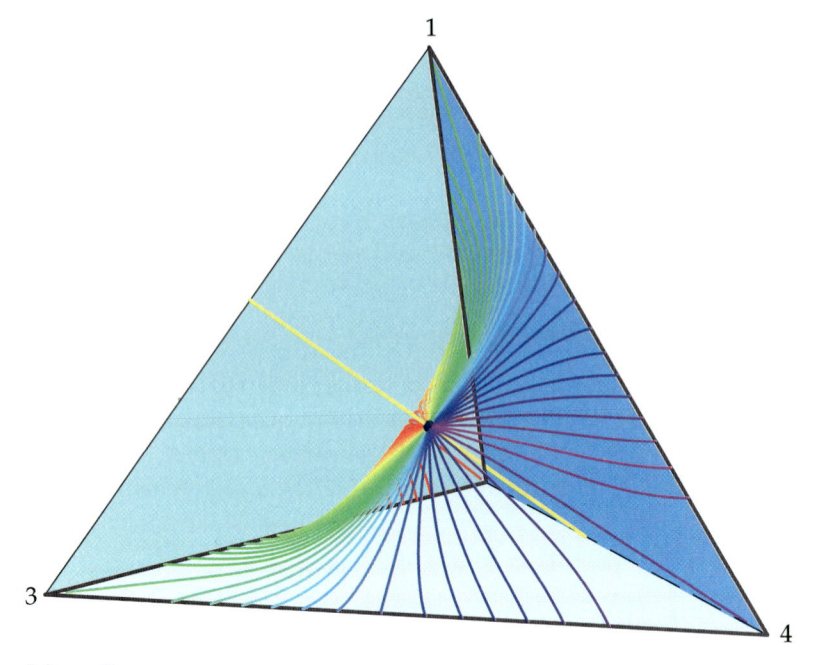

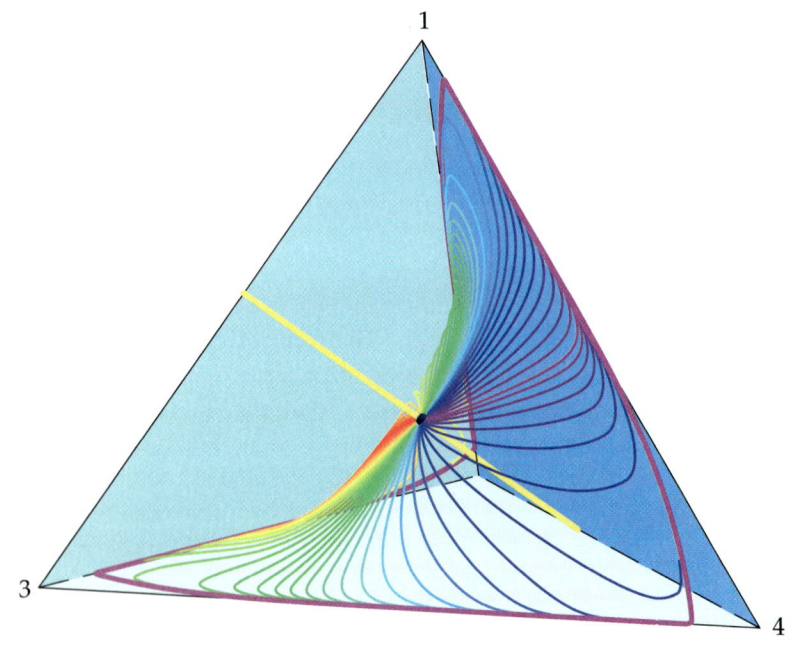

(b) $\varepsilon = \frac{1}{10}$

Figure 9.4
The Smith dynamic in game F^ε.

Nonconvergence of Evolutionary Dynamics

time, the unique Nash equilibrium of F^ε is the central state x^*. This establishes the following result.

Proposition 9.2.5 *Let $V_{(\cdot)}$ be an evolutionary dynamic that satisfies (C), (PC), and (NS), let F^ε be given by (9.12), and let $\delta > 0$. Then for $\varepsilon > 0$ suffficiently small, solutions to $\dot{x} = V_{F^\varepsilon}(x)$ from all initial conditions x with $f(x) > -\frac{1}{8} + \delta$ converge to an attractor γ^ε on which f exceeds $-\delta$; in particular, γ^ε contains neither Nash equilibria nor rest points.*

9.2.3 Mismatching Pennies

Mismatching Pennies is a three-player normal form game in which each player has two strategies, Heads and Tails. Player p receives a payoff of 1 for choosing a different strategy than player $p+1$ and a payoff of 0 otherwise, where players are indexed modulo 3.

Let F be the population game generated by matching in Mismatching Pennies; then for each population $p \in \mathcal{P} = \{1, 2, 3\}$, we have

$$F^p(x) = \begin{pmatrix} F_H^p(x) \\ F_T^p(x) \end{pmatrix} = \begin{pmatrix} x_T^{p+1} \\ x_H^{p+1} \end{pmatrix}.$$

The unique Nash equilibrium of F is the central state $x^* = ((\frac{1}{2}, \frac{1}{2}), (\frac{1}{2}, \frac{1}{2}), (\frac{1}{2}, \frac{1}{2}))$. Since there are two strategies per player, it will simplify the analysis to let $y^p = x_H^p$ be the proportion of population p players choosing Heads, and to focus on the new state variable $y = (y^1, y^2, y^3) \in Y = [0, 1]^3$ (see exercise 9.2.8).

Example 9.2.3: The Replicator Dynamic for Mismatching Pennies After the change of variable, the replicator dynamic $\dot{y} = \hat{V}_F(y)$ for Mismatching Pennies takes the form

$$\dot{y} = \begin{pmatrix} \dot{y}^1 \\ \dot{y}^2 \\ \dot{y}^3 \end{pmatrix} = \begin{pmatrix} y^1(1-y^1)(1-2y^2) \\ y^2(1-y^2)(1-2y^3) \\ y^3(1-y^3)(1-2y^1) \end{pmatrix}.$$

The derivative matrices for an arbitrary state y and for the equilibrium state $y^* = (\frac{1}{2}, \frac{1}{2}, \frac{1}{2})$ are

$$D\hat{V}(y) = \begin{pmatrix} (1-2y^1)(1-2y^2) & -2y^1(1-y^1) & 0 \\ 0 & (1-2y^2)(1-2y^3) & -2y^2(1-y^2) \\ -2y^3(1-y^3) & 0 & (1-2y^3)(1-2y^1) \end{pmatrix} \quad \text{and} \quad D\hat{V}(y^*) = \begin{pmatrix} 0 & -\frac{1}{2} & 0 \\ 0 & 0 & -\frac{1}{2} \\ -\frac{1}{2} & 0 & 0 \end{pmatrix}.$$

$D\hat{V}(y^*)$ is a circulant matrix with an eigenvalue of $-\frac{1}{2}$ corresponding to eigenvector $\mathbf{1}$, and eigenvalues of $\frac{1}{4} \pm \frac{\sqrt{3}}{4}i$ corresponding to eigenvectors $(-1, -1, 2) \pm i(-\sqrt{3}, \sqrt{3}, 0)$; note that $\mathbf{1}$, $(-1, -1, 2)$, and $(-\sqrt{3}, \sqrt{3}, 0)$ are mutually orthogonal. The phase diagram for the replicator dynamic is a *spiral saddle*; interior solutions on the diagonal where $y^1 = y^2 = y^3$ head directly toward y^*, and all other orbits

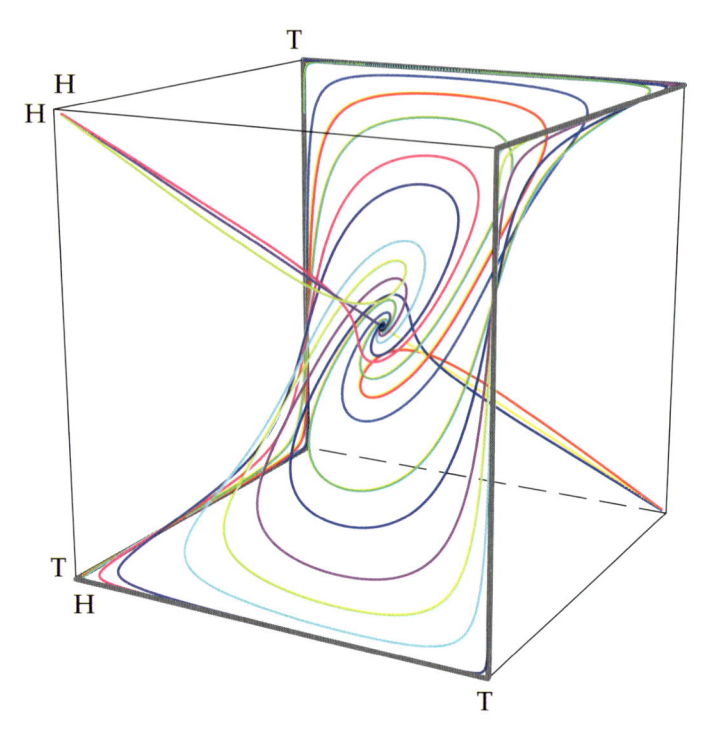

Figure 9.5
The replicator dynamic in Mismatching Pennies.

are attracted to a two-dimensional manifold containing an unstable spiral. This is depicted in figure 9.5, where behavior in populations 1, 2, and 3 is measured on the left-right, front-back, and top-bottom axes, respectively. Solutions on the manifold containing the unstable spiral converge to a six-segment heteroclinic cycle; this cycle agrees with the best response cycle of the underlying normal form game. ◆

Example 9.2.4: The Best Response Dynamic in Mismatching Pennies The analysis of the best response dynamic in Mismatching Pennies is very similar to the corresponding analysis for monocyclic games (see example 9.2.2). Divide the state space $Y = [0, 1]^3$ into eight octants in the natural way. Then the two octants corresponding to vertices *HHH* and *TTT* are backward invariant, and solutions starting in any of the remaining six octants proceed through those octants according to the best response cycle of the underlying game (see exercise 9.2.6). As figure 9.6 illustrates, almost all solutions to the best response dynamic converge to a Shapley polygon: here, a six-sided closed orbit in the interior of Y. ◆

Nonconvergence of Evolutionary Dynamics

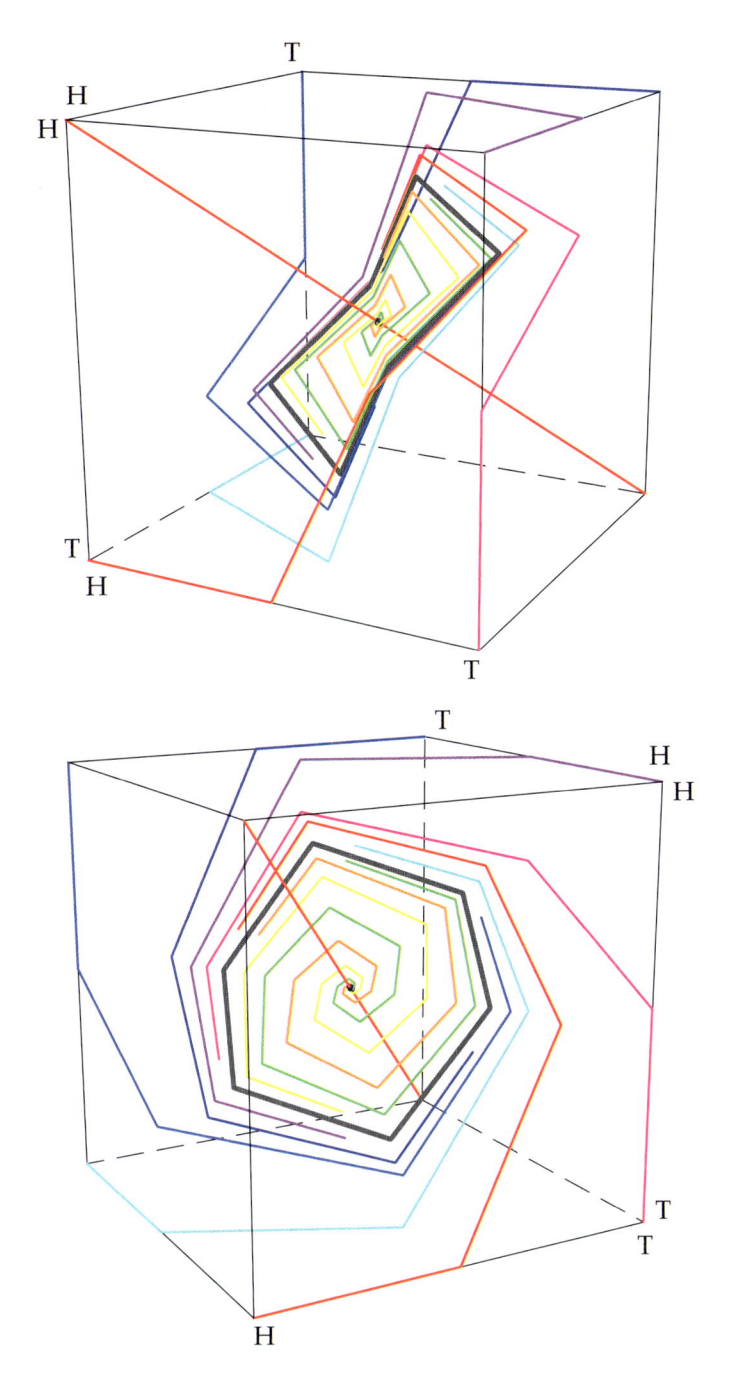

Figure 9.6
The best response dynamic in Mismatching Pennies (two viewpoints).

Exercise 9.2.6

i. Give an explicit formula for the best response dynamic for Mismatching Pennies in terms of the state variable $y \in Y = [0, 1]^3$.

ii. Prove that octants HHH and TTT described in the previous example are backward invariant.

iii. Prove that solutions starting in any of the remaining octants proceed through those octants according to the best response cycle of the underlying game. ◇

The following proposition shows that the previous two examples are not exceptional.

Proposition 9.2.7 *Let $V_{(\cdot)}$ be an evolutionary dynamic that is generated by a C^1 revision protocol ρ and that satisfies Nash stationarity (NS). Let F be Mismatching Pennies, and suppose that the unique Nash equilibrium x^* of F is a hyperbolic rest point of $\dot{x} = V_F(x)$. Then x^* is unstable under V_F, and there is an open, dense, full measure set of initial conditions from which solutions to V_F do not converge.*

Proposition 9.2.7 is remarkable in that it does not require the dynamic to satisfy a payoff monotonicity condition. Instead, it takes advantage of the fact that by definition, the revision protocol for population p does not condition on the payoffs of other populations. In fact, the specific payoffs of Mismatching Pennies are not important to obtain the instability result; any three-player game whose unique Nash equilibrium is interior works equally well. The proof of the proposition makes these points clear.

Proof For ε close to 0, let F^ε be generated by a perturbed version of Mismatching Pennies in which player 3's payoff for playing H when player 1 plays T is not 1, but $\frac{1+2\varepsilon}{1-2\varepsilon}$. Then, like Mismatching Pennies itself, F^ε has a unique Nash equilibrium, here given by $((\frac{1}{2} + \varepsilon, \frac{1}{2} - \varepsilon), (\frac{1}{2}, \frac{1}{2}), (\frac{1}{2}, \frac{1}{2}))$.

For convenience, let us argue in terms of the state variable $y = (x_H^1, x_H^2, x_H^3) \in Y = [0, 1]^3$ (see exercise 9.2.8). If $\dot{y} = \hat{V}_{F^\varepsilon}(y)$ is the dynamic $\dot{x} = V_{F^\varepsilon}(x)$ expressed in terms of y, then Nash stationarity (NS) says that

$$\hat{V}_{F^\varepsilon}(\tfrac{1}{2} + \varepsilon, \tfrac{1}{2}, \tfrac{1}{2}) = 0 \tag{9.13}$$

whenever $|\varepsilon|$ is small. Now by definition, the law of motion for population 1 does not depend directly on payoffs in the other populations, regardless of the game at hand (see equation (9.10)). Therefore, since changing the game from F^ε to F^0 does not alter population 1's payoff function, equation (9.13) implies that

$$\hat{V}^1_{F^0}(\tfrac{1}{2} + \varepsilon, \tfrac{1}{2}, \tfrac{1}{2}) = 0$$

whenever $|\varepsilon|$ is small. This observation and the fact that the dynamic is differentiable at $y^* = (\frac{1}{2}, \frac{1}{2}, \frac{1}{2})$ imply that

$$\frac{\partial \hat{V}_{F^0}^1}{\partial y^1}(y^*) = 0.$$

Repeating this argument for the other populations shows that the trace of $D\hat{V}_{F^0}(y^*)$, and hence the sum of the eigenvalues of $D\hat{V}_{F^0}(y^*)$, is 0. Since y^* is a hyperbolic rest point of $\hat{V}_{F^0}$, it follows that some eigenvalue of $D\hat{V}_{F^0}(y^*)$ has positive real part, and so that y^* is unstable under $\hat{V}_{F^0}$. Thus, the stable manifold theorem (see appendix 8.C) implies that the set of initial conditions from which solutions converge to y^* is of dimension at most 2, and that its complement is open, dense, and of full measure in Y. ∎

Exercise 9.2.8 Let X be the state space for a p population game with two strategies per population, and let $Y = [0,1]^p$, so that $TY = \mathbf{R}^p$.

i. Show that the change of variable $h: X \to Y$ has inverse $h^{-1}: Y \to X$, where

$$h(x) = \begin{pmatrix} x_1^1 \\ \vdots \\ x_1^p \end{pmatrix} \quad \text{and} \quad h^{-1}(y) = \begin{pmatrix} y^1 \\ 1-y^1 \\ \vdots \\ y^p \\ 1-y^p \end{pmatrix}.$$

ii. Show that the derivative of h at x, $Dh(x): TX \to TY$, and the derivative of h^{-1} at y, $Dh^{-1}(y): TY \to TX$, can be written as $Dh(x)z = Mz$ and $Dh^{-1}(y)\zeta = \tilde{M}\zeta$ for some matrices $M \in \mathbf{R}^{p \times 2p}$ and $\tilde{M} \in \mathbf{R}^{2p \times p}$. Show that if M is viewed as a linear map from TX to TY, then its inverse is $\tilde{M}$.

iii. Fix a C^1 vector field $V: X \to TX$, and define the new vector field $\hat{V}: Y \to TY$ by $\hat{V}(y) = h(V(h^{-1}(y)))$. Show that the dynamics $\dot{x} = V(x)$ and $\dot{y} = \hat{V}(y)$ are linearly conjugate under H, that is, $\{x_t\}$ solves the former equation if and only if $\{h(x_t)\}$ solves the latter.

iv. Let x^* be a rest point of V, and let $y^* = h(x^*)$ be the corresponding rest point of $\hat{V}$. Show that the eigenvalues of $DV(x^*)$ with respect to TX are identical to the eigenvalues of $D\hat{V}(y^*)$ with respect to TY. What is the relation between the corresponding pairs of eigenvectors? ◇

9.2.4 The Hypnodisk Game

The virtue of proposition 9.2.7 is that apart from hyperbolicity of equilibrium, virtually no assumptions about the evolutionary dynamic $V_{(\cdot)}$ are needed to establish nonconvergence. Now, if one is willing to introduce a payoff monotonicity

(a) The potential function

(b) The projected payoff vector field

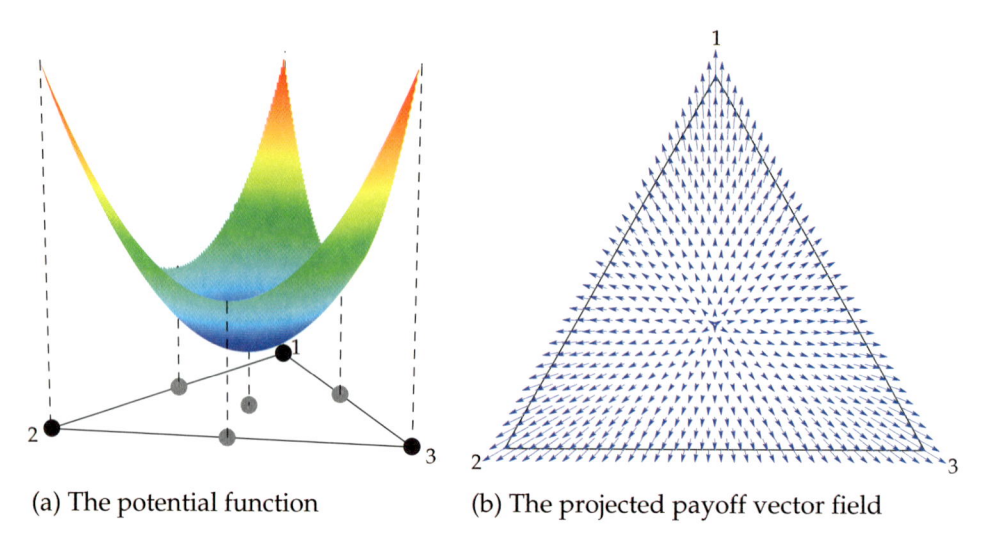

Figure 9.7
A coordination game.

condition, namely, positive correlation (PC), then one can obtain a nonconvergence without smoothness conditions and using a two-dimensional state variable rather than a three-dimensional one as in Mismatching Pennies. This low dimensionality turns out to be crucial for studying the survival of dominated strategies in section 9.4.

The construction is based on potential games. Figure 9.7 presents the potential function and projected payoff vector field of the coordination game

$$F^C(x) = Cx = \begin{pmatrix} 1 & 0 & 0 \\ 0 & 1 & 0 \\ 0 & 0 & 1 \end{pmatrix} \begin{pmatrix} x_1 \\ x_2 \\ x_3 \end{pmatrix} = \begin{pmatrix} x_1 \\ x_2 \\ x_3 \end{pmatrix}.$$

By the analysis in chapter 3, solutions to any evolutionary dynamic $\dot{x} = V_{F^C}(x)$ satisfying conditions (NS) and (PC) ascend the potential function $f^C(x) = \frac{1}{2}x'Cx = \frac{1}{2}((x_1)^2 + (x_2)^2 + (x_3)^2)$ (figure 9.7a), or equivalently, travel at acute angles to the projected payoff vectors (figure 9.7b). It follows that solutions to V_{F^C} from most initial conditions converge to the strict Nash equilibria at the vertices of X.

As a second example, suppose that agents are matched to play the anticoordination game $-C$. Figure 9.8 presents the resulting population game $F^{-C}(x) = -Cx = -x$ and its concave potential function $f^{-C}(x) = -\frac{1}{2}x'Cx = -\frac{1}{2}((x_1)^2 + (x_2)^2 + (x_3)^2)$. Both parts of the figure reveal that under any evolutionary dynamic satisfying

Nonconvergence of Evolutionary Dynamics

(a) The potential function

(b) The projected payoff vector field

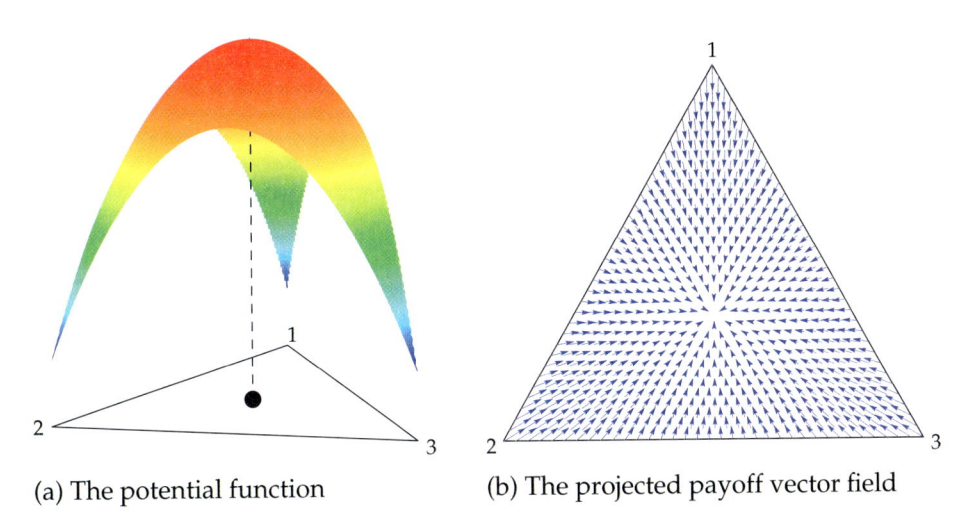

Figure 9.8
An anticoordination game.

conditions (NS) and (PC), all solution trajectories converge to the unique Nash equilibrium $x^* = (\frac{1}{3}, \frac{1}{3}, \frac{1}{3})$.

The construction of the hypnodisk game $H: X \to \mathbf{R}^3$ is easiest to describe in geometric terms. Begin with the coordination game $F^C(x) = Cx$ pictured in figure 9.7b. Then draw two circles centered at state $x^* = (\frac{1}{3}, \frac{1}{3}, \frac{1}{3})$ with radii $0 < r < R < \frac{1}{\sqrt{6}}$, as shown in figure 9.9a; the second inequality ensures that both circles are contained in the simplex. Twist the portion of the vector field lying outside of the inner circle in a clockwise direction, excluding larger and larger circles as the twisting proceeds, so that the outer circle is reached when the total twist is 180° (figure 9.9b).

Exercise 9.2.9 Provide an explicit formula for the resulting population game $H(x)$. ◇

What does this construction accomplish? Figure 9.9b reveals that inside the inner circle, H is identical to the coordination game F^C. Thus, solutions to dynamics satisfying (NS) and (PC) starting at states other than x^* in the inner circle must leave the inner circle. At states outside the outer circle, H is identical to the anticoordination game F^{-C}, so solutions to dynamics satisfying (NS) and (PC) starting at states outside the outer circle must enter the outer circle. Finally, at each state x in the annulus bounded by the two circles, $H(x)$ is not a componentwise constant vector. Therefore, states in the annulus are not Nash equilibria, and so are not rest points

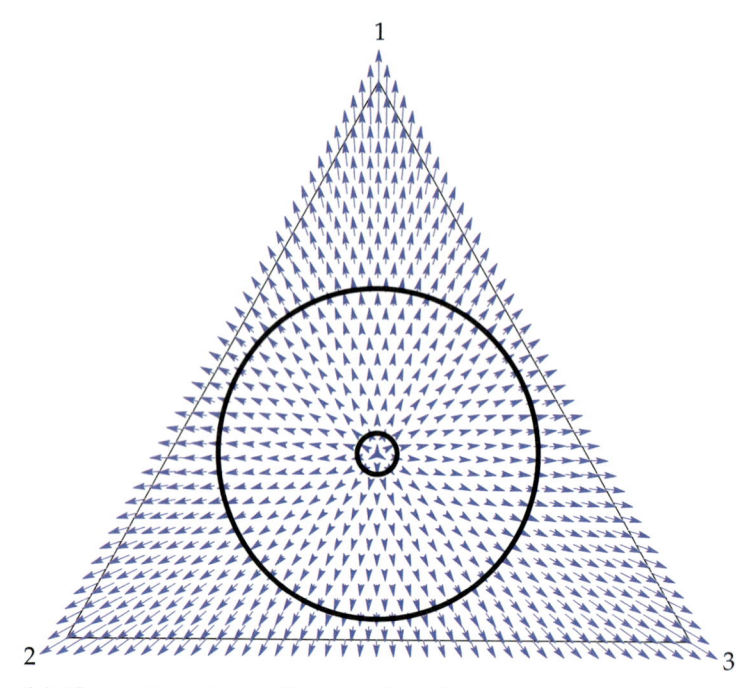

(a) The projected payoff vector field for the coordination game

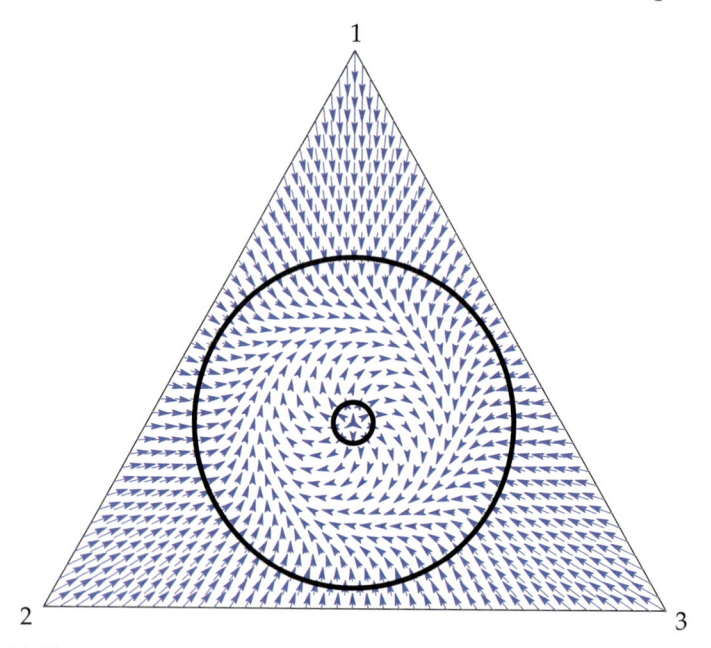

(b) The projected payoff vector field for the hypnodisk game

Figure 9.9
Construction of the hypnodisk game.

of dynamics satisfying (NS). These observations are assembled in the following proposition.

Proposition 9.2.10 *Let $V_{(\cdot)}$ be an evolutionary dynamic that satisfies (C), (NS), and (PC), and let H be the hypnodisk game. Then every solution to $\dot{x} = V_H(x)$ other than the stationary solution at x^* enters the annulus with radii r and R and never leaves, ultimately converging to a cycle therein.*

The claim of convergence to limit cycles in the final sentence of the proposition follows from the Poincaré-Bendixson theorem (theorem 9.A.5).

9.3 Chaotic Evolutionary Dynamics

All the previous phase diagrams have shown ω-limit sets with a fairly simple form; solution trajectories have converged to rest points, closed orbits, or chains of rest points and connecting orbits. For games with just two or three strategies, this is unavoidable. Clearly, all solution trajectories of continuous-time dynamics in one dimension converge to equilibrium, and in two-dimensional systems, the Poincaré-Bendixson theorem (theorem 9.A.5) indicates that these three types of ω-limit sets exhaust all possibilities.

For flows in three or more dimensions, however, ω-limit sets can be much more complicated sets known as *chaotic* (or *strange*) *attractors*. Central to most definitions of chaos is *sensitive dependence on initial conditions*: solution trajectories starting from close-together points on the attractor move apart at an exponential rate. Chaotic attractors can also be recognized in phase diagrams by their rather intricate appearance, as the following examples show.

Example 9.3.1 Consider the single-population game F generated by matching in the normal form game A:

$$F(x) = Ax = \begin{pmatrix} 0 & -12 & 0 & 22 \\ 20 & 0 & 0 & -10 \\ -21 & -4 & 0 & 35 \\ 10 & -2 & 2 & 0 \end{pmatrix} \begin{pmatrix} x_1 \\ x_2 \\ x_3 \\ x_4 \end{pmatrix}.$$

The lone interior Nash equilibrium of this game is the central state $x^* = (\frac{1}{4}, \frac{1}{4}, \frac{1}{4}, \frac{1}{4})$.

Let $\dot{x} = V_F(x)$ be the replicator dynamic for game F. One can calculate that the eigenvalues of $DV_F(x^*)$ are approximately -3.18 and $.34 \pm 1.98\,i$; thus, like the Nash equilibrium of Mismatching Pennies (example 9.2.3), the interior equilibrium x^* here is a spiral saddle with an unstable spiral.

Figure 9.10 presents the initial portion of the solution of $\dot{x} = V_F(x)$ from initial condition $x_0 = (.24, .26, .25, .25)$. This solution spirals clockwise about x^*. Near the

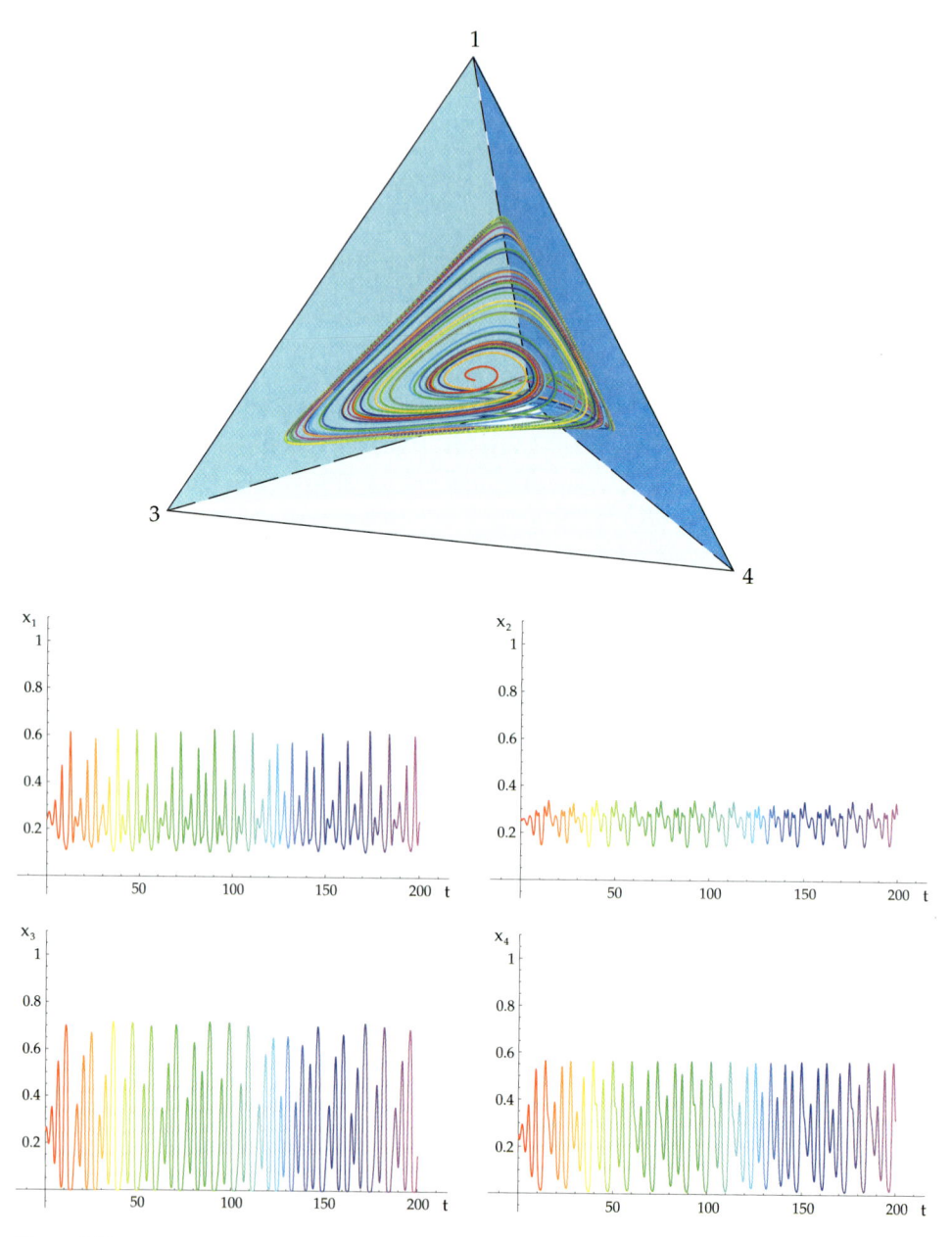

Figure 9.10
A chaotic attractor under the replicator dynamic.

Nonconvergence of Evolutionary Dynamics

rightmost point of each circuit, where the value of x_3 gets close to zero, solutions sometimes proceed along an outside path on which the value of x_3 surpasses .6. But they sometimes follow an inside path on which x_3 remains below .4, and at other times they do something in between. Which of these alternatives occurs is difficult to predict from approximate information about the previous behavior of the system.

Sensitive dependence on initial conditions is illustrated directly in figure 9.11, which tracks the solutions from two nearby initial conditions, (.47, .31, .11, .11) and (.46999, .31, .11, .11001). Apparently, the two solutions stay close together through time $t = 50$ but diverge thereafter; after time $t = 60$, the current position of one of the solutions provides little hint about the current position of the other. ◆

The scattered payoff entries in example 9.3.1 may seem to suggest that chaos only occurs in artificial examples. To counter this view, the following example shows that chaotic behavior can occur in very simple games.

Example 9.3.2: Asymmetric Rock-Paper-Scissors Suppose that two populations of agents are matched to play the two-player zero-sum game $U = (U^1, U^2)$:

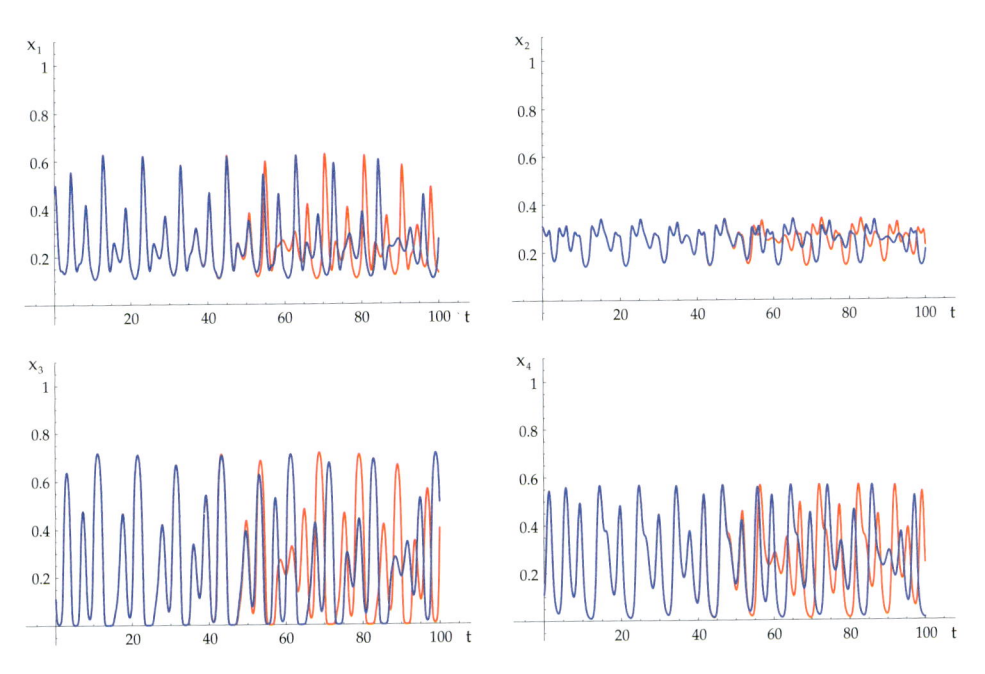

Figure 9.11
Sensitive dependence on initial conditions under the replicator dynamic.

	II		
	r	p	s
R	$\frac{1}{2}, -\frac{1}{2}$	$-1, 1$	$1, -1$
I P	$1, -1$	$\frac{1}{2}, -\frac{1}{2}$	$-1, 1$
S	$-1, 1$	$1, -1$	$\frac{1}{2}, -\frac{1}{2}$

U is an asymmetric version of Rock-Paper-Scissors in which a draw results in a half-credit win for player 1.

Figures 9.12 and 9.13 each present a single solution trajectory of the replicator dynamic for F_U. Since the social state $x = (x^1, x^2)$ is four-dimensional, it is drawn in two pieces, with x^1 represented on the left-hand side of each figure and x^2 represented on the right. Because U is a zero-sum game with Nash equilibrium $((\frac{1}{3}, \frac{1}{3}, \frac{1}{3}), (\frac{1}{3}, \frac{1}{3}, \frac{1}{3}))$, each solution of the replicator dynamic lives within a level set of $\mathcal{H}(x) = -\sum_{p \in \mathcal{P}} \sum_{i \in S^p} \log x_i^p$. In figure 9.12, whose initial condition is $((.5, .25, .25), (.5, .25, .25))$, the solution trajectory appears to follow a periodic orbit, much like those in the examples from section 9.1.1. But in figure 9.13, whose initial condition $((.5, .01, .49), (.5, .25, .25))$ is closer to the boundary of X, the solution trajectory travels around the level set of $\mathcal{H}$ in a seemingly haphazard way. Thus, despite the regularity provided by the constant of motion, the evolution of behavior in this simple game is complicated indeed. ◆

9.4 Survival of Dominated Strategies

We have considered in detail the extent to which predictions of Nash equilibrium play are supported by the behavior of evolutionary dynamics. On the positive side, chapters 5 and 6 showed that there are many dynamics whose rest points are always identical to the Nash equilibria of the underlying game, and chapter 7 showed that convergence to Nash equilibrium can be assured under many of these dynamics in particular classes of games. But the examples in section 9.2 revealed that no general guarantee of convergence to Nash equilibrium is possible, as there are games in which no reasonable dynamic leads to Nash equilibrium play.

This negative result leads us to consider a more modest question. Rather than seek evolutionary support for equilibrium play, we instead turn our attention to a more basic rationality requirement: namely, the avoidance of strategies that are strictly dominated. Section 7.4 provided some positive results on this question, showing that the best response dynamic and all imitative dynamics eliminate dominated strategies, at least along solutions starting from most initial conditions.

Nonconvergence of Evolutionary Dynamics

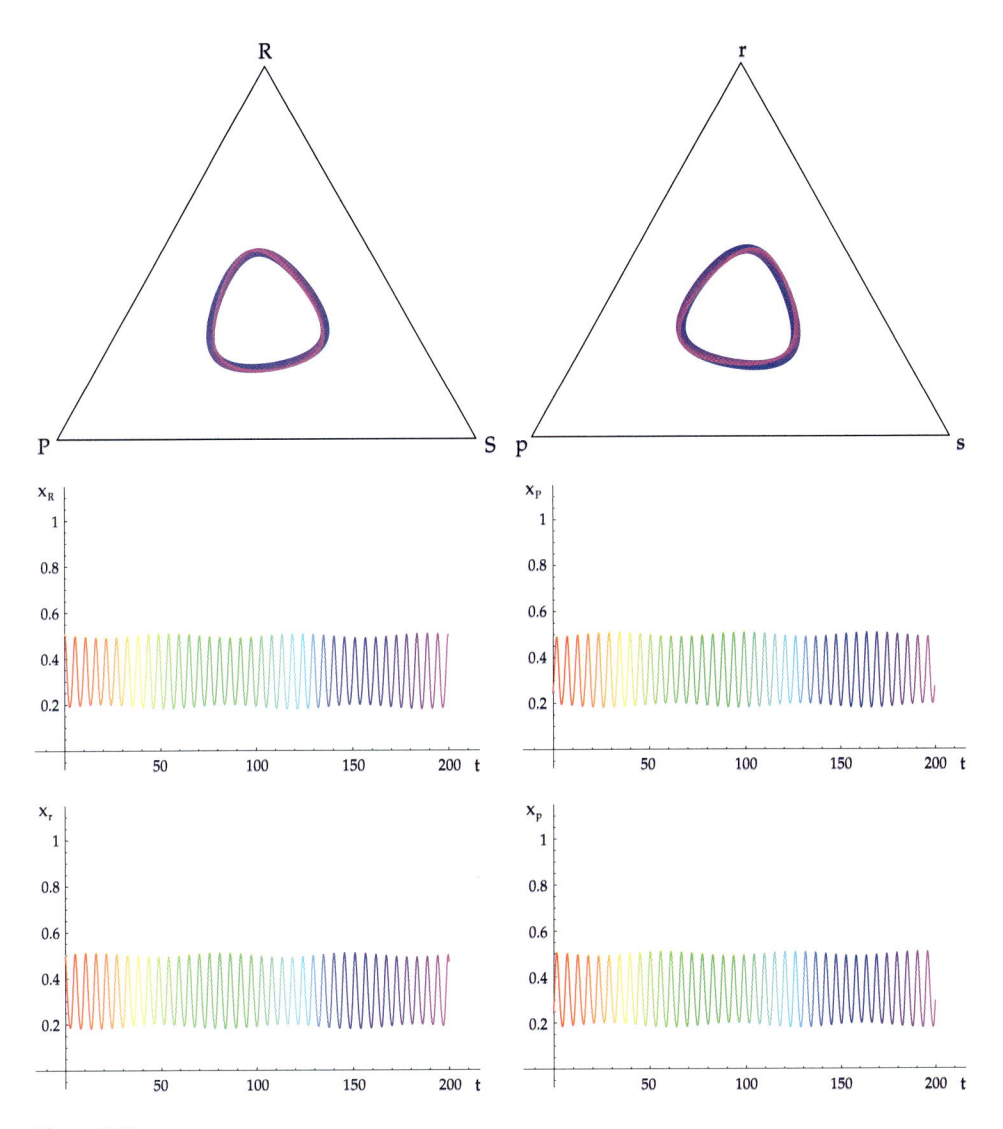

Figure 9.12
Cycling in asymmetric Rock-Paper-Scissors.

Since the elimination of strategies strictly dominated by a pure strategy is the mildest requirement employed in standard game-theoretic analyses, the results from section 7.4 may seem unremarkable. But some reflection reveals that the case for elimination of dominated strategies by evolutionary dynamics is rather tenuous. Evolutionary dynamics describe the aggregate behavior of agents who employ simple revision protocols, switching to strategies whose current payoffs are

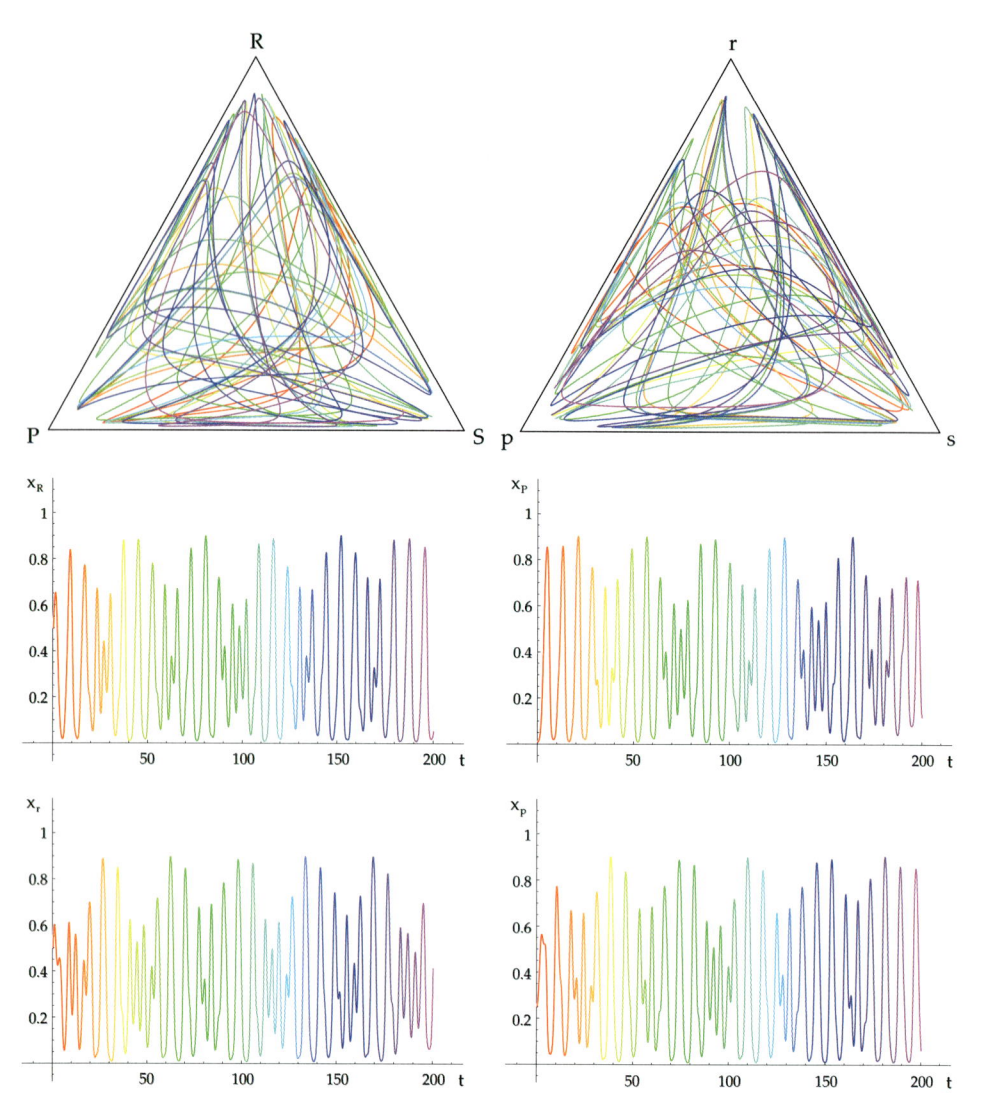

Figure 9.13
Chaos in asymmetric Rock-Paper-Scissors.

good, though not necessarily optimal. In some cases, in particular, when solutions converge, these simple rules are enough to ensure individually optimal long-run behavior. When a solution trajectory of an evolutionary dynamic converges, the payoffs to each strategy converge as well; because payoffs become fixed, even simple rules are enough to ensure that only optimal strategies are chosen. In formal terms, under Nash stationarity (NS) the limits of convergent solution trajectories must be Nash equilibria, implying that strictly dominated strategies are not chosen.

We have argued in this chapter that solutions of evolutionary dynamics need not converge, but instead may enter limit cycles or more complicated limit sets. When solutions do not converge, payoffs remain in flux. In this situation, it is not obvious whether choice rules favoring strategies whose current payoffs are relatively high will necessarily eliminate strategies that perform well at many states but that are never optimal. To the contrary, the analysis that follows demonstrates that if play remains in disequilibrium, even strategies that are strictly dominated by other pure strategies can persist indefinitely.

9.4.1 A General Survival Theorem

To turn this intuition into a formal result, we introduce one further condition on evolutionary dynamics.

Innovation: If $x \notin NE(F)$, $x_i = 0$, and $i \in \operatorname*{argmax}_{j \in S} F_j(x)$, then $(V_F)_i(x) > 0$. (IN)

Innovation (IN) requires that when a non-Nash population state includes an unused optimal strategy, this strategy's growth rate must be positive. In other words, if an unplayed strategy is sufficiently rewarding, some members of the population will discover it and select it. This condition excludes dynamics based purely on imitation; however, it includes dynamics that combine imitation with a small amount of direct selection of candidate strategies (see section 5.7 and example 9.4.3).

We are now prepared to state the survival theorem.

Theorem 9.4.1 *Suppose the evolutionary dynamic $V_{(\cdot)}$ satisfies (C), (NS), (PC), and (IN). Then there is a game F such that under $\dot{x} = V_F(x)$, along solutions from most initial conditions, there is a strictly dominated strategy played by a fraction of the population bounded away from 0.*

Theorem 9.4.1 states that evolutionary dynamics satisfying four natural requirements fail to eliminate dominated strategies in some games. In essence, the theorem shows that the dynamics studied in section 7.4 are the only ones that should be expected to eliminate dominated strategies in all games, and that even the elimination results for these dynamics are knife-edge cases.

The proof of theorem 9.4.1 makes use of the hypnodisk game from section 9.2.4. Introducing this unusual game simplifies the analysis, but the survival of dominated strategies is a broader consequence of nonconvergence and does not depend on the introduction of complicated games in any essential way (see section 9.4.2).

Proof of theorem 9.4.1 Let H be the hypnodisk game introduced in Section 9.2.4. Let F be the four-strategy game obtained from H by adding a twin to strategy 3:

$$F_i(x_1, x_2, x_3, x_4) = H_i(x_1, x_2, x_3 + x_4) \quad \text{for } i \in \{1, 2, 3\};$$

$$F_4(x) = F_3(x).$$

Strategies 3 and 4 are identical in that they always yield the same payoff and always have the same payoff consequences for other strategies. The set of Nash equilibria of F is the line segment

$$NE = \{x^* \in X : x_1^* = x_2^* = x_3^* + x_4^* = \tfrac{1}{3}\}.$$

Let

$$I = \{x \in X : (x_1 - \tfrac{1}{3})^2 + (x_2 - \tfrac{1}{3})^2 + (x_3 + x_4 - \tfrac{1}{3})^2 \leq r^2\}$$

and

$$O = \{x \in X : (x_1 - \tfrac{1}{3})^2 + (x_2 - \tfrac{1}{3})^2 + (x_3 + x_4 - \tfrac{1}{3})^2 \leq R^2\}$$

be concentric cylindrical regions in X surrounding NE, as pictured in figure 9.14. By construction, we have

$$F(x) = \tilde{C}x = \begin{pmatrix} 1 & 0 & 0 & 0 \\ 0 & 1 & 0 & 0 \\ 0 & 0 & 1 & 1 \\ 0 & 0 & 1 & 1 \end{pmatrix} \begin{pmatrix} x_1 \\ x_2 \\ x_3 \\ x_4 \end{pmatrix}$$

at all $x \in I$, so under any dynamic satisfying (PC) and (NS), solutions starting in $I - NE$ ascend the potential function $f^{\tilde{C}}(x) = \tfrac{1}{2}((x_1)^2 + (x_2)^2 + (x_3 + x_4)^2)$ until leaving the set I. At states outside the set O, we have $F(x) = -\tilde{C}x$, so solutions starting in $X - O$ ascend $f^{-\tilde{C}}(x) = -f^{\tilde{C}}(x)$ until entering O.

Lemma 9.4.2 *Suppose that $V_{(\cdot)}$ is an evolutionary dynamic that satisfies conditions (C), (NC), and (PC), and let F be the "hypnodisk with a twin" game. Then every solution to $\dot{x} = V_F(x)$ other than the stationary solutions in NE enter region $D = O - I$ and never leave.*

Define the flow from the set $U \subseteq X$ under the dynamic V_F by

$$\phi_t(U) = \{\xi \in X : \text{there is a solution } \{x_s\} \text{ to } \dot{x} = V_F(x) \text{ with } x_0 \in U \text{ and } x_t = \xi\}.$$

In words, $\phi_t(U)$ contains the time t positions of solutions to V_F whose initial conditions are in U.

Since solutions to V_F starting in $I - NE$ ascend the function $f^{\tilde{C}}$ until leaving the set I, the reverse time flow is well-defined from all such states, and NE is a *repellor*

Nonconvergence of Evolutionary Dynamics

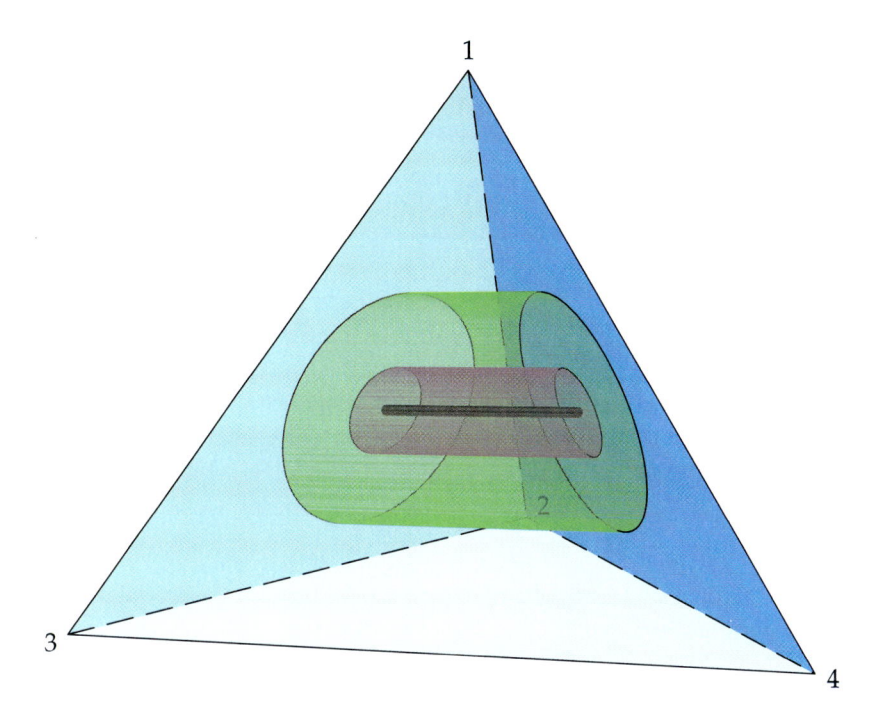

Figure 9.14
Regions O, I, and $D = O - I$.

under V_F. This means that all backward-time solutions to V_F that begin in some neighborhood U of NE converge to NE uniformly over time, or equivalently, that NE is an attractor of the time-reversed equation $\dot{y} = -V_F(y)$ (see appendix 9.B). The *dual attractor* $\mathcal{A}$ of the repellor NE is the forward-time limit of the flow of V_F starting from the complement of $\text{cl}(U)$:

$$\mathcal{A} = \bigcap_{t \geq 0} \phi_t(X - \text{cl}(U)).$$

$\mathcal{A}$ is nonempty, compact, and (both forward and backward) invariant under V_F, and lemma 9.4.2 implies that $\mathcal{A} \subset D$.

We now show that the twin strategy is used by a positive mass of agents throughout the attractor $\mathcal{A}$. Let $Z = \{x \in X: x_4 = 0\}$ be the face of X on which the twin strategy is unused.

Lemma 9.4.3 *The attractor $\mathcal{A}$ and the face Z are disjoint.*

Proof Since V_F is Lipschitz continuous and satisfies $(V_F)_i(x) \geq 0$ whenever $x_i = 0$, solutions to V_F that start in $X - Z$ cannot approach Z more than exponentially quickly, and in particular cannot reach Z in finite time (see exercise 9.4.4). Equivalently, backward solutions to V_F starting from states in Z cannot enter $\text{int}(X)$.

Suppose by way of contradiction that there exists a state ξ in $\mathcal{A} \cap Z$. Then by the previous arguments, the entire backward orbit from ξ is also contained in $\mathcal{A} \cap Z$, and hence in $D \cap Z$. Since the latter set contains no rest points by condition (PC), the Poincaré-Bendixson theorem (theorem 9.A.5) implies that the backward orbit from ξ converges to a closed orbit γ in $D \cap Z$ that circumnavigates $I \cap Z$.

By construction, the annulus $D \cap Z$ can be split into three regions: one in which strategy 1 is the best response, one in which strategy 2 is the best response, and one in which strategy 3 (and hence strategy 4) is a best response (figure 9.15). Each of these regions is bounded by a simple closed curve that intersects the inner and outer boundaries of the annulus. Therefore, the closed orbit γ, on which strategy 4 is unused, passes through the region in which strategy 4 is optimal. This contradicts innovation (IN). ∎

Exercise 9.4.4 Use Grönwall's inequality (lemma 4.A.4) to check the initial claim in the proof of the lemma. ◇

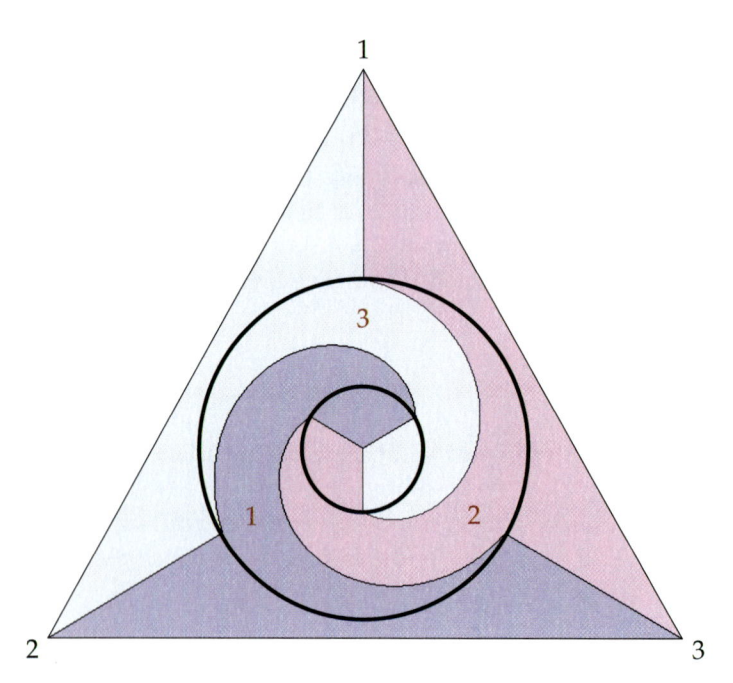

Figure 9.15
The best response correspondence of the hypnodisk game.

Nonconvergence of Evolutionary Dynamics

To complete the proof of theorem 9.4.1, we make the twin strategy feeble: that is, we uniformly reduce its payoff by $d > 0$, creating the new game

$$F^d(x) = F(x) - de_4.$$

Observe that strategy 4 is strictly dominated by strategy 3 in game F^d.

As increasing d from 0 continuously changes the game from F to F^d, doing so also continuously changes the dynamic from V_F to V_{F^d}. Thus, by theorem 9.B.5 on continuation of attractors, we have that for small d, the attractor $\mathcal{A}$ of V_F continues to an attractor $\mathcal{A}^d$ of V_{F^d} on which $x_4 > 0$; thus, so the dominated strategy survives throughout $\mathcal{A}^d$. The basin of the attractor $\mathcal{A}^d$ contains all points outside of a thin tube around the set NE of Nash equilibria of F. This completes the proof of theorem 9.4.1. ∎

9.4.2 Examples and Discussion

We conclude this chapter with some examples and exercises that demonstrate the robustness of the analysis above.

Example 9.4.1   The hypnodisk game is used as the basis for proving theorem 9.4.1 because it generates cycling under any dynamic that satisfies (NS) and (PC). But its use is not essential. Once the dynamic is fixed, one can find a simpler game that leads to cycling; then the argument based on the introduction of twin strategies can proceed as before.

We illustrate this point by constructing an example of survival under the Smith dynamic. Figure 9.16 contains the phase diagram for the Smith dynamic in the bad Rock-Paper-Scissors game

$$G(x) = Ax = \begin{pmatrix} 0 & -2 & 1 \\ 1 & 0 & -2 \\ -2 & 1 & 0 \end{pmatrix} \begin{pmatrix} x_1 \\ x_2 \\ x_3 \end{pmatrix}.$$

Evidently, the unique Nash equilibrium $x^* = (\frac{1}{3}, \frac{1}{3}, \frac{1}{3})$ is unstable, and most solution trajectories converge to a cycle located in $\text{int}(X)$.

Figure 9.17a presents the Smith dynamic in bad RPS with a twin,

$$F(x) = \tilde{A}x = \begin{pmatrix} 0 & -2 & 1 & 1 \\ 1 & 0 & -2 & -2 \\ -2 & 1 & 0 & 0 \\ -2 & 1 & 0 & 0 \end{pmatrix} \begin{pmatrix} x_1 \\ x_2 \\ x_3 \\ x_4 \end{pmatrix}. \tag{9.14}$$

The Nash equilibria of F are the states on line segment $NE = \{x^* \in X: x^* = (\frac{1}{3}, \frac{1}{3}, c, \frac{1}{3} - c)\}$, which is a repellor under the Smith dynamic. Furthermore, since Scissors and Twin always earn the same payoffs ($F_3(x) \equiv F_4(x)$), we can derive a

352   Chapter 9

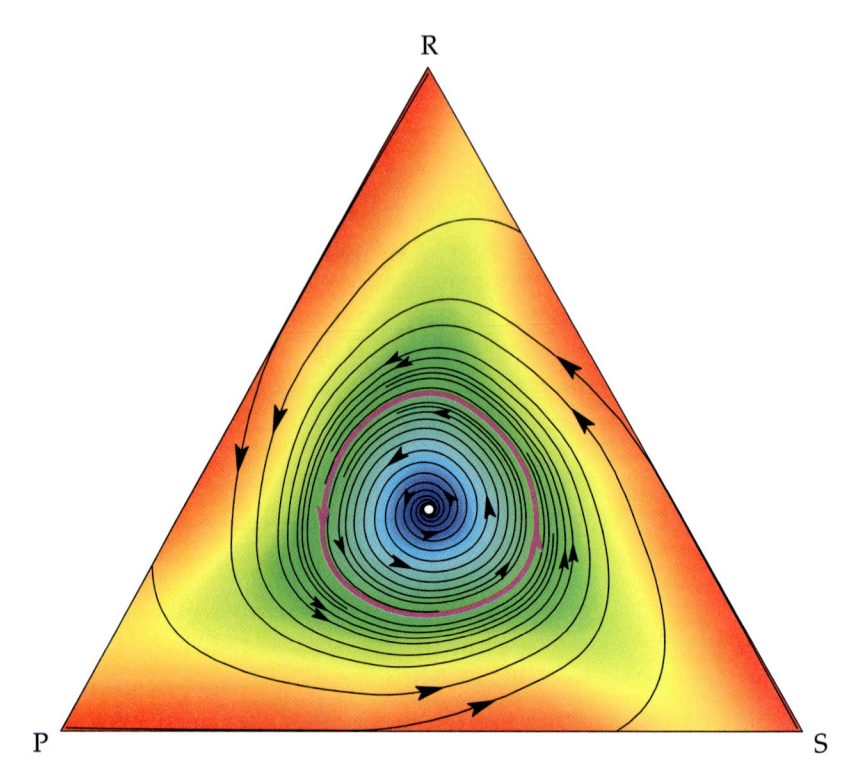

Figure 9.16
The Smith dynamic in bad RPS.

(a) Bad RPS with a twin   (b) Bad RPS with a feeble twin

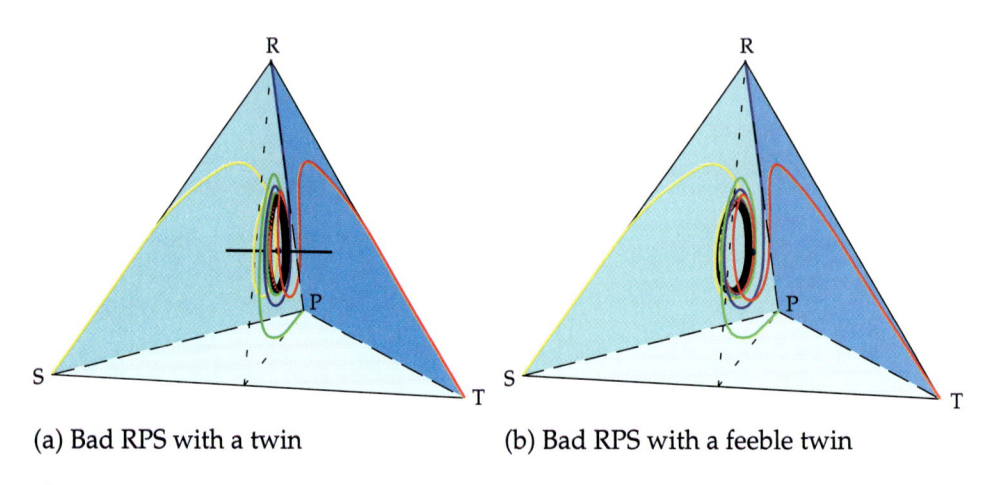

Figure 9.17
The Smith dynamic in two games.

Nonconvergence of Evolutionary Dynamics

simple expression for the rate of change of the difference between their utilization levels:

$$\dot{x}_3 - \dot{x}_4 = \left(\sum_{j \in S} x_j [F_3(x) - F_j(x)]_+ - x_3 \sum_{j \in S} [F_j(x) - F_3(x)]_+\right)$$

$$- \left(\sum_{j \in S} x_j [F_4(x) - F_j(x)]_+ - x_4 \sum_{j \in S} [F_j(x) - F_4(x)]_+\right)$$

$$= -(x_3 - x_4) \sum_{j \in S} [F_j(x) - F_4(x)]_+. \tag{9.15}$$

Intuitively, strategies lose agents at rates proportional to their current levels of use but gain strategies at rates that depend on their payoffs. Thus, when the dynamics are not at rest, the weights x_3 and x_4 move closer together. It follows that except at Nash equilibrium states, the dynamic moves toward the plane $P = \{x \in X : x_3 = x_4\}$ on which the identical twins receive equal weight (see exercise 9.4.5).

Figure 9.17b presents the Smith dynamic in bad RPS with a feeble twin,

$$F^d(x) = \tilde{A}^d x = \begin{pmatrix} 0 & -2 & 1 & 1 \\ 1 & 0 & -2 & -2 \\ -2 & 1 & 0 & 0 \\ -2-d & 1-d & -d & -d \end{pmatrix} \begin{pmatrix} x_1 \\ x_2 \\ x_3 \\ x_4 \end{pmatrix}, \tag{9.16}$$

where $d = \frac{1}{10}$. Evidently, the attractor from the previous figure moves slightly to the left, and the strictly dominated strategy Twin survives. Indeed, since the Nash equilibrium of RPS with a twin on plane P puts mass $\frac{1}{6}$ on Twin, when d is small solutions to the Smith dynamic in RPS with a feeble twin place mass greater than $\frac{1}{6}$ on the strictly dominated strategy Twin infinitely often. This lower bound is driven by the fact that in the game with an exact twin, solutions converge to plane P; thus, the bound will obtain under any dynamic that treats different strategies symmetrically. ◆

Exercise 9.4.5 Show that under the Smith dynamic in RPS with a twin, solutions from states not on the line of Nash equilibria NE converge to the plane P where the weights on Scissors and Twin are equalized. (*Hint:* Use equation (9.15) and the Poincaré-Bendixson Theorem. Take as given that the set NE is a repellor.) ◇

Example 9.4.2 The preceding analyses of survival of dominated strategies do not quantify the level of domination that is consistent with a dominated strategy maintaining a significant presence in the population. We can provide a sense of this magnitude through a numerical analysis.

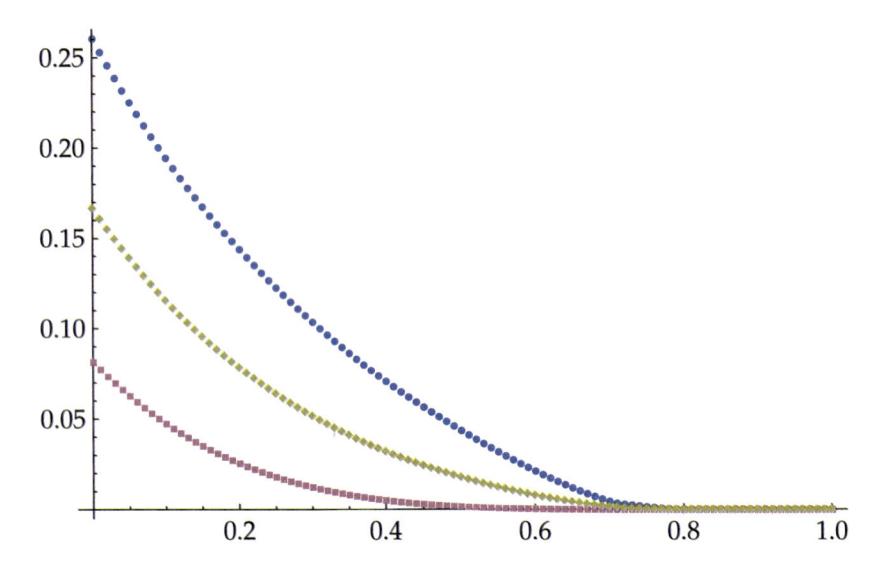

Figure 9.18
The maximum, time-average, and minimum weights on the dominated strategy under the Smith dynamic as functions of the domination level d.

Consider the behavior of the Smith dynamic in bad RPS with a feeble twin (equation (9.16)). Figure 9.18 presents the maximum, time-average, and minimum weights on the dominated strategy in the limit cycle of the Smith dynamic as functions of the domination level d. The figure shows that Twin is recurrently played by at least 10% of the population when $d \leq .31$, by at least 5% of the population when $d \leq .47$, and by at least 1% of the population when $d \leq .66$. These values of d are surprisingly large relative to the base payoff values of 0, -2, and 1. Even strategies that are dominated by a significant margin can be played in perpetuity under common evolutionary dynamics. ◆

Example 9.4.3 Theorem 7.4.4 showed that dominated strategies are eliminated along interior solutions of imitative dynamics, but theorem 9.4.1 shows that this result is not robust to small changes in these dynamics.

To understand why, consider evolution under the replicator dynamic in (standard) RPS with a twin. In standard Rock-Paper-Scissors, interior solutions of the replicator dynamic are closed orbits (see, e.g., section 9.1.1). When we introduce an exact twin, equation (7.39) implies that the ratio $\frac{x_S}{x_T}$ is constant along every solution trajectory. This is evident in figure 9.19a, which shows that the planes on which the ratio $\frac{x_S}{x_T}$ is constant are all invariant sets. If we make the twin feeble by lowering its payoff uniformly by d, we obtain the dynamics pictured in figure 9.19b. Now the ratio $\frac{x_S}{x_T}$ increases monotonically, and the dominated strategy is eliminated.

Nonconvergence of Evolutionary Dynamics

(a) RPS with a twin

(b) RPS with a feeble twin

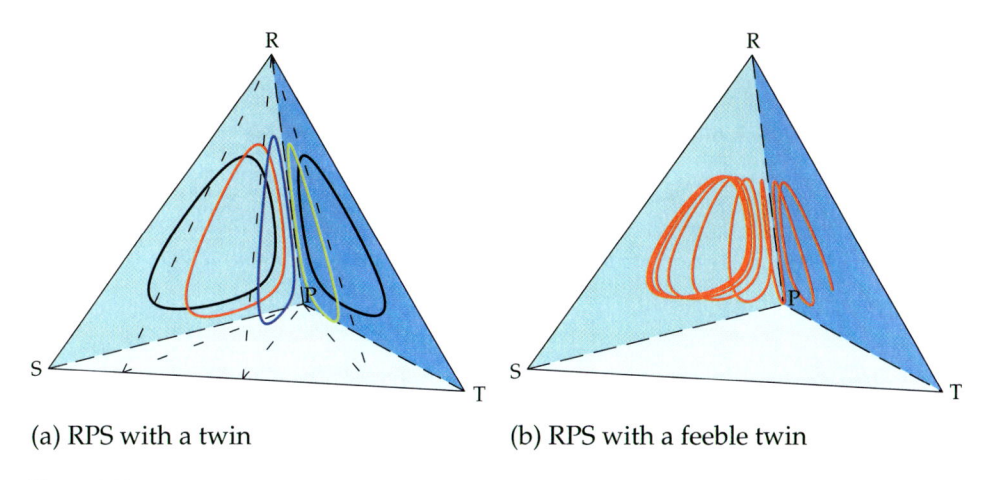

Figure 9.19
The replicator dynamic in two games.

The existence of a continuum of invariant hyperplanes under imitative dynamics in games with identical twins is crucial to this argument. At the same time, dynamics with a continuum of invariant hyperplanes are structurally unstable. If we fix the game but slightly alter the agents' revision protocol, these invariant sets can collapse, overturning the elimination result.

To make this argument concrete, suppose that instead of always following an imitative protocol, agents occasionally use a protocol based on the direct selection of candidate strategies. Such a situation is illustrated in figure 9.20a, which contains the phase diagram for bad RPS with a twin (with benefit of winning $w = 1$ and cost of losing $l = \frac{11}{10}$) under a $(\frac{9}{10}, \frac{1}{10})$ convex combination of the replicator and Smith dynamics. Whereas figure 9.19a displayed a continuum of invariant hyperplanes, figure 9.20a shows almost all solution trajectories converging to a limit cycle on the plane where $x_S = x_T$. If we make the twin feeble, the limit cycle moves slightly to the left, as in figure 9.20b, and the dominated strategy survives. ◆

Exercise 9.4.6 Show that an analogue of equation (7.39) holds for the projection dynamic on int(X). Explain why this does not imply that dominated strategies are eliminated along all solutions to the projection dynamic starting from interior initial conditions. ◇

Exercise 9.4.7 Section 7.4 showed that dominated strategies are eliminated under the best response dynamic. Explain intuitively why this result does not extend to perturbed best response dynamics, including the logit(η) dynamic with η small but positive. Using a computer, perform a numerical analysis of a well-chosen example to verify this intuition. ◇

(a) Bad RPS with a twin   (b) Bad RPS with a feeble twin

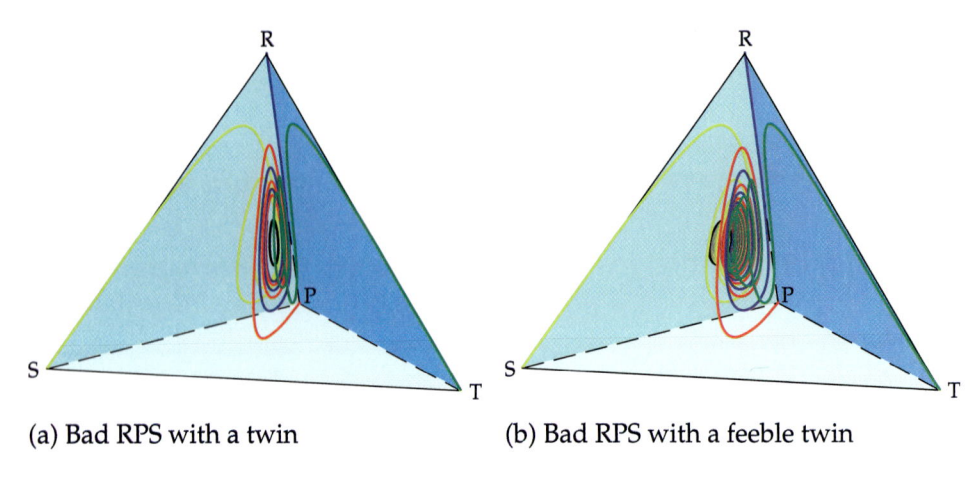

Figure 9.20
The $\frac{9}{10}$ replicator + $\frac{1}{10}$ Smith dynamic in two games.

9.A Appendix: Three Classical Theorems on Nonconvergent Dynamics

9.A.1 Liouville's Theorem

Let $V \colon \mathbf{R}^n \to \mathbf{R}^n$ be a C^1 vector field, and consider the differential equation $\dot{x} = V(x)$ with flow $\phi \colon \mathbf{R} \times \mathbf{R}^n \to \mathbf{R}^n$. Let the set $A \subset \mathbf{R}^n$ be measurable with respect to Lebesgue measure μ on $\mathbf{R}^n$. Liouville's theorem concerns the time evolution of $\mu(\phi_t(A))$, the measure (or *volume*) of the time t image of A under ϕ.

Theorem 9.A.1 Liouville's Theorem $\frac{d}{dt} \mu(\phi_t(A)) = \int_{\phi_t(A)} \operatorname{tr}(DV(x)) \, d\mu(x)$.

The quantity $\operatorname{tr}(DV(x)) = \sum_i \frac{\partial V_i}{\partial x_i}(x) \equiv \operatorname{div} V(x)$ is known as the *divergence* of V at x. According to Liouville's theorem, $\operatorname{div} V$ governs the local rates of change in volume under the flow ϕ of $\dot{x} = V(x)$. In particular, if $\operatorname{div} V = 0$ on an open set $O \subseteq \mathbf{R}^n$—that is, if V is *divergence-free* on this set—then the flow ϕ conserves volume on O.

Before proceeding with the proof of Liouville's theorem, we note that it extends immediately to cases in which the law of motion $V \colon X \to TX$ is defined on an affine set $X \subset \mathbf{R}^n$ with tangent space TX. In this case, μ represents Lebesgue measure on (the affine hull of) X. The only cautionary note is that the derivative of V at state $x \in X$ must be represented using the derivative matrix $DV(x) \in \mathbf{R}^{n \times n}$, which by definition has rows in TX. Section 3.B.3 showed how to compute this matrix: if $\hat{V} \colon \mathbf{R}^n \to \mathbf{R}^n$ is a C^1 extension of V, then $DV(x) = D\hat{V}(x) P_{TX}$, where $P_{TX} \in \mathbf{R}^{n \times n}$ is the orthogonal projection of $\mathbf{R}^n$ onto the subspace TX.

Nonconvergence of Evolutionary Dynamics

Proof Using the standard multivariate change of variable, express the measure of the set $\phi_t(A)$ as

$$\mu(\phi_t(A)) = \int_{\phi_t(A)} 1 \, d\mu(x_t) = \int_A \left| \det(D\phi_t(x_0)) \right| d\mu(x_0). \tag{9.17}$$

The derivative matrix $D\phi_t(x_0)$ in equation (9.17) captures changes in $\phi_t(x_0)$, the time t position of the solution to $\dot{x} = V(x)$ from initial condition x_0, as this initial condition is varied. It follows from arguments below that $\det(D\phi_t(x_0)) > 0$, so that the absolute value taken in equation (9.17) is unnecessary. Taking the time derivative of this equation and then differentiating under the integral sign thus yields

$$\frac{d}{dt} \mu(\phi_t(A)) = \int_A \frac{d}{dt} \det(D\phi_t(x_0)) \, d\mu(x_0). \tag{9.18}$$

Evaluating the right-hand side of equation (9.18) requires two lemmas. The first of these is stated in terms of the time-inhomogeneous linear equation

$$\dot{y}_t = DV(x_t) y_t, \tag{9.19}$$

where $\{x_t\}$ is the solution to $\dot{x} = V(x)$ from initial condition x_0. Equation (9.19) is known as the *(first) variation equation* associated with $\dot{x} = V(x)$.

Lemma 9.A.2 *The matrix trajectory $\{D\phi_t(x_0)\}_{t \geq 0}$ is the matrix solution to the first variation equation from initial condition $D\phi_0(x_0) = I \in \mathbf{R}^{n \times n}$. More explicitly,*

$$\frac{d}{dt} D\phi_t(x_0) = DV(\phi_t(x_0)) D\phi_t(x_0). \tag{9.20}$$

In other words, lemma 9.A.2 says that the column trajectories of $\{D\phi_t(x_0)\}_{t \geq 0}$ are the solutions to the first variation equation whose initial conditions are the standard basis vectors $e_1, \ldots, e_n \in \mathbf{R}^n$.

Proof By definition, the time derivative of the flow from x_0 satisfies $\frac{d}{dt} \phi_t(x_0) = V(\phi_t(x_0))$. Differentiating with respect to x_0 and then reversing the order of differentiation yields (9.20). ∎

Lemma 9.A.3 provides two basic matrix identities, the first of which is sometimes called *Liouville's formula*.

Lemma 9.A.3 *Let $M \in \mathbf{R}^{n \times n}$. Then*

i. $\det(\exp(M)) = \exp(\operatorname{tr}(M))$;
ii. $\frac{d}{dt} \det(\exp(Mt)) \big|_{t=0} = \operatorname{tr}(M)$.

Proving part (i) of the lemma is not difficult, but the intuition is clearest when M is a diagonal matrix:

$$\det\left(\exp\begin{pmatrix} \lambda_1 & \cdots & 0 \\ \vdots & \ddots & \vdots \\ 0 & \cdots & \lambda_n \end{pmatrix}\right) = \det\begin{pmatrix} e^{\lambda_1} & \cdots & 0 \\ \vdots & \ddots & \vdots \\ 0 & \cdots & e^{\lambda_n} \end{pmatrix} = \prod_i e^{\lambda_i} = \exp\left(\sum_i \lambda_i\right)$$

$$= \exp\left(\operatorname{tr}\begin{pmatrix} \lambda_1 & \cdots & 0 \\ \vdots & \ddots & \vdots \\ 0 & \cdots & \lambda_n \end{pmatrix}\right).$$

Part (ii) follows from part (i) by replacing M with Mt and differentiating.

Lemmas 9.A.2 and 9.A.3(ii) enable us to evaluate equation (9.18). First, note that lemma 9.A.2 and the linearity of the first variation equation imply that

$$D\phi_t(x_0) \approx \exp(DV(x_0)t)$$

when t is close to 0. Combining this observation with lemma 9.A.3(ii) shows that

$$\left.\frac{d}{dt}\det(D\phi_t(x_0)))\right|_{t=0} \approx \left.\frac{d}{dt}\det(\exp(DV(x_0)t))\right|_{t=0} = \operatorname{tr}(DV(x_0)).$$

By substituting this equality into equation (9.18) and noting that the focus on time $t = 0$ has been arbitrary, one obtains Liouville's theorem. ∎

Liouville's theorem can be used to prove the nonexistence of asymptotically stable sets. Since solutions in a neighborhood of such a set all approach the set, volume must be contracted in this neighborhood. It follows that a region in which divergence is non-negative cannot contain an asymptotically stable set.

Theorem 9.A.4 *Suppose* $\operatorname{div} V \geq 0$ *on the open set* $O \subseteq \mathbf{R}^n$, *and let* $A \subset O$ *be compact. Then* A *is not asymptotically stable under* $\dot{x} = V(x)$.

This theorem does not rule out the existence of Lyapunov stable sets. In fact, the example of the replicator dynamic in standard Rock-Paper-Scissors shows that such sets are not unusual when V is divergence-free.

9.A.2 The Poincaré-Bendixson and Bendixson-Dulac Theorems

We now present two classical results concerning differential equations on the plane.

The celebrated *Poincaré-Bendixson theorem* characterizes the possible long-run behaviors of such dynamics, and provides a simple way of establishing the existence of periodic orbits. Recall that a *periodic* (or *closed*) *orbit* of a differential equation is a nonconstant solution $\{x_t\}_{t \geq 0}$ such that $x_T = x_0$ for some $T > 0$.

Theorem 9.A.5 (The Poincaré-Bendixson Theorem) *Let* $V: \mathbf{R}^2 \to \mathbf{R}^2$ *be Lipschitz continuous, and consider the differential equation* $\dot{x} = V(x)$.

Nonconvergence of Evolutionary Dynamics

i. Let $x \in \mathbf{R}^2$. If $\omega(x)$ is compact, nonempty, and contains no rest points, then it is a periodic orbit.

ii. Let $Y \subset \mathbf{R}^2$. If Y is nonempty, compact, forward invariant, and contains no rest points, then it contains a periodic orbit.

Theorem 9.A.5 says that in planar systems, the only possible ω-limit sets are rest points, sequences of trajectories leading from one rest point to another (called *heteroclinic cycles* where there are multiple rest points in the sequence and *homoclinic orbits* when there is just one), and *periodic orbits*. In part (i) of the theorem, the requirement that $\omega(x)$ be compact and nonempty is automatically satisfied when the dynamic is forward invariant on a compact set (see proposition 7.A.1).

The next result, the *Bendixson-Dulac theorem*, provides a method of ruling out the existence of closed orbits in planar systems. To state this theorem, recall that a set $Y \subset \mathbf{R}^2$ is *simply connected* if it contains no holes: more precisely, if every closed curve in Y can be continuously contracted within Y to a single point.

Theorem 9.A.6 (The Bendixson-Dulac Theorem) *Let $V \colon \mathbf{R}^2 \to \mathbf{R}^2$ be C^1, and consider the differential equation $\dot{x} = V(x)$. If $\operatorname{div} V \neq 0$ throughout the simply connected set Y, then Y does not contain a closed orbit.*

Proof If γ is a closed orbit in Y, then the region R bounded by γ is invariant under ϕ. Thus

$$\frac{\mathrm{d}}{\mathrm{d}t} \mu(\phi_t(R)) = \int_{\phi_t(R)} \operatorname{div} V(x) \, \mathrm{d}\mu(x)$$

by Liouville's theorem. Since $\operatorname{div} V$ is continuous and nonzero throughout Y, its sign must be constant throughout Y. If this sign is negative, then the volume of R contracts under ϕ; if it is positive, then the volume of R expands under ϕ. Either conclusion contradicts the invariance of R under ϕ. ∎

Both results above extend to dynamics defined on two-dimensional affine spaces in the obvious way.

9.B Appendix: Attractors and Continuation

9.B.1 Attractors and Repellors

Let ϕ be a *semiflow* on the compact set $X \subset \mathbf{R}^n$, that is, $\phi \colon [0, \infty) \times X \to X$ is a continuous map with $\phi_0(x) = x$ that satisfies the group property $\phi_t(\phi_s(x)) = \phi_{s+t}(x)$ for all $s, t \geq 0$ and $x \in X$. Call the set $\mathcal{A} \subseteq X$ *forward invariant* under ϕ if $\phi_t(\mathcal{A}) \subseteq \mathcal{A}$ for all $t \geq 0$. One can verify that in this case, the sets $\{\phi_t(\mathcal{A})\}_{t \geq 0}$ are nested. Call $\mathcal{A}$ *invariant* under ϕ if $\phi_t(\mathcal{A}) = \mathcal{A}$ for all $t \in \mathbf{R}$. It is implicit in this definition that on the set $\mathcal{A}$ there is not only a semiflow but also a *flow*: on $\mathcal{A}$, the map ϕ can be extended to be well-defined and to satisfy the group property not just for times in $[0, \infty)$ but also for times in $(-\infty, \infty)$.

A set $\mathcal{A} \subseteq X$ is an *attractor* of ϕ if it is nonempty, compact, and invariant under ϕ, and if there is a neighborhood U of $\mathcal{A}$ such that

$$\lim_{t\to\infty} \sup_{x\in U} \mathrm{dist}(\phi_t(x), \mathcal{A}) = 0. \tag{9.21}$$

The set $B(\mathcal{A}) = \{x \in X : \omega(x) \subseteq \mathcal{A}\}$ is called the *basin* of $\mathcal{A}$.

The supremum operation in condition (9.21) ensures that states in the neighborhood U are attracted to $\mathcal{A}$ uniformly in time. This uniformity is important; without it, the rest point in the flow on the circle from example 7.A.2 would be an attractor. Because of the uniformity requirement, attractors differ from asymptotically stable sets (defined in section 7.A.2) only in that the latter need not be invariant.

Attractors can be defined in a number of equivalent ways. In the following proposition, the ω-limit of the set $U \subseteq X$ is defined as

$$\omega(U) = \bigcap_{t \geq 0} \mathrm{cl}\left(\bigcup_{s \geq t} \phi_s(U)\right).$$

Proposition 9.B.1 *The following statements are equivalent:*

i. $\mathcal{A}$ is an attractor of ϕ.

ii. $\mathcal{A} = \omega(U)$ for some neighborhood U of $\mathcal{A}$.

iii. $\mathcal{A} = \bigcap_{t \geq 0} \phi_t(O)$ for some open set O that satisfies $\phi_T(\mathrm{cl}(O)) \subset O$ for some $T > 0$.

iv. $\mathcal{A} = \bigcap_{t \geq 0} \phi_t(O)$ for some open, forward invariant set O that satisfies $\phi_T(\mathrm{cl}(O)) \subset O$ for some $T > 0$.

v. $\mathcal{A} = \bigcap_{t \geq 0} \phi_t(O)$ for some open, forward invariant set O that satisfies $\phi_t(\mathrm{cl}(O)) \subset O$ for all $t > 0$.

In parts (iii), (iv), and (v), the set O is known as a *weak trapping region*, a *trapping region*, and a *strongly forward invariant trapping region*, respectively.

Now suppose that $\phi \colon (-\infty, \infty) \times X \to X$ is a flow on X with attractor $\mathcal{A}$, and let U be a trapping region for $\mathcal{A}$. The set $\mathcal{A}^* = \bigcap_{t \leq 0} \phi_t(X - U)$ is known as the *dual repellor* of $\mathcal{A}$. $\mathcal{A}^*$ is the α-*limit* of a neighborhood of itself (i.e., it is the ω-limit of a neighborhood of itself under the time-reversed version of ϕ); it is also nonempty, compact, and invariant under ϕ.

The set $C(\mathcal{A}, \mathcal{A}^*) = X - (\mathcal{A} \cup \mathcal{A}^*)$ is called the *set of connecting orbits* of the attractor-repellor pair $(\mathcal{A}, \mathcal{A}^*)$. Theorem 9.B.2 shows that the behavior of the flow on this set is simple: it admits a strict Lyapunov function.

Nonconvergence of Evolutionary Dynamics

Theorem 9.B.2 *Let $(\mathcal{A}, \mathcal{A}^*)$ be an attractor-repellor pair of the flow ϕ on the compact set X. Then there exists a continuous function L: $X \to [0, 1]$ with $L^{-1}(1) = \mathcal{A}^*$ and $L^{-1}(0) = \mathcal{A}$ such that L is decreasing on $C(\mathcal{A}, \mathcal{A}^*)$ under ϕ.*

If ϕ is only a semiflow, one can still find a continuous Lyapunov function L: $X \to [0, 1]$ with $L^{-1}(0) = \mathcal{A}$ that is decreasing on $C(\mathcal{A}, \mathcal{A}^*)$.

Interestingly, the notion of chain recurrence introduced in section 7.A.1 can be characterized in terms of attractor-repellor pairs. In particular, the set $C\mathcal{R}$ of chain recurrent states of the flow ϕ consists of those states found in every attractor-repellor pair of ϕ:

Theorem 9.B.3 $C\mathcal{R} = \bigcap_{(\mathcal{A}, \mathcal{A}^*)} (\mathcal{A} \cup \mathcal{A}^*)$.

By combining theorems 9.B.2 and 9.B.3 with the fact that the number of attractor-repellor pairs of ϕ is countable, one can establish the *fundamental theorem of dynamical systems*.

Theorem 9.B.4 *Let ϕ be a flow on a compact metric space X. Then ϕ admits a Lyapunov function L: $X \to \mathbf{R}$ that is decreasing off $C\mathcal{R}$ and such that $L(C\mathcal{R})$ is a nowhere dense subset of $\mathbf{R}$.*

9.B.2 Continuation of Attractors

Consider now a one-parameter family of differential equations $\dot{x} = V^\varepsilon(x)$ in $\mathbf{R}^n$ with unique solutions $x_t = \phi_t^\varepsilon(x_0)$ such that $(\varepsilon, x) \mapsto V^\varepsilon(x)$ is continuous. Then $(\varepsilon, t, x) \mapsto \phi_t^\varepsilon(x)$ is continuous as well. Suppose that $X \subset \mathbf{R}^n$ is compact and forward invariant under the flows ϕ^ε. For $\varepsilon = 0$, we omit the superscript in ϕ.

Roughly speaking, Theorem 9.B.5 shows that each attractor of the differential equation $\dot{x} = V^0(x)$ will survive any small enough perturbation of the differential equation.

Theorem 9.B.5 *Let $\mathcal{A}$ be an attractor for ϕ with basin $B(\mathcal{A})$. Then for each small enough $\varepsilon > 0$ there exists an attractor $\mathcal{A}^\varepsilon$ of ϕ^ε with basin $B(\mathcal{A}^\varepsilon)$, such that the map $\varepsilon \mapsto \mathcal{A}^\varepsilon$ is upper-hemicontinuous and the map $\varepsilon \mapsto B(\mathcal{A}^\varepsilon)$ is lower-hemicontinuous.*

Upper-hemicontinuity cannot be replaced by continuity in this result. Consider the family of differential equations $\dot{x} = (\varepsilon + x^2)(1 - x)$ on the real line. The flow ϕ corresponding to $\varepsilon = 0$ admits $\mathcal{A} = [0, 1]$ as an attractor, but when $\varepsilon > 0$ the unique attractor of ϕ^ε is $\mathcal{A}^\varepsilon = \{1\}$. This example shows that perturbations can cause attractors to implode; the theorem shows that perturbations cannot cause attractors to explode.

Theorem 9.B.5 is a direct consequence of the following lemma.

Lemma 9.B.6 *Let $\mathcal{A}$ be an attractor for ϕ with basin $B(\mathcal{A})$, and let U_1 and U_2 be open sets satisfying $\mathcal{A} \subset U_1 \subseteq U_2 \subseteq \mathrm{cl}(U_2) \subseteq B(\mathcal{A})$. Then for each small enough $\varepsilon > 0$ there exists an attractor $\mathcal{A}^\varepsilon$ of ϕ_ε with basin $B(\mathcal{A}^\varepsilon)$, such that $\mathcal{A}^\varepsilon \subset U_1$ and $U_2 \subset B(\mathcal{A}^\varepsilon)$.*

In this lemma, one can always set $U_1 = \{x: \mathrm{dist}(x,\mathcal{A}) < \delta\}$ and $U_2 = \{x \in B(\mathcal{A}): \mathrm{dist}(x, X - B(\mathcal{A})) > \delta\}$ for some small enough $\delta > 0$.

Proof of lemma 9.B.6 Since $\mathcal{A}$ is an attractor and $\omega(\mathrm{cl}(U_2)) = \mathcal{A}$, there is a $T > 0$ such that $\phi_t(\mathrm{cl}(U_2)) \subset U_1$ for $t \geq T$. By the continuous dependence of the flow on the parameter ε and the compactness of $\phi_T(\mathrm{cl}(U_2))$, we have that $\phi_T^\varepsilon(\mathrm{cl}(U_2)) \subset U_1 \subseteq U_2$ for all small enough ε. Thus, U_2 is a weak trapping region for the semi-flow ϕ^ε, and so $\mathcal{A}^\varepsilon \equiv \omega(U_2)$ is an attractor for ϕ^ε. In addition, $\mathcal{A}^\varepsilon \subset U_1$ (since $\mathcal{A}^\varepsilon = \phi_T^\varepsilon(\mathcal{A}^\varepsilon) \subseteq \phi_T^\varepsilon(\mathrm{cl}(U_2)) \subset U_1$) and $U_2 \subset B(\mathcal{A}^\varepsilon)$. ∎

Notes

Section 9.1
The conservative properties of dynamics studied in this chapter—the existence of a constant of motion and the preservation of volume—are basic properties of Hamiltonian systems. For more on this connection, see Akin and Losert (1984) and Hofbauer (1995a; 1996); for a general introduction to Hamiltonian systems, see Marsden and Ratiu (2002). Exercises 9.1.2 and 9.1.3 are due to Schuster et al. (1981a; 1981b). Theorem 9.1.5 is due to Akin and Losert (1984) and Hofbauer (1995a), and theorem 9.1.6 is due to Hofbauer and Sigmund (1988) and Ritzberger and Weibull (1995); also see Weibull (1995).

Section 9.2
Circulant games were introduced by Hofbauer and Sigmund (1988), who called them "cyclically symmetric games"; also see Schuster et al. (1981b). The hypercycle system was proposed by Eigen and Schuster (1979) to model cyclical catalysis in a collection of polynucleotides during prebiotic evolution. Schuster, Sigmund, and Wolff (1979) introduced the term *permanent* to describe dynamics on the simplex under which the boundary is a repellor. The permanence of the hypercycle system when $n \geq 5$ was established by Hofbauer, Schuster, and Sigmund (1981); the existence of stable limit cycles in this context was proved by Hofbauer, Mallet-Paret, and Smith (1991). For further results on permanence under the replicator and related dynamics, see Hofbauer (1981a), Hutson (1984), Hofbauer and Sigmund (1988), Hutson and Schmitt (1992), Schreiber (2000), and Garay and Hofbauer (2003).

Monocyclic games were studied in the context of the replicator dynamic by Hofbauer and Sigmund (1988), who call them "essentially hypercyclic" games. The uniqueness of the interior Nash equilibrium in example 9.2.2 follows from the fact that the replicator dynamic for this game is permanent; see Hofbauer and Sigmund (1988). The analysis of the best response dynamic in this example is due to Hofbauer (1995b), Gaunersdorfer and Hofbauer (1995), and Benaïm, Hofbauer, and Hopkins (2009). Proposition 9.2.5 is due to Hofbauer and Swinkels (1996); also see Hofbauer and Sigmund (1998, sec. 8.6).

The Mismatching Pennies game was introduced by Jordan (1993) and was inspired by a 3×3 example due to Shapley (1964); see Sparrow, van Strien, and Harris (2008) and van Strien and Sparrow (2009) for recent analyses that identify chaotic behavior in Shapley's (1964) example. The analyses of the replicator and best response dynamics in Mismatching Pennies are due to Gaunersdorfer and Hofbauer (1995). Proposition 9.2.7 is due to Hart and Mas-Colell (2003). The hypnodisk game was introduced in Hofbauer and Sandholm (2010). Viossat (2007; 2008) constructed examples in which all pure strategies used in correlated equilibria vanish along some (nonconvergent) solution trajectories of various dynamics.

Nonconvergence of Evolutionary Dynamics

Section 9.3
For introductions to chaotic differential equations, see Hirsch, Smale, and Devaney (2004) at the undergraduate level or Guckenheimer and Holmes (1983) at the graduate level. Example 9.3.1 is due to Arneodo, Coullet, and Tresser (1980), who introduced it in the context of the Lotka-Volterra equations; also see Schnabl et al. (1991) and Skyrms (1992). The attractor in this example is known as a Shilnikov attractor; see Hirsch, Smale, and Devaney (2004) or Guckenheimer and Holmes (1983). Example 9.3.2 is due to Sato, Akiyama, and Farmer (2002). An early analysis of chaotic behavior under the best response dynamic is Cowan (1992); see Sparrow, van Strien, and Harris (2008), van Strien and Sparrow (2009), and van Strien (2009) for more recent analyses.

Section 9.4
This section follows Hofbauer and Sandholm (2010), who built on the work of Berger and Hofbauer (2006); the latter showed that strictly dominated strategies can survive under the BNN dynamic. For a survival result for the projection dynamic, see Sandholm, Dokumacı, and Lahkar (2008).

Appendix 9.A
For further details on Liouville's theorem, see Hartman (1964, secs. 4.1, 5.3). Theorem 9.A.4 in the text is from Weibull (1995, prop. 6.6). For treatments of the Poincaré-Bendixson theorem, see Hirsch and Smale (1974) and Robinson (1995).

Appendix 9.B
The definition of attractor in the text is from Benaïm (1999). Definition (ii) in proposition 9.B.1 is from Conley (1978), and definitions (iii), (iv), and (v) are from Robinson (1995). Theorems 9.B.2, 9.B.3, and 9.B.4 are due to Conley (1978).

Theorem 9.B.5 is part of the folklore of dynamical systems theory; compare Smale (1967, prop. 8.1). The analysis presented here is from Hofbauer and Sandholm (2010).

IV Stochastic Evolutionary Models

10 Stochastic Evolution and Deterministic Approximation

In Parts II and III of this book, we investigated the evolution of aggregate behavior under deterministic dynamics. We provided foundations for these dynamics in chapter 4. There we showed that any revision protocol ρ and population game F define a mean dynamic $\dot{x} = V_F(x)$, a differential equation that describes expected motion under the stochastic process implicitly defined by ρ and F. The focus on this deterministic equation was justified by an informal appeal to a law of large numbers; since all randomness in the evolutionary model is idiosyncratic, it should be averaged away in the aggregate as long as the population size is sufficiently large.

The goal in this chapter is to make this argument rigorous. To do so, we explicitly derive a stochastic evolutionary process—a Markov process—from a given population game F, revision protocol ρ, and finite population size N. The main result in this chapter, theorem 10.2.3, is a finite-horizon deterministic approximation theorem. The theorem shows that over any finite time span, the behavior of the stochastic evolutionary process is indeed nearly deterministic. If the population size is large enough, the stochastic process closely follows a solution trajectory of the mean dynamic with probability close to 1.

The Markov process provides a precise description of the stochastic evolution of aggregate behavior. Theorem 10.2.3 says that over moderate time spans one does not need to study the Markov process directly, as the deterministic approximation is adequate to address most questions of interest. But if one wants to understand behavior in a society over very long time spans, then the deterministic approximation theorem no longer applies, and one must study the Markov process itself. This infinite-horizon analysis is the subject of chapters 11 and 12.

Chapter 10–12 employ a variety of techniques from the theory of probability and stochastic processes, which are reviewed in the chapter appendices. These chapters consider only single-population models; the results can be extended to multipopulation models with little difficulty.

10.1 The Stochastic Evolutionary Process

Recall the model of stochastic evolution introduced in section 4.1. It considers a population of agents who recurrently play a population game $F: X \to \mathbf{R}^n$ with pure strategy set $S = \{1, \ldots, n\}$. The agents' choice procedure is described by a revision protocol $\rho: \mathbf{R}^n \times X \to \mathbf{R}_+^{n \times n}$ that takes current payoffs and population states as inputs and returns collections of conditional switch rates $\rho_{ij}(F(x), x)$ as outputs.

To set the stage for our limiting analysis, suppose that the population size is large but finite, with N members. The feasible social states therefore lie in the discrete grid $X^N = X \cap \frac{1}{N}\mathbf{Z}^n = \{x \in X : Nx \in \mathbf{Z}^n\}$.

Exercise 10.1.1 Show that X^N has cardinality $\binom{N+n-1}{n-1}$. (*Hint*: Use induction on the number of strategies n.) ◇

The stochastic process $\{X_t^N\}$ generated by F, ρ, and N is described as follows. Each agent in the society is equipped with a rate R Poisson alarm clock, where $R < \infty$ satisfies

$$R \geq \max_{x,i} \sum_{j \neq i} \rho_{ij}(F(x), x). \tag{10.1}$$

(Subject to satisfying this constraint, the choice of R is irrelevant to the approximation results.)

The ringing of a clock signals the arrival of a revision opportunity for the clock's owner. If the owner is currently playing strategy $i \in S$, he switches to strategy $j \neq i$ with probability ρ_{ij}/R. (Remember that the diagonal elements of ρ, although sometimes useful as placeholders (see equation (4.1)), play no formal role in the model.) Finally, the model respects independence assumptions that ensure that the future is independent of the past except through the present: different agents' clocks ring independently of one another, strategy choices are made independently of the timing of the clocks' rings, and as evolution proceeds, the clocks and the agents are only influenced by the history of the process by way of the current value of the social state.

In Chapter 4, we argued informally that this stochastic process is well approximated by solutions to the mean dynamic

$$\dot{x}_i = \sum_{j \in S} x_j \rho_{ji}(F(x), x) - x_i \sum_{j \in S} \rho_{ij}(F(x), x). \tag{M}$$

The rest of this chapter provides a formal defense of this approximation result.

Stochastic Evolution and Deterministic Approximation

We begin a more formal account of the stochastic evolutionary process $\{X_t^N\}$. The independence assumptions ensure that $\{X_t^N\}$ is a continuous-time Markov process on the finite state space $\mathcal{X}^N$. To describe this process explicitly, it is enough to specify its jump rates $\{\lambda_x^N\}_{x \in \mathcal{X}^N}$ and transition probabilities $\{P_{xy}^N\}_{x,y \in \mathcal{X}^N}$ (see appendix 10.C).

If the current social state is $x \in \mathcal{X}^N$, then Nx_i of the N agents are playing strategy $i \in S$. Since agents receive revision opportunities independently at exponential rate R, the basic properties of the exponential distribution (see proposition 10.A.1) imply that revision opportunities arrive in the society as a whole at exponential rate NR.

When an agent playing strategy $i \in S$ receives a revision opportunity, he switches to strategy $j \neq i$ with probability ρ_{ij}/R. Since this choice is independent of the arrivals of revision opportunities, the probability that the next revision opportunity goes to an agent playing strategy i who then switches to strategy j is

$$\frac{Nx_i}{N} \times \frac{\rho_{ij}}{R} = \frac{x_i \rho_{ij}}{R}.$$

This switch decreases the number of agents playing strategy i by 1 and increases the number playing j by 1, shifting the state by $\frac{1}{N}(e_j - e_i)$.

Summarizing this analysis yields the following observation, which specifies the parameters of the Markov process $\{X_t^N\}$.

Observation 10.1.2 *A population game F, a revision protocol ρ, a constant R satisfying (10.1), and a population size N define a Markov process $\{X_t^N\}$ on the state space $\mathcal{X}^N$. This process is described by some initial state $X_0^N = x_0^N$, the jump rates $\lambda_x^N = NR$, and the transition probabilities*

$$P_{x,x+z}^N = \begin{cases} \dfrac{x_i \rho_{ij}(F(x), x)}{R} & \text{if } z = \frac{1}{N}(e_j - e_i),\ i, j \in S,\ i \neq j, \\ 1 - \sum_{i \in S} \sum_{j \neq i} \dfrac{x_i \rho_{ij}(F(x), x)}{R} & \text{if } z = \mathbf{0}, \\ 0 & \text{otherwise.} \end{cases}$$

10.2 Finite-Horizon Deterministic Approximation

The previous section formally defined the Markov process $\{X_t^N\}$ generated by a population game F, a revision protocol ρ, and a population size N. Chapter 4 described the mean dynamic (M), an ordinary differential equation that captures the expected motion of this process; solutions $\{x_t\}$ of (M) are continuous paths through the set of social states. Can one say more precisely how the stochastic and deterministic processes are linked?

Theorem 10.2.3, the main result in this chapter, shows that when the population size N is sufficiently large, the Markov process $\{X_t^N\}$ is well approximated over finite time spans by the deterministic trajectory $\{x_t\}$.

10.2.1 Kurtz's Theorem

To begin, we state a general result on the convergence of a sequence $\{\{X_t^N\}\}_{N=N_0}^{\infty}$ of Markov processes with decreasing step sizes. Suppose that the process indexed by N takes values in the state space $\mathcal{X}^N = \{x \in X : Nx \in \mathbf{Z}^n\}$, and let $\lambda^N \in \mathbf{R}_+^{\mathcal{X}^N}$ and $P^N \in \mathbf{R}_+^{\mathcal{X}^N \times \mathcal{X}^N}$ denote the jump rate vector and transition matrix of this process.

To simplify the definitions to follow, let ζ_x^N be a random variable (defined on an arbitrary probability space) whose distribution describes the stochastic increment of $\{X_t^N\}$ from state x:

$$\mathbb{P}(\zeta_x^N = z) = P_{x,x+z}^N \tag{10.2}$$

Then define the functions $V^N : \mathcal{X}^N \to TX$, $A^N : \mathcal{X}^N \to \mathbf{R}$, and $A_\delta^N : \mathcal{X}^N \to \mathbf{R}$ by

$$V^N(x) = \lambda_x^N \, \mathbb{E}\zeta_x^N,$$

$$A^N(x) = \lambda_x^N \, \mathbb{E}\left|\zeta_x^N\right|,$$

$$A_\delta^N(x) = \lambda_x^N \, \mathbb{E}\left|\zeta_x^N \, \mathbf{1}_{\{|\zeta_x^N| > \delta\}}\right|.$$

$V^N(x)$, the product of the jump rate at state x and the expected increment per jump at x, represents the expected increment per time unit from x under $\{X_t^N\}$. V^N is thus an alternative definition of the mean dynamic of $\{X_t^N\}$. In a similar vein, $A^N(x)$ is the expected absolute displacement per time unit, and $A_\delta^N(x)$ is the expected absolute displacement per time unit due to jumps traveling further than δ.

With these definitions in hand, we can state the basic approximation result.

Theorem 10.2.1 (Kurtz's Theorem) *Let $V : X \to TX$ be a Lipschitz continuous vector field. Suppose that for some sequence $\{\delta^N\}_{N=N_0}^{\infty}$ converging to 0,*

$$\lim_{N \to \infty} \sup_{x \in \mathcal{X}^N} \left|V^N(x) - V(x)\right| = 0, \tag{10.3}$$

$$\sup_N \sup_{x \in \mathcal{X}^N} A^N(x) < \infty, \tag{10.4}$$

$$\lim_{N \to \infty} \sup_{x \in \mathcal{X}^N} A_{\delta^N}^N(x) = 0, \tag{10.5}$$

and suppose that the initial conditions $X_0^N = x_0^N$ converge to $x_0 \in X$. Let $\{x_t\}_{t \geq 0}$ be the solution to the mean dynamic

$$\dot{x} = V(x) \tag{M}$$

starting from x_0. Then for each $T < \infty$ and $\varepsilon > 0$,

$$\lim_{N \to \infty} \mathbb{P}\left(\sup_{t \in [0,T]} |X_t^N - x_t| < \varepsilon\right) = 1.$$

Fix a finite time horizon $T < \infty$ and an error bound $\varepsilon > 0$. Kurtz's theorem says that when the index N is large, nearly all sample paths of the Markov process $\{X_t^N\}$ stay within ε of a solution of the mean dynamic (M) through time T. Thus if N is large enough, then with probability close to 1, X_t^N and x_t differ by no more than ε for all t between 0 and T (figure 10.1).

What conditions are needed to reach this conclusion? Condition (10.3) demands that as N grows large, the expected displacements per time unit V^N converge uniformly to a Lipschitz continuous vector field V. Lipschitz continuity of V ensures the existence and uniqueness of solutions of the mean dynamic $\dot{x} = V(x)$. Condition

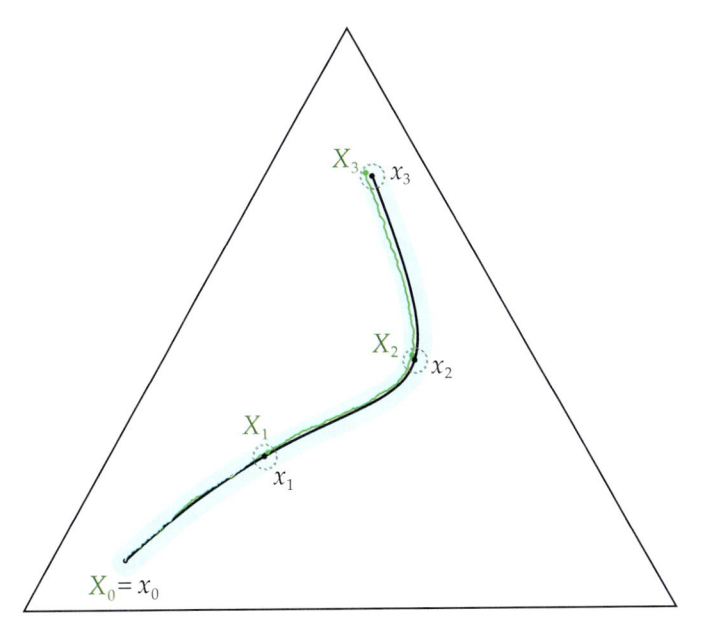

Figure 10.1
Kurtz's theorem.

(10.4) requires that the expected absolute displacement per time unit is bounded. Finally, condition (10.5) demands that jumps larger than δ^N make vanishing contributions to the motion of the processes, where $\{\delta^N\}_{N=N_0}^{\infty}$ is a sequence of constants that approaches zero.

The intuition behind Kurtz's theorem can be explained as follows. At each revision opportunity, the increment in the process $\{X_t^N\}$ is stochastic. However, the expected number of revision opportunities that arrive during the brief time interval $I = [t, t+dt]$ is of order $\lambda_x^N\, dt$. Whenever it does not vanish, this quantity grows without bound as the population size N becomes large. Conditions (10.4) and (10.5) ensure that when N is large, each increment in the state is likely to be small. This ensures that the total change in the state during time interval I is small, so that jump rates and transition probabilities vary little during this interval. Since during I there are a very large number of revision opportunities, each generating nearly the same expected increment, intuition from the law of large numbers suggests that the change in $\{X_t^N\}$ during the interval should be almost completely determined by the expected motion of $\{X_t^N\}$. This expected motion is captured by the limiting mean dynamic V, whose solutions approximate the stochastic process $\{X_t^N\}$ over finite time spans with probability close to 1.

Exercise 10.2.2 Suppose that $\{X_t^N\}$ is a Markov process on $\mathcal{X}^N = \{0, \frac{1}{N}, \frac{2}{N}, \ldots, 1\}$ with $\lambda_x^N \equiv N$. To ensure that $\frac{1}{2}$ is always a state, restrict attention to even N. Give examples of sequences of transition probabilities from state $\frac{1}{2}$ that

i. satisfy condition (10.3) of Kurtz's theorem but not conditions (10.4) or (10.5);

ii. satisfy conditions (10.3) and (10.5) but not condition (10.4);

iii. satisfy conditions (10.3) and (10.4) but not condition (10.5).

(*Hint:* It is enough to consider transition probabilities under which $V^N(\frac{1}{2}) = 0$.) Guided by your answers to parts (ii) and (iii), explain intuitively what conditions (10.4) and (10.5) require. ◇

10.2.2 Deterministic Approximation of the Stochastic Evolutionary Process

We now use Kurtz's theorem to show that the Markov processes $\{\{X_t^N\}\}_{N=N_0}^{\infty}$ defined in section 10.1 can be approximated by solutions to the mean dynamic (M) derived in section 4.2.1.

To begin, we compute the expected increment per time unit $V^N(x)$ of the process $\{X_t^N\}$. Defining the random variable ζ_x^N as in equation (10.2), we have

$$V^N(x) = \lambda_x^N \, \mathbb{E}\zeta_x^N$$

$$= NR \sum_{i \in S} \sum_{j \neq i} \frac{1}{N}(e_j - e_i) \, \mathbb{P}\left(\zeta_x^N = \frac{1}{N}(e_j - e_i)\right)$$

$$= NR \sum_{i \in S} \sum_{j \neq i} \frac{1}{N}(e_j - e_i) \frac{x_i \rho_{ij}}{R}$$

$$= \sum_{i \in S} \sum_{j \in S} (e_j - e_i) x_i \rho_{ij}$$

$$= \sum_{j \in S} e_j \sum_{i \in S} x_i \rho_{ij} - \sum_{i \in S} e_i x_i \sum_{j \in S} \rho_{ij}$$

$$= \sum_{i \in S} e_i \left(\sum_{j \in S} x_j \rho_{ji} - x_i \sum_{j \in S} \rho_{ij} \right).$$

Thus, the vector field $V^N = V$ is independent of N and is expressed more concisely as

$$V_i(x) = \sum_{j \in S} x_j \rho_{ji} - x_i \sum_{j \in S} \rho_{ij}, \tag{M}$$

as we established using a different calculation in section 4.2.1.

Conditions (10.4) and (10.5) of Kurtz's theorem require that the motions of the processes $\{X_t^N\}$ not be too abrupt. To verify these conditions, observe that since $|e_j - e_i| = \sqrt{2}$ for any distinct $i, j \in S^p$, the increments of $\{X_t^N\}$ are always either of length $\frac{\sqrt{2}}{N}$ or of length zero. If we set $\delta^N = \frac{\sqrt{2}}{N}$, this observation immediately implies condition (10.5):

$$A^N_{\frac{\sqrt{2}}{N}}(x) = \lambda_x^N \, \mathbb{E}\left|\zeta_x^N \, \mathbf{1}_{\left\{|\zeta_x^N| > \frac{\sqrt{2}}{N}\right\}}\right| = 0.$$

The observation also helps verify condition (10.4):

$$A^N(x) = \lambda_x^N \, \mathbb{E}\left|\zeta_x^N\right| \leq RN \times \frac{\sqrt{2}}{N} = \sqrt{2}R.$$

These calculations establish theorem 10.2.3, the finite-horizon deterministic approximation theorem.

Theorem 10.2.3 (Deterministic Approximation of $\{X_t^N\}$) *Let $\{\{X_t^N\}\}_{N=N_0}^{\infty}$ be the sequence of stochastic evolutionary processes defined in observation 10.1.2. Suppose that*

$V = V^N$ is Lipschitz continuous. Let the initial conditions $X_0^N = x_0^N$ converge to state $x_0 \in X$, and let $\{x_t\}_{t \geq 0}$ be the solution to the mean dynamic (M) starting from x_0. Then for all $T < \infty$ and $\varepsilon > 0$,

$$\lim_{N \to \infty} \mathbb{P}\left(\sup_{t \in [0,T]} |X_t^N - x_t| < \varepsilon \right) = 1.$$

Choose a finite time span T and two small constants δ and ε. Then for all large enough population sizes N, the probability that the process $\{X_t^N\}$ stays within ε of the deterministic trajectory $\{x_t\}$ through time T is at least $1 - \delta$.

A key requirement of theorem 10.2.3 is that V must be Lipschitz continuous, ensuring that the mean dynamic (M) admits a unique solution from every initial condition in X. This requirement is satisfied by members of the families of imitative, excess payoff, pairwise comparison, and perturbed best response dynamics (see chapters 5–6). The best response and projection dynamics, being discontinuous, are not covered by theorem 10.2.3, but deterministic approximation results that apply to these dynamics are also available (see the chapter notes).

It is well worth emphasizing that theorem 10.2.3 is a *finite-horizon* approximation result. It cannot be extended to an infinite-horizon result. To see why not, consider the logit choice protocol (example 4.3.3). Under this protocol, switches between all pairs of strategies occur with positive probability regardless of the current state. It follows that the induced Markov process $\{X_t^N\}$ is *irreducible*: there is a positive probability path between each ordered pair of states in $\mathcal{X}^N$. Irreducibility implies that every state in $\mathcal{X}^N$ is visited infinitely often with probability 1 (see chapter 11). This fact clearly precludes an infinite-horizon analogue of theorem 10.2.3. Indeed, infinite-horizon analysis of $\{X_t^N\}$ requires a different set of tools, which we develop in the next two chapters.

Example 10.2.1: Toss and Switch   Suppose that agents play a game with strategy set $S = \{L, R\}$ using the constant revision protocol ρ, where $\rho_{LL} = \rho_{LR} = \rho_{RL} = \rho_{RR} = \frac{1}{2}$. Under the simplest interpretation of this protocol, each agent receives revision opportunities at rate 1; upon receiving an opportunity, an agent flips a fair coin, switching strategies if the coin comes up Heads.

For each population size N, the protocol generates a Markov process $\{X_t^N\}$ with common jump rate $\lambda_x^N \equiv N$ and transition probabilities

$$P_{x,x+z}^N = \begin{cases} \frac{1}{2} x_R & \text{if } z = \frac{1}{N}(e_L - e_R), \\ \frac{1}{2} x_L & \text{if } z = \frac{1}{N}(e_R - e_L), \\ \frac{1}{2} & \text{if } z = \mathbf{0}. \end{cases}$$

Stochastic Evolution and Deterministic Approximation

The notation can be simplified by replacing the vector state variable $x = (x_L, x_R) \in X$ with the scalar state variable $x = x_R \in [0, 1]$. The resulting Markov process has common jump rate $\lambda_x^N \equiv N$ and transition probabilities

$$P_{x,x+z}^N = \begin{cases} \frac{1}{2}x & \text{if } z = -\frac{1}{N}, \\ \frac{1}{2}(1-x) & \text{if } z = \frac{1}{N}, \\ \frac{1}{2} & \text{if } z = 0. \end{cases}$$

Its mean dynamic is thus

$$V^N(x) = \lambda_x^N \, \mathbb{E}\zeta_x^N$$

$$= N\left(\left(-\tfrac{1}{N} \cdot \tfrac{1}{2}x\right) + \left(\tfrac{1}{N} \cdot \tfrac{1}{2}(1-x)\right)\right)$$

$$= \tfrac{1}{2} - x,$$

regardless of the population size N. To solve this differential equation, move the rest point $y = \frac{1}{2}$ to the origin using change of variable $v = x - \frac{1}{2}$. The equation

$$\dot{v} = \dot{x} = \tfrac{1}{2} - x = \tfrac{1}{2} - (v + \tfrac{1}{2}) = -v$$

has the general solution $v_t = v_0 \, e^{-t}$, implying that

$$x_t = \tfrac{1}{2} + (x_0 - \tfrac{1}{2}) e^{-t}.$$

Fix a time horizon $T < \infty$. Theorem 10.2.3 says that when N is sufficiently large, the evolutionary process is very likely to stay very close to an almost deterministic trajectory; this trajectory converges to state $x = \frac{1}{2}$, with convergence occurring at exponential rate 1.

If instead one fixes the population size N and looks at behavior over the infinite time horizon ($T = \infty$), the process eventually splits off from the deterministic trajectory, visiting all states in $\{0, \frac{1}{N}, \ldots, 1\}$ infinitely often. The infinite-horizon behavior of this process is considered in more detail in example 11.2.1. ◆

Exercise 10.2.4 Consider a population playing game F using revision protocol ρ.

i. Show that the resulting mean dynamic can be expressed as

$$\dot{x} = R(x)'x,$$

where $R(x) \in \mathbf{R}^{n \times n}$ is given by

$$R_{ij}(x) = \begin{cases} \rho_{ij}(x, F(x)) & \text{if } i \neq j, \\ -\sum_{k \neq i} \rho_{ik}(x, F(x)) & \text{if } i = j. \end{cases}$$

Note that when ρ is independent of $F(x)$ and x, as in the previous example, the matrix R is independent of x as well. In this case one obtains the linear dynamic $\dot{x} = R'x$, whose solutions can be expressed in closed form (see appendix 8.B).

ii. Suppose that $\rho_{ij} = 1$ for all i and j. Describe the parameters of the resulting Markov process $\{X_t^N\}$ and the corresponding mean dynamic. Show that solutions to the mean dynamic take the form $x_t = x^* + (x_0 - x^*)e^{-nt}$, where $x^* = \frac{1}{n}\mathbf{1}$. ◇

10.3 Extensions

10.3.1 Discrete-Time Models

It is also possible to prove deterministic approximation results for discrete-time models of stochastic evolution. To do so, we assume that the number of discrete periods that pass per unit of clock time grows with the population size N. In this situation, one can employ a discrete-time version of Kurtz's theorem, the requirements of which are direct analogues of those of theorem 10.2.1.

To obtain a deterministic approximation theorem for discrete-time Markov chains, we assume that the length of a period with respect to clock time becomes vanishingly small as the population size N increases. Let d^N be the duration of a period under the Markov chain $\{X_t^N\}$, so that this chain is initialized at time 0 and has transitions at times $d^N, 2d^N, \ldots$. Define $\{X_t^N\}$ at all times in $[0, \infty)$ by letting $X_t^N = X_{kd^N}^N$ when $t \in [kd^N, (k+1)d^N)$, making each sample path $\{X_t^N(\omega)\} = \{X_t^N(\omega)\}_{t \geq 0}$ a step function whose jumps occur at multiples of d^N.

Theorem 10.3.1 (Kurtz's Theorem in Discrete Time)   *Suppose that* $\lim_{N \to \infty} d^N = 0$. *Define the distributions of the random variables* ζ_x^N *by*

$$\mathbb{P}(\zeta_x^N = z) = \mathbb{P}(X_{(k+1)d^N}^N = x + z \mid X_{kd^N}^N = x),$$

and define the functions V^N, A^N, *and* A_δ^N *by*

$$V^N(x) = \tfrac{1}{d^N}\mathbb{E}\zeta_x^N, \qquad A^N(x) = \tfrac{1}{d^N}\mathbb{E}\left|\zeta_x^N\right|, \qquad A_\delta^N(x) = \tfrac{1}{d^N}\mathbb{E}\left|\zeta_x^N \mathbf{1}_{\{|\zeta_x^N| > \delta\}}\right|.$$

Then, mutatis mutandis, theorem 10.2.1 holds for the sequence of Markov chains $\{\{X_t^N\}\}_{N=N_0}^\infty$.

Stochastic Evolution and Deterministic Approximation

To apply the theorem, suppose that when the population size is N, each discrete time period is of duration $d^N = \frac{1}{NR}$, so that periods begin at times in the set $T^N = \{0, d^N, 2d^N, \ldots\}$. The following exercises propose two specifications of the discrete-time evolutionary process $\{X^N_t\}_{t \in T^N}$.

Exercise 10.3.2: Discrete-Time Model I: One Revision Opportunity per Period
Suppose that during each period, exactly one agent is selected at random and granted a revision opportunity, with each agent being equally likely to be chosen. The chosen agent's choices are then governed by the conditional switch probabilities ρ_{ij}/R. Using theorem 10.3.1, show that theorem 10.2.3 extends to this discrete-time model. ◇

Discrete-time models allow a possibility that continuous-time models do not: they permit many agents to switch strategies simultaneously. The next exercise shows that deterministic approximation is still possible even when simultaneous revisions by many agents are possible, so long as they are sufficiently unlikely.

Exercise 10.3.3: Discrete-Time Model II: Random Numbers of Revision Opportunities in Each Period Suppose that during each period, each agent tosses a coin that comes up Heads with probability $\frac{1}{N}$. Each agent who tosses a Head receives a revision opportunity; choices for such agents are again governed by the conditional switch probabilities ρ_{ij}/R. Use the Poisson limit theorem (propositions 10.A.4(ii) and 10.A.5) and theorem 10.3.1 to show that theorem 10.2.3 extends to this model. (*Hint*: In any given period, the number of agents whose tosses come up Heads is binomially distributed with parameters N and $\frac{1}{N}$.) ◇

10.3.2 Finite-Population Adjustments

In our model of individual choice, the revision protocol ρ was defined independently of the population size. In some cases, it is more appropriate to allow the revision protocol to depend on N in some vanishing way, for example, to account for the effects of sampling from a finite population, or for the fact that an agent whose choices are based on imitation will not imitate himself. If these effects are included, then ρ varies with N, so the normalized expected increments V^N vary with N as well. Fortunately, Kurtz's theorem allows for these sorts of effects as long as they are vanishing in size. As long as the functions V^N converge uniformly to a limiting mean dynamic V, as in condition (10.3), the finite-horizon approximation continues to hold.

Finite-population adjustments play an important role in our analyses of infinite-horizon behavior in sections 11.4 and 11.5, where they sometimes are needed to make reversibility conditions hold exactly.

10.A Appendix: The Exponential and Poisson Distributions

10.A.1 Basic Properties

A random variable T with support $[0, \infty)$ has an *exponential distribution with rate* λ, denoted $T \sim exponential(\lambda)$, if its decumulative distribution is $\mathbb{P}(T \geq t) = e^{-\lambda t}$, so that its density function is $f(t) = \lambda e^{-\lambda t}$. A Taylor approximation shows that for small $dt > 0$,

$$\mathbb{P}(T \leq dt) = 1 - e^{-\lambda dt} = 0 + \lambda e^{-\lambda \cdot 0} dt + O\left((dt)^2\right) \approx \lambda \, dt. \tag{10.6}$$

Exponential random variables are often used to model the random amount of time that passes before a certain occurrence: the arrival of a customer at a queue, the decay of a particle, and so on. The behavior of exponential random variables is often described using the metaphor of a stochastic alarm clock that rings after an exponentially distributed amount of time has passed.

Some basic properties of the exponential distribution are listed next.

Proposition 10.A.1 *Let $T_1, \ldots, T_n$ be independent with $T_i \sim exponential(\lambda_i)$. Then*

i. $\mathbb{E} T_i = \lambda_i^{-1}$;

ii. $\mathbb{P}(T_i \geq u + t \mid T_i \geq u) = \mathbb{P}(T_i \geq t) = e^{-\lambda_i t}$;

iii. *if $M_n = \min_j T_j$ and $I_n = \operatorname{argmin}_j T_j$, then $M_n \sim exponential(\sum_{i=1}^{n} \lambda_i)$, $\mathbb{P}(I_n = i) = \lambda_i / \sum_{j=1}^{n} \lambda_j$, and M_n and I_n are independent.*

Property (ii), *memorylessness*, says that if the time before one's alarm clock rings is exponentially distributed, then one's beliefs about how long from now the clock will ring do not depend on how long one has already been waiting. Together, this property and equation (10.6) say that until the time when the clock rings, the conditional probability that it rings during the next dt times units is proportional to dt:

$$\mathbb{P}(T_i \leq t + dt \mid T_i \geq t) = \mathbb{P}(T_i \leq dt) \approx \lambda_i \, dt.$$

Exponential distributions are the only continuous distributions with these properties.

Property (iii) says that given a collection of independent exponential alarm clocks, the time until the first clock rings is itself exponentially distributed, the probability that a particular clock rings first is proportional to its rate, and the time until the first ring and the ringing clock's identity are independent random variables. These facts are essential to the workings of Markov processes.

Proof Parts (i) and (ii) are easily verified. To establish part (iii), set $\lambda = \sum_{i=1}^{n} \lambda_i$, and compute the distribution of M_n as follows:

Stochastic Evolution and Deterministic Approximation

$$\mathbb{P}(M_n \geq t) = \mathbb{P}\left(\bigcap_{i=1}^n \{T_i \geq t\}\right) = \prod_{i=1}^n \mathbb{P}(T_i \geq t) = \prod_{i=1}^n e^{-\lambda_i t} = e^{-\lambda t}.$$

To prove the remaining claims in part (iii), observe that

$$\mathbb{P}\left(\bigcap_{j \neq i} \{T_i \leq T_j\} \cap \{T_i \geq t\}\right) = \int_t^\infty \left(\prod_{j \neq i} \int_{t_i}^\infty \lambda_j e^{-\lambda_j t_j}\, dt_j\right) \lambda_i e^{-\lambda_i t_i}\, dt_i \qquad (10.7)$$

$$= \int_t^\infty \left(\prod_{j \neq i} e^{-\lambda_j t_i}\right) \lambda_i e^{-\lambda_i t_i}\, dt_i$$

$$= \int_t^\infty \lambda_i e^{-\lambda t_i}\, dt_i$$

$$= (\lambda_i/\lambda) e^{-\lambda t}.$$

Setting $t = 0$ in equation (10.7) yields $\mathbb{P}(I_n = i) = \lambda_i/\lambda$, and an arbitrary choice of t shows that $\mathbb{P}(M_n \geq t, I_n = i) = \mathbb{P}(M_n \geq t)\mathbb{P}(I_n = i)$. ∎

A random variable R has a *Poisson distribution with rate* λ, denoted $R \sim Poisson(\lambda)$, if $\mathbb{P}(R = r) = e^{-\lambda} \lambda^r / r!$ for all $r \in \{0, 1, 2, \ldots\}$. Poisson random variables are used to model the number of occurrences of rare events (see propositions 10.A.3 and 10.A.4). Two of their basic properties are listed next.

Proposition 10.A.2 *If $R_1, \ldots, R_n$ are independent with $R_i \sim Poisson(\lambda_i)$, then*

i. $\mathbb{E}(R_i) = \lambda_i$;
ii. $\sum_{j=1}^n R_j \sim Poisson(\sum_{j=1}^n \lambda_j)$.

Proof To prove part (i), compute as follows:

$$\mathbb{E}(R_i) = \sum_{r=1}^\infty r\, e^{-\lambda_i} \frac{(\lambda_i)^r}{r!} = \sum_{r=1}^\infty \lambda_i e^{-\lambda_i} \frac{(\lambda_i)^{r-1}}{(r-1)!} = \lambda_i \sum_{s=0}^\infty e^{-\lambda_i} \frac{(\lambda_i)^s}{s!} = \lambda_i.$$

To prove part (ii), suppose first that $n = 2$. Then

$$\mathbb{P}(R_1 + R_2 = r) = \sum_{r_1=0}^r \mathbb{P}(R_1 = r_1)\, \mathbb{P}(R_2 = r - r_1) = \sum_{r_1=0}^r e^{-\lambda_1} \frac{(\lambda_1)^{r_1}}{r_1!} e^{-\lambda_2} \frac{(\lambda_2)^{r-r_1}}{(r-r_1)!}$$

$$= e^{-(\lambda_1+\lambda_2)} \sum_{r_1=0}^r \frac{(\lambda_1)^{r_1}(\lambda_2)^{r-r_1}}{r_1!(r-r_1)!} = e^{-(\lambda_1+\lambda_2)} \frac{(\lambda_1 + \lambda_2)^r}{r!},$$

where final equality follows from the binomial expansion

$$(\lambda_1 + \lambda_2)^r = \sum_{r_1=0}^{r} \frac{r!}{r_1!(r-r_1)!}(\lambda_1)^{r_1}(\lambda_2)^{r-r_1}.$$

Iterating yields the result for larger values of n. ∎

The exponential and Poisson distributions are fundamentally linked. Let $\{T_i\}_{i=1}^{\infty}$ be a sequence of i.i.d. *exponential*(λ) random variables. Interpret T_1 as the first time that an exponential alarm clock rings, T_2 as the interval between the first and second rings, and T_k as the interval between the $(k-1)$st and kth rings. In this interpretation, the sum $S_n = \sum_{k=1}^{n} T_k$ represents the time of the nth ring, and $R_t = \max\{n : S_n \leq t\}$ represents the number of rings through time t. Figure 10.2 illustrates a single realization of the ring time sequence $\{S_n\}_{n=1}^{\infty}$ and the number-of-rings process $\{R_t\}_{t \geq 0}$.

Proposition 10.A.3 derives the distribution of R_t, establishing a key connection between the exponential and Poisson distributions.

Proposition 10.A.3 *Under the assumptions above, $R_t \sim$ Poisson(λt).*

Proof To begin, we prove that S_n has density

$$f_n(t) = \lambda e^{-\lambda t} \frac{(\lambda t)^{n-1}}{(n-1)!}. \tag{10.8}$$

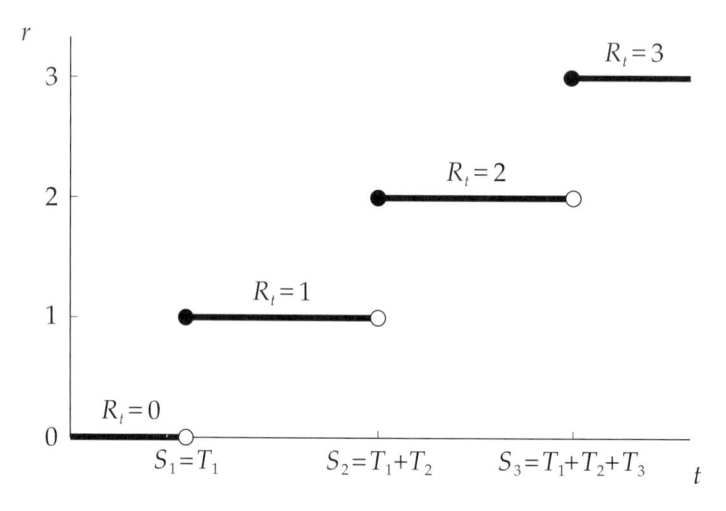

Figure 10.2
Ring times S_n and numbers of rings R_t of an exponential alarm clock.

Stochastic Evolution and Deterministic Approximation

This formula is obviously correct when $n = 1$. Suppose it is true for some arbitrary n. Then using the convolution formula $f_{X+Y}(z) = \int_{-\infty}^{\infty} f_Y(z-x) f_X(x) \, dx$ yields

$$f_{n+1}(t) = \int_0^t f_n(t-s) f_1(s) \, ds = \int_0^t \lambda \frac{(\lambda(t-s))^{n-1}}{(n-1)!} e^{-\lambda(t-s)} \times \lambda e^{-\lambda s} \, ds = \lambda e^{-\lambda t} \frac{(\lambda t)^n}{n!}.$$

Next, we show that this equation implies that S_n has cumulative distribution

$$\mathbb{P}(S_n \leq t) = \sum_{m=n}^{\infty} e^{-\lambda t} \frac{(\lambda t)^m}{m!}.$$

Since $\sum_{m=0}^{\infty} \frac{(\lambda t)^m}{m!} = e^{\lambda t}$, this statement is equivalent to

$$\mathbb{P}(S_n \leq t) = 1 - \sum_{m=0}^{n-1} e^{-\lambda t} \frac{(\lambda t)^m}{m!}.$$

Differentiating shows that this expression is in turn equivalent to the density of S_n taking form (10.8), as established above.

To complete the proof, we express the event that at least n rings have occurred by time t in two equivalent ways: $\{R_t \geq n\} = \{S_n \leq t\}$. This observation and the expression for $\mathbb{P}(S_n \leq t)$ above imply that

$$\mathbb{P}(R_t = n) = \mathbb{P}(R_t \geq n) - \mathbb{P}(R_t \geq n+1) = \mathbb{P}(S_n \leq t) - \mathbb{P}(S_{n+1} \leq t) = e^{-\lambda t} \frac{(\lambda t)^n}{n!}. \quad \blacksquare$$

10.A.2 The Poisson Limit Theorem

Proposition 10.A.3 shows that the Poisson distribution describes the number of rings of an exponential alarm clock during a fixed time span. We now establish a discrete analogue of this result.

The random variable X^p has a *Bernoulli distribution* with parameter $p \in [0,1]$, denoted $X^p \sim Bernoulli(p)$, if $\mathbb{P}(X^p = 1) = p$ and $\mathbb{P}(X^p = 0) = 1 - p$. Let $\{X_i^p\}_{i=1}^n$ be a sequence of i.i.d. $Bernoulli(p)$ random variables (e.g., coin tosses), and let $S_n^p = \sum_{i=1}^n X_i^p$ denote their sum (the number of heads in n tosses). Then S_n^p has a *binomial distribution* with parameters n and p ($S_n^p \sim binomial(n,p)$):

$$\mathbb{P}(S_n^p = s) = \binom{n}{s} p^s (1-p)^{n-s} \quad \text{for all } s \in \{0, 1, \ldots, n\}.$$

Finally, the random variable Z has a *standard normal distribution* ($Z \sim N(0,1)$) if its density function is $f(z) = \frac{1}{\sqrt{2\pi}} \exp\left(-\frac{z^2}{2}\right)$.

Proposition 10.A.4 considers the behavior of the binomial random variables S_n^p when the number of tosses n becomes large. Recall that the sequence of random variables $\{Y_n\}_{n=1}^{\infty}$ with distribution functions $\{F_n\}_{n=1}^{\infty}$ *converges in distribution* (or *converges weakly*) to the random variable Y with distribution function F (denoted $Y_n \Rightarrow Y$, or $F_n \Rightarrow F$) if $\lim_{n \to \infty} F_n(x) = F(x)$ at all points $x \in \mathbf{R}$ at which F is continuous.

Proposition 10.A.4 *Let $S_n^p \sim \text{binomial}(n,p)$. Then, as $n \to \infty$,*

i. $\dfrac{S_n^p - np}{\sqrt{np(1-p)}} \Rightarrow Z$, *where* $Z \sim N(0,1)$;

ii. $S_n^{\lambda/n} \Rightarrow R^\lambda$, *where* $R^\lambda \sim \text{Poisson}(\lambda)$.

If one increases the number of tosses n of a coin whose bias p is fixed, the *central limit theorem* says that the distribution of the number of heads S_n^p approaches a normal distribution. (In statement (i), we subtract the mean $\mathbb{E}S_n^p = np$ from S_n^p, and divide by the standard deviation $\text{SD}(S_n^p) = \sqrt{np(1-p)}$ to obtain convergence to a fixed distribution.)

Suppose instead that as one increases the number of tosses n, one decreases the probability of heads p in such a way that the expected number of heads $np = \lambda$ remains fixed. Then statement (ii), the *Poisson limit theorem*, says that the distribution of S_n^p approaches a Poisson distribution. The basic calculation needed to prove this is as follows:

$$\mathbb{P}(S_n^{\lambda/n} = s) = \frac{n!}{s!(n-s)!} \left(\frac{\lambda}{n}\right)^s \left(1 - \frac{\lambda}{n}\right)^{n-s} = \left(1 - \frac{\lambda}{n}\right)^n \frac{\lambda^s}{s!} \times \left(1 - \frac{\lambda}{n}\right)^{-s} \frac{n!}{(n-s)! \, n^s}$$

$$= P(R^\lambda = s) \times \frac{(1-\frac{\lambda}{n})^n}{e^{-\lambda}} \times \prod_{r=0}^{s-1} \frac{n-r}{n-\lambda} \to \mathbb{P}(R^\lambda = s) \quad \text{as } n \to \infty.$$

The second term of the penultimate expression is independent of s and is less than 1 (because $(1 - \frac{\lambda}{n})^n$ increases to $e^{-\lambda}$), and the final term attains its maximum over s when $s = \lfloor \lambda + 1 \rfloor$ and decreases to 1 as n grows large. Together, these observations yield the following upper bound, which is needed in exercise 10.3.3.

Proposition 10.A.5 $\mathbb{P}(S_n^{\lambda/n} = s) \leq C^\lambda \mathbb{P}(R^\lambda = s)$ *for some* $C^\lambda \in \mathbf{R}$ *independent of n and s.*

10.B Appendix: Probability Models and Their Interpretation

Appendix 10.C describes the construction and basic properties of continuous-time Markov processes on countable state spaces, the main modeling tool in the remainder of the book. In preparation, this appendix briefly reviews basic concepts from probability theory, and explains the fundamental distinction between distributional properties and sample path properties of sequences of random variables.

10.B.1 Countable Probability Models

A *countable probability model* is a pair $(\Omega, \mathbb{P})$, where the *sample space* Ω is a finite or countable set, 2^Ω is the set of all *events* (i.e., subsets of Ω), and $\mathbb{P}: 2^\Omega \to [0,1]$ is a *probability measure*, that is, a function satisfying $\mathbb{P}(\varnothing) = 0$, $\mathbb{P}(\Omega) = 1$, and *countable additivity*: if $\{A_k\}$ is a finite or countable collection of disjoint events, then $\mathbb{P}(\bigcup_k A_k) = \sum_k \mathbb{P}(A_k)$.

A *random variable* X is a function whose domain is Ω. The *distribution* of X is defined by $\mathbb{P}(X \in B) = \mathbb{P}(\omega \in \Omega : X(\omega) \in B)$ for all subsets B of the range of X. To create a finite collection of discrete random variables $\{X_k\}_{k=1}^n$, one specifies a probability model $(\Omega, \mathbb{P})$ and then defines the random variables as functions on Ω. To interpret this construction, imagine picking an ω at random from the sample space Ω according to the probability distribution $\mathbb{P}$. The value of ω so selected determines the realizations $X_1(\omega), X_2(\omega), \ldots, X_n(\omega)$ of the entire sequence of random variables $X_1, X_2, \ldots, X_n$.

Frequently one is interested in studying a sequence of random variables $\{X_k\}_{k=1}^n$ such that each X_k takes values in the same countable set R. To construct such a sequence, one can let the sample space be the set of n-vectors $\Omega = R^n$, with typical element $\omega = (\omega_1, \ldots, \omega_n)$. The random variables X_k can then be defined as *coordinate functions*: $X_k(\omega) = \omega_k$ for all $\omega \in \Omega$ and $k \in \{1, \ldots, n\}$. By choosing the probability measure $\mathbb{P}$ on Ω, one determines the joint distribution of the sequence $\{X_k\}_{k=1}^n$.

Example 10.B.1: Repeated Rolls of a Fair Die   Suppose one wants to construct a sequence of random variables $\{X_k\}_{k=1}^n$, where X_k is to represent the kth roll of a fair die. To accomplish this, let $R = \{1, 2, 3, 4, 5, 6\}$ be the set of possible results of an individual roll, and let $\Omega = R^n$. To define the probability measure $\mathbb{P}$, it is enough to let

$$\mathbb{P}(\{\omega\}) = \left(\tfrac{1}{6}\right)^n \quad \text{for all } \omega \in \Omega; \tag{10.9}$$

additivity then determines the probabilities of all other events in 2^Ω. Since

$$\mathbb{P}(X_k = x_k) = \mathbb{P}(\omega \in \Omega : X_k(\omega) = x_k) = \mathbb{P}(\omega \in \Omega : \omega_k = x_k) = \tfrac{1}{6}$$

for all $x_k \in R$, the random variables X_k have the correct marginal distributions. Moreover, if $A_k \subseteq R$ for $k \in \{1, \ldots, n\}$, it is easy to confirm that

$$\mathbb{P}\left(\bigcap_{k=1}^n \{X_k \in A_k\}\right) = \prod_{k=1}^n \mathbb{P}(X_k \in A_k),$$

so the X_k are *independent*, as desired.   ◆

Example 10.B.2: Repeated Rolls of a Die with Uncertain Bias To construct a sequence of dependent random variables, one needs to choose a probability measure $\mathbb{P}$ that is not of the product form (10.9). Suppose it is equally likely that a die is fair or that 3s and 4s occur four times as frequently as the other outcomes. To model this situation, use the sample space $\Omega = R^n$ as before, but replace the probability measure defined by (10.9) with

$$\mathbb{P}(\{\omega\}) = \tfrac{1}{2} \cdot (\tfrac{1}{6})^n + \tfrac{1}{2} \cdot \left((\tfrac{1}{3})^{N(\omega)}(\tfrac{1}{12})^{n-N(\omega)}\right),$$

where $N(\omega) = \sum_k 1_{\omega_k \in \{3,4\}}$ represents the number of 3s and 4s in the sequence ω. ◆

The *expected value* of a random variable is its integral with respect to the probability measure $\mathbb{P}$. In the case of the kth roll of a fair die,

$$\mathbb{E}X_k = \int_\Omega X_k(\omega)\,d\mathbb{P}(\omega) = \sum_{\omega \in \Omega} \omega_k\, \mathbb{P}(\{\omega\}) = \sum_{\omega_k \in R} \omega_k \left(\sum_{\omega_{-k}} \mathbb{P}(\{(\omega_k, \omega_{-k})\}) \right)$$

$$= \sum_{i=1}^{6} i \times \tfrac{1}{6} = 3\tfrac{1}{2}.$$

New random variables can be created out of old ones using functional operations. For instance, the total of the results of the n die rolls is a new random variable S_n defined by $S_n = \sum_{k=1}^{n} X_k$, or more explicitly, by $S_n(\omega) = \sum_{k=1}^{n} X_k(\omega)$ for all $\omega \in \Omega$.

10.B.2 Uncountable Probability Models and Measure Theory

The preceding constructions are sufficient for finite collections of discrete random variables, but they do not suffice when individual random variables take an uncountable number of values, or when the number of random variables is infinite. To handle these situations, the sample space Ω must be *uncountable*, that is, not expressible as a sequence of elements.

Unfortunately, uncountable sample spaces introduce a serious new technical difficulty. As an illustration, suppose one wants to construct a random variable representing a uniform draw from the unit interval. It is natural to choose $\Omega = [0,1]$ as the sample space and to define the random variable as the identity function on Ω, that is, $X(\omega) = \omega$. But then the difficulty appears: it is impossible to define a countably additive probability measure $\mathbb{P}$ that specifies the probability of *every* subset of Ω.

To resolve this problem, one choose a set of subsets $\mathcal{F} \subseteq 2^\Omega$ whose probabilities will be specified, and then introduces corresponding restrictions on the definition of a random variable. A random variable satisfying these restrictions is said to be *measurable*, and this general approach to studying functions defined on uncountable domains is known as *measure theory*.

In summary, an *uncountable probability model* consists of a triple $(\Omega, \mathcal{F}, \mathbb{P})$, where Ω is a sample space, $\mathcal{F} \subseteq 2^\Omega$ is a collection (more specifically, a σ-*algebra*) of subsets of Ω, and $\mathbb{P}: \mathcal{F} \to [0, 1]$ is a countably additive probability measure.

Example 10.B.3: Defining a Uniform Random Variable To define a random variable representing a uniform draw from the unit interval, let $\Omega = (0, 1)$, let $\mathcal{F}$ be the set of Borel sets in $(0, 1)$ (not defined here), and let $\mathbb{P}: \mathcal{F} \to [0, 1]$ be *Lebesgue measure* on Ω. $\mathbb{P}$ is the unique measure on $(\Omega, \mathcal{F})$ that agrees with the usual notion of length, in the sense that $\mathbb{P}((a, b]) = b - a$ for every interval $(a, b] \subset [0, 1]$. If $U: \Omega \to (0, 1)$ is defined by $U(\omega) = \omega$, then U is a uniform random variable on the unit interval.

The standard proof of the existence and uniqueness of Lebesgue measure is by means of a result from measure theory called the *Carathéodory extension theorem*. In the present context, this theorem shows that there is a unique way of extending $\mathbb{P}$ from the collection of half-open intervals $(a, b] \subset (0, 1)$ to the collection of all Borel sets in $(0, 1)$. ◆

Example 10.B.4: Defining a Random Variable with a Given Cumulative Distribution Function The function F is a *cumulative distribution function* if it is nondecreasing, right continuous, and satisfies $\lim_{x \to -\infty} F(x) = 0$ and $\lim_{x \to \infty} = 1$. How can one define a random variable X which has distribution F, meaning that $\mathbb{P}(X \leq x) = F(x)$ for all $x \in \mathbf{R}$?

Let $(\Omega, \mathcal{F}, \mathbb{P})$ be the probability model from the previous example, and define $X(\omega) = \sup\{y: F(y) < \omega\}$; roughly speaking, $X: (0, 1) \to \mathbf{R}$ is the inverse of $F: \mathbf{R} \to [0, 1]$. Using the right continuity of F, one can verify that $\{\omega \in \Omega: X(\omega) \leq x\} = \{\omega \in \Omega: \omega \leq F(x)\}$. Since the latter set is a Borel set, these observations imply that $\mathbb{P}(X \leq x) = \mathbb{P}(\omega \leq F(x)) = F(x)$. ◆

More generally, suppose one wants to define a (possibly infinite) collection of random variables described by some prespecified joint distributions. When is it possible to construct these random variables on some well-chosen probability space? As long as the marginal and joint distributions satisfy certain obviously necessary consistency conditions, the *Kolmogorov extension theorem* ensures the existence of a probability model on which one can define random variables with the given distributions.

10.B.3 Distributional Properties and Sample Path Properties

The reader may wonder why one should bother with the explicit construction of random variables. After all, specifying the joint distributions of the basic random variables of interest also determines the joint distributions of any random variables that can be derived from the original collection. Why not work entirely in terms of these distributions and avoid the explicit construction of the random variables altogether?

If one is only interested in the *distributional properties* of the random variables, explicit construction of the random variables is not essential. However, many key results in probability theory concern not the distributional properties of random variables, but rather their *sample path properties*. These are properties of realization sequences, that is, the sequences of values $X_1(\omega), X_2(\omega), X_3(\omega), \ldots$ that arise for each choice of $\omega \in \Omega$. We can begin to illustrate the differences between the two sorts of properties through a simple example.

Example 10.B.5 Consider the probability model $(\Omega, \mathbb{P})$ with sample space $\Omega = \{-1, 1\}$ and probability measure $\mathbb{P}(\{-1\}) = \mathbb{P}(\{1\}) = \frac{1}{2}$. Define the sequences of random variables $\{X_t\}_{t=1}^{\infty}$ and $\{\hat{X}_t\}_{t=1}^{\infty}$ as follows:

$$X_t(\omega) = \omega;$$

$$\hat{X}_t(\omega) = \begin{cases} -\omega & \text{if } t \text{ is odd,} \\ \omega & \text{if } t \text{ is even.} \end{cases}$$

If one looks only at time t marginal distributions, $\{X_t\}_{t=1}^{\infty}$ and $\{\hat{X}_t\}_{t=1}^{\infty}$ seem identical, because both sequences consist of random variables equally likely to have realizations -1 and 1. But from the sample path point of view, the two sequences are different: for either choice of ω, the sequence $\{X_t(\omega)\}_{t=1}^{\infty}$ is constant, whereas the sequence $\{\hat{X}_t(\omega)\}_{t=1}^{\infty}$ alternates between 1 and -1 forever.

These ideas are illustrated in figure 10.3, which provides graphical representations of the two sequences of random variables. In these pictures, the vertical axis represents the sample space Ω, the horizontal axis represents indices (or times) of the trials, and the interiors of the figures contain the realizations $X_t(\omega)$ and $\hat{X}_t(\omega)$.

To focus on properties of the time t marginal distributions of a sequence of random variables, we look at the *collection* of outcomes in each *vertical* section (figure 10.3a). In this respect, each X_t is identical to its partner $\hat{X}_t$, and in fact all the random variables in both sequences share the same distribution.

It is possible to distinguish between the two sequences from a distributional point of view, however, by considering their joint distributions at pairs of consecutive times t and $t+1$. From this perspective, X_t and X_{t+1} are perfectly correlated, while $\hat{X}_t$ and $\hat{X}_{t+1}$ are perfectly negatively correlated. This is a statement about the collection of outcome pairs in vertical sections of width 2 (figure 10.3b).

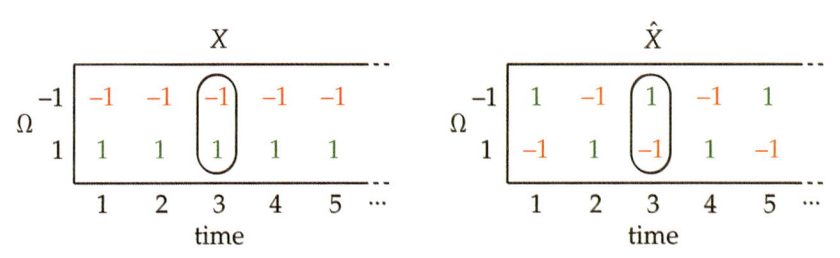

Stochastic Evolution and Deterministic Approximation

(a) Time t marginal distributions of X and $\hat{X}$

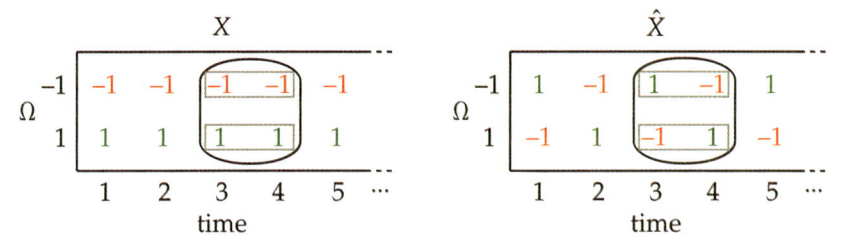

(b) Time $(t, t+1)$ joint distributions of X and $\hat{X}$

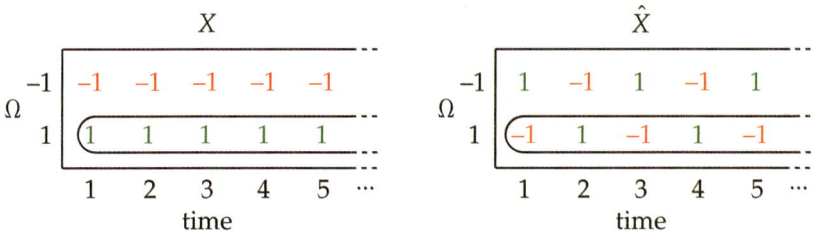

(c) Sample paths of X and $\hat{X}$

Figure 10.3
Distributional properties and sample path properties.

Finally, to focus on sample path properties, we look at the *sequences* of outcomes in each *horizontal* slice of each picture (figure 10.3c). Doing so reveals that for each ω, the sample path $\{X_t(\omega)\}_{t=1}^{\infty}$ is quite different from the sample path $\{\hat{X}_t(\omega)\}_{t=1}^{\infty}$; the former is constant, while the latter alternates forever. ◆

Intuitively, distributional properties are only meaningful from an ex ante point of view, before the realization of ω (and hence of the random variables) is known. Theorems on distributional properties constrain the probabilities of certain events, often in the limit as some parameter (e.g., the number of trials) grows large. These probability assignments are only relevant before the values of the random variables have been observed.

For their part, theorems on sample path properties typically state that with probability 1, the infinite sequence of realizations of a process must satisfy certain properties. These theorems can be interpreted as ex post statements about the random variables, since they provide information about the infinite sequence of realizations $\{X_t(\omega)\}_{t=1}^{\infty}$ that is actually observed. (To be precise, this is only true for a set of ωs that has probability 1; one cannot completely avoid referring to the ex ante point of view.)

Example 10.B.6: Properties of I.I.D. Random Variables The distinction between distributional properties and sample path properties is important for understanding the fundamental theorems about i.i.d. random variables. Let $\{X_t\}_{t=1}^{\infty}$ be a sequence of i.i.d. random variables, each of which is a function on the (uncountable) probability space $(\Omega, \mathcal{F}, \mathbb{P})$. For simplicity, assume that each X_t has mean 0 and variance 1. Then the sum $S_n = \sum_{t=1}^{n} X_t$ has mean zero and variance n, and the sample average $\bar{X}_n = S_n/n$ has mean 0 and variance $\frac{1}{n}$.

The laws of large numbers concern the convergence of the sample averages $\bar{X}_n$ as the number of trials n grows large.

The weak law of large numbers: $\quad \lim_{n \to \infty} \mathbb{P}(\omega \in \Omega : \bar{X}_n(\omega) \in [-\varepsilon, \varepsilon]) = 1 \quad$ for all $\varepsilon > 0$.

The strong law of large numbers: $\quad \mathbb{P}(\omega \in \Omega : \lim_{n \to \infty} \bar{X}_n(\omega) = 0) = 1$.

The weak law (WLLN) is a distributional result. It says that for any $\varepsilon > 0$ and $\delta > 0$, one can find a number N with this property: if the sample size n is at least N, the probability assigned to the event $\bar{X}_n \in [-\varepsilon, \varepsilon]$ is at least $1 - \delta$. (In other words, the distributions of the random variables $\bar{X}_n$ converge weakly to a point mass at zero; see exercise 12.1.4) The strong law (SLLN) is a sample path result. It says that with probability 1, the sequence of realizations of the sample average that is actually observed, $\{\bar{X}_n(\omega)\}_{n=1}^{\infty}$, is a sequence of numbers that converges to zero. (For intuition, it may be helpful to describe both of these results using pictures like those in figure 10.3.)

While the WLLN can be stated directly in terms of distributions, the SLLN only makes sense if the random variables are defined as functions on a probability space. Also, the distributional and sample path results can be distinguished by the order in which the probability $\mathbb{P}$ and the limit $\lim_{n \to \infty}$ appear; the WLLN concerns a limit of probabilities, while the SLLN concerns a "probability of a limit."

The SLLN is genuinely stronger than the WLLN, in that the conclusion of the former implies the conclusion of the latter. In general, though, distributional and sample path results address distinct aspects of a process's behavior. Consider the following pair of results, which focus on variation.

The central limit theorem: $\quad \lim_{n\to\infty} \mathbb{P}\left(\omega \in \Omega : \dfrac{S_n(\omega)}{\sqrt{n}} \in [a,b]\right) = \dfrac{1}{\sqrt{2\pi}} \int_a^b e^{-x^2/2}\, dx.$

The law of the iterated logarithm: $\quad \mathbb{P}\left(\omega \in \Omega : \limsup_{n\to\infty} \dfrac{S_n(\omega)}{\sqrt{2n \log\log n}} = 1\right) = 1.$

The central limit theorem is a distributional result: as n goes to infinity, the distributions of the normalized sums $S_n/\sqrt{n}$ converge to the standard normal distribution. This theorem allows one to approximate ex ante the probability with which the random variable $S_n/\sqrt{n}$ will take a value in any given interval $[a,b]$. The law of the iterated logarithm looks instead at variation within individual sample paths. It says that with probability 1, the sequence of realizations $\{S_n(\omega)\}_{n=1}^{\infty}$ actually observed exceeds $(1-\varepsilon)\sqrt{2n \log\log n}$ infinitely often, but exceeds $(1+\varepsilon)\sqrt{2n \log\log n}$ only finitely often. ◆

Theorems 11.A.9 and 11.A.10 in chapter 11 are generalizations of the WLLN and the SLLN for Markov processess. These results are the key to understanding the infinite-horizon behavior of our stochastic evolutionary process.

So far the focus has been on sequences of random variables, but one should also be cognizant of the distinction between distributional and sample path properties when studying limits of sequences of stochastic processes, as in section 10.2.

Example 10.B.7 Kurtz's theorem (theorem 10.2.1) provides conditions ensuring that over an initial finite time span $[0,T]$, the sequence of Markov processes $\{\{X_t^N\}\}_{N=N_0}^{\infty}$ converges to a deterministic trajectory $\{x_t\}$, in the sense that

$$\lim_{N\to\infty} \mathbb{P}\left(\omega \in \Omega : \sup_{t\in[0,T]} |X_t^N(\omega) - x_t| < \varepsilon\right) = 1. \qquad (10.10)$$

Property (10.10) might first appear to be a sample path property, but it is better regarded as a distributional property. It is a statement about a limit of probabilities, where the "random variables" $\{X^N\}_{t\in[0,T]}$ whose distributions are at issue are infinite-dimensional, taking values in the set of step functions from the time interval $[0,T]$ to the simplex X. In fact, equation (10.10) can be viewed as a statement about weak convergence of probability measures to a point mass on an appropriate function space; see the chapter notes. ◆

10.C Appendix: Countable State Markov Chains and Processes

10.C.1 Countable State Markov Chains

Markov chains and Markov processes are collections of random variables $\{X_t\}_{t\in T}$ with the property that "the future only depends on the past through the present." The focus here is on settings where these random variables take values in some finite or countable state space X. (Even if the *state space* X is countable, the random variables $X_t \colon \Omega \to X$ must be defined on a probability model with an uncountable *sample space* Ω if the set of times T is infinite whenever X has at least two elements, the set of infinite sequences $(x_1, x_2, \ldots)$ with $x_t \in X$ is an uncountable set.) The terms *Markov chain* and *Markov process* are used to distinguish between the discrete-time ($T = \{0, 1, \ldots\}$) and continuous-time ($T = [0, \infty)$) frameworks. (Some authors use these terms to distinguish between discrete and continuous state spaces.)

The sequence of random variables $\{X_t\} = \{X_t\}_{t=0}^{\infty}$ is a *Markov chain* if it satisfies the *Markov property*:

$$\mathbb{P}(X_{t+1} = x_{t+1} \mid X_0 = x_0, \ldots, X_t = x_t) = \mathbb{P}(X_{t+1} = x_{t+1} \mid X_t = x_t)$$

for all times $t \in \{0, 1, \ldots\}$ and all collections of states $x_0, \ldots, x_{t+1} \in X$ for which the conditional expectations are well defined. We only consider *temporally homogeneous* Markov chains, which are Markov chains whose one-step transition probabilities are independent of time:

$$\mathbb{P}(X_{t+1} = y \mid X_t = x) = P_{xy}.$$

The matrix $P \in \mathbf{R}_+^{X \times X}$ is the *transition matrix* for the Markov chain $\{X_t\}$. The vector $\pi \in \mathbf{R}_+^X$ defined by $\mathbb{P}(X_0 = x) = \pi_x$ is the *initial distribution* of $\{X_t\}$; when π puts all of its mass on a single state x_0, we call x_0 the *initial condition* or the *initial state*. The vector π and the matrix P fully determine the joint distributions of $\{X_t\}$ via

$$\mathbb{P}(X_0 = x_0, \ldots, X_t = x_t) = \pi_{x_0} \prod_{s=1}^{t} P_{x_{s-1} x_s}.$$

Since certain properties of Markov chains do not depend on the initial distribution π, it is sometimes left unspecified.

By definition, the one-step transition probabilities of the Markov chain $\{X_t\}$ are the elements of the matrix P:

$$\mathbb{P}(X_1 = y \mid X_0 = x) = P_{xy}.$$

The two-step transition probabilities of $\{X_t\}$ are obtained by multiplying P by itself:

$$\mathbb{P}(X_2 = y \mid X_0 = x) = \sum_{z \in X} \mathbb{P}(X_2 = y, X_1 = z \mid X_0 = x)$$

$$= \sum_{z \in X} \mathbb{P}(X_1 = z \mid X_0 = x) \, \mathbb{P}(X_2 = y \mid X_1 = z, X_0 = x)$$

$$= \sum_{z \in X} P_{xz} P_{zy}$$

$$= (P^2)_{xy}.$$

Stochastic Evolution and Deterministic Approximation

By induction, the the t-step transition probabilities of $\{X_t\}$ are given by the entries of the tth power of the transition matrix:

$$\mathbb{P}(X_t = y \mid X_0 = x) = (P^t)_{xy}.$$

10.C.2 Countable State Markov Processes: Definition and Construction

A *(temporally homogeneous) Markov process* on the countable state space X is a collection of random variables $\{X_t\} = \{X_t\}_{t \geq 0}$ with continuous time index t. This collection must satisfy the following three properties:

The (continuous-time) Markov property: $\mathbb{P}(X_{t_{k+1}} = x_{t_{k+1}} \mid X_{t_0} = x_{t_0}, \ldots, X_{t_k} = x_{t_k})$
$= \mathbb{P}(X_{t_{k+1}} = x_{t_{k+1}} \mid X_{t_k} = x_{t_k})$ for all $0 \leq t_0 < \ldots < t_{k+1}$, $x_{t_0}, \ldots, x_{t_{k+1}} \in X$
with $\mathbb{P}(X_{t_0} = x_{t_0}, \ldots, X_{t_k} = x_{t_k}) > 0$. (MP)

Temporal homogeneity: $\mathbb{P}(X_{t+u} = y \mid X_t = x) = P_{xy}(u)$ for all $t, u \geq 0$, $x, y \in X$. (TH)

Right continuity and left limits: For every $\omega \in \Omega$, the sample path
$\{X_t(\omega)\}_{t \geq 0}$ is continuous from the right and has left limits, that is,
$\lim_{s \downarrow t} X_s(\omega) = X_t(\omega)$ for all $t \in [0, \infty)$, and $\lim_{s \uparrow t} X_s(\omega)$ exists for all $t \in (0, \infty)$.
(RCLL)

Conditions (MP) and (TH) are restrictions on the (joint) distributions of $\{X_t\}$, while condition (RCLL) is a restriction on the sample paths of $\{X_t\}$.

There are two reasons for introducing restrictions on the behavior of sample paths. First, when Markov processes are used as models, restrictions like (RCLL) are natural requirements for the sample paths of the process. Second, (RCLL) is often needed to ensure that certain events whose probabilities are of interest are in fact measurable. The trouble arises here because the set of times $[0, \infty)$ is uncountable, and the probability measure $\mathbb{P}$ only satisfies countable additivity. Thus, if (RCLL) does not hold, sets like $Z = \{\omega \in \Omega : X_t(\omega) \neq 0 \text{ for some } t \geq 0\}$ need not be measurable. But if (RCLL) does hold, then Z is essentially determined by the behavior of the process $\{X_t\}$ at rational times $t \in \mathbf{Q}$; because $\mathbf{Q}$ is countable, Z can be shown to be measurable.

Processes satisfying the distributional requirements (MP) and (TH) must take this form: there must be an initial distribution $\pi \in \mathbf{R}_+^X$, a *jump rate vector* $\lambda \in \mathbf{R}_+^X$, and a transition matrix $P \in \mathbf{R}_+^{X \times X}$ such that

1. the initial distribution of the process is given by $\mathbb{P}(X_0 = x) = \pi_x$;

2. when the process is in state x, the random time before the next jump is exponentially distributed with rate λ_x;

3. the state at which a jump from x lands follows the distribution $\{P_{xy}\}_{y \in \mathcal{X}}$ (the landing state can be x itself if $P_{xx} > 0$);

4. times between jumps are independent of each other and independent of the past conditional on the current state.

The objects π, λ, and P implicitly define the joint distributions of the random variables $\{X_t\}$, so the Kolmogorov extension theorem (see section 10.B.2) implies that a collection of random variables with these joint distributions exists (i.e., can be defined as functions on some well-chosen probability space). However, Kolmogorov's theorem does not ensure that the random variables so constructed satisfy the sample path continuity property (RCLL).

Fortunately, it is not too difficult to construct the process $\{X_t\}$ explicitly. Let $\{Y_k\}_{k=0}^{\infty}$ be a discrete-time Markov chain with initial distribution π and transition matrix P, and let $\{T_k\}_{k=1}^{\infty}$ be a sequence of i.i.d. *exponential*(1) random variables that are independent of the Markov chain $\{Y_k\}$. (Since both of these collections are countable, questions of sample path continuity do not arise; the existence of these random variables as functions defined on a common probability space is ensured by Kolmogorov's theorem.)

Define the random *jump times* $\{\tau_n\}_{n=0}^{\infty}$ by $\tau_0 = 0$ and

$$\tau_n = \sum_{k=1}^{n} \frac{T_k}{\lambda_{Y_{k-1}}}, \quad \text{so that } \tau_n - \tau_{n-1} = \frac{T_n}{\lambda_{Y_{n-1}}}.$$

Finally, define the process $\{X_t\}_{t \geq 0}$ by

$$X_t = Y_n \quad \text{when } t \in [\tau_n, \tau_{n+1}).$$

The process $\{X_t\}$ begins at some initial state $X_0 = Y_0 = y_0$. It remains there for the random duration $\tau_1 \sim exponential(\lambda_{y_0})$, at which point a transition to some new state $X_{\tau_1} = Y_1 = y_1$ occurs; the process then remains at y_1 for the random duration $\tau_2 - \tau_1 \sim exponential(\lambda_{y_1})$, at which point a transition to $X_{\tau_2} = Y_2 = y_2$ occurs; and so on. By construction, the sample paths of $\{X_t\}$ are right continuous with left limits, and it is easy to check that the joint distributions of $\{X_t\}$ are the ones desired.

Example 10.C.1: The Poisson Process Consider a Markov process $\{X_t\}$ with state space $\mathcal{X} = \mathbb{Z}_+$, initial condition $X_0 = 0$, jump rates $\lambda_x = \lambda > 0$ for all $x \in \mathcal{X}$, and transition matrix $P_{xy} = 1_{\{y=x+1\}}$ for all $x, y \in \mathcal{X}$. Under this process, jumps arrive randomly at the fixed rate λ, and every jump increases the state by exactly one unit. A Markov process fitting this description is called a *Poisson process*.

Stochastic Evolution and Deterministic Approximation 393

By the definition of this process,

The waiting times $\tau_n - \tau_{n-1}$ are i.i.d. with
$$\tau_n - \tau_{n-1} \sim exponential(\lambda) \ (n \in \{1, 2, \ldots\}). \tag{P1}$$

In fact, it can be shown that under the sample path continuity condition (RCLL) and other mild technical requirements, condition (P1) is equivalent to

The increments $X_{t_k} - X_{t_{k-1}}$ are independent random variables, and
$$(X_{t_k} - X_{t_{k-1}}) \sim Poisson \ (\lambda(t_k - t_{k-1})) \ (0 < t_1 < \ldots < t_\ell). \tag{P2}$$

Proposition 10.A.3 established part of this result; it showed that if condition (P1) holds, then $X_t \sim Poisson(\lambda t)$ for all $t > 0$. But the present result says much more. A "pure birth process" whose waiting times are i.i.d. exponentials is not only Poisson distributed at each time t; in fact, all *increments* of the process are Poisson distributed, and nonoverlapping increments are stochastically independent. Conversely, if one begins with the assumption that the increments of the process are independent and Poisson, then the waits between jumps must be i.i.d. and exponential. ◆

10.C.3 Countable State Markov Processes: Transition Probabilities

The time t transition probabilities of a countable state Markov process can be expressed in an appealingly simple form. We focus here on the case of a finite state space X, but versions of the results also hold when X is countably infinite.

Let $\{X_t\}$ be a Markov process with jump rates $\lambda \in \mathbf{R}_+^X$ and transition matrix $P \in \mathbf{R}_+^{X \times X}$, and define
$$P_{xy}(t) = \mathbb{P}(X_t = y \mid X_0 = x)$$

to be the time t transition probability from state x to state y. (To prevent the notations for the transition matrix P and the time t transition probabilities $P(t)$ from overlapping, the collection of the latter is always referred to as $\{P(t)\}_{t \geq 0}$.) It is clear that $P(0) = I$, the identity matrix. Note as well that since $\{X_t\}$ is a temporally homogeneous Markov process, we have

$$\begin{aligned} P_{xy}(s+t) &= \mathbb{P}(X_{s+t} = y \mid X_0 = x) \\ &= \sum_{z \in X} \mathbb{P}(X_s = z \mid X_0 = x) \, \mathbb{P}(X_{s+t} = y \mid X_s = z, X_0 = x) \\ &= \sum_{z \in X} \mathbb{P}(X_s = z \mid X_0 = x) \, \mathbb{P}(X_t = y \mid X_0 = z) \\ &= \sum_{z \in X} P_{xz}(s) P_{zy}(t). \end{aligned}$$

Expressing this result in matrix form, we conclude that the matrix trajectory $\{P(t)\}_{t\geq 0}$ is a *semigroup*:

$$P(s+t) = P(s)P(t) \quad \text{for all } s, t \geq 0. \tag{10.11}$$

The key tool for studying the transition probabilities of a Markov process is its *generator*,

$$Q = \text{diag}(\lambda)(P - I) \in \mathbf{R}^{X \times X}.$$

Since the row sums of P are 1, the entries of Q can be expressed as

$$Q_{xy} = \begin{cases} \lambda_x P_{xy} & \text{if } x \neq y, \\ -\lambda_x \sum_{z \neq x} P_{xz} & \text{if } x = y. \end{cases}$$

Thus, for $x \neq y$, Q_{xy} represents the rate of transitions from x to y, while $-Q_{xx}$ represents the total rate of transitions away from x.

To put the generator to work, notice that when $\tau > 0$ is small, so that it is very unlikely that more than one transition has occurred by time τ, we have

$$P_{xy}(\tau) = \mathbb{P}(X_\tau = y \mid X_0 = x) \approx \begin{cases} \tau \lambda_x P_{xy} & \text{if } x \neq y, \\ 1 - \tau \lambda_x \sum_{z \neq x} P_{xz} & \text{if } x = y, \end{cases}$$

or, in matrix notation,

$$P(\tau) \approx I + \tau Q. \tag{10.12}$$

This equation explains why Q is sometimes referred to as the *infinitesimal generator* of $\{X_t\}$.

Using the semigroup property (10.11) and expression (10.12), one can informally derive an exact expression for the transition probabilities of $\{X_t\}$. Dividing the time interval $[0, t]$ into n subintervals of length $\frac{t}{n}$ and then applying (10.11) and (10.12) in turn yields

$$P(t) = P(\tfrac{1}{n}t)^n \approx \left(I + \tfrac{1}{n}Q\right)^n. \tag{10.13}$$

Taking n to infinity, the analogy with the scalar formula $\lim_{n \to \infty} (1 + \frac{q}{n})^n = e^q$ suggests that the right-hand side of equation (10.13) should converge to the matrix exponential e^{Qt} (see section 8.B.2). And indeed, one can establish rigorously that the transition probabilities can be expressed as

$$P(t) = e^{Qt} \equiv \sum_{k=0}^{\infty} \frac{(Qt)^k}{k!}. \tag{10.14}$$

There are two ways of expressing (10.14) in differential form. Theorem 8.B.2 says that (10.14) is a solution of the *backward equation*, which is the matrix differential equation $\dot{P}(t) = QP(t)$. At the same time, since the matrices Q and $P(t) = e^{Qt}$ commute, one can rewrite the previous equation as $\dot{P}(t) = P(t)Q$. This is known as the *forward equation*. The trajectory $P(t) = e^{Qt}$ is the unique solution to each of these linear differential equations from initial condition $P(0) = I$. In section 11.A.7, the backward equation is used to characterize stationary distributions of Markov processes.

Notes

Sections 10.2 and 10.3
Theorems 10.2.1 and 10.3.1 first appeared in Kurtz (1970). See Ethier and Kurtz (1986, ch. 11) for an advanced textbook treatment.

The first formal results in the game theory literature akin to theorem 10.2.3 focused on specific revision protocols. Boylan (1995) showed how evolutionary processes based on random matching schemes converge to deterministic trajectories when the population size grows large. Binmore, Samuelson, and Vaughan (1995), Börgers and Sarin (1997), and Schlag (1998) considered particular models of evolution that converge to the replicator dynamic. Binmore and Samuelson (1999) proved a general deterministic approximation result for discrete-time models of evolution under a somewhat restrictive timing assumption. Sandholm (2003) used Kurtz's theorem to prove a general finite-horizon convergence result. That paper also showed that after spatial normalization, the behavior of $\{X_t^N\}$ near rest points of the mean dynamic can be approximated by a diffusion. The strongest deterministic approximation results can be found in Benaïm and Weibull (2003; 2009). These authors established an exponential bound on the probability of deviations of $\{X_t^N\}$ from solutions of the mean dynamic. They also established results relating the infinite-horizon behavior of $\{X_t^N\}$ to the mean dynamic (see chapter 12 in the present text). These results rely on the assumption that the mean dynamic is Lipschitz continuous, but analogous results can be established when the mean dynamic is not a differential equation, but differential inclusion; see Roth and Sahdholm (2010), which built on work by Benaïm, Hofbauer, and Sorin (2005) in a related context.

While we focus on the evolution of the distribution of behavior, Tanabe (2006) proved results about the evolution of the strategy profile, that is, about the joint distribution of individual agents' choice trajectories. Suppose that at time 0, the N agents' choices of strategies from S are i.i.d. Then as N grows large, each agent's random choice trajectory converges in distribution to v, the distribution of a certain time-inhomogeneous Markov process—a so-called *McKean process*—taking values in S. Furthermore, the joint distribution of any k individuals' choice trajectories converges to the k-fold product of the measure v. This means that the independence of the k individuals' choices at time 0 persists over any finite time span, a phenomenon sometimes called *propagation of chaos*; see Sznitman (1991). One can further show that the empirical distribution of the N agents' choice trajectories also converges to the measure v. Since the time t marginal of this empirical distribution is none other than our state variable X_t^N, theorem 10.2.3 implies that the collection of time t marginals of v is none other than the solution to the mean dynamic (M).

Appendices 10.A, 10.B, 10.C
Billingsley (1995) and Durrett (2005) are excellent graduate-level probability texts. The former provides more thorough coverage of the topics considered in this chapter and contains an especially clear treatment of the Poisson process. Norris (1997), Brémaud (1999), and Stroock (2005) are all excellent books on Markov chains and Markov processes. The first is at an undergraduate level, the last at a graduate level, and the middle one somewhere in between. For more on Kurtz's theorem and weak convergence, see Durrett (1996, ch. 8).

11 Stationary Distributions and Infinite-Horizon Behavior

The central result of chapter 10 established that over finite time spans, when the population size is sufficiently large, the stochastic evolutionary process $\{X_t^N\}$ follows a nearly deterministic path, closely shadowing a solution trajectory of the corresponding mean dynamic (M). But over longer time spans—that is, if we fix the population size N and consider the process at large values of t—the random nature of the process must assert itself. In particular, if the process is generated by a *full support revision protocol*, one that always assigns positive probabilities to transitions to all neighboring states in $\mathcal{X}^N$, then $\{X_t^N\}$ must visit all states in $\mathcal{X}^N$ infinitely often. Evidently, an *infinite-horizon* analogue of theorem 10.2.3 cannot hold. To make predictions about play over very long time spans, we need new techniques for characterizing the infinite-horizon behavior of the stochastic evolutionary process.

In finite-horizon analyses the basic object of study is the mean dynamic (M), an ordinary differential equation derived from the Markov process $\{X_t^N\}$. In infinite-horizon analyses the corresponding object is the *stationary distribution* μ^N of the process $\{X_t^N\}$. A stationary distribution is defined by the property that a process whose initial condition is described by this distribution will continue to be described by this distribution at all future times. If $\{X_t^N\}$ is generated by a full support revision protocol, then its stationary distribution μ^N is not only unique, but also describes the infinite-horizon behavior of $\{X_t^N\}$ regardless of this process's initial distribution. In principle, one can use the stationary distribution to form predictions about a population's very-long-run behavior that do not depend on its initial behavior. This contrasts sharply with predictions based on the mean dynamic (M), which generally require knowledge of the initial state.

Section 11.1 begins the formal development of these ideas by introducing full support revision protocols and the related notion of *irreducibility* for the stochastic evolutionary process $\{X_t^N\}$. A typical feature of full support revision protocols is their inclusion of at least a small level of noise, which ensures that revising agents have at least some small probability of choosing each available strategy. We then define the stationary distribution μ^N of the process $\{X_t^N\}$ and review results from probability theory that link this distribution to the infinite-horizon behavior of the process. Finally, we introduce a condition on Markov processes called *reversibility*, which requires that the process look the same whether it is run forward or backward in time.

Stationary distributions of reversible Markov processes often take an especially simple form. Taking advantage of this fact, the remainder of the chapter focuses on the two settings in which the evolutionary process $\{X_t^N\}$ is known to be reversible: two-strategy games under arbitrary revision protocols (section 11.2) and potential games under exponential revision protocols (sections 11.4 and 11.5).

In principle, the stationary distribution μ^N could spread its mass over a wide range of states in the state space $\mathcal{X}^N$, in which case the prediction of play that it offers, while independent of initial behavior, would be rather diffuse. But the analyses in this chapter show that if the population size is not too small, and the amount of noise in agents' decisions is not too large, then μ^N will typically concentrate its mass on a single region in $\mathcal{X}^N$, for instance, the states corresponding to a neighborhood of a stable rest point of the relevant mean dynamic. In such cases the infinite-horizon analysis truly provides a unique prediction of play.

Summing up, we now have two approaches to forecasting behavior in population games. Finite-horizon predictions, based on the mean dynamic (M), depend on the initial population state; infinite-horizon predictions, using the stationary distribution μ^N, are independent of the initial population state. The choice between these two approaches in various applications should depend on the time span of interest, with long enough time horizons pointing toward the infinite-horizon analysis. But how long is long enough? This question is addressed in section 11.3, which investigates the time spans required for infinite-horizon analyses to become useful for predictions. Even if a population is of moderate size or the level of noise in agents' choices only somewhat small, the amounts of time needed before infinite-horizon analyses will yield meaningful predictions can be of astronomical magnitudes. For this reason, we feel that in typical economic applications, the history-dependent predictions provided by the mean dynamic are most appropriate. Further discussion of this point, including descriptions of environments in which infinite-horizon analysis may be apt, is offered in the text.

The analyses in this chapter are developed using the theory of finite-state Markov processes, particularly those tools related to stationary distributions and infinite-horizon behavior of these processes. Appendix 11.A offers a detailed presentation of the relevant mathematical techniques. It can be read as an independent unit or used as a reference while working through the main text.

11.1 Irreducible Evolutionary Processes

11.1.1 Full Support Revision Protocols

We begin with a brief review of the construction of the stochastic evolutionary process $\{X_t^N\}$ presented in section 10.1, again focusing on the single-population setting. A population of N agents recurrently plays the population game $F: X \to \mathbf{R}^n$. The agents are equipped with independent rate R Poisson alarm clocks and employ the revision protocol $\rho: \mathbf{R}^n \times X \to \mathbf{R}_+^{n \times n}$. When an i player's clock rings, he switches to strategy $j \neq i$ with probability $\rho_{ij}(F(x), x)/R$.

This model defines a Markov process $\{X_t^N\}$ on the discrete state space $\mathcal{X}^N = X \cap \frac{1}{N}\mathbf{Z}^n = \{x \in X: Nx \in \mathbf{Z}^n\}$. The process is characterized by the common jump rate $\lambda_x^N \equiv NR$ and the transition probabilities

$$P_{xy}^N = \begin{cases} \dfrac{x_i \rho_{ij}(F(x), x)}{R} & \text{if } y = x + \frac{1}{N}(e_j - e_i), j \neq i, \\ 1 - \displaystyle\sum_{i \in S}\sum_{j \neq i} \dfrac{x_i \rho_{ij}(F(x), x)}{R} & \text{if } y = x, \\ 0 & \text{otherwise,} \end{cases} \quad (11.1)$$

where R is large enough to ensure that transition probabilities are well-defined (see equation (10.1)). To introduce the possibility of unique infinite-horizon predictions, we now assume in addition that the conditional switch rates are bounded away from zero: there is a positive constant $\underline{R}$ such that

$$\rho_{ij}(F(x), x) \geq \underline{R} \quad \text{for all } i, j \in S, x \in X. \tag{11.2}$$

We refer to a revision protocol that satisfies condition (11.2) as having *full support*.

Full support protocols usually include some form of perturbation to ensure that all strategies are always chosen with positive probability. The next two examples consider two full support extensions of best response protocols. In each case, one can interpret the choice of a suboptimal strategy as the result of a mistake, of a noisy observation of payoffs, or of conscious experimentation.

Example 11.1.1: Best Response with Mutations Under *best response with mutations* at *mutation rate* $\varepsilon > 0$, called BRM(ε) for short, a revising agent switches to his current best response with probability $1 - \varepsilon$, and chooses a strategy uniformly at random (or *mutates*) with probability $\varepsilon > 0$. Thus, if the game has two strategies, each yielding different payoffs, a revising agent will choose the optimal strategy with probability $1 - \frac{\varepsilon}{2}$ and will choose the suboptimal strategy with probability $\frac{\varepsilon}{2}$.

To complete the specification of the protocol, one must specify what a non-mutating agent does when there are multiple optimal strategies. A common setup has an agent who does not mutate stick with his current strategy if it is optimal and otherwise choose at random among the optimal strategies. ◆

Exercise 11.1.1 Compute the mean dynamic for the BRM protocol, focusing on states at which the best response is unique. ◇

Example 11.1.2: Logit Choice Of the revision protocols underlying the six basic dynamics studied in chapters 5 and 6, the only one satisfying the full support condition (11.2) is the logit choice protocol with noise level $\eta > 0$ (see example 6.2.1):

$$\rho_{ij}(\pi) = \frac{\exp(\eta^{-1}\pi_j)}{\sum_{k \in S} \exp(\eta^{-1}\pi_k)}. \tag{11.3}$$

For intuition, it is useful to rewrite the logit choice protocol as

$$\rho_{ij}(\pi) = \frac{\exp(\eta^{-1}(\pi_j - \pi_{k*}))}{\sum_{k \in S} \exp(\eta^{-1}(\pi_k - \pi_{k*}))}, \tag{11.4}$$

where k^* is an optimal strategy under π. Then as η approaches zero, the denominator of (11.4) converges to a constant (namely, the number of optimal strategies under π), so as η^{-1} approaches infinity, $\rho_{ij}(\pi, x)$ vanishes at exponential rate $\pi_{k*} - \pi_j$. ◆

The mutation rate $\varepsilon \in (0, 1)$ from the BRM protocol directly specifies the probability of a suboptimal choice, while the noise level $\eta \in (0, \infty)$ of the logit protocol appears as an exponent in the formula for the choice probability. One can move between these parameterizations using the transformation $\varepsilon \mapsto \eta = -(\log \varepsilon)^{-1}$, an increasing function from $(0, 1)$ onto $(0, \infty)$, and its inverse $\eta \mapsto \varepsilon = \exp(-\eta^{-1})$. As the next exercise shows, these transformations shuttle the noise parameter between the base and the exponent of the expression for $\rho_{ij}(\pi)$. These transformations are used frequently when studying stochastic stability (see sections 12.3.1 and 12.A.5).

Exercise 11.1.2

i. Express the BRM rule in terms of the noise parameter η.
ii. Express the logit choice rule in terms of the noise parameter ε. ◇

As their noise parameters approach zero, both the BRM and logit protocols come to resemble the exact best response protocol, the protocol underlying the deterministic best response dynamic (see section 6.1). But this similarity masks a fundamental qualitative difference between the two protocols. Under best response with mutations, the probability of choosing a particular suboptimal strategy is independent of the payoff consequences of doing so; mutations do not favor alternative strategies with higher payoffs over those with lower payoffs. In contrast, since the logit protocol is defined using payoff perturbations that are symmetric across strategies, more costly mistakes are less likely to be made.

The probabilities of suboptimal choices under both the BRM and logit protocols are small when the noise level is small. One might expect the precise specification of these probabilities to be of little consequence. If one is interested in finite-horizon behavior, so that the mean dynamic (M) forms the basis for predictions, this impression is largely correct (see, for instance, theorem 9.B.5). But predictions of infinite-horizon behavior hinge on the relative probabilities of rare events (see section 11.2.3 and chapter 12). As a consequence, seemingly minor differences in choice probabilities can lead to entirely different predictions of behavior.

While mutations are commonly employed in combination with a best response rule, they are also a natural complement to imitative rules.

Example 11.1.3: Imitative Logit Choice with (and without) Mutations The protocol

$$\rho_{ij}(\pi, x) = \frac{x_j \exp(\eta^{-1}\pi_j)}{\sum_{k \in S} x_k \exp(\eta^{-1}\pi_k)} + \varepsilon \tag{11.5}$$

augments the i-logit protocol (see example 5.4.7) by adding rare mutations. Since $\exp(\eta^{-1}\pi_j)$ is always positive, the conditional switch rates to all strategies currently in use are positive even when $\varepsilon = 0$. We take advantage of this property in Section 11.4.3, which introduces a modification of the basic model under which the process $\{X_t^N\}$ generated by protocol (11.5) is irreducible even without mutations. ◆

11.1.2 Stationary Distributions and Infinite-Horizon Behavior

The full support assumption (11.2) ensures that at each revision opportunity, every strategy in S has a positive probability of being chosen by the revising agent. Therefore, there is a positive probability that the process $\{X_t^N\}$ will transit from any given state x to any other state y within a finite number of periods. A Markov process with this property is said to be *irreducible*.

Below we summarize some basic results on the infinite-horizon behavior of irreducible Markov processes. These results provide the foundation for all subsequent analyses. A detailed presentation of the relevant theory is offered in appendix 11.A.

Suppose that $\{X_t\}_{t \geq 0}$ is an irreducible Markov process on the finite state space $\mathcal{X}$, where the process has equal jump rates $\lambda_x \equiv \ell$ and transition matrix P. Theorem 11.A.8 shows that there is a unique probability vector $\mu \in \mathbf{R}_+^{\mathcal{X}}$ satisfying

$$\sum_{x \in \mathcal{X}} \mu_x P_{xy} = \mu_y \quad \text{for all } y \in \mathcal{X}. \tag{11.6}$$

The vector μ is called the *stationary distribution* of the process $\{X_t\}$. Equation (11.6) says that if the process $\{X_t\}$ is run from initial distribution μ, then at the random time of the first jump, the distribution of the process is also μ. Moreover, if we use the notation $\mathbb{P}_\pi(\cdot)$ to represent $\{X_t\}$ being run from initial distribution π, then equation (11.52) shows that

$$\mathbb{P}_\mu(X_t = x) = \mu_x \quad \text{for all } x \in \mathcal{X}, t \geq 0. \tag{11.7}$$

In other words, if the process starts off in its stationary distribution, it remains in this distribution at all subsequent times t.

Equation (11.7) is relevant if $\{X_t\}$ starts off in its stationary distribution. But what happens to this process if it starts in an arbitrary initial distribution π? Theorem 11.A.9 shows that as t grows large, the time t distribution of $\{X_t\}$ converges to μ:

$$\lim_{t \to \infty} \mathbb{P}_\pi(X_t = x) = \mu_x \quad \text{for all } x \in \mathcal{X}. \tag{11.8}$$

Thus, from the ex ante point of view, the probable locations of the process $\{X_t\}$ at sufficiently distant future times are essentially determined by μ.

To describe long-run behavior from an ex post point of view, we need to consider the behavior of the process's sample paths. Here again, the stationary distribution plays the central role. Theorem 11.A.10 states that along almost every sample path, the proportion of time spent at each state in the long run is described by μ:

$$\mathbb{P}_\pi \left(\lim_{T \to \infty} \frac{1}{T} \int_0^T \mathbf{1}_{\{X_t = x\}} \, dt = \mu_x \right) = 1 \quad \text{for all } x \in \mathcal{X}. \tag{11.9}$$

Equation (11.9) can also be summarized by saying that the limiting empirical distribution of $\{X_t\}$ is almost surely equal to μ.

11.1.3 Reversibility

In general, computing the stationary distribution of a Markov process means finding an eigenvector of a matrix, a task that is computationally daunting unless the state space, and hence the dimension of the matrix, is small. But there is a special class of Markov processes whose stationary distributions are easy to compute. A constant jump rate Markov process $\{X_t\}$ is said to be *reversible* if it admits a *reversible distribution*: a probability distribution μ on $\mathcal{X}$ that satisfies the *detailed balance conditions*:

$$\mu_x P_{xy} = \mu_y P_{yx} \quad \text{for all } x, y \in \mathcal{X}. \tag{11.10}$$

A process satisfying this condition is called reversible because, probabilistically speaking, it looks the same whether time is run forward or backward (see appendix section 11.A.6). Since summing the equality in (11.10) over x yields condition (11.6), a reversible distribution is also a stationary distribution.

There are two classes of environments in which the stochastic evolutionary process $\{X_t^N\}$ is known to be reversible: two-strategy games under arbitrary revision protocols, and potential games under exponential protocols. These two settings are studied in the next section and in sections 11.4–11.5.

11.2 Stationary Distributions for Two-Strategy Games

When the population plays a game with just two strategies, the state space $\mathcal{X}^N$ is a grid in the simplex in $\mathbf{R}^2$, and so is linearly ordered. In this case, regardless of the (full support) revision protocol the agents employ, one can compute the stationary distribution of the process $\{X_t^N\}$ explicitly. We derive this distribution in theorem 11.2.3. We then compute the stationary distributions of a few examples, previewing the equilibrium selection results to come in Chapter 12.

Let $F: X \to \mathbf{R}^2$ be a two-strategy game with strategy set $S = \{0, 1\}$, let $\rho: \mathbf{R}^2 \times X \to \mathbf{R}^{2\times 2}$ be a full support revision protocol, and let N be a finite population size. These objects define a Markov process $\{X_t^N\}$ on the state space $\mathcal{X}^N$.

While population states in game F are elements of $X = \{x \in \mathbf{R}_+^2 : x_0 + x_1 = 1\}$, the simplex in $\mathbf{R}^2$, it is convenient to identify state x with the weight $\chi \equiv x_1$ that it places on strategy 1. With this notational device, the state space of the Markov process $\{X_t^N\}$ becomes $\mathcal{X}^N = \{0, \frac{1}{N}, \ldots, 1\}$, a uniformly spaced grid in the unit interval. We will also write $F(\chi)$ for $F(x)$ and $\rho(\pi, \chi)$ for $\rho(\pi, x)$ whenever it is convenient to do so.

11.2.1 Birth and Death Processes

Because agents in our model switch strategies sequentially, transitions of the process $\{X_t^N\}$ are always between adjacent states. Since in addition states are linearly ordered, $\{X_t^N\}$ falls into a class of Markov processes called birth and death processes. These processes are quite amenable to explicit calculations, as we now illustrate by deriving a simple expression for the stationary distribution μ^N.

A constant jump rate Markov process $\{X_t^N\}$ on the state space $\mathcal{X}^N = \{0, \frac{1}{N}, \ldots, 1\}$ is a *birth and death process* if the only positive probability transitions move the state one step to the right, move the state one step to the left, or leave the state unchanged. This implies that there are vectors $p^N, q^N \in \mathbf{R}^{\mathcal{X}^N}$ with $p_1^N = q_0^N = 0$ such that the transition matrix of $\{X_t^N\}$ takes the form

$$P_{\chi y}^N \equiv \begin{cases} p_\chi^N & \text{if } y = \chi + \frac{1}{N}, \\ q_\chi^N & \text{if } y = \chi - \frac{1}{N}, \\ 1 - p_\chi^N - q_\chi^N & \text{if } y = \chi, \\ 0 & \text{otherwise.} \end{cases}$$

Clearly, the process $\{X_t^N\}$ is irreducible if $p_\chi^N > 0$ for $\chi < 1$ and $q_\chi^N > 0$ for $\chi > 0$, as we henceforth assume.

Because of their simple transition structure, birth and death chains are reversible. For the transition matrix above, the reversibility conditions (11.10) reduce to

$$\mu_\chi^N q_\chi^N = \mu_{\chi-1/N}^N p_{\chi-1/N}^N \quad \text{for } \chi \in \{\tfrac{1}{N}, \ldots, 1\}.$$

Applying this formula inductively shows that the stationary distribution of $\{X_t^N\}$ satisfies

$$\frac{\mu_\chi^N}{\mu_0^N} = \prod_{j=1}^{N\chi} \frac{p_{(j-1)/N}^N}{q_{j/N}^N} \quad \text{for } \chi \in \{\tfrac{1}{N}, \ldots, 1\}. \tag{11.11}$$

That the weights in μ^N sum to 1 implies that

$$\mu_0^N = \left(\sum_{i=0}^{N} \prod_{j=1}^{i} \frac{p_{(j-1)/N}^N}{q_{j/N}^N} \right)^{-1}, \tag{11.12}$$

where the empty product equals 1.

Example 11.2.1: Toss and Switch Revisited Example 10.2.1 considered a population of size N whose members are equipped with rate 1 Poisson alarm clocks. Each agent responds to the ringing of her clock by flipping a fair coin and switching strategies if the coin comes up Heads. The resulting Markov process $\{X_t^N\}$ is irreducible, with constant jump rate $\lambda_\chi^N \equiv N$ and positive transition probabilities $p_\chi^N = \tfrac{1}{2}(1-\chi)$ and $q_\chi^N = \tfrac{1}{2}\chi$.

Example 10.2.1 showed that the mean dynamic of this process is $\dot{\chi} = \tfrac{1}{2} - \chi$. Solutions of this dynamic are of the form $\chi_t = \tfrac{1}{2} + (\chi_0 - \tfrac{1}{2})e^{-t}$, so the dynamic is an exponential contraction toward the central state $\chi^* = \tfrac{1}{2}$. Now fix a time horizon $T < \infty$ and an error bound $\varepsilon > 0$. Then theorem 10.2.3 says that if the population size N is large enough, the value of the random variable X_t^N will stay within ε of $\chi_t = \tfrac{1}{2} + (\chi_0 - \tfrac{1}{2})e^{-t}$ for all times t in the interval $[0, T]$ with probability at least $1 - \varepsilon$ (see figure 10.1).

Now fix the population size N, and consider the behavior of the process $\{X_t^N\}$ over a very long time horizon. As discussed in section 11.1.2, the limiting distribution and the limiting empirical distribution of $\{X_t^N\}$ are given by its stationary distribution μ^N. Using formulas (11.11) and (11.12), it is easy to show that this distribution is given by

$$\mu_\chi^N = \frac{1}{2^N} \binom{N}{N\chi} \quad \text{for all } \chi \in \mathcal{X}^N = \{0, \tfrac{1}{N}, \ldots, 1\}.$$

In other words, μ^N describes a binomial distribution with parameters N and $\tfrac{1}{2}$, but with outcomes (in $\mathcal{X}^N$) representing the proportion rather than the number of

Stationary Distributions and Infinite Horizon Behavior

successful trials. Figure 11.1 illustrates μ^N for population sizes $N = 100$ and $N = 10{,}000$.

If N is not small, the central limit theorem implies that μ^N is approximately normal with mean $\frac{1}{2}$ and variance $\frac{1}{4N}$. In this case, after enough time has passed, all states in $\mathcal{X}^N$ will have been visited many times, but the vast majority of periods will have been spent at states where the two strategies are used in nearly equal proportions. ◆

Exercise 11.2.1

i. Suppose that in the previous example, revising agents flip a coin that comes up Heads with probability $h \in (0, 1)$ and switch strategies when Heads occurs. What are the mean dynamic of $\{X_t^N\}$ and the stationary distribution of $\{X_t^N\}$ in this case?

ii. Suppose that revising agents flip a coin that comes up Heads with probability $h \in (0, 1)$ and choose strategy 1 when Heads occurs and strategy 0 otherwise. What are the mean dynamic of $\{X_t^N\}$ and the stationary distribution of $\{X_t^N\}$ in this case? ◇

Exercise 11.2.2: Toss and Switch with n Strategies   Consider the n-strategy version of the Toss and Switch process: an agent whose clock rings randomizes uniformly over the n available strategies. Verify that this process is reversible with stationary distribution

$$\mu_x^N = \frac{1}{n^N} \frac{N!}{\prod_{k=1}^n (Nx_k)!} \quad \text{for all } x \in \mathcal{X}^N.$$
◇

11.2.2 The Stationary Distribution of the Evolutionary Process

We now use formula (11.11) to compute the stationary distribution of the stochastic evolutionary process, maintaining the assumption that the process is generated by a full support revision protocol. It follows from the analysis in section 11.1 that the process $\{X_t^N\}$ has constant jump rates $\lambda_x^N = NR$ and that its upward and downward transition probabilities are given by

$$p_x^N = (1-x) \cdot \tfrac{1}{R} \rho_{01}(F(x), x); \tag{11.13}$$

$$q_x^N = x \cdot \tfrac{1}{R} \rho_{10}(F(x), x). \tag{11.14}$$

Substituting formulas (11.13) and (11.14) into equation (11.11) yields

$$\frac{\mu_x^N}{\mu_0^N} = \prod_{j=1}^{Nx} \frac{p_{(j-1)/N}^N}{q_{j/N}^N} = \prod_{j=1}^{Nx} \frac{(1 - \frac{j-1}{N}) \cdot \frac{1}{R} \rho_{01}(F(\frac{j-1}{N}), \frac{j-1}{N})}{\frac{j}{N} \cdot \frac{1}{R} \rho_{10}(F(\frac{j}{N}), \frac{j}{N})} \quad \text{for } x \in \{\tfrac{1}{N}, \tfrac{2}{N}, \ldots, 1\}.$$

Simplifying this expression leads to the following result.

(a) $N = 100$

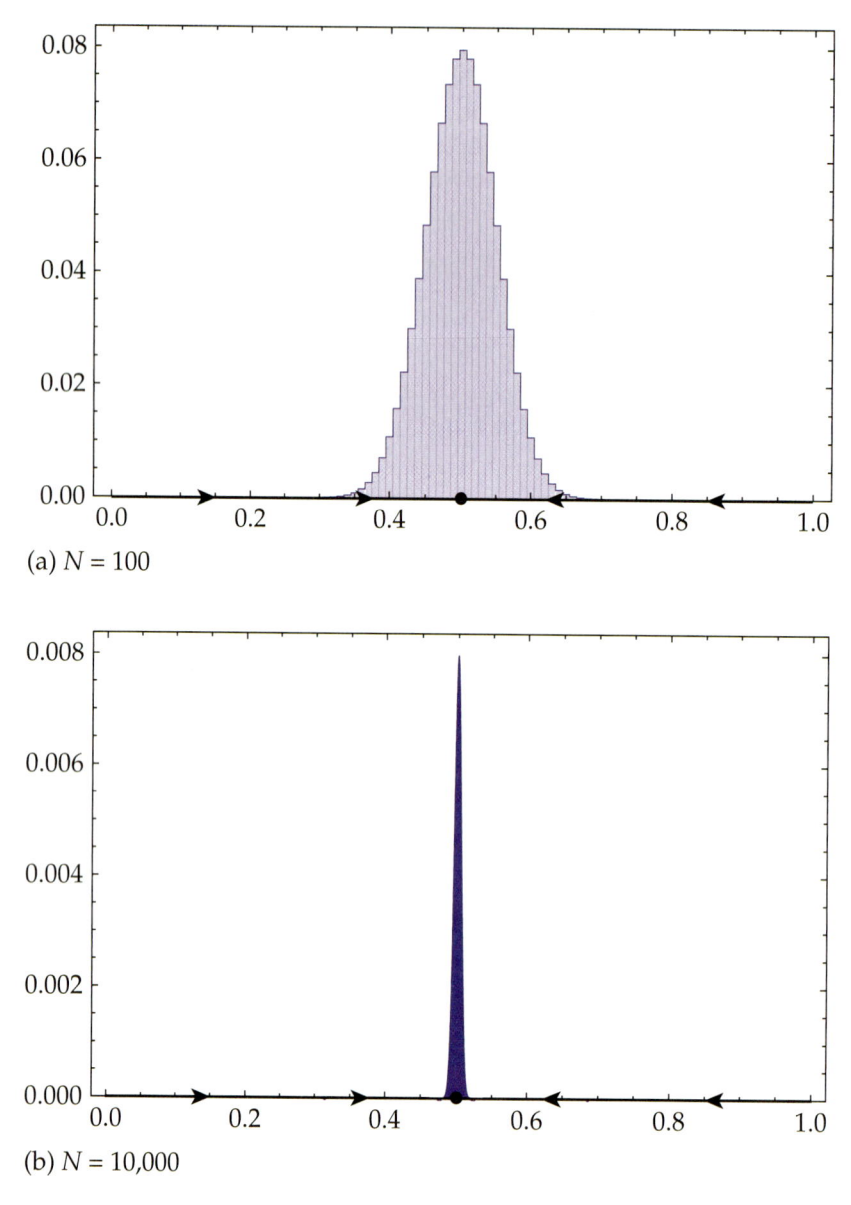

(b) $N = 10,000$

Figure 11.1
Mean dynamics and stationary distributions for Toss and Switch.

Stationary Distributions and Infinite Horizon Behavior

Theorem 11.2.3 *Suppose that a population of N agents plays the two-strategy game F using the full support revision protocol ρ. Then the stationary distribution for the evolutionary process $\{X_t^N\}$ on $\mathcal{X}^N$ is given by*

$$\frac{\mu_x^N}{\mu_0^N} = \prod_{j=1}^{N\chi} \frac{N-j+1}{j} \cdot \frac{\rho_{01}(F(\frac{j-1}{N}), \frac{j-1}{N})}{\rho_{10}(F(\frac{j}{N}), \frac{j}{N})} \quad \text{for } \chi \in \{\tfrac{1}{N}, \tfrac{2}{N}, \ldots, 1\},$$

with μ_0^N determined by the requirement that $\sum_{\chi \in \mathcal{X}^N} \mu_\chi^N = 1$.

11.2.3 Examples

The power of infinite-horizon analysis lies in its ability to generate unique predictions of play even in games with multiple strict equilibria. We illustrate this idea by computing stationary distributions for two-strategy coordination games under the BRM and logit rules. In all cases, these distributions place most of their mass near a single equilibrium, but the two rules need not select the same equilibrium.

To obtain unique predictions of infinite-horizon behavior, it is generally enough either that the population size not be too small, or that the noise level in agents' choices not be too large. But one can obtain cleaner and more general results by studying the limiting behavior of the stationary distribution as the population size approaches infinity, the noise level approaches zero, or both. This approach to studying infinite-horizon behavior, known as *stochastic stability theory*, is the subject of chapter 12.

Example 11.2.2: Stag Hunt The symmetric normal form coordination game

$$A = \begin{pmatrix} h & h \\ 0 & s \end{pmatrix}$$

with $s > h > 0$ is known as *Stag Hunt*. By way of interpretation, imagine that each agent in a match must decide whether to hunt for Hare or for Stag. Hunting for Hare ensures a payoff of h regardless of the match partner's choice. Hunting for Stag can generate a payoff of $s > h$ if the opponent does the same, but results in a zero payoff otherwise. Each of the two strategies has distinct merits. Coordinating on Stag yields higher payoffs than coordinating on Hare. But the payoff to Hare is certain, whereas the payoff to Stag depends on the choice of one's partner.

Suppose that a population of agents is repeatedly matched to play Stag Hunt. If χ denotes the proportion of agents playing Stag; then the payoffs in the resulting population game are $F_H(\chi) = h$ and $F_S(\chi) = s\chi$. This population game has three Nash equilibria: two pure equilibria and the mixed equilibrium $\chi^* = \frac{h}{s}$. We henceforth suppose that $h = 2$ and $s = 3$, so that the mixed equilibrium places mass $\chi^* = \frac{2}{3}$ on Stag.

Suppose that agents follow the best response with mutations protocol with mutation rate $\varepsilon = .10$. The resulting mean dynamic,

$$\dot{x} = \begin{cases} \frac{\varepsilon}{2} - x & \text{if } x < \frac{2}{3}, \\ (1 - \frac{\varepsilon}{2}) - x & \text{if } x > \frac{2}{3}, \end{cases}$$

has stable rest points at $x = .05$ and $x = .95$. The basins of attraction of these rest points meet at the mixed equilibrium $x^* = \frac{2}{3}$. Note that the rest point that approximates the all-Hare equilibrium has the larger basin of attraction.

Figure 11.2a presents this mean dynamic underneath the stationary distribution μ^N for $N = 100$, which is computed using the formula derived in theorem 11.2.3. While the mean dynamic has two stable equilibria, nearly all of the mass in the stationary distribution is concentrated on states where between 88 and 100 agents choose Hare. Thus, while coordinating on Stag is efficient, the safe strategy Hare is selected by the stochastic evolutionary process.

Suppose instead that agents use the logit rule with noise level $\eta = .25$. The mean dynamic is then the logit dynamic,

$$\dot{x} = \frac{\exp(3x\eta^{-1})}{\exp(2\eta^{-1}) + \exp(3x\eta^{-1})} - x,$$

which has stable rest points at $x \approx .0003$ and $x \approx .9762$, and an unstable rest point at $x \approx .7650$, so the basin of attraction of the almost-all-Hare rest point $x \approx .0003$ is even larger than under BRM. The resulting stationary distribution (figure 11.2b), places nearly all of its mass on states where either 99 or 100 agents choose Hare, in rough agreement with the result for the BRM(.10) rule. ◆

Why does most of the mass in the stationary distribution become concentrated around a single equilibrium? The stochastic evolutionary process $\{X_t^N\}$ typically moves in the direction indicated by the mean dynamic. If the process begins in the basin of attraction of a rest point or other attractor of this dynamic, then the initial period of evolution generally results in convergence to and lingering near this locally stable set.

However, since BRM and logit choice lead to irreducible evolutionary processes, this cannot be the end of the story. Indeed, the process $\{X_t^N\}$ eventually reaches all states in $\mathcal{X}^N$, and in fact visits all states in $\mathcal{X}^N$ infinitely often. This means that the process at some point must leave the basin of the stable set visited first; it then enters the basin of a new stable set, at which point it is extremely likely to head directly to the set itself. The evolution of the process continues in this fashion, with long periods near each attractor punctuated by sudden jumps between them.

Which states are visited most often over the infinite horizon is determined by the *relative* unlikelihoods of these rare but inevitable transitions between stable sets. In

Stationary Distributions and Infinite Horizon Behavior

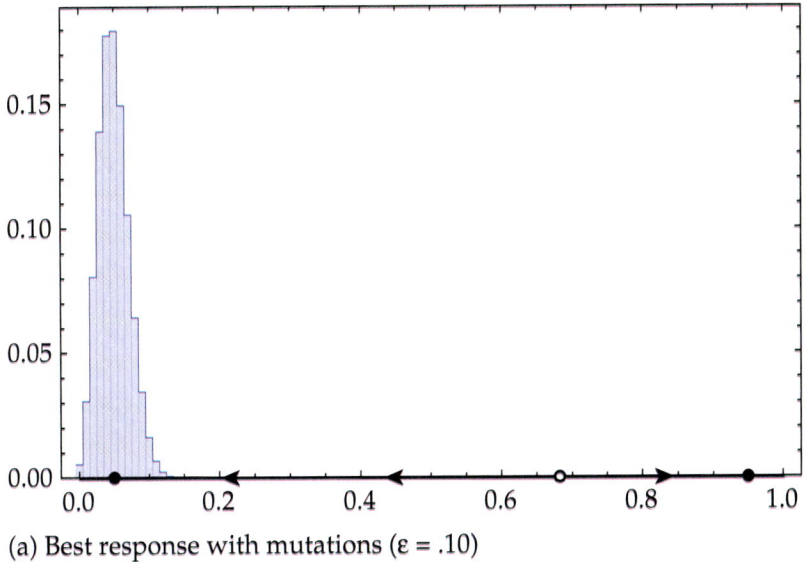

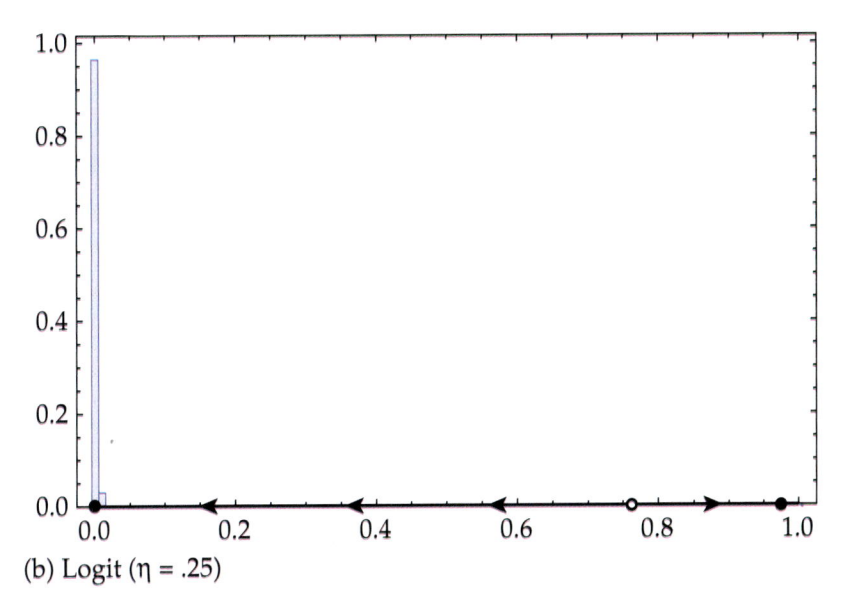

(a) Best response with mutations ($\varepsilon = .10$)

(b) Logit ($\eta = .25$)

Figure 11.2
Stationary distribution weights μ_χ for Stag Hunt ($h = 2, s = 3, N = 100$).

the previous examples, the transitions from the Stag rest point to the Hare rest point and from the Hare rest point to the Stag rest point are both very unlikely events. But for purposes of determining the stationary distribution, what matters is that in relative terms, the former transitions are much more likely than the latter. This enables us to conclude that over very long time spans, the evolutionary process will spend most periods at states where most agents play Hare.

While theorem 11.2.3 makes it easy to compute the stationary distributions in the previous example, it obscures the forces that underlie equilibrium selection. The analyses of stochastic stability in chapter 12 allow one to determine the limit behavior of the stationary distribution as the noise level becomes small even in cases in which there is no simple expression for the distribution itself. This is accomplished in section 12.5 by studying the asymptotic probabilities of transitions between stable sets, as suggested by the discussion above.

At the same time, the fact that transitions out of the basin of any stable set are very low probability events suggests that the predictions provided by the stationary distribution may only be relevant in extremely long-running interactions. We verify and discuss this point in section 11.3.

Example 11.2.3: Nonlinear Stag Hunt Now consider a version of the Stag Hunt game in which payoffs depend nonlinearly on the population state. Payoffs in this game are defined by $F_H(x) = h$ and $F_S(x) = sx^2$, with x representing the proportion of agents playing Stag. The population game F has three Nash equilibria: the pure equilibria $x = 0$ and $x = 1$ and the mixed equilibrium $x^* = \sqrt{h/s}$. We focus on the case in which $h = 2$ and $s = 7$, so that $x^* = \sqrt{2/7} \approx .5345$.

Suppose first that a population of 100 agents play this game using the BRM(.10) rule. Figure 11.3a presents the resulting mean dynamic beneath a graph of the stationary distribution μ^{100}. The mean dynamic has rest points at $x = .05$, $x = .95$, and $x^* \approx .5345$, so the almost-all-Hare rest point again has the larger basin of attraction. As was true in the linear Stag Hunt (see example 11.2.2), the stationary distribution generated by the BRM(.10) rule in this nonlinear Stag Hunt places nearly all of its mass on states where at least 88 agents choose Hare.

Figure 11.3b presents the mean dynamic and the stationary distribution μ^{100} for the logit rule with $\eta = .25$. The rest points of the logit(.25) dynamic are $x \approx .0003$, $x \approx 1$, and $x \approx .5398$, so the almost-all-Hare rest point once again has the larger basin of attraction. Nevertheless, the stationary distribution μ^{100} places virtually all of its mass on the state in which all 100 agents choose Stag.

To summarize, the prediction for very-long-run behavior under the BRM(.10) rule is inefficient coordination on Hare, while the prediction under the logit(.25) rule is efficient coordination on Stag. ◆

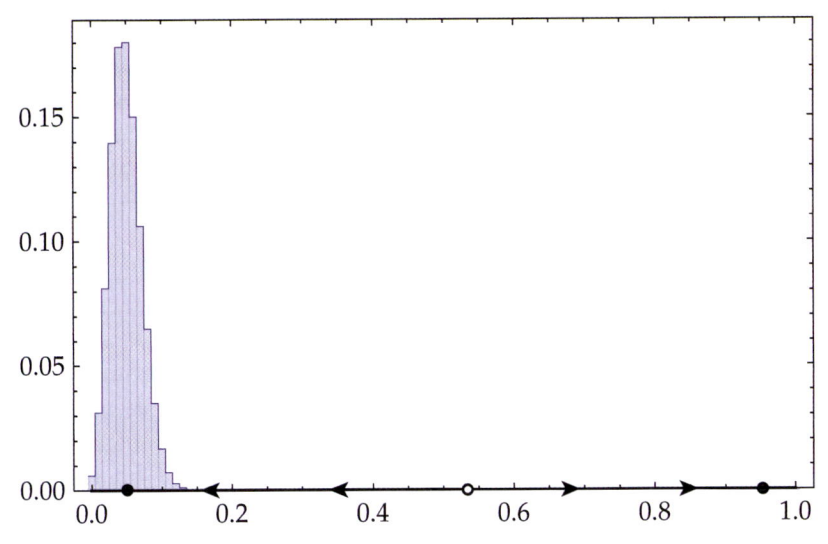

Stationary Distributions and Infinite Horizon Behavior

(a) Best response with mutations ($\varepsilon = .10$)

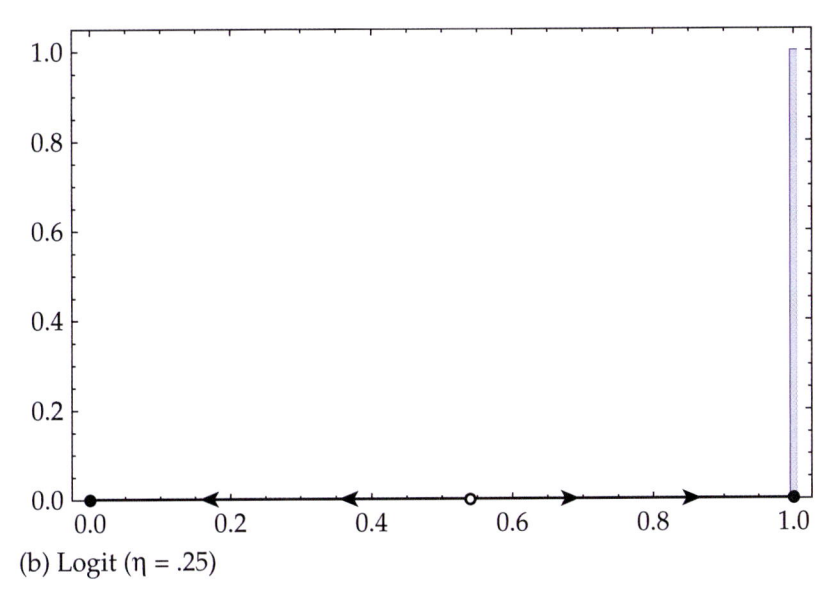

(b) Logit ($\eta = .25$)

Figure 11.3
Stationary distribution weights μ_χ for Nonlinear Stag Hunt ($h = 2, s = 7, N = 100$).

For the intuition behind this discrepancy in predictions, recall the discussion in section 11.1.1 about the key difference between the logit and BRM protocols: under logit choice, the probability of a mistake depends on its payoff consequences, whereas under BRM, it does not. As we argue in Chapter 12, the latter observation implies that under BRM, the probabilities of escaping from the basins of attraction of stable sets, and hence the identities of the states predominating in the very long run, depend only on the sizes and the shapes of the basins (see chapter 12). In the current one-dimensional example, these shapes are always line segments, so only the sizes of the basins matter; since the almost-all-Hare state has the larger basin, it is selected under the BRM rule.

On the contrary, the probability of escaping a stable equilibrium under logit choice depends not only on the shape and size of its basin, but also on the payoff differences that must be overcome during the journey. In the nonlinear Stag Hunt game, the basin of the almost-all-Stag equilibrium is smaller than that of the almost-all-Hare equilibrium. But because the payoff advantage of Stag over Hare in the former's basin tends to be much larger than the payoff advantage of Hare over Stag in the latter's, it is more difficult for the population to escape the all-Stag equilibrium than the all-Hare equilibrium. As a result, the population spends virtually all periods coordinating on Stag over the infinite horizon.

The process of escaping from the basin of a stable rest point can be compared to an attempt to swim upstream. Under BRM, the stream is steady, so the difficulty of a given excursion is proportional to distance. Under logit choice, the strength of the stream is variable, so the difficulty of an excursion depends on how this strength varies over the distance traveled. In general, the probability of escaping from a stable set is determined by both the distance that must be traveled and the varying strength of the oncoming flow.

11.3 Waiting Times and Infinite-Horizon Prediction

In order to place credence in the history-independent prediction provided by the stationary distribution, the relevant time horizon in the application at hand must be sufficiently long to justify an appeal to this distribution. This section shows that the lengths of time needed for history-independent predictions to be relevant are often extremely long, too long be of use in economic applications. After presenting some examples, we offer some suggestions about when infinite-horizon predictions are likely to be of practical use.

11.3.1 Examples

In cases where the mean dynamic has a globally asymptotically stable state, the stationary distribution μ^N will concentrate its mass around this state, at least when

Stationary Distributions and Infinite Horizon Behavior

the population size is large (see section 12.6 for a formal analysis). Example 11.3.1 considers such a case.

Example 11.3.1: Toss and Switch Again Examples 10.2.1 and 11.2.1 considered the Toss and Switch process $\{X_t^N\}$, which is defined by the constant jump rate $\lambda_\chi^N \equiv N$ and positive transition probabilities $p_\chi^N = \frac{1}{2}(1-\chi)$ and $q_\chi^N = \frac{1}{2}\chi$. The mean dynamic of this process, $\dot{\chi} = \frac{1}{2} - \chi$, is a contraction toward the rest point $\chi^* = \frac{1}{2}$, and its stationary distribution is approximately normal with mean $\frac{1}{2}$ and variance $\frac{1}{4N}$. Thus, the larger the population size N, the more concentrated around the rest point $\chi^* = \frac{1}{2}$ the stationary distribution becomes.

Now suppose the process $\{X_t^N\}$ begins in state $\chi = 0$. How long will it take before the agents are nearly equally divided between the two strategies? Using equation (11.44) from section 11.A.3, one can compute the expected time before the process reaches state .45, and the expected time before it reaches state .5, considering population sizes of 100, 1,000, and 10,000. The results are reported in table 11.1. Evidently, an equal distribution between the strategies is achieved very quickly, even when the population size is large.

For further insight, compare the numbers in the table to predictions of waiting times based on the mean dynamic. (This comparison is not always justified; see exercise 11.3.1.) The general solution to the mean dynamic is $\chi_t = \frac{1}{2} + (\chi_0 - \frac{1}{2})e^{-t}$. If the dynamic is run from state $\chi_0 = 0$, the time T that state $\chi_T = .45$ is reached satisfies $\chi_T = \frac{1}{2} - \frac{1}{2}e^{-T}$, and hence $T = \log 10 \approx 2.3026$. This is very close to the expected waiting time of 2.2977 for the 10,000 agent process.

Because the mean dynamic is continuous, it requires an infinite amount of time to reach the rest point $\chi^* = \frac{1}{2}$ from any state other than χ^*. Nevertheless, because of the random fluctuations in the process $\{X_t^N\}$, the expected time for this process to travel from state 0 to state $\frac{1}{2}$ remains quite small even when $N = 10,000$. ◆

In cases where the mean dynamic (M) has multiple asymptotically stable sets, one can reach similar but weaker conclusions about the time required to reach an asymptotically stable state from an initial condition in that state's basin of attraction: Suppose that x_0 is in the basin of x^*, and the initial conditions $X_0^N = x_0^N$ converge to x_0. Then it follows immediately from theorem 10.2.3 that for any $\varepsilon > 0$,

Table 11.1
Expected Wait to Reach State χ from State 0 in Toss and Switch

	N=100	N=1,000	N=10,000
$\chi = .45$	2.0389	2.2588	2.2977
$\chi = .50$	2.9378	4.0891	5.2403

there is a finite time T such that

$$\lim_{N\to\infty} \mathbb{P}(|X_T^N - x^*| < \varepsilon) = 1. \tag{11.15}$$

(To see why this is weaker than the conclusions of example 11.3.1, see exercise 11.3.1.)

Now imagine that the mean dynamic (M) has multiple stable sets and that a neighborhood of just one of these sets receives the preponderance of the mass in the stationary distribution μ^N. To use this fact as the basis for an infinite-horizon prediction, one should believe that if the population begins play near some other stable set of (M), it will transit to the one selected by μ^N within some reasonable amount of time. But the lengths of time that such transitions require can be extraordinary.

Example 11.3.2: Stag Hunt Revisited Example 11.2.2 presented stationary distributions for evolution in the Stag Hunt game

$$A = \begin{pmatrix} 2 & 2 \\ 0 & 3 \end{pmatrix} \tag{11.16}$$

under the BRM and logit protocols. In particular, figure 11.2a showed that with a population size of 100 under the BRM(.10) protocol, virtually all of the weight in the stationary distribution is placed in the vicinity of state $x = .05$, where most agents play the safe strategy Hare. Still, if more than $x^* = \frac{2}{3}$ of the population initially plays Stag, the expected motion of the process is toward state $x = .95$, at which nearly all agents play Stag. The results discussed in section 11.1.2 show that after a long enough time has passed, the empirical distribution of the process $\{X_t^N\}$ will be close to its stationary distribution, implying that the population will have spent most periods coordinating on Hare. How much time must pass before this infinite-horizon analysis is relevant?

Table 11.2 reports the expected amount of time before a process starting at state $x = .95$ reaches a state less than $x^* = \frac{2}{3}$, so that it is out of the basin of attraction of the all-Stag equilibrium. This is shown for two mutation rates (.10 and .01) and three population sizes (100, 1,000, and 10,000). All the expected waiting times are large. For perspective on some the size of the numbers in the table, note that the age

Table 11.2
Expected Wait before Escaping the Basin of Attraction of almost-all-Stag under BRM(ε)

	$N = 100$	$N = 1{,}000$	$N = 10{,}000$
$\varepsilon = .1$	3.03×10^{17}	7.33×10^{171}	1.59×10^{1720}
$\varepsilon = .01$	1.23×10^{50}	2.60×10^{492}	1.43×10^{4920}

of the universe is currently estimated to be 1.37×10^{10} years, or about 4.33×10^{17} seconds. ◆

This example shows that the expected amount of time to leave the basin of a stable rest point, including a rest point that is not selected by the stationary distribution, can be extremely large. This calls into question whether the stationary distribution is relevant in applications.

Exercise 11.3.1 The *expected* time to reach a stable rest point from a point *in its own basin of attraction* can also be surprisingly large. Suppose again that 100 agents use the BRM(.10) protocol during recurrent play of the Stag Hunt game (11.16). Remember that an agent who mutates chooses his strategy randomly; the probability that a revising agent chooses the suboptimal strategy is .05. Also, recall that the mean dynamic has stable rest points at $x = .05$ and $x = .95$, with the division point between the basins of attraction occurring at state $x^* = \frac{2}{3}$.

i. Using one of the formulas from example 11.A.5 (and a computer!), show that if play begins in state $x = .20$, the expected time required before the almost-all-Hare state $x = .05$ is first reached is about 8.36. (Since the formulas in example 11.A.5 are for Markov chains, and the continuous-time evolutionary process $\{X_t^N\}_{t \geq 0}$ has constant jump rate $N = 100$, the result of the Markov chain calculation must be divided by 100 to obtain the correct expected hitting time for the Markov process; see the discussion following proposition 11.A.3.)

ii. Show that if play begins in state $x = .80$, the expected time required before the almost-all-Stag state $x = .95$ is first reached is about 2.44×10^{32}.

iii. Using equation (11.46) from example 11.A.6, show that if play begins in state .80, then the probability of reaching state .05 before state .95 is about 1.32×10^{-7}, in accordance with the deterministic approximation theorem and equation (11.15).

iv. At first glance, the claims in (ii) and (iii) may seem inconsistent with one another. Explain in words how they can both be true. ◇

While the discussion above focuses on hitting times, one can also gauge the amount of time needed before the stationary distribution becomes relevant by determining how quickly the time t distributions of the evolutionary process approach the stationary distribution. See section 11.A.8 for a brief presentation of the relevant techniques.

11.3.2 Discussion

Example 11.3.2 shows that the amount of time needed to escape from the basin of attraction of a stable equilibrium can be extraordinarily large, even when the population size and noise parameters are not extreme. In fact, it is possible to show that the expected time required to escape the basin of a stable equilibrium grows exponentially both in the population size N and in the inverse noise level η^{-1} (which corresponds to $-\log \varepsilon$ in the BRM(ε) model; see section 11.1.1). This waiting time problem only becomes more acute in stochastic stability analysis (see chapter 12), which studies the limiting behavior of the stationary distributions of the stochastic evolutionary process as the population size N goes to infinity and the noise level η goes to zero. Taking these limits enables one to obtain cleaner and more general selection results than are obtainable without taking limits. At the same time, taking limits in N and η guarantees that the waiting time problem will be especially severe. No formal analyses of waiting times in models of stochastic evolution are given in this book; see the chapter notes for references where such analyses can be found.

What are the implications for predicting behavior in applications? Noting the size of the numbers in table 11.2, it seems hard to avoid the conclusion that in economic environments with at least moderate population sizes and at most moderate amounts of idiosyncratic noise in agents' decisions, the predictions of infinite-horizon analysis do not hold force within any relevant time span. Therefore, the history-dependent predictions provided by the mean dynamic (M) seem the most appropriate ones to utilize. In most cases this means giving up the possibility of unique predictions that do not require knowledge of past behavior, but there is little to gain in making unique predictions that are as likely as not to be incorrect.

Are there environments in which infinite-horizon predictions are appropriate? One possibility lies in modeling biological evolution. With simple organisms, generation lengths are very short, mutation rates can be measured precisely, and the time spans of interest may last thousands of years. For human decision makers, small populations and large noise levels would make waiting times lower, so infinite-horizon predictions could be more apt. At the same time, when populations are small, one may doubt the appropriateness of the standing assumptions that agents are anonymous and myopic. Also, large noise levels impose a strong inward force on the mean dynamic (see example 6.2.2); in cases where this dynamic already admits a globally asymptotically stable state, infinite-horizon analysis provides limited additional predictive power.

In seeking further scope for infinite-horizon predictions, it is worth bearing in mind that every economic model is an abstraction from the application it represents, trading off descriptive accuracy for ease of analysis and interpretation. One therefore should not be too hasty to discard a model with some clearly unrealistic

Stationary Distributions and Infinite Horizon Behavior

implications if those implications might be absent from a more detailed though possibly less tractable model.

In the case of the stochastic evolutionary processes studied in this book, the long waiting times for transitions between equilibria are due to these transitions' requiring the contemporaneous occurrence of many independent, low probability events. There are plausible alternative models in which the requirements for transitions are much less unlikely to be met.

One possibility lies in replacing the global interaction structure used in this book with structures in which each agent only interacts with a small, fixed subset of his opponents. For instance, agents might live in distinct locations and only interact with neighbors. Alternatively, agents might be linked through a network (based on friendship, say, or collaboration) and only interact with those to whom they have a direct connection. In such cases, simultaneous changes in strategy by agents in a single small neighborhood can spread contagiously throughout the entire population. Since a small number of revisions can set off a population-wide transition between equilibria, the wait until a transition occurs need not be long. Local interaction and network models are beyond the scope of this book; see the chapter notes for references to the literature.

Waiting times could also be greatly reduced by allowing correlation in agents' randomized choices. As a simple example, suppose that the common level of noise in agents' decisions varies with time. Then during periods of high noise levels, transitions between equilibria might not be especially unlikely, even as over time the overall proportion of suboptimal choices remains very small.

Of course, for the properties of these alternative models to be relevant to the current study, one would need to know that they generated qualitatively similar predictions of strategic behavior. Little is known about how the predictions of the various models compare, so one cannot say whether these models could be used to address the waiting time problem in a convincing way. The important point here is more limited, namely, that the existence of very long waiting times in our basic model does not imply that the infinite-horizon predictions provided by this model cannot be useful.

11.4 Model Adjustments for Finite Populations

This chapter is the first in the book to focus directly on behavior in populations of a finite size N without taking N to infinity. This means that individual agents are no longer negligible; a change in strategy by a single agent alters the population state. In this section, we modify our earlier definitions of games and revision protocols to account for finite-population effects. In some cases these changes are matters of modeling precision, or even of convenience. In others, most notably, logit evolution in potential games, these modifications are needed to ensure reversibility, which in turn allows us to obtain exact results without recourse to large population or small noise limits.

11.4.1 Finite-Population Games

When there are N agents in the population choosing strategies from the set $S = \{1, \ldots, n\}$, the population state is an element of the set $X^N = \{x \in X : Nx \in \mathbf{Z}^n\}$, a uniform grid in the simplex in $\mathbf{R}^n$. An N-agent *finite-population game* can therefore be identified with its payoff function $F^N : X^N \to \mathbf{R}^n$, where as usual, $F_i^N(x) \in \mathbf{R}$ is the payoff to strategy i when the population state is $x \in X^N$. Notice that only the values that F_i^N takes on the set $X_i^N = \{x \in X^N : x_i > 0\}$ are of consequence, since at the remaining states strategy i is unplayed.

Example 11.4.1: Matching without Self-Matching Example 2.2.1 defined the population game F generated by matching in the symmetric normal form game $A \in \mathbf{R}^{n \times n}$ by $F_i(x) = \sum_{j \in S} A_{ij} x_j = (Ax)_i$, so that $F(x) = Ax$. When agents are infinitesimal, this is the only definition that makes sense. But when there are only a finite number of agents, this definition implicitly assumes that agents can be matched against themselves. To specify payoffs without self-matching, observe that when the population state is x, each strategy i player faces Nx_j opponents playing strategy $j \neq i$, but only $Nx_i - 1$ opponents playing strategy i, making the effective population state $\frac{1}{N-1}(Nx - e_i)$. The expected payoff to a strategy i player at population state x is therefore

$$F_i^N(x) = \tfrac{1}{N-1}(A(Nx - e_i))_i = (Ax)_i + \tfrac{1}{N-1}\left((Ax)_i - A_{ii}\right). \qquad \blacklozenge \quad (11.17)$$

To be able to say that a continuous-population game is close to a large finite-population game, we require a notion of convergence for a sequence of finite-population games $\{F^N\}_{N=N_0}^{\infty}$ to a limit game $F : X \to \mathbf{R}^n$. A natural notion of convergence for such a sequence of functions is *uniform convergence*, which requires that

$$\lim_{N \to \infty} \max_{x \in X^N} |F^N(x) - F(x)| = 0. \qquad (11.18)$$

Thus, equation (11.17) implies that the sequence of finite-population games $\{F^N\}$ generated by matching without self-matching in A converges uniformly to the limit game $F(x) = Ax$.

Stationary Distributions and Infinite Horizon Behavior

State $x \in \mathcal{X}^N$ is a *Nash equilibrium* of F^N if no player can obtain a higher payoff by switching strategies:

$$[x_i > 0 \Rightarrow F_i^N(x) \geq F_j^N(x + \tfrac{1}{N}(e_j - e_i))] \quad \text{for all } i, j \in S.$$

This condition accounts for the fact that after an agent switches from strategy i to strategy j, the population has one less i player and one more j player. Since the set of population states $\mathcal{X}^N$ is not convex, Kakutani's Fixed point theorem cannot be used to prove existence of Nash equilibria (cf. theorem 2.1.1). Indeed, it is easy to construct examples of finite population games with no (pure) Nash equilibria.

Exercise 11.4.1

i. Construct a finite-population game with no Nash equilibrium.

ii. Suppose the sequence of finite-population games $\{F^N\}_{N=N_0}^\infty$ converges uniformly to the limit game $F: X \to \mathbf{R}^n$. Show that the Nash equilibrium correspondence of this sequence is upper-hemicontinuous at infinity: if $\{N^k\}_{k=1}^\infty$ is a sequence with $\lim_{k\to\infty} N^k = \infty$, x^{N^k} is a Nash equilibrium of F^{N^k}, and $\lim_{k\to\infty} x^{N^k} = x$, then x is a Nash equilibrium of F as defined in chapter 2. ◇

11.4.2 Clever Payoff Evaluation

If a population has N members, an agent who switches from strategy i to strategy j when the state is x changes the state to $x + \tfrac{1}{N}(e_j - e_i)$. If this agent wants to compare his current payoff $F_i^N(x)$ to the payoff he will obtain after switching, the relevant comparison is not to $F_j^N(x)$, but rather to $F_j^N(x + \tfrac{1}{N}(e_j - e_i))$. It is often convenient to assume that agents account for this change when deciding whether to switch strategies. Agents who do so are said to use *clever payoff evaluation*, whereas those who do not are said to use *simple payoff evaluation*.

To formalize this idea, define the set of *diminished population states* by $\mathcal{X}_-^N = \{z \in \mathbf{R}_+^n : \sum_{i \in S} z_i = \tfrac{N-1}{N} \text{ and } Nz \in \mathbf{Z}^n\}$. Each diminished population state describes the behavior of the opponents of one member of a population of size N. Then, given a game $F^N: \mathcal{X}^N \to \mathbf{R}^n$, define the *clever payoff function* $\check{F}^N: \mathcal{X}_-^N \to \mathbf{R}^n$ by

$$\check{F}_k^N(z) = F_k^N(z + \tfrac{1}{N}e_k). \tag{11.19}$$

Thus, the clever payoff vector $\check{F}^N(z)$ describes the current payoff opportunities of an agent whose *opponents'* behavior distribution is $z \in \mathcal{X}_-^N$. Finally, an agent using revision protocol $\rho = \rho(\pi, x)$ in game F^N is *clever* if at state x, his conditional switch rate from i to j is not $\rho_{ij}(F^N(x), x)$, but rather

$$\rho_{ij}(\check{F}^N(x - \tfrac{1}{N}e_i), x). \tag{11.20}$$

This notation for clever payoffs is used in section 11.5 when studying evolution in potential games. When considering two-strategy games, where the notation $x \equiv x_1$ is used to refer to the proportion of agents choosing strategy 1, it is easier to describe clever choice directly, without introducing expressions (11.19) and (11.20).

Example 11.4.2 Consider the symmetric normal form game with strategy set $S = \{0,1\}$ and payoff matrix

$$A = \begin{pmatrix} a & b \\ c & d \end{pmatrix}.$$

Suppose a population of N agents are matched without self-matching to play A, as in example 11.4.1. Following the convention from section 11.2 of writing $x \equiv x_1 = 1 - x_0$, we can express the strategies' expected payoffs as

$$F_0^N(x) = \frac{N(1-x)-1}{N-1}a + \frac{Nx}{N-1}b = \frac{1}{N-1}\left(Nx(b-a) + (N-1)a\right),$$

$$F_1^N(x) = \frac{N(1-x)}{N-1}c + \frac{Nx-1}{N-1}d = \frac{1}{N-1}\left(Nx(d-c) + Nc - d\right).$$

A simple agent prefers strategy 1 to strategy 0 whenever $F_1^N(x) > F_0^N(x)$. But a clever agent currently playing strategy 0 prefers strategy 1 whenever $F_0^N(x) < F_1^N(x + \frac{1}{N})$, and a clever agent playing strategy 1 prefers strategy 0 whenever $F_1^N(x) < F_0^N(x - \frac{1}{N})$.

The comparison made by a clever strategy 0 player at state x is the same one made by a clever strategy 1 player at state $x + \frac{1}{N}$, since both players have $N(1-x) - 1$ opponents playing strategy 0 and Nx playing strategy 1. ◆

For any fixed game A, the difference between simple and clever payoff evaluations becomes inconsequential when the population size N is large enough. But the exercises that follow show that for any given N, there are games in which simple and clever payoff evaluation always lead to opposite recommendations for play.

Exercise 11.4.2

i. Let A be a symmetric two-strategy normal form game in which strategy 1 strictly dominates strategy 0 ($c > a$ and $d > b$). Show that under matching without self-matching, clever agents always want to switch from strategy 0 to strategy 1 and never want to switch from strategy 1 to strategy 0.

ii. Now suppose that agents are playing the game

$$A = \begin{pmatrix} 0 & 3N-2 \\ 1 & 3N \end{pmatrix}.$$

How will simple agents behave in this game? Provide intuition for your result. ◇

Exercise 11.4.3 Suppose that agents are matched *with* self-matching in the Prisoner's Dilemma game

$$A = \begin{pmatrix} 3N & 0 \\ 3N+2 & 1 \end{pmatrix}.$$

What happens in this game if agents use simple payoff evaluation? What if they use clever payoff evaluation? Provide intuition for your results. ◊

11.4.3 Committed Agents and Imitative Protocols

The general infinite-population specification of an imitative revision protocol is

$$\rho_{ij}(\pi, x) = x_j r_{ij}(\pi, x). \tag{11.21}$$

The x_j term in (11.21) represents the random choice of whom to imitate; the x appearing as an argument of the conditional imitation rate $r_{ij}(\pi, x)$ can be used to allow for repeated sampling (see example 5.4.5).

In a finite-population setting, using the actual state x as the argument of ρ has the effect of allowing each player to imitate himself. To avoid self-imitation, we change the second input of ρ_{ij} from $x \in \mathcal{X}^N$ to $\frac{Nx - e_i}{N-1} \in \mathcal{X}^{N-1}$, which describes the distribution of strategies among the $N - 1$ opponents of the revising i player. The main effect of removing the revising agent from the population he samples is minor: it increases the rate at which agents switch strategies by a factor of $\frac{N}{N-1}$.

We now consider a small modification of the imitative model that has large effects on predictions of play. As we have often noted, purely imitative protocols satisfy extinction: unused strategies are never subsequently chosen. In the present context, this means that the stochastic evolutionary process $\{X_t^N\}$ has multiple recurrent classes and hence many stationary distributions. Suppose we alter our basic model to ensure that there is always at least one agent playing each strategy. Then if conditional imitation rates r_{ij} are always positive, the process $\{X_t^N\}$ will be irreducible, and so will possess a unique stationary distribution.

The simplest and least intrusive way to accomplish this is to assume that in addition to the N standard agents, there are also n committed agents, one for each of the n strategies in S. The ith committed agent always plays strategy i; he never receives revision opportunities. If we let the state variable $x \in \mathcal{X}^N$ represent the behavior of the standard (uncommitted) agents, and exclude self-imitation, we obtain a revision protocol of the form $\rho_{ij}(\pi, \frac{Nx + 1 - e_i}{N + n - 1})$. We continue to express payoffs $F^N : \mathcal{X}^N \to \mathbf{R}^n$ as a function of the behavior of the standard agents. Had we started with a function $G^N : \mathcal{X}^{N+n} \to \mathbf{R}^n$ that expressed payoffs as a function of the aggregate behavior of both kinds of agents, we could obtain F^N as $F^N(x) = G^N(\frac{Nx+1}{N+n})$.

The fraction of committed agents approaches zero as the population size becomes large. But introducing these agents into the analysis leads to completely different predictions of infinite-horizon behavior.

Example 11.4.3 Suppose that a standard agent who receives a revision opportunity picks an opponent at random and imitates him: that is, let $r_{ij} \equiv 1$, so that $\rho_{ij}(\pi, x) = x_j$. Without committed agents, the resulting stochastic evolutionary process converges with probability 1 to one of the n pure states $e_1, \ldots, e_n$. But with a single committed agent for each strategy, the process $\{X_t^N\}$ is irreducible, and so admits a unique stationary distribution μ^N. In fact, the process is reversible, and its stationary distribution is the uniform distribution on $\mathcal{X}^N$.

Since the only positive probability transitions are between pairs of adjacent states, establishing reversibility with a uniform stationary distribution reduces to verifying that $P_{xy}^N = P_{yx}^N$ for all such pairs $x \in \mathcal{X}^N$ and $y = x + \frac{1}{N}(e_j - e_i)$. Letting $z = x - \frac{1}{N}e_i = y - \frac{1}{N}e_j \in \mathcal{X}_-^N$ represent the behavior of the revising player's opponents, we compute as follows:

$$P_{xy}^N = x_i \cdot \rho_{ij}(\pi, \tfrac{Nx+1-e_j}{N+n-1}) \tag{11.22}$$

$$= x_i \cdot \frac{Nx_j + 1}{N+n-1}$$

$$= \frac{Nz_i + 1}{N} \cdot \frac{Nz_j + 1}{N+n-1}$$

$$= \frac{Nz_j + 1}{N} \cdot \frac{Nz_i + 1}{N+n-1}$$

$$= y_j \cdot \frac{Ny_i + 1}{N+n-1}$$

$$= y_j \cdot \rho_{ji}(\pi, \tfrac{Ny+1-e_i}{N+n-1})$$

$$= P_{yx}^N.$$

It follows from exercise 10.1.1 that the mass on each state $x \in \mathcal{X}^N$ is $\mu_x^N = \frac{1}{\#\mathcal{X}^N} = \binom{N+n-1}{n-1}^{-1}$. ◆

Example 11.4.4 Suppose that N standard agents and $n = 2$ committed agents play the two-strategy game F^N, employing an imitative protocol of the form

Stationary Distributions and Infinite Horizon Behavior

$$\rho_{01}(\pi,x) = (1-x)\,r_{01}(\pi,x),$$

$$\rho_{10}(\pi,x) = x\,r_{10}(\pi,x).$$

As usual, $x \in [0,1]$ denotes the proportion of agents choosing strategy 1. If r_{01} and r_{10} are positive-valued, the resulting evolutionary process is irreducible. Adjusting equation (11.11) to account for the presence of the committed agents, we find that the stationary distribution of the evolutionary process is described by

$$\frac{\mu_x^N}{\mu_0^N} = \prod_{j=1}^{Nx} \frac{p_{(j-1)/N}^N}{q_{j/N}^N}$$

$$= \prod_{j=1}^{Nx} \frac{\frac{N-j+1}{N}}{\frac{j}{N}} \cdot \frac{\frac{1}{R}\rho_{01}(F^N(\frac{j-1}{N}),\frac{j}{N+1})}{\frac{1}{R}\rho_{10}(F^N(\frac{j}{N}),\frac{j}{N+1})}$$

$$= \prod_{j=1}^{Nx} \frac{\frac{N-j+1}{N}}{\frac{j}{N}} \cdot \frac{\frac{j}{N+1}}{\frac{N-j+1}{N+1}} \cdot \frac{r_{01}(F^N(\frac{j-1}{N}),\frac{j}{N+1})}{r_{10}(F^N(\frac{j}{N}),\frac{j}{N+1})}$$

$$= \prod_{j=1}^{Nx} \frac{r_{01}(F^N(\frac{j-1}{N}),\frac{j}{N+1})}{r_{10}(F^N(\frac{j}{N}),\frac{j}{N+1})}. \quad (11.23)$$

Thus, the stationary distribution weights can be expressed in terms of the conditional imitation rates alone. ◆

Further consequences of adding committed agents to stochastic imitative models are considered in the next section.

Exercise 11.4.4 Exercise 11.2.2 presented the stationary distribution for the *n*-strategy Toss and Switch process, under which revising agents randomize uniformly over the available strategies. Write the mean dynamic generated by this process and the process defined in example 11.4.3, and use these dynamics to provide an intuitive explanation for the differences between the stationary distributions of the two processes. ◇

11.5 Potential Games and Exponential Protocols

The analysis of infinite-horizon behavior in two-strategy games is greatly simplified by the fact that in this context, the Markov process $\{X_t^N\}$ is a birth and death chain, and hence reversible. Beyond two-strategy settings, the only other context in which $\{X_t^N\}$ is known to be reversible is that of potential games, with agents employing one of a number of revision protocols under which conditional switch rates are exponential functions of payoffs.

11.5.1 Finite-Population Potential Games

The definitions and characterizations of continuous-population potential games in chapter 3 relied on tools from calculus. This section introduces definitions of full potential games and potential games for finite populations, and connects these definitions with the continuous-population definitions from chapter 3 by means of convergence results. Much of this section is comprised of exercises establishing various links between potential games defined in the two contexts.

Section 3.1 introduced the notion of a full potential function, a function whose partial derivatives equal the payoffs of the underlying game. To ensure the existence of these partial derivatives, the full potential function was defined on the positive orthant, a full-dimensional set in $\mathbf{R}^n$.

To define full potential games for finite populations, we introduce a discrete analogue of this device. As in section 11.4.2, let $\mathcal{X}_-^N = \{Z \in \mathbf{R}_+^n : \sum_{i \in S} z_i = \frac{N-1}{N}$ and $Nz \in \mathbf{Z}^n\}$ be the set of diminished population states, so that each $z \in \mathcal{X}_-^N$ describes the behavior of the opponents of one member of a population of size N. We call a finite-population game $F^N : \mathcal{X}^N \to \mathbf{R}^n$ a *full potential game* if it admits a *full potential function*: a function $f^N : \mathcal{X}^N \cup \mathcal{X}_-^N \to \mathbf{R}$ such that

$$F_i^N(x) = f^N(x) - f^N(x - \tfrac{1}{N}e_i) \quad \text{for all } x \in \mathcal{X}^N, \; i \in S. \tag{11.24}$$

One can describe condition (11.24) as requiring the payoff to strategy i to be determined by the ith discrete partial derivative of the function $\frac{1}{N} f^N$.

Exercise 11.5.1 Formalize and verify this last statement. ◇

Exercise 11.5.2: Matching in Common Interest Games Let the symmetric normal form game $A \in \mathbf{R}^{n \times n}$ be a common interest game (i.e., $A = A'$). Example 3.1.1 showed that when an infinite population is matched to play A, the resulting population game $F(x) = Ax$ is a full potential game with full potential function $f(x) = \tfrac{1}{2} x' A x$.

i. Let $F^N(x) = Ax$ be the finite-population game obtained via matching with self-matching. Verify that F^N is a full potential game with full potential function

$$f^N(x) = \tfrac{1}{2} \left(N x' A x + \sum_{k \in S} A_{kk} x_k \right).$$

ii. Now let F^N be the finite-population game obtained via matching without self-matching, as defined in equation (11.17). Verify that this F^N is also a full potential game, but with full potential function

$$f^N(x) = \tfrac{1}{2}\tfrac{N}{N-1}\left(N x'Ax - \sum_{k \in S} A_{kk} x_k\right).$$

Note that in each case, the functions $\tfrac{1}{N} f^N$ converge to f as N grows large.   ◇

Exercise 11.5.3: Congestion Games   Example 2.2.4 defined the continuous-population congestion game $F: \mathbf{R}_+^n \to \mathbf{R}$ by

$$F_i(x) = -\sum_{\phi \in \Phi_i} c_\phi(u_\phi(x)),$$

where Φ_i is the set of facilities (or links) used by strategy (or path) i, $c_\phi: \mathbf{R}_+ \to \mathbf{R}$ is the cost function of facility ϕ, and $u_\phi(x) = \sum_{i \in S: \phi \in \Phi_i} x_i$ is the utilization level of facility ϕ at state x. Example 3.1.2 showed that this game is a full potential game with full potential function

$$f(x) = -\sum_{\phi \in \Phi} \int_0^{u_\phi(x)} c_\phi(z)\, dz.$$

Apart from the change in domain, the definition of the finite-population congestion game $F^N: \mathcal{X}^N \to \mathbf{R}^n$ is identical to that of F. Show that F^N is also a full potential game, with full potential function

$$f^N(x) = -\sum_{\phi \in \Phi_i} \sum_{k=1}^{Nu_\phi(x)} c_\phi(\tfrac{k}{N}).$$ ◇

The continuous-population definition of a potential game (see section 3.2) uses a potential function that is only defined on the original set of population states, and that only determines the game's relative payoffs. Extending this notion to the present setting, we call a finite-population game $F^N: \mathcal{X}^N \to \mathbf{R}^n$ a *potential game* if it admits a *potential function*: in this case, a function $f^N: \mathcal{X}^N \to \mathbf{R}$ such that

$$F_j^N(x + \tfrac{1}{N}(e_j - e_i)) - F_i^N(x) = f^N(x + \tfrac{1}{N}(e_j - e_i)) - f^N(x) \quad \text{for all } x \in \mathcal{X}_i^N, \, i, j \in S.$$
(11.25)

Equation (11.25) says that when an agent switches from strategy i to strategy j, the change in his payoff is equal to the change in potential. This definition closely resembles the definition of normal form potential games in exercise 3.2.7, a connection that we examine in exercise 11.5.17(ii).

Exercise 11.5.4: Two-Strategy Games   Let F^N be a two-strategy game with strategy set $S = \{0, 1\}$. Verify that F^N is a finite-population potential game with potential function

$$f^N(x) = \sum_{j=1}^{Nx_1} \left(F_1^N(x) - F_0^N(x + \tfrac{1}{N}(e_0 - e_1)) \right).\qquad\diamond$$

Exercise 11.5.5: Equilibrium and Evolutionary Dynamics for Finite-Population Potential Games

i. Suppose that F^N is a potential game with potential function f^N. Show that $x \in X^N$ is a Nash equilibrium of F^N (as defined in section 11.4.1) if and only if x is a local maximizer of f^N. (Be sure to define "local maximizer of f^N".) It follows that in finite-population potential games, Nash equilibria exist.

ii. Argue that if agents in a finite-population potential game F^N switch to better-performing strategies sequentially, the population state will converge to a Nash equilibrium of F^N after a finite number of switches. $\diamond$

Theorem 3.2.9 showed that despite first appearances, the continuous-population definitions of full potential games and potential games are essentially equivalent. In the finite-population case, it is clear that every full potential game is a potential game, and theorem 11.5.6 establishes that the two definitions are in fact equivalent. Fortunately, the proof in this discrete setting requires much less effort.

Theorem 11.5.6 *Let F^N be a potential game with potential function $f^N \colon X^N \to \mathbf{R}$. Then there is an extension $\tilde{f}^N \colon X^N \cup X_-^N \to \mathbf{R}$ off that is a full potential function for F^N. Therefore, F^N is a potential game if and only if it is a full potential game.*

Proof Let $\tilde{f}(x) = f(x)$ when $x \in X^N$, and for each $z \in X_-^N$, let

$$\tilde{f}^N(z) = \tilde{f}^N(z + \tfrac{1}{N}e_1) - F_1^N(z + \tfrac{1}{N}e_1). \qquad (11.26)$$

Rearranging this expression shows that condition (11.24) holds when $i = 1$. To verify that it holds for an arbitrary strategy i, use equations (11.25) and (11.26) (with $z = x - \tfrac{1}{N}e_i$) to compute as follows:

$$F_i^N(x) = F_1^N(x + \tfrac{1}{N}(e_1 - e_i)) - \tilde{f}^N(x + \tfrac{1}{N}(e_1 - e_i)) + \tilde{f}^N(x)$$

$$= \left(\tilde{f}^N(x + \tfrac{1}{N}(e_1 - e_i)) - \tilde{f}^N(x - \tfrac{1}{N}e_i) \right) - \tilde{f}^N(x + \tfrac{1}{N}(e_1 - e_i)) + \tilde{f}^N(x)$$

$$= \tilde{f}^N(x) - \tilde{f}^N(x - \tfrac{1}{N}e_i). \qquad \blacksquare$$

By virtue of theorem 11.5.6, there is no need for the term "full potential game" in the finite-population setting. (This term is needed in the continuous-population setting, where potential games and full potential games have different domains.)

Of course, potential functions and full potential functions must still be distinguished when populations are finite.

All the developments in this section suggest that the finite-population and continuous-population definitions of potential games are different expressions of the same idea. To formalize this intuition, let $\{F^N\}_{N=N_0}^\infty$ be a sequence of finite-population potential games with full potential functions $\{f^N\}_{N=N_0}^\infty$, and let the function $f \colon \mathbf{R}_+^n \to \mathbf{R}$ be C^1. We call the sequence of rescaled full potential functions $\{\frac{1}{N} f^N\}$ *Lipschitz convergent* with limit f if there is a vanishing sequence $\{K^N\}_{N=N_0}^\infty$ such that

$$\left|\left(\tfrac{1}{N} f^N(x) - f(x)\right) - \left(\tfrac{1}{N} f^N(y) - f(y)\right)\right| \leq K^N |x-y| \quad \text{for all } x, y \in \mathcal{X}^N \cup \mathcal{X}_-^N. \tag{11.27}$$

In words, condition (11.27) requires the differences $\frac{1}{N} f^N - f$ to be Lipschitz continuous, with Lipschitz constants that approach zero as N grows large. The rescaling of the potential functions reflects the fact that the values of f^N are of order N and so must be shrunk by a factor of $\frac{1}{N}$ for convergence to be feasible.

Theorem 11.5.7 shows that a sequence of finite-population potential games $\{F^N\}$ converges uniformly to a continuous full potential game if and only if the corresponding sequence of rescaled full potential functions $\{\frac{1}{N} f^N\}$ is Lipschitz convergent. Exercise 11.5.10 provides the analogous result for potential functions defined on $\mathcal{X}^N$ only.

Theorem 11.5.7 *Let $\{F^N\}_{N=N_0}^\infty$ be a sequence of finite-population potential games with full potential functions $\{f^N\}_{N=N_0}^\infty$.*

i. *Suppose that $\{\frac{1}{N} f^N\}$ is Lipschitz convergent with C^1 limit $f \colon \mathbf{R}_+^n \to \mathbf{R}$, and define $F \colon \mathbf{R}_+^n \to \mathbf{R}^n$ by $F(x) = \nabla f(x)$. Then $\{F^N\}$ converges uniformly to $F|_X$.*

ii. *Suppose that $\{F^N\}$ converges uniformly to $F \colon X \to \mathbf{R}^n$ and that F admits a full potential function $f \colon \mathbf{R}_+^n \to \mathbf{R}$, in the sense that $F(x) = \nabla f(x)$ for all $x \in X$. Then $\{\frac{1}{N} f^N\}$ is Lipschitz convergent with limit f.*

Exercise 11.5.8 Prove theorem 11.5.7. (*Hint:* If $f \colon \mathbf{R}_+^n \to \mathbf{R}$ is C^1, the mean value theorem implies that there is a point y^N on the line segment from x to $x - \frac{e_i}{N}$ such that $f(x) - f(x - \frac{e_i}{N}) = \frac{1}{N} \frac{\partial f}{\partial x_i}(y^N)$. Combine this fact with compactness arguments.) ◇

Exercise 11.5.9

i. Lipschitz convergence is unaffected by the addition of constant terms to the potential functions f^N and f. Show that if these functions are normalized so that $f^N(e_1) = f(e_1) = 0$, and if the resulting sequence $\{\frac{1}{N} f^N\}$ is Lipschitz convergent with limit f, then the sequence $\{\frac{1}{N} f^N\}$ converges uniformly to f.

ii. Show that the uniform convergence of $\{\frac{1}{N}f^N\}$ to f does not imply the Lipschitz convergence of $\{\frac{1}{N}f^N\}$ to f. (*Hint:* Suppose that $f^N(e_1) = 0$ and that $f^N(x) = \sqrt{N}$ for $x \in \mathcal{X}^N \cup \mathcal{X}_-^N - \{e_1\}$.) ◇

Exercise 11.5.10 Let $\{F^N\}_{N=N_0}^\infty$ be a sequence of finite-population potential games with potential functions $\{f^N\}_{N=N_0}^\infty$. (Thus f^N has domain $\mathcal{X}^N$.)

i. Suppose that $\{\frac{1}{N}f^N\}$ is Lipschitz convergent with C^1 limit $f\colon X \to \mathbf{R}$, and define $F\colon X \to \mathbf{R}^n$ by $F(x) = \nabla f(x)$. Show that $\{\Phi F^N\}$ converges uniformly to F, where $\Phi = I - \frac{1}{n}\mathbf{1}\mathbf{1}'$ is the orthogonal projection of $\mathbf{R}^n$ onto TX.

ii. Suppose that $\{\Phi F^N\}$ converges uniformly to $F\colon X \to \mathbf{R}^n$ and that F admits potential function $f\colon X \to \mathbf{R}$. Show that $\{\frac{1}{N}f^N\}$ is Lipschitz convergent with limit f. ◇

11.5.2 Exponential Revision Protocols

Exponential revision protocols are divided into two classes according to whether agents choose candidate strategies directly or through imitation. We consider the direct version first.

Definition   *The protocol $\rho\colon \mathbf{R}^n \to \mathbf{R}_+^{n \times n}$ is a* direct exponential protocol *with noise level η if*

$$\rho_{ij}(\pi) = \frac{\exp(\eta^{-1}\psi(\pi_i, \pi_j))}{d_{ij}(\pi)}, \tag{11.28}$$

where the functions $\psi\colon \mathbf{R}^2 \to \mathbf{R}$ and $d\colon \mathbf{R}^n \to (0, \infty)^{n \times n}$ satisfy

$$\psi(\pi_i, \pi_j) - \psi(\pi_j, \pi_i) = \pi_j - \pi_i, \tag{11.29}$$

$$d_{ij}(\pi) = d_{ji}(\pi). \tag{11.30}$$

The definition of a direct exponential protocol is broad: it allows agents' choice procedures to take a wide range of qualitative forms depending on the specification of the functions ψ and d. For instance, under condition (11.29), the function ψ can reflect the following sorts of dependence of switch rates on payoffs:

Positive dependence on candidate payoff: $\psi(\pi_i, \pi_j) = \pi_j$.

Negative dependence on current payoff: $\psi(\pi_i, \pi_j) = -\pi_i$.

Positive dependence on payoff difference: $\psi(\pi_i, \pi_j) = \frac{1}{2}(\pi_j - \pi_i)$.

Positive dependence on positive payoff difference: $\psi(\pi_i, \pi_j) = [\pi_j - \pi_i]_+$.

Negative dependence on negative payoff difference: $\psi(\pi_i, \pi_j) = -[\pi_j - \pi_i]_-$.

Thus, exponential protocols allow switching rates to be determined by the desirability of the payoff of the candidate strategy, by dissatisfaction with the payoff of

Stationary Distributions and Infinite Horizon Behavior

the current strategy, or with comparisons of the payoffs of both strategies. The information requirements of an exponential protocol can be quite modest: for instance, the second option in the list only requires the agent to know his own current payoff.

Different choices of the function d can be used to reflect different reference groups that agents employ when considering a switch. The symmetry condition (11.30) says that when an i player considers switching to strategy j, he employs the same comparison group as a j player who considers switching to i. Consider the case in which $\psi(\pi_i, \pi_j) = \pi_j$. If

$$d_{ij}(\pi) = \sum_{k \in S} \exp(\eta^{-1} \pi_k),$$

so that agents use the full set of strategies as the comparison group, we obtain the *logit protocol*

$$\rho_{ij}(\pi) = \frac{\exp(\eta^{-1} \pi_j)}{\sum_{k \in S} \exp(\eta^{-1} \pi_k)}.$$

If instead $d_{ij}(\pi) = \exp(\eta^{-1} \pi_i) + \exp(\eta^{-1} \pi_j)$, so that the comparison group only contains the current and candidate strategies, we obtain the *pairwise logit protocol*

$$\rho_{ij}(\pi) = \frac{\exp(\eta^{-1} \pi_j)}{\exp(\eta^{-1} \pi_i) + \exp(\eta^{-1} \pi_j)}.$$

Of course, there are many further choices of ψ and ρ that satisfy the requirements above.

Exercise 11.5.11 Show that ρ is a direct exponential protocol if and only if

$$\log \frac{\rho_{ij}(\pi)}{\rho_{ji}(\pi)} = \eta^{-1}(\pi_j - \pi_i) \quad \text{for all } \pi \in \mathbf{R}^n. \qquad \diamond \quad (11.31)$$

Under a direct exponential protocol, it is as if agents choose candidate strategies from a list of all available strategies. Under an imitative exponential protocol, agents instead choose candidate strategies by observing the choice of an opponent.

Definition *The protocol $\rho \colon \mathbf{R}^n \times X \to \mathbf{R}_+^{n \times n}$ is an* imitative exponential protocol *with noise level η if*

$$\rho_{ij}(\pi, x) = x_j \frac{\exp(\eta^{-1} \psi(\pi_i, \pi_j))}{d_{ij}(\pi, x)}, \qquad (11.32)$$

where the functions $\psi\colon \mathbf{R}^2 \to \mathbf{R}$ and $d\colon \mathbf{R}^n \times X \to (0, \infty)^{n \times n}$ satisfy conditions (11.29) and

$$d_{ij}(\pi, x) = d_{ji}(\pi, x). \tag{11.33}$$

Of course, one has the same flexibility in specifying imitative exponential protocols as in specifying direct protocols. Again consider the case in which $\psi(\pi_i, \pi_j) = \pi_j$. If

$$d_{ij}(\pi, x) = \sum_{k \in S} x_k \exp(\eta^{-1} \pi_k),$$

we obtain the *i*-logit protocol from Example 11.1.3:

$$\rho_{ij}(\pi, x) = \frac{x_j \exp(\eta^{-1} \pi_j)}{\sum_{k \in S} x_k \exp(\eta^{-1} \pi_k)}.$$

If instead $d_{ij}(\pi, x) = x_i \exp(\eta^{-1} \pi_i) + x_j \exp(\eta^{-1} \pi_j)$, we obtain the *pairwise i-logit protocol*:

$$\rho_{ij}(\pi, x) = \frac{x_j \exp(\eta^{-1} \pi_j)}{x_i \exp(\eta^{-1} \pi_i) + x_j \exp(\eta^{-1} \pi_j)}.$$

11.5.3 Reversibility and Stationary Distributions

We now establish our main results on infinite-horizon behavior in potential games. The first of these, theorem 11.5.12, shows that if clever agents employ a direct exponential protocol, the stochastic evolutionary process $\{X_t^N\}$ is reversible. The stationary distribution weight $\mu^N(x)$ is proportional to the product of two terms. The first term is a multinomial coefficient and represents the number of ways of assigning the N agents to strategies in S so that each strategy i is played by precisely Nx_i agents. The second term is an exponential function of the value of potential at state x. Thus, the value of μ_x^N balances the value of potential at state x with the likelihood that state x would arise if agents were assigned to strategies at random.

Theorem 11.5.12 *Let F^N be a finite-population potential game with potential function f^N. Suppose that agents are clever and follow a direct exponential protocol with noise level η. Then the stochastic evolutionary process $\{X_t^N\}$ is reversible with stationary distribution*

$$\mu_x^N = \frac{1}{K^N} \frac{N!}{\prod_{k \in S}(Nx_k)!} \exp(\eta^{-1} f^N(x)) \tag{11.34}$$

for $x \in X^N$, where K^N is determined by the requirement that $\sum_{x \in X^N} \mu_x^N = 1$.

Proof To verify the reversibility condition (11.10), it is enough to check that the equality $\mu_x^N P_{xy}^N = \mu_y^N P_{yx}^N$ holds for pairs of states that are adjacent, in the sense that $y = x + \frac{1}{N}(e_j - e_i)$. To do so, note first that $z = x - \frac{1}{N}e_i = y - \frac{1}{N}e_j \in X_-^N$ represents both the distribution of opponents for an i player at state x, and the distribution of opponents of a j player at state y. Thus, in both cases, a clever player who is revising will consider the payoff vector $\check{F}^N(z)$ defined by $\check{F}_k^N(z) = F_k^N(z + \frac{1}{N}e_k)$ for all $k \in S$ (see equation (11.19)).

Now, by the definition of the potential function f^N,

$$f^N(y) - f^N(x) = F_j^N(y) - F_i^N(x) = \check{F}_j^N(z) - \check{F}_i^N(z). \tag{11.35}$$

Therefore, writing $\check{\pi} = \check{F}^N(z)$ and using equations (11.35), (11.29), and (11.30) to obtain the third equality below, we have

$$\mu_x^N P_{xy}^N = \mu_x^N \cdot x_i \, \rho_{ij}(\check{\pi})$$

$$= \frac{1}{K^N} \frac{N!}{\prod_{k \in S}(Nx_k)!} \exp(\eta^{-1} f^N(x)) \cdot x_i \, \frac{\exp(\eta^{-1} \psi(\check{\pi}_i, \check{\pi}_j))}{d_{ij}(\check{\pi})}$$

$$= \frac{1}{K^N} \frac{(N-1)!}{\prod_{k \in S}(Nz_k)!} \exp(\eta^{-1}(f^N(y) - \check{\pi}_j + \check{\pi}_i)) \, \frac{\exp(\eta^{-1}(\psi(\check{\pi}_j, \check{\pi}_i) + \check{\pi}_j - \check{\pi}_i))}{d_{ji}(\check{\pi})}$$

$$= \frac{1}{K^N} \frac{N!}{\prod_{k \in S}(Ny_k)!} \exp(\eta^{-1} f^N(y)) \cdot y_j \, \frac{\exp(\eta^{-1} \psi(\check{\pi}_j, \check{\pi}_i))}{d_{ji}(\check{\pi})}$$

$$= \mu_y^N \cdot y_j \, \rho_{ji}(\check{\pi})$$

$$= \mu_y^N P_{yx}^N. \quad \blacksquare$$

Theorem 11.5.13 considers evolution in potential games when clever agents employ imitative exponential protocols, assuming that there is one committed agent playing each of the n strategies in S. The stochastic evolutionary process $\{X_t^N\}$ is again reversible. This time, the stationary distribution weight μ_x^N is directly proportional to $\exp(\eta^{-1} f^N(x))$; no additional terms are required. Section 12.2 explores the consequences of this distinction for predictions about infinite-horizon behavior.

Theorem 11.5.13 *Let F^N be a finite-population potential game with potential function f^N. Suppose that there are N clever agents who follow an imitative exponential protocol with* noise level η, and that there is one committed agent for each strategy. Then the stochastic evolutionary process $\{X_t^N\}$ is reversible with stationary distribution

$$\mu_x^N = \frac{1}{\kappa^N} \exp(\eta^{-1} f^N(x)) \tag{11.36}$$

for $x \in X^N$, where κ^N is determined by the requirement that $\sum_{x \in X^N} \mu_x^N = 1$.

Proof As before, let $y = x + \frac{1}{N}(e_j - e_i)$, let $z = x - \frac{1}{N} e_i = y - \frac{1}{N} e_j \in X_-^N$, and let $\check{\pi} = \check{F}^N(z)$. Then, noting as in equation (11.22) that

$$x_i \frac{Nx_j + 1}{N + n - 1} = \frac{Nz_i + 1}{N} \cdot \frac{Nz_j + 1}{N + n - 1} = \frac{Nz_j + 1}{N} \cdot \frac{Nz_i + 1}{N + n - 1} = y_j \cdot \frac{Ny_i + 1}{N + n - 1},$$

equations (11.35), (11.29), and (11.33) yield

$$\mu_x^N P_{xy}^N = \mu_x^N \cdot x_i \, \rho_{ij}(\check{\pi}, \tfrac{Nx+1-e_i}{N+n-1})$$

$$= \frac{1}{\kappa^N} \exp(\eta^{-1} f^N(x)) \cdot x_i \, \frac{Nx_j + 1}{N + n - 1} \, \frac{\exp(\eta^{-1} \psi(\check{\pi}_i, \check{\pi}_j))}{d_{ij}(\check{\pi}, \tfrac{Nx+1-e_i}{N+n-1})}$$

$$= \frac{1}{\kappa^N} \exp(\eta^{-1}(f^N(y) - \check{\pi}_j + \check{\pi}_i)) \cdot x_i \, \frac{Nx_j + 1}{N + n - 1} \, \frac{\exp(\eta^{-1}(\psi(\check{\pi}_j, \check{\pi}_i) + \check{\pi}_j - \check{\pi}_i))}{d_{ij}(\check{\pi}, \tfrac{Nz+1}{N+n-1})}$$

$$= \frac{1}{\kappa^N} \exp(\eta^{-1} f^N(y)) \cdot y_j \, \frac{Ny_i + 1}{N + n - 1} \, \frac{\exp(\eta^{-1} \psi(\check{\pi}_j, \check{\pi}_i))}{d_{ji}(\check{\pi}, \tfrac{Ny+1-e_j}{N+n-1})}$$

$$= \mu_y^N \cdot y_j \, \rho_{ji}(\check{\pi}, \tfrac{Ny+1-e_j}{N+n-1})$$

$$= \mu_y^N P_{yx}^N. \qquad \blacksquare$$

Exercise 11.5.14 Describe the qualitative differences between stationary distributions (11.34) and (11.36) when the noise level η is large. Building on your answer to exercise 11.4.4, relate the differences between the stationary distributions to differences between the process's mean dynamics. ◇

Exercise 11.5.15 Show that if clever payoff evaluation is replaced with simple payoff evaluation in either of the previous two theorems, the resulting stochastic evolutionary process is not reversible. ◇

Exercise 11.5.16 Use the birth and death chain formula from theorem 11.2.3 to give alternative proofs of theorems 11.5.12 and 11.5.13 in the case where F^N is a two-strategy game. (Recall from exercise 11.5.4 that every two-strategy game is a potential game.) ◇

Exercise 11.5.17 This exercise provides an alternative proof of theorem 11.5.12 by way of normal form potential games. Recall from exercise 3.2.7 that the N-player normal form game $U = (U^1, \ldots, U^N)$ with strategy sets $S^1, \ldots, S^N$ is a potential game if it admits a potential function $V: \prod_p S^p \to \mathbf{R}$, which is a function satisfying

$$U^p(\hat{s}^p, s^{-p}) - U^p(s) = V(\hat{s}^p, s^{-p}) - V(s) \quad \text{for all } s \in \prod_p S^p, \hat{s}^p \in S^p, p \in \mathcal{P}.$$

i. Define a stochastic evolutionary process $\{Y_t^N\}$ on the set of pure strategy profiles $\prod_p S^p$ by assuming that each of the N players receives revision opportunities at rate 1, and that each follows a direct exponential protocol with noise level η when such opportunities arise. Show that if U is a normal form potential game with potential function V, then the process $\{Y_t^N\}$ is reversible, and that its stationary distribution ν^N is defined by $\nu^N(s) \propto \exp(\eta^{-1} V(s))$.

Now suppose that players in the game U are *indistinguishable*: all N players share the same strategy set $S^p = S \equiv \{1, \ldots, n\}$, and each player's payoffs are defined by the same function of the player's own strategy and the overall distribution of strategies $\xi(s) \in \mathcal{X}^N$, defined by $\xi_i(s) = \#\{p \in \{1, \ldots, N\}: s^p = i\}/N$. This means that there is a finite-population game $F^N: \mathcal{X}^N \to \mathbf{R}^n$ that represents U, in the sense that $U^p(s) = F_{s^p}^N(\xi(s))$ for all $s \in S$.

ii. Suppose again that U is a normal form potential game with potential function V. Show that if players in U are indistinguishable, then V is measurable with respect to $\mathcal{X}^N$, in the sense that $V(\hat{s}) = V(s)$ whenever $\xi(\hat{s}) = \xi(s)$. Also, show that the finite-population game F^N is a potential game, and that its potential function $f^N: \mathcal{X}^N \to \mathbf{R}$ is given by $f^N(x) = V(s)$, where s is any strategy profile in $\xi^{-1}(x)$.

iii. Let $\{Y_t^N\}$ be the evolutionary process on $\mathcal{X}^N$ defined in part (i). Show that under the assumptions of part (ii), the process $\{\xi(Y_t^N)\}$ is a Markov process on $\mathcal{X}^N$ with the same jump rates and transition probabilities as the process $\{X_t^N\}$ from theorem 11.5.12. Finally, use part (i) to prove directly that the stationary distribution of $\{\xi(Y_t^N)\}$ is given by equation (11.34). ◇

In Chapter 12, we turn our attention to stochastic stability analysis, which concerns the limiting behavior of the stationary distributions as the noise level becomes small or the population size becomes large. Since the reversible settings we focused on in this chapter allow the stationary distribution to be described explicitly, we not only will compute the limiting stationary distributions for these settings, but also will establish precise results on the asymptotics of the stationary distributions.

Once we move beyond the reversible cases, simple expressions for the stationary distributions are no longer available. We therefore introduce new techniques to determine the stochastically stable states.

11.A Appendix: Long-Run Behavior of Markov Chains and Processes

In appendix 10.C, we defined (discrete-time) Markov chains and (continuous-time) Markov processes on a countable state space, and showed how to construct them on an appropriate probability space $(\Omega, \mathcal{F}, \mathbb{P})$. The present appendix turns to the long-run behavior of Markov chains and processes that take values in a *finite* state space. Apart from the issue of periodicity, which is particular to the discrete-time setting, the discrete-time and continuous-time theories are quite similar, although certain concepts have somewhat different formulations in the two cases.

In this appendix, $\{X_t\}_{t=0}^{\infty}$ denotes a Markov chain with transition matrix $P \in \mathbf{R}^{X \times X}$ on the finite state space X, and $\{X_t\}_{t \geq 0}$ denotes a Markov process on X with transition matrix $P \in \mathbf{R}^{X \times X}$ and jump rate vector $\lambda \in \mathbf{R}^X$. The shorthand $\{X_t\}$ is used to refer to both cases. When we need to refer to initial conditions, we use the notations $\mathbb{P}_x(\cdot) \equiv \mathbb{P}(\cdot \mid X_0 = x)$ and $\mathbb{P}_\pi(\cdot) \equiv \sum_{x \in X} \pi_x \mathbb{P}(\cdot \mid X_0 = x)$ to describe the behavior of $\{X_t\}$ when it is run from initial state $x \in X$ or from initial distribution $\pi \in \mathbf{R}^X$.

11.A.1 Communication, Recurrence, and Irreducibility

To begin, we introduce a partial order on the finite set X that describes feasible multistep transitions under the transition matrix P. State y is *accessible* from state x, written $x \rightsquigarrow y$, if for some $n \geq 0$ there is a sequence of states $x = x_0, x_1, \ldots, x_n = y$ such that $P_{x_{i-1}, x_i} > 0$ for all $i \in \{1, \ldots, n\}$. Letting $n = 0$ ensures that each state is accessible from itself. We write $x \leftrightsquigarrow y$ to indicate that x and y are mutually accessible, in the sense that $x \rightsquigarrow y$ and $y \rightsquigarrow x$.

Accessibility defines a partial order on the set X. The equivalence classes under this order, referred to as *communication classes*, are the maximal sets of (pairwise) mutually accessible states.

To identify the states that $\{X_t\}$ can visit in the long run, define a set of states $R \subseteq X$ to be *closed* if the process cannot leave it:

$$[x \in R, x \rightsquigarrow y] \Rightarrow y \in R.$$

If R is a communication class, then R is closed if and only if it is minimal under the partial order $\rightsquigarrow$, where this order is viewed as "pointing downward" (figure 11.4). Once $\{X_t\}$ enters a closed communication class, it remains in that class forever.

Stationary Distributions and Infinite Horizon Behavior

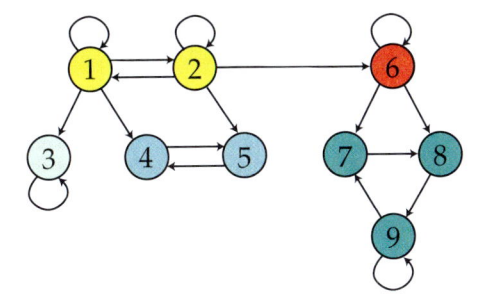

Figure 11.4
Feasible transitions between the states of a Markov chain. Members of the same communication class are shown in the same color. Members of recurrent classes are shown in shades of blue.

Example 11.A.1 Suppose that $\{X_t\}$ has state space $X = \{1,2,3,4,5,6,7,8,9\}$ and transition matrix

$$P = \begin{pmatrix} .4 & .3 & .2 & .1 & 0 & 0 & 0 & 0 & 0 \\ .5 & .1 & 0 & 0 & .3 & .1 & 0 & 0 & 0 \\ 0 & 0 & 1 & 0 & 0 & 0 & 0 & 0 & 0 \\ 0 & 0 & 0 & 0 & 1 & 0 & 0 & 0 & 0 \\ 0 & 0 & 0 & 1 & 0 & 0 & 0 & 0 & 0 \\ 0 & 0 & 0 & 0 & 0 & .8 & .1 & .1 & 0 \\ 0 & 0 & 0 & 0 & 0 & 0 & 0 & 1 & 0 \\ 0 & 0 & 0 & 0 & 0 & 0 & 0 & 0 & 1 \\ 0 & 0 & 0 & 0 & 0 & 0 & .9 & 0 & .1 \end{pmatrix}.$$

The feasible transitions of $\{X_t\}$ are represented in figure 11.4. $\{X_t\}$ has five communication classes: $\{1,2\}$, $\{3\}$, $\{4,5\}$, $\{6\}$, and $\{7,8,9\}$. Of these, $\{3\}$, $\{4,5\}$, and $\{7,8,9\}$ are closed. ◆

If the process $\{X_t\}$ begins in a communication class that is not closed (e.g., the class $\{1,2\}$ in example 11.A.1), it is possible for it to remain in this class for an arbitrarily long finite amount of time. But with probability 1, the process will leave the class after some finite amount of time, and once it leaves it can never return. Of course, once $\{X_t\}$ enters a closed communication class, it remains in that class forever.

To express these ideas more precisely, call state x *transient* if $\mathbb{P}_x(\{t: X_t = x\}$ is unbounded$) = 0$, and call state x *recurrent* if $\mathbb{P}_x(\{t: X_t = x\}$ is unbounded$) = 1$.

Theorem 11.A.1 *Let $\{X_t\}$ be a Markov chain or Markov process on a finite set X. Then*

i. every state in X is either transient or recurrent; and

ii. a state is recurrent if and only if it is a member of a closed communication class.

In light of this result, a closed communication class R is commonly referred to as a *recurrent class*.

By virtue of theorem 11.A.1, the infinite-horizon behavior of the process $\{X_t\}$ can be understood by focusing on cases in which the entire state space $\mathcal{X}$ forms a single recurrent class. (In effect, we are focusing on the behavior of the original process after it enters a recurrent class.) When all of $\mathcal{X}$ forms a single recurrent class, $\{X_t\}$ is said to be *irreducible*.

To illustrate irreducibility, we introduce an example that we will revisit throughout this appendix.

Example 11.A.2: Birth and Death Chains   A *birth and death chain* is a Markov chain $\{X_t\}_{t=0}^{\infty}$ on the state space $\mathcal{X} = \{0, 1, \ldots, N\}$ (or some other finite set endowed with a linear order) under which all transitions move the state one step to the right, move the state one step to the left, or leave the state unchanged. It follows that there are vectors $p, q \in \mathbf{R}^{\mathcal{X}}$ with $p_N = q_0 = 0$ such that

$$P_{ij} = \begin{cases} p_i & \text{if } j = i+1, \\ q_i & \text{if } j = i-1, \\ 1 - p_i - q_i & \text{if } j = i, \\ 0 & \text{otherwise.} \end{cases} \qquad (11.37)$$

A birth and death chain is thus a Markov chain with a tridiagonal transition matrix. It is irreducible if and only if $p_k > 0$ for $k < N$ and $q_k > 0$ for $k > 0$. The behavior of irreducible birth and death chains is studied in examples 11.A.4, 11.A.5, 11.A.6, and 11.A.10. ◆

Section 11.1 introduced the notion of a full support revision protocol in order to ensure that under the stochastic evolutionary process $\{X_t^N\}$, every population state in $\mathcal{X}$ is accessible from every other. Put differently, the full support condition ensures that the stochastic evolutionary process is irreducible.

11.A.2   Periodicity

In the discrete-time case, the behavior of a Markov chain $\{X_t\}_{t=0}^{\infty}$ within a recurrent class depends on the period structure of that class. The *period* of the recurrent state x is defined as $\gcd(\{t \geq 1 : \mathbb{P}_x(X_t = x) > 0\})$, that is, it is the greatest common divisor of the set of times at which the chain can revisit x if it is run from x. It can be shown that states from the same recurrent class have the same period, so it makes sense to speak of the period of the class itself.

Example 11.A.3   The Markov chain defined in example 11.A.1 has three recurrent classes: $\{3\}$, $\{4, 5\}$, and $\{7, 8, 9\}$. Clearly, the period of state 3 is 1, and the period of states 4 and 5 is 2. Since $P_{99} > 0$, a process run from initial state 9 can remain there

Stationary Distributions and Infinite Horizon Behavior

for any finite number of periods; thus state 9 has period 1, as do the other states in its class. ◆

This example illustrates a simple and useful fact: if any state x in a recurrent class has $P_{xx} > 0$, then all states in this class are of period 1.

If the Markov chain $\{X_t\}$ is irreducible, then all of its states have the same period. If this common period is greater than 1, $\{X_t\}$ is *periodic*; if instead the common period is 1, $\{X_t\}$ is *aperiodic*.

Theorem 11.A.2 describes how periodicity constrains the t step transition probabilities of an irreducible Markov chain. Part (i) of the theorem observes that the state space can be partitioned into sets that the chain must pass through sequentially. Part (ii) of the theorem implies that any t step transition not forbidden by part (i) will have positive probability if t is large enough.

Theorem 11.A.2 *Let $\{X_t\}_{t=0}^{\infty}$ be an irreducible Markov chain with period d. Then there is a partition $C_0, C_1, \ldots, C_{d-1}$ of X such that (i) $[x \in C_i$ and $P_{xy}^t > 0]$ implies that $y \in C_{(i+t) \bmod d}$, and (ii) $x, y \in C_i$ implies that $P_{xy}^{n \cdot d} > 0$ for all n large enough.*

Example 11.A.4: Birth and Death Chains: Periodicity Let $\{X_t\}_{t=0}^{\infty}$ be a birth and death chain on the state space $X = \{0, 1, \ldots, N\}$ (see example 11.A.2). If the probability of staying still is zero at every state (i.e., if $p_0 = q_N = 1$ and $p_k + q_k = 1$ for $k \in \{1, \ldots, N-1\}$), then the chain has period 2, with C_0 containing the even states and C_1 the odd states. Otherwise, the chain is aperiodic. ◆

Let us note again that periodicity is a discrete-time phenomenon. Since the jump times of continuous-time Markov processes follow exponential distributions, periodic behavior is impossible.

11.A.3 Hitting Times and Hitting Probabilities

To this point, the discussion of the behavior of Markov chains and processes has been qualitative, focusing only on the possibility or impossibility of transitions between given pairs of states over various lengths of time. We now turn to the quantitative analysis of these processes, addressing the likelihoods of these transitions.

We start by considering hitting times. Let $\{X_t\}$ be an irreducible Markov chain or Markov process on the finite state space X, and let Z be a subset of X. The *hitting time* of Z, denoted T_Z, is the random time at which the process first takes a value in Z: that is, $T_Z = \inf\{t \geq 0: X_t \in Z\}$.

Fix the set $Z \subseteq X$, and let $w_x = \mathbb{E}_x T_Z$ denote the expected time to hit Z if $\{X_t\}$ is run from state x. By definition, $w_z = 0$ whenever $z \in Z$. The expected hitting times for other initial conditions admit a pleasingly simple characterization.

Proposition 11.A.3 *Let $\{X_t\}$ be an irreducible Markov chain or process, let $Z \subseteq X$, and let $\{w_x\}_{x \notin Z}$ be the collection of expected times to hit Z starting from states outside Z.*

i. If $\{X_t\}_{t=0}^{\infty}$ is a Markov chain with transition matrix P, then $\{w_x\}_{x \notin Z}$ is the unique solution to the linear equations

$$w_x = 1 + \sum_{y \notin Z} P_{xy} w_y \quad \text{for all } x \notin Z. \tag{11.38}$$

ii. If $\{X_t\}_{t \geq 0}$ is a Markov process with jump rate vector λ and transition matrix P, then $\{w_x\}_{x \notin Z}$ is the unique solution to the linear equations

$$w_x = \lambda_x^{-1} + \sum_{y \notin Z} P_{xy} w_y \quad \text{for all } x \notin Z. \tag{11.39}$$

Let us first consider the discrete-time case (proposition 11.A.3(i)). If the Markov chain begins at state $x \notin Z$, then the expected time to reach the set Z is the sum of 1, representing the period now being spent at x, and the expected time to reach Z from the state that occurs next. Since a transition into Z means that the wait is over, one need only account for transitions to states outside of Z, including the null transition that stays at x. This is precisely what condition (11.38) requires.

In the continuous-time case (proposition 11.A.3(ii)), the time until the first transition from state x is exponentially distributed with rate λ_x. This generates a mean contribution of λ_x^{-1} to the time to reach Z, accounting for the difference between conditions (11.38) and (11.39). If the jump rate vector λ is constant, then the mean hitting times are those from the discrete-time case multiplied by the common value of λ_x^{-1}, representing the mean time between transitions. Using the generator $Q = \text{diag}(\lambda)(P - I)$ of the Markov process (see section 10.C.3 or 11.A.7), condition (11.39) can be expressed concisely as

$$-\sum_{y \notin Z} Q_{xy} w_y = 1 \quad \text{for all } x \notin Z.$$

Example 11.A.5: Birth and Death Chains: Expected Hitting Times Let $\{X_t\}_{t=0}^{\infty}$ be an irreducible birth and death chain on $X = \{0, 1, \ldots, N\}$ as defined in example 11.A.2. To compute the expected hitting times to reach a given state $z \in X$, substitute the definition (11.37) of the transition probabilities into condition (11.38); some rearranging yields

$$(p_k + q_k)w_k - p_k w_{k+1} - q_k w_{k-1} = 1. \tag{11.40}$$

To find the expected hitting time of z from an initial state x below z, one must solve the collection of equalities (11.40) with k ranging from 0 to $z-1$. This problem is

Stationary Distributions and Infinite Horizon Behavior

a second-order linear difference equation with variable coefficients and boundary conditions $w_z = 0$ and $q_0 = 0$.

To solve it, define for $k \in \{1, \ldots, z\}$ the first differences $d_k = w_k - w_{k-1}$, so that

$$w_x = w_0 + \sum_{k=1}^{x} d_k. \tag{11.41}$$

Equation (11.40) says that

$$d_k = \frac{q_{k-1}}{p_{k-1}} d_{k-1} - \frac{1}{p_{k-1}}, \tag{11.42}$$

so the terminal condition $q_0 = 0$ implies that $d_1 = -1/p_0$. Repeated substitution of the expressions for $d_{k-1}, d_{k-2}, \ldots, d_1$ given by (11.42) into (11.42) itself yields

$$d_k = -\sum_{j=1}^{k} \frac{1}{p_{j-1}} \prod_{i=j}^{k-1} \frac{q_i}{p_i}, \tag{11.43}$$

where the empty product equals 1. Equation (11.41), the terminal condition $w_z = 0$, and equation (11.43) together imply that

$$w_0 = -\sum_{k=1}^{z} d_k = \sum_{k=1}^{z} \sum_{j=1}^{k} \frac{1}{p_{j-1}} \prod_{i=j}^{k-1} \frac{q_i}{p_i}.$$

Combining this with equation (11.41) yields the general formula for the expected hitting times,

$$w_x = \sum_{k=x+1}^{z} \sum_{j=1}^{k} \frac{1}{p_{j-1}} \prod_{i=j}^{k-1} \frac{q_i}{p_i} \quad \text{for } x \in \{0, \ldots, z-1\}. \tag{11.44}$$

A similar argument combining (11.40) and the boundary conditions $w_z = 0$ and $p_N = 0$ yields an expression for the expected hitting time of z from a state y above z:

$$w_y = \sum_{k=z+1}^{y} \sum_{j=k}^{N} \frac{1}{q_j} \prod_{i=k}^{j-1} \frac{p_i}{q_i} \quad \text{for } y \in \{z+1, \ldots, N\}. \tag{11.45}$$

One can also derive an expression for the expected hitting time of the set $\{a, b\}$ from an initial state in between, but this expression is not as simple as the two previous ones. ◆

Example 11.A.6: Birth and Death Chains: Hitting Probabilities One can also express the probability that a birth and death chain reaches state a before state b using a simple formula. To state this formula concisely, let $\{X_t\}$ be an irreducible birth and death chain on $\mathcal{X} = \{0, 1, \ldots, N\}$, and define the increasing function $\phi : \mathcal{X} \to \mathbf{R}_+$ inductively via

$$\phi_0 = 0, \qquad \phi_1 = 1, \qquad \phi_{k+1} = \phi_k + \frac{\prod_{i=1}^k q_i}{\prod_{i=1}^k p_i} = \sum_{j=0}^k \prod_{i=1}^j \frac{q_i}{p_i},$$

where the empty product again equals 1. If $a < x < b$, one can show that

$$\mathbb{P}_x(T_a < T_b) = \frac{\phi_b - \phi_x}{\phi_b - \phi_a}. \tag{11.46}$$

For intuition, note that ϕ is defined so that

$$\mathbb{E}(\phi_{X_{t+1}} \mid \phi_{X_t} = \phi_k) = \mathbb{E}(\phi_{X_{t+1}} \mid X_t = k) = p_k \phi_{k+1} + (1 - p_k - q_k)\phi_k + q_k \phi_{k-1} = \phi_k.$$

(This equality says that $\{\phi_{X_t}\}$ is a *martingale*.) If $T = T_{\{a,b\}}$ denotes the hitting time of the set $\{a, b\}$, one can prove (using the *optional stopping theorem*) that

$$\mathbb{E}_x(\phi_{X_T}) = \phi_x.$$

In other words, the expected value of the process $\{\phi_{X_t}\}$ at the (random) time it hits the set $\{a, b\}$ is the same as the process's initial value. Evaluating the previous expectation yields

$$\phi_a \mathbb{P}_x(T_a < T_b) + \phi_b \mathbb{P}_x(T_b < T_a) = \phi_x,$$

which can be rearranged to obtain (11.46).   ◆

11.A.4 The Perron-Frobenius Theorem

Many key properties of irreducible finite-state Markov chains can be viewed as consequences of the *Perron-Frobenius theorem*, a basic result from matrix analysis. To present this theorem in its usual language, we call a transition matrix $P \in \mathbf{R}^{\mathcal{X} \times \mathcal{X}}$ (i.e., a non-negative matrix with row sums equal to 1) a *stochastic matrix*, and call such a matrix *irreducible* or *aperiodic* according to whether the induced Markov chain has these properties. Non-negative matrices that are both irreducible and aperiodic are sometimes referred to as *primitive*.

Theorem 11.A.4 (Perron-Frobenius)   *Suppose that the matrix $P \in \mathbf{R}^{\mathcal{X} \times \mathcal{X}}$ is stochastic and irreducible. Then*

Stationary Distributions and Infinite Horizon Behavior

i. 1 is an eigenvalue of P of algebraic multiplicity 1, and no eigenvalue of P has modulus greater than 1.

ii. The vector $\mathbf{1}$ is a right eigenvector of P corresponding to eigenvalue 1, that is, $P\mathbf{1} = \mathbf{1}$.

iii. There is a probability vector μ with positive components that is a left eigenvector of P corresponding to eigenvalue 1; thus, $\mu'P = \mu'$.

Suppose in addition that P is aperiodic, and hence primitive. Then

iv. All eigenvalues of P other than 1 have modulus less than 1.

v. The matrix powers P^t converge to the matrix $\mathbf{1}\mu'$ as t approaches infinity.

vi. If λ_2 is the eigenvalue of P with the second-largest modulus, and $r \in (|\lambda_2|, 1)$, then for some $c > 0$,

$$\max_{ij} \left|(P^t - \mathbf{1}\mu')_{ij}\right| \leq c\, r^t \quad \text{for all } t \geq 1.$$

If P is (real or complex) diagonalizable, this statement remains true when $r = |\lambda_2|$.

In sections 11.A.5 and 11.A.8 all these statements are interpreted as descriptions of properties of irreducible Markov chains.

11.A.5 Stationary Distributions for Markov Chains

Sections 11.A.5 and 11.A.6 consider stationary distributions for discrete-time Markov chains. Section 11.A.7 shows that the basic formulas for the continuous-time case are identical to those for the discrete-time case when the jump rates λ_x are the same for each state, as is the case for the stochastic evolutionary process studied in the text.

Let $\{X_t\}_{t=0}^{\infty}$ be a Markov chain with finite state space $\mathcal{X}$ and transition matrix P. A probability distribution $\mu \in \mathbf{R}^{\mathcal{X}}$ is a *stationary distribution* of $\{X_t\}_{t=0}^{\infty}$ if

$$\mu'P = \mu'. \tag{11.47}$$

More explicitly, μ is a stationary distribution if

$$\sum_{x \in \mathcal{X}} \mu_x P_{xy} = \mu_y \quad \text{for all } y \in \mathcal{X}. \tag{11.48}$$

To interpret these conditions, decompose the probability of the chain's being at state y at time 1 as follows:

$$\sum_{x \in \mathcal{X}} \mathbb{P}(X_0 = x)\, \mathbb{P}(X_1 = y \mid X_0 = x) = \mathbb{P}(X_1 = y).$$

Comparing the previous two equations reveals that if X_0 is distributed according to the stationary distribution μ, then X_1 is also distributed according to μ, and so, by the Markov property, is every subsequent X_t.

In general, a finite-state Markov chain must admit at least one stationary distribution, and it may admit many. For instance, if the transition matrix P is the identity matrix, so that each state defines its own recurrent class, then every probability distribution on X is a stationary distribution. But if a Markov chain is irreducible, definition (11.47) and parts (i) and (iii) of theorem 11.A.4 imply that its stationary distribution is unique.

Theorem 11.A.5 *If the Markov chain $\{X_t\}$ is irreducible, it admits a unique stationary distribution.*

Example 11.A.7 By focusing on the three irreducible closed sets from example 11.A.1, one can define three irreducible Markov chains with transition matrices

$$P = (1), \qquad P = \begin{pmatrix} 0 & 1 \\ 1 & 0 \end{pmatrix}, \qquad P = \begin{pmatrix} 0 & 1 & 0 \\ 0 & 0 & 1 \\ .9 & 0 & .1 \end{pmatrix}.$$

In the first case the stationary distribution is trivial, in the second case it is $\mu = (\frac{1}{2}, \frac{1}{2})$, and in the third case it is $\mu = (\frac{9}{28}, \frac{9}{28}, \frac{10}{28})$. ◆

If the Markov chain $\{X_t\}$ is not irreducible, then there is a unique stationary distribution μ^R corresponding to each of the chain's recurrent classes R, and the set of stationary distributions of $\{X_t\}$ is the convex hull of these μ^R. Intuitively, by specifying the weight placed on μ^R in the convex combination, one can choose the probability that the process begins in recurrent class R; to maintain stationarity, the relative weights on states in R must be in the proportions given by μ^R.

One can interpret the stationary distribution weights of irreducible Markov chains in terms of expected return times. If the Markov chain $\{X_t\}$ is run from initial condition x, the random variable $T_x = \inf\{t \geq 1 : X_t = x\}$ is called the *return time* of state x. (Note that if $X_1 = x$, then the return time is 1 even though the chain has not actually left state x.)

Proposition 11.A.6 *If the Markov chain $\{X_t\}$ is irreducible with stationary distribution μ, then $\mathbb{E}_x T_x = \mu_x^{-1}$ for all $x \in X$.*

Thus, the higher the weight on x in the stationary distribution, the less time expected to pass before a chain starting at x returns to this state.

11.A.6 Reversible Markov Chains

In general, computing the stationary distribution of an irreducible Markov chain means finding an eigenvector of its transition matrix, a task that is computationally demanding when the state space is large. Fortunately, there are many interesting examples in which the stationary distribution satisfies a property that is both stronger and easier to check. The Markov chain $\{X_t\}$ is *reversible* if it admits a *reversible distribution*: that is, a probability distribution μ that satisfies the *detailed balance conditions*

$$\mu_x P_{xy} = \mu_y P_{yx} \quad \text{for all } x, y \in \mathcal{X}. \tag{11.49}$$

Summing this equation over $x \in \mathcal{X}$ yields equation (11.48), so a reversible distribution is also a stationary distribution.

To understand why reversibility is so named, imagine running the Markov chain $\{X_t\}$ from initial distribution μ and observing two consecutive frames from a film of the chain. Suppose these frames display the realizations x and y. According to equation (11.49), the probability that the chain is first at state x and next at state y, $\mu_x P_{xy}$, is equal to the probability that the chain is first at state y and next at state x, $\mu_y P_{yx}$. Put differently, the probability of observing (x, y) is the same whether the film is running forward or backward. It is easy to verify that this property extends to any finite sequence of realizations.

Example 11.A.8 In example 11.A.7, the first two Markov chains are reversible, but the third is not. If the states are labeled 7, 8, and 9 and the film shows state 7 and then state 8, one can conclude that it is running forward; compare figure 11.4. ◆

Example 11.A.9: Random Walks on Graphs Let $\mathcal{G} = (\mathcal{X}, \mathcal{E})$ be a connected undirected graph with node set $\mathcal{X}$ and edge set $\mathcal{E} \subseteq \{\{x, y\}: x, y \in \mathcal{X}, x \neq y\}$. Let $d_x = \#\{E \in \mathcal{E}: x \in E\}$ be the *degree* of node x (i.e., the number of edges containing x), and let $D = \sum_{x \in \mathcal{X}} d_x$. Let $\{X_t\}$ be a Markov chain on $\mathcal{X}$ with transition probabilities

$$P_{xy} = \begin{cases} 1/d_x & \text{if } \{x, y\} \in \mathcal{E}, \\ 0 & \text{otherwise.} \end{cases}$$

Evidently, $\{X_t\}$ is irreducible and reversible with stationary distribution $\mu_x = d_x/D$. ◆

Example 11.A.10: Birth and Death Chains: Reversibility and the Stationary Distribution Birth and death chains (example 11.A.2) are always reversible. Since only adjacent transitions are possible, the detailed balance conditions (11.49) reduce to $\mu_k q_k = \mu_{k-1} p_{k-1}$ for $k \in \{1, \ldots, N\}$. Applying this formula inductively and noting that stationary distribution weights sum to 1, one obtains an explicit formula for this distribution:

$$\mu_k = \mu_0 \prod_{i=1}^{k} \frac{p_{i-1}}{q_i} \quad \text{for } k \in \{1, \ldots, N\}, \quad \text{and} \quad \mu_0 = \left(\sum_{k=0}^{N} \prod_{i=1}^{k} \frac{p_{i-1}}{q_i} \right)^{-1},$$

where, as always, the empty product equals 1. ◆

11.A.7 Stationary Distributions and Reversibility for Markov Processes

The notions of stationarity and reversibility are equally important in the continuous-time setting, where they are most easily studied using the generator of the Markov process. Section 10.C.3 described the transition probabilities of the Markov process $\{X_t\}_{t \geq 0}$ using the matrix semigroup $\{P(t)\}_{t \geq 0}$, where $P_{xy}(t) = \mathbb{P}(X_t = y \mid X_0 = x)$. The generator of $\{X_t\}_{t \geq 0}$ is the matrix $Q = \operatorname{diag}(\lambda)(P - I)$, where $\lambda \in \mathbf{R}_+^X$ and $P \in \mathbf{R}_+^{X \times X}$ are the vector of jump rates and the transition matrix of the Markov process, respectively. Equation (10.14) showed that the generator and the transition probabilities are related by $P(t) = e^{Qt}$, which is the matrix solution to the *backward equation* $\dot{P}(t) = QP(t)$ from initial condition $P(0) = I$.

Proposition 11.A.7 introduces two equivalent definitions of the stationary distribution for a Markov process.

Proposition 11.A.7 *Let $\{X_t\}_{t \geq 0}$ be a Markov process on the finite state space X with semigroup $\{P(t)\}_{t \geq 0}$ and generator Q, and let μ be a probability distribution on X. Then the following conditions are equivalent:*

$$\mu' Q = \mathbf{0}'; \tag{11.50}$$

$$\mu' P(t) = \mu' \quad \text{for all } t \geq 0. \tag{11.51}$$

When these conditions hold, μ is a stationary distribution of $\{X_t\}_{t \geq 0}$.

Condition (11.51) can be written explicitly as

$$\mathbb{P}_\mu(X_t = x) = \mu_x \quad \text{for all } x \in X, t \geq 0. \tag{11.52}$$

In other words, if $\{X_t\}$ is run with the stationary distribution μ as its initial distribution, then it continues to follow distribution μ at all times $t \geq 0$.

Proof of proposition 11.A.7 Premultiplying the backward equation by the probability distribution μ yields

$$\frac{d}{dt}(\mu' P(t)) = \mu' \dot{P}(t) = \mu' Q P(t). \tag{11.53}$$

Thus, if $\mu' Q = \mathbf{0}'$, then $\frac{d}{dt}(\mu' P(t)) = \mathbf{0}'$, which with $\mu' P(0) = \mu' I = \mu'$ implies (11.51). To establish the other direction, note that (11.51) and (11.53) imply that $\mathbf{0}' = \frac{d}{dt}(\mu' P(t)) = \mu' Q P(t)$; since $P(0) = I$, we conclude that $\mu' Q = \mathbf{0}'$. ∎

To obtain a condition that more closely resembles the discrete-time stationarity condition (11.47), one can substitute the definition of Q into equation (11.50) to obtain

$$(\mu \bullet \lambda)' P = (\mu \bullet \lambda), \tag{11.54}$$

Stationary Distributions and Infinite Horizon Behavior

where $\bullet$ denotes the componentwise product: $(\mu \bullet \lambda)_i = \mu_i \lambda_i$. If the jump rate vector λ is constant, then equation (11.54) reduces to the discrete-time condition $\mu'P = \mu'$ from equation (11.47).

Equation (11.54) suggests that the basic properties of the stationary distribution in the continuous-time setting should parallel those in the discrete-time setting as long as the jump rates are accounted for correctly. Suppose, for instance, that the Markov process $\{X_t\}$ is irreducible. If we fix $\alpha \in (0, (\max_x \lambda_x)^{-1}]$, then it is easy to verify that $\alpha Q + I$ is an irreducible stochastic matrix. Theorem 11.A.4(iii) thus implies that there is a unique probability vector μ satisfying $\mu'(\alpha Q + I) = \mu'$, or equivalently, $\mu'Q = \mathbf{0}'$.

Theorem 11.A.8 *If the Markov process $\{X_t\}$ is irreducible, it admits a unique stationary distribution.*

To link stationary distribution weights and expected return times, suppose that the process $\{X_t\}_{t \geq 0}$ is started at state x, and define the return time of state x as $T_x = \inf\{t \geq \tau_1 : X_t = x\}$, where τ_1 is the first jump time of the process. (Note that the state need not actually change at time τ_1). If the Markov process $\{X_t\}_{t \geq 0}$ is irreducible, it can be shown that $\mathbb{E}_x T_x = (\mu_x \lambda_x)^{-1}$.

Finally, a Markov process is *reversible* if it admits a *reversible distribution* μ, which here means that

$$\mu_x \lambda_x P_{xy} = \mu_y \lambda_y P_{yx} \quad \text{for all } x, y \in \mathcal{X}. \tag{11.55}$$

Summing this equation over x yields the stationarity condition (11.54). Again, equation (11.55) reduces to the discrete-time condition $\mu_x P_{xy} = \mu_y P_{yx}$ from equation (11.49) if jump rates are constant.

11.A.8 Convergence in Distribution

The fundamental results of the theory of finite-state Markov chains and processes establish various senses in which the infinite-horizon behavior of irreducible processes is independent of their initial conditions and characterizable in terms of their stationary distributions. As with i.i.d. random variables, there are distinct results on distributional properties and on sample path properties; the former are considered here, and the latter in appendix section 11.A.9. For a general discussion of the distinction between distributional and sample path properties, see section 10.B.3.

The basic distributional result, theorem 11.A.9, provides conditions under which the time t distributions of a Markov chain or process converge to its stationary distribution. In the continuous-time setting, irreducibility is sufficient for convergence in distribution; in the discrete-time setting, aperiodicity is also required.

Theorem 11.A.9 (Convergence in Distribution) *Suppose that $\{X_t\}$ is either an irreducible aperiodic Markov chain or an irreducible Markov process, and that its stationary distribution is μ. Then for any initial distribution π, we have*

$$\lim_{t \to \infty} \mathbb{P}_\pi(X_t = x) = \mu_x \quad \text{for all } x \in X.$$

In the discrete-time case, theorem 11.A.9 is an immediate consequence of theorem 11.A.4(v):

$$\lim_{t \to \infty} \mathbb{P}_\pi(X_t = x) = \lim_{t \to \infty} (\pi' P^t)_x = (\pi' \mathbf{1} \mu')_x = \mu_x.$$

Theorem 11.A.9 shows that after a long enough time has passed, the time t distribution of $\{X_t\}$ will be close to its stationary distribution. But it does not indicate how long one must wait before this limit result becomes relevant. The answer can be found in theorem 11.A.4(vi), which shows that the rate of convergence to the stationary distribution is determined by the second-largest eigenvalue modulus of the transition matrix P. We illustrate this conclusion informally by way of two examples.

Example 11.A.11 Consider the two-state Markov chain $\{X_t\}$ with transition matrix

$$P = \begin{pmatrix} 1-a & a \\ b & 1-b \end{pmatrix}.$$

To ensure that this chain is irreducible and aperiodic, suppose that $a, b > 0$ and that $a + b < 2$. The eigenvalues of P are $\lambda_1 = 1$ and $\lambda_2 = 1 - a - b$, and the associated left eigenvectors are

$$\mu \equiv \begin{pmatrix} \frac{b}{a+b} \\ \frac{a}{a+b} \end{pmatrix} \quad \text{and} \quad \begin{pmatrix} -1 \\ 1 \end{pmatrix},$$

respectively. Of course, since $\mu' P = \mu'$, μ is the stationary distribution of $\{X_t\}$.

Now let

$$L = \begin{pmatrix} \frac{b}{a+b} & \frac{a}{a+b} \\ -1 & 1 \end{pmatrix}$$

be the matrix whose rows are the left eigenvectors of P, and let $\Lambda = \text{diag}(\lambda)$. Then the matrix form of the left eigenvector equation for P is $LP = \Lambda L$. Since L is invertible, $P = L^{-1} \Lambda L$ is diagonalizable. In fact, since $PL^{-1} = L^{-1}\Lambda$, the columns of

$$R \equiv L^{-1} = \begin{pmatrix} 1 & \frac{-a}{a+b} \\ 1 & \frac{b}{a+b} \end{pmatrix}$$

are the right eigenvectors of P.

Stationary Distributions and Infinite Horizon Behavior 447

The t step transitions of the Markov chain are described by the tth power of P, which can be evaluated as follows:

$$P^t = (R\Lambda L)^t \tag{11.56}$$

$$= R\Lambda^t L$$

$$= \begin{pmatrix} 1 & -\frac{a}{a+b} \\ 1 & \frac{b}{a+b} \end{pmatrix} \begin{pmatrix} (\lambda_1)^t & 0 \\ 0 & (\lambda_2)^t \end{pmatrix} \begin{pmatrix} \frac{b}{a+b} & \frac{a}{a+b} \\ -1 & 1 \end{pmatrix}$$

$$= (\lambda_1)^t \mathbf{1}\mu' + (\lambda_2)^t \begin{pmatrix} \frac{-a}{a+b} \\ \frac{b}{a+b} \end{pmatrix} \begin{pmatrix} -1 & 1 \end{pmatrix}$$

$$= \mathbf{1}\mu' + (\lambda_2)^t \begin{pmatrix} \frac{a}{a+b} & \frac{-a}{a+b} \\ -\frac{b}{a+b} & \frac{b}{a+b} \end{pmatrix}.$$

Thus, if the chain begins at initial distribution π, its time t distribution is

$$\pi' P^t = \mu' + (\lambda_2)^t \begin{pmatrix} \frac{\pi_1 a - \pi_2 b}{a+b} & \frac{-\pi_1 a + \pi_2 b}{a+b} \end{pmatrix}.$$

In conclusion, the distribution of the Markov chain converges to the stationary distribution μ at geometric rate $|\lambda_2| = |1 - a - b|$. ◆

Some simple observations about matrix multiplication will be useful in the next example. For any matrices $A, B \in \mathbf{R}^{n \times n}$, one can write

$$AB = AIB = \sum_{k=1}^{n} A(e_k e_k')B = \sum_{k=1}^{n} (Ae_k)(e_k'B). \tag{11.57}$$

In other words, to compute the product AB, take the "outer product" of the kth column of A and the kth row of B, and then sum over k. (For a different derivation of (11.57), recall that the ijth term of AB is $\sum_k A_{ik} B_{kj}$; (11.57) expresses this fact in matrix form.) If a diagonal matrix $D = \text{diag}(d)$ is interposed between A and B, one obtains a similar expression, used implicitly in (11.56):

$$ADB = \sum_{k=1}^{n} d_k (Ae_k)(e_k'B). \tag{11.58}$$

Example 11.A.12 Let P be the transition matrix of an irreducible aperiodic Markov chain, and suppose that P is (real or complex) diagonalizable. Then, as in the previous example, $P = R\Lambda L = R\,\text{diag}(\lambda)L$, where λ is the vector of eigenvalues of P, the rows of L are left eigenvectors, and the columns of $R = L^{-1}$ are right eigenvectors. As before the t step transition probabilities are $P^t = R\Lambda^t L$, which, using equation (11.58), can be rewritten as

$$P^t = R\Lambda^t L = \sum_{k=1}^{n} (\lambda_k)^t (Re_k)(e'_k L). \tag{11.59}$$

The Perron-Frobenius theorem says that 1 is an eigenvalue of P with algebraic multiplicity 1 and that all other eigenvalues of P have modulus less than 1. Moreover, the left and right eigenvectors corresponding to eigenvalue 1 are the stationary distribution μ and the constant vector $\mathbf{1}$. Thus, if the eigenvalues are ordered so that $1 = \lambda_1 > |\lambda_2| \geq |\lambda_3| \geq \ldots \geq |\lambda_n| > -1$, then $e'_1 L = \mu'$ and $Re_1 = \mathbf{1}$. (To see that Re_1 is $\mathbf{1}$ rather than some multiple of $\mathbf{1}$, note that $LR = I$, implying that $\mu' Re_1 = e'_1 LRe_1 = I_{11} = 1$.)

Using these observations, rewrite equation (11.59) as

$$P^t = \mathbf{1}\mu' + \sum_{k=2}^{n} (\lambda_k)^t (Re_k)(e'_k L).$$

Evidently, the rate of convergence of $\{X_t\}$ to its stationary distribution is determined by the second-largest eigenvalue modulus of P. ◆

11.A.9 Ergodicity

Having considered distributional properties, we turn to sample path properties, which describe the behavior of almost every sequence of realizations of the Markov chain or process. (The distinction between these two kinds of properties is discussed in section 10.B.3.) Theorem 11.A.10 shows that if $\{X_t\}$ is an irreducible Markov chain or process, then for almost all realizations of $\omega \in \Omega$, the proportion of time that the sample path $\{X_t(\omega)\}$ spends in each state x converges; the limit is the weight μ_x that state x holds in the stationary distribution. If $\{X_t\}_{t=0}^{\infty}$ is an i.i.d. sequence, with each X_t having distribution μ, this conclusion can be obtained by applying the strong law of large numbers to the sequence of indicator random variables $\{1_{\{X_t=x\}}\}_{t=0}^{\infty}$. Theorem 11.A.10 reveals that Markov dependence is enough for this implication to hold.

Theorem 11.A.10 (Ergodicity).

i. Suppose that $\{X_t\}_{t=0}^{\infty}$ is an irreducible Markov chain with stationary distribution μ. Then for any initial distribution π,

$$\mathbb{P}_\pi \left(\lim_{T \to \infty} \frac{1}{T} \sum_{t=0}^{T-1} 1_{\{X_t=x\}} = \mu_x \right) = 1 \quad \text{for all } x \in \mathcal{X}.$$

Stationary Distributions and Infinite Horizon Behavior

ii. Suppose that $\{X_t\}_{t \geq 0}$ is an irreducible Markov process with stationary distribution μ. Then for any initial distribution π,

$$\mathbb{P}_\pi \left(\lim_{T \to \infty} \frac{1}{T} \int_0^T 1_{\{X_t = x\}} \, dt = \mu_x \right) = 1 \quad \text{for all } x \in X.$$

While irreducible aperiodic Markov chains converge in distribution and are ergodic, the latter two properties are distinct in general. For instance, a Markov chain that is irreducible but not aperiodic will still be ergodic, but it will not converge in distribution in the sense described in theorem 11.A.9. Conversely, a Markov chain whose transition matrix is the identity matrix trivially converges in distribution to its initial distribution, but it is not ergodic in the sense of theorem 11.A.10.

Notes

Section 11.1
The best response with mutations model was introduced by Kandori, Mailath, and Rob (1993). Models of imitation with mutations were studied by Binmore and Samuelson (1997), Fudenberg and Imhof (2006; 2008) Fudenberg and Hojman (2009), and Sandholm (2010e). See the chapter 12 notes for further references.

The analysis in this chapter and the next focuses on irreducible processes, but there is a distinct branch of the literature on stochastic evolution that looks at reducible processes, focusing on whether they converge to sets that are closed under better or best replies. For the relevant set-valued solution concepts, see Basu and Weibull (1991) and Voorneveld (2004; 2005), and for models of dynamics, see Young (1993a, 1998b), Hurkens (1995), Monderer and Shapley (1996b), Friedman and Mezzetti (2001), Kukushkin (2004), Josephson and Matros (2004), Dindoš and Mezzetti (2006), Josephson (2008) and Marden et al. (2009).

Section 11.2
Stationary distributions for models of stochastic evolution in two-strategy games were studied by Binmore, Samuelson, and Vaughan (1995), Binmore and Samuelson (1997), Young (1998b), Blume (2003), and Sandholm (2007c; 2010c; 2010e). Toss and Switch (examples 11.2.1 and 11.3.1) is a slight modification of the Ehrenfest urn model from statistical physics; see Brémaud (1999). The "swimming upstream" analogy following example 11.2.3 appeared in related contexts in Fudenberg and Harris (1992), Kandori (1997), and Binmore and Samuelson (1997).

Section 11.3
Ellison (1993; 2000) and Beggs (2005) (also see Kandori, Mailath, and Rob 1993 and Binmore, Samuelson, and Vaughan 1995) studied the rate of growth of waiting times as the noise level becomes small; Benaïm and Weibull (2003, lemma 3) (also see Benaïm and Sandholm 2010) considered the rate of growth as the population size becomes large.

For local interaction models, see Ellison (1993; 2000), Blume (1993; 1995), Morris (2000), Nowak and May (1992; 1993), Nowak (2006), Szabó and Fáth (2007), and the references therein. For evolution in games on networks, see Blume (1997) and books by Goyal (2007), Vega-Redondo (2007), and Jackson (2008).

Section 11.4
The distinction between simple and clever payoff evaluations was noted in Sandholm (1998). Exercise 11.4.2(ii) is due to Rhode and Stegeman (1996). Committed agents for imitative dynamics were introduced in Sandholm (2010e).

Section 11.5
Blume (1993; 1997; 2003) demonstrated the usefulness in evolutionary game theory of condition (11.31), the origins of which are in statistical mechanics. Normal form potential games were introduced in Monderer and Shapley (1996b); see also Hofbauer and Sigmund (1988). The definition of finite-population full potential games and theorem 11.5.7(i) are from Sandholm (2001a). Exercise 11.5.17(i) is due to Blume (1997). For recent work on evolution in normal form games under variations on the logit choice rule, see Alós-Ferrer and Netzer (2010), Marden and Shamma (2008), and Okada and Tercieux (2009).

Appendix 11.A
Most of the material presented here, except equations (11.44) and (11.45), can be found in standard references on Markov chains and processes; see Norris (1997), Brémaud (1999), and Stroock (2005). Durrett (2005, ch. 5) also offers a clear presentation of Markov chains. For more on the Perron-Frobenius theorem, see Seneta (1981) or Horn and Johnson (1985).

12   Limiting Stationary Distributions and Stochastic Stability

Chapter 11 began the study of the infinite-horizon behavior of stochastic evolutionary processes generated by full support revision protocols. Any such process admits a unique stationary distribution, which describes the behavior of the process over very long time spans regardless of the initial population state. Even when the underlying game has multiple strict equilibria, the stationary distribution is often concentrated in the vicinity of just one of them if the noise level η is small or the population size N is large. In these cases, the population state so selected provides a unique prediction of infinite horizon play.

The analyses in chapter 11 considered fixed evolutionary processes $\{X_t^{N,\eta}\}$, defined by particular choices of η and N. The stationary distribution $\mu^{N,\eta}$ of such a process necessarily places positive mass on every state in $\mathcal{X}^N$. Thus, if the values of η and N are held fixed, it is not possible to obtain clean selection results. Furthermore, actually computing the stationary distribution for fixed choices of η and N is generally a difficult task. Unless the evolutionary process is reversible, one cannot usually expect to do more than calculate this distribution numerically, making it difficult to prove analytical results about the underlying process.

In this chapter, we circumvent both of these difficulties by allowing the parameters η and N to approach their limiting values. While each fixed stationary distribution $\mu^{N,\eta}$ has full support on $\mathcal{X}^N$, the limit of a sequence of stationary distributions may converge to a point mass at a single state; thus, taking limits in η and N allows us to obtain exact equilibrium selection results. And although computing a particular stationary distribution requires solving a large linear system, the limiting stationary distribution can often be found without explicitly computing any of the stationary distributions along the sequence. Moving to a limiting analysis permits us not only to reach novel conclusions about the reversible environments studied in chapter 11, but also to extend the analysis beyond those convenient environments.

Taking η and N to their limiting values is useful for obtaining equilibrium selection results, but it also exacerbates the waiting time problem studied in section 11.3. Since in practice these parameters are not at their limits, the rationale for the limiting analyses performed in this chapter is analytical convenience. Before applying the selection results developed here, one should assess whether the time span of interest in the application is commensurate with the waiting times needed to generate equilibrium selection at the relevant parameter values. If not, the use of the infinite-horizon analysis is not warranted.

Population states that retain mass in a limiting stationary distribution are said to be *stochastically stable*. There are a number of different definitions of stochastic stability, depending on which limits are taken—just η, just N, η followed by N, or N followed by η—and what should count as retaining mass. Section 12.1 introduces a variety of definitions of stochastic stability and uses examples to illustrate the differences among them. It also explains how the modeler's choice of which limits to take, and in which order, is governed by the application at hand. Taking only the small noise limit, or taking this limit first, emphasizes the rarity of suboptimal play as the key force behind equilibrium selection. Taking only the large population limit, or taking it first, emphasizes the effects of large numbers of conditionally independent decisions in driving equilibrium selection.

It is not always easy to know which of these forces should be viewed as the primary one. A main goal in this chapter is to identify settings in which the small noise and large population limits agree. When this is the case, the modeler is spared the difficulty of adjudicating between discrepant predictions about very-long-run behavior.

Sections 12.2–12.4 revisit the reversible environments studied in chapter 11. Using the explicit formulas for stationary distributions developed earlier, we not only identify the limiting stationary distribution in each environment but also characterize the asymptotics of the stationary distribution as the parameters approach their limits.

When agents play a potential game using an exponential revision protocol, the stationary distribution $\mu^{N,\eta}$ must take one of two forms, with the form depending only on whether the protocol is direct or imitative (see section 11.5). The asymptotics of the stationary distribution in these environments is the subject of section 12.2.

Section 12.3 considers evolution in two-strategy games under noisy best response protocols. The examples in chapter 11 showed that even in this simple strategic setting, seemingly similar revision protocols can lead to different equilibrium selections. Here we derive simple formulas describing the asymptotics of the stationary distribution. We then use these formulas to identify conditions under which all noisy best response protocols select the same stochastically stable state. Finally, we describe general conditions under which the small noise and large population asymptotics agree, so that the choice of which limit to emphasize is inconsequential.

Limiting Stationary Distributions and Stochastic Stability

Section 12.4 studies evolution in two-strategy games under imitative protocols, both with and without mutations. In this context, the asymptotics of the stationary distribution can depend on the order in which limits in the population size N and mutation rate ε are taken. However, introducing just two committed agents, one for each strategy, ensures agreement between the double limits. Equilibrium selection can be surprisingly sensitive to the specification of the revision protocol: we present two imitative protocols whose common mean dynamic is the replicator dynamic, but which generate different stochastically stable states in a range of simple games.

The remainder of the chapter considers limiting stationary distributions in environments that are not necessarily reversible, so that tractable formulas for the stationary distribution are not available. Section 12.5 and appendix 12.A focus on small noise limits. The methods explored identify the stochastically stable states by constructing certain graphs on the state space X^N. Each edge is assigned a *cost*, which captures the rate of decay of the edge's traversal probability as the noise level approaches zero. Questions about stochastic stability can be answered by comparing the overall costs of particular well-chosen graphs, obviating the need to compute stationary distributions.

Section 12.6 and appendix 12.B consider large population limits, providing infinite-horizon complements to the finite-horizon approximation results obtained in chapter 10. As the population size grows large, all mass in the stationary distribution becomes concentrated around the so-called Birkhoff center of the mean dynamic (M). Thus, only those states satisfying a natural notion of recurrence under (M) are candidates for stochastic stability in the large population limit. By combining certain global restrictions on the mean dynamic—that (M) admits a global Lyapunov function, or that it defines a cooperative differential equation—with nondegeneracy conditions on the stochastic process itself, one can refine the previous result: the mass in the stationary distribution can only become concentrated around stable rest points of the mean dynamic.

Compared to those in the rest of the book, the developments presented in sections 12.5 and 12.6 are rather incomplete. Although the graph-theoretic tools for studying small noise stochastic stability are quite general, to date they have served as the basis for relatively few general selection results, at least in the model studied in this book. (See the chapter notes for section 12.5 for applications in other game-theoretic environments.) In a similar vein, the results in section 12.6 do not indicate which state or states are selected in the large population limit, despite the fact that in typical cases, the stationary distribution should concentrate its mass on a single asymptotically stable set. To sum up, there are many interesting open questions about stochastic stability analysis for games, and much work remains to be done to answer them.

12.1 Definitions of Stochastic Stability

We begin by introducing some definitions of stochastic stability. As in chapters 10–11, we keep the notation manageable by focusing on the single-population case.

In the stochastic evolutionary model from section 11.1, a population of size N recurrently plays a population game F^N, with agents receiving revision opportunities via independent Poisson alarm clocks. An agent's choice upon receiving a revision opportunity is governed by a full support revision protocol ρ^η, where $\eta > 0$ denotes the noise level. The full support assumption ensures that the resulting stochastic evolutionary process $\{X_t^{N,\eta}\}$ is irreducible, and so admits a unique stationary distribution $\mu^{N,\eta}$ on the state space $\mathcal{X}^N$. As explained in section 11.1.2, the stationary distribution captures the infinite-horizon behavior of the process $\{X_t^{N,\eta}\}$ in two distinct senses: it is both the process's limiting distribution and its limiting empirical distribution.

When the parameters η and N are fixed, the stationary distribution $\mu^{N,\eta}$ places positive mass on every state in $\mathcal{X}^N \subset \mathcal{X}$. But as either or both of these parameters approach their extremes, the stationary distribution may concentrate its mass on one small set of states, even in cases where the mean dynamic of the process admits multiple stable sets. The population states around which the mass in the stationary distribution accumulates are said to be *stochastically stable*. The following sections formalize this concept.

12.1.1 Small Noise Limits

We begin with the mathematically simplest setting for stochastic stability analysis by fixing the population size N and taking the noise level η to zero. Taking the small noise limit emphasizes the rarity of suboptimal choices over the magnitude of the population as the force behind equilibrium selection.

Because N is fixed, each stationary distribution in the collection $\{\mu^{N,\eta}\}_{\eta \in (0,\bar\eta]}$ is a probability measure on the same finite state space, $\mathcal{X}^N$, making stochastic stability easy to define. State $x \in \mathcal{X}^N$ is *stochastically stable in the small noise limit* if

$$\lim_{\eta \to 0} \mu_x^{N,\eta} > 0. \tag{12.1}$$

When the sequence $\{\mu^{N,\eta}\}_{\eta \in (0,\bar\eta]}$ converges to a point mass at state x, state x is *uniquely stochastically stable*. (Exercise 12.1.1 notes one subtlety about this definition.)

Section 12.5 and appendix 12.A provide general conditions under which the sequence $\{\mu^{N,\eta}\}_{\eta \in (0,\bar\eta]}$ converges to a limiting distribution $\mu^{N,*}$ as η approaches zero. When this limiting distribution exists, its support is the set of stochastically stable states.

Limiting Stationary Distributions and Stochastic Stability

Exercise 12.1.1 Construct a collection of stationary distributions $\{\mu^{N,\eta}\}_{\eta \in (0,\bar\eta]}$ under which the only stochastically stable state is not uniquely stochastically stable in the sense of the preceding definition. (*Hint:* The limiting distribution $\mu^{N,*}$ need not exist.) ◇

It is sometimes more convenient to work with a more inclusive notion of stochastic stability, one stated in terms of the exponential rates of decay of stationary distribution weights (see section 12.A.5). Consider the equation

$$\lim_{\eta \to 0} \eta \log \mu_x^{N,\eta} = r_x^N, \tag{12.2}$$

where $r_x^N \leq 0$. This equation is equivalent to the requirement that

$$\mu_x^{N,\eta} = \exp\left(\eta^{-1}(r_x^N + o(1))\right), \tag{12.3}$$

where $o(1)$ represents a term that approaches zero as η approaches zero. Both (12.2) and (12.3) say that r_x^N is the exponential rate of decay of the stationary distribution weight on state x as η^{-1} approaches infinity. With this in mind, we say that state $x \in \mathcal{X}^N$ is *weakly stochastically stable in the small noise limit* if

$$\lim_{\eta \to 0} \eta \log \mu_x^{N,\eta} = 0. \tag{12.4}$$

Put differently, state x is weakly stochastically stable if as η^{-1} approaches infinity, $\mu_x^{N,\eta}$ does not vanish at an exponential rate. This weight may remain positive, but it also may converge to zero at a subexponential pace.

The following proposition links the preceding definitions of stochastic stability.

Proposition 12.1.2

i. *Every stochastically stable state is weakly stochastically stable.*

ii. *Suppose that the limit in (12.2) exists for each state in $\mathcal{X}^N$ and that only state x is weakly stochastically stable. Then state x is uniquely stochastically stable.*

Exercise 12.1.3

i. Verify both parts of proposition 12.1.2.

ii. Show by example that without the assumption about the existence of the limits in (12.2), proposition 12.1.2(ii) is no longer true. ◇

12.1.2 Large Population Limits

By defining stochastic stability in terms of the small noise limit, one takes the vanishing probability of suboptimal behavior to be the source of equilibrium selection. An alternative approach, one more in keeping with the analyses earlier in the book, fixes the noise level and examines the behavior of the stationary distributions as the population size grows large. This approach emphasizes the role of the population's magnitude in determining equilibrium selection.

Defining stochastic stability for large population limits is complicated by the fact that as the population size N grows, the state spaces X^N vary, becoming increasingly fine grids in the simplex X. State $x \in X$ is *stochastically stable in the large population limit* if for every (relatively) open set $O \subseteq X$ containing x,

$$\lim_{N \to \infty} \mu^{N,\eta}(O) > 0. \tag{12.5}$$

If this limit is always equal to 1, x is *uniquely stochastically stable*. The warning in exercise 12.1.1 about the meaning of uniqueness applies equally well here.

Exercise 12.1.4 The natural notion of convergence for the sequence of stationary distributions $\{\mu^{N,\eta}\}_{N=N_0}^{\infty}$ is *weak convergence*, which requires that there be a probability measure $\mu^{*,\eta}$ such that for every open set $O \subseteq X$,

$$\liminf_{N \to \infty} \mu^{N,\eta}(O) \geq \mu^{*,\eta}(O).$$

Show that state x is uniquely stochastically stable if and only if $\mu^{*,\eta}$ exists and is equal to a point mass at state x. ◇

As in the context of small noise limits, it is useful here to introduce a less demanding notion of stochastic stability based on exponential rates of decay. Sections 12.2 and 12.3 establish limits of the form

$$\lim_{N \to \infty} \max_{x \in X^N} \left| \tfrac{\eta}{N} \log \mu_x^{N,\eta} - r^\eta(x) \right| = 0, \tag{12.6}$$

where r^η is a continuous function from X to $\mathbf{R}_-$. Condition (12.6) is equivalent to the requirement that

$$\mu_x^{N,\eta} = \exp\bigl(\eta^{-1} N\bigl(r^\eta(x) + o(1)\bigr)\bigr) \quad \text{uniformly in } x \in X^N, \tag{12.7}$$

where $o(1)$ represents a term that converges to zero uniformly in x as N approaches infinity. Both (12.6) and (12.7) say that as N approaches infinity, the exponential rate of decay of the stationary distribution weights on states close to x is approximately $\eta^{-1} r^\eta(x)$. If $r^\eta(x) = 0$, state x is *weakly stochastically stable in the large population limit*.

As in the case of small noise limits, there are links between our notions of stochastic stability for the large population limit.

Proposition 12.1.5 *Suppose that condition* (12.6) *holds for some continuous function* r^η. *Then*

i. *every stochastically stable state is weakly stochastically stable;*

ii. *if only one state is weakly stochastically stable, this state is uniquely stochastically stable.*

The corresponding results for the small noise setting were immediate, but this proposition requires a proof.

Proof To prove part (i), we first show that $m^\eta = \max_{x \in X} r^\eta(x)$ equals 0. Suppose to the contrary that m^η is negative. Since exercise 10.1.1 says that $\#X^N = \binom{N+n-1}{n-1} < (N+n)^n$, equation (12.7) implies that for large enough N, we have

$$\mu^{N,\eta}(X^N) \leq \#X^N \cdot \exp\left(\eta^{-1} N \cdot \tfrac{m^\eta}{2}\right) < (N+n)^n \exp\left(\eta^{-1} N \cdot \tfrac{m^\eta}{2}\right).$$

Since m^η is negative, the last expression vanishes as N grows large, contradicting that $\mu^{N,\eta}$ is a probability measure on X^N.

Now suppose that m^η is positive. Then since r^η is continuous, there is a neighborhood of the maximizer of r^η on which r^η exceeds $\tfrac{2m^\eta}{3}$. Once N is large enough, this neighborhood must contain at least one state y^N from X^N, and equation (12.7) implies that for large enough N, $\mu^{N,\eta}_{y^N} \geq \exp\left(\eta^{-1} N \cdot \tfrac{m^\eta}{3}\right)$. This expression grows without bound as N grows large, again contradicting that $\mu^{N,\eta}$ is a probability measure, and allowing us to conclude that $m^\eta = \max_{x \in X} r^\eta(x) = 0$.

We now prove part (i) by establishing the contrapositive. Suppose that state x is not weakly stochastically stable: $r^\eta(x) < 0$. Since r^η is continuous, there is an open set $O \subset X$ containing x and a constant $\delta > 0$ such that $r^\eta(y) < -\delta$ for all $y \in O$. Equation (12.7) then implies that for large enough N,

$$\mu^{N,\eta}_y \leq \exp\left(\eta^{-1} N \left(r^\eta(y) + \tfrac{\delta}{2}\right)\right) < \exp\left(-\eta^{-1} N \cdot \tfrac{\delta}{2}\right), \quad \text{when } y \in X^N \cap O.$$

Thus

$$\mu^{N,\eta}(O) < \#X^N \cdot \exp\left(-\eta^{-1} N \cdot \tfrac{\delta}{2}\right) < (N+n)^n \exp\left(-\eta^{-1} N \cdot \tfrac{\delta}{2}\right).$$

This implies that $\lim_{N \to \infty} \mu^{N,\eta}(O) = 0$. Since state x is in O, it cannot be stochastically stable.

To prove part (ii), suppose that state x is the only weakly stochastically stable state, and let $O \subset X$ be an open set containing x. Since $X - O$ is closed, there is a $\delta > 0$ such that $r^\eta(y) < -\delta$ for all $y \in X - O$. Repeating the argument from the proof of part (i) shows that $\mu^{N,\eta}(X - O)$ approaches zero as N grows large, and hence that $\mu^{N,\eta}(O)$ approaches 1 as N grows large. Therefore, state x is uniquely stochastically stable. This completes the proof of the proposition. ∎

12.1.3 Double Limits

The small noise and large population limits emphasize two different forces that could drive equilibrium selection. In applications, it may not be self-evident which of these forces is the central one. Since this point is moot when both limits generate the same predictions, it is natural to look for settings in which the small noise and large population limits agree.

To do so, one must first account for the fact that the small noise and large population limits are not directly comparable. The former concerns a sequence of probability distributions on a fixed finite grid in the simplex, whereas the latter considers a sequence of distributions on finer and finer grids. Moreover, for there to be any chance of agreement, one must take each limit while fixing the other parameter at a value "close to its limit": there is no reason to expect predictions generated by the small noise limit at small population sizes to agree with predictions generated by the large population limit at high noise levels.

The most convenient way of handling both of these issues is to consider double limits. For instance, state $x \in X$ is *stochastically stable in the small noise double limit* if for every open set $O \subseteq X$ containing x,

$$\lim_{N \to \infty} \lim_{\eta \to 0} \mu^{N,\eta}(O) > 0. \tag{12.8}$$

If this limit is always equal to 1, state x is *uniquely stochastically stable*. Since in (12.8) the population size N is held fixed while the noise level η is taken to zero, this double limit describes the behavior of the small noise limit at large population sizes.

In the same way, state $x \in X$ is *stochastically stable in the large population double limit* if for every open set $O \subseteq X$ containing x,

$$\lim_{\eta \to 0} \lim_{N \to \infty} \mu^{N,\eta}(O) > 0. \tag{12.9}$$

If this limit is always equal to 1, x is *uniquely stochastically stable*. Evidently, the double limit (12.9) describes the behavior of the large population limit at small noise levels.

As with single limits, one can consider weaker notions of stochastic stability defined in terms of exponential rates of decay. For instance, suppose that for some continuous function $r \colon X \to \mathbf{R}_-$,

$$\lim_{N \to \infty} \lim_{\eta \to 0} \max_{x \in X^N} \left| \tfrac{\eta}{N} \log \mu_x^{N,\eta} - r(x) \right| = 0. \tag{12.10}$$

Then when the population size N is sufficiently large, the exponential rate of decay of $\mu_x^{N,\eta}$ as η^{-1} approaches infinity is approximately $Nr(x)$. Similarly, if there is a continuous function $\hat{r}\colon X \to \mathbf{R}_-$ such that

$$\lim_{\eta \to 0} \lim_{N \to \infty} \max_{x \in X^N} \left| \tfrac{\eta}{N} \log \mu_x^{N,\eta} - \hat{r}(x) \right| = 0, \qquad (12.11)$$

then for small η, as N approaches infinity, the exponential rate of decay of the stationary distribution weights on states near x is approximately $\eta^{-1}\hat{r}(x)$.

Exercise 12.1.6 Write precise statements justifying these interpretations of conditions (12.10) and (12.11). ◇

For either double limit, state x is *weakly stochastically stable* if its limiting rate of decay, $r(x)$ or $\hat{r}(x)$, is equal to zero. As in proposition 12.1.5, one can show that if the function r or $\hat{r}$ is continuous, then every stochastically stable state is weakly stochastically stable, and that if only one state is weakly stochastically stable, it is uniquely stochastically stable.

Exercise 12.1.7 Prove these extensions of proposition 12.1.5 to the cases of small noise and large population double limits. ◇

Exercise 12.1.8 Consider the small noise double limit $\mu^{\dagger,*} = \lim_{N \to \infty} \lim_{\eta \to 0} \mu^{N,\eta}$, interpreting each limit in the sense of weak convergence of probability measures (see exercise 12.1.4).

i. Show that if $\mu^{\dagger,*}$ is a point mass at state x, then x is uniquely stochastically stable.

ii. Construct a collection of probability measures $\{\mu^{N,\eta}\}$ for which state x is uniquely stochastically stable in the small noise double limit, but for which $\mu^{\dagger,*}$ does not exist. ◇

In cases where the rate of decay functions r and $\hat{r}$ are identical, the double limits agree in a very strong sense. Not only do the small noise and large population limits agree about which state will predominate in the long run; they also agree about the degrees of unlikelihood of all the other states.

The next three sections focus on the reversible settings studied in chapter 11: potential games under exponential revision protocols and two-strategy games under arbitrary protocols. Starting from the explicit formulas for the fixed-parameter stationary distributions, we are able to derive simple expressions for the rates at which the stationary distribution weights decay. We show that when agents employ noisy best response protocols, or when they employ imitative protocols in the presence of committed agents, the rate of decay functions do not depend on the order in which the small noise and large population limits are taken. Thus, in these settings, which limit is emphasized has little bearing on infinite-horizon predictions.

It is an open question whether these agreements between the double limits persist beyond the reversible settings. The analyses of small noise limits in section 12.5 and of large population limits in section 12.6 take some necessary first steps toward answering this question.

12.1.4 Double Limits: A Counterexample

Before studying environments in which the two double limits agree, we demonstrate that this agreement cannot be taken for granted.

Example 12.1.1 Consider a population of agents who are matched to play the symmetric normal form game with strategy set $S = \{0, 1\}$ and payoff matrix

$$A = \begin{pmatrix} 1 & 2 \\ 3 & 1 \end{pmatrix}.$$

The unique Nash equilibrium of the population game $F(x) = Ax$ is the mixed equilibrium $x^* = (x_0^*, x_1^*) = (\frac{1}{3}, \frac{2}{3})$. To simplify notation, self-matching is allowed, but the analysis is virtually identical without it.

Suppose that agents employ the following revision protocol, which combines imitation of successful opponents and mutations:

$$\rho_{ij}^\varepsilon(\pi, x) = x_j \pi_j + \varepsilon.$$

We simplify again by allowing agents to imitate themselves; this too has a negligible effect on the results. The protocol ρ^ε generates the mean dynamic

$$\dot{x}_i = V_i^\varepsilon(x) = x_i \hat{F}_i(x) + 2\varepsilon \left(\tfrac{1}{2} - x_i\right), \tag{12.12}$$

which is the sum of the replicator dynamic and an order ε term that points toward the center of the simplex. When $\varepsilon = 0$, this dynamic is simply the replicator dynamic; the Nash equilibrium $x^* = (\frac{1}{3}, \frac{2}{3})$ attracts solutions from all interior initial conditions, and the pure states e_0 and e_1 are unstable rest points. When $\varepsilon > 0$, the two boundary rest points disappear, leaving a globally stable rest point that is near x^* but slightly closer to the center of the simplex.

Using the formulas from theorem 11.2.3, one can compute the stationary distribution $\mu^{N,\varepsilon}$ of the process $\{X_t^{N,\varepsilon}\}$ generated by F and ρ^ε for any fixed values of N and ε. Four instances are presented in figure 12.1. The notation is streamlined in the usual way, letting $\chi = x_1$ denote the fraction of agents choosing strategy 1.

Figure 12.1a presents the stationary distribution when $\varepsilon = .1$ and $N = 100$. This distribution is drawn above the phase diagram of the mean dynamic (12.12), whose global attractor appears at $\hat{\chi} \approx .6296$. The stationary distribution $\mu^{N,\varepsilon}$ has its mode at state $\chi = .64$ but is dispersed rather broadly about this state.

Limiting Stationary Distributions and Stochastic Stability

(a) $N = 100$, $\varepsilon = .1$

(b) $N = 10{,}000$, $\varepsilon = .1$

(c) $N = 100$, $\varepsilon = 10^{-5}$

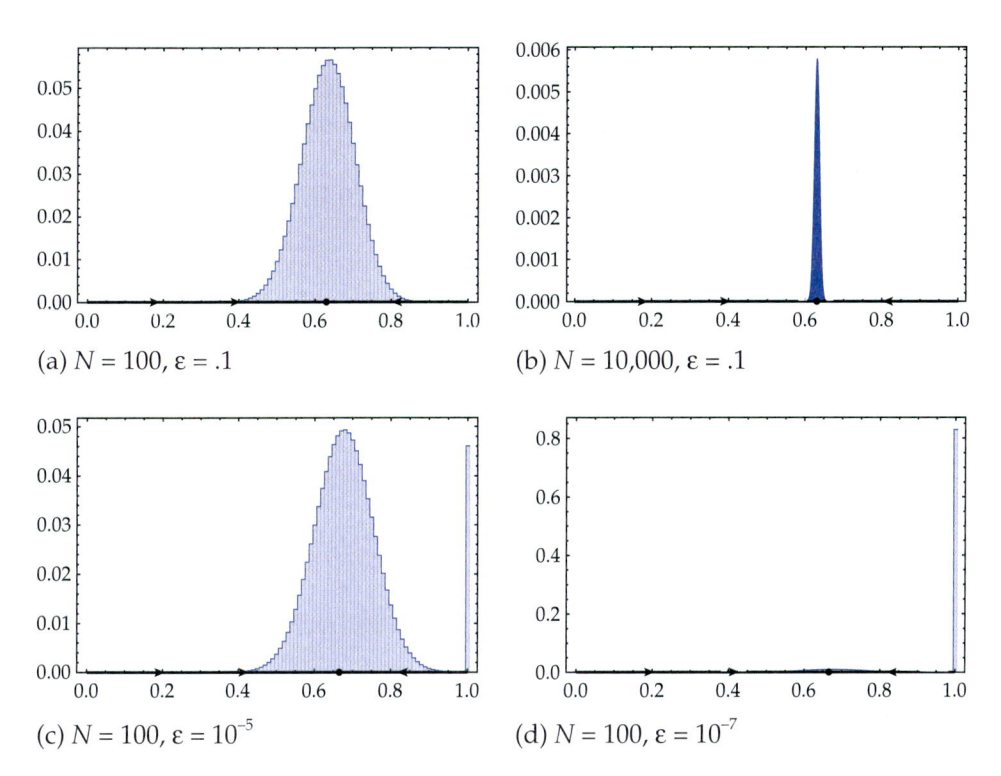

(d) $N = 100$, $\varepsilon = 10^{-7}$

Figure 12.1
Stationary distribution weights $\mu_\chi^{N,\varepsilon}$ in an anticoordination game under imitation with mutations.

Figure 12.1b presents the stationary distribution and mean dynamic when $\varepsilon = .1$ and $N = 10{,}000$. Increasing the population size moves the mode of the distribution to state $\chi = .6300$, and, more important, causes the distribution to exhibit much less dispersion around the modal state. This numerical analysis suggests that in the large population limit, the stationary distribution $\mu^{N,\varepsilon}$ will approach a point mass at $\hat{\chi} \approx .6296$, the global attractor of the relevant mean dynamic. This conjecture is confirmed in section 12.4.1.

As the noise level ε approaches zero, the rest point of the mean dynamic approaches the Nash equilibrium $\chi^* = \frac{2}{3}$. Therefore, if after taking N to infinity we take ε to zero, we obtain the double limit

$$\lim_{\varepsilon \to 0} \lim_{N \to \infty} \mu^{N,\varepsilon} = \delta_{\chi^*}, \qquad (12.13)$$

where the limits refer to weak convergence of probability measures (see exercise 12.1.4), and δ_{χ^*} denotes the point mass at state χ^*.

The remaining pictures illustrate the effects of setting very small mutation rates. When $N = 100$ and $\varepsilon = 10^{-5}$ (figure 12.1c), most of the mass in $\mu^{100,\varepsilon}$ falls in a bell-shaped distribution centered at state $\chi = .68$, but a mass of $\mu_1^{100,\varepsilon} \approx .0460$ sits in isolation at the boundary state $\chi = 1$. When ε is reduced to 10^{-7} (figure 12.1d), this boundary state commands most of the weight in the distribution ($\mu_1^{100,\varepsilon} \approx .8286$).

This numerical analysis suggests that when the mutation rate approaches zero, the stationary distribution will approach a point mass at state 1. This conjecture, too, is confirmed in section 12.4.1. Increasing the population size does not alter this result, so for the small noise double limit, we obtain

$$\lim_{N \to \infty} \lim_{\varepsilon \to 0} \mu^{N,\varepsilon} = \delta_1, \qquad (12.14)$$

where δ_1 denotes the unit point mass at state 1.

Comparing equations (12.13) and (12.14) reveals that the large population double limit and the small noise double limit disagree. ◆

In the preceding example, the (single and double) large population limits agree with the predictions of the mean dynamic, but the small noise limits do not. Still, the behavior of the latter limits is easy to explain. Starting from any interior state, and from the boundary as well when $\varepsilon > 0$, the expected motion of the process $\{X_t^{N,\varepsilon}\}$ is toward the interior rest point of the mean dynamic V^ε. But when ε is zero, the boundary states 0 and 1 become rest points of V^ε and are absorbing states of $\{X_t^{N,\varepsilon}\}$; in fact, they are the only recurrent states of the zero-noise process. Therefore, when $\varepsilon = 0$, the process $\{X_t^{N,\varepsilon}\}$ reaches either state 0 or state 1 in finite time and then remains at that state forever.

If instead ε is positive, the boundary states are no longer absorbing, and they are far from any rest point of the mean dynamic. But once the process $\{X_t^{N,\varepsilon}\}$ reaches such a state, it can only depart by way of a mutation. Thus, if the population size N is fixed and ε is extremely small, a journey from an interior state to a boundary state—here a journey against the flow of the mean dynamic—is more likely than an escape from a boundary state by way of a single mutation. It follows that in the small noise limit, the stationary distribution must become concentrated on the boundary states regardless of the nature of the mean dynamic. (In fact, it will typically become concentrated on just one of these states; see section 12.4.1.)

As this discussion indicates, the prediction provided by the small noise limit does not become a good approximation of behavior at fixed values of N and ε unless ε is so small that lone mutations are much more rare than excursions from the interior of $\mathcal{X}^N$ to the boundary. In figures 12.1c and 12.1d, which consider a modest population size of $N = 100$, a mutation rate of $\varepsilon = 10^{-5}$ is not small enough to yield agreement with the prediction of the small noise limit, although a mutation

Limiting Stationary Distributions and Stochastic Stability

rate of $\varepsilon = 10^{-7}$ yields a closer match. With larger population sizes, the relevant mutation rates would be even smaller.

This example suggests that in economic contexts, where the probabilities of mutations may not be especially small, the large population limit is more likely to be the relevant one in cases where the predictions of the two limits disagree. In biological contexts, where mutation rates may indeed be quite small, the choice between the limits seems less clear.

12.2 Exponential Protocols and Potential Games

To begin the analysis of the asymptotics of the stationary distribution, we consider populations of agents who play potential games using exponential protocols. Section 11.5 showed that for fixed values of η and N, the stationary distributions $\mu^{N,\eta}$ arising in this setting take only two forms, one for direct protocols and one for imitative protocols. For this reason, the focus is on the mechanics of the limiting analysis, and on the differences between the predictions generated by the various limits discussed above.

Recall from section 11.5 that $F^N \colon X^N \to \mathbf{R}^n$ is a finite-population potential game with potential function $f^N \colon X^N \to \mathbf{R}$ if

$$F_j^N(x + \tfrac{1}{N}(e_j - e_i)) - F_i^N(x) = f^N(x + \tfrac{1}{N}(e_j - e_i)) - f^N(x) \quad \text{for all } x \in X_i^N, i, j \in S.$$

Theorem 11.5.12 showed that if clever agents play F^N recurrently using a direct exponential protocol, then the stationary distribution of the resulting evolutionary process takes the form

$$\mu_x^{N,\eta} = \frac{1}{K^N} \frac{N!}{\prod_{k \in S}(Nx_k)!} \exp(\eta^{-1} f^N(x)) \quad \text{for all } x \in X^N, \tag{12.15}$$

where K^N is determined by the requirement that the stationary distribution weights sum to 1. Similarly, theorem 11.5.13 showed that if clever agents play F^N recurrently using an imitative exponential protocol, and if in addition there is one committed agent for each strategy in S, then the stationary distribution of the evolutionary process takes the form

$$\mu_x^N = \frac{1}{\kappa^N} \exp(\eta^{-1} f^N(x)) \quad \text{for all } x \in X^N. \tag{12.16}$$

The remainder of this section studies the asymptotic behavior of these distributions as η and N approach their limiting values.

One new piece of notation is handy for describing the rates of decay of stationary distribution weights. If $g \colon C \to \mathbf{R}$ is a continuous real-valued function on the compact set C (below either $\mathcal{X}^N$ or X), we define the function $\Delta g \colon C \to \mathbf{R}_-$ by

$$\Delta g(x) = g(x) - \max_{y \in C} g(y). \tag{12.17}$$

Thus, Δg is obtained from g by shifting its values uniformly, doing so in such a way that the maximum value of Δg is zero.

12.2.1 Direct Exponential Protocols: The Small Noise Limit

We begin by studying small noise asymptotics. Equation (12.15) immediately implies that

$$\frac{\mu_x^{N,\eta}}{\mu_y^{N,\eta}} = \frac{\prod_{k \in S}(Ny_k)!}{\prod_{k \in S}(Nx_k)!} \exp\left(\eta^{-1}(f^N(x) - f^N(y))\right) \quad \text{for all } x, y \in \mathcal{X}^N. \tag{12.18}$$

Taking logarithms of both sides of (12.18) and multiplying by the noise level η, we have

$$\lim_{\eta \to 0} \eta \log \frac{\mu_x^{N,\eta}}{\mu_y^{N,\eta}} = \lim_{\eta \to 0} \left((f^N(x) - f^N(y)) + \eta \log\left(\frac{\prod_{k \in S}(Ny_k)!}{\prod_{k \in S}(Nx_k)!}\right)\right)$$

$$= f^N(x) - f^N(y). \tag{12.19}$$

Thus, when the noise level is small, the multinomial terms become inconsequential compared to the potential function values. This observation is enough to identify the maximizers of the potential function f^N as the stochastically stable states.

Theorem 12.2.1 *Suppose that clever agents using a direct exponential protocol play a finite-population potential game F^N with potential function f^N. Then in the small noise limit, the stochastically stable states are those in* $\mathrm{argmax}_{x \in \mathcal{X}^N} f^N(x)$.

By combining equation (12.19) with the fact that the stationary distribution weights on stochastically stable states have a zero rate of decay, we obtain the following characterization of the rates of decay at all states.

Theorem 12.2.2 *Under the assumptions of theorem 12.2.1,*

$$\lim_{\eta \to 0} \eta \log \mu_x^{N,\eta} = \Delta f^N(x) \quad \text{for all } x \in \mathcal{X}^N. \tag{12.20}$$

Theorem 12.2.2 says that as η^{-1} approaches infinity, the stationary distribution weight $\mu_x^{N,\eta}$ vanishes at exponential rate $\Delta f^N(x)$. This rate is the difference between the value of the potential function at x and its maximal value.

Proof of theorem 12.2.2 Let x_*^N be a maximizer of f^N on $\mathcal{X}^N$. If we could show that

$$\lim_{\eta \to 0} \eta \log \mu_{x_*^N}^{N,\eta} = 0, \tag{12.21}$$

Limiting Stationary Distributions and Stochastic Stability

it would follow from equation (12.19) that

$$\lim_{\eta \to 0} \eta \log \mu_x^{N,\eta} = \lim_{\eta \to 0} \left(\eta \log \frac{\mu_x^{N,\eta}}{\mu_{e_1}^{N,\eta}} - \eta \log \frac{\mu_{x_*^N}^{N,\eta}}{\mu_{e_1}^{N,\eta}} + \eta \log \mu_{x_*^N}^{N,\eta} \right)$$

$$= \left(f^N(x) - f^N(e_1) \right) - \left(f^N(x_*^N) - f^N(e_1) \right)$$

$$= \Delta f^N(x), \tag{12.22}$$

proving the theorem.

The argument used to establish (12.21) follows the same lines as the first part of the proof of proposition 12.1.5. First, suppose contrary to (12.21) that there is a sequence $\{\eta^k\}$ converging to zero along which the limit in (12.21) is $-c < 0$. In this case, the reasoning in equation (12.22) implies that

$$\lim_{\eta^k \to 0} \eta^k \log \mu_x^{N,\eta^k} = \Delta f^N(x) - c \leq -c \quad \text{for all } x \in \mathcal{X}^N.$$

It follows that for η^k far enough along the sequence, we have

$$\sum_{x \in \mathcal{X}^N} \mu_x^{N,\eta^k} = \sum_{x \in \mathcal{X}^N} \exp\left(\frac{1}{\eta^k} \cdot \eta^k \log \mu_x^{N,\eta^k} \right) \leq \#\mathcal{X}^N \cdot \exp\left(-\frac{c}{2\eta^k} \right),$$

The last expression vanishes as k grows large, contradicting the fact that μ^{N,η^k} is a probability measure.

Next, suppose contrary to (12.21) that there is a sequence $\{\eta^k\}$ converging to zero along which the limit in (12.21) is $c > 0$. Then by definition, there is a sequence $\{\delta^k\}$ converging to zero such that $\mu_{x_*^N}^{N,\eta^k} = \exp((\eta^k)^{-1}(c + \delta^k))$. This expression grows without bound as k grows large, contradicting the fact that each μ^{N,η^k} is a probability measure. This completes the proof of the theorem. ∎

12.2.2 Direct Exponential Protocols: The Large Population Limit

The analysis of the large population limit is more complicated than that of the small noise limit, owing to the dependence of the state space $\mathcal{X}^N$ on the population size N (see section 12.1.2). We must contend with this and two further issues on the way to our next result, theorem 12.2.3.

First, to obtain any sort of limit result, we must consider a sequence of potential games $\{F^N\}_{N=N_0}^{\infty}$ that "settle down" in some sense. Theorem 12.2.3 requires the rescaled potential functions $\{\frac{1}{N} f^N\}_{N=N_0}^{\infty}$ to converge uniformly to a limit function $f: \mathcal{X} \to \mathbf{R}$. This requirement is rather weak: theorem 11.5.7 and the subsequent exercises showed that the requirement is necessary but not sufficient for the potential games themselves to converge.

Second, taking the large population limit does not cause the multinomial term from equation (12.15) to vanish, as it did with the small noise limit. Theorem 12.2.3 shows that this term can be captured using the logit potential function $f^\eta \colon X \to \mathbf{R}$. This function, first presented in equation (7.5), is given by

$$f^\eta(x) = f(x) - \eta \sum_{i \in S} x_i \log x_i$$

where $0 \log 0 = 0$ as usual. The second term in f^η, given by η times the entropy function $h(x) = -\sum_{i \in S} x_i \log x_i$, increases the value of f^η at states representing "more random" probability distributions, the more so the higher the value of the noise level η.

The original use of f^η in theorem 7.1.4 was as a strict Lyapunov function for the logit(η) dynamic. In the present context, as N grows large, the stationary distribution weights $\mu_x^{N,\eta}$ decay at rates determined by $\frac{1}{\eta} \Delta f^\eta$.

Theorem 12.2.3 *Let $\{F^N\}_{N=N_0}^\infty$ be a sequence of finite-population potential games whose rescaled potential functions $\{\frac{1}{N} f^N\}_{N=N_0}^\infty$ converge uniformly to the C^1 function $f \colon X \to \mathbf{R}$. Suppose that agents are clever and employ a direct exponential protocol with noise level $\eta > 0$. Then the sequence of stationary distributions $\{\mu^{N,\eta}\}_{N=N_0}^\infty$ satisfies*

$$\lim_{N \to \infty} \max_{x \in X^N} \left| \tfrac{\eta}{N} \log \mu_x^{N,\eta} - \Delta f^\eta(x) \right| = 0. \tag{12.23}$$

Corollary 12.2.4 *Under the conditions of theorem 12.2.3, state x is weakly stochastically stable in the large population limit if and only if $x \in \operatorname{argmax}_{y \in X} f^\eta(y)$.*

Proof of theorem 12.2.3 Equation (12.18) says that for any $x \in X^N$,

$$\frac{\mu_x^{N,\eta}}{\mu_{e_1}^{N,\eta}} = \frac{N!}{\prod_{i \in S} (Nx_i)!} \exp\!\left(\eta^{-1}\!\left(f^N(x) - f^N(e_1)\right)\right). \tag{12.24}$$

By Stirling's formula (see the chapter notes), $N! = \sqrt{2\pi N}\, N^N \exp(-N + \frac{\theta^N}{N})$ for some $\theta^N \in [0, \frac{1}{12}]$. Therefore, letting $S(x) = \{i \in S \colon x_i > 0\}$ and $n(x) = \#S(x)$, we can rewrite (12.24) as

$$\frac{\mu_x^{N,\eta}}{\mu_{e_1}^{N,\eta}} = \frac{\sqrt{2\pi N}\, N^N \exp(-N + \frac{\theta^N}{N})}{\prod_{i \in S(x)} \sqrt{2\pi N x_i}\, (Nx_i)^{Nx_i} \exp(-Nx_i + \frac{\theta^{Nx_i}}{Nx_i})} \exp\!\left(\eta^{-1}\!\left(f^N(x) - f^N(e_1)\right)\right)$$

$$= \exp\!\left(\eta^{-1}\!\left(f^N(x) - f^N(e_1)\right)\right) \left(\prod_{i \in S(x)} x_i^{-(Nx_i + 1/2)} \right) \cdot \frac{1}{(2\pi N)^{(n(x)-1)/2}} \exp\!\left(\frac{\theta^N}{N} - \sum_{i \in S(x)} \frac{\theta^{Nx_i}}{Nx_i} \right).$$

Limiting Stationary Distributions and Stochastic Stability

Taking logarithms and multiplying by $\frac{\eta}{N}$ yields

$$\frac{\eta}{N} \log \frac{\mu_x^{N,\eta}}{\mu_{e_1}^{N,\eta}} = \frac{1}{N} f^N(x) - \frac{1}{N} f^N(e_1) - \eta \sum_{i \in S(x)} x_i \log x_i$$
$$+ \frac{\eta}{N}\left(\frac{\theta^N}{N} - \sum_{i \in S(x)} \left(\frac{\theta^{Nx_i}}{Nx_i} + \frac{1}{2}\log x_i\right) - \frac{n(x)-1}{2} \log 2\pi N\right).$$

Since any $x \in X^N$ with $x_i > 0$ satisfies $x_i \geq \frac{1}{N}$, it follows that

$$\left|\frac{1}{N}\sum_{i \in S(x)}\left(\frac{\theta^{Nx_i}}{Nx_i} + \frac{1}{2}\log x_i\right)\right| \leq \left|\frac{n(x)}{12N}\right| + \left|\frac{n(x)}{2N}\log\frac{1}{N}\right|.$$

Combining the last three equations, and using the facts that $\{\frac{1}{N} f^N\}$ converges uniformly to f and that $f^\eta(e_1) = f(e_1)$, we have

$$\lim_{N \to \infty} \max_{x \in X^N} \left|\frac{\eta}{N} \log \frac{\mu_x^{N,\eta}}{\mu_{e_1}^{N,\eta}} - (f^\eta(x) - f^\eta(e_1))\right| = 0. \tag{12.25}$$

The argument that (12.25) implies (12.23) is similar to the proof of theorem 12.2.2. ∎

Theorem 12.2.3 shows how both the rates of decay of the stationary distribution weights and the location of the stochastically stable state depend on the noise level η. The larger is η, the more weight that f^η places on the entropy term, and hence the better the prospects for visitation for states far from the boundary of the simplex. This point is illustrated in the next example.

Example 12.2.1 Suppose that agents are matched to play 123 Coordination (see examples 3.1.5, 6.2.2, and 7.1.3):

$$A = \begin{pmatrix} 1 & 0 & 0 \\ 0 & 2 & 0 \\ 0 & 0 & 3 \end{pmatrix}.$$

Whether the population is finite or continuous, and whether self-matching is allowed or prohibited, the resulting population game is a potential game. In the continuous-population case, the potential function of the potential game is the convex function

$$f(x) = \frac{1}{2}\left((x_1)^2 + 2(x_2)^2 + 3(x_3)^2\right),$$

which is illustrated in figure 3.1. The potential functions for the finite-population games are described in exercise 11.5.2.

Suppose that agents are clever and employ a direct exponential protocol with noise level $\eta > 0$. Theorem 12.2.3 says that as the population size N grows large, the rates of decay of the stationary distribution weights are determined by the logit potential function

$$f^\eta(x) = \tfrac{1}{2}((x_1)^2 + 2(x_2)^2 + 3(x_3)^2) - \eta(x_1 \log x_1 + x_2 \log x_2 + x_3 \log x_3)$$
$$= f(x) + \eta\, h(x).$$

The function f^η is the weighted sum of the convex potential function f and the concave entropy function h, with the weight on the latter given by the noise level η.

At larger values of η, f^η is dominated by its entropy term. This is illustrated in figure 12.2, which presents a graph and contour plot of f^η when $\eta = 1.5$. Here f^η appears concave. Its unique maximizer, and hence the uniquely stochastically stable state in the large population limit, is $x^* \approx (.2114, .2596, .5290)$, which puts significant weight on all three strategies. Thus, if the revision protocol is noisy, then in the infinite horizon, the population tends to congregate at states at which all three strategies are common.

More moderate noise levels balance the contributions of f and h to f^η. This is illustrated in figure 12.3, which presents a graph and contour plot of f^η when $\eta = .6$. This logit potential function does not look especially concave or convex. The uniquely stochastically stable state, $x^* \approx (.0072, .0073, .9855)$, places nearly all weight on strategy 3. There is another local maximum of f^η at $x^2 \approx (.0502, .8864, .0634)$, which by theorem 8.2.4 is a locally stable rest point of the deterministic logit dynamic. Thus, if the process $\{X_t^{N,\eta}\}$ starts off near x^2, it is likely to approach x^2 and then remain there for a large amount of time. Nevertheless, x^2 is not stochastically stable, and the stationary distribution weights on nearby states decay at rates of about

$$\tfrac{1}{\eta}\Delta f^\eta(x^2) = \tfrac{1}{.6}(f^\eta(x^*) - f^\eta(x^2)) \approx \tfrac{10}{6}(1.5084 - 1.0522) = .7603.$$

When η is small, f^η closely resembles the original potential function f. Figure 12.4 presents a graph and contour plot of f^η when $\eta = .2$; these pictures are very similar to the pictures of f in figure 3.1. In addition to the stochastically stable state $x^* \approx e_3$, the function f^η has local maxima at states $x^2 \approx e_2$ and $x^1 \approx (.9841, .0078, .0081)$. The rates of decay of the stationary distribution weights near the latter two states are

$$\tfrac{1}{\eta}\Delta f^\eta(x^2) = \tfrac{1}{.2}(f^\eta(x^*) - f^\eta(x^2)) \approx 5(1.5 - 1) = 2.5;$$

$$\tfrac{1}{\eta}\Delta f^\eta(x^1) = \tfrac{1}{.2}(f^\eta(x^*) - f^\eta(x^1)) \approx 5(1.5 - .5029) = 4.9855. \qquad \blacklozenge$$

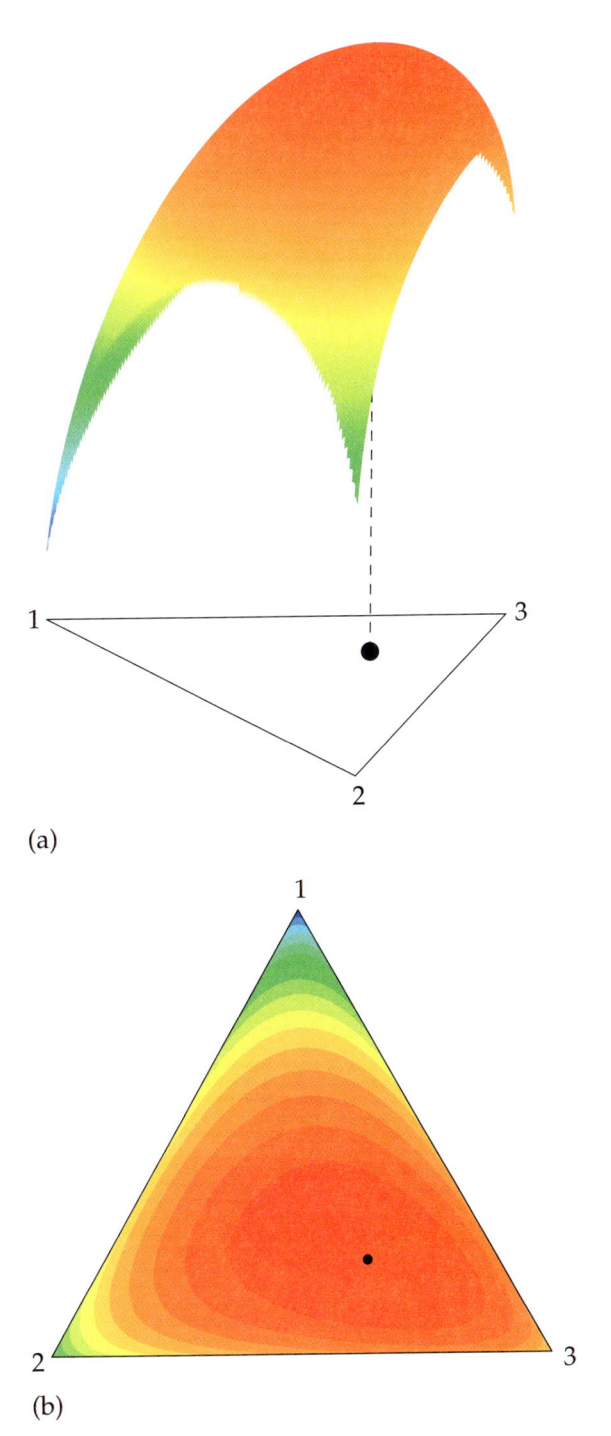

Figure 12.2
Graph (a) and contour plot (b) of the logit(1.5) potential function for 123 Coordination.

(a)

(b)

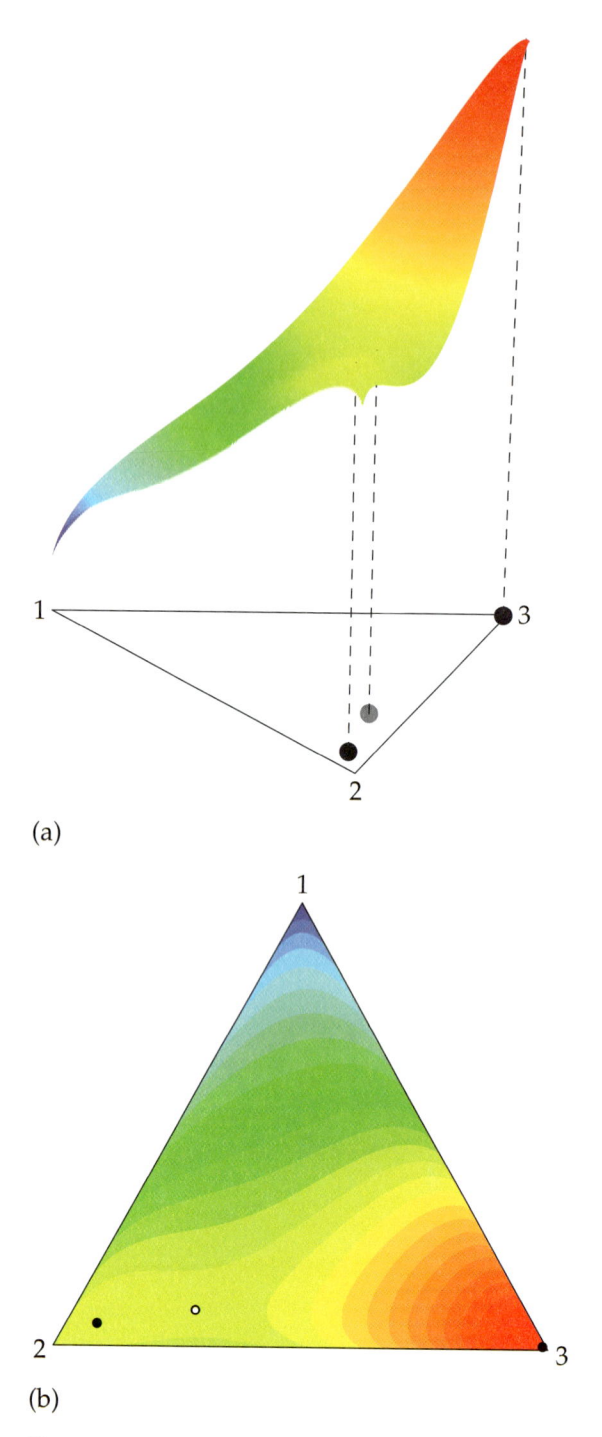

Figure 12.3
Graph (a) and contour plot (b) of the logit(.6) potential function for 123 Coordination.

(a)

(b)

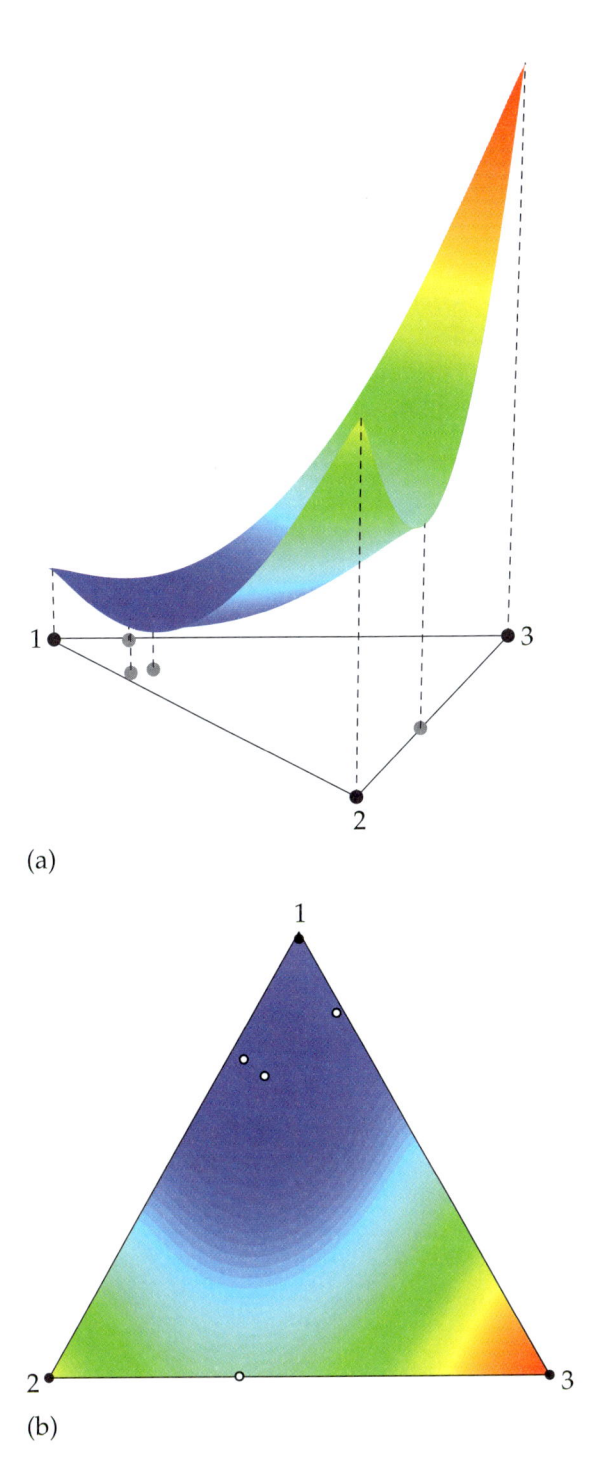

Figure 12.4
Graph (a) and contour plot (b) of the logit(.2) potential function for 123 Coordination.

12.2.3 Direct Exponential Protocols: Double Limits

As noted in section 12.1.3, the best way to compare the predictions of the small noise and large population limits is to compare the two double limits: the small noise double limit, whose interior limit has η approaching zero, and the large population double limit, whose interior limit has N approaching infinity. In the current setting, the behavior of the double limits is easily deduced from the previous theorems, along with the facts that the sequences of functions $\{\frac{1}{N}\Delta f^N\}_{N=N_0}^{\infty}$ and $\{\Delta f^\eta\}_{\eta \in (0,\bar{\eta}]}$ converge uniformly to f.

Corollary 12.2.5 *Under the conditions of theorem 12.2.3, the stationary distributions $\mu^{N,\eta}$ satisfy*

i. $\lim\limits_{N \to \infty} \lim\limits_{\eta \to 0} \max\limits_{x \in \mathcal{X}^N} \left| \frac{\eta}{N} \log \mu_x^{N,\eta} - \Delta f(x) \right| = 0$ and

ii. $\lim\limits_{\eta \to 0} \lim\limits_{N \to \infty} \max\limits_{x \in \mathcal{X}^N} \left| \frac{\eta}{N} \log \mu_x^{N,\eta} - \Delta f(x) \right| = 0.$

Corollary 12.2.5 says that when agents play potential games using direct exponential protocols, the predictions generated by the small noise and large population limits agree in a strong sense. In both cases, when the other parameter is held fixed at a value "close to its limit", the rates of decay of stationary distribution weights are approximately described by differences in the potential function f. Thus, the choice between the two analyses has limited consequences for forecasts of infinite-horizon behavior.

12.2.4 Imitative Exponential Protocols with Committed Agents

We close this section by computing limiting stationary distributions for potential games under imitative exponential protocols, assuming that there is one committed agent for each available strategy. The analysis follows a similar path to the previous one, but starting from the stationary distribution formula (12.16) rather than (12.15). The only difference between these formulas is that formula (12.15) for the direct protocol contains a multinomial term, whereas formula (12.16) for the imitative protocol does not. This not only makes the analysis of the imitative case simpler, but also alters the prediction of behavior in the large population limit.

Equation (12.16) implies that under an imitative exponential protocol, ratios between stationary distribution weights are given by

$$\frac{\mu_x^{N,\eta}}{\mu_y^{N,\eta}} = \exp\left(\eta^{-1}\left(f^N(x) - f^N(y)\right)\right) \quad \text{for all } x, y \in \mathcal{X}^N.$$

This implies in turn that

$$\frac{\eta}{N} \log \frac{\mu_x^{N,\eta}}{\mu_y^{N,\eta}} = \frac{1}{N} \left(f^N(x) - f^N(y)\right).$$

Limiting Stationary Distributions and Stochastic Stability

From here, the same argument used to prove theorem 12.2.2 yields the following result.

Theorem 12.2.6 *Suppose that clever agents using an imitative exponential protocol play a finite-population potential game F^N with potential function f^N, and that there is one committed agent for each strategy in F^N. Then for all $\eta \in X^N$,*

$$\lim_{\eta \to 0} \eta \log \mu_x^{N,\eta} = \Delta f^N(x).$$

Together, theorems 12.2.2 and 12.2.6 show that in the small noise limit, infinite-horizon behaviors under direct and imitative protocols look the same. The explanation is simple: the stationary distributions (12.15) and (12.16) only differ by the inclusion in the former of the multinomial term, a term that becomes inconsequential when the noise level is sufficiently small.

For the large population limit, theorem 12.2.3 shows that under direct exponential protocols, the rates of decay of the stationary distribution weights are described by $\frac{1}{\eta}\Delta f^\eta$. Example 12.2.1 shows that high noise levels lead to predictions far from what one would expect from the potential function f alone.

In the imitative case, the absence of the multinomial term from (12.16) means that an entropy term is no longer needed to describe the large population asymptotics. Theorem 12.2.7 shows that as N grows large, the stationary distribution weights of the stochastic process $\{X_t^N\}$ decay at rates determined not by $\frac{1}{\eta}\Delta f^\eta$, but by $\frac{1}{\eta}\Delta f$. Thus, while higher noise levels lead to lower exponential rates of decay, they do not introduce any distortions of potential.

Theorem 12.2.7 *Let $\{F^N\}_{N=N_0}^\infty$ be a sequence of finite-population potential games whose rescaled potential functions $\{\frac{1}{N}f^N\}_{N=N_0}^\infty$ converge uniformly to the C^1 function $f \colon X \to \mathbf{R}$. Suppose that agents are clever and employ an imitative exponential protocol with noise level $\eta > 0$, and that there is one committed agent for each strategy in F^N. Then the sequence of stationary distributions $\{\mu^{N,\eta}\}_{N=N_0}^\infty$ satisfies*

$$\lim_{N \to \infty} \max_{x \in X^N} \left| \tfrac{\eta}{N} \log \mu_x^{N,\eta} - \Delta f(x) \right| = 0.$$

Corollary 12.2.8 *Under the conditions of theorem 12.2.7, state x is weakly stochastically stable in the large population limit if and only if $x \in \mathrm{argmax}_{y \in X} f(y)$.*

The fact that imitative protocols lead to cleaner equilibrium selection results than direct protocols may be unexpected, but recalling our earlier results on deterministic dynamics makes this conclusion less surprising. For instance, whereas section 6.2 concluded that the logit dynamic violates positive correlation (PC), and that its rest points are perturbed equilibria rather than Nash equilibria, section 5.4 established that the imitative logit dynamic (example 5.4.7) satisfies (PC), and that its rest points include all Nash equilibria of the underlying game. Evidently, by enabling agents to take advantage of their opponents' experiences, imitative protocols generate aggregate behavior that respects the incentives in the underlying game. This is so even when agents employing the protocol barely distinguish between strategies with high and low payoffs.

Exercise 12.2.9 To verify that the double limits agree in this context, state and prove an analogue of corollary 12.2.5 for imitative exponential protocols with committed agents. ◇

Of course, without committed agents, the results for imitative protocols would be very different, even if the irreducibility of the evolutionary process were ensured in some other way (see example 12.1.1 and section 12.4.1).

12.3 Noisy Best Response Protocols in Two-Strategy Games

This section turns to the other reversible setting discussed in chapter 11: two-strategy games. Since here reversibility places no restrictions on the form of the revision protocol, the equilibrium selection results are not preordained; in many games, different protocols lead to different stochastically stable states.

We begin by defining a general class of noisy best response protocols. In doing so, we introduce the important notion of the *cost* of a suboptimal choice, which is defined as the rate of decay of the probability of making this choice as the noise level approaches zero. Using this notion, we derive simple formulas that characterize the asymptotics of the stationary distribution under the various limits in η and N, and we offer a necessary and sufficient condition for an equilibrium to be uniquely stochastically stable under every noisy best response protocol.

Sections 12.3 and 12.4 employ our usual notation for two-strategy games. State x is identified with the weight $\chi \equiv x_1$ that it places on strategy 1, so that the state space becomes $\mathcal{X}^N = \{0, \frac{1}{N}, \ldots, 1\} \subset [0, 1]$; also, $F(\chi)$ is substituted for $F(x)$, and $\rho(\pi, \chi)$ for $\rho(\pi, x)$, whenever doing so is convenient. Many of the proofs use the dominated convergence theorem to justify switching the order of limits and integration; see the chapter notes for references on this result.

12.3.1 Noisy Best Response Protocols and Their Cost Functions
Noisy best response protocols can be expressed as

$$\rho_{ij}^\eta(\pi) = \sigma^\eta(\pi_j - \pi_i), \tag{12.26}$$

for some function $\sigma^\eta \colon \mathbf{R} \to (0, 1)$. When a strategy i player using such a protocol receives a revision opportunity, she switches to strategy $j \neq i$ with a probability that

Limiting Stationary Distributions and Stochastic Stability

only depends on the payoff advantage of strategy j over strategy i. To justify its name, the protocol σ^η should recommend optimal strategies with high probability when the noise level is small:

$$\lim_{\eta \to 0} \sigma^\eta(a) = \begin{cases} 1 & \text{if } a > 0, \\ 0 & \text{if } a < 0. \end{cases}$$

To place further structure on the probabilities of suboptimal choices, we impose restrictions on the rates at which the probabilities $\sigma^\eta(a)$ of choosing a suboptimal strategy approach zero as η approaches zero. We define the *cost* of switching to a strategy with payoff *disadvantage* $d \in \mathbf{R}$ by

$$\kappa(d) = -\lim_{\eta \to 0} \eta \log \sigma^\eta(-d). \tag{12.27}$$

By unpacking this expression, we can write the probability of switching to a strategy with payoff disadvantage d when the noise level is η as

$$\sigma^\eta(-d) = \exp\left(-\eta^{-1}(\kappa(d) + o(1))\right),$$

where $o(1)$ represents a term that vanishes as η approaches zero. Thus, $\kappa(d)$ is the exponential rate of decay of the choice probability $\sigma^\eta(-d)$ as η^{-1} approaches infinity. (Section 12.5.1 introduces a more restrictive notion of cost that is also common in the literature; see that section and section 12.A.5 for further discussion.)

We constrain our class of protocols in the following way.

Definition *The noisy best response protocol* (12.26) *is* regular *if*

i. *the limit in* (12.27) *exists for all* $d \in \mathbf{R}$, *with convergence uniform on compact intervals;*

ii. κ *is nondecreasing;*

iii. $\kappa(d) = 0$ *whenever* $d < 0$;

iv. $\kappa(d) > 0$ *whenever* $d > 0$.

Conditions (ii)–(iv) impose restrictions on the rates of decay of switching probabilities. Condition (ii) requires the rate of decay to be nondecreasing in the payoff disadvantage of the alternative strategy. Condition (iii) requires the switching probability of an agent currently playing the suboptimal strategy to have rate of decay zero; the condition is satisfied when the probability is bounded away from zero, although this is not necessary for the condition to hold. Finally, condition (iv) requires the probability of switching from the optimal strategy to the suboptimal one to have a positive rate of decay. These conditions are consistent with having either $\kappa(0) > 0$ or $\kappa(0) = 0$. Thus, when both strategies earn the same payoff, the probability that a revising agent opts to switch strategies can converge to zero with a positive rate of decay, as in example 12.3.1, or can be bounded away from zero, as in examples 12.3.2 and 12.3.3.

We now present the three leading examples of noisy best response protocols.

Example 12.3.1: Best Response with Mutations   The best response with mutations (BRM) protocol with noise level $\eta\,(= -(\log \varepsilon)^{-1})$ (example 11.1.1) is defined by

$$\sigma^\eta(a) = \begin{cases} 1 - \exp(-\eta^{-1}) & \text{if } a > 0, \\ \exp(-\eta^{-1}) & \text{if } a \leq 0. \end{cases}$$

In this specification, an indifferent agent only switches strategies in the event of a mutation. Since for $d \geq 0$ we have $-\eta \log \sigma^\eta(-d) = 1$, protocol σ^η is regular with cost function

$$\kappa(d) = \begin{cases} 1 & \text{if } d \geq 0, \\ 0 & \text{if } d < 0. \end{cases}$$
◆

Example 12.3.2: Logit choice   The *logit choice protocol* with noise level $\eta > 0$ (examples 6.2.1 and 11.1.2) is defined by

$$\sigma^\eta(a) = \frac{\exp(\eta^{-1} a)}{\exp(\eta^{-1} a) + 1}.$$

For $d \geq 0$, we have $-\eta \log \sigma^\eta(-d) = d + \eta \log(\exp(-\eta^{-1} d) + 1)$. It follows that σ^η is regular with cost function

$$\kappa(d) = \begin{cases} d & \text{if } d > 0, \\ 0 & \text{if } d \leq 0. \end{cases}$$
◆

Example 12.3.3: Probit Choice   The logit choice protocol can be derived from a random utility model in which the strategies' payoffs are perturbed by i.i.d. double exponentially distributed random variables (see example 6.2.3). The *probit choice protocol* assumes instead that the payoff perturbations are i.i.d. normal random variables with mean 0 and variance η. Thus

$$\sigma^\eta(a) = \mathbb{P}(\sqrt{\eta}\, Z + a > \sqrt{\eta}\, Z'),$$

where Z and Z' are independent and standard normal. It follows that

$$\sigma^\eta(a) = \Phi\!\left(\frac{a}{\sqrt{2\eta}}\right), \tag{12.28}$$

where Φ is the standard normal distribution function.

A well-known approximation of Φ (see the chapter notes) tells us that when $z < 0$,

… Limiting Stationary Distributions and Stochastic Stability

$$\Phi(z) = K(z) \exp(\tfrac{-z^2}{2}) \tag{12.29}$$

for some $K(z) \in (\frac{-1}{\sqrt{2\pi}\,z}(1-\frac{1}{z^2}), \frac{-1}{\sqrt{2\pi}\,z})$. It follows that $K(z) \in (\frac{-1}{2\sqrt{2\pi}\,z}, \frac{-1}{\sqrt{2\pi}\,z})$ whenever $z < -\sqrt{2}$. Also, one can verify directly that (12.29) holds with $K(z) \in [e \cdot \Phi(-\sqrt{2}), \tfrac{1}{2}]$ whenever $z \in [-\sqrt{2}, 0]$.

Now equations (12.28) and (12.29) imply that

$$-\eta \log \sigma^{\eta}(-d) = -\eta \log \Phi\left(\tfrac{-d}{\sqrt{2\eta}}\right) = \tfrac{1}{4}d^2 - \eta \log K\left(\tfrac{-d}{\sqrt{2\eta}}\right) \tag{12.30}$$

when $d \geq 0$, with our earlier estimates showing that

$$\eta \log K\left(\tfrac{-d}{\sqrt{2\eta}}\right) \in \left(\tfrac{1}{2}\eta \log \eta - \eta \log 2\sqrt{\pi}\,d,\ \tfrac{1}{2}\eta \log \eta - \eta \log \sqrt{\pi}\,d\right) \quad \text{if } d > 2\sqrt{\eta};$$

$$\eta \log K\left(\tfrac{-d}{\sqrt{2\eta}}\right) \in \left[\eta\left(1 + \log \Phi(-\sqrt{2})\right),\ \eta \log \tfrac{1}{2}\right] \quad \text{if } d \in [0, 2\sqrt{\eta}].$$

Thus, for any $D > 0$ and any $\delta > 0$, we have $|\eta \log K(\tfrac{-d}{\sqrt{2\eta}})| < \delta$ for all $d \in [0, D]$ when $\eta > 0$ is sufficiently small. We conclude from equation (12.30) that σ^{η} is regular with cost function

$$\kappa(d) = \begin{cases} \tfrac{1}{4}d^2 & \text{if } d > 0, \\ 0 & \text{if } d \leq 0. \end{cases}$$
◆

12.3.2 The Small Noise Limit

We now investigate the asymptotics of the stationary distribution $\mu^{N,\eta}$, starting with the small noise limit. For convenience, we continue to assume clever payoff evaluation; the alternative assumption has only minor effects on the small noise limit (see exercise 12.3.2) and no effect at all on the large population limit or the double limits.

After accounting for clever payoff evaluation (see section 11.4.2, especially equations (11.19) and (11.20)), theorem 11.2.3 says that the stationary distribution $\mu^{N,\eta}$ for the game F^N under protocol σ^{η} satisfies

$$\eta \log \frac{\mu_x^{N,\eta}}{\mu_0^{N,\eta}} = \eta \log \left(\prod_{j=1}^{N\chi} \frac{(N-j+1)}{j} \cdot \frac{\rho_{01}^{\eta}(\check{F}^N(\tfrac{j-1}{N}), \tfrac{j-1}{N})}{\rho_{10}^{\eta}(\check{F}^N(\tfrac{j-1}{N}), \tfrac{j}{N})} \right)$$

$$= \sum_{j=1}^{N\chi} \left(-\eta \log \sigma^{\eta}\left(F_0^N(\tfrac{j-1}{N}) - F_1^N(\tfrac{j}{N})\right) + \eta \log \sigma^{\eta}\left(F_1^N(\tfrac{j}{N}) - F_0^N(\tfrac{j-1}{N})\right) \right.$$

$$\left. + \eta \log \tfrac{N-j+1}{j} \right). \tag{12.31}$$

With this motivation, we define the *relative cost function* $\tilde{\kappa}: \mathbf{R} \to \mathbf{R}$ by

$$\tilde{\kappa}(d) = \lim_{\eta \to 0} \left(-\eta \log \sigma^\eta(-d) + \eta \log \sigma^\eta(d) \right) \tag{12.32}$$

$$= \kappa(d) - \kappa(-d)$$

$$= \begin{cases} \kappa(d) & \text{if } d > 0, \\ 0 & \text{if } d = 0, \\ -\kappa(-d) & \text{if } d \leq 0. \end{cases}$$

The assumptions on κ imply that $\tilde{\kappa}$ is nondecreasing, sign-preserving ($\text{sgn}(\tilde{\kappa}(d)) = \text{sgn}(d)$), and odd ($\tilde{\kappa}(d) = -\tilde{\kappa}(-d)$). Now, equations (12.31) and (12.32) imply that

$$\lim_{\eta \to 0} \eta \log \frac{\mu_\chi^{N,\eta}}{\mu_0^{N,\eta}} = \sum_{j=1}^{N\chi} \left(\kappa\left(F_1^N(\tfrac{j}{N}) - F_0^N(\tfrac{j-1}{N})\right) - \kappa\left(F_0^N(\tfrac{j}{N}) - F_1^N(\tfrac{j-1}{N})\right) \right)$$

$$= \sum_{j=1}^{N\chi} \tilde{\kappa}\left(F_1^N(\tfrac{j}{N}) - F_0^N(\tfrac{j-1}{N})\right).$$

Therefore, if we define the function $I^N: X^N \to \mathbf{R}$ by

$$I^N(\chi) = \sum_{j=1}^{N\chi} \tilde{\kappa}\left(F_1^N(\tfrac{j}{N}) - F_0^N(\tfrac{j-1}{N})\right), \tag{12.33}$$

then an easy modification of the proof of theorem 12.2.2 yields the following result.

Theorem 12.3.1 *Suppose that N clever agents play a two-strategy game F^N using a regular noisy best response protocol with cost function κ. Then for all $\chi \in X^N$,*

$$\lim_{\eta \to 0} \eta \log \mu_\chi^{N,\eta} = \Delta I^N(\chi). \tag{12.34}$$

For intuition, it is worth comparing this result to the corresponding result for potential games and direct exponential protocols, theorem 12.2.2. In both cases, taking the small noise limit causes the combinatorial term to vanish, leaving only a term that depends on payoff differences. But in equation (12.34), the payoff differences are transformed by the relative cost function $\tilde{\kappa}$, which determines how these differences influence the asymptotics of the stationary distribution. In the case of logit choice, example 12.3.2 shows that $\tilde{\kappa}$ is the identity function, and so the analysis here agrees with theorem 12.2.2.

Theorem 12.3.1 can be used to prove equilibrium selection results for finite-population games, but this is postponed until section 12.5 to delay some picky accounting for finite-population effects that is needed to obtain exact selection results. Instead, the study of equilibrium selection in two-strategy games is continued using results on double limits (see theorem 12.3.5).

Exercise 12.3.2 State and prove the analogue of theorem 12.3.1 for simple agents. ◇

12.3.3 The Large Population Limit

The description of the large population limit requires a few additional assumptions and definitions. First, we suppose that the sequence of two-strategy games $\{F^N\}_{N=N_0}^\infty$ converges uniformly to a continuous-population game F; we assume throughout that $F\colon [0,1] \to \mathbf{R}^2$ is a continuous function. Second, we let

$$F_\Delta(x) \equiv F_1(x) - F_0(x)$$

denote the payoff advantage of strategy 1 at state x in the limit game. Third, we let

$$\tilde\sigma^\eta(a) = \frac{\sigma^\eta(a)}{\sigma^\eta(-a)} \tag{12.35}$$

be the ratio of the probability of switching to a strategy with payoff advantage a to the probability of switching to a strategy with payoff advantage $-a$. Finally, we define the function $I^\eta\colon [0,1] \to \mathbf{R}$ by

$$I^\eta(x) = \int_0^x \eta \log \tilde\sigma^\eta(F_\Delta(y))\,\mathrm{d}y - \eta\left(x \log x + (1-x)\log(1-x)\right), \tag{12.36}$$

where $0 \log 0 = 0$.

Theorem 12.3.3 *Let $\{F^N\}_{N=N_0}^\infty$ be a sequence of two-strategy games that converges uniformly to the continuous-population game F. Suppose that agents are clever and employ regular noisy best response protocol σ^η. Then the sequence of stationary distributions $\{\mu^{N,\eta}\}_{N=N_0}^\infty$ satisfies*

$$\lim_{N\to\infty} \max_{x\in\mathcal{X}^N} \left| \tfrac{\eta}{N} \log \mu_x^{N,\eta} - \Delta I^\eta(x) \right| = 0.$$

Proof Equations (12.31) and (12.35) imply that

$$\frac{\eta}{N} \log \frac{\mu_x^{N,\eta}}{\mu_0^{N,\eta}} = \frac{\eta}{N} \sum_{j=1}^{Nx} \left(\log \tilde\sigma^\eta\!\left(F_1^N(\tfrac{j}{N}) - F_0^N(\tfrac{j-1}{N})\right) + \log \tfrac{N-j+1}{N} - \log \tfrac{j}{N} \right). \tag{12.37}$$

Since σ^η is bounded away from zero, and since $0 \geq \log\!\left(\tfrac{\lceil Nx \rceil}{N}\right) \geq \log(x)$ and $0 \geq \log\!\left(\tfrac{N - \lceil Nx\rceil + 1}{N}\right) \geq \log(1-x)$ for $x \in (0,1)$, the dominated convergence theorem implies that the Riemann sum in (12.37) converges to an integral. In particular, we have

$$\lim_{N \to \infty} \frac{\eta}{N} \log \frac{\mu_x^{N,\eta}}{\mu_0^{N,\eta}} = \int_0^x \eta \left(\log \tilde{\sigma}^\eta (F_1(y) - F_0(y)) + \log(1-y) - \log(y) \right) dy$$

$$= \int_0^x \eta \log \tilde{\sigma}^\eta (F_\Delta(y)) \, dy - \eta \left(x \log x + (1-x) \log(1-x) \right)$$

$$= I^\eta(x),$$

with the limit, which is taken over those N for which $x \in \mathcal{X}^N$, being uniform in x. The remainder of the proof is similar to that of theorem 12.2.2. ∎

Once again, there are similarities between this result and the corresponding result for potential games and direct exponential protocols, theorem 12.2.3. As in the earlier result, the function I^η describing rates of decay is the sum of two terms: a term that depends on payoff differences in the limit game and an entropy term. Also, the function I^η serves as a Lyapunov function for the relevant mean dynamic; compare theorem 7.1.4 to Exercise 12.3.4. But as was the case in the previous theorem, the payoff differences appearing in I^η are transformed to account for the influence of the protocol σ^η.

Exercise 12.3.4

i. Compute the mean dynamic obtained when agents use noisy best response protocol σ^η to play population game F.

ii. Prove that I^η is a global strict Lyapunov function for this mean dynamic. ◇

12.3.4 Double Limits

Stating the results for double limits requires one final definition. Given a continuous-population game F and a noisy best response protocol with cost function κ, we define the *ordinal potential function* $I \colon [0, 1] \to \mathbf{R}$ by

$$I(x) = \int_0^x \tilde{\kappa}(F_\Delta(y)) \, dy, \tag{12.38}$$

where the relative cost function $\tilde{\kappa}$ is defined in equation (12.32). Observe that by marginally adjusting the state x so as to increase the mass on the optimal strategy, one increases the value of I at rate $\tilde{\kappa}(a)$, where a is the optimal strategy's payoff advantage. Thus, the ordinal potential function combines information about payoff differences with the costs of the associated suboptimal choices.

Limiting Stationary Distributions and Stochastic Stability

Example 12.3.4 If ρ^η represents best response with mutations (example 12.3.1), then the ordinal potential function (12.38) becomes the *signum potential function*

$$I_{\text{sgn}}(x) = \int_0^x \text{sgn}(F_\Delta(y))\,dy.$$

The slope of this function at state x is 1, -1, or 0, according to whether the optimal strategy at x is strategy 1, strategy 0, or both. ◆

Example 12.3.5 If ρ^η represents logit choice (example 12.3.2), then (12.38) becomes the usual potential function

$$I_1(x) = \int_0^x F_\Delta(y)\,dy,$$

(see example 3.2.3), whose slope at state x is just the payoff difference at x. ◆

Example 12.3.6 If ρ^η represents probit choice (example 12.3.3), then (12.38) becomes the *quadratic potential function*

$$I_2(x) = \int_0^x \tfrac{1}{4}\langle F_\Delta(y)\rangle^2\,dy,$$

where $\langle a \rangle^2 = \text{sgn}(a)\,a^2$ is the signed square function. The values of I_2 again depend on payoff differences, but relative to the logit case, larger payoff differences play a more important role. This contrast can be traced to the fact that at small noise levels, the double exponential distribution has fatter tails than the normal distribution; compare example 12.3.3. ◆

Theorem 12.3.5 shows that under either double limit, the rates of decay of the stationary distribution are captured by the ordinal potential function I. Since the double limits agree, the predictions of infinite-horizon behavior under noisy best response rules do not depend on whether equilibrium selection is driven by the small noise or large population limit.

Theorem 12.3.5 *Under the conditions of theorem 12.3.3, the stationary distributions $\mu^{N,\eta}$ satisfy*

i. $\lim_{N\to\infty} \lim_{\eta\to 0} \max_{x\in\mathcal{X}^N} \left|\tfrac{\eta}{N}\log \mu_x^{N,\eta} - \Delta I(x)\right| = 0$

ii. $\lim_{\eta\to 0} \lim_{N\to\infty} \max_{x\in\mathcal{X}^N} \left|\tfrac{\eta}{N}\log \mu_x^{N,\eta} - \Delta I(x)\right| = 0.$

Proof To prove part (i), one uses the dominated convergence theorem to show that the Riemann sums $\tfrac{1}{N}I^N(x)$ converge uniformly to the integrals $I(x)$, in the sense that

$$\lim_{N\to\infty} \max_{x\in X^N} \left|\tfrac{1}{N} I^N(x) - I(x)\right| = 0.$$

This uniform convergence implies that

$$\lim_{N\to\infty} \max_{y\in X^N} \tfrac{1}{N} I^N(y) = \max_{y\in[0,1]} I(y),$$

and hence that

$$\lim_{N\to\infty} \max_{x\in X^N} \left|\tfrac{1}{N}\Delta I^N(x) - \Delta I(x)\right| = \lim_{N\to\infty} \max_{x\in X^N} \left|\left(\tfrac{1}{N} I^N(x) - \tfrac{1}{N} I^N(x_*^N)\right) - \left(I(x) - I(x_*)\right)\right| = 0,$$

where x_*^N and x_* maximize I^N and I, respectively. Since the limit in equation (12.34) is uniform (because X^N is finite), we have

$$\lim_{\eta\to 0} \max_{x\in X^N} \left|\tfrac{\eta}{N} \log \mu_x^{N,\eta} - \Delta I(x)\right|$$

$$\leq \lim_{\eta\to 0} \max_{x\in X^N} \left|\tfrac{\eta}{N} \log \mu_x^{N,\eta} - \tfrac{1}{N}\Delta I^N(x)\right| + \lim_{\eta\to 0} \max_{x\in X^N} \left|\tfrac{1}{N}\Delta I^N(x) - \Delta I(x)\right|$$

$$= \max_{x\in X^N} \left|\tfrac{1}{N}\Delta I^N(x) - \Delta I(x)\right|.$$

Combining this inequality with the previous equation yields

$$\lim_{N\to\infty} \lim_{\eta\to 0} \max_{x\in X^N} \left|\tfrac{\eta}{N} \log \mu_x^{N,\eta} - \Delta I(x)\right| \leq \lim_{N\to\infty} \max_{x\in X^N} \left|\tfrac{1}{N}\Delta I^N(x) - \Delta I(x)\right| = 0,$$

which proves part (i) of the theorem. The proof of part (ii) of the theorem is similar. ∎

12.3.5 Stochastic Stability: Examples

By theorem 12.3.5 (and the definitions in section 12.1.3), the states that are weakly stochastically stable in the double limits are those that maximize the ordinal potential function I; if this function has a unique maximizer, that state is uniquely stochastically stable. We now investigate in greater detail how a game's payoff function and the revision protocol's cost function interact to determine the stochastically stable states.

Since stochastic stability analysis is most interesting when it selects among multiple strict equilibria, we focus here on coordination games. The two-strategy population game $F: [0, 1] \to \mathbf{R}^2$ is a *coordination game* if there is a state $x^* \in (0, 1)$ such that

$$\mathrm{sgn}(\Delta F(x)) = \mathrm{sgn}(x - x^*) \quad \text{for all } x \neq x^*.$$

Any ordinal potential function I for a coordination game is quasi-convex, with local maximizers at each boundary state. Because $I(0) \equiv 0$ by definition, theorem 12.3.5 implies the following result.

Corollary 12.3.6 *Assume the conditions of theorem 12.3.3, and suppose that the limit game F is a coordination game. Then state 1 is uniquely stochastically stable in both double limits if $I(1) > 0$, while state 0 is uniquely stochastically stable in both double limits if $I(1) < 0$.*

The next two examples, which revisit two games introduced in chapter 11, show that the identity of the stochastically stable state may or may not depend on the revision protocol the agents employ.

Example 12.3.7: Stag Hunt Revisited In Example 11.2.2, considered stochastic evolution in the Stag Hunt game

$$A = \begin{pmatrix} h & h \\ 0 & s \end{pmatrix},$$

where $s > h > 0$. When a continuous population of agents are matched to play this game, their expected payoffs are given by $F_H(x) = h$ and $F_S(x) = sx$, where x denotes the proportion of agents playing Stag. This coordination game has two pure Nash equilibria and a mixed Nash equilibrium that puts weight $x^* = \frac{h}{s}$ on Stag.

Figure 12.5 presents normalized versions of the ordinal potentials for the BRM, logit, and probit protocols in this game:

$$I_{\text{sgn}}(x) = |x - x^*| - x^*;$$

$$I_1(x) = \tfrac{s}{2}x^2 - hx;$$

$$I_2(x) = \begin{cases} -\tfrac{s^2}{12}x^3 + \tfrac{hs}{4}x^2 - \tfrac{h^2}{4}x & \text{if } x \leq x^*, \\ \tfrac{s^2}{12}x^3 - \tfrac{hs}{4}x^2 + \tfrac{h^2}{4}x - \tfrac{h^3}{6s} & \text{if } x > x^*. \end{cases}$$

The normalized potential functions ΔI_{sgn}, ΔI_1, and ΔI_2 are drawn for two specifications of payoffs: $h = 2$ and $s = 3$ (figure 12.5a) and $h = 2$ and $s = 5$ (figure 12.5b). For any choices of $s > h > 0$ and any protocol, ΔI is symmetric about its minimizer, the mixed Nash equilibrium $x^* = \frac{h}{s}$. As a result, the three protocols always agree about equilibrium selection: the all-Hare equilibrium is uniquely stochastically stable when $x^* > \tfrac{1}{2}$ (or equivalently, when $2h > s$), and the all-Stag equilibrium is uniquely stochastically stable when the reverse inequality holds. ◆

Example 12.3.8: Nonlinear Stag Hunt Revisited Example 11.2.3 considered the Nonlinear Stag Hunt game with payoff functions $F_H(x) = h$ and $F_S(x) = sx^2$, with x representing the proportion of agents playing Stag. This game has two pure Nash equilibria and a mixed equilibrium at $x^* = \sqrt{h/s}$. The payoffs and mixed equilibria for $h = 2$ and various choices of s are graphed in figure 12.6.

(a) $h = 2, s = 3$

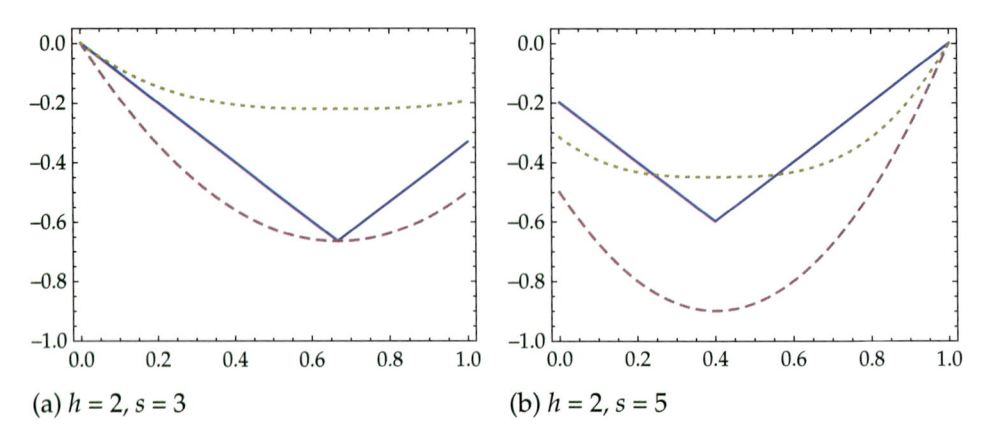

(b) $h = 2, s = 5$

Figure 12.5
The ordinal potentials ΔI_{sgn} (blue), ΔI_1 (purple), and ΔI_2 (yellow) for Stag Hunt.

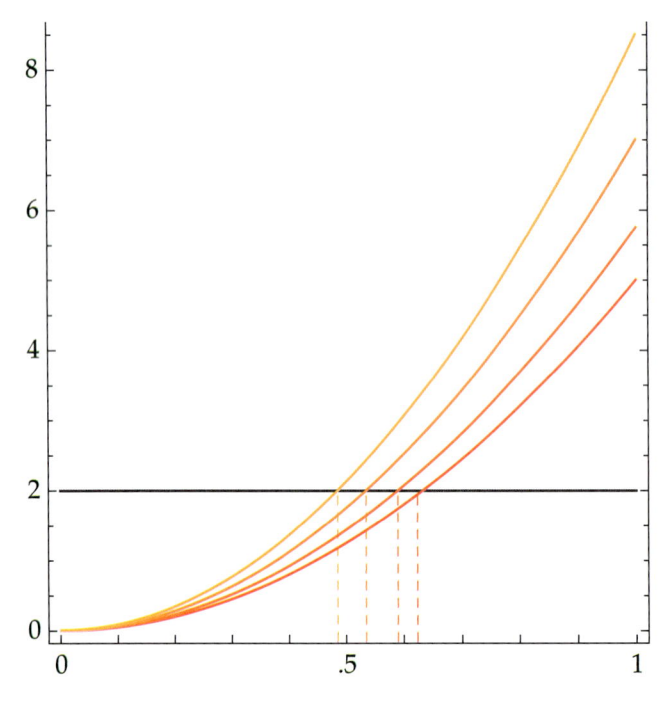

Figure 12.6
Payoffs and mixed equilibria in nonlinear Stag Hunt ($h = 2, s = 5, 5.75, 7, 8.5$).

The ordinal potentials for the BRM, logit, and probit models are given by

$$I_{\text{sgn}}(x) = |x - x^*| - x^*;$$

$$I_1(x) = \tfrac{s}{3}x^3 - hx;$$

$$I_2(x) = \begin{cases} -\tfrac{s^2}{20}x^5 + \tfrac{hs}{6}x^3 - \tfrac{h^2}{4}x & \text{if } x \leq x^*, \\ \tfrac{s^2}{20}x^5 - \tfrac{hs}{6}x^3 + \tfrac{h^2}{4}x - \tfrac{4h^2 x^*}{15} & \text{if } x > x^*. \end{cases}$$

Figure 12.7 presents the functions ΔI_{sgn}, ΔI_1, and ΔI_2 for $h = 2$ and for various choices of s.

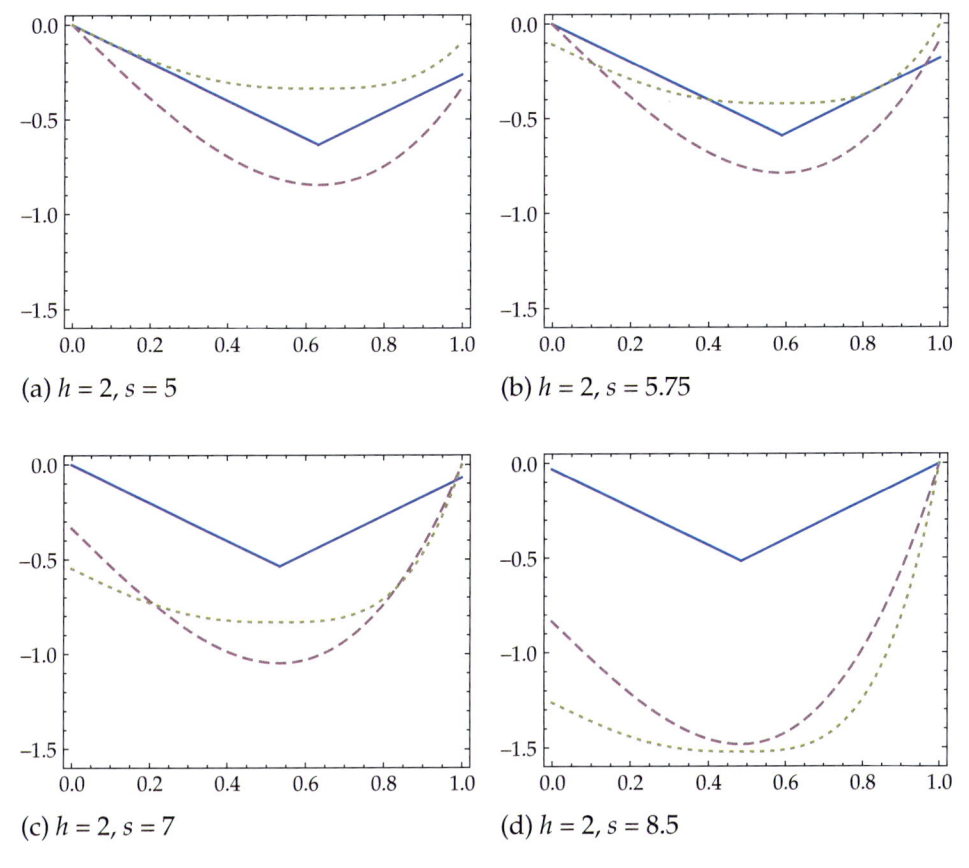

(a) $h = 2$, $s = 5$

(b) $h = 2$, $s = 5.75$

(c) $h = 2$, $s = 7$

(d) $h = 2$, $s = 8.5$

Figure 12.7
The ordinal potentials ΔI_{sgn} (blue), ΔI_1 (purple), and ΔI_2 (yellow) for Nonlinear Stag Hunt.

When s is at its lowest level of 5, coordination on Stag is at its least attractive. Since $x^* = \sqrt{2/5} \approx .6325$, the basin of attraction of the all-Hare equilibrium is considerably larger than that of the all-Stag equilibrium. Figure 12.7a illustrates that coordination on Hare is stochastically stable under all three protocols.

If one makes coordination on Stag somewhat more attractive by increasing s to 5.75, the mixed equilibrium becomes $x^* = \sqrt{2/5.75} \approx .5898$. The all-Hare equilibrium remains stochastically stable under the BRM and logit rules, but all-Stag becomes stochastically stable under the probit rule (figure 12.7b).

Increasing s further, to 7, shifts the mixed equilibrium closer to the midpoint of the unit interval ($x^* = \sqrt{2/7} \approx .5345$). The BRM rule continues to select all-Hare, while the probit and logit rules both select all-Stag (figure 12.7c).

Finally, when $s = 8.5$, the all-Stag equilibrium has the larger basin of attraction ($x^* = \sqrt{2/8.5} \approx .4851$). At this point, coordination on Stag becomes attractive enough that all three protocols select the all-Stag equilibrium (figure 12.7d).

As the value of s increases, why does the transition to selecting all-Stag occur first for the probit rule, then for the logit rule, and finally for the BRM rule? Figure 12.6 shows that increasing s not only shifts the mixed Nash equilibrium to the left but also markedly increases the payoff advantage of Stag at states where it is optimal. Since the cost function of the probit rule is the most sensitive to payoff differences, its equilibrium selection changes at the lowest level of s. The next selection to change is that of the (moderately sensitive) logit rule, and the last is the selection of the (insensitive) BRM rule. ◆

Exercise 12.3.7

i. Construct a two-strategy coordination game in which the logit protocol selects a different equilibrium than the BRM and probit protocols.

ii. Construct a two-strategy game in which the BRM, logit, and probit protocols each generates a distinct equilibrium selection. (Evidently the game cannot be a coordination game.) ◇

12.3.6 Risk Dominance, Stochastic Dominance, and Stochastic Stability

Building on these examples, we now seek general conditions on payoffs that ensure stochastic stability under all noisy best response protocols.

Example 12.3.7 shows that in the Stag Hunt game with linear payoffs, the noisy best response rules considered always select the equilibrium with the larger basin of attraction. The reason for this is easy to explain. Linearity of payoffs, along with the fact that the relative cost function $\tilde{\kappa}$ is sign-preserving and odd (see equation (12.32)), implies that the ordinal potential function I is symmetric about the mixed equilibrium x^*, where it attains its minimum value. If, for example, x^* is less than

… Limiting Stationary Distributions and Stochastic Stability

$\frac12$, so that pure equilibrium 1 has the larger basin of attraction, then $I(1)$ exceeds $I(0)$, implying that state 1 is uniquely stochastically stable. Similarly, if x^* exceeds $\frac12$, then $I(0)$ exceeds $I(1)$, and state 0 is uniquely stochastically stable.

With this motivation, we call strategy i *strictly risk dominant* in the two-strategy coordination game F if the set of states where it is the unique best response is larger than the corresponding set for strategy $j \neq i$. If F has mixed equilibrium $x^* \in (0,1)$, then strategy 0 is strictly risk dominant if $x^* > \frac12$, and strategy 1 is strictly risk dominant if $x^* < \frac12$. If the relevant inequality holds weakly in either case, the strategy is *weakly risk dominant*.

The foregoing arguments yield the following result, in which we denote by e_i the state at which all agents play strategy i.

Corollary 12.3.8 *Assume the conditions of theorem 12.3.3, and suppose that the limit game F is a coordination game with linear payoffs. Then*

i. State e_i is weakly stochastically stable under every noisy best response protocol if and only if strategy i is weakly risk dominant in F;

ii. If strategy i is strictly risk dominant in F, then state e_i is uniquely stochastically stable under every noisy best response protocol.

Example 12.3.8 suggests that in games with nonlinear payoffs, risk dominance only characterizes stochastic stability under the BRM rule. In any coordination game with mixed equilibrium x^*, the ordinal potential function for the BRM rule is $I_{\text{sgn}}(x) = |x - x^*| - x^*$. This function is minimized at x^*, and increases at a unit rate as one moves away from x^* in either direction, reflecting the fact that under the BRM rule, the probability of a suboptimal choice is independent of its payoff consequences. Clearly, whether $I_{\text{sgn}}(1)$ is greater than $I_{\text{sgn}}(0)$ depends only on whether x^* is less than $\frac12$.

Corollary 12.3.9 *Assume the conditions of theorem 12.3.3, and suppose that the limit game F is a coordination game and that σ^η is the BRM rule. Then*

i. state e_i is weakly stochastically stable if and only if strategy i is weakly risk dominant in F;

ii. if strategy i is strictly risk dominant in F, then state e_i is uniquely stochastically stable.

Once one moves beyond the BRM rule and linear payoffs, risk dominance is no longer necessary or sufficient for stochastic stability. We therefore introduce a refinement of risk dominance that serves this role.

To work toward this new definition, observe that any function on the unit interval $[0,1]$ can be viewed as a random variable by regarding the interval as a sample space endowed with Lebesgue measure λ. With this interpretation in mind, we define the *advantage distribution* of strategy i to be the cumulative distribution function of the payoff advantage of strategy i over the alternative strategy $j \neq i$:

$$G_i(a) = \lambda(\{x \in [0,1]: F_i(x) - F_j(x) \leq a\}).$$

We let $\bar{G}_i$ denote the corresponding decumulative distribution function:

$$\bar{G}_i(a) = \lambda(\{x \in [0,1]: F_i(x) - F_j(x) > a\}) = 1 - G_i(a).$$

In words, $\bar{G}_i(a)$ is the measure of the set of states at which the payoff to strategy i exceeds the payoff to strategy j by more than a.

One can restate the definition of risk dominance in terms of the advantage distribution.

Observation 12.3.10 *Let F be a coordination game. Then strategy i is weakly risk dominant if and only if $\bar{G}_i(0) \geq \bar{G}_j(0)$, and strategy i is strictly risk dominant if and only if $\bar{G}_i(0) > \bar{G}_j(0)$.*

Our refinement of risk dominance requires not only that strategy i be optimal at a larger set of states than strategy j, but also that strategy i have a payoff advantage of at least a at a larger set of states than strategy j for every $a \geq 0$. More precisely, strategy i is *weakly stochastically dominant* in the coordination game F if $\bar{G}_i(a) \geq \bar{G}_j(a)$ for all $a \geq 0$. If in addition $\bar{G}_i(0) > \bar{G}_j(0)$, strategy i is *strictly stochastically dominant*. The notion of stochastic dominance for strategies we propose here is obtained by applying the usual definition of stochastic dominance from utility theory (see the chapter notes) to the strategies' advantage distributions.

Exercise 12.3.11 Consider the Nonlinear Stag Hunt game from examples 12.3.8 and 11.2.3, with payoff functions $F_H(x) = h$ and $F_S(x) = sx^2$.

i. Plot $\bar{G}_H$ and $\bar{G}_S$ when $h = 2$ and $s = 5$. Is either strategy stochastically dominant?

ii. Plot $\bar{G}_H$ and $\bar{G}_S$ when $h = 2$ and $s = 8.5$. Is either strategy stochastically dominant? ◇

Theorem 12.3.12 shows that stochastic dominance is both sufficient and necessary to ensure stochastic stability under every noisy best response rule.

Theorem 12.3.12 *Assume the conditions of theorem 12.3.3, and suppose that the limit game F is a coordination game. Then*

i. state e_i is weakly stochastically stable under every noisy best response protocol if and only if strategy i is weakly stochastically dominant in F;

ii. if strategy i is strictly stochastically dominant in F, then state e_i is uniquely stochastically stable under every noisy best response protocol.

Limiting Stationary Distributions and Stochastic Stability

The idea behind theorem 12.3.12 is simple. The definitions of I, $\tilde{\kappa}$, κ, F_Δ, and G_i imply that

$$I(1) = \int_0^1 \tilde{\kappa}(F_\Delta(y)) \, dy \tag{12.39}$$

$$= \int_0^1 \kappa(F_1(y) - F_0(y)) \, dy - \int_0^1 \kappa(F_0(y) - F_1(y)) \, dy$$

$$= \int_{-\infty}^\infty \kappa(a) \, dG_1(a) - \int_{-\infty}^\infty \kappa(a) \, dG_0(a).$$

As we have seen, whether state e_1 or state e_0 is stochastically stable depends on whether $I(1)$ is greater than or less than $I(0) = 0$. This in turn depends on whether the value of the first integral in the final line of (12.39) exceeds the value of the second integral. Since the cost function κ is monotone, theorem 12.3.12 reduces to a variation on the standard characterization of first-order stochastic dominance, namely, that distribution G_1 stochastically dominates distribution G_0 if and only if $\int \kappa \, dG_1 \geq \int \kappa \, dG_0$ for every nondecreasing function κ.

Proof of theorem 12.3.12 Again view $[0, 1]$ as a sample space by endowing it with Lebesgue measure, and define $Y_i \colon [0, 1] \to \mathbf{R}_+$ by

$$Y_i(\omega) = \sup\{a \colon G_i(a) < \omega\}.$$

Then Y_i is a random variable with distribution G_i (see example 10.B.4). It thus follows from equation (12.39) that

$$I(1) = \int_0^1 \kappa(Y_1(\omega)) \, d\omega - \int_0^1 \kappa(Y_0(\omega)) \, d\omega. \tag{12.40}$$

By construction,

$Y_i(\omega) < 0$ when $\omega \in [0, G_i(0-))$;

$Y_i(\omega) = 0$ when $\omega \in [G_i(0-), G_i(0)]$;

$Y_i(\omega) > 0$ when $\omega \in (G_i(0), 1]$;

and

$$G_1(0) - G_1(0-) = \lambda(\{x \in [0, 1] \colon F_1(x) = F_0(x)\}) = G_0(0) - G_0(0-).$$

Thus, since κ equals 0 on $(-\infty, 0)$, we can rewrite (12.40) as

$$I(1) = \int_{G_1(0-)}^{1} \kappa(Y_1(\omega))\,d\omega - \int_{G_0(0-)}^{1} \kappa(Y_0(\omega))\,d\omega$$

$$= \int_{G_1(0)}^{1} \kappa(Y_1(\omega))\,d\omega - \int_{G_0(0)}^{1} \kappa(Y_0(\omega))\,d\omega. \tag{12.41}$$

To prove the "if" direction of part (i) of the theorem, suppose without loss of generality that strategy 1 is weakly stochastically dominant in F. Then $G_1(a) \leq G_0(a)$ for all $a \geq 0$, so the definition of Y_i implies that $Y_1(\omega) \geq Y_0(\omega)$ for all $\omega \in [G_1(0), 1]$. Since κ is nondecreasing and non-negative, it follows from equation (12.41) that $I(1) \geq I(0)$, and hence that state 1 is weakly stochastically stable.

To prove part (ii), suppose without loss of generality that strategy 1 is strictly stochastically dominant in F. Then $G_1(a) \leq G_0(a)$ for all $a \geq 0$ and $G_1(0) < G_0(0)$. In this case, we not only have that $Y_1(\omega) \geq Y_0(\omega)$ for all $\omega \in [G_1(0), 1]$, but also that $Y_1(\omega) > 0$ when $\omega \in (G_1(0), G_0(0)]$. Since κ is nondecreasing, and since it is positive on $(0, \infty)$, it follows from equation (12.41) that

$$I(1) \geq \int_{G_1(0)}^{G_0(0)} \kappa(Y_1(\omega))\,d\omega > 0 = I(0),$$

and hence that state 1 is uniquely stochastically stable.

Finally, to prove the "only if" direction of part (i), suppose without loss of generality that strategy 1 is not weakly stochastically dominant in F. Then $G_1(b) > G_0(b)$ for some $b \geq 0$. Now consider a noisy best response protocol with cost function

$$\kappa(a) = \begin{cases} 0 & \text{if } a \leq 0, \\ 1 & \text{if } a \in (0, b], \\ k & \text{if } a > b, \end{cases}$$

where $k > G_1(b)/(G_1(b) - G_0(b))$. Then

$$\int_{-\infty}^{\infty} \kappa(a)\,dG_i(a) = (G_i(b) - G_i(0)) + k\,(1 - G_i(b)).$$

Therefore, equation (12.39) implies that

$$I(1) = ((G_1(b) - G_1(0)) - (G_0(b) - G_0(0))) + k\,((1 - G_1(b)) - (1 - G_0(b)))$$

$$\leq G_1(b) + k\,(G_0(b) - G_1(b))$$

$$< 0,$$

implying that state e_1 is not weakly stochastically stable. This completes the proof of the theorem. ∎

Limiting Stationary Distributions and Stochastic Stability

Exercise 12.3.13 Derive corollary 12.3.8 from theorem 12.3.12 by showing that in linear coordination games, risk dominance and stochastic dominance are equivalent. ◇

12.4 Imitative Protocols in Two-Strategy Games

We now shift our focus from noisy best response protocols to imitative protocols. We begin by developing the basic insight from example 12.1.1, showing that under imitative protocols with mutations, the double limits of the stationary distribution $\mu^{N,\varepsilon}$ in the population size N and mutation rate ε need not agree: while the large population double limit can select any state as stochastically stable, the small noise double limit can only select boundary states. We then alter the basic model by introducing one committed agent for each strategy. Doing so yields an irreducible evolutionary process even when mutations are absent and ensures that the two double limits agree when mutations are present. To conclude the section, we demonstrate how the stochastically stable state can vary with the choice of imitative protocol, even across protocols generating the same mean dynamic, and even in games with linear payoffs.

12.4.1 Imitative Protocols with Mutations

We start by defining the class of protocols to be studied. The protocol

$$\rho_{ij}^{\varepsilon}(\pi, x) = x_j r_{ij}(\pi, x) + \varepsilon \qquad (12.42)$$

is a *positive imitative protocol with mutations* if the functions r_{01} and r_{10} that determine conditional imitation rates are continuous and positive-valued (and hence bounded away from zero on compact sets), and if the mutation rate ε is positive. If instead $\varepsilon = 0$, (12.42) is a *positive imitative protocol without mutations*. As in section 5.4, we will assume that net conditional imitation rates are monotone. This condition, which was defined for n-strategy games in equation (5.7), reduces in the two-strategy case to

$$\pi_j \geq \pi_i \Leftrightarrow r_{ij}(\pi, x) \geq r_{ji}(\pi, x) \text{ for } i, j \in \{0, 1\}. \qquad (12.43)$$

To simplify the notation, we assume that the conditional switch rates $r_{ij}(\pi, x) = r_{ij}(\pi)$ do not depend directly on the population state; however, none of the results require this restriction.

Suppose there are no committed agents. Then in order for the process $\{X_t^{N,\varepsilon}\}$ to be irreducible, the mutation rate ε must be positive. If this is so, the stationary distribution $\mu^{N,\varepsilon}$ satisfies

$$\frac{\mu_x^{N,\varepsilon}}{\mu_0^{N,\varepsilon}} = \prod_{j=1}^{Nx} \frac{p_{(j-1)/N}^N}{q_{j/N}^N}$$

$$= \prod_{j=1}^{Nx} \frac{\frac{N-j+1}{N}}{\frac{j}{N}} \cdot \frac{\frac{1}{R}\rho_{01}(F^N(\frac{j-1}{N}), \frac{j-1}{N-1})}{\frac{1}{R}\rho_{10}(F^N(\frac{j}{N}), \frac{j-1}{N-1})}$$

$$= \prod_{j=1}^{Nx} \frac{N-j+1}{j} \cdot \frac{\frac{j-1}{N-1} r_{01}(F^N(\frac{j-1}{N})) + \varepsilon}{\frac{N-j}{N-1} r_{10}(F^N(\frac{j}{N})) + \varepsilon} \tag{12.44}$$

for $x \in \{\frac{1}{N}, \frac{2}{N}, \ldots, 1\}$. (We have assumed that there is no self-imitation, but the alternative assumption leads to similar results; see example 11.4.4.)

Theorem 12.4.1 describes the asymptotics of the stationary distribution in ε and N for both orders of limits. This result is stated in terms of the ordinal potential function $J: [0,1] \to \mathbf{R}$, defined by

$$J(x) = \int_0^x \log \frac{r_{01}(F(y))}{r_{10}(F(y))} \, dy. \tag{12.45}$$

As with the ordinal potential I defined in equation (12.38), marginally increasing the mass on the optimal strategy here increases the value of J; this follows directly from monotonicity condition (12.43).

Theorem 12.4.1 employs one new definition: the collection $\{\alpha^\varepsilon\}_{\varepsilon \in (0,\bar{\varepsilon}]}$ is *of exact order ε* as ε approaches zero, denoted $\alpha^\varepsilon \in \Theta(\varepsilon)$, if there is an interval $[a,b] \subset (0,\infty)$ such that $\alpha^\varepsilon/\varepsilon \in [a,b]$ for all ε close enough to zero.

Theorem 12.4.1 *Let $\{F^N\}_{N=N_0}^\infty$ be a sequence of two-strategy population games that converges uniformly to the continuous-population game F. Suppose that agents employ a positive imitative protocol with mutations. Then the stationary distributions $\mu^{N,\varepsilon}$ satisfy*

i. $\lim_{N\to\infty} \lim_{\varepsilon \to 0} \frac{1}{N} \log \frac{\mu_1^{N,\varepsilon}}{\mu_0^{N,\varepsilon}} = J(1)$, and $\frac{\mu_x^{N,\varepsilon}}{\mu_0^{N,\varepsilon}}$ and $\frac{\mu_x^{N,\varepsilon}}{\mu_1^{N,\varepsilon}}$ *are in* $\Theta(\varepsilon)$ *when* $x \in X^N - \{0,1\}$;

ii. $\lim_{\varepsilon \to 0} \lim_{N\to\infty} \max_{x \in X^N} \left| \frac{1}{N} \log \mu_x^{N,\varepsilon} - \Delta J(x) \right| = 0$.

Theorem 12.4.1 formalizes and develops the intuitions introduced in example 12.1.1. Part (i) shows that in the small noise double limit, all of the mass in the stationary distribution becomes concentrated on the boundary states. In fact, as long as $J(1) \neq 0$, it becomes concentrated on just one boundary state: state 1 if $J(1) > 0$, or state 0 if $J(1) < 0$. But part (ii) shows that in the large population double limit, a stochastically stable state must be one that maximizes J on the unit interval; no favoritism is shown toward boundary states in this case.

Limiting Stationary Distributions and Stochastic Stability

Exercise 12.4.2 To verify that theorem 12.4.1(ii) agrees with the large population limit, derive the mean dynamic associated with protocol (12.42) when $\varepsilon = 0$, and show that the function J is a strict Lyapunov function for this dynamic on the open interval $(0, 1)$. ◇

Proof of theorem 12.4.1 To prove the first statement in part (i), observe that

$$\frac{\mu_1^{N,\varepsilon}}{\mu_0^{N,\varepsilon}} = \prod_{j=1}^{N} \frac{N-j+1}{j} \cdot \frac{\frac{j-1}{N-1} r_{01}(F^N(\frac{j-1}{N})) + \varepsilon}{\frac{N-j}{N-1} r_{10}(F^N(\frac{j}{N})) + \varepsilon}$$

$$= \frac{N\varepsilon}{r_{10}(F^N(\frac{1}{N})) + \varepsilon} \cdot \prod_{j=2}^{N-1} \frac{N-j+1}{j} \cdot \frac{\frac{j-1}{N-1} r_{01}(F^N(\frac{j-1}{N})) + \varepsilon}{\frac{N-j}{N-1} r_{10}(F^N(\frac{j}{N})) + \varepsilon} \cdot \frac{r_{01}(F^N(\frac{N-1}{N})) + \varepsilon}{N\varepsilon}$$

$$= \prod_{j=1}^{N-1} \frac{N-j}{j} \cdot \frac{\frac{j}{N-1} r_{01}(F^N(\frac{j}{N})) + \varepsilon}{\frac{N-j}{N-1} r_{10}(F^N(\frac{j}{N})) + \varepsilon}.$$

Since the troublesome $N\varepsilon$ terms have been eliminated, none of the terms in the final product converge to zero or infinity. Indeed, we have

$$\lim_{\varepsilon \to 0} \log \frac{\mu_1^{N,\varepsilon}}{\mu_0^{N,\varepsilon}} = \log \left(\prod_{j=1}^{N-1} \frac{N-j}{j} \cdot \frac{\frac{j}{N-1} r_{01}(F^N(\frac{j}{N}))}{\frac{N-j}{N-1} r_{10}(F^N(\frac{j}{N}))} \right) = \sum_{j=1}^{N-1} \log \frac{r_{01}(F^N(\frac{j}{N}))}{r_{10}(F^N(\frac{j}{N}))},$$

so the dominated convergence theorem implies that

$$\lim_{N \to \infty} \lim_{\varepsilon \to 0} \frac{1}{N} \log \frac{\mu_1^{N,\varepsilon}}{\mu_0^{N,\varepsilon}} = \lim_{N \to \infty} \frac{N-1}{N} \cdot \frac{1}{N-1} \sum_{j=1}^{N-1} \log \frac{r_{01}(F^N(\frac{j}{N}))}{r_{10}(F^N(\frac{j}{N}))} = J(1).$$

To prove the second statement in part (i), observe that for $\chi \in \mathcal{X}^N - \{0, 1\}$, we have

$$\frac{\mu_\chi^{N,\varepsilon}}{\mu_0^{N,\varepsilon}} = \prod_{j=1}^{N\chi} \frac{N-j+1}{j} \cdot \frac{\frac{j-1}{N-1} r_{01}(F^N(\frac{j-1}{N})) + \varepsilon}{\frac{N-j}{N-1} r_{10}(F^N(\frac{j}{N})) + \varepsilon}$$

$$= \frac{N\varepsilon}{r_{10}(F^N(\frac{1}{N})) + \varepsilon} \cdot \prod_{j=2}^{N\chi} \frac{N-j+1}{j} \cdot \frac{\frac{j-1}{N-1} r_{01}(F^N(\frac{j-1}{N})) + \varepsilon}{\frac{N-j}{N-1} r_{10}(F^N(\frac{j}{N})) + \varepsilon}.$$

Since all terms except the initial $N\varepsilon$ approach positive constants as ε approaches zero, the claim follows. The analysis of $\mu_\chi^{N,\varepsilon}/\mu_1^{N,\varepsilon}$ is similar.

We prove part (ii). Equation (12.44) reveals that

$$\frac{1}{N} \log \frac{\mu_x^{N,\varepsilon}}{\mu_0^{N,\varepsilon}} = \frac{1}{N} \sum_{j=1}^{Nx} \left(\log \frac{\frac{N-j+1}{N}}{\frac{j}{N}} + \log \frac{\frac{j-1}{N-1} r_{01}(F^N(\frac{j-1}{N})) + \varepsilon}{\frac{N-j}{N-1} r_{10}(F^N(\frac{j}{N})) + \varepsilon} \right).$$

Thus, the dominated convergence theorem implies that

$$\lim_{N \to \infty} \frac{1}{N} \log \frac{\mu_x^{N,\varepsilon}}{\mu_0^{N,\varepsilon}} = \int_0^x \left(\log \frac{1-y}{y} + \log \frac{y \, r_{01}(F(y)) + \varepsilon}{(1-y) r_{10}(F(y)) + \varepsilon} \right) dy.$$

(For the first integrand, see the proof of theorem 12.3.3.) A second application of the dominated convergence theorem then yields

$$\lim_{\varepsilon \to 0} \lim_{N \to \infty} \frac{1}{N} \log \frac{\mu_x^{N,\varepsilon}}{\mu_0^{N,\varepsilon}} = \int_0^x \left(\log \frac{1-y}{y} + \log \frac{y \, r_{01}(F(y))}{(1-y) r_{10}(F(y))} \right) dy$$

$$= \int_0^x \log \frac{r_{01}(F(y))}{r_{10}(F(y))} \, dy$$

$$= J(x).$$

Since all limits are uniform in x, an argument similar to the proof of theorem 12.2.2 completes the proof of part (ii). ∎

This analysis confirms that in the absence of committed players, the small noise and large population double limits yield different predictions. As we noted after example 12.1.1, we are inclined to favor the prediction of the large population double limit in most economic applications, but feel that either double limit could be useful in biological applications.

Before proceeding, we should note that in games with $n > 2$ strategies, when agents use imitative protocols with mutations, the small noise limit is far easier to evaluate than the large population limit. If the population size N is fixed and ε is small enough, the process $\{X_t^{N,\varepsilon}\}$ will spend nearly all periods at vertices of the simplex X. Moreover, sojourns between vertices will nearly always travel along the edges of X, and on each of these ($\binom{n}{2}$) edges, the process $\{X_t^{N,\varepsilon}\}$ is essentially a birth and death process. By developing this observation, one can analyze the small noise limit of $\{X_t^{N,\varepsilon}\}$ by studying an auxiliary Markov chain with just n states, and with transition probabilities governed by the behavior of the ($\binom{n}{2}$) birth and death processes. (See the chapter notes for references that carry out this analysis.)

12.4.2 Imitative Protocols with Committed Agents

Now suppose that there is one committed agent playing each strategy. This assumption ensures that the stochastic evolutionary process is irreducible, even in the

Limiting Stationary Distributions and Stochastic Stability

absence of mutations. Theorem 12.4.3 and its proof show that the large population asymptotics of the stationary distribution take a very simple form.

Theorem 12.4.3 *Let $\{F^N\}_{N=N_0}^{\infty}$ be a sequence of two-strategy population games that converges uniformly to the continuous-population game F. Suppose that the N standard agents employ a positive imitative protocol without mutations, and that there is one committed agent for each strategy. Then the sequence of stationary distributions $\{\mu^N\}_{N=N_0}^{\infty}$ satisfies*

$$\lim_{N \to \infty} \max_{x \in X^N} \left| \tfrac{1}{N} \log \mu_x^N - \Delta J(x) \right| = 0. \tag{12.46}$$

Proof As noted in example 11.4.4, the stationary distribution μ^N satisfies

$$\frac{\mu_x^N}{\mu_0^N} = \prod_{j=1}^{Nx} \frac{p_{(j-1)/N}^N}{q_{j/N}^N}$$

$$= \prod_{j=1}^{Nx} \frac{\frac{N-j+1}{N}}{\frac{j}{N}} \cdot \frac{\frac{1}{R} \rho_{01}(F^N(\frac{j-1}{N}), \frac{j}{N+1})}{\frac{1}{R} \rho_{10}(F^N(\frac{j}{N}), \frac{j}{N+1})}$$

$$= \prod_{j=1}^{Nx} \frac{\frac{N-j+1}{N}}{\frac{j}{N}} \cdot \frac{\frac{j}{N+1}}{\frac{N-j+1}{N+1}} \cdot \frac{r_{01}(F^N(\frac{j-1}{N}))}{r_{10}(F^N(\frac{j}{N}))}$$

$$= \prod_{j=1}^{Nx} \frac{r_{01}(F^N(\frac{j-1}{N}))}{r_{10}(F^N(\frac{j}{N}))}. \tag{12.47}$$

Since r_{01} and r_{10} are both bounded and bounded away from zero, the dominated convergence theorem implies that

$$\lim_{N \to \infty} \frac{1}{N} \log \frac{\mu_x^N}{\mu_0^N} = \lim_{N \to \infty} \frac{1}{N} \sum_{j=1}^{Nx} \log \frac{r_{01}(F^N(\frac{j-1}{N}))}{r_{10}(F^N(\frac{j}{N}))} = J(x) \tag{12.48}$$

and that convergence is uniform in x. The remainder of the proof is similar to that of theorem 12.2.2. ∎

The following theorem, whose proof is left as an exercise, shows that when committed agents are present, introducing rare mutations has no significant impact on the conclusions of theorem 12.4.3, regardless of the order in which the limits in ε and N are taken, making the choice between the orders of limits inconsequential.

Theorem 12.4.4 *Let $\{F^N\}_{N=N_0}^{\infty}$ be a sequence of two-strategy population games that converges uniformly to F. Suppose that the N standard agents employ a positive imitative* *protocol with mutations, and that there is one committed agent for each strategy. Then the stationary distributions $\mu^{N,\varepsilon}$ satisfy*

i. $\lim_{N\to\infty} \lim_{\varepsilon\to 0} \max_{x\in\mathcal{X}^N} \left|\frac{1}{N}\log\mu_x^{N,\varepsilon} - \Delta J(x)\right| = 0$ *and*

ii. $\lim_{\varepsilon\to 0} \lim_{N\to\infty} \max_{x\in\mathcal{X}^N} \left|\frac{1}{N}\log\mu_x^{N,\varepsilon} - \Delta J(x)\right| = 0.$

Exercise 12.4.5   Prove theorem 12.4.4.   ◇

Exercise 12.4.6   Show that theorems 12.4.3 and 12.4.4 remain true if there are $k_0 \geq 1$ committed agents playing strategy 0 and $k_1 \geq 1$ committed agents playing strategy 1.   ◇

12.4.3   Imitative Protocols, Mean Dynamics, and Stochastic Stability

Once committed agents are introduced, the asymptotics of the stationary distribution are the same for either order of limits and agree with those of the large population limit alone when mutations are absent. Thus, for a given game and imitative protocol, the stochastically stable states are defined unambiguously. For simplicity, consider the large population limit when mutations are absent. In this case, stochastic stability is defined as in equation (12.5), and proposition 12.1.5 and theorem 12.4.3 imply that a unique maximizer of the ordinal potential function J is uniquely stochastically stable.

Section 12.3 showed that by virtue of their different levels of sensitivity to payoff disadvantages, different noisy best response protocols can generate different stochastically stable states. Before noise levels reach their limit, dissimilarities among the protocols also manifest themselves in small differences among their mean dynamics. One might therefore expect that variation among protocols' stochastically stable states can always be linked back to variation among their mean dynamics.

We now demonstrate that under imitative protocols, mean dynamics alone are not enough to identify the stochastically stable state. We consider two imitative protocols that generate the replicator dynamic as their mean dynamic, and show that in a range of linear games, the two protocols generate different stochastically stable states.

Example 12.4.1: Stochastic Imitation in Boar Hunt   The symmetric normal form game

$$A = \begin{pmatrix} h & h \\ b & B \end{pmatrix}$$

with $b < h < B$ is called *Boar Hunt*. The strategies in this coordination game are hunting for Hare (strategy 0) and hunting for Boar (strategy 1). As in the Stag Hunt game (examples 11.2.2 and 12.3.7), hunting for Hare yields a certain payoff of h, while coordinating on hunting for Boar yields the highest possible payoff. But unlike in Stag Hunt, either strategy in Boar Hunt can be risk dominant. If a population of agents are matched to play Boar Hunt, the resulting population game has payoffs $F_0(x) = h$ and $F_1(x) = b(1-x) + Bx$. In addition to the all-Hare ($x = 0$) and all-Boar ($x = 1$) equilibria, there is a mixed equilibrium in which fraction $x^* = \frac{h-b}{B-b}$ of the population hunts for Boar.

Since Boar Hunt is a coordination game, the ordinal potential J induced by any imitative protocol satisfying monotonicity condition (12.43) must be maximized at state 0, state 1, or both. Theorem 12.4.3 then implies that the all-Hare equilibrium is uniquely stochastically stable if $J(1) < J(0) \equiv 0$, while the all-Boar equilibrium is uniquely stochastically stable if $J(1) > 0$.

Now suppose that agents employ an imitative protocol whose conditional imitation rates take one of the following two forms:

$$r_{ij}(\pi) = M - \pi_i, \tag{12.49}$$

$$r_{ij}(\pi) = \pi_j - m, \tag{12.50}$$

where $M > B$ and $m < b$. These protocols are linear specifications of imitation driven by dissatisfaction (example 5.4.3) and imitation of success (example 5.4.4), respectively. Both protocols generate the replicator dynamic as their mean dynamic regardless of the game at hand.

Because both the population game F and the revision protocols (12.49) and (12.50) are linear, the corresponding ordinal potential functions J_D and J_S are easy to evaluate. Evaluating these functions at state 1, we find that

$$J_D(1) = \int_0^1 \log \frac{M - F_0(y)}{M - F_1(y)} \, dy = \log \frac{M - h}{M - B} + \frac{M - b}{B - b} \log \frac{M - B}{M - b} + 1;$$

$$J_S(1) = \int_0^1 \log \frac{F_1(y) - m}{F_0(y) - m} \, dy = \log \frac{B - m}{h - m} + \frac{b - m}{B - b} \log \frac{B - m}{b - m} + 1.$$

To make this example more concrete, fix $m = 0$, $b = 1$, $h = 2$, $B = 3$, and $M = 4$. Then the mixed Nash equilibrium of F is $x^* = \frac{h-b}{B-b} = \frac{1}{2}$, implying that neither strategy is strictly risk dominant; clearly, the all-Boar equilibrium $x = 1$ is payoff dominant. The normalized functions ΔJ_D and ΔJ_S for this case are graphed in figure 12.8. Since $J_D(1) = -\frac{3}{2}\log 3 + \log 2 + 1 \approx .0452$, imitation driven by dissatisfaction (12.49) leads to the selection of the payoff dominant all-Boar equilibrium, $x = 1$. But since $J_S(1) = -J_D(1) \approx -.0452$, imitation of success (12.50) leads to the selection of the payoff dominated all-Hare equilibrium, $x = 0$. Evidently, the same qualitative results obtain in any game with similar payoff values, implying that either protocol can select or fail to select a strictly risk dominant equilibrium. To

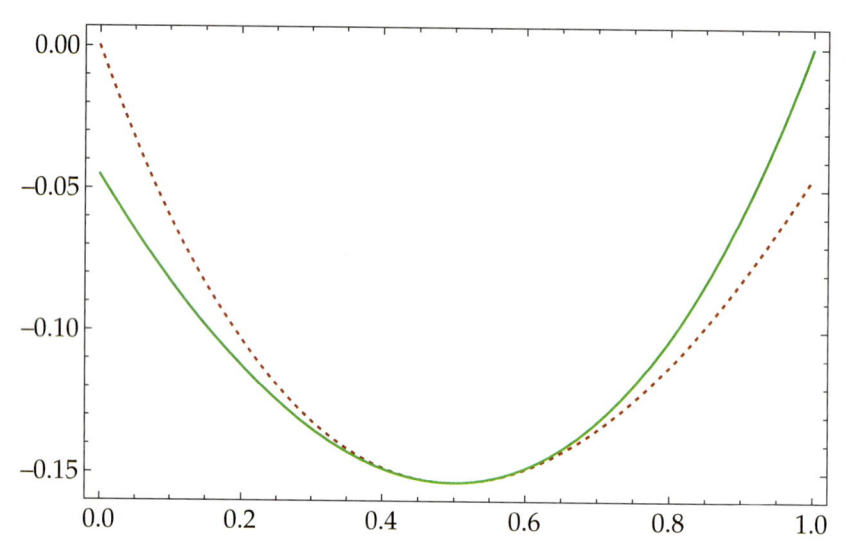

Figure 12.8
The ordinal potentials ΔJ_D (green) and ΔJ_S (red) when $m = 0, b = 1, h = 2, B = 3, M = 4$.

sum up, protocols (12.49) and (12.50) both generate the replicator dynamic as their mean dynamic, but can select different stochastically stable states in simple games.

This discrepancy can be traced to the different ways in which the conditional imitation rates r_{ij} influence the evolutionary process's mean dynamic and stationary distribution. Since the mean dynamic describes the expected increments of the process, its values depend on differences between the conditional imitation rates r_{01} and r_{10}:

$$\dot{x} = (1-x)x\, r_{01}(F(x)) - x(1-x)\, r_{10}(F(x)) = x(1-x)\big(r_{01}(F(x)) - r_{10}(F(x))\big).$$

For its part, the stationary distribution is the limiting distribution of the stochastic process, and so is determined by the products of the process's one-step transition probabilities. Because of this, the stationary distribution weights depend on the ratios of r_{01} and r_{10}, or equivalently, on the differences between the logarithms of r_{01} and r_{10} (see equations (12.47) and (12.48)).

This last observation can be used to explain the discrepant equilibrium selection results. To begin, write

$$J(1) = \int_0^1 \log \frac{r_{01}(F(y))}{r_{10}(F(y))}\, dy$$

$$= \int_0^1 \log r_{01}(F(y))\, dy - \int_0^1 \log r_{10}(F(y))\, dy. \qquad (12.51)$$

The all-Boar equilibrium is stochastically stable if $J(1) > J(0) = 0$, which is true when the first integral in (12.51) is larger than the second. Similarly, the all-Hare equilibrium is stochastically stable if the second integral in (12.51) is larger than the first.

Observe that as x increases from 0 to 1, the payoff to Hare is constant at $F_0(x) = 2$, while the payoff to Boar, $F_1(x) = 2x + 1$, is uniformly distributed between 1 and 3. The identity of the stochastically stable state is driven by which direction of imitation, Hare to Boar or Boar to Hare, is determined by the constant payoff.

Consider each protocol in turn. Under imitation driven by dissatisfaction (12.49), the conditional imitation rates are given by $r_{01}(x) = M - F_0(x) = 2$ and $r_{10}(x) = 4 - F_1(x)$. If $F_1(x)$ is viewed as a random variable with a *uniform*[1, 3] distribution, then $r_{10}(x)$ has a *uniform*[1, 3] distribution as well. Thus, since the logarithm function is concave, Jensen's inequality implies that the first integral in (12.51) is larger than the second, and hence that the all-Boar equilibrium is stochastically stable. Intuitively, the conditional imitation probabilities in each direction have the same mean, but only those from Boar to Hare are variable. The Boar to Hare transition is therefore less likely than its opposite, and so the all-Boar equilibrium is selected.

Under imitation of success (12.50), the conditional imitation rates are given by $r_{01}(x) = F_1(x) - m = F_1(x)$ and $r_{10}(x) = F_0(x) - m = 2$. This time, the conditional imitation probabilities from Boar to Hare are fixed, while those from Hare to Boar are variable; the latter transition is therefore less likely, and the all-Hare equilibrium is stochastically stable. ◆

In order to obtain robust equilibrium selection results under imitative protocols, one must place additional structure on the manner in which conditional imitation rates depend on the payoffs of an agent's current and prospective strategies. See the chapter notes for references to work in this direction.

12.5 Small Noise Limits

To this point, the analyses of infinite-horizon behavior have focused on settings that generate reversible processes, so that stationary distributions can be described by simple formulas. Beyond these settings, working directly from exact expressions for the stationary distribution becomes a much less promising path. Fortunately, there are techniques that allow one to determine the limiting stationary distributions directly, without the intermediate step of computing stationary distributions for fixed parameter values.

This section introduces general techniques for evaluating stochastic stability in the small noise limit, based on the construction of certain graphs on the state space X^N. These techniques are then used to prove specific equilibrium selection results. A full development of the methods applied here can be found in appendix

12.A. The methods used to study large population limits are drawn from stochastic approximation theory; these are treated in section 12.6 and appendix 12.B.

12.5.1 Noisy Best Response Protocols and Cost Functions

We consider a fixed population of N agents who play an n-strategy population game, employing a noisy best response protocol $\sigma^\varepsilon \colon \mathbf{R}^n \to \mathbf{R}^{n \times n}_+$. We assume throughout that $\sum_{j \in S} \sigma^\varepsilon_{ij}(\pi) = 1$ for all $i \in S$ and $\pi \in \mathbf{R}^n$, and that $\sigma^\varepsilon_{ij}(\pi) > 0$ whenever $\varepsilon > 0$.

As in section 12.3.1, we impose restrictions on the behavior of the choice probabilities $\sigma^\varepsilon_{ij}(\pi)$ as ε approaches zero, expressing these restrictions in terms of costs. Here we follow most of the literature in using a definition of costs, (12.52), that is somewhat more restrictive than the one introduced in section 12.3.1. The restrictions placed on the values of costs, (12.53) and (12.54), are rather weak.

Suppose that for every ordered pair (i, j) of distinct strategies and every payoff vector $\pi \in \mathbf{R}^n$, there are constants $a_{ij}(\pi) > 0$ and $\kappa_{ij}(\pi) \geq 0$ such that

$$\sigma^\varepsilon_{ij}(\pi) = (a_{ij}(\pi) + o(1))\, \varepsilon^{\kappa_{ij}(\pi)}, \quad \text{where} \tag{12.52}$$

$$\kappa_{ij}(\pi) = 0 \quad \text{when } \{j\} = \mathrm{argmax}_{k \in S}\, \pi_k, \tag{12.53}$$

$$\kappa_{ij}(\pi) > 0 \quad \text{when } j \notin \mathrm{argmax}_{k \in S}\, \pi_k. \tag{12.54}$$

Then $\kappa \colon \mathbf{R}^n \to \mathbf{R}^{n \times n}_+$ is the *cost function* associated with protocol σ^ε.

The limit used in (12.52) to define costs $\kappa_{ij}(\pi)$ is more demanding than the limit (12.27) used in section 12.3.1. To see this, apply the change of parameter $\varepsilon = \exp(-\eta^{-1})$ to rewrite (12.52) as

$$\sigma^\eta_{ij}(\pi) = (a_{ij}(\pi) + o(1)) \exp(-\eta^{-1} \kappa_{ij}(\pi)). \tag{12.55}$$

It follows from (12.55) that

$$-\lim_{\eta \to 0} \eta \log \sigma^\eta_{ij}(\pi) = \lim_{\eta \to 0} \left(\kappa_{ij}(\pi) - \eta \log(a_{ij}(\pi) + o(1)) \right) = \kappa_{ij}(\pi), \tag{12.56}$$

in agreement with condition (12.27). We discuss the differences between these definitions later in this section and in section 12.A.5.

Conditions (12.53) and (12.54) are minimal requirements for (12.52) to be considered a noisy best response protocol; (12.53) says that switching to the unique optimal strategy has zero cost, and (12.54) says that switching to any suboptimal strategy has a positive cost. (As in section 12.3.1, there is some flexibility in specifying the cost of switching to an optimal strategy when more than one exists; compare examples 12.5.1 and 12.5.2.) There are certainly other requirements that are natural to impose on κ (e.g., monotonicity and symmetry), but these conditions are not taken up here. As with those of revision protocols, the diagonal elements of the cost function κ are just placeholders, so changing their values has no effect on the analyses.

Limiting Stationary Distributions and Stochastic Stability

We now derive the cost functions for the BRM and logit protocols, using the restrictive definition of costs from equation (12.52) and allowing for games with more than two strategies. Write $S^*(\pi) = \text{argmax}_{k \in S} \pi_k$ for the set of optimal strategies at π; $n^*(\pi) = \#S^*(\pi)$ for the number of such strategies; and $k^*(\pi) \in S^*(\pi)$ for an arbitrary optimal strategy. The argument π is omitted from these notations when doing so will not cause confusion.

Example 12.5.1: Best Response with Mutations   Under the BRM(ε) protocol (example 11.1.1), a revising agent switches to a current best response with probability $1 - \varepsilon$ and chooses a strategy at random with probability ε. There are various ways to specify what happens in the event of a tie; here we assume that if a mutation does not occur, an agent playing an optimal strategy does not switch, while an agent not playing an optimal strategy chooses at random among such strategies. In sum, we have

$$\sigma^\varepsilon_{ij}(\pi) = \begin{cases} (1-\varepsilon) + \frac{1}{n}\varepsilon & \text{if } \pi_i = \pi_{k^*} \text{ and } j = i, \\ \frac{1}{n^*}(1-\varepsilon) + \frac{1}{n}\varepsilon & \text{if } \pi_i < \pi_j = \pi_{k^*}, \\ \frac{1}{n}\varepsilon & \text{if } \max\{\pi_i, \pi_j\} < \pi_{k^*}, \text{ or if } \pi_i = \pi_{k^*} \text{ and } j \neq i. \end{cases}$$

If we consider only its off-diagonal elements, the cost function for the BRM protocol takes a simple form:

$$\text{when } i \neq j, \; \kappa_{ij}(\pi) = \begin{cases} 0 & \text{if } \pi_i < \pi_j = \max_{k \in S} \pi_k, \\ 1 & \text{otherwise.} \end{cases} \quad \blacklozenge$$

Example 12.5.2: Logit Choice   The logit(η) protocol is

$$\sigma^\eta_{ij}(\pi) = \frac{\exp(\eta^{-1}\pi_j)}{\sum_{k \in S} \exp(\eta^{-1}\pi_k)}.$$

Performing the change of variable $\eta = -(\log \varepsilon)^{-1}$ and rearranging, we obtain

$$\sigma^\varepsilon_{ij}(\pi) = \frac{\varepsilon^{-\pi_j}}{\sum_{k \in S} \varepsilon^{-\pi_k}}$$

$$= \frac{\varepsilon^{\pi_{k^*} - \pi_j}}{n^* + \sum_{k \notin S^*} \varepsilon^{\pi_{k^*} - \pi_k}}$$

$$= \frac{1}{n^*}\left(1 - \frac{\sum_{k \notin S^*} \varepsilon^{\pi_{k^*} - \pi_k}}{n^* + \sum_{k \notin S^*} \varepsilon^{\pi_{k^*} - \pi_k}}\right) \varepsilon^{\pi_{k^*} - \pi_j}.$$

Therefore, the cost function for the logit rule is

$$\kappa_{ij}(\pi) = \max_{k \in S} \pi_k - \pi_j. \qquad \blacklozenge$$

A few comments are in order here about the two different limits used to define costs: condition (12.27) and condition (12.52). Since (12.52) is more demanding than (12.27), it allows one to prove slightly stronger results in cases where both apply: condition (12.52) leads to results about stochastic stability, whereas (12.27) leads to results about weak stochastic stability. Of course, because (12.52) is more demanding, it rules out certain protocols that (12.27) allows, most notably the probit choice protocol, which presents some novel properties in the *n*-strategy case (see example 12.A.1 and the chapter notes). But one can perform versions of the analyses in this section with costs defined as in (12.27); see section 12.A.5.

12.5.2 Limiting Stationary Distributions via Trees

In the present model of stochastic evolution, a population of N agents repeatedly plays a population game $F^N \colon X^N \to \mathbf{R}^n$. Each agent receives revision opportunities according to a rate 1 Poisson process. When such an opportunity arises, an agent decides what to do next by employing a noisy best response protocol $\sigma^\varepsilon \colon \mathbf{R}^n \to \mathbf{R}_+^{n \times n}$. We assume that agents are clever, in that they account for the effect of their own choices on the population state when assessing the payoffs of other strategies. Thus, if the population state is x, and an i player considers switching to strategy j, he evaluates the payoffs of the latter strategy as $\check{F}_j^N(x - \tfrac{1}{N}e_i) = F_j^N(x + \tfrac{1}{N}(e_j - e_i))$ (see section 11.4.2). Assuming that agents are clever leads to cleaner selection results but is not essential to the analysis.

Under these assumptions, the stochastic evolutionary process $\{X_t^\varepsilon\}$ has transition probabilities of the form

$$P_{xy}^\varepsilon = \begin{cases} x_i\, \sigma_{ij}^\varepsilon(\check{F}(x - \tfrac{1}{N}e_i)) & \text{if } y = x + \tfrac{1}{N}(e_j - e_i),\, j \neq i, \\ \sum_{i \in S} x_i\, \sigma_{ii}^\varepsilon(\check{F}(x - \tfrac{1}{N}e_i)) & \text{if } y = x, \\ 0 & \text{otherwise.} \end{cases}$$

The unique stationary distribution of this process is denoted by μ^ε.

We now introduce a notion of cost for one-step transitions of the process $\{X_t^\varepsilon\}$. For distinct states $x, y \in X^N$, the *cost* c_{xy} of the transition from x to y is the rate of decay of the transition probability P_{xy}^ε as ε approaches zero; the cost is defined to be infinite if the transition is impossible. Evidently, transition costs for the present model take the form

$$c_{xy} = \begin{cases} \kappa_{ij}(\check{F}(z)) & \text{if } x = z + \tfrac{1}{N}e_i \text{ and } y = z + \tfrac{1}{N}e_j \neq x, \\ \infty & \text{otherwise.} \end{cases}$$

Limiting Stationary Distributions and Stochastic Stability

These transition costs provide a simple way of computing the limiting stationary distribution $\mu^* = \lim_{\varepsilon \to 0} \mu^\varepsilon$. The key result is presented concisely here; complete details can be found in sections 12.A.1 and 12.A.2.

Consider two types of directed graphs on X^N. First, a *path* from $x \in X^N$ to $y \neq x$ is a directed graph $\{(x, x_1), (x_1, x_2), \ldots, (x_{l-1}, y)\}$ on X^N whose edges lead from x to y without hitting any node more than once. Second, a *tree* with *root* $x \in X^N$, also called an *x-tree*, is a directed graph on X^N with no outgoing edges from x, exactly one outgoing edge from each $y \neq x$, and a path, necessarily unique, from each $y \neq x$ to x. Denote a typical x-tree by τ_x, and let T_x denote the set of x-trees on X^N.

The characterization of the limiting stationary distribution, theorem 12.5.1, requires a definition of costs for trees. Given a directed graph γ on X^N, we define its *cost* $C(\gamma)$ as the sum of the costs of the edges it contains:

$$C(\gamma) = \sum_{(y,z) \in \gamma} c_{yz}. \tag{12.57}$$

C_x^* is the lowest cost of any x-tree, and C^* is the lowest cost of any tree on X^N.

$$C_x^* = \min_{\tau_x \in T_x} C(\tau_x), \quad \text{and} \quad C^* = \min_{x \in X} C_x^*.$$

The next theorem follows from theorem 12.A.2 and corollary 12.A.3.

Theorem 12.5.1 *Consider the collection of processes $\{\{X_t^\varepsilon\}_{t \geq 0}\}_{\varepsilon \in [0, \bar{\varepsilon}]}$ on the state space X^N, and let $\{\mu^\varepsilon\}_{\varepsilon \in [0, \bar{\varepsilon}]}$ be their stationary distributions. Then*

i. $\mu^* = \lim_{\varepsilon \to 0} \mu^\varepsilon$ *is a stationary distribution of* $\{X_t^0\}$ *with support* $\{x \in X^N : C_x^* = C^*\}$;

ii. *for each* $x \in X^N$, *there is a constant* $b_x > 0$ *such that* $\mu_x^\varepsilon = b_x \varepsilon^{C_x^* - C^*} + o(\varepsilon^{C_x^* - C^*})$.

Part (i) of the theorem shows that the stochastically stable states are precisely those that admit minimal-cost trees. Part (ii) of the theorem reveals that the stationary distribution weight on each other state decays at a rate determined by its cost disadvantage relative to the stochastically stable states.

According to theorem 12.5.1, one can show that state x is uniquely stochastically stable by proving that for any other state $y \neq x$ and any y-tree τ_y, there is an x-tree whose cost is less than $C(\tau_y)$. In fact, since μ^* is a stationary distribution of the zero-noise process, only the recurrent states of this process are candidates for stochastic stability, making it sufficient to consider trees rooted at recurrent states.

In some settings, this direct approach to assessing stochastic stability works perfectly well; we demonstrate this next. In other settings, it is preferable to employ simpler criteria for stochastic stability that can be deduced from theorem 12.5.1 but that do not require the explicit construction of x-trees. We develop this approach in sections 12.5.4 and 12.5.5.

12.5.3 Two-Strategy Games and Risk Dominance

We now illustrate the use of Theorem 12.5.1 in the simplest possible setting: two-strategy games.

Let $F: X^N \to \mathbf{R}^2$ be an N-agent, two-strategy population game, and identify state x with the weight $x \equiv x_1$ that it places on strategy 1. Because the state space $X^N = \{0, \frac{1}{N}, \ldots, 1\}$ is linearly ordered, and since only transitions to adjacent states have positive probability, each state $x \in X^N$ admits a unique tree with finite cost, namely,

$$\tau_x = \{(0, \tfrac{1}{N}), \ldots, (x - \tfrac{1}{N}, x), (x + \tfrac{1}{N}, x), \ldots, (1, \tfrac{N-1}{N})\}.$$

(figure 12.9). Therefore, state x is stochastically stable if and only if $C_x^* = C(\tau_x)$ is minimal, where

$$C(\tau_x) = \sum_{k=0}^{Nx-1} c_{k/N,(k+1)/N} + \sum_{k=Nx+1}^{N} c_{k/N,(k-1)/N}$$

$$= \sum_{k=0}^{Nx-1} \kappa_{01}(F_0(\tfrac{k}{N}), F_1(\tfrac{k+1}{N})) + \sum_{k=Nx+1}^{N} \kappa_{10}(F_0(\tfrac{k-1}{N}), F_1(\tfrac{k}{N})).$$

Example 12.5.3: Stag Hunt Once More   Consider the Stag Hunt game from examples 11.2.2 and 12.3.7:

$$A = \begin{pmatrix} h & h \\ 0 & s \end{pmatrix},$$

where $s > h > 0$. This game has two pure Nash equilibria and one mixed Nash equilibrium. Let $h = 4$ and $s = 7$, so that the mixed equilibrium puts weight $x^* = \frac{4}{7}$ on Stag. If N agents are matched without self-matching to play this game, the expected payoffs to Hare and Stag are $F_H^N(x) = 4$ and $F_S^N(x) = \frac{Nx-1}{N-1} \cdot 7$.

Suppose that $N = 15$. Then since $F_H^N(\tfrac{8}{15}) = 4 = F_S^N(\tfrac{9}{15})$, a clever agent with exactly 8 opponents playing Stag is indifferent; other numbers of opponents playing Stag lead to a strict preference for one strategy or the other. Notice that the mixed Nash equilibrium of A lies between states $\tfrac{8}{15}$ and $\tfrac{9}{15}$.

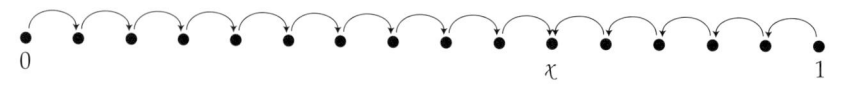

Figure 12.9
The lone x-tree whose cost is finite.

Limiting Stationary Distributions and Stochastic Stability

Under any noisy best response rule, states 0 and 1 are the only recurrent states and hence the only candidates for stochastic stability. Thus, by theorem 12.5.1, the stochastic stability analysis reduces to a comparison of $C(\tau_0)$ and $C(\tau_1)$.

Figure 12.10 presents trees τ_0 and τ_1 and labels the edges in these trees with their costs under the BRM rule. Each edge in τ_0 points toward the state below it, and so represents a switch by one agent from strategy 1 to strategy 0. Edges starting at states $x \geq \frac{9}{15}$ require switching away from an optimal strategy and so have cost 1; the remaining states do not and so have cost 0. (Edge $(\frac{9}{15}, \frac{8}{15})$ has cost 1 because of the assumption that indifferent agents do not switch without mutating.) It follows that $C(\tau_0) = \#\{\frac{9}{15}, \ldots, 1\} = 7$. By similar logic, the cost of τ_1 under the BRM rule is $C(\tau_1) = \#\{0, \ldots, \frac{8}{15}\} = 9$. Since $C(\tau_0) = 7 < 9 = C(\tau_1)$, state 0 is stochastically stable under the BRM rule.

Figure 12.11 labels the edges in τ_0 and τ_1 with their costs under the logit rule. The cost of an edge representing a switch to an optimal strategy is still zero, but the cost of an edge representing a switch to a suboptimal strategy now equals that strategy's payoff disadvantage. Summing the edge costs in each tree, we find that $C(\tau_0) = 10\frac{1}{2} < 18 = C(\tau_1)$. Thus, state 0 is also stochastically stable under the logit rule. ◆

In Section 12.3.6, we introduced weak and strict risk dominance for infinite-population games, and showed that when stochastic stability is defined in terms of double limits, strict risk dominance implies unique stochastic stability if payoffs are linear (corollary 12.3.8) or if agents use the BRM protocol (corollary 12.3.9). We now establish versions of these results for the finite-population setting, where only the small noise limit is taken. Since the state space is discrete, we will need to use slightly stronger definitions and evaluate a number of slightly different cases to obtain exact results.

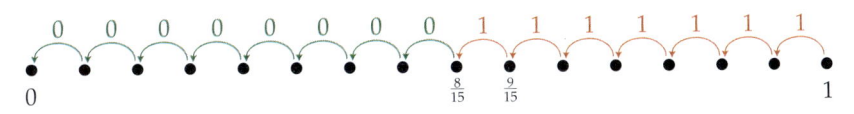

(a) τ_0 and its edge costs

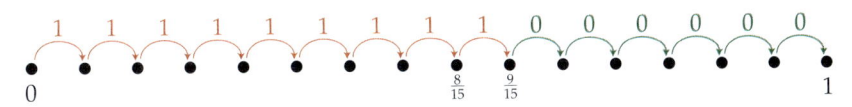

(b) τ_1 and its edge costs

Figure 12.10
Trees and BRM edge costs in Stag Hunt ($h = 4$, $s = 7$, $N = 15$).

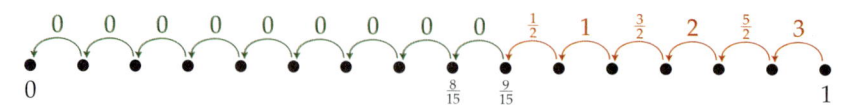

(a) τ_0 and its edge costs

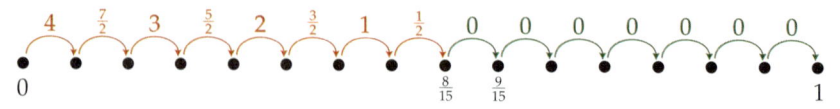

(b) τ_1 and its edge costs

Figure 12.11
Trees and logit edge costs in Stag Hunt ($h = 4, s = 7, N = 15$).

We begin by introducing three definitions of risk dominance for the two-strategy game F^N. Let $y \in X^{N-1}$ represent the proportion of an agent's opponents playing strategy 1. Strategy 1 is *weakly risk dominant* if

$$F_1^N\left(\tfrac{N-1}{N}y + \tfrac{1}{N}\right) \overset{\geq}{>} F_0^N\left(\tfrac{N-1}{N}y\right) \quad \text{for all } y \in X^{N-1} \text{ with } y \overset{\geq}{>} \tfrac{1}{2}. \tag{12.58}$$

Strategy 1 is *strictly risk dominant* if

$$F_1^N\left(\tfrac{N-1}{N}y + \tfrac{1}{N}\right) > F_0^N\left(\tfrac{N-1}{N}y\right) \quad \text{for all } y \in X^{N-1} \text{ with } y \geq \tfrac{1}{2}. \tag{12.59}$$

And strategy 1 is *strongly risk dominant* if

$$F_1^N\left(\tfrac{N-1}{N}y + \tfrac{1}{N}\right) \overset{\geq}{>} F_0^N\left(\tfrac{N-1}{N}y\right) \quad \text{for all } y \in X^{N-1} \text{ with } y \overset{\geq}{>} \tfrac{1}{2}\tfrac{N-2}{N-1}. \tag{12.60}$$

Exercise 12.5.2 Define weak, strict, and strong risk dominance for strategy 0 in a way that agrees with the preceding definitions. ◇

The first two definitions correspond to the definitions of weak and strict risk dominance in section 12.3.6. The main novelties here are that the appropriate state variable is the distribution of opponent's behavior, and that the effect of the agent's own choice on the population state is taken into account in the payoff comparison. The more demanding notion of strong risk dominance is precisely what is needed to obtain an exact selection result under the BRM protocol.

Because conditions (12.58)–(12.60) only consider points y in X^{N-1} (rather than in all of $[0, 1]$), there is some overlap among the definitions. The form of the overlap depends on whether N is odd or even.

Exercise 12.5.3

i. Show that when N is odd, strong and strict risk dominance are equivalent and are more demanding than weak risk dominance.

ii. Show that when N is even, strict and weak risk dominance are equivalent and are less demanding than strong risk dominance. ◇

Exercise 12.5.4: Matching and Risk Dominance in Normal Form Games Consider the symmetric normal form game with strategy set $S = \{0, 1\}$ and payoffs

$$A = \begin{pmatrix} a & b \\ c & d \end{pmatrix}.$$

Suppose that $a > c$ and $d > b$, so that A is a coordination game with mixed equilibrium $x^* = \frac{a-c}{a-b-c+d}$. Strategy 1 is strictly risk dominant in the normal form game A if $x^* < \frac{1}{2}$, and strategy 0 is strictly risk dominant in A if $x^* > \frac{1}{2}$.

Let $F^N \colon \mathcal{X}^N \to \mathbf{R}^2$ be the game obtained when N agents are matched without self-matching to play A, as described in example 11.4.2:

$$F_0^N(x) = \tfrac{N(1-x)-1}{N-1}a + \tfrac{Nx}{N-1}b;$$

$$F_1^N(x) = \tfrac{N(1-x)}{N-1}c + \tfrac{Nx-1}{N-1}d.$$

i. Let the preceding equations define F_0^N and F_1^N for all $x \in [0, 1]$. Show that strategy 1 is strictly risk dominant in A if and only if

$$F_1^N\!\left(\tfrac{N-1}{N}y + \tfrac{1}{N}\right) > F_0^N\!\left(\tfrac{N-1}{N}y\right) \quad \text{when } y \in [\tfrac{1}{2}, 1],$$

which is condition (12.59) strengthened to allow y to be outside of $\mathcal{X}^{N-1}$.

ii. Suppose that N is odd. Using part (i), show that strategy 1 is strictly risk dominant in A if and only if it is strictly risk dominant in F^N, as defined in condition (12.59).

iii. Suppose that N is even. Show that strategy 1's being strongly risk dominant in F^N implies that it is strictly risk dominant in A and that this in turn implies that strategy 1 is strictly risk dominant in F^N. Then show that the two converse implications are false. ◇

The two-strategy finite-population game F^N is a *coordination game* if there is a threshold $y^* \in (0, 1)$ such that

$$\operatorname{sgn}\!\left(F_1^N\!\left(\tfrac{N-1}{N}y + \tfrac{1}{N}\right) - F_0^N\!\left(\tfrac{N-1}{N}y\right)\right) = \operatorname{sgn}(y - y^*) \quad \text{for all } y \in \mathcal{X}^{N-1}. \tag{12.61}$$

Thus, a clever agent prefers strategy 1 if more than fraction y^* of his opponents play strategy 1, and prefers strategy 0 if less than fraction y^* play strategy 1. (In the matching context of exercise 12.5.4, one can let y^* equal x^*, the weight on strategy 1 in the mixed equilibrium of A.) If y^* is not in $\mathcal{X}^{N-1}$, it is not uniquely determined and can be replaced by any other point in the interval $(y_-^*, y_+^*) = (\frac{1}{N-1}\lfloor(N-1)y^*\rfloor, \frac{1}{N-1}\lceil(N-1)y^*\rceil)$ without affecting condition (12.61). The end points of this interval are adjacent states in $\mathcal{X}^{N-1}$, and they are uniquely determined.

Theorem 12.5.5 establishes the connection between risk dominance and stochastic stability under the BRM rule. The proof of the theorem can be viewed as a discrete version of the corresponding analysis from section 12.3, where the length of each basin of attraction was measured by differences in the signum potential I_{sgn}; here these lengths are measured by counting states. The discreteness of the state space leads to slightly stronger conditions for stochastic stability, and also requires the evaluation of a number of similar cases in order to prove the result.

Theorem 12.5.5 *Let F^N be a two-strategy coordination game, and suppose that agents are clever and employ the BRM protocol. Then*

i. if strategy 1 is weakly risk dominant, then state e_1 is stochastically stable;

ii. if strategy 1 is strongly risk dominant, then state e_1 is uniquely stochastically stable.

Proof Part (i) is left as an exercise. To prove part (ii), let y^* be a threshold for the game F^N, as defined in equation (12.61), and suppose first that $y^* \notin \mathcal{X}^{N-1}$. Then letting $y_+^* = \frac{1}{N-1}\lceil(N-1)y^*\rceil \in \mathcal{X}^{N-1}$, and letting $1[s]$ equal 1 if statement s is true and 0 otherwise, we have

$$c_{x, x + \frac{1}{N}} = \kappa_{01}(F_0^N(x), F_1^N(x + \tfrac{1}{N}))$$

$$= 1[F_0^N(x) \geq F_1^N(x + \tfrac{1}{N})]$$

$$= 1[x \leq \tfrac{N-1}{N} y_+^* - \tfrac{1}{N}];$$

$$c_{x, x - \frac{1}{N}} = \kappa_{10}(F_0^N(x - \tfrac{1}{N}), F_1^N(x))$$

$$= 1[F_0^N(x - \tfrac{1}{N}) \leq F_1^N(x)]$$

$$= 1[x \geq \tfrac{N-1}{N} y_+^* + \tfrac{1}{N}],$$

where the final equalities follow from condition (12.61). This shows that every state except states 0 and 1 has an outgoing zero-cost edge (and that state $\frac{N-1}{N}y_+^*$ has two of them). Thus states 0 and 1 are the only recurrent states, and hence the only candidates for stochastic stability. The costs of the relevant trees are

$$C(\tau_1) = \sum_{k=0}^{N-1} c_{k/N,(k+1)/N}$$

$$= \#\{x \in X^N : x \leq \tfrac{N-1}{N} y_+^* - \tfrac{1}{N}\}$$

$$= \#\{z \in \mathbf{Z} : 0 \leq z \leq (N-1) y_+^* - 1\}$$

$$= (N-1) y_+^*;$$

$$C(\tau_0) = \sum_{k=1}^{N} c_{k/N,(k-1)/N}$$

$$= \#\{x \in X^N : x \geq \tfrac{N-1}{N} y_+^* + \tfrac{1}{N}\}$$

$$= \#\{z \in \mathbf{Z} : (N-1) y_+^* + 1 \leq z \leq N\}$$

$$= (N-1)(1 - y_+^*) + 1.$$

If N is odd, then strategy 1 is strongly risk dominant if and only if $y_+^* \leq \tfrac{1}{2}$; if N is even, the relevant inequality is $y^* \leq \tfrac{N-2}{2(N-1)}$. Both conditions imply that $C(\tau_1) < C(\tau_0)$. Therefore, by theorem 12.5.1, state e_1 is uniquely stochastically stable.

Next, suppose that $y^* \in X^{N-1}$. Then

$$c_{x,x+\frac{1}{N}} = \kappa_{01}(F_0^N(x), F_1^N(x + \tfrac{1}{N})) = \mathbf{1}[x \leq \tfrac{N-1}{N} y^*];$$

$$c_{x,x-\frac{1}{N}} = \kappa_{10}(F_0^N(x - \tfrac{1}{N}), F_1^N(x)) = \mathbf{1}[x \geq \tfrac{N-1}{N} y^* + \tfrac{1}{N}].$$

Thus, states 0 and 1 are again the only ones with no outgoing zero-cost edge (although in this case no state has two such edges). Now

$$C(\tau_1) = \sum_{k=0}^{N-1} c_{k/N,(k+1)/N} = (N-1) y^* + 1;$$

$$C(\tau_0) = \sum_{k=1}^{N} c_{k/N,(k-1)/N} = (N-1)(1 - y^*) + 1.$$

If N is odd, then strategy 1 is strongly risk dominant if and only if $y^* \leq \tfrac{N-3}{2(N-1)}$; if N is even, the relevant inequality is again $y^* \leq \tfrac{N-2}{2(N-1)}$. Both of these conditions imply that $C(\tau_1) < C(\tau_0)$, and hence that state e_1 is uniquely stochastically stable. This completes the proof of part (ii) of the theorem. ∎

Exercise 12.5.6

i. Prove part (i) of theorem 12.5.5.

ii. Prove that the converse of part (ii) of theorem 12.5.5 is also true.   ◇

Exercise 12.5.7 Show that Theorem 12.5.5 remains true without the assumption that F^N is a coordination game. ◇

Exercise 12.5.8 To focus on cost functions that agree with those in section 12.3, suppose that

$$\kappa_{01}(c, c-d) = \kappa_{10}(c-d, c) = \hat{\kappa}(d) \quad \text{for all } c, d \in \mathbf{R},$$

where $\hat{\kappa}\colon \mathbf{R} \to \mathbf{R}_+$ is nondecreasing, zero on $(-\infty, 0)$, and positive on $(0, \infty)$. Verify that under these assumptions, theorems 12.5.1 and 12.3.1 agree, in the sense that they single out the same states as stochastically stable. (*Hint:* It is enough to show that $C(\tau_x) - C(\tau_y) = I^N(y) - I^N(x)$ for all $x, y \in X^N$.) ◇

Exercise 12.5.9 Let F^N be the population game generated by matching in the two-strategy coordination game A, and suppose that agents are clever and employ a noisy best response rule whose cost function satisfies the conditions from exercise 12.5.8.

i. Show that state e_i is stochastically stable if and only if strategy i is weakly risk dominant.

ii. Show that if $\hat{\kappa}$ is increasing on $\mathbf{R}_+$, then state e_i is uniquely stochastically stable if and only if strategy i is strictly risk dominant. Explain in words why strict risk dominance is sufficient for unique stochastic stability here, whereas strong risk dominance was needed under the BRM rule. ◇

12.5.4 The Radius-Coradius Theorem

A key advantage of the graph-theoretic approach to stochastic stability analysis is that it can be applied in nonreversible settings. To explore this possibility, we introduce a new sufficient condition for stochastic stability that is derived from theorem 12.5.1, but is often easier to apply.

For the intuition behind the new condition, examine figures 12.10 and 12.11, which present the trees τ_0 and τ_1, along with the edge costs generated by a Stag Hunt game under the BRM and logit protocols. To prove that state 0 is stochastically stable under these protocols, we showed that in each case, the cost of τ_0 is lower than the cost of τ_1.

We now suggest an alternative interpretation for this analysis. Each figure shows that the cost of traveling from state 0 to a point from which state 1 can be reached for free exceeds the cost of traveling from state 1 to a point from which state 0 can be reached for free. That is, the tree analysis can be recast as one that compares the cost of escaping the basin of attraction of state 0 to the cost of returning to this equilibrium from state 1. If the former cost is greater than the latter, state 0 is stochastically stable.

Limiting Stationary Distributions and Stochastic Stability

This intuition is the basis for the *radius-coradius theorem*, which is presented next. The proof and extensions of this result are provided in sections 12.A.3 and 12.A.4.

As in section 12.5.2, suppose that N clever agents repeatedly play a population game $F^N: \mathcal{X}^N \to \mathbf{R}^n$, responding to revision opportunities by applying a noisy best response protocol σ^ε with cost function κ. Let $\{X_t^\varepsilon\}$ denote the resulting Markov process on $\mathcal{X}^N$.

Now let $\hat{\mathcal{X}} \subseteq \mathcal{X}$ denote the set of recurrent states of the zero-noise process $\{X_t^0\}$. For distinct x and y in $\hat{\mathcal{X}}$, define Π_{xy} to be the set of paths $\pi = \{(x, x_1), (x_1, x_2), \ldots, (x_{l-1}, y)\}$ through $\mathcal{X}$ such that $x_i \notin \hat{\mathcal{X}}$ for all $i \in \{1, \ldots, l-1\}$.

Next, let $\mathfrak{R}$ denote the set of recurrent classes of $\{X_t^0\}$. For distinct recurrent classes $R, S \in \mathfrak{R}$, define the *cost* of a transition from R to S by

$$c_{RS} = \min_{x \in R} \min_{y \in S} \min_{\pi \in \Pi_{xy}} C(\pi),$$

where $C(\pi)$ is the sum of the edge costs along path π, as defined in equation (12.57). Evidently, c_{RS} is the lowest cost of any path from a state in R to a state in S.

We now introduce notions of difficulty of escape from and ease of return to the basin of attraction of a recurrent class. The *radius* of recurrent class R,

$$\mathrm{rad}(R) = \min_{S \neq R} c_{RS},$$

is the minimal cost of a transition from R to another recurrent class. It therefore measures the difficulty of exiting the basin of attraction of R.

To define the notion of ease of return, let Π_{SR} denote the set of paths $\pi = \{(S, Q_1), (Q_1, Q_2), \ldots, (Q_{l-1}, R)\}$ in $\mathfrak{R}$ from S to R. Then the *coradius* of recurrent class R is given by

$$\mathrm{corad}(R) = \max_{S \neq R} \min_{\pi \in \Pi_{SR}} \sum_{(Q, Q') \in \pi} c_{QQ'}.$$

In other words, the coradius of R describes the total cost of reaching recurrent class R from the most disadvantageous initial class S, allowing that route to involve stops in other recurrent classes, and assuming that the path taken from each class to the next has as low a cost as possible.

Theorem 12.5.10 says that if the difficulty of escaping from R, as measured by $\mathrm{rad}(R)$, exceeds the difficulty of returning to R, as measured by $\mathrm{corad}(R)$, then R is the set of stochastically stable states.

Theorem 12.5.10 *Let $\{\{X_t^\varepsilon\}_{t=0}^\infty\}_{\varepsilon \in [0, \bar{\varepsilon}]}$ be a regular collection of Markov chains. If R is a recurrent class of $\{X_t^0\}$ with $\mathrm{rad}(R) > \mathrm{corad}(R)$, then R is the set of stochastically stable states.*

This result follows directly from theorem 12.A.6. Section 12.A.4 contains the proof of this and more general results.

12.5.5 Half-Dominance

Theorem 12.5.5 says that in two-strategy games, strong risk dominance is sufficient for equilibrium selection under the BRM rule. We now use the radius-coradius theorem obtain an extension of this result for games with arbitrary numbers of strategies.

In a two-strategy game, a risk dominant strategy is one that is optimal whenever it is played by at least half of an agent's opponents. Our generalization of risk dominance for n-strategy games, called *half-dominance*, retains this crucial property.

The following three definitions of half-dominance parallel the definitions of risk dominance given in section 12.5.3. Let F^N be an n-strategy, finite-population game. Strategy i is *weakly half-dominant* in F^N if

$$F_i^N\left(\tfrac{N-1}{N}y + \tfrac{1}{N}e_i\right) \gtreqless F_j^N\left(\tfrac{N-1}{N}y + \tfrac{1}{N}e_j\right) \quad \text{for all } y \in X^{N-1} \text{ with } y_i \gtreqless \tfrac{1}{2} \text{ and all } j \neq i. \tag{12.62}$$

Strategy i is *strictly half-dominant* if

$$F_i^N\left(\tfrac{N-1}{N}y + \tfrac{1}{N}e_i\right) > F_j^N\left(\tfrac{N-1}{N}y + \tfrac{1}{N}e_j\right) \quad \text{for all } y \in X^{N-1} \text{ with } y_i \geq \tfrac{1}{2} \text{ and all } j \neq i. \tag{12.63}$$

Finally, strategy i is *strongly half-dominant* if

$$F_i^N\left(\tfrac{N-1}{N}y + \tfrac{1}{N}e_i\right) \gtreqless F_j^N\left(\tfrac{N-1}{N}y + \tfrac{1}{N}e_j\right) \quad \text{for all } y \in X^{N-1} \text{ with } y_i \gtreqless \tfrac{1}{2}\tfrac{N-2}{N-1} \text{ and all } j \neq i. \tag{12.64}$$

The statements in the next exercise are the analogues of those made about risk dominance in exercise 12.5.3.

Exercise 12.5.11

i. Show that when N is odd, strong and strict half-dominance are equivalent and are more demanding than weak half-dominance.

ii. Show that when N is even, strict and weak half-dominance are equivalent and are less demanding than strong half-dominance. ◇

Exercise 12.5.12: Matching, Pairwise Risk Dominance, and Half-Dominance

Let $A \in \mathbf{R}^{n \times n}$ be a symmetric normal form game.

i. Strategy i is *strictly half-dominant* in A if $(Ax)_i > (Ax)_j$ whenever $x_i \geq \tfrac{1}{2}$. Fix a population size N, and let F^N be generated by matching without self-matching in A (see example 11.4.1):

Limiting Stationary Distributions and Stochastic Stability

$$F_i^N(x) = \tfrac{1}{N-1}(A(Nx - e_i))_i = (Ax)_i + \tfrac{1}{N-1}\left((Ax)_i - A_{ii}\right).$$

Suppose this equation is used to define F^N throughout X. Show that strategy i is strictly half-dominant in A if and only if

$$F_i^N(\tfrac{N-1}{N}y + \tfrac{1}{N}e_i) > F_j^N(\tfrac{N-1}{N}y + \tfrac{1}{N}e_j) \quad \text{for all } y \in X \text{ with } y_i \geq \tfrac{1}{2} \text{ and all } j \neq i,$$

which is condition (12.63) strengthened to allow y to lie outside of X^{N-1}.

ii. Strategy i *strictly pairwise risk dominates* strategy j in A if $A_{ii} + A_{ij} > A_{ji} + A_{jj}$. Construct a symmetric normal form coordination game in which strategy i strictly pairwise risk dominates every other strategy $j \neq i$, but in which strategy i is not strictly half-dominant in A.

iii. A satisfies the *marginal bandwagon property* if $A_{ii} - A_{ji} > A_{ik} - A_{jk}$ for all $i, j, k \in S$, so that the loss associated with playing strategy j rather than strategy i is worst when one's opponent in a match plays strategy i. Suppose that every pure strategy of A is a symmetric Nash equilibrium. Show that if strategy i strictly pairwise risk dominates every other strategy, and A satisfies the marginal bandwagon property, then strategy i is strictly half-dominant in A.

iv. Show that the conclusion of part (iii) remains true even without the restriction that all pure strategies generate symmetric Nash equilibria. (*Hint:* Show that under the marginal bandwagon property, any pure strategy that does not generate a symmetric Nash equilibrium is strictly dominated by another pure strategy.) ◇

Theorem 12.5.13 shows that strong half-dominance implies stochastic stability under the BRM rule.

Theorem 12.5.13 *Suppose that clever agents play a finite-population game F^N using the BRM rule. If strategy i is strongly half-dominant in F^N, then state e_i is uniquely stochastically stable.*

The intuition behind this result is simple. At a first approximation, that strategy i is strongly half-dominant means that it is the unique best response whenever it is played by at least fraction α of the population, where $\alpha < \tfrac{1}{2}$. Since there are N agents in the population, $N(1 - \alpha)$ is an approximate lower bound on the number of mutations need to escape the basin of attraction of equilibrium e_i. This lower bound is the radius of $\{e_i\}$. By the same token, $N\alpha$ is an approximate upper bound on the number of mutations needed to reach the basin of e_i from any outside state. This upper bound is the coradius of $\{e_i\}$. Since $\alpha < \tfrac{1}{2}$, the radius of $\{e_i\}$ is larger than its coradius, implying that e_i is the unique stochastically stable state.

This heuristic analysis contains a number of loose arguments. The proof below makes these arguments precise.

Proof First, assume that N is odd, so that there are states in $\mathcal{X}^N$ with $x_i = \frac{N-1}{2N}$ and $x_i = \frac{N+1}{2N}$, and suppose that $j \neq i$. If x is a state with $x_i \geq \frac{N-1}{2N}$, then at least fraction $\frac{N}{N-1} \cdot \frac{N-1}{2N} = \frac{1}{2}$ of a j player's opponents play strategy i. Similarly, if x is a state with $x_i \geq \frac{N+1}{2N}$, then at least fraction $\frac{N}{N-1}(\frac{N+1}{2N} - \frac{1}{N}) = \frac{1}{2}$ of an i player's opponents play strategy i. Since i is strongly half-dominant, it follows that

$$c_{xy} = 0 \quad \text{when } x_i \geq \tfrac{N-1}{2N} \text{ and } y = x + \tfrac{1}{N}(e_i - e_j); \tag{12.65}$$

$$c_{xy} = 1 \quad \text{when } x_i \geq \tfrac{N+1}{2N} \text{ and } y = x + \tfrac{1}{N}(e_j - e_i). \tag{12.66}$$

Statement (12.65) implies that the only state x that satisfies $x_i \geq \frac{N-1}{2N}$ and is a recurrent state of the zero-noise process is state e_i. Therefore, if y is a recurrent state other than e_i, and $\pi \in \Pi_{e_i y}$, then π must contain edges of the form $(z, z + \frac{1}{N}(e_k - e_i))$ with z_i taking every value in the set $\{1, \frac{N-1}{N}, \ldots, \frac{N+1}{2N}\}$. By (12.66), each such edge has cost 1. It follows that $\mathrm{rad}(\{e_i\}) \geq \#\{1, \frac{N-1}{N}, \ldots, \frac{N+1}{2N}\} = \frac{N+1}{2N}$.

Now let y be a recurrent state other than e_i. Let $\hat{\pi} \in \Pi_{ye_i}$ be a path in which every edge is of the form $(z, z + \frac{1}{N}(e_i - e_k))$. When $z_i \geq \frac{N-1}{2N}$, (12.65) implies that each such edge has cost zero. It follows that $C(\hat{\pi}) \leq \#\{0, \frac{1}{N}, \ldots, \frac{N-3}{2N}\} = \frac{N-1}{2N}$. Since this is true of every recurrent state other than e_i, it must be that $\mathrm{corad}(\{e_i\}) \leq \frac{N-1}{2N}$. Thus $\mathrm{rad}(\{e_i\}) \geq \frac{N+1}{2N} > \frac{N-1}{2N} \geq \mathrm{corad}(\{e_i\})$, and so theorem 12.5.10 implies that state e_i is uniquely stochastically stable.

Next, assume that N is even, so that there are states in $\mathcal{X}^N$ with $x_i = \frac{1}{2}$, and suppose that $j \neq i$. If x is a state with $x_i \geq \frac{1}{2}$, then at least fraction $\frac{N}{N-1}(\frac{1}{2} - \frac{1}{N}) = \frac{N-2}{2(N-1)}$ of an i player's opponents and at least fraction $\frac{N}{2(N-1)}$ of a j player's opponents are playing i. Since strategy i is strongly half-dominant, it follows that

$$c_{xy} = 0 \quad \text{when } x_i \geq \tfrac{1}{2} \text{ and } y = x + \tfrac{1}{N}(e_i - e_j);$$

$$c_{xy} = 1 \quad \text{when } x_i \geq \tfrac{1}{2} \text{ and } y = x + \tfrac{1}{N}(e_j - e_i).$$

Modifications of previous arguments show that $\mathrm{rad}(\{e_i\}) \geq \frac{N}{2} + 1$ and that $\mathrm{corad}(\{e_i\}) \leq \frac{N}{2}$, so theorem 12.5.10 again implies that state e_i is uniquely stochastically stable. ∎

The graph-theoretic approach developed in this section has been fruitful for stochastic stability analysis in settings beyond those considered here; in particular, models of extensive form games and local interaction have been handled successfully with these techniques (see the chapter notes). In the present setting of simultaneous-move population games, few results exist beyond those already presented. Still, the existing tools seem sufficient to develop further equilibrium selection results, making this a natural direction for future research.

… Limiting Stationary Distributions and Stochastic Stability

12.6 Large Population Limits

This section considers infinite-horizon behavior in the large population limit. Theorem 10.2.3 showed that over any finite time interval $[0, T]$, the sample paths of the stochastic evolutionary process $\{X_t^N\}$ are very likely to stay very close to a solution trajectory of the mean dynamic (M) once the population size N is large enough. This deterministic approximation is not valid over the infinite horizon. For instance, if $\{X_t^N\}$ is irreducible, it must visit every state in $\mathcal{X}^N$ infinitely often; this behavior cannot be approximated by a solution to an ordinary differential equation.

Although the infinite-horizon analogue of theorem 10.2.3 is false, one still expects the mean dynamic to impose restrictions on infinite-horizon behavior: while all states in $\mathcal{X}^N$ are visited infinitely often, states that are visited frequently should correspond to possible long-run behaviors of the mean dynamic, at least when N is large enough. After all, if state x is "transient" under (M), then a stochastic process visiting x is very likely to shadow the solution trajectory of (M) leading away from x, and it cannot return to x without an excursion against the flow of (M).

To formalize this intuition, we study the behavior of the stationary distribution μ^N as N approaches infinity. Section 12.6.1 shows that under quite general conditions, the mass in μ^N can only accumulate on states that are recurrent under (M). It follows that in settings where the mean dynamic has a globally attracting state—for instance, in strictly stable games under a variety of revision protocols—this state is uniquely stochastically stable. Section 12.6.2 offers more refined results, showing that in potential games and supermodular games, under perturbed best response protocols, the mass in μ^N can only accumulate on states that are locally stable rest points of (M). The results in these sections bring together ideas developed throughout the book: the well-behaved classes of games from part I, the analyses of deterministic dynamics from parts II and III, and the study of infinite-horizon behavior under stochastic dynamics from part IV.

12.6.1 Convergence to Recurrent States of the Mean Dynamic

Fix a population size N, and let $\{X_t^N\}$ be the stochastic evolutionary process generated by a population game F^N and a Lipschitz continuous revision protocol ρ. As in section 10.2.1, let ζ_x^N be a random variable whose distribution describes the stochastic increment of $\{X_t^N\}$ from state x:

$$\mathbb{P}(\zeta_x^N = z) = P_{x,x+z}^N = \mathbb{P}\left(X_{\tau_{k+1}}^N = x + z \,\middle|\, X_{\tau_k}^N = x\right),$$

where τ_k is the kth jump time of the process $\{X_t^N\}$. Until Section 12.6.2, we need not assume that the process $\{X_t^N\}$ is irreducible, and we can allow the transition probabilities of the process $\{X_t^N\}$ to be influenced by the finite-population effects (see exercise 12.6.1).

Suppose that as N grows large, the sequence of games $\{F^N\}_{N=N_0}^{\infty}$ converges uniformly to a Lipschitz continuous, continuous-population game $F\colon X \to \mathbf{R}^n$. It follows that the transition laws of the processes $\{\{X_t^N\}_{t\geq 0}\}_{N=N_0}^{\infty}$ converge: there is a collection of random variables $\{\zeta_x\}_{x \in X}$ taking values in $\{z \in \mathbf{R}^n : z = e_j - e_i$ for some $i, j \in S\}$ whose transition probabilities are Lipschitz continuous in x, and that satisfy

$$\lim_{N\to\infty} \max_{x \in \mathcal{X}^N} \max_{i,j \in S} \left| \mathbb{P}(\zeta_x^N = \tfrac{1}{N}(e_j - e_i)) - \mathbb{P}(\zeta_x = e_j - e_i) \right| = 0. \tag{12.67}$$

In other words, $N\zeta_x^N$ converges in distribution to ζ_x, with convergence uniform over X.

Exercise 12.6.1 Verify that condition (12.67) holds, even allowing for finite-population effects, including clever payoff evaluation, no self-imitation, and fixed numbers of committed agents for each strategy (see section 11.4). ◇

As in section 10.2.1, let $V^N(x) = N\,\mathbb{E}\zeta_x^N$ be the expected increment per time unit of the process $\{X_t^N\}$. Then condition (12.67) implies that V^N converges uniformly to the Lipschitz continuous function $V\colon X \to TX$ defined by $V(x) = \mathbb{E}\zeta_x$. Moreover, theorem 10.2.3 says that over any finite time interval, if N is large enough, the process $\{X_t^N\}$ is well approximated by an appropriate solution of the mean dynamic,

$$\dot{x} = V(x). \tag{M}$$

To describe infinite-horizon behavior in the large population limit, recall from section 7.A.1 that state $x \in X$ is a *recurrent point* of (M) ($x \in \mathcal{R}$) if $x \in \omega(x)$, so that x is contained in its own ω-limit set. The closure $\mathrm{cl}(\mathcal{R})$ of the set of recurrent points is called the *Birkhoff center* of (M). The first result states that when the population size is large, any stationary distribution of $\{X_t^N\}$ must concentrate its mass near this set.

Theorem 12.6.2 *Under the preceding assumptions, let $\{\mu^N\}_{N=N_0}^{\infty}$ be any sequence of stationary distributions for the Markov processes $\{X_t^N\}_{N=N_0}^{\infty}$, and let $O \subseteq X$ be an open set containing $\mathrm{cl}(\mathcal{R})$. Then $\lim_{N\to\infty} \mu^N(O) = 1$.*

This result is a consequence of theorem 12.B.1 in appendix 12.B.

Theorem 12.6.2 provides an infinite-horizon complement to the finite-horizon approximation result, theorem 10.2.3. Theorem 12.6.2 does not say that the process $\{X_t^N\}$ will shadow any particular solution trajectory of (M) indefinitely, but it does show that when the population size is large, the vast majority of time in the very long run will be spent near recurrent points of (M). Together, theorems 10.2.3 and 12.6.2 help justify the focus on the mean dynamic in parts II and III of this book.

Since the Birkhoff center contains rest points, closed orbits, and more complicated limit sets of the mean dynamic, theorem 12.6.2 is usually not enough to identify the stochastically stable states. However, if the mean dynamic has a globally attracting state x^*, then $\mathcal{R} = \{x^*\}$, so the theorem implies that x^* is uniquely stochastically stable. This general result is presented in section 12.B.1 (see corollary 12.B.2); some implications for stochastic evolution in stable games are discussed here. For part (ii) of the following theorem, recall that the set of perturbed equilibria $PE(F, v)$ consists of the rest points of the perturbed best response dynamic generated by F and v (see section 6.2).

Corollary 12.6.3 *Suppose the conditions of theorem 12.6.2 hold.*

i. Let F be a strictly stable game with unique Nash equilibrium x^*, and let ρ be a revision protocol that generates an integrable excess payoff dynamic or an impartial pairwise comparison dynamic. Then μ^N converges weakly to a point mass at x^*, and so x^* is uniquely stochastically stable.

ii. Let F be a stable game, and let ρ be a perturbed best response protocol generated by an admissible deterministic perturbation v. Then μ^N converges weakly to a point mass at the unique perturbed equilibrium $\tilde{x} \in PE(F, v)$, and so $\tilde{x}$ is uniquely stochastically stable.

Proof Theorems 7.2.6 and 7.2.9 show that in a strictly stable game, the unique Nash equilibrium x^* is globally asymptotically stable under any integrable excess payoff dynamic and any impartial pairwise comparison dynamic. Similarly, theorem 7.2.8 shows that in a stable game, any perturbed best response dynamic generated by an admissible deterministic perturbation has a unique and globally asymptotically stable rest point. The corollary follows immediately from these results and theorem 12.6.2. ∎

12.6.2 Convergence to Stable Rest Points of the Mean Dynamic

In cases where the mean dynamic has multiple components of recurrent states, theorem 12.6.2 does not reveal which of these components receives mass in the limiting stationary distribution. Still, components that are unstable seem like poor candidates for this role. If the process $\{X_t^N\}$ moves off the component, then obeying the mean dynamic (M) will draw the process away from the component, and will make it difficult for the process to return to the component.

For this argument to be sound, it must be the case that when the process visits, say, an unstable rest point of (M), it does not stop moving entirely; rather, there must be enough random motion that the process can leave the immediate neighborhood of the rest point, after which the pull of the mean dynamic will take the process still further away. Without this random motion, the process might reach an unstable rest point of the mean dynamic and stay there forever. This is precisely what happens, for instance, if agents use an imitative protocol (without mutations or committed agents) in a game with no pure Nash equilibria (see example 12.B.1). Of the families of continuous revision protocols from chapters 5 and 6—imitative, excess payoff, pairwise comparison, and perturbed best response—only the last exhibits the nondegeneracy needed to prove that unstable rest points cannot retain mass in the stationary distributions.

While one might expect such nondegeneracy to be sufficient to rule out unstable rest points, it is not. For instance, one can construct deterministic dynamics whose recurrent states are all locally unstable (see example 12.B.2); in this case, theorem 12.6.2 says that unstable states are the only candidates for stochastic stability. To ensure that the mass in μ^N does not accumulate at unstable rest points, the mean dynamic must be well-behaved in some global sense, as is true if it admits a global Lyapunov function (see appendix 7.B) or if it is a cooperative differential equation (see appendix 7.C), so that examples of the sort just mentioned are ruled out. Section 12.B.2 states general results along these lines; here we present implications for perturbed best response processes.

To employ existing results, we must define the process $\{X_t^N\}$ more restrictively than in in section 12.6.1; in particular, transition probabilities cannot depend on N. In the notation of the previous section, we require that

$$\mathbb{P}\big(\zeta_x^N = \tfrac{1}{N}(e_j - e_i)\big) = \mathbb{P}\big(\zeta_x = e_j - e_i\big) \quad \text{for all } i,j \in S, x \in \mathcal{X}^N, N \geq N_0.$$

For this restriction to hold, payoffs must be independent of the population size ($F^N = F$), and there cannot be finite-population effects of the sorts introduced in section 11.4.

With these additional restrictions in place, we can state our result. Below, $PE(F,v)$ again denotes the set of perturbed equilibria for the pair (F,v), and $LS(F,v)$ denotes the set of Lyapunov stable states under the perturbed best response dynamic generated by F and v.

Theorem 12.6.4 *Suppose that the conditions of theorem 12.6.2 and the additional restrictions noted above hold.*

i. Let F be a potential game, and let ρ be a perturbed best response protocol generated by an admissible deterministic perturbation v. Suppose $PE(F,v)$ is finite. If O is an open set containing $LS(F,v)$, then $\lim_{N\to\infty} \mu^N(O) = 1$.

ii. Let F be an irreducible supermodular game, and let ρ be a perturbed best response protocol generated by an admissible stochastic perturbation ε. Let v be the corresponding deterministic perturbation, whose existence is ensured by theorem 6.2.1. If O is an open set containing $LS(F,v)$, then $\lim_{N\to\infty} \mu^N(O) = 1$.

Limiting Stationary Distributions and Stochastic Stability

Proof Theorem 7.1.4 shows that under the conditions of part (i), the function $\tilde{f}(x) = f(x) - v(x)$ is a strict global Lyapunov function for the perturbed best response dynamic. Moreover, that ρ is a perturbed best response protocol implies that the process $\{X_t^N\}$ is nondegenerate at every rest point x of the perturbed best response dynamic, in the sense that span(support(ζ_x)) = TX. The conclusion of part (i) therefore follows from theorem 12.B.4.

Observation 7.3.5 and theorem 7.3.7 show that under the conditions of part (ii), the perturbed best response dynamic is strongly cooperative and hence irreducible (see appendix 7.C). The conclusion of part (ii) then follows from example 12.B.3 and theorem 12.B.5. ∎

Theorem 12.6.4 represents an improvement on earlier results, but it still is not enough to identify the stochastically stable states in cases with multiple stable rest points. Accomplishing this would require evaluating the asymptotic probabilities of motions of $\{X_t^N\}$ against the flow of the mean dynamic that lead to transitions among its stable rest points. (The situation is analogous to theorem 12.A.5, but it is more complex because it concerns the large population limit rather the small noise limit.) It is known that the asymptotic transition probabilities can be obtained as solutions to certain optimal control problems, which describe paths through X that minimize the "costs" of transitions between stable rest points. However, solving these optimal control problems seems difficult, at least outside of the reversible cases studied in sections 12.2 and 12.3. See the chapter notes for further discussion and references.

Another unanswered question concerns the agreement of the small noise and large population double limits. Sections 12.2 and 12.3 showed that these double limits agree in many (though not all) reversible cases, allowing predictions of infinite-horizon behavior without assessments of whether the rarity of mistakes or the averaging generated by large populations drives equilibrium selection. Although it seems natural to expect this agreement to extend to nonreversible but otherwise well-behaved settings, whether and when it does so is not yet known.

12.A Appendix: Trees, Escape Paths, and Stochastic Stability

Appendix 11.A showed that an irreducible Markov chain $\{X_t\}$ on a finite state space X admits a unique stationary distribution μ, and that μ is both the limiting distribution and the limiting empirical distribution of the process. The present appendix investigates limits of the stationary distribution as the parameters describing the Markov chain approach their extremes.

Under small noise limits, the state space of the Markov chain stays fixed, but the transition probabilities approach some limiting values as the noise level vanishes.

The analysis is most interesting when the Markov chains corresponding to positive noise levels are irreducible (and so have unique stationary distributions) while the chain corresponding to the zero-noise limit is not irreducible (and so has multiple recurrent classes and stationary distributions). Then as the noise level approaches zero, the corresponding sequence of unique stationary distributions converges, and its limit is a stationary distribution of the limiting Markov chain. In this way, the limiting analysis typically singles out one recurrent class of the limiting chain. The states in this class are said to be *stochastically stable*.

We begin the analysis by showing how the stationary distribution of an irreducible Markov chain on the finite state space X can be represented in terms of trees whose nodes are in X. We then introduce Markov chains with a noise parameter, and shows how the tree characterization of the stationary distribution can be used to determine the set of stochastically stable states. All results are presented in a discrete-time setting, but apply immediately to continuous-time Markov processes with constant jump rates (see section 11.A.7).

12.A.1 The Markov Chain Tree Theorem

Let $\{X_t\}$ be an irreducible Markov chain on the finite state space X. Let $P \in \mathbf{R}_+^{X \times X}$ be its transition matrix, and let $\mu \in \mathbf{R}_+^X$ be its unique stationary distribution: $\mu'P = \mu'$.

The Markov chain tree theorem characterizes μ in terms of certain graphs defined on the state space X. We view X as a set of *nodes* that can be connected by *directed edges*, which are ordered pairs $(x, y) \in X \times X$ with $x \neq y$. A *directed graph* g on X can be identified with a set of directed edges.

Five special types of directed graphs are important in the analysis. Four are introduced here, and the fifth in the proof of theorem 12.A.1. A *walk* from x to y is a directed graph $\{(x, x_1), (x_1, x_2), \ldots, (x_{l-1}, y)\}$ whose directed edges traverse a route connecting x to y. A *path* from x to $y \neq x$ is a walk from x to y with no repeated nodes. A *cycle* is a walk from x to itself that contains no other repeated nodes.

A *tree* with *root* x, also called an *x-tree*, is a directed graph with no outgoing edges from x, exactly one outgoing edge from each $y \neq x$, and a unique path from each $y \neq x$ to x. Denote a typical x-tree by τ_x, and let T_x denote the set of x-trees on X.

Now, define the vector $v \in \mathbf{R}_+^X$ by

$$v_x = \sum_{\tau_x \in T_x} \prod_{(y,z) \in \tau_x} P_{yz}. \tag{12.68}$$

The scalar v_x is obtained by taking the product of the transition probabilities associated with each x-tree and summing the results over all x-trees. The irreducibility of $\{X_t^N\}$ implies that at least one of the summands is positive and hence that v_x itself is positive.

Limiting Stationary Distributions and Stochastic Stability

In fact, much more is true. The following theorem establishes that the positive vector v is proportional to the stationary distribution of $\{X_t\}$.

Theorem 12.A.1 (The Markov Chain Tree Theorem) *Let $\{X_t\}$ be an irreducible Markov chain with transition matrix $P \in \mathbf{R}_+^{X \times X}$ and stationary distribution μ. Define the vector v via equation (12.68). Then v is a positive multiple of μ.*

Proof Let G_x be the set of directed graphs γ_x on X such that (1) each $y \in X$ has exactly one outgoing edge in γ_x; (2) γ_x contains a unique cycle; and (3) the unique cycle contains x. The proof of the theorem is based on the observation that the set G_x can be represented in two distinct ways as disjoint unions of trees augmented by a single edge:

$$G_x = \bigcup_{y \neq x} \bigcup_{\tau_y \in T_y} \tau_y \cup \{(y, x)\}; \tag{12.69}$$

$$G_x = \bigcup_{\tau_x \in T_x} \bigcup_{y \neq x} \tau_x \cup \{(x, y)\}. \tag{12.70}$$

In (12.69), one takes each τ_y tree with $y \neq x$ and constructs a graph $\gamma_x \in G_x$ by adding an edge from y to x. In (12.70), one takes each τ_x tree and each $y \neq x$, and constructs a graph $\gamma_x \in G_x$ by adding an edge from x to y.

Let ψ be the analogue of v whose components are obtained by taking the sum over graphs in G_x rather than over trees in T_x:

$$\psi_x = \sum_{\gamma_x \in G_x} \prod_{(y,z) \in \gamma_x} P_{yz}.$$

Using (12.69) and (12.70), one obtains two new expressions for ψ in terms of v and P:

$$\sum_{y \neq x} v_y P_{yx} = \psi_x = v_x \sum_{y \neq x} P_{xy}.$$

Adding $v_x P_{xx}$ to the first and last expressions yields

$$\sum_{y \in X} v_y P_{yx} = v_x,$$

or equivalently, $v'P = v'$. Since the stationary distribution of $\{X_t^N\}$ is unique, and since v is positive, v must be a positive multiple of μ. ∎

12.A.2 Limiting Stationary Distributions via Trees

We now consider the long-run behavior of perturbed Markov chains, whose transition probabilities include small noise terms. These noise terms ensure that the perturbed Markov chains are irreducible, even in cases where the unperturbed chain is not. It is natural to expect the stationary distributions of the perturbed chains to place most of their weight on the recurrent classes of the unperturbed chain. But, more interestingly, one typically finds nearly all of this weight being placed on just one recurrent class of the unperturbed chain. The members of this recurrent class are said to be *stochastically stable*. In summary, by introducing a small amount of noise to the transition probabilities, one can obtain unique history-independent predictions about infinite-horizon behavior in settings where multiple history-dependent predictions would otherwise prevail.

It is possible to carry out the analysis in this section under restrictions on the transition probabilities weaker than those specified in condition (12.71) below. That approach is pursued in section 12.A.5.

Let $\{\{X_t^\varepsilon\}_{t=0}^\infty\}_{\varepsilon \in (0,\bar{\varepsilon}]}$ be a parameterized collection of Markov chains on the finite state space $\mathcal{X}$. The transition matrices $P^\varepsilon \in \mathbf{R}_+^{\mathcal{X} \times \mathcal{X}}$ of these chains are assumed to vary continuously in ε. In addition, for each pair of distinct states x and $y \neq x$, we assume that if $P_{xy}^0 = 0$, and if $P_{xy}^{\hat{\varepsilon}} > 0$ for some $\hat{\varepsilon} \in (0, \bar{\varepsilon}]$, then the collection $\{P_{xy}^\varepsilon\}_{\varepsilon \in (0,\bar{\varepsilon}]}$ satisfies

$$P_{xy}^\varepsilon = a_{xy}\varepsilon^k + o(\varepsilon^k) \quad \text{for some } a_{xy} > 0 \text{ and some } k > 0. \tag{12.71}$$

(Recall that $o(\varepsilon^k)$ represents a remainder function $r: (0, \bar{\varepsilon}] \to \mathbf{R}$ satisfying $\lim_{\varepsilon \to 0} r(\varepsilon)/\varepsilon^k = 0$, so that $r(\varepsilon)$ approaches zero faster than ε^k approaches zero.) In words, we have assumed that each positive but vanishing off-diagonal component of the transition matrix has a leading term that is mononomial in ε. Finally, we assume that when ε is positive, the chain $\{X_t^\varepsilon\}$ is irreducible, and so admits a unique stationary distribution $\mu^\varepsilon \in \mathbf{R}_+^\mathcal{X}$. When these assumptions are met, we say that the collection $\{\{X_t^\varepsilon\}_{t=0}^\infty\}_{\varepsilon \in [0,\bar{\varepsilon}]}$ is *regular*.

Next, we define the *cost* c_{xy} of the transition from state x to state $y \neq x$ for the regular collection $\{\{X_t^\varepsilon\}_{t=0}^\infty\}_{\varepsilon \in [0,\bar{\varepsilon}]}$:

$$c_{xy} = \begin{cases} 0 & \text{if } P_{xy}^0 > 0, \\ k & \text{if } P_{xy}^\varepsilon = a_{xy}\varepsilon^k + o(\varepsilon^k), \\ \infty & \text{if } P_{xy}^\varepsilon = 0 \text{ for all } \varepsilon \in [0, \bar{\varepsilon}]. \end{cases} \tag{12.72}$$

By regularity, this definition covers all possible cases.

We now extend the notion of cost to graphs on $\mathcal{X}$. Given an x-tree τ_x, define the *cost* $C(\tau_x)$ of this tree to be the sum of the costs of the edges it contains:

$$C(\tau_x) = \sum_{(y,z) \in \tau_x} c_{yz}.$$

Finally, let C_x^* be the lowest cost of any x-tree, and let C^* be the minimum value of C_x^* over all states in $\mathcal{X}$:

Limiting Stationary Distributions and Stochastic Stability

$$C_x^* = \min_{\tau_x \in T_x} C(\tau_x) \quad \text{and} \quad C^* = \min_{x \in X} C_x^*.$$

With these preliminaries in hand, we can state the following result on the limiting behavior of the stationary distributions μ^ε.

Theorem 12.A.2 *Let $\{\{X_t^\varepsilon\}_{t=0}^\infty\}_{\varepsilon \in [0, \bar{\varepsilon}]}$ be a regular collection of Markov chains with transition costs c_{xy}, and let μ^ε be the stationary distribution of $\{X_t^\varepsilon\}$. Then*

i. $\mu^* = \lim_{\varepsilon \to 0} \mu^\varepsilon$ *exists;*

ii. μ^* *is a stationary distribution of $\{X_t^0\}$;*

iii. $\mu_x^* > 0$ *if and only if $C_x^* = C^*$.*

State $x^* \in X$ is said to be *stochastically stable* if it receives positive mass in the limiting stationary distribution μ^*. According to theorem 12.A.2, state x^* is stochastically stable if and only if there is an x^*-tree whose cost is minimal. Part (ii) of the theorem says that the limiting stationary distribution μ^* is a stationary distribution of the unperturbed process $\{X_t^0\}$. Thus, the perturbations provide a selection among the recurrent classes of this unperturbed process; μ^* either puts positive mass on all states in a given recurrent class of $\{X_t^0\}$, or it puts zero mass on all states in this class (compare theorem 11.A.5 and the subsequent discussion).

The following argument not only establishes theorem 12.A.2 but also provides an explicit expression for the limiting stationary distribution.

Proof of theorem 12.A.2 To begin, marshal the previous definitions to show that

$$\prod_{(y,z) \in \tau_x} P_{yz}^\varepsilon = \prod_{(y,z) \in \tau_x} \left(a_{yz} \varepsilon^{c_{yz}} + o(\varepsilon^{c_{yz}}) \right) = A_{\tau_x} \varepsilon^{C(\tau_x)} + o(\varepsilon^{C(\tau_x)}), \quad \text{where } A_{\tau_x} = \prod_{(y,z) \in \tau_x} a_{yz}.$$

Thus, defining $v^\varepsilon \in \mathbf{R}_+^X$ as in (12.68), we have

$$v_x^\varepsilon = \sum_{\tau_x \in T_x} \prod_{(y,z) \in \tau_x} P_{yz}^\varepsilon = \alpha_x \varepsilon^{C_x^*} + o(\varepsilon^{C_x^*}), \quad \text{where } \alpha_x = \sum_{\tau_x : C(\tau_x) = C_x^*} A_{\tau_x}.$$

Theorem 12.A.1 says that

$$\mu_x^\varepsilon = \frac{v_x^\varepsilon}{\sum_{y \in X} v_y^\varepsilon} = \frac{\alpha_x \varepsilon^{C_x^*} + o(\varepsilon^{C_x^*})}{\sum_{y \in X} \left(\alpha_y \varepsilon^{C_y^*} + o(\varepsilon^{C_y^*}) \right)}. \tag{12.73}$$

Taking limits yields

$$\mu_x^* \equiv \lim_{\varepsilon \to 0} \mu_x^\varepsilon = \begin{cases} \dfrac{\alpha_x}{\sum_{y: C_y^* = C^*} \alpha_y} & \text{if } C_x^* = C^*, \\ 0 & \text{if } C_x^* > C^*, \end{cases}$$

which proves parts (i) and (iii) of the theorem.

Finally, since $\mu_x^* = \lim_{\varepsilon \to 0} \mu_x^\varepsilon$ exists, since $\lim_{\varepsilon \to 0} P^\varepsilon = P^0$, and since $(\mu^\varepsilon)' P^\varepsilon = (\mu^\varepsilon)'$ for all $\varepsilon \in (0, \bar{\varepsilon}]$, a straightforward continuity argument shows that $(\mu^*)' P^0 = (\mu^*)'$, proving part (ii) of the theorem. ∎

In addition to identifying the stochastically stable states, the proof of theorem 12.A.2 establishes rates of decay for the stationary distribution weights on other states.

Corollary 12.A.3 *Under the conditions of theorem 12.A.2, there are constants $b_x > 0$ such that $\mu_x^\varepsilon = b_x \varepsilon^{C_x^* - C^*} + o(\varepsilon^{C_x^* - C^*})$.*

12.A.3 Limiting Stationary Distributions via Trees on Recurrent Classes

Since in the end μ^* provides a selection from the recurrent classes of the limit chain $\{X_t^0\}$, it is natural to seek a version of theorem 12.A.2 stated in terms of trees whose nodes are not the states in X, but rather the recurrent classes of $\{X_t^0\}$. Because there are generally far fewer recurrent classes than states, such a result could be significantly easier to apply than theorem 12.A.2. After obtaining an auxiliary result, we establish the desired characterization in theorem 12.A.5.

To begin, let $\hat{X} \subseteq X$ denote the set of recurrent states of $\{X_t^0\}$. For each $\varepsilon \in (0, \bar{\varepsilon}]$, define the *censored chain* $\{\hat{X}_k^\varepsilon\}_{k=0}^\infty$ to be a process that records the values of the process $\{X_t^\varepsilon\}$ when it visits states in $\hat{X}$. More precisely, let T_k^ε denote the (random) time that $\{X_t^\varepsilon\}$ makes its kth visit to $\hat{X}$, and then set $\hat{X}_k^\varepsilon = X_{T_k^\varepsilon}^\varepsilon$.

One can verify that $\{\hat{X}_k^\varepsilon\}$ is indeed a Markov chain that inherits irreducibility from the original chain. Using theorem 11.A.10, one can obtain an expression for the stationary distribution $\hat{\mu}^\varepsilon$ of the censored chain in terms of that of the original chain:

$$\hat{\mu}_x^\varepsilon = \frac{\mu_x^\varepsilon}{\sum_{y \in \hat{X}} \mu_y^\varepsilon} \quad \text{for all } x \in \hat{X}.$$

Since theorem 12.A.2 implies that $\lim_{\varepsilon \to 0} \mu_z^\varepsilon = 0$ whenever $z \notin \hat{X}$, we can conclude that the masses in the distributions $\hat{\mu}^\varepsilon$ converge to those in the original limiting stationary distribution μ^*:

$$\lim_{\varepsilon \to 0} \hat{\mu}_x^\varepsilon = \mu_x^* \quad \text{for all } x \in \hat{X}. \tag{12.74}$$

In light of equation (12.74), we can determine the limiting stationary distribution μ^* by applying the analysis from section 12.A.2 to the censored chain $\{\hat{X}_k^\varepsilon\}$. For $x, y \in \hat{X}$, let W_{xy} be the set of walks $\{(x, x_1), (x_1, x_2), \ldots, (x_{l-1}, y)\}$ from x to y such that $x_i \notin \hat{X}$ for all $i \in \{1, \ldots, l-1\}$. Then the transition probabilities of the censored chain $\{\hat{X}_k^\varepsilon\}$ are given by

Limiting Stationary Distributions and Stochastic Stability

$$\hat{P}^\varepsilon_{xy} = \sum_{w \in W_{xy}} \prod_{(z,z') \in w} P^\varepsilon_{zz'}.$$

By regularity, it follows that for some $\hat{a}_{xy} > 0$, we have

$$\hat{P}^\varepsilon_{xy} = \hat{a}_{xy} \varepsilon^{\hat{c}_{xy}} + o(\varepsilon^{\hat{c}_{xy}}), \quad \text{where } \hat{c}_{xy} = \min_{w \in W_{xy}} \sum_{(z,z') \in w} c_{zz'}. \tag{12.75}$$

In words, the cost of the transition from x to y in the censored chain is the minimum cost of a walk from x to y in the original chain.

To obtain a slightly simpler characterization of the transition cost $\hat{c}_{xy}$ in (12.75), notice that one of the walks in W_{xy} that achieves the minimum in (12.75) will be a path, that is, a walk that visits no state more than once. Thus, letting Π_{xy} denote the set of paths $\pi = \{(x,x_1),(x_1,x_2),\ldots,(x_{l-1},y)\}$ through X such that $x_i \notin \hat{X}$ for all $i \in \{1,\ldots,l-1\}$, we can write

$$\hat{c}_{xy} = \min_{\pi \in \Pi_{xy}} \sum_{(z,z') \in \pi} c_{zz'}. \tag{12.76}$$

Now let $\hat{t}_x$ denote an x-tree with nodes in $\hat{X}$, and let $\hat{T}_x$ denote the set of such trees. If we define

$$\hat{C}(\hat{t}_x) = \sum_{(y,z) \in \hat{t}_x} \hat{c}_{yz}, \quad \hat{C}^*_x = \min_{\hat{t}_x \in \hat{T}_x} \hat{C}(\hat{t}_x) \quad \text{and} \quad \hat{C}^* = \min_{y \in \hat{X}} \hat{C}^*_y,$$

then theorem 12.A.2 and equation (12.74) yield the following result.

Corollary 12.A.4 *Under the assumptions of theorem 12.A.2, $\mu^*_x > 0$ if and only if $\hat{C}^*_x = \hat{C}^*$.*

Had we attempted to define a censored process directly on the set $\mathfrak{R}$ of recurrent classes of $\{X^0_t\}$, we would have encountered a difficulty: unless each recurrent class is a singleton, this process need not have the Markov property. Nevertheless, a few simple observations allow a move from corollary 12.A.4, which characterizes stochastic stability using graphs on the set of recurrent states $\hat{X}$, to a characterization via graphs on the set of recurrent classes $\mathfrak{R}$.

We note a few simple consequences of the fact that transitions between states in the same recurrent class have zero cost. First, any minimal-cost x-tree $\hat{t}_x$ must have these two properties: (1) for each recurrent class R that does not contain x, $\hat{t}_x$ has exactly one edge from a state in R to a state outside R; and (2) $\hat{t}_x$ has no edges from any state in R_x, the recurrent class that contains x, to a state outside R_x. For instance, if $\hat{t}_x$ had two states $y,z \in R$ with edges to states outside R, then replacing the outgoing edge from z with an edge from z to y would result in a new x-tree with lower cost than $\hat{t}_x$. Second, the minimal cost $\hat{C}^*_x$ is the same for all states in the same recurrent class. For if $x, y \in R_x$ and $\hat{\tau}_x$ is a minimal-cost x-tree, we can construct a y-tree $\hat{\tau}_y$ with $C(\hat{\tau}_y) \leq C(\hat{\tau}_x)$ from $\hat{\tau}_x$ by deleting the outgoing edge from y and adding an edge from x to y. (In fact, property 2 implies that both the new edge from x and the deleted edge from y have zero cost, and so that $C(\hat{\tau}_y) = C(\hat{\tau}_x)$.)

These observations imply that in applying corollary 12.A.4, one can treat all nodes in a given recurrent class as a unit by replacing trees on recurrent states with trees on recurrent classes. To state this idea precisely, define the cost c_{RS} of a transition from recurrent class R to recurrent class $S \neq R$ by

$$c_{RS} \equiv \min_{x \in R} \min_{y \in S} \hat{c}_{xy} = \min_{x \in R} \min_{y \in S} \min_{\pi \in \Pi_{xy}} \sum_{(z,z') \in \pi} c_{zz'}. \tag{12.77}$$

Let τ_R be an R-tree with nodes in $\mathfrak{R}$, the set of recurrent classes of $\{X_t^0\}$, and let T_R be the set of such trees. Using formulation (12.77) of transition costs, define

$$C(\tau_R) = \sum_{(Q,Q') \in \tau_R} c_{QQ'}, \qquad C_R^* = \min_{\tau_R \in T_R} C(\tau_R), \qquad C^* = \min_{R \in \mathfrak{R}} C_R^*.$$

Then corollary 12.A.4, the preceding observations, and some bookkeeping are enough to establish the following result.

Theorem 12.A.5 *Let $\{\{X_t^\varepsilon\}_{t=0}^\infty\}_{\varepsilon \in [0,\bar{\varepsilon}]}$ be a regular collection of Markov chains with transition costs c_{xy}, let μ^ε be the stationary distribution of $\{X_t^\varepsilon\}$, and let $\mu^* = \lim_{\varepsilon \to 0} \mu^\varepsilon$. Then* support$(\mu^*) = \bigcup \{R \in \mathfrak{R} : C_R^* = C^*\}$.

The reuse of the notation C^* from theorem 12.A.2 is intentional: one can show that the minimal cost generated by a tree on $\mathcal{X}$ equals the minimal cost generated by a tree on $\mathfrak{R}$.

In applying theorem 12.A.5, keep in mind that in computing the edge costs c_{RS}, one need only consider paths in the set Π_{xy}, that is, paths with only transient states (i.e., states in $\mathcal{X} - \hat{\mathcal{X}}$) as intermediate states. The theorem can be formulated without this constraint (see the chapter notes), but the present formulation is sometimes easier to apply. To understand why, suppose that the lowest-cost path from recurrent class S to recurrent class R is by way of a third recurrent class Q. Then when theorem 12.A.5 is applied, the minimal-cost R-tree will not include an edge from S to R, since a lower-cost tree can always be obtained by instead including the edge from S to Q. In other words, it is enough to consider direct paths when determining edge costs, since the advantages of any fruitful indirect paths are reaped when the minimal-cost trees are found.

12.A.4 Radius-Coradius Theorems

Theorem 12.A.5 characterizes stochastic stability in terms of minimal-cost trees whose nodes are recurrent classes. In examples with few recurrent classes, this

Limiting Stationary Distributions and Stochastic Stability

result is easy to apply, as one can find the minimal-cost trees by computing the cost of every possible tree and then determining which cost is smallest. But if there are more than a few recurrent classes, exhaustive search quickly becomes intractable. As an alternative, one can look for sufficient conditions for stochastic stability that are easy to check, because they obviate the need to explicitly determine the minimal-cost tree in the cases where they apply.

The sufficient conditions we consider are defined in terms of the radius and coradius of a recurrent class. For any pair of recurrent classes $(R, S) \in \mathfrak{R} \times \mathfrak{R}$, define the cost c_{RS} of the transition from R to S as in equation (12.77). The *radius* of recurrent class R,

$$\text{rad}(R) = \min_{S \neq R} c_{RS},$$

is the minimal cost of a transition from R to another recurrent class. Thus, the radius provides a simple measure of the difficulty of escaping from R.

Our sufficient conditions for stability also require a measure of the difficulty of returning to R from other recurrent classes. To define this measure, let Π_{SR} denote the set of (nonrepeating) paths $\pi = \{(S, Q_1), (Q_1, Q_2), \ldots, (Q_{l-1}, R)\}$ through $\mathfrak{R}$ that lead from S to R. Then the *coradius* of recurrent class R is given by

$$\text{corad}(R) = \max_{S \neq R} \min_{\pi \in \Pi_{SR}} C(\pi), \quad \text{where } C(\pi) = \sum_{(Q,Q') \in \pi} c_{QQ'}.$$

In words, the coradius of R describes the total cost of reaching R from the most disadvantageous initial class S, assuming that the route taken from S to R has as low a cost as possible.

Theorem 12.A.6 provides our first sufficient condition for stochastic stability.

Theorem 12.A.6 *Let $\{\{X_t^\varepsilon\}_{t=0}^\infty\}_{\varepsilon \in [0, \bar{\varepsilon}]}$ be a regular collection of Markov chains with transition costs c_{xy}, let μ^ε be the stationary distribution of $\{X_t^\varepsilon\}$, and let $\mu^* = \lim_{\varepsilon \to 0} \mu^\varepsilon$. If $R \in \mathfrak{R}$ is a recurrent class of $\{X_t^0\}$ with $\text{rad}(R) > \text{corad}(R)$, then $\text{support}(\mu^*) = R$.*

Theorem 12.A.6 says that if the difficulty of escaping from R, as measured by $\text{rad}(R)$, exceeds the difficulty of returning to R, as measured by $\text{corad}(R)$, then R is the set of stochastically stable states. This result follows immediately from the more general theorem 12.A.7.

To obtain this more powerful sufficient condition for stochastic stability, we introduce the notions of modified cost and modified coradius. The *modified cost* of edge (Q, Q') is

$$\bar{c}_{QQ'} = c_{QQ'} - \min_{\hat{Q} \neq Q} c_{Q\hat{Q}} = c_{QQ'} - \text{rad}(Q).$$

The modified cost of path $\pi = \{(Q_0, Q_1), (Q_1, Q_2), \ldots, (Q_{l-1}, Q_l)\}$ is

$$C^-(\pi) = c_{Q_0 Q_1} + \sum_{i=1}^{l-1} c^-_{Q_i Q_{i+1}}.$$

Note the use of the original cost rather than the modified cost for the first edge in the path. Finally, the *modified coradius* of recurrent class R is

$$\operatorname{corad}^-(R) = \max_{S \neq R} \min_{\pi \in \Pi_{SR}} C^-(\pi).$$

An intuition for these definitions is as follows. According to theorem 12.A.5, the states in recurrent class R are stochastically stable if and only if there is a minimal-cost R-tree. By definition, every R-tree τ_R must contain an edge departing from every recurrent class $Q \neq R$, and every S-tree τ_S must contain an edge departing from every recurrent class $Q \neq S$. Thus, for each $Q \notin \{R, S\}$, both τ_R and τ_S will contain an edge whose cost is at least $\operatorname{rad}(Q)$. Since the costs represented by these radii must appear in both trees, they can be factored out when comparing the costs of τ_R and τ_S themselves. This factoring out is precisely what the notions of modified cost and modified coradius accomplish.

Theorem 12.A.7 Let $\{\{X_t^\varepsilon\}_{t=0}^\infty\}_{\varepsilon \in [0, \bar{\varepsilon}]}$ be a regular collection of Markov chains with transition costs c_{xy}, let μ^ε be the stationary distribution of $\{X_t^\varepsilon\}$, and let $\mu^* = \lim_{\varepsilon \to 0} \mu^\varepsilon$. If $R \in \mathfrak{R}$ is a recurrent class of $\{X_t^0\}$ with $\operatorname{rad}(R) > \operatorname{corad}^-(R)$, then $\operatorname{support}(\mu^*) = R$.

Proof Let $S \in \mathfrak{R} - \{R\}$, and let τ_S be an S-tree. If we can show that there is an R-tree τ_R with $C(\tau_R) < C(\tau_S)$, then the result follows from theorem 12.A.5.

Let $\pi^* = \{(S, Q_1), (Q_1, Q_2), \ldots, (Q_{l-1}, R)\}$ be a path from S to R satisfying

$$\pi^* \in \operatorname*{argmin}_{\pi \in \Pi_{SR}} C^-(\pi),$$

so that $C^-(\pi^*) \leq \operatorname{corad}^-(R)$. To construct τ_R, we start with the tree τ_S, delete each edge leading out from nodes $Q_1, \ldots, Q_{l-1}$, and R, and then add all edges in path π^*.

We now verify that τ_R is an R-tree. Clearly, τ_R has exactly one outgoing edge from each $Q \neq R$ and no outgoing edges from R. To verify that there is path from each $Q \neq R$ to R, it is enough to observe that the sequence of edges leading from Q through subsequent nodes must hit path π. If it did not, it would enter a cycle consisting entirely of nodes outside of path π. The edges in this cycle would then all be in τ_S, contradicting that τ_S is a tree.

Now, since τ_R and τ_S only differ in their outgoing edges from S, R, and $Q_1, \ldots Q_{l-1}$, and since $C^-(\pi^*) \leq \operatorname{corad}^-(R)$, we have

Limiting Stationary Distributions and Stochastic Stability

$$c(\tau_R) - c(\tau_S) \leq C(\pi^*) - \left(\sum_{i=1}^{l-1} \operatorname{rad}(Q_i) + \operatorname{rad}(R)\right)$$

$$= \left(C^-(\pi^*) + \sum_{i=1}^{l-1} \operatorname{rad}(Q_i)\right) - \left(\sum_{i=1}^{l-1} \operatorname{rad}(Q_i) + \operatorname{rad}(R)\right)$$

$$\leq \operatorname{corad}^-(R) - \operatorname{rad}(R)$$

$$< 0.$$

Since we assumed at the outset that $\operatorname{rad}(R) > \operatorname{corad}^-(R)$, the proof is complete. ∎

It can be shown that when $\operatorname{rad}(R) > \operatorname{corad}^-(R)$, the expected time to reach R from any other recurrent class is of asymptotic order no greater than $\varepsilon^{-\operatorname{corad}^-(R)}$; see the chapter notes for references.

12.A.5 Lenient Transition Costs and Weak Stochastic Stability

Section 12.A.2 defined regular Markov chains to be those whose vanishing transition probabilities satisfy condition (12.71), a condition that can be rewritten as

$$P_{xy}^\varepsilon = (a_{xy} + o(1))\,\varepsilon^k. \tag{12.78}$$

Here $k \geq 0$ is the cost of the transition, a_{xy} is a positive constant, and $o(1)$ is a term that vanishes as ε approaches zero.

In some settings, condition (12.78) is too strong to apply, making it useful to replace it with the following more lenient requirement:

$$P_{xy}^\varepsilon = \varepsilon^{k+o(1)}. \tag{12.79}$$

It is easy to verify that condition (12.78) implies condition (12.79), but that the converse implication does not hold (see example 12.A.1).

Condition (12.79) is more commonly expressed after the change of parameter $\varepsilon \mapsto \eta \equiv -(\log \varepsilon)^{-1}$, so that the noise level η appears in an exponent. In this formulation, (12.78) becomes

$$P_{xy}^\eta = (a_{xy} + o(1))\exp(-\eta^{-1}k), \tag{12.80}$$

where $o(1)$ now represents a term that vanishes as η approaches zero. For its part, equation (12.79) becomes

$$P_{xy}^\eta = \exp\!\left(-\eta^{-1}(k + o(1))\right), \tag{12.81}$$

which can be expressed equivalently as

$$-\lim_{\eta \to 0} \eta \log P_{xy}^\eta = k. \tag{12.82}$$

The analysis in section 12.3 shows that the lenient definition (12.82) of transition costs is the natural one for studying the small noise asymptotics of the stationary distribution. The lenient definition of transition costs also broadens the class of noisy best response rules that are susceptible to analysis.

Example 12.A.1: Probit Choice In example 12.3.3, agents' decisions are based on *probit choice*: revising agents choose an optimal response after the payoffs to each strategy are subjected to i.i.d. normal perturbations with mean zero and variance η. Suppose that at state x in a two-strategy game, the payoff to strategy i exceeds that of strategy j by $d > 0$. Then the probability of a transition from state x to state $y = x + \frac{1}{N}(e_j - e_i)$ under probit choice is

$$P_{xy}^\eta = x_i \cdot k^\eta(d) \exp\left(-\frac{d^2}{4\eta}\right) \quad \text{for some } k^\eta(d) \in \left(\frac{\sqrt{\eta}}{\sqrt{\pi}d}\left(1 - \frac{2\eta}{d^2}\right), \frac{\sqrt{\eta}}{\sqrt{\pi}d}\right).$$

This transition probability does not satisfy (12.80), but it satisfies (12.81) with transition cost $k = \frac{1}{4}d^2$. ◆

What are the implications of allowing lenient transition costs? Let $\{\{X_t^\eta\}_{t=0}^\infty\}_{\eta \in [0,\bar{\eta}]}$ be a parameterized collection of Markov chains on the finite state space X. Suppose that the chain $\{X_t^\eta\}$ is irreducible when η is positive, and that the transition matrices $P^\eta \in \mathbf{R}_+^{X \times X}$ vary continuously in η. Finally, suppose that for each pair of distinct states x and $y \neq x$, if $P_{xy}^0 = 0$ and $P_{xy}^{\hat{\eta}} > 0$ for some $\hat{\eta} > 0$, then the sequence $\{P_{xy}^\eta\}_{\eta \in (0,\bar{\eta}]}$ satisfies (12.82) for some $k \geq 0$. If these conditions are met, we call the collection of Markov chains *weakly regular*, and we define the (*lenient*) *cost* of the transition from state x to state $y \neq x$ by

$$c_{xy} = -\lim_{\eta \to 0} \eta \log P_{xy}^\eta, \tag{12.83}$$

adopting the convention that $-\log 0 = \infty$.

One can prove analogues of the results from sections 12.A.2–12.A.4 using lenient transition costs, but at the cost of losing some borderline selection results. If we recreate the proof of theorem 12.A.2 with transition costs defined as in equation (12.83), then in place of equation (12.73) we obtain

$$\mu_x^\eta = \frac{\exp(-\eta^{-1}(C_x^* + o(1)))}{\sum_{y \in X} \exp(-\eta^{-1}(C_y^* + o(1)))}. \tag{12.84}$$

It does not follow from this that a state x with $C_x^* = C^*$ is stochastically stable, in the sense that $\lim_{\eta \to 0} \mu_x^\eta > 0$. But equation (12.84) does imply that for all x and y in X, we have

$$-\lim_{\eta \to 0} \eta \log \frac{\mu_x^\eta}{\mu_y^\eta} = C_x^* - C_y^*;$$

then using the argument used to prove theorem 12.2.2, one can conclude that

$$-\lim_{\eta \to 0} \eta \log \mu_x^\eta = C_x^* - C^*. \tag{12.85}$$

We call state $x \in X$ *weakly stochastically stable* if the limit in (12.85) is equal to zero, or equivalently, if as η^{-1} approaches infinity, μ_x^η does not vanish at an exponential rate. Equation (12.85) shows that x is weakly stochastically stable if and only if $C_x^* = C^*$.

Sections 12.A.2–12.A.4 presented a variety of sufficient conditions for stochastic stability in regular collections of Markov chains. The preceding discussion implies that in each case, there is a corresponding sufficient condition for weak stochastic stability in weakly regular collections of Markov chains as long as transition costs are defined using (12.83) rather than (12.72). In general, the limiting stationary distribution of such a collection need not exist. But proposition 12.1.2 shows that if there is only one weakly stochastically stable state, then the limiting stationary distribution exists and is a point mass at this state; in the parlance of section 12.1.1, such a state is *uniquely stochastically stable*.

This argument can be extended to obtain conditions for the selection of a unique recurrent class in a weakly regular collection of Markov chains. In particular, if there is a unique recurrent class R of the zero-noise chain that satisfies a sufficient condition for stochastic stability from theorem 12.A.5, 12.A.6, or 12.A.7, then R is the set of stochastically stable states. For instance, if $\mathrm{rad}(R) > \mathrm{corad}^-(R)$, with costs defined as in (12.83), then R is the set of stochastically stable states.

12.B Appendix: Stochastic Approximation Theory

Stochastic approximation theory studies stochastic processes whose increments are small and whose expected increments can be described by a mean dynamic. The basic aim of the theory is to link the infinite-horizon behavior of the stochastic processes to various sorts of recurrent sets of the deterministic mean dynamic.

The theory distinguishes between two main settings. In the case of *decreasing step sizes*, one considers a single stochastic process whose increments become smaller as time passes. This is the case when the state variable represents a time-averaged quantity, or, alternatively, the proportions of balls of different colors in an urn to which balls are added in each period. A fundamental result from this theory shows that the sample paths of the stochastic process converge almost surely to components of the *chain recurrent set* of the mean dynamic, defined in section 7.A.1. See the chapter notes for references and further discussion.

In the case of *constant step sizes*, one considers a sequence of stochastic processes indexed by a parameter that determines the size of the increments of the process. Here the goal of the theory is to link the stationary distributions of the processes with small step sizes to the recurrent states of the mean dynamic (M).

The remainder of this appendix presents results from the constant step size theory. Section 12.B.1 shows that under quite general conditions, when the step size is sufficiently small, the stationary distributions of the stochastic processes concentrate their mass near recurrent states of (M). If the processes exhibit enough random variation, then some recurrent states, for instance, unstable rest points, would seem to be unlikely candidates for retaining stationary distribution mass. Section 12.B.2 describes conditions on the mean dynamic and the stochastic processes themselves ensuring that mass concentrates only on stable rest points of (M).

12.B.1 Convergence to the Birkhoff Center

We follow the development of the deterministic approximation results in section 10.2. For each $N \geq N_0$, corresponding to a step size of $\frac{1}{N}$, suppose that the process $\{X_t^N\}_{t \geq 0}$ takes values in the state space $X^N = \{x \in X: Nx \in \mathbf{Z}^n\}$. Let $\lambda^N \in \mathbf{R}_+^{X^N}$ and $P^N \in \mathbf{R}_+^{X^N \times X^N}$ denote the jump rate vector and transition matrix of this process. Let ζ_x^N be a random variable whose distribution describes the stochastic increment of $\{X_t^N\}$ from state x:

$$\mathbb{P}(\zeta_x^N = z) = P_{x,x+z}^N = \mathbb{P}\left(X_{\tau_{k+1}}^N = x + z \,\big|\, X_{\tau_k}^N = x\right),$$

where τ_k is the time of the process's kth jump. The expected increment per time unit of the process $\{X_t^N\}$ is described by $V^N: X \to TX$, defined by $V^N(x) = \lambda_x^N \mathbb{E}\zeta_x^N$.

As in theorem 10.2.1, we assume that there is a Lipschitz continuous vector field $V: X \to TX$ such that the functions V^N converge uniformly to V:

$$\lim_{N \to \infty} \sup_{x \in X^N} |V^N(x) - V(x)| = 0.$$

In addition, we assume that there is a constant $c < \infty$ such that $|\zeta_x^N| \leq \frac{c}{N}$ with probability 1, which implies that the remaining conditions of theorem 10.2.1 hold. Therefore, if the initial conditions $X_0^N = x_0^N$ converge to $x_0 \in X$, and if $\{x_t\}_{t \geq 0}$ denotes the corresponding solution to the mean dynamic

$$\dot{x} = V(x), \tag{M}$$

then for each $T < \infty$ and $\varepsilon > 0$, we have

$$\lim_{N \to \infty} \mathbb{P}\left(\sup_{t \in [0,T]} |X_t^N - x_t| < \varepsilon \right) = 1. \tag{12.86}$$

Theorem 10.2.1 is a statement about finite-horizon behavior: the time span $T < \infty$ is fixed in advance, and (12.86) says that when N is large enough, the stochastic process $\{X_t^N\}$ is very likely to mirror the deterministic trajectory through time T.

Limiting Stationary Distributions and Stochastic Stability

In order to state an infinite-horizon approximation result, we must review a few definitions from section 7.A.1. Let $\{x_t\} = \{x_t\}_{t\geq 0}$ be the solution of the mean dynamic (M) from initial condition x_0. The ω-*limit* of this solution trajectory is the set of all points that the trajectory approaches arbitrarily closely infinitely often:

$$\omega(x_0) = \left\{ y \in X \colon \text{there exists } \{t_k\}_{k=1}^{\infty} \text{ with } \lim_{k\to\infty} t_k = \infty \text{ such that } \lim_{k\to\infty} x_{t_k} = y \right\}. \tag{12.87}$$

State $x \in X$ is a *recurrent point* of (M) ($x \in \mathcal{R}$) if $x \in \omega(x)$. The *Birkhoff center* of (M) is the closure $\mathrm{cl}(\mathcal{R})$ of the set of recurrent points.

Since the processes $\{X_t^N\}$ are not assumed to be irreducible, each of these processes may admit multiple stationary distributions. Theorem 12.B.1 says that if we fix any sequence $\{\mu^N\}_{N=N_0}^{\infty}$ of stationary distributions, then all stationary distributions far enough along the sequence place most of their mass near the Birkhoff center of (M).

Theorem 12.B.1 *Let $\{\mu^N\}_{N=N_0}^{\infty}$ be any sequence of stationary distributions for the Markov processes $\{X_t^N\}_{N=N_0}^{\infty}$, and let $O \subseteq X$ be an open set containing $\mathrm{cl}(\mathcal{R})$. Then $\lim_{N\to\infty} \mu^N(O) = 1$.*

Theorem 12.B.1 has strong implications in settings in which the mean dynamic has a unique recurrent point. Recall that the *point mass* at state $x \in X$, denoted δ_x, is the probability measure on X that satisfies $\delta_x(A) = 1$ if $x \in A$ and $\delta_x(A) = 0$ otherwise. Also, the sequence of measures $\{\mu^N\}_{N=N_0}^{\infty}$ *converges weakly* to the point mass δ_x if $\lim_{N\to\infty} \mu^N(O) = 1$ for every (relatively) open set $O \subseteq X$ containing x (see exercise 12.1.4).

Corollary 12.B.2 *Let $\{\mu^N\}_{N=N_0}^{\infty}$ be any sequence of stationary distributions for the Markov processes $\{X_t^N\}_{N=N_0}^{\infty}$, and suppose that the mean dynamic (M) admits a unique recurrent point, x^*. Then the sequence $\{\mu^N\}$ converges weakly to the point mass δ_{x^*}.*

Under additional regularity assumptions, it can be shown that if the state space is dilated by a factor of $\sqrt{N}$, then the stationary distributions μ^N converge to a multivariate normal distribution centered at x^* (see the chapter notes).

12.B.2 Sufficient Conditions for Convergence to Stable Rest Points

Theorem 12.B.1 does not rule out the possibility that the stationary distributions μ^N concentrate their mass near unstable rest points or other unstable invariant sets of the mean dynamic. This section presents conditions under which the stationary distributions must concentrate their mass near stable rest points of (M).

As of this writing, the following results require additional structure on the Markov processes $\{\{X_t^N\}_{t\geq 0}\}_{N=N_0}^{\infty}$. We say that this collection has *homogeneous transitions* if the distribution of the rescaled stochastic increment $\lambda_x^N \zeta_x^N$ is independent of N. In this case, we let ζ_x denote a random variable with the same distribution as $\lambda_x^N \zeta_x^N$. It follows that the expected increment per time unit $V^N(x) = \lambda_x^N \mathbb{E}\zeta_x^N = V(x)$ is independent of N. We maintain the assumption from section 12.B.1 that V is Lipschitz continuous.

To rule out convergence to unstable rest points, we must assume in addition that the process $\{X_t^N\}$ exhibits enough random motion near these points. The next example illustrates this idea.

Example 12.B.1 Consider a birth and death process $\{X_t^N\}$ on $\mathcal{X}^N = \{0, \frac{1}{N}, \ldots, 1\}$ with common jump rate $\lambda_x^N \equiv N$ and transition probabilities

$$p_x^N = p_x = (1-x)(1-(1-x)^2);$$
$$q_x^N = q_x = x(1-x^2).$$

An interpretation of this process is as follows. When a jump time occurs, one agent from the population is selected at random. This agent then samples two members of the population. If at least one of them is playing the other strategy, the agent switches to that strategy.

Since the product of the jump rate ($\lambda_x^N = N$) and the step size ($\frac{1}{N}$) is 1, the mean dynamic for this process for any N is

$$\dot{x} = p_x - q_x = x(1-x)(1-2x). \tag{12.88}$$

Under this dynamic, the rest point $x^* = \frac{1}{2}$ attracts all initial conditions in $(0,1)$, and the boundary rest points 0 and 1 are unstable. Nevertheless, the only recurrent states of the process are states 0 and 1. Thus, for any value of N, every stationary distribution μ^N of the process $\{X_t^N\}$ places all of its mass on unstable rest points of the mean dynamic (12.88). ◆

The example shows that if x is a rest point of the mean dynamic (M) at which the process $\{X_t^N\}$ stops moving (that is, if $P(\zeta_x = 0) = 1$), then the point mass δ_x is a stationary distribution of $\{X_t^N\}$ even if x is unstable under (M). But while x being a rest point of (M) means that the *expected* increment $\mathbb{E}\zeta_x^N$ is null, the actual increment ζ_x^N need not be. As long as the process $\{X_t^N\}$ churns enough to wander slightly away from the rest point x, the force of the mean dynamic will push it still further away, and will make it very difficult for the process to return.

To formalize this idea, we say that the collection $\{\{X_t^N\}_{t \geq 0}\}_{N=N_0}^\infty$ is *nondegenerate* at rest point x if $\mathrm{span}(\mathrm{support}(\zeta_x)) = TX$, so that the directions of random motions around the rest point x span the tangent space of X. Notice that nondegeneracy is only possible for interior rest points; if from a boundary state there is a positive probability of motion into the interior, this state cannot be a rest point.

Even if an unstable rest point is nondegenerate, it is still possible for the stationary distribution to become concentrated around this point. The following example does not satisfy the standing assumptions about the form of the state space or the homogeneity of the processes, but it illustrates the idea in a simple way.

Example 12.B.2 Consider a dynamic $\dot{x} = V(x)$ on the unit circle that moves clockwise except at a single rest point x^* (see example 7.A.2), and let $\{X_t^N\}_{N=N_0}^{\infty}$ be a sequence of Markov processes that are defined on grids in the unit circle, and whose mean dynamics V^N converge to V. If the process $\{X_t^N\}$ is nondegenerate at x^*, then churning ensures that whenever the process reaches x^*, it eventually wanders a non-negligible distance past x^*. Once this happens, the process resumes its clockwise motion around the circle until it returns to a neighborhood of x^*, where the churning then resumes. Since x^* is the sole recurrent point of the mean dynamic, theorem 12.B.1 says that the stationary distributions μ^N converge weakly to the point mass δ_{x^*} as N approaches infinity. ◆

Ruling out examples of this sort requires assumptions about the global behavior of the mean dynamic, assumptions ensuring that there is no easy way for the Markov process to return to an unstable rest point. One possibility is to require the mean dynamic to generate a so-called simple flow. As a partner to the ω-limit set $\omega(x_0)$ for initial condition $x_0 \in X$ under the mean dynamic $\dot{x} = V(x)$, define the α-*limit set* $\alpha(x_0)$ to be the ω-limit set of the time-reversed equation $\dot{x} = -V(x)$. The set $\alpha(x_0)$ is nonempty only if the solution of the mean dynamic from x_0 exists in X for all backward time. We say that (M) generates a *simple flow* if the set $\bigcup_{x \in X} (\alpha(x) \cup \omega(x))$ of all α- and ω-limit points of (M) is finite. In a simple flow, each solution trajectory converges to one of a finite number of rest points, as does each backward-time solution that does not leave X. Simple flows do not contain closed orbits, limit cycles, chaotic attractors, or other complicated limit sets.

To formalize the requirement that there be no easy way for the Markov process to return to the rest point x^* after leaving its vicinity, define an *orbit chain* to be a sequence $\{x^k\}_{k=1}^{K}$ of rest points of (M) with connecting forward orbits $\{\gamma_k\}_{k=1}^{K-1}$, meaning that $x^k = \alpha(\gamma^k)$ and $x^{k+1} = \omega(\gamma^k)$ for all $k \in \{1, \ldots, K-1\}$. The rest point x^* is *orbit chain unstable* if there is an orbit chain leading from x^* to another rest point y^* and no orbit chain leading back. Otherwise x^* is *orbit chain stable*.

Theorem 12.B.3 *Suppose that the collection $\{\{X_t^N\}_{t \geq 0}\}_{N=N_0}^{\infty}$ has homogeneous transitions and is nondegenerate at every rest point of (M) that is not Lyapunov stable. Suppose further that (M) generates a simple flow on X. If $\{\mu^N\}$ is a sequence of stationary distributions for the Markov chains $\{X_t^N\}$, and if $O \subseteq X$ is an open set containing the orbit chain stable equilibria of (M), then $\lim_{N \to \infty} \mu^N(O) = 1$.*

For an application of this result, recall from section 7.1 that the C^1 function $L\colon X \to \mathbf{R}$ is a *strict Lyapunov function* for V if $\dot L(x) \equiv \nabla L(x)'V(x) \geq 0$ for all $x \in X$, with equality only at rest points of V. It is easy to see that any dynamic with a finite number of rest points that admits a strict Lyapunov function generates a simple flow. This observation and theorem 12.B.3 yield the following result.

Theorem 12.B.4 *Suppose that the collection $\{\{X^N_t\}_{t\geq 0}\}^\infty_{N=N_0}$ has homogeneous transitions and that it is nondegenerate at every rest point of the mean dynamic* (M) *that is not Lyapunov stable. In addition, suppose that $RP(V)$ is finite and that* (M) *admits a strict Lyapunov function $L\colon X \to \mathbf{R}$. Let $\{\mu^N\}^\infty_{N=N_0}$ be a sequence of stationary distributions for the Markov chains, and let $O \subseteq X$ be an open set containing all Lyapunov stable rest points of* (M). *Then $\lim_{N\to\infty} \mu^N(O) = 1$.*

Since in this theorem the dynamic (M) has a finite number of rest points and admits a strict Lyapunov function, its Lyapunov stable rest points and its asymptotically stable rest points are identical.

One can also prove that the stationary distributions μ^N concentrate their mass near stable rest points of (M) when (M) is cooperative and irreducible. Since such dynamics can admit complicated unstable invariant sets, a global form of nondegeneracy is needed to reach the desired conclusion. For each state $x \in X$, define $\Sigma_x = \mathbb{E}\zeta_x\zeta'_x - \mathbb{E}\zeta_x\mathbb{E}\zeta'_x \in \mathbf{R}^{n\times n}$ to be the covariance matrix generated by the random vector ζ_x. The collection $\{\{X^N_t\}_{t\geq 0}\}^\infty_{N=N_0}$ is *globally nondegenerate* if there is a $c > 0$ such that $\mathrm{Var}(z'\zeta_x) \equiv z'\Sigma_x z \geq c$ for all unit-length $z \in TX$ and all $x \in X$.

Example 12.B.3 verifies that stochastic evolutionary processes generated by perturbed best response protocols satisfy global nondegeneracy.

Example 12.B.3 Let $\{\{X^N_t\}_{t\geq 0}\}^\infty_{N=N_0}$ be the collection of stochastic evolutionary processes generated by the game F and the protocol $\rho(\pi, x) = \tilde M(x)$, where $\tilde M\colon \mathbf{R}^n \to \mathrm{int}(X)$ is a continuous perturbed maximizer function. If we write $\tilde B \equiv \tilde M \circ F$, then the distribution of the normalized increment ζ_x can be expressed as

$$\mathbb{P}(\zeta_x = z) = \begin{cases} x_i \tilde B_j(x) & \text{if } z = e_j - e_i, \\ \sum_{i\in S} x_i \tilde B_i(x) & \text{if } z = \mathbf{0}, \\ 0 & \text{otherwise.} \end{cases}$$

It follows that

$$\mathbb{E}\zeta_x = \tilde B(x) - x \quad \text{and} \quad \mathbb{E}\zeta_x\zeta'_x = \mathrm{diag}(\tilde B(x)) + \mathrm{diag}(x) - \tilde B(x)x' - x\tilde B(x)',$$

and hence that

$$\Sigma_x = \mathbb{E}\zeta_x\zeta'_x - \mathbb{E}\zeta_x\mathbb{E}\zeta'_x = \mathrm{diag}(\tilde B(x)) - \tilde B(x)\tilde B(x)' + \mathrm{diag}(x) - xx'.$$

Limiting Stationary Distributions and Stochastic Stability

Now let

$$b = \min_{x \in X} \min_{i \in S} \tilde{B}_i(x).$$

Since X is compact and F and $\tilde{M}$ are continuous, b is positive. Moreover, if z is a unit-length vector in TX, we have

$$z' \Sigma_x z = \sum_{i \in S} (z_i)^2 \tilde{B}_i(x) - \left(\sum_{i \in S} z_i \tilde{B}_i(x) \right)^2 + \sum_{i \in S} (z_i)^2 x_i - \left(\sum_{i \in S} z_i x_i \right)^2$$

$$= \sum_{i \in S} \tilde{B}_i(x) \left(z_i - \sum_{j \in S} z_j \tilde{B}_j(x) \right)^2 + \sum_{i \in S} x_i \left(z_i - \sum_{j \in S} z_j x_j \right)^2$$

$$\geq b \sum_{i \in S} \left(z_i - \sum_{j \in S} z_j \tilde{B}_j(x) \right)^2$$

$$= b \left(\sum_{i \in S} (z_i)^2 + n \left(\sum_{j \in S} z_j \tilde{B}_j(x) \right)^2 \right)$$

$$> b.$$

Thus the collection $\{\{X_t^N\}_{t \geq 0}\}_{N=N_0}^\infty$ is globally nondegenerate. ◆

We now present the final stochastic approximation result.

Theorem 12.B.5 *Suppose that the collection $\{\{X_t^N\}_{t \geq 0}\}_{N=N_0}^\infty$ has homogeneous transitions and is globally nondegenerate, and suppose that the mean dynamic (M) is affinely conjugate to a C^1, cooperative, irreducible differential equation. If $\{\mu^N\}_{N=N_0}^\infty$ is a sequence of stationary distributions of the Markov chains $\{X_t^N\}$, and if $O \subseteq X$ is an open set containing all Lyapunov stable rest points of (M), then $\lim_{N \to \infty} \mu^N(O) = 1$.*

Notes

Section 12.1
Stochastic stability analysis was introduced to game theory by Foster and Young (1990), Kandori, Mailath, and Rob (1993), and Young (1993a); these authors defined stochastic stability using the small noise limit. Stochastic stability in the large population limit and in the double limits was studied by Binmore, Samuelson, and Vaughan (1995), Binmore and Samuelson (1997), Benaïm and Weibull (2003), and Sandholm (2010c; 2010e). Example 12.1.1 is essentially due to Binmore and Samuelson (1997).

Section 12.2
For the exact form of Stirling's formula used in the proof of theorem 12.2.3, see Lang (1997).

Section 12.3
Sections 12.3.1–12.3.6 follow Sandholm (2010c), which built on earlier papers by Blume (2003) and Sandholm (2007c); also see Maruta (2002). The definition of noisy best response protocols is essentially

due to Blume (2003). Evolutionary game models of probit choice can be found in Ui (1998), Myatt and Wallace (2003), and Dokumacı and Sandholm (2007b). For the approximation of normal distribution tail probabilities used in example 12.3.3, see Durrett (2005, theorem 1.1.3). See Billingsley (1995) or Folland (1999) for the dominated convergence theorem, and see Sandholm (2010c, appendix) for details on how to apply it in the proofs of theorems 12.3.3 and 12.3.5.

Ordinal potential functions were introduced in the context of normal form games by Monderer and Shapley (1996b). Corollary 12.3.8 is due to Blume (2003), and corollary 12.3.9 is essentially due to Kandori, Mailath, and Rob (1993). For more on stochastic dominance in utility theory, see Border (2001).

Section 12.4
This section follows Sandholm (2010e), which built on the work of Binmore, Samuelson, and Vaughan (1995) and Binmore and Samuelson (1997). The latter papers introduced multiple limits to the study of stochastic stability and established a version of theorem 12.4.1.

For the results described in the text on equilibrium selection in n-strategy games under imitative protocols with mutations and results on equilibrium selection under the frequency-dependent Moran process, see Fudenberg and Imhof (2006; 2008). For applications of the latter results, see Nowak et al. (2004), Taylor et al. (2004), and Fudenberg et al. (2006), as well as surveys by Nowak (2006) and Traulsen and Hauert (2009).

Binmore and Samuelson (1997) obtained equilibrium selection results along the lines described at the end of section 12.4 for imitative protocols driven by dissatisfaction, providing conditions under which an equilibrium that is both risk dominant and payoff dominant is stochastically stable. Maruta (2002) characterized the effects of different forms of payoff dependence in direct revision protocols on stochastic stability results.

Section 12.5
The use of minimal cost trees to determine small noise stochastically stable states was introduced to game theory by Kandori, Mailath, and Rob (1993) and Young (1993a), building on ideas developed in Freidlin and Wentzell (1998). These two papers and most of their successors focus on the BRM model; exceptions include Ui (1998), Myatt and Wallace (2003), Alós-Ferrer and Netzer (2010), Marden and Shamma (2008), and Dokumacı and Sandholm (2007b).

Selection of risk dominant equilibrium in the BRM model was established in Kandori, Mailath, and Rob (1993); the risk dominance concept itself is due to Harsanyi and Selten (1988). The importance of clever agents for obtaining exact finite population selection results was noted in Sandholm (1998); see also Rhode and Stegeman (1996). Robson and Vega-Redondo (1996) and Bergin and Lipman (1996) studied alternative noisy best response models in which Kandori, Mailath, and Rob's (1993) selection result fails to hold. Robles (1998) and Sandholm and Pauzner (1998) showed that decreasing mutation rates and growing populations can abrogate history-independent predictions in stochastic evolutionary models.

The radius-coradius theorem is due to Ellison (2000). The notion of half-dominance first appeared in Morris, Rob, and Shin (1995). Exercise 12.5.12 is due to Kandori and Rob (1998). Theorem 12.5.13 is due to Maruta (1997), Kandori and Rob (1998), and Ellison (2000). Algorithms for determining the stochastically stable state in supermodular games were presented in Kandori and Rob (1995) and Beggs (2005).

A considerable body of work on stochastic stability in extensive form games is not considered here; see the chapter 1 notes for references.

Section 12.6
Theorem 12.6.2 is due to Benaïm (1998) and Benaïm and Weibull (2009). Theorem 12.6.4 is due to Hofbauer and Sandholm (2007).

The probabilities of transitions of the stochastic evolutionary process between stable rest points of the mean dynamic can be evaluated in the large population limit using techniques from large deviations theory. This analysis can then used to evaluate the asymptotics of waiting times and of the stationary distribution. Benaïm and Sandholm (2010), building on the frameworks of Dupuis (1988) and Freidlin and Wentzell (1998), develop this general approach and provide complete large deviations analyses of evolution in two-strategy games and in potential games under logit choice.

Appendix 12.A

Theorem 12.A.1 is an old and often-rediscovered result from Markov chain theory; see Aldous and Fill (2001, ch. 9 notes) for some historical remarks. This theorem was first used to compute limiting stationary distributions by Freidlin and Wentzell (1998) in the context of stochastically perturbed differential equations. The results presented in Section 12.A.2 for Markov chains on finite state spaces are due to Kandori, Mailath, and Rob (1993) and Young (1993a).

Young (1993a; 1998b) introduced the notion of a regular collection of Markov chains that is employed here, and also provided characterizations of limiting stationary distributions by way of trees on recurrent classes, as considered in Section 12.A.3. The analogue of theorem 12.A.5 stated in Young (1993a; 1998b) requires one to consider indirect paths between recurrent classes (see the discussion after theorem 12.A.5) and is proved using a tree-surgery argument that is rather different than the argument employed here. The statement of theorem 12.A.5 provided here, which uses only direct paths, was proposed in Kandori and Rob (1995).

The radius-coradius theorems in section 12.A.4 are modifications of results of Ellison (2000), whose analysis also considered waiting times for transitions between recurrent classes. More refined results on waiting times can be found in Beggs (2005).

Appendix 12.B

Basic references on stochastic approximation theory with decreasing step sizes and fixed step sizes are Benaïm (1999) and Benaïm (1998), respectively. The decreasing step size results are the basic tool for studying the model of learning in games known as stochastic fictitious play, in which the state variable describes the time-averaged play of n players who recurrently play an n-player normal form game. References include Fudenberg and Kreps (1993), Kaniovski and Young (1995), Benaïm and Hirsch (1999a), Hofbauer and Sandholm (2002), Benaïm, Hofbauer, and Sorin (2005; 2006), Benaïm, Hofbauer, and Hopkins (2009) and Benaïm and Faure (2010). Pemantle (2007) surveyed results on this and related processes.

Theorem 12.B.1 follows from Benaïm (1998, corollary 3.2). For asymptotic normality, see Kurtz (1976, theorem 2.7) and Ethier and Kurtz (1986, sec. 11.2). Theorem 12.B.3 follows from Benaïm (1998, theorem 4.3), and theorem 12.B.5 follows from Benaïm and Hirsch (1999b, theorem 1.5).

References

Abraham, R., and J. Robbin. 1967. *Transversal Mappings and Flows*. New York: W. A. Benjamin.

Abreu, D., and R. Sethi. 2003. Evolutionary stability in a reputational model of bargaining. *Games and Economic Behavior* 44: 195–216.

Agastya, M. 2004. Stochastic stability in a double auction. *Games and Economic Behavior* 48: 203–222.

Akin, E. 1979. *The Geometry of Population Genetics*. Berlin: Springer.

———. 1980. Domination or equilibrium. *Mathematical Biosciences* 50: 239–250.

———. 1990. The differential geometry of population genetics and evolutionary games. In *Mathematical and Statistical Developments of Evolutionary Theory*, ed. S. Lessard, 1–93. Dordrecht: Kluwer.

———. 1993. *The General Topology of Dynamical Systems*. Providence, R.I.: American Mathematical Society.

Akin, E., and V. Losert. 1984. Evolutionary dynamics of zero-sum games. *Journal of Mathematical Biology* 20: 231–258.

Aldous, D., and J. A. Fill. 2001. Reversible Markov chains and random walks on graphs. Unpublished manuscript, University of California, Berkeley, and Johns Hopkins University.

Alós-Ferrer, C., and A. B. Ania. 2005. The evolutionary stability of perfectly competitive behavior. *Economic Theory* 26: 497–516.

Alós-Ferrer, C., A. B. Ania, and K. R. Schenk-Hoppé. 2000. An evolutionary model of Bertrand oligopoly. *Games and Economic Behavior* 33: 1–19.

Alós-Ferrer, C., G. Kirchsteiger, and M. Walzl. 2010. On the evolution of market institutions: The platform design paradox. *Economic Journal* 120: 215–243.

Alós-Ferrer, C., and N. Netzer. 2010. The logit response dynamics. *Games and Economic Behavior* 68: 413–427.

Alós-Ferrer, C., and S. Weidenholzer. 2006. Imitation, local interactions, and efficiency. *Economics Letters* 93: 163–168.

———. 2007. Partial bandwagon effects and local interactions. *Games and Economic Behavior* 61: 179–197.

———. 2008. Contagion and efficiency. *Journal of Economic Theory* 143: 251–274.

Anderlini, L., and A. Ianni. 1996. Path dependence and learning from neighbors. *Games and Economic Behavior* 13: 141–177.

Anderson, S. P., A. de Palma, and J.-F. Thisse. 1992. *Discrete Choice Theory of Product Differentiation*. Cambridge, Mass.: MIT Press.

Ania, A. B. T. Tröger, and A. Wambach. 2002. An evolutionary analysis of insurance markets with adverse selection. *Games and Economic Behavior* 40: 153–184.

Arneodo, A., P. Coullet, and C. Tresser. 1980. Occurrence of strange attractors in three-dimensional Volterra equations. *Physics Letters* 79A: 259–263.

Arslan, G., J. R. Marden, and J. S. Shamma. 2007. Autonomous vehicle target assignment: A game-theoretical formulation. *ASME Journal of Dynamic Systems, Measurement and Control* 129: 584–596.

Aubin, J.-P. 1991. *Viability Theory*. Boston: Birkhäuser.

Aubin, J.-P., and A. Cellina. 1984. *Differential Inclusions*. Berlin: Springer.

Avriel, M. 1976. *Nonlinear Programming: Analysis and Methods*. Englewood Cliffs, N.J.: Prentice-Hall.

Balder, E. J. 2002. A unifying pair of Cournot-Nash equilibrium existence results. *Journal of Economic Theory* 102: 437–470.

Balkenborg, D., J. Hofbauer, and C. Kuzmics. 2008. Refined best-response correspondence and dynamics. Unpublished manuscript, University of Exeter, Northwestern University, and University of Vienna.

Balkenborg, D., and K. H. Schlag. 2001. Evolutionarily stable sets. *International Journal of Game Theory* 29: 571–595.

———. 2007. On the evolutionary selection of sets of Nash equilibria. *Journal of Economic Theory* 133: 295–315.

Banerjee, A., and J. W. Weibull. 2000. Neutrally stable outcomes in cheap-talk coordination games. *Games and Economic Behavior* 32: 1–24.

Basu, K., and J. W. Weibull. 1991. Strategy sets closed under rational behavior. *Economics Letters* 36: 141–146.

Beckmann, M., C. B. McGuire, and C. B. Winsten. 1956. *Studies in the Economics of Transportation*. New Haven, Conn.: Yale University Press.

Beggs, A. W. 2005. Waiting times and equilibrium selection. *Economic Theory* 25: 599–628.

Ben-Shoham, A., R. Serrano, and O. Volij. 2004. The evolution of exchange. *Journal of Economic Theory* 114: 310–328.

Benaïm, M. 1998. Recursive algorithms, urn processes, and the chaining number of chain recurrent sets. *Ergodic Theory and Dynamical Systems* 18: 53–87.

———. 1999. Dynamics of stochastic approximation algorithms. In *Séminaire de Probabilités XXXIII*, ed. J. Azéma, M. Émery, M. Ledoux, and M. Yor, 1–68. Berlin: Springer.

Benaïm, M, and M. Faure. 2010. Stochastic approximations, cooperative dynamics, and supermodular games. Unpublished manuscript, Université de Neuchâtel.

References

Benaïm, M., and M. W. Hirsch. 1999a. Mixed equilibria and dynamical systems arising from fictitious play in perturbed games. *Games and Economic Behavior* 29: 36–72.

———. 1999b. On stochastic approximation algorithms with constant step size whose average is cooperative. *Annals of Applied Probability* 30: 850–869.

Benaïm, M., J. Hofbauer, and E. Hopkins. 2009. Learning in games with unstable equilibria. *Journal of Economic Theory* 144: 1694–1709.

Benaïm, M., J. Hofbauer, and W. H. Sandholm. 2008. Robust permanence and impermanence for stochastic replicator dynamics. *Journal of Biological Dynamics* 2: 180–195.

Benaïm, M., J. Hofbauer, and S. Sorin. 2005. Stochastic approximations and differential inclusions. *SIAM Journal on Control and Optimization* 44: 328–348.

———. 2006. Stochastic approximations and differential inclusions: Applications. *Mathematics of Operations Research* 31: 673–695.

Benaïm, M., and W. H. Sandholm. 2010. Large deviations, reversibility, and equilibrium selection under evolutionary game dynamics. Unpublished manuscript, Université de Neuchâtel and University of Wisconsin.

Benaïm, M., and J. W. Weibull. 2003. Deterministic approximation of stochastic evolution in games. *Econometrica* 71: 873–903.

———. 2009. Mean-field approximation of stochastic population processes in games. Unpublished manuscript, Université de Neuchâtel and Stockholm School of Economics.

Berger, U. 2005. Fictitious play in $2 \times n$ games. *Journal of Economic Theory* 120: 139–154.

———. 2007a. Brown's original fictitious play. *Journal of Economic Theory* 135: 572–578.

———. 2007b. Two more classes of games with the continuous-time fictitious play property. *Games and Economic Behavior* 60: 247–261.

———. 2008. Learning in games with strategic complementarities revisited. *Journal of Economic Theory* 143: 292–301.

Berger, U., and J. Hofbauer. 2006. Irrational behavior in the Brown–von Neumann–Nash dynamics. *Games and Economic Behavior* 56: 1–6.

Bergin, J., and B. L. Lipman. 1996. Evolution with state-dependent mutations. *Econometrica* 64: 943–956.

Bhaskar, V. 1998. Noisy communication and the evolution of cooperation. *Journal of Economic Theory* 82: 110–131.

Bhatia, N. P., and G. P. Szegö. 1970. *Stability Theory of Dynamical Systems*. Berlin: Springer.

Billingsley, P. 1995. *Probability and Measure*. 3d ed. New York: Wiley.

Binmore, K., J. Gale, and L. Samuelson. 1995. Learning to be imperfect: The ultimatum game. *Games and Economic Behavior* 8: 56–90.

Binmore, K., and L. Samuelson. 1997. Muddling through: Noisy equilibrium selection. *Journal of Economic Theory* 74: 235–265.

———. 1999. Evolutionary drift and equilibrium selection. *Review of Economic Studies* 66: 363–393.

Binmore, K., L. Samuelson, and R. Vaughan. 1995. Musical chairs: Modeling noisy evolution. *Games and Economic Behavior* 11: 1–35. Erratum, 21 (1997), 325.

Binmore, K., L. Samuelson, and H. P. Young. 2003. Equilibrium selection in bargaining models. *Games and Economic Behavior* 45: 296–328.

Bishop, D. T., and C. Cannings. 1978. A generalized war of attrition. *Journal of Theoretical Biology* 70: 85–124.

Bisin, A., and T. Verdier. 2001. The economics of cultural transmission and the dynamics of preferences. *Journal of Economic Theory* 97: 298–319.

Björnerstedt, J., and J. W. Weibull. 1996. Nash equilibrium and evolution by imitation. In *The Rational Foundations of Economic Behaviour*, ed. K. J. Arrow, E. Colombatto, M. Perlman, and C. Schmidt, 155–181. New York: St. Martin's Press.

Blume, A., Y.-G. Kim, and J. Sobel. 1993. Evolutionary stability in games of communication. *Games and Economic Behavior* 5: 547–575.

Blume, L. E. 1993. The statistical mechanics of strategic interaction. *Games and Economic Behavior* 5: 387–424.

———. 1995. The statistical mechanics of best response strategy revision. *Games and Economic Behavior* 11: 111–145.

———. 1997. Population games. In *The Economy as an Evolving Complex System*, ed. W. B. Arthur, S. N. Durlauf, and D. A. Lane, vol. 2, 425–460. Reading, Mass.: Addison-Wesley.

———. 2003. How noise matters. *Games and Economic Behavior* 44: 251–271.

Bomze, I. M. 1986. Noncooperative two-person games in biology: A classification. *International Journal of Game Theory* 15: 31–57.

———. 1990. Dynamical aspects of evolutionary stability. *Monatshefte für Mathematik* 110: 189–206.

———. 1991. Cross-entropy minimization in uninvadable states of complex populations. *Journal of Mathematical Biology* 30: 73–87.

———. 2002. Regularity versus degeneracy in dynamics, games, and optimization: A unified approach to different aspects. *SIAM Review* 44: 394–414.

Bomze, I. M., and B. M. Pötscher. 1989. *Game Theoretical Foundations of Evolutionary Stability*. Berlin: Springer.

Bomze, I. M., and J. W. Weibull. 1995. Does neutral stability imply Lyapunov stability? *Games and Economic Behavior* 11: 173–192.

Border, K. C. 2001. Comparing probability distributions. Unpublished manuscript, California Institute of Technology.

Börgers, T., and R. Sarin. 1997. Learning through reinforcement and the replicator dynamics. *Journal of Economic Theory* 77: 1–14.

Boyce, D. E., H. S. Mahmassani, and A. Nagurney. 2005. A retrospective on Beckmann, McGuire, and Winsten's *Studies in the Economics of Transportation*. *Papers in Regional Science* 84: 85–103.

References

Boylan, R. T. 1995. Continuous approximation of dynamical systems with randomly matched individuals. *Journal of Economic Theory* 66: 615–625.

Braess, D. 1968. Über ein paradoxen der verkehrsplanung. *Unternehmensforschung* 12: 258–268. Translated by D. Braess, A. Nagurney, and T. Walkobinger as "On a Paradox of Traffic Planning," *Transportation Science* 39 (2005), 446–450.

Brémaud, P. 1999. *Markov Chains: Gibbs Fields, Monte Carlo Simulation, and Queues*. New York: Springer.

Brown, G. W. 1949. Some notes on computation of games solutions. Report P-78. Rand Corporation.

———. 1951. Iterative solutions of games by fictitious play. In *Activity Analysis of Production and Allocation*, ed. T. C. Koopmans et al., 374–376. New York: Wiley.

Brown, G. W., and J. von Neumann. 1950. Solutions of games by differential equations. In *Contributions to the Theory of Games I*, ed. H. W. Kuhn and A. W. Tucker, 73–79. Annals of Mathematics Studies 24. Princeton, N.J.: Princeton University Press.

Bulow, J., and P. Klemperer. 1999. The generalized war of attrition. *American Economic Review* 89: 175–189.

Burke, M. A., and H. P. Young. 2001. Competition and custom in economic contracts: A case study of Illinois agriculture. *American Economic Review* 91: 559–573.

Cabrales, A. 1999. Adaptive dynamics and the implementation problem with complete information. *Journal of Economic Theory* 86: 159–184.

———. 2000. Stochastic replicator dynamics. *International Economic Review* 41: 451–481.

Cabrales, A., and G. Ponti. 2000. Implementation, elimination of weakly dominated strategies, and evolutionary dynamics. *Review of Economic Dynamics* 3: 247–282.

Cabrales, A., and R. Serrano. 2007. Implementation in adaptive better-response dynamics. Unpublished manuscript, Universidad Carlos III and Brown University.

Carmona, G., and K. Podczeck. 2009. On the existence of pure-strategy equilibria in large games. *Journal of Economic Theory* 144: 1300–1319.

Cesa-Bianchi, N., and G. Lugosi. 2006. *Prediction, Learning, and Games*. Cambridge: Cambridge University Press.

Chamberland, M., and R. Cressman. 2000. An example of dynamic (in)consistency in symmetric extensive form evolutionary games. *Games and Economic Behavior* 30: 319–326.

Conley, C. 1978. *Isolated Invariant Sets and the Morse Index*. Providence, R.I.: American Mathematical Society.

Cooper, R. W. 1999. *Coordination Games: Complementarities and Macroeconomics*. Cambridge: Cambridge University Press.

Correa, J. R., A. S. Schulz, and N. E. Stier-Moses. 2004. Selfish routing in capacitated networks. *Mathematics of Operations Research* 29: 961–976.

———. 2008. A geometric approach to the price of anarchy in nonatomic congestion games. *Games and Economic Behavior* 64: 457–469.

Cournot, A. A. 1838. *Recherches sur les Principes Mathématiques de la Théorie des Richesses*. Paris: Hachette. Trans. N. T. Bacon. 1898. London: Macmillan.

Cowan, S. G. 1992. Dynamical systems arising from game theory. Ph.D. diss., University of California, Berkeley.

Cressman, R. 1992. *The Stability Concept of Evolutionary Game Theory: A Dynamic Approach.* Berlin: Springer.

———. 1995. Evolutionary game theory with two groups of individuals. *Games and Economic Behavior* 11: 237–253.

———. 1996a. Evolutionary stability in the finitely repeated prisoner's dilemma game. *Journal of Economic Theory* 68: 234–248.

———. 1996b. Frequency-dependent stability for two-species interactions. *Theoretical Population Biology* 49: 189–210.

———. 1997. Local stability of smooth selection dynamics for normal form games. *Mathematical Social Sciences* 34: 1–19.

———. 2000. Subgame monotonicity in extensive form evolutionary games. *Games and Economic Behavior* 32: 183–205.

———. 2003. *Evolutionary Dynamics and Extensive Form Games.* Cambridge, Mass.: MIT Press.

———. 2005. Stability of the replicator equation with continuous strategy space. *Mathematical Social Sciences* 50: 127–147.

———. 2006. Uninvadability in N-species frequency models for resident-mutant systems with discrete or continuous time. *Theoretical Population Biology* 69: 253–262.

———. 2009. Continuously stable strategies, neighborhood superiority, and two-player games with continuous strategy space. *International Journal of Game Theory* 38: 221–247.

Cressman, R., J. Garay, and J. Hofbauer. 2001. Evolutionary stability concepts for n-species frequency-dependent interactions. *Journal of Theoretical Biology* 211: 1–10.

Cressman, R., and J. Hofbauer. 2005. Measure dynamics on a one-dimensional continuous trait space: Theoretical foundations for adaptive dynamics. *Theoretical Population Biology* 67: 47–59.

Cressman, R., J. Hofbauer, and F. Riedel. 2006. Stability of the replicator equation for a single-species with multi-dimensional continuous trait space. *Journal of Theoretical Biology* 239: 273–288.

Cressman, R., and K. H. Schlag. 1998. On the dynamic (in)stability of backwards induction. *Journal of Economic Theory* 83: 260–285.

Crouzeix, J.-P. 1998. Characterizations of generalized convexity and generalized monotonicity: A survey. In *Generalized Convexity, Generalized Monotonicity: Recent Results*, ed. J.-P. Crouzeix, J. E. Martinez Legaz, and M. Volle, 237–256. Dordrecht: Kluwer.

Crow, J. F., and M. Kimura. 1970. *An Introduction to Population Genetics Theory.* New York: Harper and Row.

Dafermos, S., and F. T. Sparrow. 1969. The traffic assignment problem for a general network. *Journal of Research of the National Bureau of Standards B* 73: 91–118.

Dawid, H., and W. B. MacLeod. 2008. Hold-up and the evolution of investment and bargaining norms. *Games and Economic Behavior* 62: 26–52.

References

Dawkins, R. 1976. *The Selfish Gene.* Oxford: Oxford University Press.

———. 1982. *The Extended Phenotype.* Oxford: Oxford University Press.

Dekel, E., J. C. Ely, and O. Yilankaya. 2007. Evolution of preferences. *Review of Economic Studies* 74: 685–704.

Dekel, E., and F. Gul. 1997. Rationality and knowledge in game theory. In *Advances in Economics and Econometrics: Theory and Applications*, ed. D. M. Kreps and K. F. Wallis, vol. 1, 87–172. Cambridge: Cambridge University Press.

Demichelis, S., and F. Germano. 2000. On the indices of zeros of Nash fields. *Journal of Economic Theory* 94: 192–217.

———. 2002. On (un)knots and dynamics in games. *Games and Economic Behavior* 41: 46–60.

Demichelis, S., and K. Ritzberger. 2003. From evolutionary to strategic stability. *Journal of Economic Theory* 113: 51–75.

Demichelis, S., and J. W. Weibull. 2008. Language, meaning, and games: A model of communication, coordination, and evolution. *American Economic Review* 98: 1292–1311. Corrigendum, 99 (2009), 2277.

Dindoš, M., and C. Mezzetti. 2006. Better-reply dynamics and global convergence to Nash equilibrium in aggregative games. *Games and Economic Behavior* 54: 261–292.

Dokumacı, E., and W. H. Sandholm. 2007a. Schelling redux: An evolutionary model of residential segregation. Unpublished manuscript, University of Wisconsin.

———. 2007b. Stochastic evolution with perturbed payoffs and rapid play. Unpublished manuscript, University of Wisconsin.

Droste, E., C. Hommes, and J. Tuinstra. 2002. Endogenous fluctuations under evolutionary pressure in Cournot competition. *Games and Economic Behavior* 40: 232–269.

Dugatkin, L. A., and H. K. Reeve, eds. 1998. *Game Theory and Animal Behavior.* Oxford: Oxford University Press.

Dupuis, P. 1988. Large deviations analysis of some recursive algorithms with state dependent noise. *Annals of Probability* 16: 1509–1536.

Dupuis, P., and A. Nagurney. 1993. Dynamical systems and variational inequalities. *Annals of Operations Research* 44: 9–42.

Durrett, R. 1996. *Stochastic Calculus: A Practical Introduction.* Boca Raton: CRC Press.

Durrett, R. 2005. *Probability: Theory and Examples.* 3d ed. Belmont, Calif.: Brooks-Cole.

Eigen, M., and P. Schuster. 1979. *The Hypercycle: A Principle of Natural Self-Organization.* Berlin: Springer.

Ellingsen, T., and J. Robles. 2002. Does evolution solve the hold-up problem? *Games and Economic Behavior* 39: 28–53.

Ellison, G. 1993. Learning, local interaction, and coordination. *Econometrica* 61: 1047–1071.

———. 2000. Basins of attraction, long-run equilibria, and the speed of step-by-step evolution. *Review of Economic Studies* 67: 17–45.

Ellison, G., and D. Fudenberg. 2000. Learning purified mixed equilibria. *Journal of Economic Theory* 90: 84–115.

Ely, J. C. 2002. Local conventions. *Advances in Theoretical Economics* 2 (1), article 1.

Ely, J. C., and W. H. Sandholm. 2005. Evolution in Bayesian games. I: Theory. *Games and Economic Behavior* 53: 83–109.

Ely, J. C., and O. Yilankaya. 2001. Nash equilibrium and the evolution of preferences. *Journal of Economic Theory* 97: 255–272.

Eshel, I. 1983. Evolutionary and continuous stability. *Journal of Theoretical Biology* 103: 99–111.

Eshel, I., L. Samuelson, and A. Shaked. 1998. Altruists, egoists, and hooligans in a local interaction model. *American Economic Review* 88: 157–179.

Eshel, I., and E. Sansone. 2003. Evolutionary and dynamic stability in continuous population games. *Journal of Mathematical Biology* 46: 445–459.

Ethier, S. N., and T. G. Kurtz. 1986. *Markov Processes: Characterization and Convergence*. New York: Wiley.

Fisher, R. A. 1930. *The Genetical Theory of Natural Selection*. Oxford: Clarendon Press.

Folland, G. B. 1999. *Real Analysis: Modern Techniques and Their Applications*. 2d ed. New York: Wiley.

Foster, D. P., and H. P. Young. 1990. Stochastic evolutionary game dynamics. *Theoretical Population Biology* 38: 219–232. Corrigendum, 51 (1997), 77–78.

———. 1998. On the nonconvergence of fictitious play in coordination games. *Games and Economic Behavior* 25: 79–96.

Freidlin, M. I., and A. D. Wentzell. 1998. *Random Perturbations of Dynamical Systems*. 2d ed. New York: Springer.

Friedberg, S. H., A. J. Insel, and L. E. Spence. 1989. *Linear Algebra*. 2d ed. Englewood Cliffs, N.J.: Prentice-Hall.

Friedman, D. 1991. Evolutionary games in economics. *Econometrica* 59: 637–666.

Friedman, D., and D. N. Ostrov. 2008. Conspicuous consumption dynamics. *Games and Economic Behavior* 64: 121–145.

Friedman, D., and D. N. Ostrov. 2010. Gradient dynamics in population games: Some basic results. Unpublished manuscript, UC Santa Cruz.

Friedman, J. W., and C. Mezzetti. 2001. Learning in games by random sampling. *Journal of Economic Theory* 98: 55–84.

Friesz, T. L., D. Bernstein, N. J. Mehta, R. L. Tobin, and S. Ganjalizadeh. 1994. Day-to-day dynamic network disequilibria and idealized traveler information systems. *Operations Research* 42: 1120–1136.

Fudenberg, D., and C. Harris. 1992. Evolutionary dynamics with aggregate shocks. *Journal of Economic Theory* 57: 420–441.

Fudenberg, D., and D. Hojman. 2009. Stochastic stability in large populations. Unpublished manuscript, Harvard University.

References

Fudenberg, D., and L. A. Imhof. 2006. Imitation processes with small mutations. *Journal of Economic Theory* 131: 251–262.

———. 2008. Monotone imitation dynamics in large populations. *Journal of Economic Theory* 140: 229–245.

Fudenberg, D., and D. M. Kreps. 1993. Learning mixed equilibria. *Games and Economic Behavior* 5: 320–367.

Fudenberg, D., and D. K. Levine. 1998. *Theory of Learning in Games*. Cambridge, Mass.: MIT Press.

Fudenberg, D., M. A. Nowak, C. Taylor, and L. A. Imhof. 2006. Evolutionary game dynamics in finite populations with strong selection and weak mutation. *Theoretical Population Biology* 70: 252–363.

Fudenberg, D., and J. Tirole. 1991. *Game Theory*. Cambridge, Mass.: MIT Press.

Garay, B. M., and J. Hofbauer. 2003. Robust permanence for ecological differential equations, minimax, and discretizations. *SIAM Journal on Mathematical Analysis* 34: 1007–1039.

Gaunersdorfer, A., and J. Hofbauer. 1995. Fictitious play, Shapley polygons, and the replicator equation. *Games and Economic Behavior* 11: 279–303.

Gilboa, I., and A. Matsui. 1991. Social stability and equilibrium. *Econometrica* 59: 859–867.

Goeree, J. K., C. A. Holt, and T. R. Palfrey. 2008. Quantal response equilibrium. In *The New Palgrave Dictionary of Economics,* ed. L. E. Blume and S. N. Durlauf. 2d ed. Basingstoke, U.K.: Palgrave Macmillan.

Golman, R., and S. E. Page. 2009. Basins of attraction and equilibrium selection under different learning rules. *Journal of Evolutionary Economics* 20: 49–75.

Gordon, W. B. 1972. On the diffeomorphisms of Euclidean space. *American Mathematical Monthly* 79: 755–759. Addendum, 80 (1973): 674–675.

Gorodeisky, Z. 2008. Stochastic approximation of discontinuous dynamics. Unpublished manuscript, Hebrew University.

———. 2009. Deterministic approximation of best-response dynamics for the matching pennies game. *Games and Economic Behavior* 66: 191–201.

Goyal, S. 2007. *Connections: An Introduction to the Economics of Networks*. Princeton, N.J.: Princeton University Press.

Goyal, S., and M.C.W. Janssen. 1997. Nonexclusive conventions and social coordination. *Journal of Economic Theory* 77: 34–57.

Guckenheimer, J., and P. Holmes. 1983. *Nonlinear Oscillations, Dynamical Systems, and Bifurcations of Vector Fields*. Berlin: Springer.

Guth, W. 1995. An evolutionary approach to explaining cooperative behavior by reciprocal incentives. *International Journal of Game Theory* 24: 323–344.

Guth, W., and M. E. Yaari. 1992. Explaining reciprocal behavior in simple strategic games: An evolutionary approach. In *Explaining Process and Change: Approaches to Evolutionary Economics*, ed. U. Witt, 23–34. Ann Arbor: University of Michigan Press.

Haigh, J. 1975. Game theory and evolution. *Advances in Applied Probability* 7: 8–11.

Hamilton, W. D. 1967. Extraordinary sex ratios. *Science* 156: 477–488.

———. 1996. *Narrow Roads of Gene Land.* Vol. 1. Oxford: W. H. Freeman/Spektrum.

Hammerstein, P., and R. Selten. 1994. Game theory and evolutionary biology. In *Handbook of Game Theory with Economic Applications,* ed. R. J. Aumann and S. Hart, vol. 2, 929–993. Amsterdam: Elsevier.

Harker, P. T., and J.-S. Pang. 1990. Finite-dimensional variational inequality and nonlinear complementarity problems: A survey of theory, algorithms, and applications. *Mathematical Programming* 48: 161–220.

Harsanyi, J. C. 1973. Games with randomly disturbed payoffs: A new rationale for mixed-strategy equilibrium points. *International Journal of Game Theory* 2: 1–23.

Harsanyi, J. C., and R. Selten. 1988. *A General Theory of Equilibrium Selection in Games.* Cambridge, Mass.: MIT Press.

Hart, S. 2002. Evolutionary dynamics and backward induction. *Games and Economic Behavior* 41: 227–264.

———. 2005. Adaptive heuristics. *Econometrica* 73: 1401–1430.

Hart, S., and A. Mas-Colell. 2001. A general class of adaptive strategies. *Journal of Economic Theory* 98: 26–54.

———. 2003. Uncoupled dynamics do not lead to Nash equilibrium. *American Economic Review* 93: 1830–1836.

Hartman, P. 1964. *Ordinary Differential Equations.* New York: Wiley.

Hauert, C. 2007. VirtualLabs in evolutionary game theory. Software. ⟨http://www.univie.ac.at/virtuallabs⟩.

Heifetz, A., C. Shannon, and Y. Spiegel. 2007. What to maximize if you must. *Journal of Economic Theory* 133: 31–57.

Helbing, D. 1992. A mathematical model for behavioral changes by pair interactions. In *Economic Evolution and Demographic Change: Formal Models in Social Sciences,* ed. G. Haag, U. Mueller, and K. G. Troitzsch, 330–348. Berlin: Springer.

Henry, C. 1973. An existence theorem for a class of differential equations with multivalued right-hand side. *Journal of Mathematical Analysis and Applications* 41: 179–186.

Herold, F., and C. Kuzmics. 2009. Evolutionary stability of discrimination under observability. *Games and Economic Behavior* 67: 542–551.

Herz, A.V.M. 1994. Collective phenomena in spatially extended evolutionary games. *Journal of Theoretical Biology* 169: 65–87.

Hewitt, E., and K. Stromberg. 1965. *Real and Abstract Analysis.* Berlin: Springer.

Hines, W.G.S. 1980. Three characterizations of population strategy stability. *Journal of Applied Probability* 17: 333–340. Correction, R. Cressman and W.G.S. Hines, 21 (1984), 213–214.

———. 1987. Evolutionary stable strategies: A review of basic theory. *Theoretical Population Biology* 31: 195–272.

References

Hino, Y. 2010. An improved algorithm for detecting potential games. *International Journal of Game Theory*, forthcoming.

Hiriart-Urruty, J.-B., and C. Lemaréchal. 2001. *Fundamentals of Convex Analysis.* Berlin: Springer.

Hirsch, M. W. 1988. Systems of differential equations that are competitive or cooperative. III: Competing species. *Nonlinearity* 1: 51–71.

Hirsch, M. W., and S. Smale. 1974. *Differential Equations, Dynamical Systems, and Linear Algebra.* San Diego, Calif.: Academic Press.

Hirsch, M. W., S. Smale, and R. L. Devaney. 2004. *Differential Equations, Dynamical Systems, and an Introduction to Chaos.* Amsterdam: Elsevier.

Hofbauer, J. 1981a. A general cooperation theorem for hypercycles. *Monatshefte für Mathematik* 91: 233–240.

———. 1981b. On the occurrence of limit cycles in the Volterra-Lotka equation. *Nonlinear Analysis* 5: 1003–1007.

———. 1985. The selection mutation equation. *Journal of Mathematical Biology* 23: 41–53.

———. 1995a. Imitation dynamics for games. Unpublished manuscript, University of Vienna.

———. 1995b. Stability for the best response dynamics. Unpublished manuscript, University of Vienna.

———. 1996. Evolutionary dynamics for bimatrix games: A Hamiltonian system? *Journal of Mathematical Biology* 34: 675–688.

———. 2000. From Nash and Brown to Maynard Smith: Equilibria, dynamics, and ESS. *Selection* 1: 81–88.

Hofbauer, J., and E. Hopkins. 2005. Learning in perturbed asymmetric games. *Games and Economic Behavior* 52: 133–152.

Hofbauer, J., and L. A. Imhof. 2009. Time averages, recurrence, and transience in the stochastic replicator dynamics. *Annals of Applied Probability* 19: 1347–1368.

Hofbauer, J., J. Mallet-Paret, and H. L. Smith. 1991. Stable periodic solutions for the hypercycle system. *Journal of Dynamics and Differential Equations* 3: 423–436.

Hofbauer, J., J. Oechssler, and F. Riedel. 2009. Brown–von Neumann–Nash dynamics: The continuous strategy case. *Games and Economic Behavior* 65: 406–429.

Hofbauer, J., and W. H. Sandholm. 2002. On the global convergence of stochastic fictitious play. *Econometrica* 70: 2265–2294.

———. 2007. Evolution in games with randomly disturbed payoffs. *Journal of Economic Theory* 132: 47–69.

———. 2009. Stable games and their dynamics. *Journal of Economic Theory* 144: 1665–1693.

———. 2010. Survival of dominated strategies under evolutionary dynamics. *Theoretical Economics*, forthcoming.

Hofbauer, J., P. Schuster, and K. Sigmund. 1979. A note on evolutionarily stable strategies and game dynamics. *Journal of Theoretical Biology* 81: 609–612.

———. 1981. Competition and cooperation in catalytic self-replication. *Journal of Mathematical Biology* 11: 155–168.

Hofbauer, J., and K. Sigmund. 1988. *Theory of Evolution and Dynamical Systems*. Cambridge: Cambridge University Press.

———. 1998. *Evolutionary Games and Population Dynamics*. Cambridge: Cambridge University Press.

———. 2003. Evolutionary game dynamics. *Bulletin of the American Mathematical Society, New Series* 40: 479–519.

Hofbauer, J., and G. Sorger. 1999. Perfect foresight and equilibrium selection in symmetric potential games. *Journal of Economic Theory* 85: 1–23.

Hofbauer, J., and S. Sorin. 2006. Best response dynamics for continuous zero-sum games. *Discrete and Continuous Dynamical Systems B* 6: 215–224.

Hofbauer, J., S. Sorin, and Y. Viossat. 2009. Time average replicator and best-reply dynamics. *Mathematics of Operations Research* 34: 263–269.

Hofbauer, J., and J. M. Swinkels. 1996. A universal Shapley example. Unpublished manuscript, University of Vienna and Northwestern University.

Hofbauer, J., and J. W. Weibull. 1996. Evolutionary selection against dominated strategies. *Journal of Economic Theory* 71: 558–573.

Hopkins, E. 1999. A note on best response dynamics. *Games and Economic Behavior* 29: 138–150.

———. 2002. Two competing models of how people learn in games. *Econometrica* 70: 2141–2166.

Hopkins, E., and R. M. Seymour. 2002. The stability of price dispersion under seller and consumer learning. *International Economic Review* 43: 1157–1190.

Horn, R. A., and C. R. Johnson. 1985. *Matrix Analysis*. Cambridge: Cambridge University Press.

Huck, S., and J. Oechssler. 1999. The indirect evolutionary approach to explaining fair allocations. *Games and Economic Behavior* 28: 13–24.

Hurkens, S. 1995. Learning by forgetful players. *Games and Economic Behavior* 11: 304–329.

Hutson, V. 1984. A theorem on average Lyapunov functions. *Monatshefte für Mathematik* 98: 267–275.

Hutson, V., and K. Schmitt. 1992. Permanence and the dynamics of biological systems. *Mathematical Biosciences* 111: 1–71.

Imhof, L. A. 2005. The long-run behavior of the stochastic replicator dynamics. *Annals of Applied Probability* 15: 1019–1045.

Jackson, M. O. 2008. *Social and Economic Networks*. Princeton, N.J.: Princeton University Press.

Jacobsen, H. J., M. Jensen, and B. Sloth. 2001. Evolutionary learning in signalling games. *Games and Economic Behavior* 34: 34–63.

Jordan, J. S. 1993. Three problems in learning mixed-strategy Nash equilibria. *Games and Economic Behavior* 5: 368–386.

Josephson, J. 2008. Stochastic better-reply dynamics in finite games. *Economic Theory* 35: 381–389.

References

Josephson, J., and A. Matros. 2004. Stochastic imitation in finite games. *Games and Economic Behavior* 49: 244–259.

Kandori, M. 1997. Evolutionary game theory in economics. In *Advances in Economics and Econometrics: Theory and Applications*, ed. D. M. Kreps and K. F. Wallis, vol. 1, 243–277. Cambridge: Cambridge University Press.

Kandori, M., G. J. Mailath, and R. Rob. 1993. Learning, mutation, and long-run equilibria in games. *Econometrica* 61: 29–56.

Kandori, M., and R. Rob. 1995. Evolution of equilibria in the long run: A general theory and applications. *Journal of Economic Theory* 65: 383–414.

———. 1998. Bandwagon effects and long-run technology choice. *Games and Economic Behavior* 22: 84–120.

Kandori, M., R. Serrano, and O. Volij. 2008. Decentralized trade, random utility, and the evolution of social welfare. *Journal of Economic Theory* 140: 328–338.

Kaniovski, Y. M., and H. P. Young. 1995. Learning dynamics in games with stochastic perturbations. *Games and Economic Behavior* 11: 330–363.

Khan, M. A., and Y. Sun. 2002. Non-cooperative games with many players. In *Handbook of Game Theory with Economic Applications*, ed. R. J. Aumann and S. Hart, vol. 3, 1761–1808. Amsterdam: Elsevier.

Kim, Y.-G., and J. Sobel 1995. An evolutionary approach to pre-play communication. *Econometrica* 63: 1181–1193.

Kimura, M. 1958. On the change of population fitness by natural selection. *Heredity* 12: 145–167.

Koçkesen, L., E. A. Ok, and R. Sethi. 2000. The strategic advantage of negatively interdependent preferences. *Journal of Economic Theory* 92: 274–299.

Kojima, F. 2006a. Risk dominance and perfect foresight dynamics in n-player games. *Journal of Economic Theory* 128: 255–273.

———. 2006b. Stability and instability of the unbeatable strategy in dynamic processes. *International Journal of Economic Theory* 2: 41–53.

Kojima, F., and S. Takahashi. 2007. Anti-coordination games and dynamic stability. *International Game Theory Review* 9: 667–688.

———. 2008. p-dominance and perfect foresight dynamics. *Journal of Economic Behavior and Organization* 67: 689–701.

Kosfeld, M. 2002. Stochastic strategy adjustment in coordination games. *Economic Theory* 20: 321–339.

Koutsoupias, E., and C. Papadimitriou. 1999. Worst-case equilibria. In *Proceedings of the 16th Annual Symposium on Theoretical Aspects of Computer Science (STACS '99)*, 404–413. Lecture Notes in Computer Science 1563. Berlin: Springer.

Krantz, S. G., and H. R. Parks. 1999. *The Geometry of Domains in Space*. Boston: Birkhäuser.

Krishna, V., and T. Sjöström. 1998. On the convergence of fictitious play. *Mathematics of Operations Research* 23: 479–511.

Kuhn, H. W. 2003. *Lectures on the Theory of Games*. Princeton, N.J.: Princeton University Press.

Kukushkin, N. S. 2004. Best response dynamics in finite games with additive aggregation. *Games and Economic Behavior* 48: 94–110.

Kuran, T., and W. H. Sandholm. 2008. Cultural integration and its discontents. *Review of Economic Studies* 75: 201–228.

Kurtz, T. G. 1970. Solutions of ordinary differential equations as limits of pure jump Markov processes. *Journal of Applied Probability* 7: 49–58.

———. 1976. Limit theorems and diffusion approximations for density dependent Markov processes. In *Stochastic Systems, Modeling Identification and Optimization I*, ed. R.J.B. Wets, 67–78 .Mathematical Programming Study 5. Amsterdam: Elsevier.

Kuzmics, C. 2004. Stochastic evolutionary stability in extensive form games of perfect information. *Games and Economic Behavior* 48: 321–336.

Lahkar, R. 2008. The dynamic instability of dispersed price equilibria. Unpublished manuscript, Institute for Financial Management and Research.

Lahkar, R., and W. H. Sandholm. 2008. The projection dynamic and the geometry of population games. *Games and Economic Behavior* 64: 565–590.

Lahkar, R. and R. M. Seymour. 2008. The evolution of mixed strategies in population games. Unpublished manuscript, Institute for Financial Management and Research and University College London.

Lang, S. 1997. *Undergraduate Analysis*. 2d ed. New York: Springer.

Lax, P. D. 2007. *Linear Algebra and Its Applications*. 2d ed. New York: Wiley.

Leonard, R. J. 1994. Reading Cournot, reading Nash: The creation and stabilization of Nash equilibrium. *Economic Journal* 104: 492–511.

Luce, R. D., and H. Raiffa. 1957. *Games and Decisions: Introduction and Critical Survey*. New York: Wiley.

Mailath, G. J. 1998. Do people play Nash equilibrium? Lessons from evolutionary game theory. *Journal of Economic Literature* 36: 1347–1374.

Mailath, G. J., and L. Samuelson. 2006. *Repeated Games and Reputations: Long-Run Relationships*. Oxford: Oxford University Press.

Marden, J. R., G. Arslan, and J. S. Shamma. 2009. Cooperative control and potential games. *IEEE Transactions on Systems, Man and Cybernetics. Part B: Cybernetics* 39: 1393–1407.

Marden, J. R., and J. S. Shamma. 2008. Revisiting log-linear learning: Asynchrony, completeness and a payoff-based implementation. Unpublished manuscript, Georgia Institute of Technology and California Institute of Technology.

Marden, J. R., H. P. Young, G. Arslan, and J. S. Shamma. 2009. Payoff-based dynamics for multi-player weakly acyclic games. *SIAM Journal on Control and Optimization* 48: 373–396.

Marsden, J. E., and T. S. Ratiu. 2002. *Introduction to Mechanics and Symmetry: A Basic Exposition of Classical Mechanical Systems*. 2d ed. Berlin: Springer.

Maruta, T. 1997. On the relationship between risk dominance and stochastic stability. *Games and Economic Behavior* 19: 221–234.

References

———. 2002. Binary games with state dependent stochastic choice. *Journal of Economic Theory* 103: 351–376.

Mas-Colell, A. 1984. On a theorem of Schmeidler. *Journal of Mathematical Economics* 13: 201–206.

Mathevet, L. 2007. Supermodular Bayesian implementation: Learning and incentive design. *Theoretical Economics*, forthcoming.

Matsui, A. 1991. Cheap-talk and cooperation in a society. *Journal of Economic Theory* 54: 245–258.

———. 1992. Best response dynamics and socially stable strategies. *Journal of Economic Theory* 57: 343–362.

Matsui, A., and K. Matsuyama. 1995. An approach to equilibrium selection. *Journal of Economic Theory* 65: 415–434.

Matsui, A., and D. Oyama. 2006. Rationalizable foresight dynamics. *Games and Economic Behavior* 56: 299–322.

Maynard Smith, J. 1972. Game theory and the evolution of fighting. In *On Evolution*, 8–28. Edinburgh: Edinburgh University Press.

———. 1974. The theory of games and the evolution of animal conflicts. *Journal of Theoretical Biology* 47: 209–221.

———. 1982. *Evolution and the Theory of Games*. Cambridge: Cambridge University Press.

Maynard Smith, J., and G. R. Price. 1973. The logic of animal conflict. *Nature* 246: 15–18.

McFadden, D. 1981. Econometric models of probabilistic choice. In *Structural Analysis of Discrete Data with Econometric Applications*, ed. C. F. Manski and D. McFadden, 198–272. Cambridge, Mass.: MIT Press.

McKelvey, R. D., and T. R. Palfrey. 1995. Quantal response equilibria for normal form games. *Games and Economic Behavior* 10: 6–38.

Miękisz, J. 2004. Statistical mechanics of spatial evolutionary games. *Journal of Physics A* 37: 9891–9906.

———. 2008. Evolutionary game theory and population dynamics. In *Multiscale Problems in the Life Sciences*, ed. V. Capasso and M. Lachowicz, 269–316. Berlin: Springer.

Milgrom, P., and J. Roberts. 1990. Rationalizability, learning, and equilibrium in games with strategic complementarities. *Econometrica* 58: 1255–1278.

———. 1991. Adaptive and sophisticated learning in normal form games. *Games and Economic Behavior* 3: 82–100.

Milgrom, P., and C. Shannon. 1994. Monotone comparative statics. *Econometrica* 62: 157–180.

Milgrom, P., and R. J. Weber. 1985. Distributional strategies for games with incomplete information. *Mathematics of Operations Research* 10: 619–632.

Milnor, J. W. 1965. *Topology from the Differentiable Viewpoint*. Princeton, N.J.: Princeton University Press.

Minty, G. J. 1967. On the generalization of a direct method of the calculus of variations. *Bulletin of the American Mathematical Society* 73: 315–321.

Miyasawa, K. 1961. On the convergence of the learning process in 2×2 non-zero-sum two-person games. Research memorandum 33, Econometric Research Program, Princeton University.

Möbius, M. M. 2000. The formation of ghettos as a local interaction phenomenon. Unpublished manuscript, Massachusetts Institute of Technology.

Monderer, D., and A. Sela. 1997. Fictitious play and no-cycling conditions. Unpublished manuscript, Technion (Israel Institute of Technology).

Monderer, D., and L. S. Shapley. 1996a. Fictitious play property for games with identical interests. *Journal of Economic Theory* 68: 258–265.

———. 1996b. Potential games. *Games and Economic Behavior* 14: 124–143.

Montgomery, J. 2009. Intergenerational cultural transmission as an evolutionary game. *American Economic Journal: Microeconomics*, forthcoming.

Moran, P.A.P. 1962. *The Statistical Processes of Evolutionary Theory.* Oxford: Clarendon Press.

Morris, S. 2000. Contagion. *Review of Economic Studies* 67: 57–78.

Morris, S., R. Rob, and H. S. Shin. 1995. p-dominance and belief potential. *Econometrica* 63: 145–157.

Myatt, D. P., and C. C. Wallace. 2003. A multinomial probit model of stochastic evolution. *Journal of Economic Theory* 113: 286–301.

———. 2008a. An evolutionary analysis of the volunteer's dilemma. *Games and Economic Behavior* 62: 67–76.

———. 2008b. When does one bad apple spoil the barrel? An evolutionary analysis of collective action. *Review of Economic Studies* 75: 499–527.

———. 2009. Evolution, teamwork, and collective action: Production targets in the private provision of public good. *Economic Journal* 119: 61–90.

Myerson, R. 1991. *Game Theory: Analysis of Conflict.* Cambridge, Mass.: Harvard University Press.

Nachbar, J. H. 1990. "Evolutionary" selection dynamics in games: Convergence and limit properties. *International Journal of Game Theory* 19: 59–89.

Nagurney, A. 1999. *Network Economics: A Variational Inequality Approach.* 2d ed. Dordrecht: Kluwer.

Nagurney, A., and D. Zhang. 1996. *Projected Dynamical Systems and Variational Inequalities with Applications.* Dordrecht: Kluwer.

———. 1997. Projected dynamical systems in the formulation, stability analysis, and computation of fixed demand traffic network equilibria. *Transportation Science* 31: 147–158.

Nash, J. F. 1950a. Equilibrium points in n-person games. *Proceedings of the National Academy of Sciences* 36: 48–49.

———. 1950b. Non-cooperative games. Ph.D. diss., Princeton University. Reprinted in *The Essential John Nash*, ed. H. W. Kuhn and S. Nasar, 51–83, Princeton, N.J., Princeton University Press, 2002.

Nash, J. F. 1951. Non-cooperative games. *Annals of Mathematics* 54: 287–295.

Nemytskii, V. V., and V. V. Stepanov. 1960. *Qualitative Theory of Differential Equations.* Princeton, N.J.: Princeton University Press.

References

Nöldeke, G., and L. Samuelson. 1993. An evolutionary analysis of backward and forward induction. *Games and Economic Behavior* 5: 425–454.

———. 1997. A dynamic model of equilibrium selection in signaling markets. *Journal of Economic Theory* 73: 118–156.

Norman, T.W.L. 2008. Dynamically stable sets in infinite strategy spaces. *Games and Economic Behavior* 62: 610–627.

Norris, J. R. 1997. *Markov Chains*. Cambridge: Cambridge University Press.

Nowak, M. A. 2006. *Evolutionary Dynamics: Exploring the Equations of Life*. Cambridge, Mass.: Harvard University Press.

Nowak, M. A., and R. M. May. 1992. Evolutionary games and spatial chaos. *Nature* 359: 826–829.

———. 1993. The spatial dilemmas of evolution. *International Journal of Bifurcation and Chaos* 3: 35–78.

Nowak, M. A., A. Sasaki, C. Taylor, and D. Fudenberg. 2004. Emergence of cooperation and evolutionary stability in finite populations. *Nature* 428: 646–650.

Oechssler, J., and F. Riedel. 2001. Evolutionary dynamics on infinite strategy spaces. *Economic Theory* 17: 141–162.

———. 2002. On the dynamic foundation of evolutionary stability in continuous models. *Journal of Economic Theory* 107: 223–252.

Ok, E. A. 2007. *Real Analysis with Economic Applications*. Princeton, N.J.: Princeton University Press.

Ok, E. A., and F. Vega-Redondo. 2001. On the evolution of individualistic preferences: An incomplete information scenario. *Journal of Economic Theory* 97: 231–254.

Okada, D., and O. Tercieux. 2009. Log-linear dynamics and local potential. Unpublished manuscript, Rutgers University and Paris School of Economics.

Osborne, M. 2004. *An Introduction to Game Theory*. Oxford: Oxford University Press.

Oyama, D. 2002. p-dominance and equilibrium selection under perfect foresight dynamics. *Journal of Economic Theory* 107: 288–310.

Oyama, D., S. Takahashi, and J. Hofbauer. 2008. Monotone methods for equilibrium selection under perfect foresight dynamics. *Theoretical Economics* 3: 155–192.

Oyama, D., and O. Tercieux. 2009. Iterated potential and robustness of equilibria. *Journal of Economic Theory* 144: 1726–1769.

Oyama, D., W. H. Sandholm, and O. Tercieux. 2010. Sampling best response dynamics and deterministic equilibrium selection. Unpublished manuscript, Hitotsubashi University, University of Wisconsin, and Paris School of Economics.

Papadimitriou, C. H. 2001. Algorithms, games, and the Internet. In *Proceedings of the 33d Annual ACM Symposium on Theory of Computing (STOC '01)*, 749–753.

Patriksson, M. 1994. *The Traffic Assignment Problem: Models and Methods*. Utrecht: VSP.

Pawlowitsch, C. 2008. Why evolution does not always lead to an optimal signaling system. *Games and Economic Behavior* 63: 203–226.

Pemantle, R. 2007. A survey of random processes with reinforcement. *Probability Surveys* 4: 1–79.

Pohley, H.-J., and B. Thomas. 1983. Nonlinear ESS models and frequency dependent selection. *BioSystems* 16: 87–100.

Ponti, G. 2000. Cycles of learning in the centipede game. *Games and Economic Behavior* 30: 115–141.

Rhode, P., and M. Stegeman. 1996. A comment on "Learning, mutation, and long-run equilibria in games." *Econometrica* 64: 443–449.

Ritzberger, K. 1994. The theory of normal form games from the differentiable viewpoint. *International Journal of Game Theory* 23: 207–236.

———. 2002. *Foundations of Noncooperative Game Theory.* Oxford: Oxford University Press.

Ritzberger, K., and J. W. Weibull. 1995. Evolutionary selection in normal form games. *Econometrica* 63: 1371–1399.

Roberts, A.W., and D. E. Varberg. 1973. *Convex Functions.* New York: Academic Press.

Robinson, C. 1995. *Dynamical Systems: Stability, Symbolic Dynamics, and Chaos.* Boca Raton, Fla.: CRC Press.

Robinson, J. 1951. An iterative method of solving a game. *Annals of Mathematics* 54: 296–301.

Robles, J. 1998. Evolution with changing mutation rates. *Journal of Economic Theory* 79: 207–223.

———. 2008. Evolution, bargaining, and time preferences. *Economic Theory* 35: 19–36.

Robson, A. 1990. Efficiency in evolutionary games: Darwin, Nash, and the secret handshake. *Journal of Theoretical Biology* 144: 379–396.

Robson, A., and F. Vega-Redondo. 1996. Efficient equilibrium selection in evolutionary games with random matching. *Journal of Economic Theory* 70: 65–92.

Rockafellar, R. T. 1970. *Convex Analysis.* Princeton, N.J.: Princeton University Press.

Rosenthal, R. W. 1973. A class of games possessing pure strategy Nash equilibria. *International Journal of Game Theory* 2: 65–67.

Roth, G., and W. H. Sandholm. 2010. Stochastic approximations with constant step size and differential inclusions. Université de Neuchâtel and University of Wisconsin.

Roughgarden, T. 2005. *Selfish Routing and the Price of Anarchy.* Cambridge, Mass.: MIT Press.

Roughgarden, T. 2009. Intrinsic robustness of the price of anarchy. In *Proceedings of the 41st Annual ACM Symposium on Theory of Computing (STOC '09)*, 513–522. New York: ACM.

Roughgarden, T., and E. Tardos. 2002. How bad is selfish routing? *Journal of the ACM* 49: 236–259.

———. 2004. Bounding the inefficiency of equilibria in nonatomic congestion games. *Games and Economic Behavior* 49: 389–403.

Samuelson, L. 1994. Stochastic stability in games with alternative best replies. *Journal of Economic Theory* 64: 35–65.

References

———. 1997. *Evolutionary Games and Equilibrium Selection.* Cambridge, Mass.: MIT Press.

Samuelson, L., and J. Zhang. 1992. Evolutionary stability in asymmetric games. *Journal of Economic Theory* 57: 363–391.

Sandholm, W. H. 1998. Simple and clever decision rules in a model of evolution. *Economics Letters* 61: 165–170.

———. 2001a. Potential games with continuous player sets. *Journal of Economic Theory* 97: 81–108.

———. 2001b. Preference evolution, two-speed dynamics, and rapid social change. *Review of Economic Dynamics* 4: 637–639.

———. 2002. Evolutionary implementation and congestion pricing. *Review of Economic Studies* 69: 81–108.

———. 2003. Evolution and equilibrium under inexact information. *Games and Economic Behavior* 44: 343–378.

———. 2005a. Excess payoff dynamics and other well-behaved evolutionary dynamics. *Journal of Economic Theory* 124: 149–170.

———. 2005b. Negative externalities and evolutionary implementation. *Review of Economic Studies* 72: 885–915.

———. 2006. A probabilistic interpretation of integrability for game dynamics. Unpublished manuscript, University of Wisconsin.

———. 2007a. Evolution in Bayesian games. II: Stability of purified equilibria. *Journal of Economic Theory* 136: 641–667.

———. 2007b. Pigouvian pricing and stochastic evolutionary implementation. *Journal of Economic Theory* 132: 367–382.

———. 2007c. Simple formulas for stationary distributions and stochastically stable states. *Games and Economic Behavior* 59: 154–162.

———. 2008. "Strategic Learning and Its Limits" by H. Peyton Young. Book Review. *Games and Economic Behavior* 63: 417–420.

———. 2009a. Evolutionary game theory. In *Encyclopedia of Complexity and Systems Science,* ed. R. A. Meyers, 3176–3205. Heidelberg: Springer.

———. 2009b. Large population potential games. *Journal of Economic Theory* 144: 1710–1725.

———. 2010a. Decompositions and potentials for normal form games. *Games and Economic Behavior*, forthcoming.

———. 2010b. Local stability under evolutionary game dynamics. *Theoretical Economics* 5: 27–50.

———. 2010c. Orders of limits for stationary distributions, stochastic dominance, and stochastic stability. *Theoretical Economics* 5: 1–26.

———. 2010d. Pairwise comparison dynamics and evolutionary foundations for Nash equilibrium. *Games* 1: 3–17.

———. 2010e. Stochastic imitative game dynamics with committed agents. Unpublished manuscript, University of Wisconsin.

Sandholm, W. H., E. Dokumacı, and F. Franchetti. 2010. Dynamo: Diagrams for evolutionary game dynamics. Software. <http://www.ssc.wisc.edu/~whs/dynamo>.

Sandholm, W. H., E. Dokumacı, and R. Lahkar. 2008. The projection dynamic and the replicator dynamic. *Games and Economic Behavior* 64: 666–683.

Sandholm, W. H., and A. Pauzner. 1998. Evolution, population growth, and history dependence. *Games and Economic Behavior* 22: 84–120.

Sato, Y., E. Akiyama, and J. D. Farmer. 2002. Chaos in learning a simple two-person game. *Proceedings of the National Academy of Sciences* 99: 4748–4751.

Schlag, K. H. 1998. Why imitate, and if so, how? A boundedly rational approach to multi-armed bandits. *Journal of Economic Theory* 78: 130–156.

Schmeidler, D. 1973. Equilibrium points of non-atomic games. *Journal of Statistical Physics* 7: 295–300.

Schnabl, W., P. F. Stadler, C. Forst, and P. Schuster, 1991. Full characterization of a strange attractor: Chaotic dynamics in low-dimensional replicator systems. *Physica D* 48: 65–90.

Schreiber, S. J. 2000. Criteria for C^r robust permanence. *Journal of Differential Equations* 162: 400–426.

Schuster, P., and K. Sigmund. 1983. Replicator dynamics. *Journal of Theoretical Biology* 100: 533–538.

Schuster, P., K. Sigmund, J. Hofbauer, and R. Wolff. 1981a. Self-regulation of behaviour in animal societies. I: Symmetric contests. *Biological Cybernetics* 40: 1–8.

———. 1981b. Self-regulation of behaviour in animal societies. II: Games between two populations without self-interaction. *Biological Cybernetics* 40: 9–15.

Schuster, P., K. Sigmund, J. Hofbauer, R. Wolff, R. Gottlieb, and P. Merz. 1981c. Self-regulation of behaviour in animal societies. III: Games between two populations with self-interaction. *Biological Cybernetics* 40: 16–25.

Schuster, P., K. Sigmund, and R. Wolff. 1979. Dynamical systems under constant organization. III. Cooperative and competitive behavior of hypercycles. *Journal of Differential Equations* 32: 357–368.

Selten, R. 1980. A note on evolutionarily stable strategies in asymmetric animal conflicts. *Journal of Theoretical Biology* 84: 93–101.

Seneta, E. 1981. *Non-negative Matrices and Markov Chains.* 2d ed. New York: Springer.

Sethi, R. 1999. Evolutionary stability and media of exchange. *Journal of Economic Behavior and Organization* 40: 233–254.

Sethi, R., and E. Somanathan. 1996. The evolution of social norms in common property resource use. *American Economic Review* 86: 766–788.

———. 2001. Preference evolution and reciprocity. *Journal of Economic Theory* 97: 273–297.

Shahshahani, S. 1979. A new mathematical framework for the study of linkage and selection. *Memoirs of the American Mathematical Society*, 211.

Shapley, L. S. 1964. Some topics in two person games. In *Advances in Game Theory*, ed. M. Dresher, L. S. Shapley, and A. W. Tucker, 1–28. Princeton, N.J.: Princeton University Press.

Sheffi, Y. 1985. *Urban Transportation Networks: Equilibrium Analysis with Mathematical Programming Methods*. Englewood Cliffs, N.J.: Prentice-Hall.

Sigmund, K. 2010. *The Calculus of Selfishness*. Princeton, N.J.: Princeton University Press.

Skyrms, B. 1990. *The Dynamics of Rational Deliberation*. Cambridge, Mass.: Harvard University Press.

———. 1992. Chaos in game dynamics. *Journal of Logic, Language, and Information* 1: 111–130.

———. 2002. Signals, evolution, and the explanatory power of transient information. *Philosophy of Science* 69: 407–428.

Slade, M. E. 1994. What does an oligopoly maximize? *Journal of Industrial Economics* 42: 45–51.

Smale, S. 1967. Differentiable dynamical systems. *Bulletin of the American Mathematical Society* 73: 747–817.

Smirnov, G. V. 2002. *Introduction to the Theory of Differential Inclusions*. Providence, R.I.: American Mathematical Society.

Smith, H. L. 1995. *Monotone Dynamical Systems: An Introduction to the Theory of Competitive and Cooperative Systems*. Providence, R.I.: American Mathematical Society.

Smith, M. J. 1984. The stability of a dynamic model of traffic assignment: An application of a method of Lyapunov. *Transportation Science* 18: 245–252.

Sparrow, C., S. van Strien, and C. Harris. 2008. Fictitious play in 3×3 games: The transition between periodic and chaotic behavior. *Games and Economic Behavior* 63: 259–291.

Stroock, D.W. 2005. *An Introduction to Markov Processes*. Berlin: Springer.

Swinkels, J. M. 1992. Evolutionary stability with equilibrium entrants. *Journal of Economic Theory* 57: 306–332.

———. 1993. Adjustment dynamics and rational play in games. *Games and Economic Behavior* 5: 455–484.

Szabó, G., and G. Fáth. 2007. Evolutionary games on graphs. *Physics Reports* 446: 97–216.

Sznitman, A. 1991. Topics in propagation of chaos. In *Ecole d'Eté de Probabilités de Saint-Flour*, ed. P. L. Hennequin, vol. 19, 167–251. Berlin: Springer.

Takahashi, S. 2008. Perfect foresight dynamics in games with linear incentives and time symmetry. *International Journal of Game Theory* 37: 15–38.

Tanabe, Y. 2006. The propagation of chaos for interacting individuals in a large population. *Mathematical Social Sciences* 51: 125–152.

Taylor, C., D. Fudenberg, A. Sasaki, and M. A. Nowak. 2004. Evolutionary game dynamics in finite populations. *Bulletin of Mathematical Biology* 66: 1621–1644.

Taylor, P. D. 1979. Evolutionarily stable strategies with two types of players. *Journal of Applied Probability* 16: 76–83.

Taylor, P. D., and L. Jonker. 1978. Evolutionarily stable strategies and game dynamics. *Mathematical Biosciences* 40: 145–156.

Thomas, B. 1984. Evolutionary stability: States and strategies. *Theoretical Population Biology* 26: 49–67.

———. 1985. On evolutionarily stable sets. *Journal of Mathematical Biology* 22: 105–115.

Topkis, D. 1979. Equilibrium points in non-zero-sum n-person submodular games. *SIAM Journal on Control and Optimization* 17: 773–787.

———. 1998. *Supermodularity and Complementarity.* Princeton, N.J.: Princeton University Press.

Trapa, P. E., and M. A. Nowak. 2000. Nash equilibria for an evolutionary language game. *Journal of Mathematical Biology* 41: 172–188.

Traulsen, A., and C. Hauert. 2009. Stochastic evolutionary game dynamics. In *Reviews of Nonlinear Dynamics and Complexity,* ed. H. G. Schuster, vol. 2, 25–61. New York: Wiley.

Tröger, T. 2002. Why sunk costs matter for bargaining outcomes: An evolutionary approach. *Journal of Economic Theory* 102: 28–53.

Tsakas, E., and M. Voorneveld. 2009. The target projection dynamic. *Games and Economic Behavior* 67: 708–719.

Ui, T. 1998. Robustness of stochastic stability. Unpublished manuscript, Bank of Japan.

———. 2000. A Shapley value representation of potential games. *Games and Economic Behavior* 31: 121–135.

van Damme, E. 1991. *Stability and Perfection of Nash Equilibria.* 2d ed. Berlin: Springer.

van Strien, S. 2009. Hamiltonian flows with random walk behavior originating from zero-sum games and fictitious play. Unpublished manuscript, University of Warwick.

van Strien, S., and C. Sparrow. 2009. Fictitious play in 3×3 games: Chaos and dithering behavior. Unpublished manuscript, University of Warwick.

Vega-Redondo, F. 1996. *Evolution, Games, and Economic Behaviour.* Oxford: Oxford University Press.

———. 1997. The evolution of Walrasian behavior. *Econometrica* 65: 375–384.

———. 2007. *Complex Social Networks.* Cambridge: Cambridge University Press.

Vickers, G. T., and C. Cannings. 1987. On the definition of an evolutionarily stable strategy. *Journal of Theoretical Biology* 129: 349–353.

Viossat, Y. 2007. The replicator dynamics does not lead to correlated equilibria. *Games and Economic Behavior* 59: 397–407.

———. 2008. Evolutionary dynamics may eliminate all strategies used in correlated equilibria. *Mathematical Social Sciences* 56: 27–43.

Vives, X. 1990. Nash equilibrium with strategic complementarities. *Journal of Mathematical Economics* 19: 305–321.

———. 2000. *Oligopoly Pricing: Old Ideas and New Tools.* Cambridge, Mass.: MIT Press.

References

———. 2005. Complementarities and games: New developments. *Journal of Economic Literature* 43: 437–479. Corrigendum, 44 (2006), 3.

von Neumann, J., and O. Morgenstern. 1944. *Theory of Games and Economic Behavior*. Princeton, N.J.: Prentice-Hall.

Voorneveld, M. 2004. Preparation. *Games and Economic Behavior* 48: 403–414.

———. 2005. Consistent retracts and preparation. *Games and Economic Behavior* 51: 228–232.

Wardrop, J. G. 1952. Some theoretical aspects of road traffic research. *Proceedings of the Institution of Civil Engineers*, pt II, vol. 1, 325–378.

Wärneryd, K. 1993. Cheap talk, coordination, and evolutionary stability. *Games and Economic Behavior* 5: 532–546.

Weibull, J. W. 1994. The "as if" approach to game theory: Three positive results and four obstacles. *European Economic Review* 38: 868–881.

———. 1995. *Evolutionary Game Theory*. Cambridge, Mass.: MIT Press.

———. 1996. The mass action interpretation. Excerpt from "The work of John Nash in game theory: Nobel Seminar, December 8, 1994." *Journal of Economic Theory* 69: 165–171.

———. 2002. What have we learned from evolutionary game theory so far? Unpublished manuscript, Stockholm School of Economics.

Young, H. P. 1993a. The evolution of conventions. *Econometrica* 61: 57–84.

———. 1993b. An evolutionary model of bargaining. *Journal of Economic Theory* 59: 145–168.

———. 1998a. Conventional contracts. *Review of Economic Studies* 65: 773–792.

———. 1998b. *Individual Strategy and Social Structure*. Princeton, N.J.: Princeton University Press.

———. 2001. The dynamics of conformity. In *Social Dynamics*, ed. S. N. Durlauf and H. P. Young, 133–153. Cambridge, Mass.: MIT Press.

———. 2004. *Strategic Learning and Its Limits*. Oxford: Oxford University Press.

Zeeman, E. C. 1980. Population dynamics from game theory. In *Global Theory of Dynamical Systems*, ed. Z. Nitecki and C. Robinson, 472–497. Lecture Notes in Mathematics 819. Berlin: Springer.

Zhang, J. 2004a. A dynamic model of residential segregation. *Journal of Mathematical Sociology* 28: 147–170.

———. 2004b. Residential segregation in an all-integrationist world. *Journal of Economic Behavior and Organization* 24: 533–550.

Zusai, D. 2010. The tempered best response dynamic. Unpublished manuscript, University of Wisconsin.

Notation Index

Symbol	Description	Page
A	payoff matrix for a symmetric normal form game	25
$\mathcal{A}$	attractor	331
$\mathcal{A}^*$	dual repellor	360
b^p	pure best response correspondence for population p	23
$b_x(y)$	invasion barrier of state x against state y	276
B^p	mixed best response correspondence	23
$\tilde{B}^p$	perturbed best response function for population p	189
$\underline{B}^p(x)$	minimal mixed best response to state x for population p	99
$\bar{B}^p(x)$	maximal mixed best response to state x for population p	99
$B(\mathcal{A})$	basin of attractor $\mathcal{A}$	331
c_ϕ	cost function for facility ϕ	28
c_{xy}	cost of transition from state x to state y	502
c_{xy}^-	lenient cost of transition from state x to state y	530
c_{QR}	cost of transition from recurrent class Q to recurrent class R	511
c_{QR}^-	modified cost of transition from recurrent class Q to recurrent class R	527
$\bar{C}$	social cost function	68
C_x^*	minimal cost of any x-tree	503
C^*	minimal cost of any tree	503
$C(\phi)$	set of initial conditions from which flow ϕ converges	267
$C(\gamma)$	cost of graph γ	503
$C^-(\pi)$	modified cost of path π	528

C_i^p	cost function for strategy $i \in S^p$	68
$C_{[0,T]}$	space of continuous functions on $[0, T]$	234
$C\mathcal{R}$	set of chain recurrent states	262
D	deterministic evolutionary dynamic	129
e^A	matrix exponential	311
e_i	standard basis vector in $\mathbf{R}^n$	23
e_i^p	standard basis vector in $\mathbf{R}^n$	55
$\mathbb{E}$	expectation operator	384
$E_{x^*}(x)$	squared distance of x from x^*	233
f	full potential function	54
f	potential function	73
$\tilde{f}$	perturbed potential function	227
f^η	logit potential function	227
f^N	finite-population potential function	424
F	population game/payoff function	23
$\bar{F}$	aggregate payoff function	23
$\mathcal{F}$	set of Lipschitz continuous population games	129
$\mathcal{F}$	σ-algebra	385
F^N	finite-population game/payoff function	418
$\check{F}^N$	clever payoff function	419
F^p	payoff function for population p	23
$\bar{F}^p$	average payoff function for population p	23
$\hat{F}^p$	excess payoff function for population p	125
$\tilde{F}^p$	virtual payoff function for population p	197
F_i^p	payoff function for strategy $i \in S^p$	23
G	Lyapunov function for the best response dynamic in a stable game	243
$\tilde{G}$	Lyapunov function for perturbed best response dynamics in a stable game	244
$\tilde{G}^\eta$	Lyapunov function for the logit dynamic in a stable game	284
G_{x^*}	Lyapunov function for the best response dynamic for ESS x^*	289
G_i	advantage distribution of strategy i	488

Notation Index

$\bar{G}_i$	decumulative advantage distribution of strategy i	488
G_i^p	percentage growth rate function for strategy $i \in S^p$	162
h	entropy function	466
H	Akin transformation	229
H_{x*}	Lyapunov function for the replicator dynamic in a strictly stable game	234
i	strategy	22
I	ordinal potential function	480
$I_F(x)$	set of states that can strictly invade state x	85
$\bar{I}_F(x)$	set of states that can weakly invade state x	85
J	ordinal potential function	492
L	Lyapunov function	223
$L(X, Y)$	set of linear maps from X to Y	101
$L_s^2(X, Y)$	set of symmetric bilinear maps from $X \times X$ to Y	101
m^p	mass of population p	22
$\tilde{M}$	perturbed maximizer function	189
$\bar{M}$	restriction of $\tilde{M}$ to $\mathbf{R}_0^n$	190
M^p	maximizer correspondence for population p	178
$\tilde{M}^p$	perturbed maximizer function for population p	188
n	number of strategies for the society	22
n^p	number of strategies for population p	22
N	population size	121
$NX(x)$	normal cone of X at x	41
p	population	22
p	number of populations	22
p_i	transition probability for birth and death chain	436
p_x^N	transition probability for N-agent birth and death process	403
P	transition matrix of Markov chain or process	390
$\mathcal{P}$	society	22
$\mathbb{P}$	probability measure	383
P_Z	orthogonal projection onto subspace Z	46
P^N	transition matrix for $\{X_t^N\}$	369

P^N_{xy}	transition probability for $\{X^N_t\}$	369
$\mathbb{P}_x$	probability measure for Markov chain or process run from state x	434
$P(t)$	matrix of time t transition probabilities of Markov process	393
q_i	transition probability for birth and death chain	436
q^N_x	transition probability for N-agent birth and death process	403
Q	generator of Markov process	394
r	rate of decay function for double limits	458
r^N_x	rate of decay of $\mu^{N,\eta}_x$ in noise level η	455
$r^\eta(x)$	rate of decay of $\mu^{N,\eta}_x$ in population size N	456
$r_{ij}(\pi, x)$	conditional imitation rate from strategy i to strategy j	126
R	agents' clock rate	121
R	replicator dynamic	229
$\mathcal{R}$	set of recurrent states	261
$\mathfrak{R}$	set of recurrent classes	511
$\mathbf{R}^n_I$	set of vectors in $\mathbf{R}^n$ with all nonzero components in I	282
$\mathbf{R}^{np}_0$	tangent space of X^p	34
$\mathbf{R}^{np}_*$	complement of int $(\mathbf{R}^{np}_-)$	166
s^p	strategy for player p	22
S	set of pure strategy profiles	26
$S(x)$	support of state x	234
S^p	set of strategies for population or player p	22
S^{-p}	set of strategy profiles of player p's opponents	26
$\mathcal{T}$	set of continuous forward-time trajectories	129
T_x	set of x-trees	503
TX	tangent space of X	34
TX^p	tangent space of X^p	34
$TX(x)$	tangent cone of X at x	40
u_ϕ	utilization level of facility ϕ	28
U	normal form game	26
U^p	payoffs of player p	26
v	admissible deterministic perturbation	189

Notation Index

v_i^p	standard basis vector in $\mathbf{R}^{n^p}$	99
V	potential function for a normal form potential game	75
V	vector field defining a differential equation	131
V_F	mean dynamic in game F	130
W^p	auxiliary function for player p for a normal form potential game	75
x	social state	23
χ	population state in a two-strategy game	182
χ	social state after stochastic dominance transformation	254
$\underline{x}$	minimal social state	99
$\bar{x}$	maximal social state	99
x^p	population state	22
χ^p	population state after stochastic dominance transformation	254
$\underline{x}^p$	minimal population state	99
$\bar{x}^p$	maximal population state	99
x_i^p	mass of agents playing strategy $i \in S^p$	22
$\hat{x}_i^p$	percentage of agents playing strategy $i \in S^p$	153
$\{x_t\}$	deterministic solution trajectory	132
X	set of social states	23
X^p	set of population states	22
X_v	set of pure social states	23
X_y	set of states whose supports contain the support of y	234
X_v^p	set of pure population states	22
$\mathcal{X}$	portion of radius 2 sphere in $\mathbf{R}_+^n$	228
$\mathcal{X}$	state space of a Markov chain or process	390
X^N	set of social states in an N-agent population game	121
X_-^N	set of diminished population states	419
X_i^N	set of population states with at least one strategy i player	418
$\{X_t\}$	Markov chain or process	389
$\{X_t^N\}$	stochastic evolutionary process	369
$\{X_t^\varepsilon\}$	stochastic evolutionary process	502
$\{X_t^{N,\eta}\}$	stochastic evolutionary process	451

$\{X_t^{N,\varepsilon}\}$	stochastic evolutionary process	491
z	tangent vector in TX	34
z^p	tangent vector in TX^p	34
$\alpha(\xi)$	α-limit of the solution trajectory with initial condition ξ	535
γ^p	revision potential for population p	237
Γ	Lyapunov function for excess payoff dynamics in a stable game	241
δ_x	point mass at x	533
Δ	shift operator	464
Δ^p	set of mixed strategies for population p	23
ε	admissible stochastic perturbation	189
ε	mutation rate	399
ζ_x	normalized stochastic increment from state x	516
ζ_x^N	stochastic increment from state x	370
η	noise level	188
ι_n	nth root of unity	327
κ	cost function for noisy best response protocol	475
κ	cost function for noisy best response protocol, restrictive definition	500
$\tilde{\kappa}$	relative cost function for noisy best response protocol	478
λ	jump rate vector of Markov process	391
λ	Lebesgue measure	487
λ^p	rate of motion for population p under a target protocol	124
λ_x^N	jump rate for $\{X_t^N\}$	369
$\tilde{\mu}$	perturbed maximum function	215
μ	maximum function	243
μ	Lebesgue measure	324
μ	stationary distribution of a Markov chain or process	401
μ^N	stationary distribution of $\{X_t^N\}$	397
μ^ε	stationary distribution of $\{X_t^\varepsilon\}$	503
μ^*	limit of stationary distributions μ^ε	503
$\mu^{N,\eta}$	stationary distribution of $\{X_t^{N,\eta}\}$	451

Notation Index

$\mu^{N,\varepsilon}$	stationary distribution of $\{X_t^{N,\varepsilon}\}$	491
$\mu^{N,*}$	small noise limit of $\mu^{N,\eta}$	454
$\mu^{*,\eta}$	large population limit of $\mu^{N,\eta}$	456
Ξ	orthogonal projection onto $(TX^p)^\perp$	48
Ξ	orthogonal projection onto $TX^\perp$	48
π	payoff vector	126
π	initial distribution of Markov chain or process	390
$\hat{\pi}$	excess payoff vector	126
π^p	payoff vector for population p	121
Π_C	closest point projection onto set C	50
Π_{xy}	set of paths from state x to state y	511
Π_{QR}	set of paths from recurrent class Q to recurrent class R	511
ρ	profile of revision protocols	121
ρ^p	revision protocol for population p	121
$\rho_{ij}^p(\pi^p, x^p)$	conditional switch rate from strategy $i \in S^p$ to strategy $j \in S^p$	121
$\rho^p(\phi)$	set of population p strategies requiring facility ϕ	28
Υ_{x^*}	multiple of the mass on strategies outside the support of x^*	285
ϕ	facility	28
ϕ	flow	134
ϕ	semiflow	135
Φ	set of facilities	28
Φ	orthogonal projection onto TX^p	34
Φ	orthogonal projection onto TX	35
Φ_i^p	set of facilities required by strategy $i \in S^p$	28
σ^p	exact target protocol for population p	124
σ^η	noisy best response protocol with noise level η	474
σ^ε	noisy best response protocol with mutation rate ε	500
Σ	stochastic dominance operator on X^p	94
Σ	stochastic dominance operator on X	94
$\tilde{\Sigma}$	difference operator with range X^p	95
$\tilde{\Sigma}$	difference operator with range X	95
τ^p	target protocol for population p	124

τ_n	nth jump time of a Markov process	392
τ_x	x-tree	503
Ψ	Lyapunov function for pairwise comparison dynamics in a stable game	246
Ψ_{x^*}	Lyapunov function for pairwise comparison dynamics for ESS x^*	286
ω	element of sample space	383
$\omega(\xi)$	ω-limit of the solution trajectory with initial condition ξ	224
$\omega(U)$	ω-limit of the set of solution trajectories with initial conditions in U	360
Ω	null operator on TX	96
Ω	sample space	383
$\Omega(V_F)$	set of ω-limit points of $\dot{x} = V_F(x)$	224
$\mathbf{1}$	vector of ones	34
$\ll$	strong inequality	266

Mathematical Notations, Definitions, and Conventions

The sets of integers, real numbers, and complex numbers are denoted $\mathbf{Z}$, $\mathbf{R}$, and $\mathbf{C}$, respectively. $\mathbf{R}_+ = [0, \infty)$ is the set of *nonnegative* real numbers, and $(0, \infty)$ is the set of *positive* real numbers. Similarly, $\mathbf{R}_- = (-\infty, 0]$ is the set of *nonpositive* real numbers, and $(-\infty, 0)$ is the set of *negative* real numbers.

$\mathbf{R}^n$ denotes the set of column vectors consisting of n real entries, while $\mathbf{R}^{m \times n}$ denotes the set of matrices with m rows and n columns of real entries. For vectors and matrices with nonnegative components, we write $\mathbf{R}^n_+$ and $\mathbf{R}^{n \times n}_+$, respectively. $\mathbf{1} \in \mathbf{R}^n$ is the column vector whose entries are all 1, and $\mathbf{0} \in \mathbf{R}^n$ is the column vector whose entries are all 0. The Euclidean length of the vector $x \in \mathbf{R}^n$ is denoted $|x| = \sqrt{\sum_i (x_i)^2}$.

When writing vector or matrix equations, we are careful to distinguish between a column vector $x \in \mathbf{R}^n$ and its transpose, the row vector x'. However, when we define a specific column vector in the text, we generally do not indicate transposition. For instance, to define the the column vector $x^* \in \mathbf{R}^2$ whose entries are both $\frac{1}{2}$, we write $x^* = (\frac{1}{2}, \frac{1}{2})$.

Notation Index

The interior, boundary, closure, and convex hull of the set A are denoted $\mathrm{int}(A)$, $\mathrm{bd}(A)$, $\mathrm{cl}(A)$, and $\mathrm{conv}(A)$, respectively. The notation $\subset$ denotes strict set inclusion, and $\subseteq$ denotes weak set inclusion.

When defining a function from the set A to the set B, we write $f: A \to B$. When defining correspondences (i.e., set-valued functions), we write $f: A \rightrightarrows B$. A function $f: \mathbf{R} \to \mathbf{R}$ is *nondecreasing* if $x < y$ implies that $f(x) \leq f(y)$; if $x < y$ implies that $f(x) < f(y)$, then f is *increasing*. *Nonincreasing* and *decreasing* functions are defined similarly.

Index

Note: Page numbers in *italics* indicate definitions or statements of theorems.

Accessibility, *434*
Acuteness, *166*, 167–169, 236, 239
Additive random utility model, 189
Admissible deterministic perturbation, *189–190*
Admissible stochastic perturbation, *189*
Advantage distribution, *487–488*
Affine calculus, 108–115
Affine combination, *44*
Affine conjugacy, 255
Affine hull, 32–33, *45*
Affine space, *44*, 45
Aggregate monotone percentage growth rates, *164*
Aggregate payoff, *23*, 56–57
Akin transformation, *229*, 230–232
α-limit, *360*, *535*
Anonymity, 3–4, 21
Applications, xxiii, 2–3, 16, 21
Arms race, 98
Asymptotic stability, *262*, 265–266
  vs. attractors, 331
  global, 233, *262*
Attracting set, *262*, 263–265
  globally, 241, *262*
Attractor, *331*, *360*
  vs. asymptotically stable set, 331
  characterizations of, 360
  dual, *360–361*
Attractor-repellor pairs, *360–361*
  and chain recurrence, 361
Average payoff, *23*, 56

Backward equation, *395*, 444
Banach fixed point theorem, 133

Basins of attraction, *331*, *360*
  escape from (*see* Escape from basins of attraction)
  variation across dynamics, 184–186
Bayesian games, 16
Beckmann, Martin, 6
Bendixson-Dulac theorem, *359*
Bertrand competition, 97
Best response correspondence
  mixed, *23*, 98–100, 179
  pure, *23*, 98–100
Best response dynamic, 9, 150–152, 177–178, *179*, 180–187
  chaotic behavior under, 363
  construction of solutions, 178–186
  discontinuity of, 150, 187
  elimination of iteratively dominated strategies, 222–223, 258–259
  existence of solutions, 179
  and fictitious play, 216
  global convergence in potential games, 222–224
  global convergence in stable games, 242–244, 248–250
  incentive properties, 186–187
  local stability of ESS, 283, 285–286, 289–290
  local stability of Nash equilibria in potential games, 274
  Lyapunov functions for, 181
  nonuniqueness of solutions, 179–185
  simple solution of, 251
  stable cycles under, 329–330, 334–336
Bilinear
  form, 81
  map, 105

Biological modeling, 13–15, 21
  derivations of the replicator dynamic, 158, 160, 175
  and stochastic stability, 416, 463, 494
Birkhoff center, *261*, 453, *516*, 532, *533*
Birth and death chains, *436*, 437–440, 443. *See also* Birth and death processes
Birth and death processes, *403*, 404–405. *See also* Birth and death chains
BNN dynamic. *See* Brown-von Neumann-Nash dynamic
Braess's paradox, 62
Brown, George W., 138, 216
Brown-von Neumann-Nash dynamic, *128–129*, 143–144, 150–152, *167*, 172–173, 248–250. *See also* Excess payoff dynamics

Calculus, 100–115
  on affine spaces, 108–115
Carathéodory extension theorem, 385
Carathéodory solution, 179, 200, *205*
Cauchy-Schwarz inequality, *306*
Censored Markov chain, *524*
Central limit theorem, *382*, 388
Chain recurrence, *262*, 361, 531
  and stochastic approximation theory, 531
Chain rule, *100*, 104
Chaotic behavior under game dynamics, 11, 319, 341–346, 363
Clever payoff evaluation, *419*, 420–421, 430–433, 463, 502
Clever payoff function, *419*, 502
Closed orbits, 151–152, 358–359
Committed agents, 421–423, 431–432, 472–474
Communication classes, *434*
  closed, *434*
  partial order on, 434–435
  recurrent, *436*
Componentwise product, *103*–104
Conditional imitation rates, *153*
  monotonicity of, 153, 401
Conditional switch rates, 119, *121*
Cone, 39–40, 50–51
  normal (*see* Normal cone)
  polar, 39–40, 50–51
  tangent, 38–39, *40*, 41–44, 65–66, 130–131
Congestion games, 2, 21, 26, *27–28*, 51, 56–57, 60–64, 115–116, 425. *See also* Full potential games; Potential games
  cost function, 28
  facility, 28
  finite-population, *425*
  inefficiency bounds for, 68–71
  isoelastic, *66*, 67–68
  link, 27
  modeling externalities using, 28
  path, 27
  as potential games, 56–57
  utilization level, *28*
Conservative properties of game dynamics, 319–327
Constant games, *77*, 78–79
Constant of motion, *233*, 235
Continuation of attractors, 331, 361
  and game dynamics, 330–333, 351
Convergence
  in distribution, *382*
  weak, *382*, *456*, 459, *533*
Convex combination, *44*
Convex hull, *44*
Convex set
  dimension of, *46*
  tangent space of, *46*
Cooperative differential equations, 222, 255–256, 266, 267–268
  generic convergence to equilibrium, 268
  irreducible, *266*
  minimal and maximal rest points of, 267
  and stochastic approximation theory, 518–519, 536–537
  strongly, 255–256, *266*
  strong monotonicity of semiflow, 266
Coordinate function, *383*
Coradius, *511*, 513–514, *527*
Correspondence
  bounded, *205*
  convex-valued, *205*
  nonempty, *205*
  upperhemicontinuous, *205*
Cost
  of a graph, *503*, 522
  of a suboptimal choice, 474, *475*, 476, *500*, 501–502, 510
  of a transition, 453, *502*, *511*, 519, *522*, 527–530
Countable additivity, *383*, 391
Courant-Fischer theorem, 304
Cournot, Antoine Augustin, 6
Cournot competition, 57
Cumulative distribution function, *385*
Cyclical behavior under game dynamics, 11, 151–152, 236–237, 319, 327–330

Index

Danskin's envelope theorem, 243, 268
Darwinian fitness, 13–15, 160
Data requirements, 140, 142–144, 150, 169, 172–173
Decumulative distribution function, 94
Derivative, *100–101*
  directional, *102*
  of functions on affine spaces, 111–113
  higher-order, 105–106
  as a linear map, 100–101, 111–113
  partial, *101*, 102
Derivative matrix, *101*
Detailed balance conditions, *402*, 443
Deterministic approximation, 9–12, 120, 122, *367–372*, *373–374*, *375–377*, 395, 414–415, 515, 532
  and differential equations, 367–372, *373–374*, *375–377*
  and differential inclusions, 179, 395
  and infinite horizon behavior, and, 414–415, 515
Deterministic evolutionary dynamics, 1, 9–11, 120, *129–130*, 139. *See also* Dynamics
  derivation from revision protocols, 130–131
  existence and forward invariance, 130–131
  families of, 140, 148, 150–153
  Lipschitz continuity in initial conditions, 131
  uniqueness of solutions, 131
Diffeomorphism, *315*
Differentiability, *100–101*, 111
  class C^1, *101*, 112
  class C^k, *106*, 112–113
  continuous, *101*, 112
  of functions on closed sets, 106–107
Differentiable conjugacy, *315*
Differentiably strictly convex function, *190*
Differential equations, *131*, *132–137*, *308–315*
  on compact convex sets, 135–137
  continuity of solutions in initial conditions, 134
  cooperative (*see* Cooperative differential equations)
  existence and uniqueness of solutions, 133–137, 207
  exponential growth and decay, 132–133
  flows of, *134*
  gradient systems, *228*, 229–232
  incompressible, *324*
  initial value problems, *132*
  linear (*see* Linear differential equations)
  linearization near rest points (*see* Linearization of differential equations)
  maximal time interval of solutions, 134
  reparameterization of time, 158
  solutions of, *132*, 133–137
  stability concepts for, 262, 314
  volume-preserving, *324*
Differential inclusions, 179, *205*, 206–208
  on closed convex sets, 205–206
  defined by projections, 207–208
  existence of Carathéodory solutions, 179, *205*
  good upper hemicontinuous, *205*
  properties of solution sets, 179, 206–207
  stability concepts for, 262
Differentiation as a linear operation, 103
Diminished population state, *419*, 424
Diminishing returns, *252*, 253
Direct sum, *46*
Displacement vector, *31*, 32–34
Distribution, *383*
  Bernoulli, *381*
  binomial, *381*
  double exponential, *194*
  exponential, *378*, 379–381, 392–393
  function, *385*
  joint, 387–389
  marginal, *383*, 386–387
  Poisson, *379*, 380–382, 393
  standard normal, *381*
  uniform, *385*
Divergence, *325*, *356*
Divergence-free, *325*, *356*
Dominance solvability, 222–223, 257, *258*, 259–260
Dominated strategies, *258*
  elimination of, 222–223, 257–260, 347
  iteratively, 222–223
  survival of, 8, 223, 319–320, 344–356
Double limits. *See* Stochastic stability, double limits; Stationary distribution asymptotics, double limits
Duality, 109–111, 209. *See also* Involution
Dual repellor, *360–361*
Dynamics. *See also* Deterministic evolutionary dynamics
  antitarget, *128*
  best response (*see* Best response dynamic)
  Brown-von Neumann-Nash (*see* Brown-von Neumann-Nash dynamic)
  exact target, *124*, 125, 178

Dynamics (cont.)
  excess payoff (*see* Excess payoff dynamics)
  hybrid, 141, *173*, 174–175
  imitative (*see* Imitative dynamics)
  imitative logit, *158*, 159
  integrable target, 235–245
  logit (*see* Logit dynamic)
  pairwise comparison (*see* Pairwise comparison dynamics)
  perturbed best response (*see* Perturbed best response dynamics)
  projection (*see* Projection dynamic)
  replicator (*see* Replicator dynamic)
  sampling best response, 217
  separable target, 237
  Smith (*see* Smith dynamic)
  target, *124*, 125, 222
  target projection, 217
  tempered best response, 217
  variable rate logit, *196*
Dynamo, xxii

Economic modeling, 2–3, 13–15
  and stochastic stability, 416–417, 463, 494
Edge, 443, *520*
Ehrenfest urn model, 449
Eigenvalues, *300*, 301–306
  algebraic multiplicity, *300–301*
  eigenspace associated with, *301*
  geometric multiplicity, *301*
Entropy function, *195*, *466*
Equilibrium. *See* Nash equilibrium; Rest points of evolutionary game dynamics; Restricted equilibrium; Perturbed equilibrium
Equilibrium selection. *See* Stochastic stability; Unique predictions in stochastic evolutionary models
Escape from basins of attraction, 408, 410, 412, 486, 499, 510–511, 519, 529
  "swimming upstream", 412, 449
  waiting times until, 410, 412–417, 529
ESS. *See* Evolutionarily stable state
Euclidean isometry, *302*
Euler's Theorem, *104*
Event, *383*
Evolutionarily stable state, 6, 11, 14, 81–82, 271, 275, *276–278*, 279–299
  characterizations of, 276–282
  Cressman, *280*, 281, 316
  globally (*see* Globally evolutionarily stable state)

  and Nash equilibrium, 277–282
  regular, *281*
  regular Taylor, 271, 275, *282*, 283, 291–297
  and stable games, 271, 282–283, 285–286
  Taylor, *280*, 281
Evolutionarily stable strategy. *See* Evolutionarily stable state
Evolutionary dynamics
  deterministic (*see* Deterministic evolutionary dynamics)
  foundations (*see* Foundations for evolutionary dynamics)
  stochastic (*see* Stochastic evolutionary process)
  topology and, 217
Evolutionary game theory, meaning of the term, 14–15
Evolutionary process. *See* Deterministic evolutionary dynamics; Stochastic evolutionary process
Excess payoff, *125*, 126, 143–144, 166–167
Excess payoff dynamics, 140–141, 150, 165, *166*, 167–169, 196, 222. *See also* Brown-von Neumann-Nash dynamic
  global convergence in potential games, 222–224
  global convergence in stable games, 222, 241–242
  integrable, *241*, 242
  local stability of ESS, 283, 285–286, 289–290
  local stability of Nash equilibria in potential games, 273–274
Expected value, *384*
Exponential revision protocols, *428–429*, *430–433*, *463–474*
  in potential games, 430–433, 463–474
Extensive form games, xxii, 518, 538
Externalities, 2–3, 5–6, 21, 27–29, 53, 67, 85, 97
  self-defeating, *80*
Externality pricing, 58
Externality symmetry, 55, 73
  full, *55*
Extinction, *160–161*

Farkas's lemma, *111*
Fictitious play, 216
  stochastic, 217, 539
Finite-horizon deterministic approximation. *See* Deterministic approximation
Finite intersection property, 93
Finite-population adjustments, 377, 417–423

Index

Finite-population games, *418*, 419
  convergence of sequences of, 418
  matching without self-matching, 418
  potential (*see* Finite-population potential games)
Finite-population potential games, 423, *424–425*, 426–428, 430–433, 463
  convergence of, 427–428, 465
  and exponential revision protocols, 430–433, 463–474
  full, *424*, 426–427
  Nash equilibria of, 426
  and normal form potential games, 433
First variation equation, *357*
Fisher, Ronald A., 17
Fitness, 13–15, 160
Flow, 134, 330–331, 348, 359, *360*
  simple, *535*
Forward equation, *395*
Forward invariant, 135, *359*
Foundations for evolutionary dynamics, 8–9, 11–12, 119–120. *See also* Revision protocol
Frequency-dependent Moran process, 158, 175, 538
Full externality symmetry, *55*
Full population games, 54. *See also* Population games, with entry and exit
Full potential function, *54*, 55
  concave, 60
Full potential games, 53, *54*, 55–71. *See also* Potential games
  characterization of, 54
  concave, 60
  efficiency in, 66–71
  examples of, 55–62
  finite-population, *424*, 426–427
  homogeneous, *66*, 67–68
  Nash equilibria of, 58–66
  positively homogeneous, *67*, 68
  relation to potential games, 76–77
Fundamental theorem of algebra, 300
Fundamental theorem of calculus, *100*, *107*
Fundamental theorem of dynamical systems, 262, *361*
Fundamental theorem of linear algebra, *110–111*, 300

Game
  anticoordination, 183, 269, 338–339
  arms race, 98
  Bayesian, 16
  Bertrand oligopoly, 97
  Boar Hunt, *496*, 497–499
  circulant, *327*, 328–333
  common interest, *55–56*, 66, 71–72, 115, 424–425
  congestion (*see* Congestion games)
  constant, *77*, 78–79
  with continuous strategy sets, xxii
  Cournot competition, 57
  dominance solvable, 222, *258*
  extensive form, xxii, 518, 538
  Hawk-Dove, 29–31, 36–37, 51, 80
  hypnodisk, 337–338, *339–340*, 341, 347–351
  Matching Pennies, 156, 157, 249–250
  Mismatching Pennies, *333*, 334–337
  monocyclic, *329*, 330
  multi-zero-sum, *83*, 320
  negative dominant diagonal, *85*, 116
  nonlinear Stag Hunt, 410–412, 484–486, 488
  normal form (*see* Normal form games)
  null stable, *79*, 83–84, 233, 235
  12 Coordination, 29–31, 36–37, 146–147, 182
  123 Coordination (*see* 123 Coordination)
  passive, *77*, 78–79
  population (*see* Population games)
  potential (*see* Potential games)
  psuedostable, *91*
  pure coordination, 338
  repeated, 137
  Rock-Paper-Scissors (*see* Rock-Paper-Scissors)
  stable (*see* Stable games)
  Stag Hunt, *407*, 408–409, 414–415, 483–484, 504–506
  strictly stable, *79*, 83–84, 232–235
  supermodular (*see* Supermodular games)
  three-strategy, 29–31, 34–38, 42–43
  two-strategy (*see* Two-strategy games)
  war of attrition, 83, 116
  Zeeman's, *184*, 185, 292–293
  zero-sum, *83*, 320–322
Generator, *394*, 444
GESS. *See* Globally evolutionarily stable state
Global convergence, 6, 11, 221–260
  in dominance solvable games, 222–223, 257–260
  in potential games, 221–228
  in stable games, 222, 232–250
  in supermodular games, 222, 249, 251–257

Global inverse function theorem, 212
Globally asymptotically stable set, 233, *262*, 265–266
Globally attracting set, 241, *262*
Globally evolutionarily stable state, *87*, 88–91, 233–235
Globally neutrally stable state, *87*, 88–93
GNSS. *See* Globally neutrally stable state
Gradient, *101*, 102
  of a function on an affine space, *112*
Gradient systems, *228*, 229–232
Graphs, 443, 453, 499
  cycle, *520*
  directed, *520*
  edge, 443, *520*
  node, 443, *520*
  path, *503*, *520*
  random walks on, *443*
  tree, *503*, *520*
  walk, *520*
Grönwall's inequality, *135*, 208, 260, 350

Half-dominance, 512
  and stochastic stability, 513–514
  strict, *512*
  strong, *512*
  weak, *512*
Hamilton, William D., 17, 116
Hamiltonian systems, 362
Hartman-Grobman theorem, *314*
Hausdorff metric, 188
Hessian matrix, *106*, *112–113*
Heteroclinic cycle, 151–152, *359*
Heteroclinic orbit, 151–152
Heuristic learning in games, xxii. *See also* Fictitious play
Hines's lemma, 291, *307–308*
Hitting probability, 440
Hitting time, *437*, 438–439, 442
Homeomorphism, *313*
Homoclinic orbit, *359*
Homogeneous functions, 66–71, *104*, 105
  Euler's Theorem, *104*
Homogeneous transitions, *533–534*
Hybrid dynamics, 141, *173*, 174–175
Hyperbolic rest point, *314*
Hypercycle system, *328*, 329

i-logit dynamic. *See* Imitative logit dynamic
Imitative dynamics, 140, 150, *153–165*. *See also* Replicator dynamic
  elimination of iteratively dominated strategies, 222–223, 259–260
  and extinction, 160–161
  global convergence in potential games, 224–225
  instability of non-Nash rest points, 272–273
  local stability of Nash equilibria in potential games, 273–274, 290–297
  monotone percentage growth rates, *162–163*, 259, 272
  and restricted equilibrium, 164–165
  slow motion toward and away from boundary, 161–162
  support invariance, 161–162
Imitative logit dynamic, *158*, 159
Imitative revision protocols, 9, 126–128, 140, 142–143, 153–158, 421–423
  and committed agents, 421–423
  exponential, *429*, 430–433
  imitation driven by dissatisfaction, *127*, 143, *154–155*
  imitation of success, *127*, 143, *155*
  imitation of success with repeated sampling, *155–156*, 157–158
  imitation via pairwise comparisons, *154*
  imitative logit, *158*, 430
  with mutations, 401, *491*
  pairwise imitative logit, *430*
  pairwise proportional imitation, *126*, 143, *154*
Impartial pairwise comparison dynamics, *246*, 247–248
Improvement step, *252*
Independence, 383
Individual negligibility, 3, 21
Inertia, 8, 17, 120–121, 141
Inescapable set, *264*
Infinitesimal generator, *394*, 444
Initial distribution, *390–391*, 434
Initial state, *390–391*, 434
Innovation, 347
Integrability, 55, 73, 108, 238
  of functions on affine spaces, 113–115
  of revision protocols, 222, 237, 238–240
  triangular, 74
Invariant set, *134*, *251*, *262*, *359*
Invasion, 85–90, 276–278
  strict, *85*, 86
  weak, *85*, 86
Invasion barrier, 276, 277
  uniform, *276*, 277

Index

Involution, 40. *See also* Duality
Irreducibility, 12, 374, 397, 401, *436*, 445–449, 454
  and uniqueness of the stationary distribution, 401, 442, 454
Isolated set of Nash equilibria, 273
Iteratively dominated strategies. *See* Dominated strategies

Jacobian matrix. *See* Derivative matrix
Jensen's inequality, 234, 499
Jonker, Leo, 14
Jordan canonical form, *305*, 306

Kakutani fixed point theorem, 24
k-BNN dynamics, *167*
Kolmogorov extension theorem, 385, 392
k-Smith dynamics, *170*
Kuhn-Tucker conditions and Nash equilibrium, 59–60, 64–66, 115
Kurtz's theorem, *370–371*, *372–373*, 377, 389. *See also* Deterministic approximation
  in discrete time, 376

Large deviations theory, 538–539
Large population limit. *See* Stochastic stability, large population limit; Stationary distribution asymptotics, large population limit
Law of cosines, 145
Laws of large numbers, 372, *388*
Law of the iterated logarithm, *389*
Learning in games, xxii. *See also* Fictitious play
Lebesgue measure, 385
Legendre pair, *210*
Legendre transform, 191, 208, *209*, 210, *211*, 212, 214–215
Lenient transition cost, 529, *530*
Limit cycles under game dynamics, *See* Cyclical behavior under game dynamics
Limiting stationary distributions, 12–13, 451–539. *See also* Stationary distribution asymptotics; Stochastic stability
Linear
  form, *109*, 110–111
  isomorphism, *109*
  map, 46, *101*
Linear differential equations, *308*, 309–313
  center, 310–311
  contractions, *311*
  expansions, *312*
  explicit solutions of, 310–311

  flow of, *11*, 312
  hyperbolic, *312*
  improper node, 309–310
  matrix exponentials and, *311*, 312
  saddle, 309
  sink, *312*
  source, *312*
  stability theory for, 312–313
  stable node, 309
  stable spiral, 309–310
  stable subspace, *313*
  unstable node, 309
  unstable spiral, 309–310
  unstable subspace, *313*
Linearization of differential equations, 290–291, 313–315
  Hartman-Grobman theorem, *314*
  stable manifold theorem, 315
Linearization of game dynamics, 271, 290–299
  and nonconvergence, 327–329, 336–337, 341
Linear stability, 290, *314*
Linear subspace, *44*
Liouville's formula, *357*, 358
Liouville's theorem, 325, *356*, 357–359
Lipschitz continuity, *133*, 142
  local, *133*
Lipschitz convergence of finite-population games, *427*, 428
Local interactions, xxii, 449, 514
  reduced waiting times under, 417
Local maximizer set, *273*
Local stability under differential equations, 10–11, 290–291, 313–315
  and game dynamics, 10–11, 271–299
Logit choice function, *128*, *188*, 191, 194–196. *See also* Revision protocol, logit
  derivations of, 194–195
  derivative of, 195
  potential function for, 195,
Logit dynamic, *128*, 143, 150–152, *153*, 248–250
  connections with the replicator dynamic, 299, 317
  examples, 191–194
  incentive properties, 196–198
  local stability of ESS, 284–285, 298–299
  variable rate, *196*
Logit equilibrium, *191*, 192–194, 210
Logit potential function, 225, *227*, 228, 466–471
Lotka-Volterra equation, *160*, 363

Lyapunov functions, 137, 181, 221–222, 232–250, 262, 271, 282–290, 320–323, 329, 480, 536
  and local stability of ESS, 282–290
  stability analysis via, 262–266
  for stable games, 232–250
  and stochastic approximation theory, 518–519, 536
  strict, 221, 223, 232, 536
Lyapunov stability, 241, 262, 263

Marginal bandwagon property, 513
Markov chains, 389, 390, 391, 434–443, 445–449
  aperiodic, 437, 446–449
  censored, 524
  convergence in distribution, 445–448
  convergence of empirical distributions, 402, 448–449
  ergodicity, 448–449
  hitting times, 437–439, 442
  vs. Markov processes, 390
  periodic, 437
  rates of convergence to stationary distribution, 446–448
  return times, 442
  temporal homogeneity, 390
  transition probabilities, 390–391
Markov chain tree theorem, 521
Markov processes, 367, 391, 392–395, 434–440, 444–449
  birth and death processes, 403, 404–405
  construction of, 392
  convergence in distribution, 402, 445–446
  convergence of empirical distributions, 402, 448–449
  ergodicity, 402, 448–449
  for game dynamics (see Stochastic evolutionary process)
  generator, 394
  hitting times, 437, 438–439
  jump rates, 391–392, 434
  jump times, 392
  vs. Markov chains, 390
  return times, 445
  right continuity and left limits, 391
  sample paths of, 391
  semigroup, 394, 444
  temporal homogeneity, 391
  transition probabilities, 393–395, 444
Markov property, 390–391
Martingale, 440

Matrix, 299–308
  aperiodic, 440, 441
  characteristic polynomial of, 300
  circulant, 327
  congruent, 304
  derivative (see Derivative matrix)
  determinant of, 300
  diagonalizable, 302
  eigenvectors and eigenvalues of, 300, 301–306 (see also Eigenvalues)
  generalized eigenvector of, 306, 313
  Hessian, 106, 112–113
  idempotent, 47, 48–50
  inertia of, 304
  inverse, 300
  irreducible, 440, 441
  Jacobian (see Derivative matrix)
  kernel, 299
  as a linear map, 46, 101
  normal, 303
  nullity of, 299
  nullspace of, 299
  orthogonal, 302, 304
  primitive, 440, 441
  range of, 299
  rank of, 299, 300
  real diagonalizable, 302
  real Jordan, 303, 305
  rotation, 301
  similarity of, 302
  singular value decomposition of, 306
  singular values of, 306, 307
  skew-symmetric, 303, 322
  spectral norm of, 306
  spectral theorem, 303–304
  stochastic, 440, 441
  symmetric, 47–50, 303
  trace of, 300
Matrix exponential, 311, 312, 394–395
Maximizer correspondence, 178–179, 242–243
  integrability of, 243
Maximum function, 243
Maynard Smith, John, 2, 5–7, 13–14, 17, 116, 275
Maynard Smith replicator dynamic, 156, 157–158, 175
McGuire, C. Bartlett, 6
Mean dynamics, 10, 120, 122–123, 124, 125, 139, 367–368, 515–519, 532
  derivations of, 123, 372–373
  examples of, 125–129

Index

and limiting stationary distributions, 515–519, 531–537
Measurability, 385, 391
Measure zero, *205*
Microfoundations, 8–9, 11–12, 119–120. *See also* Revision protocol
Minmax theorem, 92–93
Mixed strategists, 275, 280
Modified coradius, *528*
Modified cost, *527*
Monotone percentage growth rates, *162–163*, 259, 272
  alternative names for, 175
  and positive correlation, 163
Monotonicity
  of dynamics in payoffs, 10, 144–145, 175, 235–236, 240
  of net conditional imitation rates, *153*
  of percentage growth rates (*see* Monotone percentage growth rates)
Moran process, 158, 175, 538
Moreau decomposition theorem, 50, *51*, 202, 207–208, 233
Morgenstern, Oskar, 2, 4, 6
Multilinear map, 26, 106
Mutation, 399, 401
Mutation rate, 399–401
  conversion to noise level, 400, 500, 529
Myopia, 8, 17, 120–121, 141
Myopic adjustment dynamic, 175

Nash, John F., 2, 5
Nash equilibrium, *24*, 27
  and ESS, 277–282
  excess payoff characterization of, 168
  existence of, 6, 24, 53, 99, 138
  in finite-population games, *418*
  foundations and justification, evolutionary, 8–11, 13–15, 24, 119, 139–146, 221, 344
  foundations and justification, traditional, 7–8, 13–15, 17, 24, 119, 139, 178
  geometry of, 42–44, 51, 64–66
  global convergence to, 6, 11, 221–260
  mass action interpretation of, 2, 5, 17
  maximal, *99*
  minimal, *99*
  normal cone characterization of, *42*, 43–44, 51, 65–66, 146, 202
  of potential games, 58–66
  purification of, 317
  quasistrict, *281*, 282
  refinements of, 13–15
  selection among multiple, 12–13
Nash stationarity, 10, 140–141, *145*, 146–147, 150, 172–175, 221
  of best response dynamic, 186–187
  of excess payoff dynamics, 167–169
  of hybrid dynamics, 173–174
  of pairwise comparison dynamics, 169–173
  of projection dynamic, 202
Natural selection, 13–15, 160
Neighborhood, *262*
Network congestion. *See* Congestion games
Neutrally stable state, *81–82*
  globally (*see* Globally neutrally stable state)
Node, 443, *520*
Noise level, 128, 158–159
  conversion to mutation rate, 400, 500, 529
Nonconvergence of game dynamics, 11, 271, 319–356
Nondegeneracy, 517–518, 534–537
  global, *536*, 537
  at rest points, *534*
Normal cone, 38–40, *41*, 42–44
  characterization of Nash equilibrium, *42*, 43–44, 51, 65–66
Normal form games, 4, *25–26*, 55–56
  continuous player sets, 16–17
  diminishing returns, *252*, 253
  matching in, 5, 15, *25–26*, 27
  multipopulation matching in, *26*, 27, 84, 326–327
  nondegenerate, *252*
  potential, *71*, *75*, 115–116, 433
  random vs. complete matching in, 25
  supermodular, 97, 251–253
NS. *See* Nash stationarity
NSS. *See* Neutrally stable state
Null stable games, *79*, 83–84, 233, 235

Ω-limit, *224*, *261*, 263–265, *533*
  properties, 261
  of a set, *360*
12 Coordination, *29–31*, 36–37, 146–147, 182
123 Coordination, *37–38*
  basic dynamics in, 224–228
  best response dynamic in, 183–184
  drawing of, 37–38
  global convergence in, 224–228
  limiting stationary distributions in, 467–471
  logit dynamic in, 191–194
  logit potential function of, 228, 467–471

123 Coordination (cont.)
  positive correlation in, 147–149
  potential function of, 59–61, 224–226
  transported replicator dynamic in, 230–232
Optional stopping theorem, 440
Orbit
  closed, *358*, 359
  heteroclinic, *359*
  homoclinic, *359*
  periodic, *358*, 359
Orbit chain, *535*
Orbit chain unstable, *535*
Orders of limits
  in population size and noise level (*see*
    Stationary distribution asymptotics,
    agreement of double limits; Stationary
    distribution asymptotics, disagreement of
    double limits)
  in population size and time horizon, 11–12, 397
Ordinal potential function, *480*, 481–486, 492,
  497–498
Ordinary differential equations. *See* Differential
  equations
Ordinary least squares, 49–50
Orthogonal complement, *44*
Orthogonal projection, 31, 34–39, *46*, 47–51,
  109–110, 112–115
Orthogonal translation vector, *44*, 112–115
Ostrowski's theorem, 304

Pairwise comparison dynamics, 141, 150, *170*,
  171–172. *See also* Smith dynamic
  global convergence in potential games,
    222–224
  global convergence in stable games, 246–248
  impartial, 246–248
  local stability of ESS, 283, 285–290
  local stability of Nash equilibria in potential
    games, 273–274
Passive games, *77*, 78–79
Path, *503*, *520*
Payoff, 23
  aggregate, *23*, 56–57
  average, *23*, 56
  excess, *125*, 126, 143–144, 166–167
  function, 23
  projected, 36–39, 43–44, 72–73, 76–78, 148
  relative, 35, 74, 78–79
  virtual, *197*, 198
PC. *See* Positive correlation
Peano's theorem, 133

Percentage growth rates, *162*
  aggregate monotone, *164*
  monotone, *163*
  sign-preserving, *164*
Perfect foresight dynamics, 17, 137
Period, *436*
Periodicity, 436–437
Periodic orbit, *358*, 359
Periodic orbits under game dynamics. *See*
  Cyclical behavior under game dynamics
Permanence, 362
Perron-Frobenius theorem, *440–441*
Perturbed best response dynamics, 150, 177, 187,
  188–*189*, 190–198, 222, 253–257. *See also* Logit
  dynamic
  almost global convergence in supermodular
    games, 222, 249, 253–257
  global convergence in potential games,
    227–228
  global convergence in stable games, 222,
    244–245
  local stability of ESS, 283–285
  local stability of perturbed equilibria in
    potential games, 274–275
  local stability via linearization, 297–299
  and stochastic fictitious play, 217
Perturbed best response function, *189*, 222
  monotonicity of, 222
Perturbed equilibrium, *196*, 217, 518
  in experimental economics, 187–188, 217
Perturbed maximizer functions, 187–193,
  212–216. *See also* Logit choice function
  characterizations of, 216
  derived from deterministic perturbations,
    189–190, 195–196, 212–216
  derived from stochastic perturbations, *189*,
    190, 195–196, 212–216, 254–255
  integrability of, 215–216, 244
  representation theorem, 190–191, 212–215
Perturbed maximum functions, *215*, 216, 244
Perturbed stationarity, *197*
Picard-Lindelöf theorem, *133*, 207
Playing the field, 2, 5, 25–26
Poincaré-Bendixson theorem, 341, 350, 353,
  358–359
Poincaré-Hopf theorem, 194
Point mass, 461, *533*
Poisson alarm clock, 121, 380
Poisson limit theorem, 377, 381, *382*
Poisson process, 392–393
Polar cone, *39*, 40

Index

Polytope, 4, 40
Population games, 1, 3–6, 21, *22–23*, 24–44
  basic properties of, 3–4, 21
  classes of, 5–6, 53
  drawing, 29–38
  with entry and exit, 64, 93
  with finite populations (*see* Finite-population games)
  full, *54*
  geometry of, 29–44
Population mass, *22*
Population size, *121*
Population states, *22*, 46
  diminished, *419*, 424
  with finite populations, 121, 368
  maximal, *99*, 254
  minimal, *99*
  pure, *22*
  stochastic dominance order on, *94*, 99
Populations, 3, 21, *22*
  finite vs. continuous, 3–4, 22
  largeness of, 3, 21, 119–121
  monomorphic, 275, 280
  polymorphic, 275, 280
Positive correlation, 10, 140–141, *144–145*, 146–150, 172–175, 238–240
  under the best response dynamic, 186–187
  under excess payoff dynamics, 167–169
  geometric interpretation of, 145–149
  under hybrid dynamics, 173–174
  under imitative dynamics, 163
  under pairwise comparison dynamics, 169–172
  probabilistic interpretation of, 144–145
  under the projection dynamic, 202
  virtual, *198*
Potential functions, 54–55, *73*, *108*, *425*
  and affine spaces, 113–115
  concave, 60
  full, *54*, 55, *424*, *425*–427
  and integrability, 55, 73, 108, 113–115
  local maximizers of, 58–62, 75, 273–275, 426
  as Lyapunov functions, 221–228
  and Nash equilibria, 58–66, 75, 426
  ordinal, *480*, 481–486, 492, 497–498
  quadratic, *481*
  signum, *481*
Potential games, 5–6, 11, 24, 53–72, *73*, 74–79, 221–232, 423–428, 430–433, 452, 463–474
  characterizations of, 54, 73–74
  concave, 60, 84–85

efficiency in, 66–71
  with entry and exit, 64
  examples of, 55–62, 71–72, 74–75
  and exponential revision protocols, 430–433, 463–474
  finite-population (*see* Finite-population potential games)
  full (*see* Full potential games)
  global convergence in, 221–228
  gradient systems for, 228–232
  and limiting stationary distributions, 518–519
  local stability and local maximization of potential in, 273–275
  Nash equilibria of, 58–66, 426
  normal form, *71*, *75*, 115–116, 433
  relation to full potential games, 76–77
Price of anarchy. *See* Congestion games, inefficiency bounds for
Price, George R., 11, 116, 275
Probability measure, *383*, *385*
Probability model
  countable, *383*
  uncountable, *385*
Probit choice function, *476–477*, 530. *See also* Revision protocol, probit
Product rule, *100*, *103–104*
Projected payoff, 36–39, 43–44, 72–73, 76–78, 148
Projection
  closest point, 47, *50–51*
  orthogonal (*see* Orthogonal projection)
  subspace, onto a, *46*, 47
Projection dynamic, 145, 150–153, 177–178, 198, *199*, 200–205
  connections with the replicator dynamic, 150–152, 202–205
  constants of motion for null stable games, 235, 248–250, 320–322
  existence and uniqueness of solutions, 200–201
  global convergence in potential games, 222–224
  global convergence in strictly stable games, 232–233
  gradient systems for potential games, 228
  incentive properties, 202
  local stability of ESS, 282–283, 292
  local stability of Nash equilibria in potential games, 273–274
  nonuniqueness of backward solutions, 151–153

Projection dynamic (cont.)
  preservation of volume in null stable games, 326–327
  revision protocol for, 202–205
Propagation of chaos, 395
Protocol. *See* Revision protocol
Pseudostable games, 91
Psuedoconcave function, 91
Purification of Nash equilibrium, 317

Quadratic form, 81
Quantal response equilibrium. *See* Perturbed equilibrium; Logit equilibrium
Quasistrict equilibrium, *281*, 282

Radius, *511*, 513–514, *527*
Radius-coradius theorems, *511*, 513–514, 526, *527*–*528*, 529, 531
Random variables, *383*, 385
  construction of, 385
  distributional properties, 386–389
  i.i.d., 388–389
  realizations, 383, 387–389
  sample path properties, 386–389
Rationality, 7, 13–15, 17
Rayleigh-Ritz theorem, *304*
Real Jordan canonical form, *305*, 306
Recurrence under differential equations, 224, 260, *261*, 262, 515, *516*, 517
Recurrent class, *436*, 523–526
Recurrent state, *435*, 436
Regular collection of Markov chains, *522*
  weakly, *530*
Regular noisy best response protocol, *475*
Relative consumption effects, 98
Relative entropy, *234*
Relative payoff, 35, 74, 78–79
Reparameterization of time, 158
Repeated games, 137
Repellor, *348*–*349*
Replicator dynamic, 9, *126*, 127–128, 137–138, 150–152, *154*, 155, 164–165, 172–173
  chaotic behavior, 341–346
  connections with the logit dynamic, 299, 317
  connections with the Lotka-Volterra equation, 160, 363
  connections with the projection dynamic, 150–152, 202–205
  constants of motion for null stable games, 235, 248–250, 320–322
  convergence of time averages, 322–324
  examples, 146–149
  gradient systems for potential games, 228–232
  local stability of ESS, 282–283, 291–295
  Maynard Smith, *156*, 157–158
  permanence under, 362
  preservation of volume in null stable games, 324–326
  stable cycles under, 328–329, 333–334
Rest points of differential equations, 313–314
  hyperbolicity of, *314*
  linear instability of, *314*
  linear stability of, *314*
Rest points of evolutionary game dynamics, 145–146
  and restricted equilibria, 164–165
Restricted equilibrium, *164*–*165*
Return map, *330*
Return time, *442*, *445*
Reversibility, 12, 377, 398, 402–404, 430–434, 442–443, 452
  interpretation, 443
Reversible distribution, *402*, *443*, *445*
Revision potential, *237*, 241, 243–244
Revision protocol, 1, 8–9, 119–120, *121*, 122–131, 139
  best response, *178*
  best response with mutations (BRM) *399*–*400*, *401*, 476, 481, 501
  comparison to the average payoff, *128*–*129*
  continuity for, 139–142, 150
  data requirements for, 140, 142–144, 150, 169, 172–173
  direct, 9, *128*, 129
  exact, *122*
  exact target, *124*, *125*, 143, 178
  exponential, *428*–*429*, 430–433, 463–474
  full support, *397*, *399*, 400–401, 436, 451, 454
  hybrid, 9, 141, *173*, 174–175
  imitation with mutations, 401, *491*
  imitative (*see* Imitative revision protocols)
  information requirements for, 139–144, 150
  integrable target, 222, *237*, 238–240
  logit, *128*, 400–401, 429, 476, 481, 501–502 (*see also* Logit choice function; Revision protocol, exponential)
  noisy best response, 474–476, 500
  pairwise comparison, *129*
  pairwise logit, *429*
  pairwise proportional imitation, *126*, 143, *154*

Index

perturbed best response, *188*, 518–519
probit, *476–477*, 481, 502, 530
separable target, *168*, *237*, 238
target, *124*, 125, 143–144, 166–167, 235–245
Riemannian metric, 268
Riemann sum, 479–482
Riesz representation theorem, *109*
Risk dominance, *487*, 491, 497, 505–510
  pairwise, *513*
  and stochastic stability, 487, 508–510
  strict, *487*, 505, *506*
  strong, *506*
  weak, *487*, 505, *506*
Rock-Paper-Scissors, *82*
  asymmetric, 343–346
  bad, *82*
  basic dynamics in, 151–153, 261, 321, 351–356, 358
  best response dynamic in, 180–182, 184
  chaotic behavior in, 343–346
  as a circulant game, 327
  cyclical behavior in, 236–237, 321, 351–356, 358
  drawing, 37–39
  GNSS and GESS in, 90–92
  good, *82*
  hybrid dynamics in, 174–175, 354–356
  projection dynamic in, 200–201
  as a stable game, 82–83, 90–92
  standard, *82*
Roles, 3, 21. *See also* Populations
Root, *503*, *520*
Roots of unity, *327*

Sample path, 371, 386–389
  of a Markov process, 391
Sample space, *383*, 385, 390
Search models, 29, 97
Self-defeating externalities, *80*
Selfish routing. *See* Congestion games
Self-matching, 418, 420–421
Semiflow, *135*, 330–331
  monotone, *266*, 359, 360
  strongly monotone, *266*, 267–268
Sensitive depenence on initial conditions, 341
Separating hyperplane theorem, 40
Sex ratios, evolution of, 17, 116
Shapley polygon, *329*, 334
Sign preservation, *167*, *170*, 246–247
Simple flow, *535*
Simple payoff evaluation, *419*

Simply connected set, *359*
Small noise limit. *See* Stochastic stability, small noise limit; Stationary distribution asymptotics, small noise limit
Smith, Michael J., 138, 269
Smith dynamic, *129*, 150–152, *170*, 172–173, 248–250. *See also* Pairwise comparison dynamics
Social states, 4, *23*, 46
  feasible changes in, 74, 78–79 (*see also* Tangent space)
  maximal, *99*, 254, 256
  minimal, *99*, 256
  pure, *22*
  stochastic dominance order on, *94*, 99
Society, 3, *22*
Spectral theorem, *303–304*
Stable games, 5–6, 11, 24, 53, *79*, 80–93, 221–222, 232–250
  characterization of, 80–81
  constants of motion for, 235, 248–250, 320–322
  with entry and exit, 93
  and evolutionarily stable states 271, 282–283, 285–286
  examples of, 80–85
  global convergence in, 222, 232–250
  globally neutrally stable states in, 90–93
  invasion in, 85–90
  limiting stationary distributions in, 517
  Lyapunov functions for, 233–234, 241–250
  Nash equilibria of, 90–93
  null, *79*, 83–84, 233, 235
  stochastic stability in, 517
  strictly, *79*, 83–84, 232–235
Stable manifold, 315
Stable manifold theorem, 315, 331
State space, 390
Stationary distribution asymptotics, 451–539
  agreement and disagreement of double limits, 452–453, 492–496, 519
  double limits, 452, 472, 481–482, 492–496
  graph-theoretic evaluation of, 503
  under imitative protocols with committed agents, 494–499
  under imitative protocols with mutations, 491–494
  large population limit, 452–453, 456, 515–519, 531–537, 479–480, 465–471, 473
  and mean dynamics, 460–463, 473–474
  under noisy best response protocols, 477–486

Stationary distribution asymptotics (cont.)
  small noise limit, 452–453, 455, 464–465, 473, 477–479, 499–514, 519–531
  tree analysis of, 521–526, 530–531
  in two-strategy games, 452–453, 474, 477–499
Stationary distributions, 12–13, 397, 401, *402*, *441*, 442, 444–445
  and infinite horizon prediction, 11–12, 397
  limiting (*see* Limiting stationary distributions)
  and mean return times, 442, 445
  time until relevance of predictions, 398, 412–417, 451–452
  tree characterization of, 521, 530
  for two-strategy games, 405, *407*, 408–412
Steepness at the boundary, 190, *208*, *210*
Stirling's formula, 466
Stochastic approximation theory, 515–519, 531–537
  asymptotic normality, 533
  constant step size, 531–537
  convergence to the Birkhoff center, 516, 532–533
  convergence to recurrent states, 516, 532–533
  convergence to stable rest points, 533–537
  and cooperative differential equations, 536–537
  decreasing step size, 531
  Lyapunov functions and, 536
  nondegeneracy and, 517–518, 534–537
Stochastic dominance, 94, 254, 488–491
  and stochastic stability, 488–490
  strict, *488*
  weak, *488*
Stochastic evolutionary process, 11–13, 119–122, 367–368, *369*, 502
  discrete time specifications, 376–377
  unique predictions of infinite-horizon behavior (*see* Unique predictions in stochastic evolutionary models)
Stochastic fictitious play, 217, 539
Stochastic stability, 13, 407, 451–453, *454–459*, 460–521, *522*, 523–531
  agreement and disagreement of double limits, 452–453, 459–463, 492–496, 519
  under best response with mutations, 487, 508–510
  choice of limits, 452, 455–456
  dependence on revision protocol, 483–486, 496–499
  double limits, 452, *458*, 459–463, 472, 483, 492–496

  graph-theoretic evaluation of, 503
  and half-dominance, 513–514
  under imitative protocols with committed agents, 494–499
  under imitiative protocols with mutations, 460–463, 491–494
  independence of revision protocol, 486–491
  large population limit, 452, 455, *456*, 457, 465–471, 473, 515–519
  and mean dynamics, 460–463, 473–474
  under noisy best response protocols, 483–491, 504–505, 508–510, 513–514
  in potential games under exponential protocols, 452, 463–474
  via radius-coradius theorems, 511, 526–529, 531
  and risk dominance, 487, 508–510
  small noise limit, 452–453, *454–455*, 464–465, 473, 494, 499–514, 519–531
  in stable games, 517
  and stochastic dominance, 488–490
  tree analysis of, 521–526, 530–531
  in two-strategy games, 452–453, 459–463, 474, 486–491, 496–499, 504–510
  unique, *454*, 455, *456*, 457, *458*, 459, *531*
  waiting time critique, 416–417
  weak, *455–456*, 457, 459, 502, *531*
Strategies, 22
  continuous sets of, xxii
  twin, 348
Strategy distributions. *See* Population states; Social states
Strictly dominated strategies. *See* Dominated strategies
Strictly stable games, *79*, 83–84, 232–235
Strong law of large numbers, *388*, 389
Strongly monotone semiflow, 266, 267–268
  generic convergence to equilibrium, 268
  minimal and maximal rest points, 267
Strongly positive, *266*
Subdifferential, 243, 269
Subspace, *44*
Supermodular games, 5–6, 11, 24, 53, *94*, 95–100, 221–222
  almost global convergence of perturbed best response dynamics, 222, 249, 253–257
  characterizations of, 94–96
  examples of, 97–98
  global convergence of the best response dynamic, 222, 249, 251–257
  irreducible, 255–257

Index

and limiting stationary distributions, 518–519
monotonicity of best responses, 98–99, 222
monotonicity of perturbed best responses, 222
Nash equilibria in, 99–100
normal form, *97*, 251–253
Support invariance, 161–162
Sylvester's law of inertia, *304*

Tangent cone, 38–39, *40*, 41–44, 65–66, 130–131
Tangent space
  of an affine space, *44*
  of a convex set, *46*
  of the set of population states, 31, 34, *46*, 48–49
  of the set of social states, 31, 34, *46*, 49
Tangent vector, *31*, 32–34
Taylor, Peter D., 14
Taylor's formula, *106*
Theorem of the maximum, 284, 316
Topological conjugacy, *313–314*
Toss and Switch, *374*, 375, 404–406, 413, 423
Transient state, *435*, 436
Transition matrix, *390–391*
Trapping region, *360*
Tree, *503*, *520*
  root, *503*, *520*
Two-strategy games
  anticoordination, 183
  coordination, *482*, 483–486, *507*, 508–510
  drawing, 29–32
  normal cones and Nash equilibria of, 41, 43
  12 Coordination, *29–31*, 36–37, 146–147, 182
  positive correlation in, 147
  potential, 72, 74, 425–426
  stable, 80
  stationary distribution asymptotics in, 452–453, 474, 477–499, 504–510
  stationary distributions for, 405, *407*, 408–412
  supermodular, 98

Unbeatable strategy, 116
Uncountable, 384
Uninvadable state, 316
Unique predictions in stochastic evolutionary models, 12–13, 407–412, 451–453. *See also* Stochastic stability
  waiting time critique, 398, 412–417
Unstable manifold, 315

Variational inequality problem, 43, 51
Viability theorem, 207

Virtual payoffs, *197*, 198
Virtual positive correlation, *198*, 244
von Neumann, John, 2, 4, 6, 138
von Neumann-Morgenstern utility, 25

Walk, *520*
Wardrop equilibrium, 115
Weak compatibility, 175
Weak convergence, *382*, *456*, 459, *533*
Weak law of large numbers, *388*, 389
Weak trapping region, *360*, 362
Whitney extension theorem, 76, 106–107
Winsten, Christopher B., 6
Within-population interactions, 84

Zeeman's game, *184*, 185, 292–293